JG 26

Top Guns of the Luftwaffe

Donald L. Caldwell
Foreword by Adolf Galland

Orion Books · New York

Published by Orion Books, a division of Crown Publishers, Inc., 201 East 50th Street, New York, New York 10022. Member of the Crown Publishing Group.

ORION and colophon are trademarks of Crown Publishers, Inc.

Manufactured in the United States of America

Library of Congress Cataloging-in-Publication Data

Caldwell, Donald L.
    JG 26: top guns of the Luftwaffe / by Donald L. Caldwell; foreword by Adolf Galland.
        p.   cm.
        1. Germany. Luftwaffe. Jagdgeschwader 26 "Schlageter"—History.
    2. World War, 1939-1945—Aerial operations, German.   I. Title.
    D787.C35   1991
    940.54'4943—dc20   91-2625
                                                                       CIP

ISBN 0-517-57039-4

Book Design by Shari de Miskey

10 9 8 7 6 5 4 3 2 1

First Edition

to the fighter pilots

CONTENTS

FOREWORD   xiii

ACKNOWLEDGMENTS   xvii

INTRODUCTION   xxi

1.   ORIGINS (1935–1939)   1

    The Resurgent Luftwaffe   1
    The Condor Legion   4
    Days of Peace   6
    Albert Leo Schlageter   7
    War Looms   8

2.   SITZKRIEG AND BLITZKRIEG (1 September 1939–
26 June 1940)   10

    War Begins   10
    Formation of the Third Gruppe   10
    The Geschwader's First Victory   11
    10(Nacht)/JG 26 and the Battle of the
      Helgoland Bight   12
    The Winter Doldrums   14
    The Blitzkrieg Strikes West   16

Breakthrough on the Meuse 21
The Dunkirk Evacuation 23
Operation Paula—The Air Attack on Paris 26
The End of the Campaign 28

3. JG 26 IN THE BATTLE OF BRITAIN (24 July 1940–
9 February 1941) 29

Return to Germany 29
The First Phase—Channel Attacks and Free Hunts 30
The Second Phase—Adlerangriff 35
13 August—Adlertag 38
15 August—The Luftwaffe's Black Thursday 41
18 August—The "Hardest Day" 45
Galland Takes Command 48
Decimation of the Defiants 50
The Third Gruppe in Action 53
The Third Phase—Attacks on London 59
15 September—The Battle's Climax 61
The Fourth Phase—Fighters as Bombers 64
Conclusions 67

4. THE 7TH STAFFEL IN THE MEDITERRANEAN
THEATER (February–August 1941) 72

A New Theater of War 72
The Scourge of Malta 73
Flank Duty for the Balkan Campaign 76
Back to Sicily 76
Malta Reprieved 78
Return to the Kanalfront 81

5. DEFENSE IN THE WEST (1941) 83

New Equipment 83
Cover for the Navy 85
Back to the Channel 86
The Nonstop Offensive 89

CONTENTS

	Arrival of the FW 190	98
	A Successful Summer	99
	Galland to Berlin	103

6.	ABBEVILLE KIDS AND ST. OMER BOYS (1942)	106
	One Day on the Kanalfront	106
	Winter on the Channel Coast	109
	The Channel Dash	110
	Formation of the Jabostaffeln	113
	Renewal of the British Offensive	115
	Focke-Wulf Summer	116
	The Dieppe Raid	124
	A New Enemy	129
	A Time of Trials	135

7.	SCHLAGETER FIGHTERS ON THE EASTERN FRONT (January–July 1943)	142
	The First Gruppe Leaves the Kanalfront	142
	The Situation in the North Is Stabilized	144
	The Seventh Staffel on the Leningrad Front	146
	Springtime Lull	147
	The Return	148

8.	HOLDING IN THE WEST (January–June 1943)	150
	The Jabo Effort Peaks	150
	Change of Command	153
	Battles with the RAF	156
	A Slow Buildup	160
	Arrival of the Thunderbolts	168

9.	TEMPORARY ASCENDANCY (July–December 1943)	176
	The Battles Escalate	176
	The Schweinfurt-Regensburg Raid	184
	Steady Pressure	191

Defensive Reorganization   196
The Muenster Raid   198
The Second Schweinfurt Raid   200
The Dueren Raid   202
Harder Battles   205

10. THE ALLIES COMMAND THE SKIES (January–
May 1944)   211

The War of Attrition   211
Big Week   219
The Berlin Raids   226
Jaegerschreck—Fear of Fighters   231
The First Attacks on the Oil Industry   239

11. THE INVASION FRONT (6 June–3 September 1944)   242

D-Day   242
The Defensive Plan and Its Execution   243
Hopeless Inferiority   253
Successes and Failures   261
A Black Day for the Lightnings   276
Retreat to the Reich   280

12. SUPPORT FOR THE ARMY (September–
December 1944)   284

Disorganization and Recovery   284
Operation Market Garden   290
A Dreary Autumn   296
The Battle of the Ardennes   311
III/JG 54 Returns to Combat   318

13. UNTERNEHMEN BODENPLATTE—The Attack
on Allied Airfields (1 January 1945)   323

JG 26 Gets the Word   323
I/JG 26 and III/JG 54 Attack Grimbergen   325

II/JG 26 Attacks Brussels-Evere   331
III/JG 26 Attacks Brussels-Evere   338
The Balance   340

14.   THE FINAL BATTLES (January–May 1945)   343

Attrition Continues   343
The Spirit of the Geschwader   350
Breakup and Consolidation   353
The Defenses Break   368
Himmelfahrtskommandos—Missions to Heaven   376
The Lines Close In   380

SOURCES   392

TABLE OF EQUIVALENT RANKS—GERMAN AIR FORCE,
   U.S. ARMY AIR FORCE, AND ROYAL AIR FORCE   400

GLOSSARIES:
    1. Abbreviations (non-German)   403
    2. Aviation Terms   403
    3. Aircraft Types   404
    4. German Terms   408

JG 26 Tables of Organization   413

JG 26 Victory Claims—A Statistical Summary   424

JG 26 Casualties—A Statistical Summary   426

INDEX   428

FOREWORD

Generalleutnant Adolf Galland, Ret.

I AM PLEASED TO COMPLY WITH THE AUTHOR'S REQUEST TO WRITE A foreword to this book, the first detailed history of a Luftwaffe combat unit to be written by an American in the English language. This unit, Jagdgeschwader 26 "Schlageter," JG 26, was one with which I had a long and close relationship. In my travels I am frequently reminded of the English-speaking world's continued fascination with World War II fighter combat. It is therefore surprising that only a few balanced portrayals of the German side of the air war have appeared in English. Many authors have stressed the exploits of the Experten, or aces, while paying little attention to the day-to-day activities of the fighter units and their average pilots. Before you can claim a true understanding of the air war, you must know something of the accomplishments and sacrifices of the individual combat units. This book thus attempts to fill a real gap.

After the loss of World War I, Germany could only manage to train a few dozen fighter pilots and some reconnaissance crews, contrary to the Versailles treaty. This nucleus was transferred to other assignments and used to build up the entire Luftwaffe, so that the fighter arm was understaffed and played an inferior role as a defense force from the very beginning. Fundamental mistakes were made. Great Britain was never considered as a potential adversary; later, the performance of the young Luftwaffe, which had expanded too rapidly, was totally overestimated.

After using many tricks, I was able to join the Luftwaffe fighter force, and in June 1940 I was transferred to JG 26 to take over its Third Gruppe. From that time on, JG 26 was always my favorite fighter unit in the Luftwaffe. Since my two brothers Paul and Wilhelm, both successful fighter pilots, were killed in JG 26—the former as a Staffelkapitaen (Squadron Leader) and the latter as a Gruppenkommandeur (Group Commander)—this has indeed been "my wing."

You might well wonder, as I did, why the author, who is an American and a member of the postwar generation, selected JG 26 as the subject of his book. He has told me that he originally planned to write a history of the Jagdwaffe, the Luftwaffe's fighter arm. A desire to stress the human side of Luftwaffe service forced him to narrow his scope, and his attention was ultimately drawn to JG 26, one of the best German fighter units for much of the war, and the one most respected by the Royal Air Force and the United States Army Air Force. The history of this one unit encompasses in microcosm the rise and fall of the entire German fighter arm, and it remains the Luftwaffe unit best known in the English-speaking world—although as the "Abbeville Kids" rather than by its correct designation. The author interviewed fifty former members of JG 26, from Kommodore to enlisted pilot, plus many members of the ground staff. To ensure the impartiality and completeness of the book, the official records of both sides were searched, and the true course of events in a number of air battles was reestablished for the first time. In its quest for historical objectivity, the book does not gloss over unpleasant facts, especially those concerning conditions in the late 1944–1945 Luftwaffe, after the course of the war had turned irrevocably against Germany. It is almost a miracle that the complete breakdown of pilot morale did not occur prior to D-Day in 1944, when the total collapse was more than obvious.

Even though there is an excellent German history of JG 26 in existence, written by Josef Priller and Otto Boehm, the present work is the best fulfillment that we could wish for. The book inevitably contains errors—the Luftwaffe destroyed most of its records at war's end, and men's memories of events fifty years ago must be considered fallible. Nevertheless, I feel that this book, with its unique perspective on the air war, is a suitable memorial to the fallen men of Jagdgeschwader 26 "Schlageter."

Thanks to Donald L. Caldwell, and success to his profound book, written in full fairness.

ADOLF GALLAND
January 1991

ACKNOWLEDGMENTS

MY GREATEST DEBT OF GRATITUDE IS OWED TO THE VETERANS OF THE
Geschwader whose enthusiastic cooperation made this book possible. I shall never cease to be amazed that my written appeals for assistance—which came from a stranger, a novice author, and a former enemy—were answered with such an outpouring of documents, photographs, and amazingly frank first-person accounts. I am proud that I can now call many of these men my friends. They are: Hermann Ayerle, Ernst Battmer, F. W. Bauerhenne, Guenther Bloemertz, Karl Boehm-Tettelbach, Matthias Buchmann, Joseph Buerschgens, Peter Crump, Heinz Ebeling (deceased), Georg Eder (deceased), Guenther Egli, Xaver Ellenrieder, Adolf Galland, Heinz Gehrke, Georg Genth, Adolf Glunz, Alfred Heckmann, Walter Horten, Erich Jauer, Gerhard Kemen, Gerhard Kroll, Walter Krupinski, Ottomar Kruse, Hans Kukla, Erwin Leykauf, Willi Luerding, Werner Molge, Johannes Naumann, Edu Neumann, Josef Niesmak, Wolfgang Pils, Rolf Pingel, Wolfgang Polster, Hans Prager, Hans-Werner Regenauer, Heinrich Schild, Gottfried Schmidt, Walter Schmidt, Friedrich Schneider, Gerhard Schoepfel, Rolf Schroedter (deceased), Otto Stammberger, Walter Stumpf, Siegfried Sy (deceased), Erhard Tippe, Fritz Ungar, and Gerd Wiegand. Special thanks are owed to Adolf Galland for the foreword and to Joseph Buerschgens for hand-carrying it and the manuscript across two continents.

My search for participants from the "other side," while necessarily less exhaustive, was equally rewarding. My thanks go to the following USAAF and RCAF veterans: William Beyer, William Binnebose, George Brooks, William Capron, George Carpenter, H. H. Christensen, Elmer Clarey, McCauley Clark, Darrell Cramer, Jack Curtis, Bernard Dennehy, James Doyle, Walker Mahurin, Merle Olmsted, Chet Patterson, Herman Schonenberg, Robert Seelos, Luther Smith, Rod Smith, John Truluck, George van den Heuvel, Chuck Yeager, and Hubert Zemke.

I must next acknowledge the air war historians and archivists who welcomed me into their fraternity with generous gifts of time, leads, photographs, and information. These men are: Arno Abendroth, Bernd Barbas, Steve Blake, Winfried Bock, Walt Boyne, James Crow, Joachim Eickhoff, Pat Eriksson, Vanackere Etienne, John Foreman, Werner Girbig, Steve Gotts, Peter Grimm, Ian Hawkins, Carl Hildebrandt, Jim Kitchens, Dave McFarland, Michael Meyer, Eric Mombeek, Werner Oeltjebruns, Michael Payne, Gert Poelchau, W. G. Ramsey, Jean-Louis Roba, Chris Shores, Guenter Sundermann, Helmut Terbeck, Lothair Vanoverbeke, and Tony Wood.

Thanks also go to Horst Amberg, Dagmar Herzog, Steve Jobs, Bob Jones, R. J. Lissner, Laura Muskopf, Josef Priller (fils), Bill Saunders, John Smith III, Karl-Heinz Winkler, and Steve Wozniak for their invaluable assistance.

Motorbuch Verlag has granted me permission to quote translated passages from Josef Priller's *JG 26: Geschichte eines Jagdgeschwaders*. The Bundesarchiv Bildarchiv (Koblenz) and the Imperial War Museum (London) have granted permission to reprint photographs from their collections.

I wish to acknowledge the help given me by the professional staffs of the British Public Records Office, the Bundesarchiv-Militaerarchiv (Freiburg), the Lake Jackson Public Library, the Military Archives Division of the National Archives, the United States Air Force Historical Research Center, and the United States Air Force Museum.

I further wish to thank the USAF Historical Research Center for their tangible support of this work in the form of a USAF-HRC Research Grant.

Last but by no means least, my thanks go to my wife, Jackie, for her unwavering patience and support.

I apologize to any correspondent who cannot find his story or photograph in this volume. Because of the commercial realities of the publishing business, this book has had to be cut severely in length. Additional volumes on JG 26, including a photo album and a war diary, will be published if the success of this first book warrants them.

Any book of this size and scope will contain errors of both omission and commission. I welcome correspondence with anyone who has information to share pertaining to this fascinating period in aviation history. I wish to state further that all quotations in the book that were originally written or spoken in the German language were translated into English by myself. The responsibility for any consequent errors in fact or tone is my own.

DONALD L. CALDWELL
Lake Jackson, Texas
April 1990

INTRODUCTION

ASK ANY WORLD WAR II VETERAN OF THE AMERICAN EIGHTH AIR FORCE or the Royal Air Force's Fighter Command about the Abbeville Kids, and he'll tell you stories of Goering's elite yellow-nosed fighter unit, whose ferocious, slashing attacks on the Allied bomber and fighter formations always seemed to come from the most favorable tactical position—either from head-on, or from out of the sun. Their fame was legendary; their complex of bases behind the French coast of the English Channel was to be avoided, if at all possible.

Read the official Allied histories of the air war, and you'll get a different story. The Luftwaffe had had no elite fighter units; therefore, the Abbeville Kids had never existed. Period. What was the truth? As always in war, "truth" was a flexible commodity, to be molded as needed by the propagandists. Generals rarely praise an enemy's exploits "on the record": to do so encourages an excess of respect, or even fear, for the opposition. However, Allied air intelligence, and thus the Allied High Command, kept a watchful eye from 1941 to mid-1944 on one specific German fighter unit, the one they considered to be the best in the Luftwaffe—Jagdgeschwader 26, commonly abbreviated JG 26. JG 26 gained its greatest notoriety in 1942, when its most successful subordinate unit was based at Abbeville in northern France. The nicknames "Abbeville Boys" and "Abbeville Kids" were coined by the opposing Allied aircrews. The German pilots heard the terms from captured airmen and good-naturedly adopted the names for themselves.

It is true that JG 26 was never officially designated by the Luftwaffe as an elite formation. It became one, nevertheless; initially as a result of outstanding leadership, and then as a natural outgrowth of its war station on the Channel coast, where its mission was to fend off attacks by the best aircraft and airmen that the Allies could muster. For two years, JG 26, with no more than 124 fighters under command, dominated the airspace over northern France and western Belgium. It fought against the Western Allies for the entire war and flew its last missions against the British one day before the armistice that ended the fighting on its front.

This is the story of the men behind the legend.

JG26

1
ORIGINS
1935–1939

THE RESURGENT LUFTWAFFE

THE THROATY ROAR OF AIRCRAFT ENGINES REVERBERATED FOR miles down the river valley. The Rhine barge crews looked upstream. Three dots soon became recognizable as small biplanes, in close formation. The aircraft, Heinkel He 51 fighters, were less than twenty feet above the water and left wakes in the blackish-green Rhine. As the fighters passed the barges, the men below could recognize their bright orange cowlings and waved enthusiastically. The pilots responded by gently rocking their wings and proceeded downstream. Jagdgeschwader 234, "the Rhineland's own" fighter wing, was on patrol.

The fighters had arrived the previous year, as part of the German military force that had moved into the Rhineland. Only one Jagdgruppe (fighter group) of the still-tiny Luftwaffe had participated in the operation. On 7 March 1936, Hptm. Oskar Dinort, the Gruppenkommandeur (group commander) of the Third Gruppe of Jagdgeschwader 134 (abbreviated III/JG 134), was informed of Hitler's decision to reoccupy Germany's western border states, which had remained demilitarized by treaty after the withdrawal of Allied occupation forces in 1930. The Rhineland was to return to the protection of the German Reich. Two Staffeln (squadrons) of Dinort's Gruppe were ordered to circle the cathedral of Cologne at

1

noon on 8 March and then land at the Cologne airport. A Ju 52 transport carrying ammunition for the He 51s of the Gruppe was to meet them at the airport. The mission was duly carried out, and the ammunition was loaded in the fighters. Their guns could not have been fired even if they had been needed, however, as the fighters lacked their synchronization gear.

Hitler's bluff proved successful. Germany's former enemies made no response. At this time the German Luftwaffe, itself forbidden by the Versailles treaty, was barely one year old. On 1 March 1935, the Reichsluftwaffe had been proclaimed by Adolf Hitler as the third service arm of the Wehrmacht (armed forces) of the German Reich. Hermann Goering, Air Minister in Hitler's government, was named Commander-in-Chief. On its day of origin, the new service, soon to be known both inside and outside Germany simply as the Luftwaffe (literally, air force), contained a single fighter unit. This formation, of squadron strength, had been activated at Doeberitz on 1 April 1934 and was equipped with a mixture of Arado Ar 65 and Heinkel He 51 biplane fighters.

The squadron was soon enlarged into a full two-Gruppe Jagdgeschwader (fighter wing), designated Jagdgeschwader 132, and was awarded the honor title "Richthofen," after Germany's most famous fighter pilot. The Richthofen Geschwader provided a cadre of fully trained fighter pilots to serve as flight and Staffel leaders in the rapidly expanding Jagdwaffe (fighter arm). The staff of the Reichswehr, the defense force that the Versailles treaty permitted Germany, had kept close tabs on the veteran pilots from the World War. These men were now offered commissions into senior flying command positions. Non-flying commanders and staff officers, and senior enlisted ground staff, were drafted from the 100,000-man Reichswehr. The German aviation industry had stayed current by building designs for foreign customers; for Lufthansa, the state-owned airline; and for the numerous German "sport flying" organizations. A number of enthusiastic young pilots had been trained under various subterfuges. The Jagdwaffe was therefore able to expand rapidly.

A second fighter wing, Jagdgeschwader 134 "Horst Wessel," had grown to full three-Gruppe strength by early 1936. Hptm. Dinort's III/JG 134 soon split from its parent unit. As noted above, it was ordered to move to Germany's western border regions on 8

March 1936. III/JG 134 was assigned permanent bases in the Rhineland, where it formed the nucleus of a new Geschwader which was ultimately to become JG 26. Dinort's third Staffel, the 7th (7/JG 134), left the Gruppe on 8 March, flying from Cologne to nearby Duesseldorf. This unit, renumbered 5/JG 134, remained in Duesseldorf for more than a year as an independent Jagdstaffel (fighter squadron), flying a mixture of Ar 65s, Ar 68s, and He 51s. The rest of III/JG 134, comprising the Stab (staff), the 8th and 9th Staffeln, and a newly formed 7th Staffel, settled in with their He 51s at the Cologne airport.

On 11 January 1937 a new Geschwader headquarters was activated at the Duesseldorf airport. The new unit was designated Jagdgeschwader 234, but at first commanded no flying units. On 3 March Major Werner Rentsch activated a new, independent fighter Gruppe, II/JG 234, at Duesseldorf, from a cadre provided by 5/JG 134. The Gruppe's three Staffeln (the 4th, 5th, and 6th) were equipped with Arado Ar 68 biplanes. Veterans of the period retain fond memories of the mock dogfights between the Arados of II/JG 234 and the Heinkels of III/JG 134.

III/JG 134, now under Hptm. Walter Grabmann, was redesignated I/JG 234 on 15 March 1937. Its Staffeln were renumbered, becoming the 1st, 2nd, and 3rd Staffeln of JG 234. The Gruppe was soon re-equipped with the Luftwaffe's new monoplane fighter, the Messerschmitt Bf 109B, and moved on 8 June 1937 to a new Luftwaffe airbase at Cologne-Ostheim.

II/JG 234 began receiving its Bf 109Bs in November 1937. The Geschwader was the second, after JG 132 "Richthofen," to be fully equipped with the Messerschmitt fighter. The Bf 109 was to become the world's most-produced fighter, and one of its most famous. Willy Messerschmitt's elegantly simple monoplane was a radical departure from Germany's previous fighters, both in its light construction and in its high wing loading. The first production version, the Bf 109B, was powered by a Junkers Jumo 210D inverted-vee liquid cooled engine of 720 horsepower and had a top speed of 290 mph and a service ceiling of 26,900 feet. It was armed with only three rifle-caliber machine guns, 7.9-mm MG 17s, but the wings were soon adapted to take armament, and the next models, the Bf 109C and Bf 109D, carried two MG 17s in the wings and two above the engine. Initial production rates were low, as Messerschmitt considered these variants to be only interim models until the much more powerful engines for which the fighter had been designed became available. Interim or not, the Bf 109B was superior in performance to any other fighter in service in continental Europe, a fact soon to be made manifestly plain over the Spanish battlefields.

THE CONDOR LEGION

On 25 July 1936, Adolf Hitler was approached in Berlin by a Spanish officer bearing a letter from General Francisco Franco, the leader of the Spanish Nationalist insurgents. Franco requested a few Ju 52 transports to assist him in moving his Moroccan troops across the Strait of Gibraltar to the Spanish mainland. Hitler assented at once, setting in motion an extended trial period for the Luftwaffe's men and machines that lasted for almost three years and established the doctrines that governed the Luftwaffe in the World War to come.

A full-sized German air fleet, the Condor Legion, was soon operational in Spain. The Ju 52s were flown in by air; other aid had to be smuggled past the Republican blockade in ships. The first shipload included six dismantled He 51 fighters and their pilots, led by the young Oblt. Hannes Trautloft, "on leave" from 9/JG 134 in Cologne. At least two more of the original six pilots, Lt. Herwig Knueppel and Lt. Wolf-Heinrich Freiherr von Houwald, were also from III/JG 134. During the nearly three years of the Spanish Civil War, 126 commissioned pilots and 200 enlisted pilots served in Jagdgruppe 88 (J88), the Condor Legion's fighter component. This number was equal to one-half of all the fighter pilots serving in Germany in May 1939. Thus a substantial percentage of JG 26's prewar pilots saw combat in Spain. The most famous of these men at the time of his Spanish service was Hptm. Gotthardt Handrick, the winner of the modern pentathlon in the 1936 Berlin Olympics. Handrick took command of Jagdgruppe 88 in mid-1937 and assumed command of I/JG 26 on his return to Germany in July 1938. Another JG 26 "name" who served in Spain was Adolf Galland, who in late 1937 at the age of 25 was given command of 3/J88, the third of the Gruppe's three Staffeln. Unfortunately for Galland, his Staffel was the last to be re-equipped with Bf 109s, and his tour in Spain was spent flying He 51s in the ground support role. On his return from Spain he was considered an "attack pilot" and was given command of a Staffel of Henschel Hs 123 ground assault aircraft, which he led in the Polish campaign in the fall of 1939, and from which he escaped only through subterfuge—he persuaded a flight surgeon that he could no longer fly in the open-cockpit biplanes for "medical reasons" and was ordered to a Bf 109 unit in time for the Western campaign the following spring.

Spanish service was much sought after by ambitious officers of the Jagdwaffe, promising a short, guaranteed tour of duty, a chance to gain a reputation while sharpening combat skills, and an almost guaranteed promotion upon return to the homeland. Understandably, the German pilots' opportunities in Spain were not entirely without risk. At least four pilots from JG 26's predecessor units were killed while on duty in Spain.

The development of tactical doctrine was as important to the German airmen in Spain as the testing of men and equipment. Close support of infantry, with ground control; mass bombing of population centers; large scale aerial resupply—all were tested first in Spain. Of most importance to JG 26 was the development of fighter formations and doctrine. In 1937, the Condor Legion flew in the same close formations as the rest of the world's air forces, based on the Kette of three aircraft. After its introduction to service, the Germans quickly realized that the Bf 109B, the fastest service fighter in the world, was unsuited for these close formations. Werner Moelders, Galland's successor in command of 3/J88, is credited with the development of the "finger four" Schwarm (flight) formation, so-called because the relationship of its four aircraft resembled that of the fingertips of an outstretched hand. His most important innovation, however, was the Rotte, or element of two aircraft, which became the basic fighting unit. The job of the Rottenfuehrer, or element leader, was to attack; the job of the Rottenflieger, or wingman, was to protect and follow his leader. Lateral spacing between aircraft was increased to two hundred yards, the turning radius of the Bf 109. The aircraft could thus break together, to attack, or toward one another, for mutual defense. The Schwarm was 600 yards across and was hard to maneuver as a unit until Moelders developed the cross-over turn, in which the outside aircraft of the formation made the sharpest turn. He also staggered the Schwaerme (flights) of each Staffel in altitude, which both improved the ability of the formation's pilots to sight the enemy and made the formation itself less conspicuous in the glare of the sun. The formation leader was able to control his widely spaced unit by means of radio.

Moelders's reports to the Luftwaffe High Command in 1938 and 1939 resulted in the reorganization of the Jagdwaffe from units of three aircraft, the Kette, to units of four, the Schwarm. This did not require a major change in the tables of organization, since the strength of a Staffel remained the same, twelve aircraft (four Ketten became three Schwaerme). As it was standard doctrine for the Geschwaderkommodore (wing commander) and each Gruppenkommandeur to lead flights containing their staff officers, an extra plane and pilot did have to be found for each of the staff formations. It took some time to work out these details, as the staffs were very small and contained no supernumerary flying personnel. A tactical manual by Hptm. Trautloft, who joined the staff of a fighter training school after his return from Spain, introduced the new procedures to the flying units.

DAYS OF PEACE

The peacetime routine of Jagdgeschwader 234 was similar to that of fighter units around the world—formation flying, simulated aerial combat, and firing on ground targets. Joint field exercises with the army became more frequent in the late 1930s, as it became apparent that Germany was fated to enter once again into offensive warfare. Aerial gunnery practice was a problem, as central Europe then, as now, was very crowded. A high point for the flying and ground crews of the Staffeln was the annual excursion to the Luftwaffe's North Sea training base on the island of Sylt, where the pilots could sate their aggressiveness with live firing on towed targets. "Buzz jobs," or low-altitude flights, were normally forbidden, but periodic "propaganda flights" were ordered for the purpose of impressing the local civilian population and, incidentally, the French. These flights were flown in close formation at the lowest possible altitude up the Rhine valley, from Cologne past Coblenz to Bingen. The pilots made the most of these opportunities to show off in their Heinkel and Arado biplanes, whose attractive light gray finishes were accented by garish orange trim. (From 1935 to 1937 each Jagdgeschwader painted its biplane fighters' cowlings and fuselage top decking in a characteristic color—that of JG 234 was orange.) The arrival of the Bf 109s in their somber dark green warpaint brought this ostentatious identification scheme to an end. Geschwader and Staffel emblems were soon designed and painted on the aircraft, both as a means of identification and as a demonstration of unit pride.

Major Eduard Ritter von Schleich, a World War fighter pilot known to the Allies as the "Black Knight," arrived in mid-1937 to take command of II/JG 234. Von Schleich was a Bavarian who had been knighted by Kaiser Wilhelm II after receiving Germany's highest World War I medal for heroism, the *Pour le Mérite*. He was well known for his chivalrous, courtly demeanor and proved a popular commander. His Gruppe soon moved to a newly constructed airfield near its previous home in Duesseldorf. I/JG 234 and II/JG 234 remained subordinated to JG 134 "Horst Wessel" until 1 November 1938, when the newly promoted Oberst von Schleich was named the first Kommodore of the Geschwader, which was redesignated that same day from JG 234 to JG 132. (The flying units of the prewar Luftwaffe were assigned and numbered on a geographic basis. Twice during this period the air districts were redrawn, resulting in a renumbering of the flying units.)

The original cadre of the Geschwader had played a key role in one of Hitler's first successful bluffs, the military reoccupation of the Rhineland. The local citizens, their pride in their nation and its armed forces restored, adopted the young servicemen as their own, inviting them to various civil ceremonies and parades and coming in large numbers to the numerous air shows put on for their benefit at the Cologne and Duesseldorf air bases. Eventually someone suggested that the fighter unit take the name of one of the local nationalist heroes. The suggestion was accepted with alacrity by the Luftwaffe High Command, and on 11 December 1938, with appropriate ceremony, the Geschwader officially became Jagdgeschwader 132 "Schlageter."

ALBERT LEO SCHLAGETER

Albert Leo Schlageter was a native of Schoenau, in the Black Forest. Nineteen years old when the First World War began, he enlisted in the artillery and soon was made an officer. After the Armistice, he marched his battery back in full military order to the Rhine River, where he dismissed his men. He then joined the Freikorps, a loosely organized group of paramilitary units, and in 1919 took part in the expulsion of the Bolsheviks from Riga, Lithuania. After more fighting, now against the Poles, he returned home to the Rhineland, where he soon took up arms again. His opponents this time were the French, who occupied the Rhineland while overseeing the payment of reparations under the terms of the Versailles treaty. These reparations included much of the Ruhr's coal production and industrial output and were in large part responsible for the terrible inflation that crippled Germany in the early 1920s. Schlageter was captured after blowing up a section of the Duisburg-Duesseldorf railroad track and was sentenced to death by a French military court. He was shot by a firing squad on 26 May 1923. His burial plot became a nationalist shrine. After the French troops were withdrawn, a large, slender, stainless steel cross was erected on the site, and ceremonies were held on each anniversary of his execution. The Nazis were quick to capitalize on this ready-made nationalist saga, but as Schlageter's Roman Catholicism was well known, they were unable to appropriate him totally into the Nazi canon. The Geschwader adopted as its emblem a gothic S in a shield; this was painted on each of the unit's aircraft in the period 1939–1941. Less well known is another version of the emblem, in which the S is superimposed on a slender Christian cross.

WAR LOOMS

Each member of the Geschwader was now entitled to wear a band inscribed "Jagdgeschwader Schlageter" around the right cuff of his service jacket. This mark of distinction was a real boost to morale. JG 132 was only the third fighter unit to be awarded such an honor title. One practical result of this distinction was that for propaganda, if not operational, reasons, the Schlageter unit was always among the first to receive new equipment. Re-equipment with Bf 109E-1s began in December 1938 and was complete by the end of January. This was the model of the Messerschmitt fighter in which the Schlageter pilots would shortly go to war.

The Bf 109E-1 was powered with the DB 601A, an 1100

horsepower inverted-vee liquid cooled engine from Daimler-Benz. The new engine improved the fighter's performance dramatically—top speed was increased to 342 mph and service ceiling to 34,450 feet. The only fighter in the world able to challenge these figures was the Supermarine Spitfire, which was just beginning to enter service with the Royal Air Force. The only weakness of the E-1 apparent within the Luftwaffe was its armament, which was the same as that of the earlier variants. The four 7.9-mm machine guns had to be retained until new cannon designs could be perfected.

On 1 May 1939 all Luftwaffe flying units were renumbered for the second time. JG 132 became JG 26; its official designation was now Jagdgeschwader 26 "Schlageter." Oberst von Schleich continued to command the Geschwader from Duesseldorf. Major Handrick led the Cologne-based First Gruppe, while Hptm. Werner Palm, and later Hptm. Herwig Knueppel, ran the Second Gruppe from Duesseldorf.

The Geschwader's peacetime routine had but a few short months to continue. Tension in Europe mounted throughout the summer of 1939. On 25 August, I/JG 26 was ordered to move from Cologne to Odendorf, across the Rhine in the Eifel forest. At 0100 that same day, II/JG 26 received orders to relocate "inconspicuously" from Duesseldorf to Boenninghardt, west of the Rhine near the Dutch border, and to be operational in the new location by 1815. The start of the war on 1 September thus found the Geschwader "in the field"; its mission—the air defense of the Western frontier.

2
SITZKRIEG AND
BLITZKRIEG
1 September 1939–
26 June 1940

WAR BEGINS

On the 1st of September 1939, Hitler unleashed the blitzkrieg on a half-comprehending world. The offensive components of the Luftwaffe were its Kampfgeschwader, Stukageschwader, and Zerstoerergeschwader (bomber, dive-bomber, and heavy fighter wings). These supported the army in its attack on Poland. A few Bf 109 units were used in Poland, but most were held back for defensive purposes. According to current Luftwaffe doctrine, single-engined fighters (that is, Bf 109s) were suitable for little more than point defense, while the twin-engined Bf 110 heavy fighters were capable of handling both bomber escort and air superiority missions. Jagdgeschwader 26 found itself stationed near its peacetime bases. Its stated mission was "to protect the industrial region and the western German border." The expected RAF attacks never came, and the fighter pilots found themselves sitting in their cockpits on the ground, at Sitzbereitschaft (cockpit readiness), for hours on end. Their bases faced the neutral nations of Belgium and the Netherlands, and the eager pilots were somewhat jealous of their brethren farther south, who were better positioned to come to grips with the French and the British.

FORMATION OF THE THIRD GRUPPE

The Third Gruppe of the Geschwader was established at Werl on 23 September. Its first Kommandeur left the Geschwader

10

in November and was replaced by Hptm. Ernst Freiherr von Berg. The initial strength of the Gruppe was only one Staffel; initial equipment was a mixture of obsolete Ar 68s, Ar 66s, and Kl 35s, with a handful of Bf 109Cs. The Gruppe was rapidly expanded by the time-honored expedient of carving up established units. The 2nd Staffel contributed half of its pilots and ground staff to the new 7th Staffel; the 4th Staffel apparently moved almost in total to the new 8th Staffel; while the 9th Staffel received its cadre from a Zerstoerer unit, II/ZG 26. The Gruppe was brought up to strength in aircraft in October, with the receipt of thirty Bf 109E-1s. The Geschwader's organization was now the standard one of the period—three Gruppen, each with three Staffeln numbered in a single sequence. (That is, the First Gruppe contained the 1st, 2nd, and 3rd Staffel; the Second Gruppe, the 4th, 5th, and 6th Staffel; the Third Gruppe, the 7th, 8th, and 9th Staffel.)

THE GESCHWADER'S FIRST VICTORY

On 28 September, Lt. Joseph "Jupp" Buerschgens, a 22-year-old career officer whose home was in nearby Duesseldorf, was ordered to escort a Henschel Hs 126 on a spotting mission over the Saar, far to the south of the Geschwader's usual patrol area. The 2nd Staffel pilot accompanied the reconnaissance plane as far as the border and prepared to turn back, in accordance with his orders. Just then he sighted eight French Curtiss Hawk 75As below him; beyond them were three more. They were above Germany, and thus fair game. Furthermore, they had spotted the slow Henschel and were circling for an attack. Buerschgens flipped his Messerschmitt into a quick split-S, burst past the eight circling fighters, and opened fire on the Curtiss closest to the Henschel. The French fighter shuddered and spun out, smoking. It was reported later to have crashed near Tuendorf, but Buerschgens was much too busy to watch it fall. He recovered from his power dive at 6,500 feet and zoomed to regain altitude and a position to attack the other fighters. He broke up an attack on the Henschel, which was able to make its escape after taking only seven hits.

Buerschgens now faced odds of one to ten. He utilized his Messerschmitt's superiority in vertical maneuvering to stay out of range, almost ramming one plane. His aircraft was then struck

11

several times by French fire. His throttle was shot from his hand; his radiator was holed and began to leak; bullets from behind him hissed past his head and into his instrument panel. A bullet then slammed into his right shoulder. In severe pain, Buerschgens leaned forward, pressed the stick against his body with his left hand, and dove away. He made his escape and sought to find a place to land, his visibility to the right obscured by spurting blood. He sighted a meadow in front of him, a small stream, and beyond these a German wire entanglement. He bellied his plane in smoothly; the barbed wire brought it to a halt. Buerschgens had landed in a minefield in front of the German West Wall defenses, and an army patrol had to be sent out to rescue him. His smashed shoulder required eight months to heal. While in the hospital, Jupp Buerschgens, the first pilot of the Geschwader to score an air victory, was awarded the Iron Cross Second Class.

10(NACHT)/JG 26 AND THE BATTLE OF THE HELGOLAND BIGHT

The offensive-minded Luftwaffe High Command paid very little attention to air defense in the prewar years. Night fighting was neglected almost entirely. In early September 1939, a number of night fighter Staffeln were hurriedly organized, and equipped with obsolete day fighters. Tactical doctrine was rudimentary; their mission was described as "flak support." One of these units was 10(Nacht)/JG 26. Its commander was Oblt. Johannes Steinhoff, who transferred in from the demonstration unit 1(Nachtjagd)/ LG 1. The parent Geschwader, JG 26, contributed only a few pilots. For two months, the Staffel flew evening and dawn patrols from Bonn-Hangelar in obsolescent Bf 109Cs, entirely without result.

The Sitzkrieg or "Sitting War," the "Phony War" to the Allies in the west, was fought in the air under a peculiar set of gentlemen's rules. Neither side wished to be the first to hit civilians, and thus provoke the other to reprisals. The night bombers of the RAF flew small-scale leaflet raids over Germany, while the RAF's day bombers were restricted to naval targets. The earliest RAF raids on ships at the Wilhelmshaven naval base met with some success, and the Germans beefed up their defenses. One Staffel that was moved

12

north to the area of the seaports was 10(Nacht)/JG 26, its night duties temporarily abandoned.

By mid-December, Wilhelmshaven was protected by two of the Wehrmacht's first radar units and by about one hundred Bf 109s and Bf 110s, all under the command of Obstlt. Carl Schumacher, Kommodore of JG 1. On 18 December, the staff of RAF Bomber Command scheduled a raid on warships believed to be berthed in the port, despite forecasts of crystal-clear weather. About thirty Wellington bombers took off at two-minute intervals starting at 0930 hours and after forming up headed across the North Sea. The bombers made landfall near the Danish-German border at 1230 and turned south toward Wilhelmshaven. Their planned course kept them within range of the German coastal defenses for an hour and a half. The stage was set for a massacre.

Both German radar sets were in working order, and both picked up the British formation some twenty minutes from Wilhelmshaven. The news was initially disregarded at JG 1 headquarters—"seagulls" was one reason suggested for the radar plot—and it took the full twenty minutes for the news to register "officially"; by then the bombers were passing overhead. In the interim, the frantic Luftwaffe radar officer had called the airfields directly. Only Oblt. Steinhoff's six Bf 109Cs were airborne and in a position to intercept the Wellingtons before they reached Wilhelmshaven.

Steinhoff's pilots had been well briefed on the defenses of the Wellington. It had an effective rear turret containing two .303-inch machine guns and adequate frontal armament, but it was defenseless from the beam or below. As ordered, the Messerschmitts made beam approaches, which required difficult deflection aiming. Steinhoff had to make two beam attacks on his target before the bomber burst into flames and fell inverted into the sea. His pilots fired off all their ammunition and claimed five more Wellingtons. The remaining bombers closed up their formation and passed over the docks without releasing their bombs. The ships were too close to land to be bombed, according to their orders.

By now, two more German fighter formations had closed on the struggling bombers, and the one-sided battle continued. When the last fighter turned back, ten bombers had crashed at sea or force-landed on shore. Two more ditched in the North Sea, and another three were destroyed in forced landings back in England.

13

Schumacher's pilots filed a total of thirty-four victory claims, of which twenty-six were ultimately allowed; this was almost double the actual RAF losses. The RAF claimed to have downed a dozen German fighters, while actual losses were two Bf 109s.

The German victory was not nearly as complete as it could have been. Ground control, as mentioned, was poor, and there were also problems in the air. Many attacks were not pressed to a sufficiently close range. And many fighters were damaged by the bombers' rear gunners, an indication that orders to concentrate on beam attacks had been ignored. For its part, RAF Bomber Command put as good a face on its defeat as possible, blaming it on "poor air discipline." But the British survivors knew better; news spread quickly through the still-small bomber force, and the "unofficial" word ultimately prevailed—unescorted daylight bombing raids into the heart of the German defenses were suicidal.

THE WINTER DOLDRUMS

Before the year's end, Steinhoff's 10(Nacht)/JG 26 was absorbed in a specialist night fighter Gruppe, IV(Nacht)/JG 2, leaving JG 26 and thus this history. For the Geschwader's three Gruppen of day fighters, the boring routine of standing patrols and cockpit readiness continued throughout the winter. The ground crews' monotony was broken by orders to repaint the fuselages of their Messerschmitts from dark green splinter camouflage to pale blue, appropriate to the conditions of air and ground superiority visualized by the Wehrmacht for the coming spring campaign. The first Bf 103E-3s, which were merely E-1s with increased armament, were taken on charge by the Geschwader. The two wing-mounted machine guns of the E-1 were replaced by 20-mm MG/FF cannon. Messerschmitt planned to equip the new fighter with a third 20-mm cannon, mounted between the engine cylinder banks and firing through the propeller hub. But trials revealed that the new cannon's vibrations damaged the fighter's light structure, and in fact no Bf 109E saw operational service carrying an engine cannon.

The Geschwader's pilots, all of them professional military men, were anxious to see combat. The Jagdgeschwader facing the French border were building fine records. JG 53 was especially active; Hptm. Werner Moelders of that unit scored ten personal victories during the Sitzkrieg. The Schlageter fighters' record was, in comparison, mediocre. After Buerschgens's combat, only one additional victory was scored by the Geschwader during the Sitzkrieg. It was obtained on 7 November by Lt. Joachim Muencheberg, adjutant of the Third Gruppe, who shot an RAF Blenheim light bomber into the Rhine River near Opladen.

On 9 December, Oberst von Schleich was relieved of the command of the Geschwader, in line with a policy calling for the removal of all World War I veterans from flying posts. While personally disappointing to von Schleich, the change made sense, not only from a physiological standpoint, but because the Luftwaffe suffered, then and always, from a serious lack of experienced officers for upper-level staff positions and ground commands. The Black Knight of the First World War went on to hold a number of responsible commands during the Second, ultimately reaching the rank of Generalleutnant and the position of commander of the Luftwaffe ground organization in Norway. The energetic, courtly von Schleich had imprinted the Schlageter Geschwader with his own self-confident professionalism and had served as a valuable role model for the unit's young pilots.

The new Geschwaderkommodore was Major Hugo Witt, whose military service dated back to the earliest days of the Reichswehr immediately after World War I. His career had been varied—he had suffered severe facial burns in the crash of the dirigible *Hindenburg*—and largely successful, but at age 39 his days as a combat commander were numbered. Sure enough, he was to be relieved on 24 June 1940, two days after the conclusion of the French campaign.

Luftwaffe organization during this period was still somewhat fluid. New Geschwader were being formed from formerly independent Gruppen, and other Gruppen were traded back and forth. A Jagdgeschwader had the staff to administer and to control three Gruppen; it was apparently not immediately obvious that it was more efficient to administer and control the *same* three Gruppen. I/JG 26 moved to Boenninghardt in February and was there subordinated to JG 51, although it was still treated administratively as part of its home Geschwader. The Gruppe remained under the tactical control of another Geschwader for most of the French campaign. To further complicate matters, JG 26 picked up as its third Gruppe

15

a succession of Jagdgruppen from other Geschwader. As they are of only tangential interest, and as documentation of their activities is poor, these attached Gruppen will be mentioned again only in passing. Fortunately for the historian, Gruppe-swapping as a routine policy ended with the conclusion of the French campaign in June.

THE BLITZKRIEG STRIKES WEST

As the bitter winter of 1939–1940 ended, the impatient pilots of JG 26 awaited the inevitable spring campaign with optimism. They believed their mount, the Bf 109E-3, to be the best single-engined fighter in the world. Mock dogfights that winter with the Bf 110s of ZG 26 "Horst Wessel" had further increased their confidence. The Bf 109 had proved to be a far better fighter than the twin-engined Bf 110.

An objective assessment of JG 26's likely opponents shows the pilots' self-assurance to have been well founded. The Bf 109E-3 was a proven fighter with an armament of two cannon and two machine guns, a top speed of 350 mph at 19,500 feet, and a service ceiling of 34,500 feet. No continental aircraft in front-line service offered comparable performance. The only equally matched opponent appeared to be the British Supermarine Spitfire, as yet an unknown quantity. No Spitfires were based in France; the only RAF fighters on the continent were a few obsolete Gloster Gladiators and Hawker Hurricanes, the RAF's most numerous fighter. The Hurricane model in France was armed with eight light machine guns; it had a top speed of 310 mph at 18,000 feet and a service ceiling of 33,400 feet.

Of the Germans' West European opponents, the Dutch had a well-organized air force featuring modern indigenous designs by the firm of Anthony Fokker, but their planes were pitifully few in numbers. The Belgian Air Force could be dismissed out of hand as small and ill-equipped. What of the French? Wracked by the disruptions of nationalization, the modernization of their large air force lagged far behind schedule. Alone of the new French designs, the Dewoitine D 520 was the equal on paper to the Messerschmitt, with an armament of one cannon and two machine guns and a top speed of 334 mph. However, only one Groupe de Chasse was operational with the fighter. Another new fighter, the Bloch MB 152, was proving to be a failure in service; most were grounded for various defects. The Bloch had a top speed of only 288 mph. The most numerous French fighter was the Morane Saulnier MS 406, an obsolescent design with a top speed of 304 mph. The most successful French fighter in the coming campaign was of American design and manufacture—the Curtiss Hawk 75A. This handy and robust aircraft had an armament of four machine guns and a top speed of 313 mph.

There is little information available concerning Jagdgeschwader 26's activities during the six-week campaign that resulted in the conquest of France and the Low Countries. Nevertheless, enough data can be pieced together to give a flavor of the activities of the Schlageter fighters during those spring days of long ago. The Stab and the three Gruppen of the Geschwader began the campaign from bases in their home territory of the Rhineland. They were administered by Oberst von Doering's Jagdfliegerfuehrer 2 (Fighter Command 2, abbreviated Jafue 2), which was a component of Genobst. Kesselring's Luftflotte 2. Kesselring's forces supported Genobst. von Bock's Army Group B, which was to attack the Low Countries frontally and draw the British and mobile French forces forward into Belgium, while Genobst. von Rundstedt's Army Group A cut through the "impenetrable" Ardennes forests of southern Belgium and Luxembourg, outflanking the Maginot Line, which ran along the French-German border, and splitting the Allied forces. Jafue 2 contained four Geschwader—JG 3, JG 26, JG 51, and ZG 26. Jagdgeschwader 26, with its own Second and Third Gruppen and the Third Gruppe of JG 3 under command, operated over the Netherlands for the first few days of the campaign, as did I/JG 26, which was attached to JG 51.

The primary mission of the Geschwader on the first morning of the campaign was to sweep across Fortress Holland in advance of Ju 52 transports, which were loaded with paratroopers and air-landing troops. The surviving fighter pilots recall racing across the polders in the gray dawn, light antiaircraft and small-arms tracers arcing ineffectively behind them. Five Dutch aircraft were shot down by the Schlageter fighters, and the Junkers transports' first missions were carried out without hindrance from the air.

Once the Germans had landed, however, they found themselves engaged in fierce combat. The Dutch had not been taken by surprise and fought back bravely. The airfields around Rotterdam and the Hague were soon littered with smashed Luftwaffe transports, and by noon the situation was very much in doubt. In an attempt to clear the "fog of war," Lt. Wolfgang Ludewig of 9/JG 26 was ordered to land near the Hague and ascertain the positions of an infantry division that had landed on several fields in the area that morning. Ludewig was hit by ground fire in his first attempt to land at Ypenburg. After another attempt, and still more damage, he was forced to land in the dunes outside the field. He reported to Gen. von Sponeck, as ordered, but was then unable to take off. Ludewig remained grounded for the duration of the brief Dutch campaign. He finally returned to his unit on 18 May, bearing a commendation from von Sponeck attesting to his skills as an infantryman. Since Ludewig had been carried as missing for several days, a casualty report detailing the entire episode was filed after his return. The report, unique in its dry humor, may still be found in the official files.

By the end of 11 May, the British Expeditionary Force (BEF) and the French Seventh Army had advanced halfway across Belgium and taken up their previously planned (but not fortified) positions along the Meuse and Dyle rivers. Air cover was to be provided by *Groupement 25* of the French Air Force, which contained only twenty-eight MS 406s of GC III/1 and twenty MB 152s of GC II/8, plus the four Hurricane squadrons of the Air Component of the BEF. This small force was reinforced from the Paris area by some of GC III/3's Moranes and from England by three additional Hurricane squadrons. In addition, the Curtiss Hawk 75As of GC I/4 moved forward to Antwerp. According to most sources, this latter unit belonged to *Groupement 23*, whose mission was to cover the French armies holding the hinge point of the Allied advance at the France-Luxembourg border. The transfer of one of the best French fighter units away from the Ardennes area, just as von Rundstedt's forces were advancing into it, is evidence of the skill of the Germans' deception.

It was GC I/4 that confronted JG 26 on 11 May, in the Geschwader's first major air battles of the war. The *Groupe* began the day with twenty-six aircraft. Its Hawks were hit over Antwerp by the Messerschmitts of the Third Gruppe at 1745, and again by the Second Gruppe at 1910. The German pilots claimed six victories, while suffering no casualties. The French claimed three certain victories and one probable victory over the Bf 109s but lost their commander and one enlisted pilot killed, and two other pilots wounded. In addition, many of the Hawks suffered serious damage from the Messerschmitts' cannon fire.

On the same day, fighters of 2/JG 26 encountered MS 406s from GC III/1 or GC III/3 in the Antwerp area. The Staffel destroyed one of the Moranes, but JG 26 suffered its first combat loss of the war, when Fw. Gerhard Herzog was shot down. Herzog fell into the hands of the BEF, was spirited across the Channel, and spent the rest of the war in Canada.

The favorite mission of the Jagdwaffe was the freie Jagd, or free hunt, which was simply a fighter sweep without escort responsibilities. It was an ideal task for the aggressive young pilots, especially in a fluid offensive campaign and under conditions of qualitative and quantitative superiority. Their other major assignment was the Jagdschutz, which translates as "fighter protection." At this stage of the war, this was little more than a patrol of a specified area of the front, protection being offered to any friendly bombers or reconnaissance aircraft encountered. In truth, these were the only two missions for which the Jagdgeschwader of the period were suited— they lacked the training, doctrine, and equipment for close escort, tactical reconnaissance, or ground attack. The task of bomber escort was reserved for Goering's elite twin-engined fighters, the Bf 110s of the Zerstoerergeschwader.

The freie Jagden flown on 12 May failed to make contact with the enemy. On 13 May, the Geschwader began a series of base movements. The Stab and Third Gruppe, and the attached III/JG 3, moved forward to Muenchen-Gladbach near the Dutch border, while the Second Gruppe moved to Uerdingen, also nearer the front. Meanwhile, von Bock continued his steady push through northern Belgium, while von Rundstedt's armor spearheads reached the Meuse River, around Sedan, almost unnoticed. Von Bock's forces played their diversionary role well, advancing in such strength that all available Allied air forces were drawn to oppose them. Among the new units thrown into the battle were several squadrons from RAF Fighter Command's No. 11 Group. The newest British day fighters, the Spitfire and the Defiant, had up until now been withheld from the Continent. However, on this day both saw combat over Holland—against JG 26.

Early in the morning, the six Defiants of "B" Flight, No. 264

Squadron, took off from Horsham St. Faith in easternmost England to patrol the Dutch coast. Defiants were turreted, two-man fighters with no forward-firing armament. They were given top cover by the six Spitfires of "A" flight, No. 66 Squadron. The Allied fighter pilots spotted a number of Ju 87Bs dive bombing a railroad line and attacked them successfully—ten victory credits were awarded for downed Stukas. The British fighters were then hit by the Messerschmitts of 5/JG 26. The Spitfires were successful in avoiding combat, except for one that force-landed in Belgium with combat damage. The Defiants, far slower than the German fighters, were unable to evade them and suffered severely. Five of the six were shot down. The Staffel claimed victories over seven Spitfires and one Defiant, while the true British losses were one Spitfire and five Defiants.

No. 264 Squadron's Defiants shot down one Bf 109E, that of Lt. Karl Borris. Borris, a member of JG 26 from December 1939 to V-E Day, kept a personal diary in addition to his logbook. He used his notes to compose the following account of this mission:

> The telephone shrills—orders from the Kommodore. The 5th Staffel is to take off immediately for a Jagdschutz mission in the area around Dordrecht. We hurry to our machines, take off, and roar westward. It is shortly after 0600. Clouds appear at about 2,500 meters [8,000 feet]; it is somewhat hazy. Below us lies the mouth of the Rhine. We are south of Dordrecht. Suddenly someone cries on the radio, "Aircraft right! Achtung, Spitfires!" Enemy contact with a mixed British formation . . . I bank toward a Defiant. I can clearly see the four machine guns in its turret firing; however, I do not think they can track me in a dogfight. I approach closer, and open fire at about seventy meters range. At this moment, something hits my aircraft, hard. I immediately pull up into the clouds and examine the damage. The left side of my instrument panel is shot through; a round has penetrated the Revi [reflex gunsight]; and a fuel line has obviously been hit—the cockpit is swimming in gasoline. The engine coughs and quits, starved of fuel. I push a wing over and drop from the clouds. Unbuckle, canopy off, out! I must first pull myself up against a strong headwind. I finally get out, at an altitude of about 800 meters [2,600 feet] . . . I turn a few somersaults, find the handle, and open my parachute. . . . A light northeast wind blows me toward the mouth of the Rhine. I sideslip with all my strength and land on the outermost dike wall of the last polder of the delta.

After landing all alone in a barren, deserted no-man's-land, Borris finally made it back to his home Staffel on 17 May. Fighter Command did not again send its precious Spitfires or painfully vulnerable Defiants over Holland. The former were needed at home, if the British Isles were to be defended; the crews of the latter had to be given time to devise new tactics, if they were to survive the coming battles.

The Dutch Air Force flew one of its last sorties early on the 13th. The last operational Fokker T-V medium bomber took off from Schipol at 0519 to bomb the Moerdijk bridge, escorted by two Fokker G-1 twin-boomed fighters. The bomber made two runs on the bridge at low altitude but failed to damage it. The three aircraft attempted return to Schipol at minimum altitude—in the words of the Dutch, at *"huisje-boompje-beestje,"* or house-tree-animal level. The small formation was hit by 4/JG 26 near Dordrecht, and the T-V and one G-1 were shot down in flames by the 4th's Kapitaen, Oblt. Karl Ebbighausen. The sole remaining G-1 landed at Schipol at 0559.

The First Gruppe was also active on the 13th. Around eighteen Bf 109s from this unit, probably two Staffeln, attacked six MS 406s of GC III/3 over Breda in the Netherlands. The French fighters had just intercepted a German medium bomber formation out of the cover of a rain squall. Lt. Eberhard Henrici of 1/JG 26 shot down one Morane, whose pilot was able to make a forced landing and reach the French lines. The commander of the French formation fought a prolonged, lone battle before ramming a Messerschmitt and crashing to his own death. The German victim was probably Uffz. Hermann Speck, JG 26's first combat fatality. Another 1st Staffel pilot was shot down in this engagement, but survived with wounds.

BREAKTHROUGH ON THE MEUSE

The next day, 14 May, saw the German victory secured. The Allies, finally alerted to their peril, attacked the German bridge-heads across the Meuse River with all available air forces. The Jagdgeschwader of von Massow's Jafue 3 flew 814 interception sorties, claiming eighty-nine Allied aircraft downed. By day's end, the British and French bomber squadrons had been decimated. Since all of the mobile Allied units were far to the north in Belgium, and the French had neglected to maintain a strategic reserve, the Germans could continue pouring their armor across the Meuse and on to the Channel coast, virtually unimpeded by air or ground attacks against their flanks. The Allied units to the north were heavily engaged by Army Group B and could not turn to face the new threat at their rear. The Germans had sprung their trap, and the best of the Allied formations were caught in it.

The Schlageter fighters did not benefit from the good hunting to their south. On this day, JG 26 was supporting von Bock's own attempt at a breakthrough, in the Gembloux gap between the Dyle and Meuse river lines. The 14th also brought the capitulation of the Netherlands, which permitted the Luftwaffe units still engaged in that nation, including I/JG 26, to join the main battle.

On 16 May, JG 26 saw combat over France for the first time. Over the next two days, the Geschwaderstab and the Second and Third Gruppen, with the attached III/JG 3, moved their bases forward into eastern Belgium. The 18th found them supporting von Rundstedt's panzers in their race to the Channel. The armor, part of von Kleist's Panzer Group, was cutting diagonally across von Bock's front; boundary lines on the ground or in the air meant little.

The Second Gruppe was credited with shooting down twelve Allied fighters in the Douai-Cambrai area between 1615 and 1630 that afternoon—ten MS 406s, one Hawk 75A, and one Hurricane. The Allied units have not been determined; the situation had grown so chaotic that any of a number of units could have been involved. Only one JG 26 Messerschmitt was shot down on the 18th, and its pilot was freed from the French three days later.

May 19th brought a continuation of the previous day's fighting over the front. The Second Gruppe claimed three victories, but suffered a serious loss—the unit's Kommandeur, Hptm. Herwig Knueppel, one of the original "Spaniards," and with three recent victories the most successful JG 26 unit leader, did not return that evening from a combat with fighters over Lille. He was carried as missing for two days, until his body was found. Oblt. Karl Ebbighausen, Kapitaen of 4/JG 26 and another successful air fighter, was named Knueppel's temporary replacement.

The next week brought a diminution in the air fighting but no rest for the weary ground staffs. All of the Geschwader's component units moved yet again—I/JG 26 to Antwerp, and the rest of the Geschwader to fields in far western Belgium. The British Expeditionary Force succeeded in reaching Dunkirk, its one remaining port, in good order, and began establishing a defensive perimeter, while the Royal Navy completed its hurried plans for the now inevitable evacuation. Fighter Command was instructed to provide as much protection as possible to the beleaguered infantry without jeopardizing its ability to defend the home island. Over the next few days, single RAF fighter squadrons were ordered to sweep the coast from Boulogne to Ostend. Massive dogfights on the 24th and the 27th resulted in ten victory claims by the Schlageter pilots, against no losses. Because the German fighters typically flew in Gruppe formations of forty aircraft, they invariably outnumbered the British when the two sides met. The RAF, whose largest tactical unit contained only a dozen fighters, was slow to counter with larger formations.

THE DUNKIRK EVACUATION

The first day of the evacuation, 28 May, found all of the Geschwader's constituent Gruppen active over Dunkirk. In a violent battle with sixteen fighters, pilots of the First Gruppe claimed six Spitfires shot down; one German pilot was killed. The Second Gruppe claimed two Spitfires and one Hurricane shot down over the Channel, while the Third Gruppe claimed six Hurricanes over Ostend.

Although these early battles with Spitfires had apparently ended in the Luftwaffe's favor, the German fighter pilots soon came to realize that their new opponent's capabilities were a match for those of their Messerschmitts. They gained the impression that the Spitfire had a higher ceiling than the Bf 109 and was more maneuverable at all speeds and altitudes. The better German pilots had already learned to fight Hurricanes in the vertical plane, using dive-and-zoom tactics; turning battles were to be avoided whenever possible. These tactics were even more important against Spitfires. The favorite German escape maneuver (for the next three years) was the split-S, a half-roll followed by a dive. A less popular tactic because of its effect on the pilot, but one which guaranteed a successful escape if started with sufficient altitude, was a steep pitch forward into a dive straight ahead. This maneuver drew negative gravity, which caused the carburetors of the RAF fighters' Merlin engines to cut out momentarily. The Bf 109E's DB 601A engine received fuel by direct injection, whatever its orientation; thus the German fighter could always gain distance on a pursuing Spitfire or Hurricane by diving straight ahead.

The dawn of 29 May was cloudy and overcast. There was no appreciable air activity over the beachhead until afternoon; the combats then gradually increased in scale and intensity. At 1840 an RAF formation consisting of four Spitfire and Hurricane squadrons arrived to take over the cover patrol. The two Hurricane squadrons were at 10,000 feet, while the Spitfires flew at 25,000 feet—too far apart for effective support. Worse, intersquadron communications were limited in Fighter Command to visual signals; there were no common radio frequencies among squadrons. The Hurricanes were hit from the clouds by a large force of Bf 109s—III/JG 26, possibly supplemented by III/JG 3. Before the Spitfires could intervene, they too were struck by a superior number of Messerschmitts—Hptm. Ebbighausen's II/JG 26. During the next half hour, ten British fighters went down; four Spitfires were claimed by II/JG 26, while six Hurricanes and Spitfires were credited to III/JG 26. The scattered British fighters made their way back to England as best they could, having lost one-quarter of their number. While the British fighters were engaged, the German Stukas made their most effective attack of the week on the destroyers and transports of the evacuation force, entirely unhindered by the RAF. The Schlageter Geschwader's success was won without loss, although the four RAF squadrons involved were credited with the destruction of fifteen Bf 109s.

The weather prevented any air operations on the 30th. The evacuation proceeded under cover of a thick fog bank. All three JG 26 Gruppen saw combat on the following day. The First Gruppe claimed one Spitfire, but lost two pilots; the Second Gruppe claimed one Hurricane without loss. The day's major successes belonged to the Third Gruppe. The mid-afternoon Fighter Command patrol comprised one squadron each of Spitfires, Hurricanes, and Defiants. At 1520, the Defiant crews saw a large formation of He 111s and turned toward it. As the bombers fled, the British fighters were hit by an estimated "seventy" Bf 109s, diving from the sun. This German unit is unknown; it might have been III/JG 3. The Defiants entered a defensive circle; the Messerschmitts downed one of them, and two of the Defiants then collided and crashed. The Hurricane squadron, No. 213, was heavily engaged by III/JG 26. The Gruppe shot down five Hurricanes and filed nine victory claims; the Hurricane pilots shot down two Third Gruppe aircraft, while claiming six. Lt. Joachim Muencheberg, the Third Gruppe adjutant, scored an unprecedented four victories on the 31st.

On 1 June, the Geschwader suffered five casualties, which was its largest daily total to date. Two pilots were killed, two were injured, and one was shot down behind the French lines and captured, to be released after the Armistice. Two Geschwader pilots bailed out of their Messerschmitts during the day without injury. All morning the Luftwaffe mounted heavy attacks on the beachhead and offshore shipping. At noon, the Second Gruppe took off from Chievres on a defensive sweep. They arrived over Dunkirk in time to engage a formation of Hurricanes which was approaching some Do 17s. The RAF unit was one of three Hurricane squadrons in a patrolling "wing"; all three squadrons were soon caught up in the whirling melee, which resulted in the loss of five British aircraft. The pilots of the Second Gruppe claimed six Hurricanes and one Spitfire in this battle, but only three of their claims were confirmed—an indication of the scale and severity of the combats. The Gruppe was probably the only Bf 109 unit engaged. It suffered only three losses, although the Hurricane pilots were credited with thirteen Bf 109s. Fighter Command's victory claims for the week of Dunkirk exceeded actual Luftwaffe losses by a factor of about four to one.

The JG 26 Geschwaderstab was conspicuously unsuccessful in aerial combat during the Western campaign. The number of staff officers was small, and a choice had to be made between administrative duties and combat flying. Kommodore Witt opted for the paperwork and flew very few missions. Hptm. Viktor "Pappi" Causin, the popular executive officer and a former brewer, did not fly. The other two officers, Oblt. Horten (technical officer) and Oblt. Hasselmann (adjutant), seethed in frustration. They were permitted to fly but a single mission over Dunkirk, during which dust and smoke severely restricted visibility below 10,000 feet. A dip beneath the haze revealed a scene of total chaos—the beaches were black with men and equipment; the sea was roiled by drunken ships heeling to and fro. No British aircraft could be seen. Since the fighters of JG 26 were not permitted to attack ground targets, Horten and Hasselmann returned to base.

On the 2nd, the Second Gruppe again saw hard combat. Early that morning, Hptm. Erich Noack had arrived at Chievres from a training command to take over the Gruppe. The unit reached Dunkirk at 0900, in time to join some Bf 110s in a massive battle with four RAF fighter squadrons that had succeeded in reaching an He 111 formation. The Gruppe claimed six British fighters, without loss. The evacuation continued unabated throughout the day. By nightfall, 338,226 Allied troops had reached England, and the beaches were empty of living men. Goering had failed utterly to fulfill his boast of destroying the British army from the air. However, in the excitement of the campaign, the men of the Luftwaffe had no sense of defeat; for the fighter pilots, especially, the week had been one of apparent great success.

OPERATION PAULA—THE AIR ATTACK ON PARIS

While the Dunkirk evacuation was still under way, Goering's attention turned elsewhere. On 3 June, Paris was bombed for the first time. Three hundred bombers of Luftflotten 2 and 3, under heavy fighter escort, attacked airfields in the Paris region. The French had maintained a large fighter reserve for just such an eventuality, but their defense proved surprisingly ineffective. The Schlageter Geschwader's Stab, First, and Second Gruppe took part in the raid. Major Witt led the Stabsschwarm on the mission, but had no "fighter's luck," to use the pilots' ironic term; he failed to sight a single enemy plane. The First Gruppe claimed two French fighters, while the Second claimed one, for the temporary loss of one pilot released by the French after the Armistice.

After the elimination of the Dunkirk perimeter on 4 June, the entire Geschwader moved to fields in the Calais area. Air battles over the Channel coast cost the Geschwader six pilots during the next week, but claims comfortably exceeded losses. On 6 June, Hptm. Adolf Galland arrived to take over the command of III/JG 26 from Major Ernst Freiherr von Berg, who left the Geschwader. Von Berg, a cavalry officer, had proven to be an ineffective combat leader, as well as a poor pilot—he was nicknamed the "propeller killer." Galland had gained twelve victories since April, while serving as the adjutant of JG 27. This was a fair indication of the performance to be expected from the dynamic young career officer, now that he had at last obtained a genuine combat command in a fighter unit.

On 8 June, a 7th Staffel Schwarm was attacked by Hurricanes while in the vicinity of the fluid front lines. Lt. Klaus Mietusch was forced to set his damaged aircraft down in enemy territory. He landed without injury, but a French civilian then shot him in the buttocks with a boar rifle. After Mietusch's repatriation, he had to be sent to Germany for treatment. According to his friend Jupp Buerschgens, this episode affected Mietusch profoundly; after returning to his Staffel, Mietusch flew for a while as Lt. Buerschgens's wingman while he regained his touch and taste for combat.

Buerschgens himself missed most of the French campaign. While recovering from his September 1939 injury, he served as an ordnance officer in Muenster. When he returned to JG 26, he was assigned to the 7th Staffel, where most of his friends from the 2nd Staffel had been transferred upon formation of the Third Gruppe. Jupp Buerschgens's first victory of the campaign came on 9 June. In his words:

> That afternoon we were ordered to fly a freie Jagd to Paris from our base at Capelle, north of the Seine. As we approached Paris we sighted two squadrons of enemy fighters climbing up from the city. We attacked them from above. I fastened on to the tail of one fighter, which vanished into the general air battle with a split-S. I immediately climbed away into a heavy layer of haze, which lay at about 3,000 meters [10,000 feet] and had clear skies above and below it. Flying at the upper border of the layer, I would pop out, look around for an opponent, and disappear again into the protective cloud. One time when I emerged I saw in front of me an aircraft doing just as I was—popping out, looking around, and dropping from sight again. I saw roundels, and carefully approached the enemy plane, remaining in the cloud until I had reached optimum firing distance. I opened fire with all my weapons. I saw strikes in the cockpit and on the fuselage. The enemy aircraft reared up sharply, and came past me in a flat left curve, almost at my altitude. I could see that the pilot had been hit. He was slumped forward. The machine banked more steeply, and dove over a wing. I saw it crash in a heavily populated

27

area west of Paris. I followed the plane until I was almost on the ground, dismayed and perplexed by what I had done.

In previous air battles I had always seen only the aircraft, not the men who were flying them. This time, I saw the man whom I had killed. He could just as easily have found himself behind me. I needed much longer than normal to find my airfield. My wingman landed long before me in a well-shot-up Bf 109. He had had better luck than my French opponent.

THE END OF THE CAMPAIGN

The Wehrmacht continued its inexorable advance southward through France. JG 26 moved twice more, finally basing at Villa-coublay, a large permanent airfield outside Paris. The French Air Force was hard to find. Those of its aircraft with sufficient range were flying to North Africa. II/JG 26 was awarded the honor of flying cover patrols over the armistice negotiations at Compiegne. The RAF, however, failed to put in an appearance. The Armistice was signed on 22 June. JG 26 began to move back to its permanent stations in Germany, where it was finally reunited with its First Gruppe. On 24 June, the command of the Geschwader was given to Major Gotthardt Handrick, who passed his First Gruppe to Hptm. Kurt Fischer. Major Witt's departure was sweetened by his promotion on 1 July to Oberstleutnant. He became operations officer at Jafue 2 in Le Touquet, and later in the war he held various staff positions in Africa, Norway, Silesia, and Italy.

Jagdgeschwader 26 had made a solid record for itself in the brief campaign, claiming 160 victories against seventeen of its own pilots killed in action, two lost in flying accidents, three captured by the British, and about one dozen injured. The First Gruppe claimed twenty-four victories, the Second, sixty-six, and the Third, sixty-nine. The Geschwader's score for the war to date did not approach that of the current leader, JG 53, which claimed 275 victories, but JG 26 had one of the best records during the six-week Western campaign. It spent the following month absorbing new equipment and training new pilots. The unit's battle-seasoned veterans looked forward with confidence to their next round against the RAF.

3
JG 26 IN THE BATTLE
OF BRITAIN
24 July 1940 –
9 February 1941

RETURN TO GERMANY

At the conclusion of the French campaign the German High Command ordered a pause in operations for the purposes of reorganization, planning, and possible negotiations with their sole remaining opponent, Great Britain. The fight against Britain was carried on by a small Luftwaffe force on the Pas de Calais, while JG 26 and many other Luftwaffe units returned to Germany. The Schlageter fighters found themselves back at their permanent bases on the Rhine, where from 26 June to 20 July they mounted guard against the minor threat posed by RAF Bomber Command.

All of the Geschwader's aircraft were fitted with seat and back armor before the return to combat. Attempts to implement an engine-mounted cannon in the Bf 109 were temporarily abandoned, and the model that was to carry it, the Bf 109E-3, disappeared from the JG 26 inventory. The Bf 109E-3 was replaced on Messerschmitt's production lines by the E-4. The MG FF/M cannon, originally designed for engine mounting, had a higher rate of fire than the MG FF, and supplanted the earlier cannon in the wings of the E-4. Another standard feature of the E-4 was an armored windshield.

Another significant variant, the Bf 109E-4/N, was an answer to the Jagdwaffe pilots' complaints of poor high-altitude performance.

29

This model had a modified engine, the DB 601N, with an increase in engine compression ratio from 6.9 to 8.2, boosting maximum horsepower to 1175. There was a cost for this improvement—96-octane fuel was required in the new engine instead of the standard 87 octane. High-octane fuel was always in short supply in Germany, and the E-4/N was given a restricted production run. JG 26 was one of the few Geschwader to receive this model. According to the Luftwaffe's aircraft loss returns, JG 26 fought the Battle of Britain with E-1s, E-4s, and E-4/Ns. The lightly armed E-1 was still being flown by some of the enlisted pilots in late October.

THE FIRST PHASE—CHANNEL ATTACKS
AND FREE HUNTS

On 21 July, JG 26 was ordered to the Channel coast. The Geschwader arrived at its full strength of 121 aircraft and was assigned to Genobst. Kesselring's Luftflotte 2. The three combat Gruppen occupied airfields within a few miles of the coast at Calais; the First at Audembert, the Second at Marquise-Ost, and the Third at Caffiers. When the Germans arrived, the fields were planted in grain. Their qualifications for fighter operations were merely an adequate size and flatness, attributes which were fairly uncommon in the area. Both Marquise and Caffiers had attracted the attention of the British in the First World War and had been used by them as fighter bases. JG 26 conducted operations and administration from trailers; the personnel lived in tents or in the nearby towns. The Messerschmitts were parked beneath trees, where available, but in any case under camouflaged netting held up by long poles. By 30 July, the Geschwaderstab had joined the First Gruppe at Audembert, and a Geschwader operations room had been set up in Le Colombier.

The Luftwaffe's tasks during this phase were to protect the Wehrmacht's invasion buildup on the coast and to establish aerial supremacy over the Channel. Its small but growing force was under the direct command of Oberst Johannes Fink, Kommodore at KG 2. He sought to draw Fighter Command into a battle of attrition, which if prolonged could only end in a Luftwaffe victory. Air Chief Marshal Sir Hugh Dowding, Commander-in-Chief of Fighter Command, and Air Vice Marshal Keith Park, Air Officer Commanding No. 11 Group of Fighter Command in the critical target area of southeastern England, were well aware of German intentions from radio intercepts, which had been decoded by the Ultra organization, and refused then or later to rise to the German bait. No. 11 Group was given barely one-third of Fighter Command's squadrons. The tactics devised by Park and approved by Dowding called for forward interceptions by small fighter formations. Their plan was to disrupt the bomber formations and minimize the weight of the bombing attacks, without risking the wholesale destruction of their fighter resources. Inevitably, the first phase of the battle was inconclusive. Weaknesses in the Luftwaffe's equipment soon became apparent, however, with serious implications for the Wehrmacht's plans. These shortcomings included the Ju 87's extreme vulnerability to fighter attack, the Bf 110's inadequacy in the escort role, and the Bf 109's limited combat radius.

The Bf 109 pilots were called on to fly freie Jagden, reconnaissance sorties, and various types of escort missions. At the beginning of the battle, the Geschwader fought as individual Gruppen; the Geschwader itself was considered too large to function effectively as a combat unit. The forty-aircraft Gruppe employed a powerful and flexible combat formation that was far superior to anything put up by the RAF at this time. The fighting element was the two-aircraft Rotte. The tactical unit was the Schwarm of four aircraft, which flew in Moelders's "finger four" formation. The standard Staffel formation was a broad vee containing its three Schwaerme. The Gruppe formation contained the Stab and three Staffeln, all stepped up in line astern. Fighter Command's tactical unit was still the vee of three aircraft, and its largest combat formation remained the twelve-aircraft squadron.

Typically, the German fighters would assemble over France at 15–18,000 feet and climb during the flight across the Channel to an altitude of 21–24,000 feet. The maximum duration of a Bf 109 combat mission was ninety minutes. As it took half an hour to reach England after takeoff, no more than one half hour was available for tactical operations, sufficient to reach just north of London. A red panel lamp came on at the one-quarter fuel level, urging the Bf 109 pilot to bolt for home, whatever the tactical situation. The Channel itself was a psychological burden to the German pilots. The German word for channel, Kanal, also means sewer. The English

31

Channel was soon dubbed the "Scheisskanal" (sanitary sewer). However, the efficient German air-sea rescue service was a tremendous boost to morale, at times rescuing downed pilots from the Thames Estuary itself.

The Schlageter Geschwader's first missions to England were flown on 24 July. The British, determined not to forfeit their own coastal waters, were continuing to run convoys of small colliers through the Channel and the Thames Estuary. Shortly before noon on the 24th, the British detected a German formation approaching a convoy. The raiders comprised two Staffeln of Dorniers escorted by forty Bf 109s of Major Galland's III/JG 26. The British intercepted in good time. No. 54 Squadron's Spitfires, flying from Rochford on the north coast of the Estuary, made first contact and were engaged by the Messerschmitts. Six No. 65 Sqd. Spitfires from Manston then attacked the bombers but could not close on their tight formation. Long-range fire from the Spitfires' .303-inch machine guns had no apparent effect on the Dorniers but did help prevent the Germans from doing any damage to the convoy.

The fighter combat was prolonged and vicious. Galland's Gruppe was held in close contact for so long that low fuel forced the pilots to break off the engagement and head for France. Their favorite escape maneuver, the split-S, and smoking engines fooled No. 54 Squadron's pilots into claiming six kills, plus eight probables and two damaged. The true German losses from this combat were two pilots. One pilot bailed out, but he was killed when his parachute failed to open. The other casualty was Oblt. Werner Bartels, the Third Gruppe's popular and efficient technical officer (TO). Bartels was shot down by a No. 65 Sqd. Spitfire over Margate and belly-landed near the coast, seriously wounded. Bartels was a 38-year-old former test pilot who had come to III/JG 26 that February to work on some problems with the Bf 109E and had been asked to stay on permanently. He had been named TO in May. Bartels was repatriated in 1943 and joined the Me 262 program.

That evening, Adolf Galland expressed his dissatisfaction with the performance of his Gruppe, which had claimed the destruction of only two Spitfires. One claim was Galland's; his victim was Plt. Off. Johnny Allen of No. 54 Squadron, an eight-victory ace, who was killed. The second victim, another No. 54 Sqd. Spitfire, was able to force-land; its pilot suffered minor injuries. Galland's loss of two pilots was sobering; he has stated that this first combat over England removed any doubts that the RAF would prove a most formidable opponent.

The Second Gruppe's first mission of the battle was a disaster. Their orders were to fly a freie Jagd ahead of the bomber formation, but only ten aircraft were ready at the designated time of 1225. Hptm. Erich Noack took off leading only four aircraft of the 5th Staffel and five of the 6th. While approaching Dover, Noack saw "thirty Spitfires"—actually nine, from No. 610 Squadron—above them, aborted the mission, and turned back for France. Noack's approach to the field at Marquise was too high; he pulled up to go around but stalled out and crashed over one wing. He was killed instantly. The Second Gruppe had lost its second Kommandeur to die in the young war. Oblt. Karl Ebbighausen of the 4th Staffel was named to succeed Noack.

The next day brought an improvement in Luftwaffe tactics. The Germans' newly installed radar and wireless intercept stations at Wissant allowed Oberst Fink, the tactical commander, to hit the convoys when they were at their most vulnerable. Convoy CW 8 was the first to suffer from the Germans' increased capability. Fink's primary attack force consisted of three waves of Ju 87s, each escorted by one JG 26 Gruppe. The first wave, closely escorted by Galland's Third Gruppe, found the convoy unprotected by fighters. Two flights of No. 54 Sqd. Spitfires were airborne over Dover. One flight—five planes—was ordered to intercept. The Spitfires, led by Flt. Lt. B. H. "Wonky" Way, bored straight at the Stukas and were struck immediately by the Bf 109s. Galland recalled that the Spitfires hit the Ju 87s just before the latter began to peel off in their dives. He led his Gruppe down, selected one Spitfire for himself, and hit it with a full burst of fire. The fighter caught fire and crashed into the sea near the Dover harbor mole; the British pilot (probably Way) did not get out. The small flight of Spitfires was overwhelmed before it could inflict any damage on the Ju 87s. Jupp Buerschgens recalls that the 7th Staffel dove with the Stukas and surprised a formation of Spitfires waiting for the Ju 87s to pull out of their dives. The Spitfires below were from No. 64 Squadron. The two Spitfire squadrons lost three aircraft and two of their pilots; two more Spitfires crash-landed in repairable condition. III/JG 26 claimed five Spitfires, one by Major Galland and four by pilots of the 7th Staffel.

25 July was a disappointing day for Fighter Command. Eight Spitfires were destroyed, and another seven damaged. No. 54 Squadron had lost five pilots killed and three wounded, plus twelve aircraft destroyed, in three weeks' nonstop fighting. The next day it was withdrawn to the north for a brief rest. III/JG 26 lost one pilot, killed late in the day, in return for its five victories.

By the next morning, half of Convoy CW 8 had been sunk by dive bombers or E-boats. The Admiralty canceled all sailing of merchant ships through the Straits of Dover by day. By 28 July, the Royal Navy was forced to withdraw its Dover-based destroyer forces, and on the 29th, all movement of British naval units in the Straits by day was stopped. Fink had thus won his battle. The significance of his victory was minimal, however, as only limited forces had been committed, and the Royal Air Force and the Royal Navy still possessed the means and will to cripple any invasion force.

On the 28th, Oberst Fink employed his bombers as decoys. No. 74 "Tiger" Squadron's Spitfires and No. 257 Squadron's Hurricanes were scrambled from Manston and Hawkinge at 1450 to intercept a large raid heading for Dover. (All times in this history are local German time; during this period this was one hour later than that kept by the British.) Upon the approach of the British fighters, the bomber formation wheeled around and headed for France, leaving the fighters to the attention of the strong escort—the First and Second Gruppen of JG 51, led by their new Kommodore (as of that morning), Major Werner Moelders. No. 41 Squadron was then ordered up from Manston, only to be hit by Major Galland, up sun with III/JG 26. The confused combats cost the Tigers two fighters destroyed and two damaged; No. 41 Squadron lost one damaged. The Spitfire pilots claimed four Messerschmitts destroyed, one probably destroyed, and three damaged (usually abbreviated 4-1-3 claims). Galland's Gruppe suffered no casualties. JG 51 lost two aircraft destroyed and one damaged; one of its pilots was killed, and one—Moelders—was shot in the legs. German claims totaled five Spitfires, exactly matching the total number lost and damaged. III/JG 26's share was two—Galland got one, and an 8th Staffel pilot claimed the other. In addition, Galland's wingman, Oblt. Muencheberg, caught a stray Hurricane, of No. 257 Squadron, and damaged it so badly that it was written off after its forced landing. Muencheberg was credited with its destruction.

The Luftwaffe continued to attack shipping from 26 July through 7 August, while building up its forces in northern France. JG 26 suffered no losses during this period, which was highlighted on 1 August by Kesselring's presentation of the Knight's Cross to Adolf Galland. Galland, who had seventeen aerial victories and numerous ground attacks (in Spain and Poland) to his credit, was the first Schlageter pilot so honored.

THE SECOND PHASE—ADLERANGRIFF

On 2 August the Luftwaffe High Command completed its plan for the destruction of the RAF, which was code-named Adlerangriff (Eagle Attack). Massive attacks were to be made on the infrastructure of Fighter Command in southeastern England—its airplanes, airfields, and ground organization—which would draw the whole of the British aerial defense forces to the area and lead to their destruction. The original plan called for three phases, to last a total of two weeks. On 6 August Goering set the 10th as the date of Adlertag (Eagle Day), the opening day. Bad weather would force its postponement until the 13th.

The fighting on 8 August was a continuation of the July pattern of sweeps and shipping attacks and was thus not directly associated with Adlerangriff. However, the scale and severity of the combat on this day resulted in its selection by the British as the opening day of the second phase, and for years it was regarded in Britain as the "official" opening day of the Battle of Britain. At noon, III/JG 26, along with II/JG 51 and III/JG 51, swept the Dover area in a freie Jagd. They succeeded in drawing up three squadrons of Spitfires. The British claimed the destruction of nine Bf 109s in the ensuing combat, for the loss of three Spitfires. The Germans in turn claimed nine RAF fighters. Four of these claims were by III/JG 26, which suffered the only German casualty, a fatality.

After two quiet days, the Luftwaffe returned to the offensive in strength. On the 11th a series of sweeps across Kent by Luftflotte 2's fighters succeeded in drawing a number of No. 11 Group squadrons into combat. Luftflotte 3's Bf 110s and Bf 109s provoked a similar reaction from No. 10 Group over Portland. The two sides' fighter losses for the day were nearly equal—twenty-six British for twenty-five German. It is not known whether I/JG 26 or II/JG 26 took part in these sweeps; neither Gruppe filed any claims or suffered any losses. Galland's Third Gruppe had no known successes in the air combats, and it suffered the Geschwader's only casualty of the day— the Bf 109E-1 of the 7th Staffel's Lt. Buerschgens. Over Manston, Buerschgens took several hits in his fuselage and engine from a No. 74 Sqd. Spitfire, possibly that of Squadron Leader Malan. Buerschgens made it back across the Channel but was forced to belly-land in a field near his base at Caffiers. His Messerschmitt had to be written off.

At least three Third Gruppe pilots filed claims for the destruction of barrage balloons over Dover. The British considered balloon attacks to be irresponsible displays of German arrogance; the Germans, on the other hand, felt the balloons were legitimate targets, as balloons made low-level attacks extremely hazardous. (Balloon-bashing was also great sport, especially after an otherwise unsuccessful sweep.)

The 12th of August dawned clear and stayed fair, giving the Luftwaffe an opportunity to soften up targets in southern England in advance of Adlertag. In mid-morning, after a series of perfectly executed strikes on the coastal radar stations by Erprobungsgruppe 210's Bf 110s, Kesselring ordered his Ju 87s to attack two small convoys in the Thames Estuary. The second wave was escorted by III/JG 26. Fifteen Hurricanes from Nos. 501 and 151 squadrons were able to get to the Stukas before they were in turn struck by the 109s. The Stukas jettisoned their bombs and scattered before the attack. The dogfight that followed cost the British five Hurricanes and two pilots, without loss to the Third Gruppe. Galland hung on a Hurricane's tail from 12,000 feet down to 4,500 feet, from which height he watched as it dove, trailing smoke, to crash land between Margate and Broadstairs. Their was no witness to the crash, so Galland's claim was disallowed. His claim was, in fact, valid; the pilot making the successful forced landing was No. 501 Squadron's Squadron Leader Holland. Five claims by Third Gruppe pilots are known, matching the five RAF losses.

That afternoon Manston underwent the first major attack of what was to become a weeks-long ordeal. Eighteen Do 17s of Oberst Fink's Kampfgeschwader 2 made a single pass at medium altitude, dropping a dense pattern of high explosive and fragmentation bombs. The airfield erupted in a cloud of chalk dust and smoke rising to several thousand feet. Several Spitfires were able to take off during the attack, but they were unable to catch the rapidly withdrawing Dorniers. At least three airborne squadrons were vectored to intercept the Gruppe on withdrawal. Ten Hurricanes of No. 56 Squadron, still straining for altitude, were the first to reach the Dorniers and their escort, three dozen Bf 109s of Hptm. Fischer's I/JG 26. The Messerschmitts ignored the Hurricanes, but the dense defensive fire of the bombers downed two of the British fighters. The Dorniers then returned to Arras unscathed.

Hptm. Fischer's luckless First Gruppe had not yet scored in the battle; indeed, Lt. Hans-Werner Regenauer of the 2nd Staffel states that he had not even sighted an enemy aircraft prior to 12 August. Fischer probably left the Hurricanes alone because he had already spotted No. 54 Squadron's Spitfires, which were also below the bombers when they reached the area. One section of Spitfires—three aircraft—attacked the rear of Fischer's Gruppe, but he led his unit down in a successful attack on the larger formation; the Gruppe claimed the destruction of four Spitfires. No. 54 Squadron, which had just returned to No. 11 Group from ten days rest in Scotland, lost two Spitfires, whose wounded pilots crash landed their aircraft. No. 64 Squadron arrived late to the fight and lost one Spitfire, whose pilot bailed out, wounded, while a second force-landed. Two Messerschmitts went down. One German pilot was killed; the other, Lt. Regenauer, survived. Hans-Werner Regenauer recalls:

> I was flying as Lt. Hafer's wingman, and had just fired at a Spitfire on the tail of his Messerschmitt, when someone fired at my aircraft and hit the cooling system. I hid in a cloud and headed toward the French coast. The aircraft lost altitude, and finally the engine stopped. I bailed out at about 200 meters [650 feet], and after a bath lasting about seven hours, was taken aboard an English ship.

The 12th also saw Hptm. Ebbighausen's Second Gruppe file its first victory claim of the battle; Lt. Krug of the 4th Staffel claimed a Spitfire over Margate at 1225. Galland's hard-charging Third Gruppe had taken a commanding lead in the race for aerial victories within the Geschwader, a lead it would maintain well past the end of the Battle of Britain.

The Geschwaderstab remained scoreless—Major Handrick was no more successful as a combat leader than Major Witt, which was a source of constant frustration to the TO, Oblt. Horten. There were not enough pilots for a Schwarm, the standard tactical unit, as only Handrick and Horten were available for flying duty. And although the First Gruppe shared the Stab's base at Audembert, Handrick chose not to fly with them. He believed that a Kommodore needed to keep all of his units in sight, the better to direct them; the only way to do this was to follow rather than lead them. In Horten's words:

> Handrick and I usually flew independently of the Gruppe at our field; thus we were alone. We took off later than they and missed the dances above. Bounces were not customary at that period, since the Tommies avoided fighter-versus-fighter combat whenever possible. Long chases were also uncommon. So neither Handrick nor I saw any enemy aircraft in the air.

13 AUGUST—ADLERTAG

The next day, 13 August, was the long awaited Adlertag, which initiated the heaviest week of fighting in the battle. Adlertag was a disaster for the Germans, the extent of which was not even suspected by them at the time. None of the targets chosen by Luftwaffe intelligence were vital to Fighter Command's operation. Most of the attacks were failures. The most successful from a technical standpoint was a raid by forty Ju 87s that pulverized Detling, a Coastal Command airfield. The Stukas were permitted to bomb untouched by British fighters, which had been drawn away by JG 26's freie Jagd. The Second Gruppe crossed the English coast at 25,000 feet, with the First Gruppe below them. They could see Dover's cliffs, but dense cloud cover spread out to the west at 6,000 feet. Hptm. Ebbighausen navigated blind, using his compass and clock. Karl Borris, at this time a Leutnant in the 5th Staffel, recorded the mission in his diary:

> A formation was reported below us to the left; apparently enemy fighters, as their formation of threes looked suspicious. Below us to the right was another formation, which I reported; the Komman-

deur banked toward this one. My Schwarm was flying next to the Stabsschwarm. I saw three aircraft directly below us, which I recognized as Hurricanes. The Kommandeur apparently did not see them, as he had his eye on the large formation, which was now about three miles ahead of us. I nosed over, and soon had the left fighter sitting in my crosshairs. Would the two others come after me? My emotions were stretched to the breaking point. 100 meters—70 meters—the Hurricane, with its distinctive belly radiator, loomed large in my Revi reflector sight. Now! He started to bank gently to the left. Take a lead! There he goes, already in bright flames! Away! I threw my aircraft into a left bank toward our own planes. In front of me, a 109 hung below a Hurricane, firing, but could not follow its tight turn. Sideslip beneath! 70 meters—50 meters—the aiming post crossed the Tommy's nose. I fired all four guns. Hits! Thick smoke from the wing roots; flames shot out from both sides. I broke away, and looked behind me. Somewhat below me, a Hurricane was firing in my direction. Climb! The Tommy did not follow, but cut away. Where were my comrades? I saw nothing. Over there! A machine approached me from behind. In an instant, I flipped my machine on its back and left the scene. . . .

Borris returned to Marquise alone. Many of the Second Gruppe's pilots remained unaccounted for for many hours. It turned out that the entire 6th Staffel, and four pilots of the 5th, lost their orientation in the solid cloud deck and ran out of fuel, force-landing in the area between Reims and Verdun. Borris's victories were the only ones logged by the Geschwader on Adlertag; Galland's Third Gruppe had drawn escort duty for the air-sea rescue seaplanes and speedboats.

The next day, Luftwaffe activity was much reduced from Adlertag. The first major raid of the 14th was not mounted until nearly noon. It consisted of eighty Ju 87s, supported by the three Gruppen of JG 26. Hptm. Fischer's First Gruppe had close escort responsibility, while Major Galland's Third Gruppe flew detached escort, and Hptm. Ebbighausen's Second Gruppe mission was either detached escort or a supporting freie Jagd. No. 11 Group had ample warning of the raid's approach and met it over Dover with forty-two fighters. The resulting melee involved nearly two hundred fighters, and lasted a full hour. The First Gruppe stayed with the Stukas, claimed two Spitfires, and lost one pilot. Hptm. Ebbighausen and Lt. Krug of the Second Gruppe also claimed Spitfires. The Third Gruppe scored six victories. Its Kommandeur, Major Galland, shot down a Hurricane that had reached the Stuka formation:

> I had to fire from great range, because the Ju 87 was in mortal danger. The Hurricane dove, went into cloud, then pulled up through the cloud—and at that moment I killed him.

Another Hurricane then attacked Galland; his wingman, Joachim Muencheberg, picked it off his tail. When Galland had taken over command of the Third Gruppe in June, he had inherited Muencheberg as his adjutant. Muencheberg was impatient for a combat command of his own but made the most of his opportunities. He gained four victories while flying Galland's wing, certainly one of the best scores of the period for a Rottenflieger, and testimony to Muencheberg's exceptional skills as a combat pilot.

All of the Geschwader's victories were claimed in the Folkestone-Dover area between 1330 and 1400 hours. The RAF fighters belonged to: No. 32 Squadron, which lost one Hurricane destroyed and two force-landed but repairable; No. 65 Squadron, two of whose Spitfires force-landed; No. 610 Squadron, which also had two Spitfires force-land; and No. 615 Squadron, which lost two Hurricanes with their pilots, and had another two suffer damage. The ten JG 26 claims correspond to nine downed RAF fighters, but six of the British aircraft and seven of their pilots ultimately returned to combat! It is easy to see how the German fighter pilots' victory claims, made in all good faith, could lead to serious miscalculations by the Luftwaffe High Command.

The lone JG 26 casualty in this battle has recorded his impressions. Feldwebel Gerhard Kemen had completed his flight training in June 1940, and had then reported to 1/JG 26. On the 14th,

> My 1st Staffel took off with the rest of the First Gruppe at around 1255 to escort a bomber formation to England. . . . We waited for the bombers at around 3,000 meters [10,000 feet], and then accompanied them in the direction of England. My Staffel was positioned to the left rear of the bombers. Oberleutnant Henrici, my Rottenfuehrer, flew at the rear of our Staffel, and we were thus at the end of the entire formation. As we crossed the English coast, Henrici

and I saw about four or five Hurricanes approaching us. We left the formation and attacked the British aircraft. During the battle, I found myself behind a Hurricane and opened fire. At that same moment, I was hit in the back, at the level of my shoulder harness. I must have lost consciousness immediately. When I came to, my hands were covered in oil, and I thought only of bailing out. I found the emergency release for the canopy, unfastened my parachute harness from the seat, and shot from the aircraft. Shortly thereafter, I again passed out. I don't know for how long; I came to my senses only long enough to pull the parachute handle. I can recall nothing of striking the ground, being discovered, or being transported to the hospital. I next regained consciousness in a hospital near Dover, following an operation. . . .

Gerhard Kemen was shot down by Plt. Off. R. F. Smythe of No. 32 Squadron, who was immediately shot down by a First Gruppe Messerschmitt. Smythe force-landed at Hawkinge without injury, but his Hurricane was scrapped. Kemen was transported to a Canadian POW camp in 1941, was repatriated with several other wounded JG 26 pilots in 1943, and returned to active duty in time for the final battles for the Reich—this time on a ground staff.

JG 26's escort tactics were successful; only one Ju 87 was lost, and apparently few RAF fighters even got near the vulnerable dive-bombers. Results of the attack, the vortex of the whirlwind of activity reported above, were negligible—the Dover lightship was sunk, and one Staffel of Bf 109s found the time to shoot down eight barrage balloons. The raid did serve as a massive diversion, under the cover of which the Bf 110s of EprGr 210 pummeled Manston once again.

The Schlageter pilots had every reason for satisfaction as they retold the day's experiences that evening in their quarters. Their victory claims over England had far exceeded their own losses. Bad weather was forecast for the coming morning, but from the pilots' perspective the Luftwaffe's plan was working—a few more days of favorable weather and the RAF would be driven from the skies.

15 AUGUST—THE LUFTWAFFE'S BLACK THURSDAY

Despite the German forecast of poor weather, early morning clouds over England and France burned off, and the day promised to be fair. The three Luftflotten in northern France and southern Norway were called to readiness; this would be the day to administer the long-awaited knockout blow to Fighter Command. The first buildup by Luftflotte 2 aircraft over Calais was picked up by No. 11 Group's radars shortly after 1200. The force consisted of sixty Ju 87s escorted by two Gruppen from JG 26. Their targets were the satellite airfields at Hawkinge and Lympne. Two airborne squadrons were vectored to intercept. No. 501 Squadron's Hurricanes reached the Hawkinge attack force just as the Junkers echeloned to dive. The Hurricane pilots succeeded in downing two bombers before they were in turn struck from above by the escort, which shot down two fighters. No. 54 Squadron had less luck in penetrating the Lympne attackers' fighter screen, which was provided by Major Galland's III/JG 26. Al Deere has described the scene in his autobiography, *Nine Lives*:

> It was an impressive yet frustrating sight as the dive-bombers, in perfect echelon formation, swept toward the airfield and peeled off to attack. A mere handful of Spitfires altered the picture very little as, virtually lost in the maze of 109s, they strove to interfere.

No. 54 Squadron lost two Spitfires in this battle. Major Galland, who was one of the victorious German pilots, escorted the Stukas partway back across the Channel, and then took his Gruppe back to England at 15,000 feet, on an abbreviated freie Jagd. He saw a Spitfire squadron re-forming below and led his unit on a bounce. Pieces flew off the first Spitfire he attacked, before it burst into flames. A second took hits but avoided a killing blow by Fighter Command's favorite escape maneuver, a steep climbing turn, which the 109 was unable to follow.

JG 26 was also actively involved in Luftflotte 2's second major raid of the day. Sixty of their number—probably two Gruppen, including the tireless Third—swept in over Kent in support of eighty-eight Do 17s of KG 3, which had a close escort of more than 130 Bf 109s from JG 51, JG 52, and JG 54. The bombers' targets were the Rochester and Eastchurch airfields. Both were hit hard. Seven No. 11 Group squadrons attempted to engage the bombers but were fended off by the massive escort. Only two Dorniers were lost.

A last series of raids came in late afternoon. Galland's Gruppe was assigned another free hunt, this time in support of Dorniers that hit West Malling, an airfield not currently in use by Fighter Command, instead of Biggin Hill, their briefed target. The Dorniers were not attacked by RAF fighters, which were driven off by the Messerschmitts. Over East Kent at 2015 hours, No. 151 Squadron lost five Hurricanes and two pilots to Bf 109s of III/JG 26.

Before they returned to Caffiers, Galland and Muencheberg had the opportunity to score yet another kill. Their victim was in all probability the indefatigable New Zealander, Flt. Lt. Al Deere. After a successful interception of an EprGr 210 raid, Deere stalked one of that unit's Bf 109s clear to France. About to lose his prey, Deere opened fire at extreme range—and gave his presence away. The Messerschmitt dove vertically, straight toward an airfield whose landing circuit

> . . . was infested with 109s, two of which detached themselves and turned to cut me off as, with throttle wide open, I headed home at sea level, muttering to myself "you bloody fool."

The two German aircraft split up and attacked the Spitfire in turns. Deere broke into each pass. His fighter accumulated damage all the way back across the Channel. As the coast came in sight, the Messerschmitts broke away for home. At this moment, the Spitfire's engine burst into flames. Deere half-rolled and, after some difficulty, dropped from his plane. He landed safely near Ashford.

Although German claims on the 15th exceeded true British losses by three to one, Lt. Mueller-Duehe's victory, as described by Jupp Buerschgens, is one about which there can be no doubt:

> Three pilots of the 7th Staffel—Lt. Gerhard Mueller-Duehe, Lt. Walter Blume, and myself—were returning from a mission over southern England. As we neared the French coast, we saw ahead of us a single fighter, and assumed it was one of ours. Shortly before we reached it, it turned, and we recognized it as a Spitfire.
>
> Because we were all short on fuel and ammunition, we cut across his path, hoping to shoot him down or force him to land on French soil. The fight became a low-level chase around trees and hedges, in sharp turns. The Spitfire counter-attacked; its pilot was an excellent flier. Due to lack of fuel and ammunition, first I and then Lt. Blume had to give up the pursuit; Lt. Mueller-Duehe was the last

to quit. The Spitfire was at that time headed toward England. When the last Bf 109 turned homeward, the Spitfire turned about and prepared for a landing on the French beach at Wissant. Lt. Mueller-Duehe saw this, and thought the pilot must have suffered a severe wound. After landing on our field at Caffiers, M-D jumped into a staff car, and shortly thereafter reached the Spitfire and its pilot. German Army personnel stood guard and had taken the pilot prisoner. He was very confused and unhappy, which was certainly understandable. M-D shook his hand and asked him why he had landed on the wrong side of the Channel. The British pilot confessed that he had lost his orientation completely and had thought he was landing on the English coast. German technical specialists found that the Spitfire was carrying the most modern communications equipment, better than ours; a discovery of great tactical and technical value to us.

The Spitfire was flown by Pilot Officer Ralph Roberts of No. 64 Squadron. His "new equipment" can only have been a VHF radio, so new that it had only begun to reach the RAF squadrons that month.

The Luftwaffe's effort peaked on 15 August. Never again in the battle would it fly as many sorties—more than 2,000—or suffer heavier losses. The British claimed 180 victories, against a true German loss of seventy-six, which included forty fighters. The Luftwaffe for its part claimed 111 victories on the 15th; actual Fighter Command losses totaled thirty-five. JG 26 had performed its assigned tasks with energy, skill, and exceptional success. The three Gruppen claimed a total of twenty-two victories, without loss.

Action over southern England and the Channel continued at a furious pace on the next day. III/JG 26 was apparently given the day off after its four-mission 15th. The First Gruppe flew a successful freie Jagd, claiming a Hurricane and a Spitfire without loss. Hptm. Karl Ebbighausen led his Second Gruppe up from Marquise at 1300 for a freie Jagd over Dover and Folkestone. They were hit by a squadron of Spitfires as they crossed the English coast. The Gruppe, reinforced by an unidentified Messerschmitt formation, fought back with all of its accumulated skill, and the British squadron, No. 266, was savagely treated—six Spitfires were lost, and three pilots were killed, including the CO, Squadron Leader Wilkinson, who is said to have collided with a Bf 109. Wilkinson's victory by collision was the only claim by No. 266 Squadron to be confirmed. II/JG 26 claimed two Spitfires, but lost its Kommandeur. Karl Ebbighausen's disappearance was not noticed during the fierce action, and his body was never recovered. He was the third Second Gruppe Kommandeur to be killed in three months, and was replaced by Hptm. Erich Bode, who had previously succeeded Ebbighausen as Kapitaen of the 4th Staffel.

18 AUGUST—THE "HARDEST DAY"

The Luftwaffe took a breather on the 17th. Galland was summoned to a conference at Karinhall, Goering's estate outside Berlin. On the 18th, with fair weather once again expected, Kesselring's Luftflotte 2 returned to its current task, the destruction of No. 11 Group's airfields. KG 1 was assigned Biggin Hill, while KG 76 drew Kenley. Participating in the escort were Gruppen from each of Luftflotte 2's Bf 109 and Bf 110 units: JG 3, JG 26, JG 51, JG 52, JG 54, and ZG 26. Shortly after noon, Dover radar reported the heaviest enemy buildup yet seen. By 1340, eighty-two defending fighters from ten squadrons were airborne. More than three hundred aircraft were on a collision course for east Kent.

JG 26's contribution to this raid was the Third Gruppe, today in Galland's absence, under the command of Oblt. Gerhard Schoepfel. III/JG 26 and one Gruppe from JG 3 drew the choice freie Jagd assignment, sweeping across Dover twenty-five miles ahead of the bombers.

The twelve Hurricanes of No. 501 Squadron were en route to their home field at Gravesend, after a morning's operations from their forward satellite at Hawkinge. Their pilots' thoughts of an afternoon off were shattered by orders from their controller to climb to 20,000 feet and patrol over Canterbury. They were soon seen by Gerhard Schoepfel, whose account of the ensuing combat was recorded by a war correspondent:

> We were on a freie Jagd. The Gruppe flew over Dover, gaining quite a bit of altitude. Suddenly I saw a squadron of English fighters climbing far beneath us. We had probably been reported, and the British were looking for us. The British flew over the water in a broad

arc, and then over land, in the direction of Canterbury. I led the Gruppe after them immediately. We were in a favorable position as we approached. Eight aircraft, Hurricanes, flew in front in flights of vees. Behind them was a cover flight. Its fourth aircraft was weaving—flying first left, then right. The English still had not seen us. They now had the more favorable position, since they were higher, but we attacked. I flew toward the weaving aircraft. At 100 meters I had it in front of me, and pressed the button. The fire of my cannon and machine guns literally blew the Hurricane apart. Pieces fell away, smoking and burning. The second aircraft in the cover flight was now in my sights. I repeated the same maneuver. I opened fire, and the Hurricane burst into flames. Undisturbed, the others continued spiraling upward. They had no inkling that there were Messerschmitts on their tails. Now I was behind the third aircraft. A short burst, and this one likewise fell apart. Number three! The Englishmen flew onward; still they had noticed nothing. So I took on the fourth aircraft. This time, however, I approached too closely. When I pressed the button, the Englishman exploded, so near me that pieces hit my crate. It sprayed oil so thickly on the front and right side of my canopy that I could see nothing, and had to break off the battle, which had lasted two minutes.

Schoepfel's feat was at the time unprecedented. He had destroyed four of No. 501 Squadron's dozen Hurricanes in the two-minute attack, killing one pilot and wounding the other three. What he did not make clear to the correspondent is that he had made his attack entirely alone. He had noticed immediately that the Hurricanes' spiral climb would soon put them with their backs to the sun. A single aircraft would have a good opportunity to approach this mass of airplanes undetected. So he ordered his Gruppe to stay above, in the sun, and commenced to trail the Hurricanes until they climbed past him and turned away. Schoepfel then dove to gain speed, pulled up in the first weaver's blind spot beneath it, and opened fire at close range. These tactics were so brilliantly successful that they were repeated three times; none of the four British pilots had time to radio a warning.

Luftflotte 2's afternoon targets were two more No. 11 Group airfields, those at Hornchurch and North Weald. (All four of the day's targets were sector stations, and thus the most important targets in southeastern England, but Luftwaffe Intelligence was unaware of this fact.) KG 2 was to attack Hornchurch; KG 53, North Weald. The fighter force given the freie Jagd assignment was relatively large, Bf 109s being drawn from all five Luftflotte 2 Jagdgeschwader. The close escort comprised only two Gruppen—twenty-five JG 51 Bf 109s with KG 2, and twenty ZG 26 Bf 110s with KG 53. No. 11 Group's controllers juggled the positions of nine intercepting squadrons. Several bombers were downed, and III/JG 26 apparently took position to better protect the Dorniers of KG 2. As the Hurricanes of Squadron Leader Mike Crossley's No. 32 Squadron attempted to get at the bombers, the 109s streamed down. The Hurricanes broke formation and turned to get on the tails of the diving fighters. Lt. Gerhard Mueller-Duehe's Messerschmitt was hit by a short burst of machine-gun fire. It erupted in flames, its dive steepened, and plane and pilot crashed in a field. Mueller-Duehe, a career army officer who had transferred to the Luftwaffe before the war, died a budding Experte, with six confirmed victories.

Five British pilots claimed victories after this action. Apparently, one or more took shots at Oblt. Walter Blume, who crashed, severely wounded, near Canterbury. Like Mueller-Duehe, Blume was a prewar member of the Geschwader, but he was a reservist rather than a regular officer. He was repatriated in 1943 and returned to combat, ending the war with fourteen victories. The Bf 109s gave better than they got in the dogfight, shooting down the Hurricanes of Squadron Leader Crossley and two other pilots. All three British pilots bailed out, two with burns.

The Dorniers that were the subject of No. 32 Squadron's attention flew on, unscathed. A few minutes later, an approaching front blanketed the targeted airfields with clouds. The bomber Geschwader, under orders to bomb only positively identified military targets, wheeled about without bombing. Once again JG 26 had done its job to perfection. The same could not be said for all of the German fighter units, however; the Luftwaffe suffered sixty-seven losses, including twenty Ju 87s from Luftflotte 3. The 18th of August has been tagged the "hardest day" of the Battle of Britain for its high loss total, one hundred aircraft, and the concentrated nature of its combats over southeastern England. Two results of the day's actions were the temporary withdrawal of the dive-bombers from the battle over England and an order requiring much larger, and much closer, fighter escorts for the bomber formations.

GALLAND TAKES COMMAND

Dowding's forces were given a brief respite for the next few days by heavy clouds and rain. Goering, incensed by what he believed to be the Jagdwaffe's failures, took the opportunity to make some changes in his fighter forces. The three Jagdgeschwader of Luftflotte 3—JG 2, JG 27, and JG 53—were reassigned to Luftflotte 2 and ordered to move from Cherbourg to Calais, near the decisive target area. In the stated belief that the failure of his fighters to defeat Fighter Command was due to lack of aggressiveness, Goering promoted two of his most successful Gruppenkommandeure to Geschwader commands. Adolf Galland was one of the two; Hannes Trautloft was the other. Major Galland took over JG 26 on 22 August; Gerhard Schoepfel was promoted to command the Third Gruppe and was replaced at 9th Staffel by Oblt. Ebeling. By the end of October, all eight fighter Kommodoren had been replaced by younger men.

Major Gotthardt Handrick, at 31 judged too old to lead fighters in battle, turned over the Geschwader to the 28-year-old Major Galland and left to take command of the Luftwaffe mission in Rumania. An ambitious, well-bred officer, Handrick's skills as an athlete and sportsman on the ground had not translated into equal success in the air. Highly thought of in the Luftwaffe, Handrick served in a number of senior staff and command positions, finishing the war as an Oberst in command of the 8th Jagddivision.

In a letter to the author, Adolf Galland gave the following reasons for the success of JG 26 under his command:

> The [prewar] commanders were excellent officers in peacetime, but they were not at all the best leaders in combat. Replacement of commanders was the necessary first step. From then on, every operation and mission in Geschwader strength was led by myself personally. I knew exactly what could and could not be done in large air battles. As the next step, I devised, wrote up, and carried out a Geschwader system for fighter escort of bomber formations which was well-known and liked as the best one possible.

In his postwar interrogation, Galland claimed that JG 26 and the unit he considered second best, Trautloft's JG 54 Green Hearts, were the only Jagdgeschwader able to carry out the escort function with consistently low losses. The keys were careful planning and precise execution. A Jagdgeschwader could protect at most a single Geschwader of bombers, and then only if the bombers maintained close formation. Galland held his formation leaders "personally responsible" for every bomber escorted; he required an explanation for each loss.

Jupp Buerschgens credits JG 26's success in protecting the bombers to the experience and tactical awareness of its pilots, who knew instinctively that only a flexible escort formation—that is, constantly changing in speed, altitude, direction, and distance from the bombers—could be successful. Other units interpreted their orders to maintain "close escort" more literally and, having forfeited their freedom of action, lost many more aircraft, both fighters and bombers, to the British interceptors.

Major Galland began his planned purge immediately. Hptm. Kurt Fisher was the first to go; he was replaced as Kommandeur of the First Gruppe by Hptm. Rolf Pingel, a successful leader from JG 53 and, like Galland, a "Spaniard." The Second Gruppe lost one Staffelkapitaen. The successful Third Gruppe really required no changes, but, bowing to Muencheberg's entreaties, Galland gave the eager 21-year-old command of the 7th Staffel. Oblt. Georg Beyer, an older pilot and another "Spaniard," gave up the 7th to become Galland's adjutant at Geschwader headquarters. Two weeks later, the Kapitaen of the 1st Staffel was replaced by Oblt. Eberhard Henrici.

Another novelty introduced by Galland ensured that a full Geschwader Stabsschwarm of four aircraft would be available for missions. When necessary, he borrowed as wingmen experienced enlisted pilots from the Staffeln—a practice that soon became widespread. Oblt. Horten felt that now that he was flying as wingman to a "pistol," his fortunes in the air were bound to change. He was right, inasmuch as Galland was able to find the enemy every time he took to the air. However, not being a Muencheberg, Horten soon found that it was impossible both to maintain formation with Galland and to line up on his own targets—and Galland was not about to set him up with any! Horten's only targets would be those few planes that succeeded in evading his Kommodore's aim. If one broke toward Horten, he would have a fleeting chance to fire at it. It would be a difficult deflection shot, for which he had not been trained. Consulting his manuals, Horten found to his surprise that firing at crossing targets was positively discouraged by the Luftwaffe as a waste of ammunition. The only "correct" way to line up on a target was Manfred von Richthofen's method—from directly behind it, and as close as possible. As this was inappropriate to Horten's situation, he applied his keen engineer's mind—and his previous experience in the infantry as an antiaircraft machine-gunner—to the problem and calculated some rough rules-of-thumb to allow him to judge the correct lead through his Revi reflector sight. The values he calculated appeared too large, but he resolved to test them at the first opportunity.

Return of fair weather brought a resumption of large-scale Luftwaffe bomber attacks on 24 August. Still hoping to force Fighter Command to commit its last reserves, Kesselring continued his attacks on airfields, while adding aircraft factories to the target list. It was decided (incorrectly) that radar stations were unprofitable targets, and attacks on them were stopped. III/JG 26 was one of three Gruppen assigned to escort forty Ju 88s and Do 17s. So tight was the formation that only two of the twelve RAF squadrons scrambled against it were able to penetrate the screen. One Third Gruppe Bf 109 was shot down into the Channel; its pilot was picked up by the German rescue service. Two more of the Gruppe's aircraft crash landed in France. The Geschwader succeeded in shooting down seven RAF fighters over the course of the day.

On the next day, large scale raids on No. 11 Group's airfields were successfully driven off by the defenders. Bomber losses were heavy, leading to demands for even closer escort. A number of bombs fell on London on the night of the 25th, initiating a chain of events of great significance. JG 26 shot down seven fighters and suffered no casualties. The Schlageter fighters were rested for the next two days and reentered combat on the 28th.

DECIMATION OF THE DEFIANTS

On 28 August, the by now predictable morning buildup over Calais was reported by Dover radar at 0900. It proved to consist of thirty-three bombers escorted by 120 Bf 109s. Thirty-two Hurricanes and the twelve Defiants of No. 264 Squadron were scrambled, making contact just as the bomber formation split up. Half made for Eastchurch, and the rest for Rochford; both were important Fighter Command bases on the banks of the Thames. The Third Gruppe of JG 26, led by the new Kommodore of the Geschwader, had the unenviable job of low cover for the Eastchurch raiders. The Hurricanes were engaged by the high cover. The following description of the next few minutes is based on Galland's postwar recollections:

Galland glanced up at the Heinkels and saw a tight formation of a dozen single-seaters paralleling the bombers, and just beneath them. Momentarily puzzled, Galland thought that they might be Ju 87s. Then he saw the turrets—Defiants! Employing their unique mode of attack and about to rake the defenseless bellies of the Heinkels with their forty-eight turret machine guns. Shoving his throttle forward and yanking the stick back hard, Galland pointed his machine straight up at the Defiants, followed by his Stab flight. The tight British formation was blown apart. Action was so swift that Galland couldn't keep an enemy in his sights. He found himself flying alongside a Defiant, which was immediately shot down by Oblt. Horten. After overshooting a second Defiant, which had throttled back its engine, Galland dove after a third, opening fire at one hundred yards and closing to twenty. His cannon ammunition was gone; only his two light machine guns were firing. His target was the aircraft of No. 264 Squadron's CO, Squadron Leader Garvin, and the senior ranking Defiant gunner, Flight Lieutenant Ash. Four times Ash holed the 109, but Galland finally won the contest; the Defiant's fuel tank burst into flames. As Galland broke away, Ash and Garvin succeeded in bailing out. Garvin survived with burns, but Ash hit his plane's tail and his parachute streamed. No. 264 Squadron was finished as a day fighting unit. Four Defiants were shot down and five others were damaged on this mission. The Defiant squadron was left with three serviceable aircraft and one experienced crew, and it withdrew to the north the next day.

Walter Horten's perspective was that of a wingman; his description of this battle thus differs somewhat from that of his commander:

We had searched far and near, without seeing the enemy, when Galland changed course somewhat to the right. My experience told me that he had discovered something. Then I saw a tiny moving point, and approaching it, saw it as a "mill"; . . . Since we were making considerable steam, we soon overtook it and it was recognized as a lonely, weaving Defiant. . . . We were astonished at its impudence (or stupidity). When Galland approached it from below, its turret did not move at all. We throttled back and watched. Phosphor trails passed between the two aircraft. . . . I saw no effect of the fire. I suddenly realized that I might be in for it, if the Englishman pulled up suddenly to give his gunner a clear field of fire over his tail. But just then he made an elegant turn to the left and came past me from my upper right to my lower left. I made a quick calculation for lead, and "let fly." I saw my first tracers pass close behind his tail, corrected my aim slightly, and opened fire again. The aircraft burst into flames over its entire wingspan, and fell away as a burning torch. My first, a "textbook victory," and it came about in a crossing situation!

JG 26 now faced a sterner enemy than the hapless Defiants—the implacable Kanal. Fuel lights glowing even as combat continued, the Messerschmitts broke away and streamed across Kent toward France. At least seven didn't make it and ditched in the Channel. All of their pilots were rescued uninjured. Galland soon learned, to his chagrin, that the second Rotte of his Stabsschwarm wouldn't be returning at all. Hptm. Beyer, his new adjutant, and Beyer's wingman, an enlisted pilot borrowed from the 7th Staffel, had apparently been bounced by the intercepting Hurricanes and shot down. Both came down near Canterbury and survived the war as prisoners.

The battle had entered its most critical stage for the British. Now that the Germans had moved the single-engined fighters of Luftflotte 3 to the Calais area, Kesselring had eight hundred of his most capable aircraft type, the Bf 109E, with which to wear down Fighter Command. Fighter Command had a total of 759 Hurricanes and Spitfires assigned to its squadrons on 1 September, but only 345 were in No. 11 Group—and of these, only 254 were operational.

Kesselring tried a variety of tactics over the next few days, including more airfield attacks. By now most of No. 11 Group's fields were in shambles. The fighting on the 31st was especially fierce. Fighter Command lost thirty-nine planes in aerial combat—the Luftwaffe claimed 116. Thirty-four British pilots were killed or wounded. The Luftwaffe also lost thirty-nine aircraft—the RAF claimed ninety-four—of which twenty-eight were fighters; twenty-two German fighter pilots were lost. JG 26 flew three Geschwader escorts and one freie Jagd during the day, most to the airfields on the north side of the Thames Estuary, at the extreme limit of the Bf 109's range. The Geschwader claimed twenty-two victories for the day, but lost five aircraft and pilots, its heaviest loss of pilots for any single day of the battle. In the morning, Kesselring sent four waves of bombers against the airfields, each with a massive escort of Bf 109s and Bf 110s. JG 26 was part of the escort for a Gruppe of Do 17s ordered to hit North Weald, a No. 11 Group sector station northeast of London. No. 56 Squadron's twelve Hurricanes attempted to defend their airfield but lost four fighters to the Messerschmitts, while succeeding in damaging only one German aircraft. No. 56 Squadron had to be withdrawn the next day to the relative quiet of No. 10 Group's sector in western England.

Shortly after noon, JG 26 was again airborne, this time as part of the escort for two waves of Do 17s and He 111s dispatched to attack the sector stations at Biggin Hill and Hornchurch, and the fighter airfield at Croydon. The Kenley controller was slow to react, and the airfields were all hit before the raids were intercepted. No. 85 Squadron's Hurricanes and No. 603 Squadron's Spitfires chased the raiders back across the Thames Estuary. No. 603 Squadron's Spitfire pilots, newly arrived from No. 13 Group in Scotland, claimed four Bf 109s without loss. JG 26 lost two pilots in this battle.

THE THIRD GRUPPE IN ACTION

The Third Gruppe's role in the Geschwader's third mission of 31 August has been reconstructed using information provided by Gerhard Schoepfel:

Late that afternoon Hptm. Schoepfel and his adjutant, Oblt. Haiboeck, sat in the small operations hut at the edge of their field at Caffiers, compiling the Gruppe's combat report for the morning missions. Only one plane had been lost, that of Oblt. Heinz Ebeling, Kapitaen of the 9th Staffel. He had been seen to crash land in the Channel, and the air-sea rescue (ASR) headquarters at Boulogne had already telephoned to report his safe rescue. Ebeling was at that moment returning to the airfield. Through the hut's open door, Schoepfel could see the ground crews at work. The landing ground itself was nothing but a mown grainfield, with an appreciable slope down to the dispersal area. The Bf 109s were parked in the spaces between individual trees and bushes, surrounded by walls of sandbags and camouflaged with nets. The planes were refueled, topped off with oil, and rearmed, and the three Staffeln reported the number of aircraft available for duty— between six and eight per Staffel. The total was then passed along to the Geschwader.

The skies were clear, and Schoepfel expected to be called on to fly another mission. Sure enough, the telephone behind him soon rang with orders from Major Galland. JG 26 was to escort a Geschwader of Do 17s in another attack on the airfield at Hornchurch, which was north of London and thus at the extreme limit of the Bf 109's range. The First and Second Gruppen were to fly close escort; the Third, detached escort. The bomber Geschwader would arrive on the line St. Omer-Calais at 1800–1805 hours.

Oblt. Haiboeck called the Staffel trailers and summoned the Kapitaene to a conference. The three men soon came walking up, yellow scarves around their necks and carefully crushed service caps at their sides—Joachim "Jochen" Muencheberg of the 7th Staffel, whose handsome Aryan features made him a favorite of the propaganda company photographers; Gustav "Micky" Sprick of the 8th, a flaxen-haired, even-tempered farmboy; and Heinz Ebeling of the 9th, whose flushed face bore a big smile, in marked contrast to his usual stern appearance. Ebeling had just been fished from the Channel by a Do 18 after a ninety-minute swim, and he was still feeling the effects of the tumbler of cognac he had been offered by his rescuers.

The Kapitaene accepted their assignment as detached escort with pleasure—anything was better than close escort. Schoepfel then gave them their takeoff times and sequence, the route of the bomber formation, the schedule and route of the ASR aircraft; answered questions; and dismissed them. Twenty minutes before the scheduled time of takeoff, the Staffel dispersals came to life again. The pilots, who were fully dressed in their flying suits and fur boots, arose from the lounge chairs in which they napped between missions. They were fully equipped for a water crossing. Below their knees they wore a belt containing flare cartridges. In various pockets in their suits, fastened with cord to prevent their loss during a parachute jump or a ditching, were a flare pistol, a sheathed knife, rescue flags, chocolates and glucose, and Pervitin tablets, a type of stimulant.

The pilots put on their life jackets, looked over their equipment and aircraft, checked their watches, and spoke one last time with the ground crews. After urinating behind their aircraft, they climbed into their cockpits, and with the help of the crew chiefs fastened their seat and parachute harnesses. At signals from the Staffelkapi- taene, the mechanics began turning the starter cranks. The initial dull sound grew into a loud roar; the pilots let in the clutches, and with jerky movements the propellers began to turn. Helmets were put on; throat microphones were fastened; canopies were latched. On another signal, the wheel chocks were removed, and one aircraft after another crept out from beneath the camouflage netting cov- ering its box, following the Staffel leaders.

Schoepfel led the four aircraft of his Stabsschwarm over a slight rise to the takeoff point; some twenty Messerschmitts of his Gruppe bumped along behind them. After getting the takeoff signal, Schoep- fel extended his flaps and pushed his throttle forward. His aircraft began to move. He then pushed his control stick forward; his tail wheel lifted as he sped down the hill. After a short run, the Bf 109 was free of the ground. Schoepfel quickly raised his flaps and land- ing gear, adjusted his propeller, and connected his gunsight. He banked gently to the left and watched the rest of the Gruppe lift off and join up. The formation headed inland in a shallow climb, met the bombers, and turned on course. The First and Second Gruppen arrived, split into Schwaerme, and moved into position, very near the bombers. The Third Gruppe continued climbing, and by mid- Channel was almost ten thousand feet above the bombers. At a short signal from Schoepfel, they separated to fly in Staffeln to the left, the right, and behind the bombers, keeping them just in sight. As the pilots approached the chalk cliffs of Dover, the spit of land at Dungeness pointed its sandy-yellow finger at them; in the far dis- tance they could see the Thames. The pilots scanned their instru- ments briefly; this would be their last chance to do so for a while.

As the head of the bomber formation crossed the English coast, the Dover-London flak highway sprang into action, carpeting the formation's course with puffs of black smoke. Schoepfel's element leaders kept their eyes on the northwest horizon. From past experience, they expected the first attack by the British fighter squadrons to come over Canterbury. Schoepfel turned his formation east, to better spot attacks from the favored position, out of the western sun. Muencheberg was the first to report a British fighter formation, well below the bombers. He led his 7th Staffel down in a screaming dive. Streams of smoke could be seen erupting from the Messerschmitts' guns; the last British fighter began to burn. The rest half-rolled and dove away, with Muencheberg's men in hot pursuit.

The Dornier formation still held together well. No more RAF fighters were seen until shortly before London—then a long string of Spitfires and Hurricanes erupted from a cloud. Hptm. Schoepfel's pilots headed toward them at full throttle, and burst into their midst. The Kommandeur broke up a Spitfire's attack on a Dornier with a short squirt of fire from long range. The startled British pilot broke to the right and flew right through the Messerschmitt's fire. There was an explosion; flaps and landing gear dropped; and the Spitfire dove away out of control. Schoepfel accepted Haiboeck's radioed congratulations and pointed his fighter toward France. The bombers had already dropped their bombs and turned for home. Their formation now contained large gaps; one Dornier, mortally damaged, trailed the rest. Schoepfel's Gruppe returned by Rotten and Schwaerme. The fighters were seen off by one last burst from the Dover antiaircraft guns and then found themselves back over the Channel. Far to their rear, a large formation of British fighters could be seen swarming like locusts; they would not be able to catch up. Several rescue buoys were spotted in mid-Channel, as yet unoccupied; an ASR seaplane hugged the coastline at low altitude. Caffiers was seen less than a minute after the fighters crossed the French coast. A 109 dove on the command post, rocking its wings as a sign of victory. Hptm. Schoepfel led his own Schwarm in to land. The slender fighters dropped heavily onto the uneven clay soil. Mechanics then directed the aircraft to their dispersals; their propellers came to a stop; the roaring in the pilots' ears was at last extinguished. The earth had them again.

The Staffelkapitaene soon sought out Hptm. Schoepfel and made their reports. Oblt. Muencheberg claimed one victory for his Staffel, at the cost of two pilots. Oblt. Sprick's Staffel claimed one

Spitfire, for no losses. Oblt. Ebeling celebrated his deliverance earlier in the day by shooting down two Hurricanes, but had then witnessed one of his own pilots take a direct hit from antiaircraft fire; fortunately the man was able to bail out. It had been a rough mission, and only moderately successful; several of the bombers had been seen to go down south of London, after the RAF fighters' attack. Nothing could stem the natural ebullience of Schoepfel's men, however; the mission was reflown until long past nightfall, with the aid of cigars, cognac, and much waving of the pilots' arms and hands.

The first of September was yet another day of heavy attacks on the Biggin Hill, Detling, and Eastchurch airfields. The London dock area was also bombed, in retaliation for RAF raids on Berlin, which were intended to answer the Luftwaffe's London attacks of 25 August.

JG 26 flew one mission on the first, a Geschwader escort to the London area, and filed eleven claims. The one Geschwader aircraft that failed to return was that of Oblt. Buerschgens of the 7th Staffel. Jupp Buerschgens, by now a ten-victory Experte, relates the story of his last mission:

> I led the 7th Staffel, as I had done frequently over the past several weeks. At 1300 we took off from Caffiers. Our mission was to escort a bomber formation in an attack on Kenley, an airfield near London. Flying at about 6,000 meters [19,500 feet] altitude, we reached the target without being attacked, and were only then engaged by British fighters, which were primarily interested in the bombers and Bf 110s. I was still right beside the bombers when a Spitfire immediately beneath me attacked a circling Bf 110 from behind. It was simple for me to get behind the attacker by a short maneuver. We then had a Bf 110, a Spitfire, and a Bf 109 (myself), flying in a row. While the rear gunner fired at the Spitfire and the Spitfire in turn attempted to silence the rear gunner, I found it easy to put a long burst into the Spitfire, which immediately smoked and broke away in a split-S. I had approached very near the 110, whose gunner was firing continuously, and turned away to keep from ramming it. At this moment I felt a blow beside my left foot in the cockpit, and my engine quickly came to a stop. Good Lord!—the Bf 110 gunner, seeing me pointed at him (like the Spitfire), had taken me to be another enemy, and had hit my aircraft.

Streaming a white cloud of fuel, I feathered my prop and glided unmolested in the direction of the French coast, hoping that I might reach the water of the Channel and eventually be fished out by a German rescue aircraft. The sun shone brightly; the seconds seemed like hours. Around me, the bitter combats continued to rage. Damaged German bombers, British and German fighters fell away, smoking, burning, or breaking up. Parachutes opened or failed to open—it was a gruesome but also an exciting spectacle. I had never before been able to observe such an air battle. My glide took me ever nearer the ground; I would never be able to reach the water of the Channel. I glanced at my watch; it was about 1400. I was aware that this was the end of my fighting career and tears streamed down my face. I finally crashed my loyal Bf 109 (into many pieces) near Rye, south of Folkestone, and woke up later in the hospital, suffering from back and head injuries.

About a week later, I was taken by subway to the interrogation camp in London. The caption to a photograph an English photojournalist took of me and my guards stated that I had quite a sense of humor for a German. I had cheerfully told the ticket taker that I did not need a ticket, as I had a season pass—a season that stretched into six years of imprisonment as a guest of the British king.

After resting the next day, during which the heavy attacks on Fighter Command's bases continued, JG 26 returned to action. On 3 September, North Weald, a sector station north of London, was heavily damaged by a wave of Dornier bombers. JG 26 was assigned to cover their withdrawal. Eight No. 11 Group squadrons tried unsuccessfully to reach the Dorniers as they returned across east Kent. No. 603 Squadron's eight Spitfires became embroiled with II/JG 26 over Margate. The British pilots attempted to go into line astern formation, but were hit by the Messerschmitts from above, and the battle immediately became one-on-one. After ten minutes of twisting combat, three machines had fallen in flames. One German pilot was lost; two severely burned British pilots bailed out into the Thames Estuary. One was Plt. Off. Richard Hillary, who described the battle in his wartime memoir, *Falling Through Space*. Both Spitfires were claimed by the Second Gruppe's Kommandeur, Hptm. Erich Bode, as his first victories of the war. No. 603 Squadron had now lost fourteen Spitfires destroyed, four pilots killed, and six pilots wounded; it had been the combat zone for only seven days.

JG 26's missions on the 4th and 5th of September failed to

contact the RAF. Park's controllers had strict orders not to vector squadrons to intercept Luftwaffe formations believed to contain only fighters. Some of the more optimistic German pilots believed the RAF's refusal of combat to be a sign of imminent collapse. No. 11 Group was, in fact, up to strength in aircraft. Fighter Command's shortage of pilots, especially experienced leaders, had become serious, however, and on the 6th Dowding modified his policy of resting and fighting his squadrons as units. Depleted squadrons would now be required to transfer their experienced survivors to units still in combat.

For the Germans, a string of successful or uneventful days would invariably be followed by harder fighting. The 6th was another busy day for the Schlageter pilots. In the morning, they flew a Geschwader escort for another attack on No. 11 Group's airfields. On this occasion the British were waiting, and the Third Gruppe was bounced from above by Spitfires. Oblt. Muencheberg lost all three aircraft from his 7th Staffel Schwarm. The Gruppe then became involved with Hurricanes and shot down five. Pilots of the Second Gruppe claimed two Spitfires and two Hurricanes, without loss. That afternoon the Geschwader flew another escort mission and, without loss to themselves, claimed the destruction of five British fighters.

THE THIRD PHASE—ATTACKS ON LONDON

At some point during the first week of September, Adolf Hitler, obsessed then as always with revenge, made the fateful decision that assured Great Britain's survival. At first dubious, Reichsmarschall Goering kept his peace for a few days and then gave in. Frustrated by his fighter pilots' inability to destroy Fighter Command, and by Dowding's seemingly miraculous ability to parry his bombers' thrusts with a bare minimum of defensive forces, Goering ordered his two active Luftflotten to concentrate on the one target that would surely be defended by all of Fighter Command's resources. This target was, of course, London.

Within ten days, the extent of Goering's miscalculation was plain to all of the combatants. The new strategy allowed the recovery of No. 11 Group's command and control apparatus, and the full restoration of its defensive capabilities. German losses rose. The invasion was postponed, and the Luftwaffe's mission was changed from a tactical one—gaining air supremacy over the projected battlefield of southeastern England—to a far more nebulous strategic task. Britain's will to continue the war was now to be broken by terror bombing of the civilian population. There would be no invasion.

On the afternoon of the 7th of September, Hermann Goering, having "taken over personal command of the Luftwaffe in its war against England," according to the Wehrmacht communiqué, stood with his entourage at Cap Blanc Nez while the largest Luftwaffe formation ever assembled passed overhead. Its target was London. Nearly one thousand aircraft flew toward the Thames Estuary. They were stepped from 14,000 to 23,000 feet and covered 800 square miles. JG 26 was buried far back in the last wave, flying close cover for KG 30's Ju 88s. The Schlageter fighters performed the hated close escort duty with their usual competence; KG 30 lost only one aircraft this day. JG 26 claimed the destruction of five British fighters on the mission, while losing two pilots as prisoners.

It was some time in early September that Galland made his famous request to Goering for a Geschwader of Spitfires. He was of course not speaking literally, but for the effect his insulting words would have on his commander-in-chief. Galland's point was that close escort minimized all of the Bf 109's advantages over the RAF fighters—its greater speed at high altitude and its superiority in dive-and-zoom tactics—and magnified its weaknesses—poor cockpit visibility, poor radius of action, relatively poor turning circle. Was it not the fighters' proper role to defeat Fighter Command, and thus make the invasion possible, or were they present merely to protect the bombers? Galland wanted Goering to know that he couldn't have it both ways. Galland's pilots knew only that they were being forced by their leaders to fight at a disadvantage, and referred to themselves sarcastically as Kettenhunde—chained dogs.

The heavy attacks on London continued for the next week. JG 26's missions were a mixture of close escorts, withdrawal escorts, and free hunts. The Geschwader's rate of victory claims dropped noticeably. However, the victory totals of several pilots were now nearing twenty, the nominal requirement in 1940 for the award of the coveted Knight's Cross. Hptm. Schoepfel got his twenty-first on the 11th, and his Knight's Cross the same day. His victim was a

Coastal Command Blenheim fighter from No. 235 Squadron, part of the escort for twelve Fleet Air Arm Albacore torpedo bombers that were attacking invasion shipping in Calais harbor. Oblt. Muencheberg scored his twentieth victory on 14 September and claimed the award that same day, as did Hptm. Rolf Pingel, Kommandeur of the First Gruppe.

15 SEPTEMBER—THE BATTLE'S CLIMAX

The turning point of the Battle of Britain came on a bright Sunday. The morning raid took an abnormally long time to assemble, giving Park's controllers ample time to marshal their forces. Struck by nine squadrons of Hurricanes and Spitfires over London, one hundred Dorniers scattered their bombs, swung about, and dove to full speed in desperate attempts to escape attack. Dowding's pilots, exhilarated by their success, had time for tea and sandwiches while Kesselring assembled an even larger raid over France. This consisted of 150 bombers escorted by two of Goering's very best escort units: Galland's JG 26 and Trautloft's JG 54. Their numbers were to prove woefully insufficient.

According to British sources, the bombers first circled over Maidstone and then took thirty minutes to cover the sixty miles from the coast to London—telling indications that they had missed the rendezvous with their escort. Over eastern Kent, the bomber formations were attacked by 170 fighters. The Bf 109s were hard pressed, but kept the British fighters at a distance. Galland engaged Hurricanes and Spitfires in a whirling melee for ten whole minutes, without result. Then he sighted a squadron of Hurricanes in close formation below:

> I dove from about 800 meters [2,500 feet] above them, approached at high speed, and fired at the far left aircraft in the rear flight, continuing fire until point-blank range. Finally, large pieces of metal flew off the Hurricane. As I shot past this aircraft, I found myself in the middle of the enemy squadron, which was flying in stepped formation. I immediately attacked the right-hand aircraft of the leading flight of three. Again, metal panels broke off; the aircraft nosed over and dove earthward, ablaze. The remaining English pilots were so startled that none as much as attempted to get on my

tail; rather, the entire formation scattered and dove away. Two parachutes appeared about 500 meters [1,600 feet] below our formation.

As Galland's Messerschmitts followed him away from the bombers, chaos erupted behind them. Over eastern London, the bombers were attacked head-on by no fewer than thirteen squadrons of fighters. Once again the bombers broke and scattered under the onslaught, spreading bombs over the East London suburbs. As they fled pell-mell to the southeast, it was obvious to everyone in the air that the Luftwaffe had suffered a massive defeat. The bombers had lost a quarter of their number. The battle of attrition that was to have wiped out Fighter Command was instead destroying the cream of the Luftwaffe's offensive force, the bombers that had scourged Warsaw and Rotterdam.

On 15 September, Fighter Command saved Great Britain. The fighter pilots were sure of it, the Ministry of Information tried its best to convince the civilian population of it, and two days later, Ultra confirmed it—the German aerial resupply fleet, a vital part of the invasion force, was ordered to disperse. The British were able to decode the radio message the same day it was intercepted. On the 19th, Hitler ordered the indefinite postponement of Unternehmen Seeloewe (Operation Sealion), the planned invasion of Great Britain.

For the rest of September, Kesselring tried a variety of tactics. Sperrle's Luftflotte 3 in northwestern France had switched to night bombing when its fighters were transferred to Calais. Luftflotte 2 now began night attacks as well, while sending fighters alone and fighters interspersed with bombers by day. JG 26 scored heavily during this period, whenever the British chose to do battle. On a massive freie Jagd north of the Thames Estuary on 23 September, the Geschwader's pilots claimed ten Hurricanes and Spitfires out of Jafue 2's total score of twenty-one. However, Fighter Command losses for the entire day totaled only eleven. The Geschwader's only losses were two pilots of the Third Gruppe, both of whom were shot down by Spitfires over Kent and captured. Since their crash landings were observed by their opponents, the victors are known to have been from Biggin Hill's No. 92 Squadron, which in its turn lost one Spitfire to the Third Gruppe Kommandeur, Hptm. Schoepfel.

On 24 September, Galland downed his fortieth opponent, a

Hurricane of No. 17 Squadron, over Rochester. Hitler summoned him to Berlin and awarded him the Oak Leaves to the Knight's Cross—the third Wehrmacht member to be so honored. Galland was an instinctive pilot who threw his Messerschmitt around in the air in seemingly impossible maneuvers. Nonetheless, Oblt. Horten managed to keep up with his "Kapitano" and had a successful month. In Horten's words:

> From 23 August until the end of September, I flew forty-five missions with Galland, and witnessed twenty-five of his victories. I was in a position to fire eight times. I downed seven enemy aircraft, five of them during crossing encounters from a great distance (up to one thousand meters), using only my machine guns. One Spitfire was hit from behind at fifty meters; I struck another Spitfire from the front, in a bank. In mid-September orders came down from the Chief of the General Staff that technical officers were no longer to fly combat missions. When I returned from a sortie in late September with a doublet [twin victories], the Geschwader was not able to report them. I had been grounded, along with all the other TOs. My gunnery procedure [deflection estimation] was orphaned for a while.

The Luftflotte 3 fighter units, which had reinforced Luftflotte 2 in anticipation of Unternehmen Seeloewe, returned to their bases in northwestern France on the 25th, a move followed with interest by the British radar operators. Kesselring and Sperrle ordered more attacks on aircraft factories, and Supermarine and Bristol were heavily damaged. On the last day of September, Kesselring and Sperrle returned to heavy day attacks, which were rebuffed with high losses. These proved to be the Kampfgeschwader's last large-scale day raids on England. The single-engined German fighters suffered a sharp defeat; for the destruction of thirteen British fighters, twenty-nine Bf 109s were lost, and a number of others crash-landed in France with varying degrees of damage. The often-derided Bf 110 Gruppen had one of their better days, shooting down six British fighters without loss.

For its part, JG 26 had one of its worst days of the battle, losing four pilots for only five victory claims. Galland's wingman, Hptm. Walter Kienzle, was picked off early in the day by a Spitfire. Kienzle was under consideration as a potential Gruppenkommandeur, and was thus flying in the place of honor beside (and under the eye of) the Kommodore.

Galland himself did not score until the Geschwader was returning from its third mission of the day. He spotted a Hurricane below him and dove to the attack. He approached to point-blank range and opened fire. The Hurricane exploded in flames, covering Galland's Messerschmitt in oil from wingtip to wingtip. After the return to Audembert, a piece of British sheet metal was found in the fighter's supercharger intake. A number of the Geschwader's fighters never returned, but fell into the Channel from fuel exhaustion; others reached their fields on their last drops of gasoline.

THE FOURTH PHASE—FIGHTERS AS BOMBERS

With the defeat of Goering's bomber force and the indefinite postponement of Seeloewe, the battle entered a new stage—Fighter Command was to be extended and exhausted defending against fighter-bomber raids by day, while the Kampfgeschwader destroyed England's cities and civilian morale by night. To this end, one Staffel from each Jagdgruppe was equipped with the Bf 109E-4/B, which could carry a single 250-kg (551-lb) bomb. In vain, Galland railed against this misuse of his elite Jaeger (which means both hunters and fighter pilots). He felt that his pilots were being punished for the failure of the entire Luftwaffe, that as "stopgaps and scapegoats," fighter-bombers could have no effect on the course of the war but would suffer for no purpose. Galland has described the tactics of the period, and his pilots' attitudes, in his book *Die Ersten und die Letzten*, which as *The First and the Last* has remained the most popular Luftwaffe memoir available in English:

> Each Geschwader was responsible for escorting its own bomb-carriers. The altitude for the approach was about 6,000 meters [19,500 feet]. At the start we let the Jabos (Jagdbomber or fighter-bombers) fly in bomber formation, but it was soon apparent that this let the enemy fighters concentrate fully on the bomb-carriers. We then distributed the Jabos in small units throughout the entire Geschwader formation and thus brought them in fairly safely over their target area. This type of raid had no more than nuisance value. The passive behavior toward enemy fighters; the feeling of inferiority

when we were attacked because of our lack of speed, maneuverability, and rate of climb; added to the unconvincing effect of single bombs scattered over wide areas, combined to ruin the morale of the German fighter pilot, already low because of the need to fly close escort.

The fighter-bombers' efforts, while foredoomed to failure from a strategic standpoint, did succeed in extending and frustrating No. 11 Group. The raids were exceedingly difficult to intercept, coming over at such high speeds and altitudes that only Spitfires had a chance to reach them. Park formed a special reconnaissance flight with new Spitfire IIs; their job was to shadow the elusive intruders and direct interceptions. Park finally had to order standing patrols to be flown. The defense never solved the problem to its satisfaction, and German fighter casualties were low; JG 26 lost only seven pilots during October.

Although the British mark 31 October as the official end of the battle, fighter and fighter-bomber sweeps continued until halted by the rains of winter. The British resumed the operation of their coastal convoys, and the Stukas returned to action against them; the Jagdgeschwader remaining on the Channel were called upon to escort these anti-shipping raids. JG 26 lost thirteen more pilots before year's end, including two Staffelkapitaene.

One of these was Oblt. Heinz Ebeling, who was lost on 5 November, the same day that he was awarded the Knight's Cross for "eighteen aerial victories, numerous ground attacks, and the successful and rapid conversion of the 9th Staffel to the fighter-bomber role." He collided with his wingman while on a Jabo mission to London; both men were captured near Dungeness.

On 7 November JG 26 received its first Bf 109E-7s, which had fittings for a 300-liter (79-gallon) drop tank or a 250-kg (551-lb) bomb. Possibly of decisive importance had they been available for long-range escort service in August, the E-7's capabilities were wasted in November, spreading meaningless bombs over southern England. Few details are available for the missions of the period; the routine was monotonous, even though dangerous, and the diarists had either become casualties or were too exhausted to write. Two more of the Geschwader's Experten were awarded the Knight's Cross: Oblt. Micky Sprick qualified after his twentieth victory on 1

October. Hptm. Walter Adolph, who transferred in from III/JG 27 on 4 October to replace Erich Bode as Kommandeur of the Second Gruppe, was awarded his on 13 November.

On 17 November, the Geschwader escorted the Bf 110 Jabos of EprGr 210 in a raid on Martlesham Heath. The Hurricanes of Nos. 17 and 257 Squadrons made an effective interception. No. 17 Squadron waded into the fighter-bomber formation. Obstlt. Galland shot down one of its Hurricanes, whose pilot bailed out uninjured, but the others succeeded in shooting down three Bf 110s. No. 257 Squadron took on the bulk of the Bf 109s and claimed two shot down and one probable, while losing one pilot killed and one injured, both from the guns of Galland. One JG 26 aircraft was shot down into the sea, killing Oblt. Eberhard Henrici, Kapitaen of the 1st Staffel. His replacement as Staffelkapitaen was Oblt. Josef "Pips" Priller, a successful young pilot from JG 51 who had won his Knight's Cross in that unit the previous month.

Lt. Borris's diary tells of the situation in the Second Gruppe as winter arrived:

21 November 1940

Fog and mists drifted ever more frequently from the Kanal across the land. We flew fewer missions, but they were never easy. Again and again we traveled the racecourse to London. That the English fighter squadrons were well-practiced on this track is clear. . . . Now they waited with impunity above our formations and sought out the most favorable position for attack. We had to stay in formation and wait until the Spitfires came tumbling down. . . .

By early December most of the German fighter units had withdrawn from the battlefield. Only three Jagdgeschwader remained on the Channel coast—JG 2, JG 3, and JG 26. Missions came less and less frequently. At noon on the 5th, promised reasonable flying weather, JG 26 flew a full-strength freie Jagd over Kent. The Third Gruppe bounced the Hurricanes of No. 253 Squadron and shot down one; a second British fighter was forced to land. The rest of the Geschwader met successive waves of Spitfires from Nos. 64, 75, and 92 squadrons. No. 64 Squadron lost Spitfires to Obstlt. Galland and a 5th Staffel Unteroffizier, while claiming two Messerschmitts. Squadron Leader "Sailor" Malan's No. 74 "Tiger" Squadron claimed ten Bf 109s, but only one German pilot was in fact lost over England. Another pilot, Obfw. Robert Menge, a recent transfer into the 3rd Staffel from JG 77, was badly injured by Spitfires over Folkestone, but managed to return to base. A third Bf 109 suffered combat damage and belly-landed at Wissant. Galland's victory was his 57th, making him the top-scoring pilot in the Luftwaffe.

The landing ground of the First Gruppe became so sodden from the incessant rain that the aircraft had to be supported by planks and logs. To prevent their aircraft from sinking in the mud, the entire Geschwader moved inland on 7 December, to an airfield on the plain of the Somme River that had been occupied until recently by JG 53 and ZG 26. The field was Abbeville-Drucat; by 1942 the units based here would be so highly respected by the Allies that for the rest of the war any especially aggressive and skillful German fighter formation was automatically considered by the Allied aircrews to be from the "Abbeville Kids." This winter, however, there was little military activity. The Geschwader's ground personnel were able to relax for the first time in seven months, and the first men to obtain leave headed homeward. Adolf Hitler, on a rare visit to a front-line unit, was the Geschwader's guest for Christmas dinner. On 9 February 1941, JG 26 was finally ordered to return to Germany for rest and re-equipment. For the Schlageter Geschwader the Battle of Britain had officially come to an end.

CONCLUSIONS

The Battle of Britain has become one of the most thoroughly analyzed battles in history. By consensus, the Luftwaffe lost because of failures of intelligence, leadership, and equipment, in that order. They came much closer to victory than they realized; Air Vice Marshal J. E. "Johnnie" Johnson, who was in a position to know, feels that the Luftwaffe could have won dominance over southern England with two weeks of concerted effort and could then have isolated the planned battlefield by attacks on communications targets, preparing the way for the invasion. Why didn't it happen?

The incompetence of the Luftwaffe's intelligence staff has been remarked on elsewhere at length. It never gained the slightest understanding of either the mechanism by which Fighter Command controlled its aerial forces or the extreme vulnerability of the RAF's communications links. Luftwaffe intelligence consistently misidentified factories and airfields. An especially pernicious failing was its inability to judge the claims of its own pilots on any kind of rational basis. Any airfield claimed hit by the bombers was crossed off Kesselring's target map. More to the point of this discussion, the Luftwaffe's strict requirements for confirming aerial victories were assumed to be sufficient insurance against overclaiming. The truth was quite different. An official Luftwaffe intelligence appreciation of the state of Fighter Command, issued on 17 August 1940, estimated the RAF's losses from 1 July to 15 August to have been 770 fighters. The true figure was 318; the error was more than 240 percent.

Historians who have studied the battle's claim and loss records in detail have concluded that both sides overclaimed to the same degree. However, the RAF commanders knew full well what the Germans' true losses were, from Ultra intercepts and simply by counting crashes. Their side's exaggerated claims were allowed to stand, to boost the morale of the fighter pilots and the civilian population, but had no effect whatsoever on the RAF's conduct of the battle. The German High Command, on the other hand, was led to believe by its fighter pilots' claims (and the underestimation of British production rates) that the RAF was down to its last few planes, only to have the Luftwaffe bomber formations smashed time after time by those "last fifty Spitfires."

We have all read of Goering's tirades that summer and autumn. Goering's insistence that the fighters remain chained to the bombers is said to have been the result of the bombers' high loss rates. However, this was war, and high losses were acceptable, provided they led to victory. Furthermore, Goering was a former fighter pilot, and he certainly had no great emotional attachment to the Kampfgeschwaders' "furniture vans" and their crews. There was another reason for Goering's anger. He felt personally betrayed by his fighter pilots. The Jaeger were obviously exaggerating their successes. But were the exaggerations deliberate? Goering believed that they were. The incentive was certainly there. The Luftwaffe placed more emphasis on individual victory scores than any other air force, and a Knight's Cross ribbon around the neck was a sure ticket to promotion and public adulation. Goering had no way to check his suspicions. His Chief of Intelligence, Schmid, lacked the qualifications for the job, and Goering's primary field commander, Kesselring, was a non-aviator and an inveterate optimist. The two decisions that did the most to lose the battle followed from Goering's pique. Bitter and frustrated, his glib promises to his Fuehrer shown to be worthless, Goering determined to punish his fighter pilots— first by shackling them to the bombers, where their casualties would rise without commensurate chances of success; and second, when victory claims continued high, by giving in to Hitler and abruptly changing targets to London, at the extreme limit of the Bf 109's range.

In a letter to the author, General Galland has confirmed part of this theory—Goering indeed suspected his pilots of submitting fraudulent victory claims. Galland pointed out, however, that the scores Goering saw were the early, unassessed figures, sent to Berlin each afternoon at the insistence of the High Command, and were much higher than the numbers eventually confirmed. But as we have seen, even the confirmed figures were over twice the actual RAF losses. Research for the present history has found that in several air battles JG 26's total number of confirmed victory claims was approximately equal to the number of British aircraft actually destroyed, plus the number that force-landed in repairable condition. There is no reason to assume that the German pilots' claims were not made in good faith. The Luftwaffe's error was in underestimating the ability of the RAF to return to service aircraft that were seen to go down trailing smoke and flames, apparently out of control. There is no way that such insight could have been gained at the time. Goering never again fully trusted his fighter force, and relations remained strained for the rest of the war.

In the opinion of the Wehrmacht, JG 26 had by the end of the battle become a premier formation. Galland stated in his postwar interrogation that from mid-1940 until the end of 1941, JG 26 was unquestionably the best German fighter unit. By any quantitative measure its reputation was justified. Between July and December, the Schlageter fighters claimed 285 aerial victories (forty-four by the Stab, forty-eight by the First Gruppe, seventy-four by the Second

69

Gruppe, 119 by the Third Gruppe) for the loss of fifty-six pilots killed, missing, or prisoner—a victory-to-loss ratio of 5.1 to 1. In marked contrast to other Geschwader, no JG 26 formation ever suffered such crippling losses that its combat efficiency dropped. Seven JG 26 pilots were awarded the Knight's Cross for their fighting prowess, and Galland received the Oak Leaves, the top award of the period. The end of 1940 found Galland the top scorer in the Jagdwaffe, with fifty-seven victories.

Adolf Galland's second-favorite fighter unit, Hannes Trautloft's JG 54, claimed 238 victories against forty-three losses, for an excellent claim-to-loss ratio of 5.5 to 1. The record of JG 27, a more typical Jagdgeschwader, is also available for comparison. During its tour of duty on the Channel, between July and November, it claimed 147 victories while losing sixty pilots, for a claim-to-loss ratio of 2.4 to 1. Its two Knight's Crosses were for reasons other than success in combat, and its top scorer in the battle had ten victories. It is interesting to speculate whether the rankings of the two Geschwader would have been reversed if Galland had not transferred to JG 26 in June but had remained with JG 27 for the course of the battle.

Between 10 July and 31 October, approximately 640 British fighters were shot down by the eight Jagdgeschwader engaged in the battle. Assuming that the German claims were overstated by a constant factor of two, JG 26's adjusted score becomes 142, or about one-quarter of all the German fighters' victories, almost double its quota if all eight Jagdgeschwader had scored equally. What did its success gain it? First, at Galland's insistence, a vacation in the Austrian Alps for all of his pilots, while the ground staff received home leave. Second, the newest model aircraft, and the pick of the Jagdwaffe's experienced pilots as formation leaders. And last, the honor of remaining in the west for the duration of the war, battling the best Allied aircraft and pilots.

The reader may feel that too much emphasis has been placed in this account on the "score," and not enough on its human cost. The victory count was in fact all-important to the participants at the time, and the narrative has attempted to reflect this. However, the cost was indeed high; this became more apparent as the war progressed. JG 26 suffered relatively few casualties in the Battle of Britain, about 10 percent of the total number of Bf 109 pilots lost. Of course, some JG 26 Staffeln were hit disproportionately hard—of the fourteen pilots who began the battle with the 7th Staffel, five were dead and seven were prisoners by 30 October. But the significance for Germany lay not in the number of casualties, but in their quality. Most of the German pilots lost in 1940 were professional soldiers and airmen, with extensive prewar training. Men of the caliber of Buerschgens, Ebbighausen, Ebeling, Henrici, and Mueller-Duehe were quite literally irreplaceable. The number and quality of fully trained, professional combat leaders available to the Jagdwaffe began a definite, if at first imperceptible decline that fall, while the British were reinforced by successive waves of highly trained pilots from the occupied countries, the Empire, and finally, America. The seeds of the total defeat of Germany's fighter force in 1944 were thus sown over the fields of Kent in 1940.

4

THE 7TH STAFFEL IN THE MEDITERRANEAN THEATER

February—August 1941

A NEW THEATER OF WAR

IN EARLY DECEMBER 1940, A SMALL BRITISH ARMY ADVANCED across the Egyptian border into Italian-held Libya. Within a few weeks, it became obvious in Berlin that only German help could prevent the expulsion of the Italians from the African continent. As a first step, air power was needed to neutralize the British-held island of Malta, which lay between Sicily and North Africa. The Italians had maintained an air offensive of sorts against the island for the previous six months. The British had beaten them off with a motley collection of Sea Gladiators and Hurricane Is, while slowly building up their naval and bomber forces on the island. The Luftwaffe High Command called on Fliegerkorps X, then in Norway. By year's end, in an excellent demonstration of the flexibility of air power (and efficient German staff work), some two hundred German planes had relocated from Norway to southern Italy and Sicily. On 9 January 1941, nine Ju 87s bombed ships in Marsa Scirocco Bay, Malta. The next day, the Stukas found the aircraft carrier *Illustrious* escorting a convoy and damaged her badly. The carrier limped into Malta's Grand Harbor that evening. The German bombers were back over Malta the next day; the *"Illustrious* Blitz" had begun. No longer would the Maltese watch the air battles overhead from their rooftops, keeping score as at a sporting match. The war had turned deadly.

72

Fliegerkorps X contained two Gruppen of Ju 87s, two Gruppen of Ju 88s, one Gruppe of He 111s, a Staffel of reconnaissance aircraft, and a Bf 110 Gruppe. The British aerial defense consisted of a single Hurricane squadron, No. 261. Although the Bf 110s got off to a good start, claiming three Hurricanes on 19 January without loss, a request was made for some single-engined fighter support. Thus it happened that Jagdgeschwader 26's rest period in Germany was interrupted by orders to prepare a single Staffel for transfer to the Mediterranean theater.

The 7th "Red Heart" Staffel, commanded by the 22-year-old Knight's Cross recipient, Oberleutnant Joachim Muencheberg, was chosen for the task. A forty-man detachment selected from the ground staff and maintenance crews boarded Ju 52s on 22 January and took off for the south. They were met in Rome by twelve Staffel pilots in brand-new Bf 109E-7s. On 9 February, the entire formation left Rome for its new base at Gela, Sicily.

THE SCOURGE OF MALTA

Muencheberg's men lost no time in making their presence felt. On 12 February, three Ju 88s were intercepted by four No. 261 Sqd. Hurricanes. The German bombers led the British fighters out to sea. When well strung out, the British flight was hit by Muencheberg's Staffel out of the sun. Three Hurricanes went down in flames, including that of the flight leader, who was a Wellington bomber pilot—the RAF command on Malta believed in filling leadership positions strictly on the basis of seniority, rather than experience or skill.

Although the 7th Staffel had lost almost all of its original pilot complement in the Battle of Britain, its replacements were fully trained, and Muencheberg, an intelligent leader as well as a highly skilled pilot, had briefed them well on the tactics that had proven most successful against the RAF fighters in 1940—attack from above whenever possible and never get into a turning battle. No. 261 Squadron's Hurricane Is proved to be almost helpless above 16,000 feet, and the German tactics were foolproof—they could climb above 20,000 feet on the short approach from Sicily, dive on any targets present over Malta, zoom up after a quick attack, and climb back to safety. Although radar gave the British ample

warning of the German raids, the inadequate fighter defenses on
Malta obtained results far different from those gained over southern England the previous summer. The RAF was hobbled by inferior aircraft, a prewar mentality, and a smugness resulting from
their successes over the Italians. This overconfidence would be
shattered permanently by Muencheberg and his dozen Messerschmitts.

On 16 February, the Staffel escorted StG 2's Stukas in an attack
on Luqa airfield. Muencheberg planned on this occasion to split his
formation and sandwich any defending fighters between the
Schwaerme. Eight Hurricanes met the Messerschmitts over Luqa, at
20,000 feet, and were promptly boxed in. One British flight leader
had his arm smashed by a cannon shell and had to bail out; two more
Hurricanes force-landed safely, riddled with shell holes. Muencheberg and his men were credited with three victories; the British filed
no claims.

The next Hurricane to fall was claimed by Muencheberg on 25
February. On the following day, the field at Luqa was subjected to
the most damaging raid to date. More than sixty German bombers
attacked, destroying six Wellingtons on the ground and leaving the
field unserviceable for forty-eight hours. The Messerschmitts did
their usual efficient job as escorts, claiming four Hurricanes without
loss. Five Hurricanes and three pilots were in fact lost. One of the
pilots killed was Flg. Off. Eric Taylor, the island's leading scorer at
the time, with at least seven victories. Muencheberg's report praised
the spirit of one of his opponents, who attempted to ram a Ju 88
with his blazing Hurricane before bailing out.

By the end of February, the British defenders were thoroughly
demoralized. By German count, eleven Hurricanes had been lost to
the Messerschmitts. A contemporary British account states:

> The enemy was slowly gaining air superiority and was flying
> lower and more boldly. He was neutralizing the striking power of the
> air forces on the island, and in the course of ten days nearly all the
> Royal Air Force's flight leaders were lost.

The RAF on Malta received no replacement fighters in February, and on 28 February a raid on Hal Far airfield left them
temporarily with no serviceable fighters at all. No carriers were

available to bring in reinforcements, but twelve Hurricanes managed to fly over from North Africa in March; one of them was piloted by Flg. Off. E. M. "Imshi" Mason, the top-scoring British ace of the first Libyan campaign, with fifteen claims against the Italians.

Muencheberg's Bf 109s continued their patrols over the island. On 7 March, the fighters swept across St. Paul's Bay at low altitude, strafing and badly damaging a Sunderland flying boat. They returned on the 10th, completed the destruction of the Sunderland, and heavily damaged a second.

During this period, medium bombers flying from England to reinforce Egypt and Malta crossed occupied France at night and landed on Malta soon after daylight. On the morning of 15 March, German radar detected a small formation of Wellingtons south of Sicily. A few Messerschmitts were scrambled, led by Muencheberg, who pulled up from Gela in a near-vertical climb. Wellingtons had no ventral defenses, which was well-known to the Germans, and Muencheberg thus made his attack from directly beneath the bombers, still in his steep climb. His target immediately burst into flames and fell away. Soon after this interception, the RAF withdrew its Wellingtons to North Africa, temporarily leaving the island impotent as an offensive air base.

The biggest bag by the German fighters came on 22 March, when seven Hurricanes were claimed. Eight Hurricanes had been sent up against ten Ju 88s and their escort of twelve Bf 109s. Five British pilots were killed in the resulting combat; the Germans suffered no damage or casualties.

The Red Hearts' scoring for the month was completed on the 28th, when Muencheberg returned from his 200th combat sortie claiming his 33rd victory, another Hurricane. A total of thirteen of the British fighters was claimed by the Staffel in March.

The British carrier *Ark Royal* ferried in a number of badly needed Hurricane IIs in April. The Maltese defenses still rested in the sorely tried hands of No. 261 Squadron, which had gone through two squadron leaders in the past two months. Things went somewhat easier for the defenders in April; British records state that only seven Hurricanes and three pilots were lost during the month.

FLANK DUTY FOR THE BALKAN CAMPAIGN

The British on Malta were given a short reprieve by the German invasion of Yugoslavia and Greece. The whole of Fleigerkorps X flew to Italy to support the attack. The Red Heart pilots flew their first mission over Yugoslavia on 6 April. The Staffel's assignment was to strafe the airfield at Podgorica. The field's only two defenders, Avia BH 33E biplanes, were shot down by Oblt. Muencheberg and Oblt. Mietusch. 7/JG 26 returned from Taranto after only three days to resume its harassment of Malta, accompanied by a single Stuka Gruppe.

BACK TO SICILY

Muencheberg's Staffel quickly reasserted itself over Malta. On the morning of 11 April, eight Hurricanes were scrambled; they had barely reached 10,000 feet when they were hit by the Messerschmitts. Three British pilots crash-landed their damaged fighters, the victims of Oblt. Muencheberg and his deputy, Oblt. Mietusch.

On 13 April, Flg. Off. "Imshi" Mason was patroling over Malta with his wingman, a very experienced pilot. The latter's orders were to weave constantly above and behind Mason—the concept of the "fighting pair" had not yet taken hold in No. 261 Squadron. During one of the wingman's turns, Mason dove suddenly to attack a Schwarm of Bf 109s down sun. Mason's target dove away, leaving Mason to the attention of the other three 109s, which promptly boxed him in. His wingman, in the meantime, remained above, wondering where his leader had gone. Mason was hit in the hand, and his Hurricane was shot full of holes, but it did not burn. He made a successful forced landing offshore; Oblt. Mietusch was credited with shooting him down. Mason spent some time in a hospital, left the island, and next saw combat in Iraq.

Twenty-four Hurricanes were flown to Malta from the *Ark Royal* on 27 April. The first flight of seven was led to Malta by a Sunderland. Apparently Oblt. Muencheberg, leading a sweep high above the island, saw the Sunderland approach its anchorage; it was the first of the large flying boats to be spotted in some time. Muencheberg quickly dove to wave-top height, followed by his men. Just as the Sunderland's crew made fast to the mooring buoy, the Messerschmitts streaked across the bay in trail, each firing in turn. A single pass was sufficient; before the British light flak could find the range the German fighters made their exit, leaving the Sunderland a mass of flaming wreckage on the water.

Muencheberg's 39th and 40th victories came on 1 May, within two minutes of one another. We have his own description of this battle:

> My Kette [three aircraft] was approaching the northern coast of Malta. Through the haze I suddenly noticed, quite close, a formation of Hurricanes. I immediately whipped my crate around and headed toward the sun. The Hurricanes divided into two flights of four; one reversed course, while the other headed for Malta. The Tommies had apparently not noticed us. I fell in behind the second flight.
>
> I warned my Number 3 to watch the enemy Holzauge ["wooden eye" or lookout]. I then started to work over the lead enemy aircraft, but opened fire at too great a range. The Hurricane showed only a thin trail of smoke, dove away to the right, and disappeared in the haze. The second plane now filled my sights. That fellow had obviously not seen me either, and sat there like a block of wood. My first burst tore through his fuselage, and he dove away burning brightly. I spotted my wingman Johannsen alongside me, tearing large chunks from the third Hurricane. The fourth Hurricane, the Holzauge, now banked right in front of me, trying to get on Johannsen's tail. I broke into him and scored some hits on his nose; as he dove away I was able to hit him again on a reverse course, from above. We both came around once more. The Tommy out-turned me and came out above me, on my tail. I dove steeply to the south, and at that moment saw yet another Hurricane, not one hundred meters in front of me. This one was apparently preparing to land. I instantly decided to attack. My first burst must have hit the pilot, because he took no defensive action. The airplane continued flying straight ahead, rocking slightly. I fired the last of my ammunition at less than fifty meters range. The Tommy finally fell away, its left wing blazing.
>
> I still had to make my escape. I was entirely alone and faced not only the Holzauge, who was my opponent from the earlier combat, but also, above me to the left, I could see the black and white bellies of four more Hurricanes. Just then the antiaircraft guns opened fire. I was fortunate to get out of this witch's cauldron. Later, my two comrades and I were all able to celebrate our great success together.

77

Both of Muencheberg's victims survived, with wounds. His punishment of the RAF continued. He downed five Hurricanes during the first week of May and was awarded the Oak Leaves to the Knight's Cross on the 7th, after his 43rd victory.

Malta's new air commander decided that No. 261 Squadron, until now the lone fighter squadron on the island, was beyond reclamation and disbanded it on 12 May. Most of its surviving pilots were transferred away from Malta, to squadrons elsewhere in the Mediterranean. Its battered equipment was passed to the newly formed No. 185 Squadron, while the burden of the defense passed to No. 249 Squadron, which had just flown in from the *Ark Royal*. The pilots of No. 249, an experienced Fighter Command squadron with an excellent record in the Battle of Britain, were dismayed by the condition of the defenses and by the low morale displayed by the Malta veterans.

In late May, Fliegerkorps X was ordered east to support the invasion of Crete. The Red Hearts were the last Luftwaffe aircraft to leave Sicily. Muencheberg announced his departure from the theater in typical fashion. He led eight of his Messerschmitts in a wide sweep around Malta. After dropping their auxiliary fuel tanks, they dove from 10,000 feet to 15, and swept over the island from the south. According to German accounts, this attack from an unexpected direction achieved complete surprise, and they were able to make two passes over Takali, a major fighter airfield, before the British defenses awoke. By then the Messerschmitts were on their way back to Sicily, leaving at least five of No. 249 Squadron's new Hurricanes ablaze.

MALTA REPRIEVED

By the end of May, 7/JG 26 was operational in southern Greece. Fliegerkorps X never returned to Sicily; after the Cretan campaign, most units flew to the Balkans, in preparation for the forthcoming invasion of the Soviet Union. The Red Hearts were called upon to provide flank support for the Wehrmacht's eastward movement. They were ordered to move to the Peloponnesus, in southern Greece, to defend the Balkans against Allied air attacks and to escort dive-bombers searching for shipping in the eastern Mediterranean. Soon after their arrival, however, they were greeted with further orders. A major British offensive in North Africa was in the wind, and the sole Bf 109 unit in Libya, I/JG 27, needed reinforcement. By the time 7/JG 26 arrived in Ain-el-Gazala, Libya, the British offensive had petered out, but Muencheberg's men were nonetheless given a warm welcome by I/JG 27 and its Kommandeur, Hptm. Edu Neumann.

The morning after the Red Heart ground staff arrived in Africa, a ten-man detachment was ordered forward from Ain-el-Gazala to the Egyptian border at Gambut, to set up an advanced landing ground for the Staffel. It was planned that the fighters would occupy this field during the day and fly back to the rear each night. Matthias Buchmann, a Staffel armorer, states that the men and their equipment were crowded into a single 3.5-ton Opel-Blitz truck. They promptly became lost in a small sandstorm and were then bombed by Ju 87s, which destroyed the truck and injured all the occupants to some extent. The men were between the battle lines. They were next taken under fire by British artillery and were finally rescued by a party of Italian stretcher bearers. Buchmann rates this incident as the most memorable of his entire war.

The first known aerial combat for the 7th Staffel in North Africa took place on 17 June, when Oblt. Mietusch and Uffz. Kestler shot down two Hurricanes southeast of Sidi Omar. Three days later, Oblt. Muencheberg downed a Hurricane east of Buq Buq. The Red Hearts' victims were probably pilots from the South African Air Force, which had just arrived in North Africa; the South Africans were finding the new theater far more difficult than East Africa, the site of their recent successful campaign against the Italians. The Hurricane pilots of the Desert Air Force were at even more of a disadvantage against the Germans than were their counterparts on Malta. Their aircraft were fitted with huge desert air filters, greatly reducing their maximum speed and altitude. And their tactics would have restricted them to low altitudes even if their aircraft did not—the British Army insisted on direct fighter cover, which translated into low-altitude patrols in close formation, perfect targets for the experienced German fighter pilots.

The best account of the 7th Staffel's activities during this period was drafted by Muencheberg himself, in the form of a letter to Obstlt. Galland dated 23 June:

The Peloponnesus was absolutely desolate. Unbelievably hot, much dust, quartered in tents. Cut off from any connection with the outside world. Our mission was just as shabby—attacks on naval targets in the eastern Mediterranean, in cooperation with a Stuka Gruppe. We had to fly sea reconnaissance with auxiliary tanks once or twice daily, up to 200 kilometers [120 miles] south of Crete. Two and a half hours of flying, without result, since the British fleet was sufficiently occupied off Syria. There was no air-sea rescue service at all, making things even more unpleasant. . . .

I thus welcomed the call of the Fliegerfuehrer [Air Commander] Afrika for fighter reinforcements when the battle for Sollum took a threatening turn, and transferred with six aircraft and part of the ground crew to the Tobruk area. My remaining pilots were still in Italy, bringing up the remaining aircraft, and were unable to accompany me. They are now sitting in Greece, and I have attempted to persuade Korps to permit them to join me here. Actually, I should have returned already, as the situation has stabilized, but I have received permission to stay here a while longer. . . . I dread to think of still another useless period in Greece or on Crete, where we were scheduled to move. . . . But only the stars can tell. . . .

At present I am stationed at Edu Neumann's field, and am living with him in his trailer. The heat is more tolerable here than in Greece. Innumerable flies buzz around us, and the occasional sandstorms are unpleasant. Up to now I have had no mechanical difficulties, even though our aircraft have no tropical kits. I operate in tactical cooperation with I/JG 27, but independently. Things have gone smoothly, with the splendid hospitality that is the rule among the fighter fraternity. As to our actual fighting, we have had a run of bad luck—up to now only Mietusch and I have shot down planes, both Hurricanes; Numbers 10 and 44 respectively. . . .

. . . I would like to request that you not forget us. Also, please bring this letter to the attention of my Gruppe, along with my heartiest greetings, and thank Hptm. Schoepfel and Oblt. Sprick for their letters. We have little opportunity to write here. . . .

The front stabilized after the failure of the British offensive, and combat flying was restricted to brief forays over the lines and attacks on the Malta and Tobruk convoys. On 24 June Muencheberg and three of his pilots intercepted a reconnaissance Hurricane. Muencheberg shot it down, killing the pilot. The Staffel saw escort duty on 30 June, when it accompanied eight Ju 87s in an attack on a small coastal convoy. The Stukas were intercepted by No. 1 Sqd.

SAAF, which downed two of them before the Messerschmitts intervened. One of the South African Hurricanes was shot down, killing its pilot, while two others were damaged. The Staffel's next major engagement took place on 15 July. A large air battle developed over a convoy of British lighters bound for Tobruk. Several Ju 87s were shot down. Muencheberg shot a Hurricane off the tail of a Bf 110; the British fighter crashed in flames behind the Allied lines. Two British pilots were killed in this combat. On 29 July, ten Ju 87s attacked a Tobruk convoy and were in turn hit by eight Tomahawks of No. 2 Sqd. SAAF. The South Africans shot down four Ju 87s before 7th Staffel Bf 109s could reach them. Two Tomahawks were then shot down; one pilot was killed, and the other survived as a POW. Oblt. Muencheberg was credited with both victories.

RETURN TO THE KANALFRONT

Muencheberg's fears that his Staffel would be detached permanently from its parent Geschwader were not realized. The pilots returned to JG 26 in France in late August. Their move was made quickly—Oblt. Mietusch claimed the Staffel's last Mediterranean victory, the probable destruction of a Martin Maryland bomber, on 21 August, while Oblt. Muencheberg shot down a Spitfire over northern France on 26 August. The ground crews did not make it back until the end of September. They flew by way of Greece and the Balkans. On 23 September, a Ju 52 carrying Matthias Buchmann and other ground crewmen was attacked by three Bristol Beaufighters. Two men were injured by cannon fire. The transport returned safely to Africa, but both men died there of their wounds. The 7th Staffel's first casualties in the Mediterranean theater were thus suffered at the very end of their detached service. Most ironic, the Staffel's only fatalities were these two ground crewmen. The pilots had come through the six months' operations without loss.

None of the twelve pilots known to have served in the Mediterranean with the 7th Staffel ended the war in JG 26. At least six of them were killed; three survived the war in other fighter units, or in Russian imprisonment. The other three pilots are known to have transferred from the Geschwader, but their later service history has not to date been traced. The 7th Staffel's record while in the Mediterranean theater was unique in the air war—fifty-two air victories without a single pilot casualty or aircraft loss. Although almost half of their victories, twenty-five, were claimed by Muencheberg himself, the remaining credits were distributed remarkably evenly. Twelve of the small group of pilots scored victories; no more than one or two men (to date unidentified) returned to France scoreless.

5
DEFENSE IN THE WEST
1941

NEW EQUIPMENT

THE FURLOUGH GRANTED THE GESCHWADER IN FEBRUARY WAS the only rest period the unit as a whole would receive for the entire war. At the expiration of their leaves, the personnel of JG 26 reported to their permanent bases in western Germany. In March the Stab and the First Gruppe became the Luftwaffe's first combat units to receive Messerschmitt's newest fighters, the Bf 109F-1 and Bf 109F-2. These aircraft were dramatically different in appearance from the Bf 109Es they replaced. Every aspect of the original airframe design had been examined with an eye toward improving aerodynamic efficiency. The cowling was made symmetrical and was faired into a large rounded spinner. The radiators were recessed farther into the wing and incorporated a boundary layer bypass. The horizontal tail was relocated and cantilevered to eliminate its external brace. The wingtips were rounded. The tail wheel was made retractable. All the control surfaces were redesigned, as was the supercharger air intake. The new engine intended for the Bf 109F, the Daimler-Benz DB 601E, was not ready, and the F-1 and F-2 retained the DB 601N of the Bf 109E-7. Using the same engine, the new model was superior to the old in maximum speed, rate of turn, initial climb, climb rate at altitude, and diving speed. Most important, its overall performance at altitude was improved.

The Schlageter pilots were pleased with the flying qualities of their new mounts. However, there was a price to pay. Willy Messerschmitt's designs were never noted for their robustness. The light structure of the new model cost the lives of a number of pilots. Several Bf 109F-0s of the initial production batch lost their entire tail assemblies in flight. It was found that at certain engine speeds a harmonic oscillation severe enough to rip off the tail was induced in the now-unbraced tail assembly. This problem was solved, first by external and finally by internal stiffeners, before the aircraft were cleared for service. A second structural problem did not appear until the aircraft had actually entered combat. Airplanes began returning from missions with ripples in their wing skins, indicative of hidden damage to the wing structure. Apparently neither the factory nor the RLM (German Air Ministry) thought the problem was serious, but after the wing spars of several aircraft collapsed in flight, trapping the pilots in their cockpits, Oblt. Schroedter, technical officer of the Third Gruppe, borrowed some strain gauges from Rechlin and ran his own experiments. The weak areas in the wing were identified, and local stiffeners were designed. These could not be applied in the Geschwader shops, however, and Schroedter was given the job of flying obviously damaged aircraft to the repair facility in Antwerp to have their wings replaced. Because of a shortage of combatworthy Bf 109Fs, the Geschwader's re-equipment was delayed, and I/JG 26 was forced to fly mixed formations of Bf 109Es and Bf 109Fs into the fall of 1941.

As a weight-saving measure, the armament of the Bf 109F was reduced from that of the Bf 109E. All wing armament was removed. The F-1 had two 7.92-mm MG17 machine guns in the upper cowling and one Oerlikon MG FF/M 20-mm cannon mounted between the engine cylinder banks and firing through the propeller spinner. The drum-fed MG FF/M was supplanted in the F-2 by the excellent new Mauser 15-mm MG 151 machine cannon, which was belt fed and electrically operated. It fired at 700 rounds per minute, considerably faster than the MG FF/M's 550 rounds per minute, but the weight of fire from the F-2, as well as its dispersion, was less than that from the E-4 and E-7, which had two wing-mounted MG FF/Ms and two cowl-mounted MG 17s.

COVER FOR THE NAVY

At the end of March, shortly after the Third Gruppe had exchanged its Bf 109E-7s for Bf 109Fs, the Geschwader received orders to return to France. They were to become part of Luftflotte 3, and base in Brittany, in the far western part of the country. Their prime mission was to protect German naval forces, especially the battle cruisers *Scharnhorst* and *Gneisenau*, which had recently reached harbor at Brest after a successful raid in the Atlantic. JG 26's Kommodore took the opportunity afforded by the transfer flight on 4 April to try out his new Bf 109F in combat. After his customary breakfast of red wine and raw eggs, Obstlt. Galland took off from Duesseldorf and flew to Le Touquet on the Channel coast, where he landed to refuel. He and his wingman then made a "private excursion over the British Isles." They surprised a pair of No. 91 Sqd. Spitfires, bringing down one apiece.

The next two weeks brought little combat, only an occasional interception of a Blenheim or Spitfire on reconnaissance. The bored Galland planned another excursion. On 15 April, Oberst Theo Osterkamp, Jagdfliegerfuehrer (fighter commander, usually abbreviated Jafue) in Le Touquet, was celebrating his birthday. Galland loaded the space behind his seat with a basket of lobsters and several bottles of champagne and took off from Brest with a wingman. Again he detoured over England. The sharp-eyed Galland spotted a lone Spitfire far below him and dove on it. After a long chase, the Spitfire burst into flames and crashed near Dover. Soon thereafter, an entire squadron of Spitfires was sighted climbing toward them. Again Galland achieved surprise; he opened fire on the rearmost plane from 100 yards and closed the range to thirty yards, at which point the British fighter exploded. The pair of Messerschmitts was now in the middle of the enemy formation. Galland hit a third Spitfire from close range, but neither German pilot saw it crash. Galland's wingman reached firing position behind another Spitfire, only to have his guns jam. The Germans then applied full throttle and dove for the Channel. Upon reaching Le Touquet, Galland was prevented from making a wheels-up landing by the frantically waving ground crews. But this embarrassing conclusion to the mission failed to disturb Galland's outward self-composure as he presented the undam-

aged birthday gifts to Osterkamp while reporting his latest victories.

The rest of the Geschwader saw little action. A typical mission
was a simulated ground attack, in which the pilots dropped cement
bombs on the coastal rocks. Friedrich Schneider, at that time a
brand-new enlisted pilot in the 3rd Staffel, recalls that on 26 May
the First Gruppe flew one hundred miles out to sea to escort in the
battleship *Bismarck*, which was making for Brest after her first foray
into the Atlantic. But the ship had been sunk that day by the Royal
Navy, and the German pilots were recalled. On 31 May, the
Geschwader received orders to move again, this time to the Channel coast. During their two months in Brittany, the Stab claimed
three victories (Galland's); the First Gruppe, six; and the Second
Gruppe, two; while the Third Gruppe had no "fighter's luck" and
made no claims.

BACK TO THE CHANNEL

JG 26's pilots flew to their new airfields along the Channel
coast on 1 June. Obstlt. Galland and his Stab returned to Audembert, their base the previous autumn, which was only two miles
from Oberst Osterkamp's Jafue 2 operations room. Galland resumed
his previous practice of rotating the Staffeln of his command through
Audembert at roughly two-week intervals. This permitted him to
evaluate all of the pilots of the Geschwader in turn. The Staffel at
Audembert was designated the Fuehrungsverband, or lead formation. Audembert was a very small field, but adequate for the Stabsschwarm and the single Staffel serving as Galland's Praetorian
Guard. The First Gruppe went to Clairmairais, one of several fields
near St. Omer. The Second Gruppe based at Maldegem in far
western Belgium, while the Third Gruppe went to Liegescourt,
northeast of Abbeville. None of these airfields had hard-surfaced
runways. Their grass landing grounds were usable only in good
weather but would prove adequate for the coming hunting season.

The new commanders of Fighter Command and No. 11
Group, Air Marshals Sholto Douglas and Leigh-Mallory, were more
offensively minded than their predecessors and had eagerly accepted
Marshal of the RAF Lord Trenchard's advice in late 1940 that they
should "lean toward France." Large formations of British fighters,

sometimes accompanying a small group of Bristol Blenheim light bombers, were overflying the French coast almost daily. Their objective was to entice the German fighters to come up and do battle. The Geschwader's primary mission for the next year and a half would be to defend the military installations and industrial targets in northern France and western Belgium against these incursions by the RAF.

The British code names for these missions will be a useful means of reference. "Circuses" were bomber missions with fighter escort. These proved to be the type of mission most likely to provoke a response by German fighters, and they soon evolved into highly elaborate operations. "Rhubarbs" were low-altitude probes by a maximum of four fighters, which the defenders ignored until ground strafing and bombing were added to Fighter Command's repertoire. "Rodeos" were sweeps by large formations of fighters; again, these could be safely ignored by the Germans. Last, "Roadsteads" were attacks on German Channel convoys. Flak ships proved adequate defense against the slow, poorly armed Blenheims, which were the only bombers available for the early missions.

Circus No. 1 had been flown on 10 January 1941. The scale of the British effort was small until mid-year, giving the Germans time to build up an air defense system. By June, a workable system using radar and ground control was in place, similar in concept if not in scale to that defending southern England. Although the British chose the time, course, and strength of their overflights, the true tactical initiative belonged to the Germans. The bombers posed no real threat—the bomber strength of a typical Circus was six Blenheims, each carrying a mere 1,000 pounds of bombs—and the British fighters could be attacked or not, as the immediate situation dictated. The most common British fighter in early 1941, the Spitfire II, was markedly inferior to the Bf 109F-2; the new Spitfire V was at best an even match for the German fighter. The Germans retained their superiority in the climb, the dive, and the zoom climb from a dive, which meant that they could join and break off combat at will. The British Spitfires and Hurricanes could out-turn any German fighter, but all German pilots knew this, and their rule was "one pass and away." The confident and experienced Schlageter pilots were about to begin their most successful period of the war.

While the men of JG 26 were settling into their new bases on the Channel coast, the Jagdgruppen of JG 2 "Richthofen," Luftflotte 3's other fighter unit, shifted westward to cover the Schlageter Geschwader's previous area of responsibility in western France. Luftflotte 2, along with all the other Luftwaffe fighter units in the west, returned to Germany in early June, en route to the Russian frontier. The first two weeks of June saw only desultory contact between the RAF and JG 26. By mid-June, JG 26 was fully operational and ready to oppose all RAF incursions in force. On the 16th, Hptm. Rolf Pingel's First Gruppe scored heavily against Circus No. 14. Coastal Command provided six Blenheims for a raid on Boulogne. Ten No. 11 Group fighter squadrons formed the escort. Over the target, the bombers dove to avoid the flak. Formation cohesion was lost, permitting the Messerschmitts to get to the bombers. I/JG 26 shot down two Blenheims and claimed nine Spitfires, while losing three Bf 109E-7s. The pilot of one Messerschmitt was killed; the second bailed out over the Channel and was rescued uninjured; and the third crash-landed at Audembert with 60 percent damage, equivalent to a writeoff. In other action, the 8th Staffel lost one plane and pilot. Obstlt. Galland shot down a Hurricane from the Blenheims' close escort. British claims were far in excess of German losses. No. 11 Group claimed eleven Bf 109s destroyed, five probably destroyed, and four damaged (conventionally abbreviated as 11-5-4 claims), while actual German losses were the four aircraft mentioned.

The ability of JG 26 to penetrate the escort led to larger and larger British formations. A Circus ultimately required up to twenty squadrons of fighters, some 240 aircraft, to protect a dozen or so Blenheims. The fighters were deployed as follows. First across the target were three Target Support Wings, each of three Spitfire squadrons. One paralleled the path of the bombers, overtaking them en route. The other two approached from different directions, crossing in the vicinity of the target. They then split up in flights of four, which had finally replaced sections of three in Fighter Command, and patrolled the target area until their fuel state forced them to return. The Escort Wing contained four squadrons of Spitfires or Hurricanes. Their functions can be inferred from their titles—Close Escort, Medium Escort, High Escort, and Low Escort Squadron. The obsolescent Hurricanes proved inadequate in this role and were replaced by Spitfires during the year. Above the Escort Wing was the Escort Cover Wing of three squadrons; coming along behind to mop up were the Forward Support Wing and the Rear Support Wing, each of two squadrons. The deployment of this armada required great skill by the British ground controllers and airborne wing commanders. Timing was critical because of the British fighters' short endurance. Cloudless conditions were essential at the assembly point over southern England; thus Circuses were rarely attempted other than in the spring and summer months.

The German defenders did not attempt to confront these massive formations directly. JG 26 entered combat in Staffel or Gruppe strength, rather than as a Geschwader. The German battle plan never changed—their fighters were to get off the ground quickly, gain height, and make use of sun and cloud to attack any part of the enemy "beehive" that appeared vulnerable. Oberst Osterkamp and his two Kommodoren, Galland and Major Walter Oesau of JG 2, understood that their role was to inflict maximum damage on the RAF while preserving their own limited forces. It was not required or expected that the bombers be attacked by every German intercept formation. Only the most skilled formation leaders, such as Galland himself, could judge the proper moment at which the escort could be penetrated at minimum risk in order to reach the bombers.

THE NONSTOP OFFENSIVE

At some point in this period, the British dubbed the campaign the "nonstop offensive," a term still recalled by German veterans and authors. German propagandists soon began calling it the "nonsense offensive," and the term fell into disuse by the Allies. The 21st of June brought the greatest RAF effort to date—two Circuses, each consisting of six No. 2 Group Blenheims escorted or supported by seventeen squadrons of No. 11 Group fighters. The day's claims by No. 11 Group totaled 26-7-6 Bf 109s for the loss of six fighters and two of their pilots, and one Blenheim. The actual German losses in aircraft were nine Bf 109s destroyed and four damaged. JG 26 lost three pilots killed and two more who were taken prisoner after bailing out into the Channel. JG 2 lost one pilot. The unprecedented scale of the fighting resulted in German claims that were well in excess of actual British losses—the pilots of JG 26 filed fourteen victory claims.

The 21st of June proved to be an unforgettable day for Adolf Galland. At noon, the first report of an approaching British formation reached his command post in Audembert. He ordered all three Gruppen to intercept and then raced to his own aircraft. At 1224 he took off with the Fuehrungsverband. At 11,000 feet he spotted the British formation below him; it had just bombed the airfield at St. Omer-Arques, a popular target of the period. He dove through the close escort and attacked the right Blenheim of the rear vee of three. It immediately burst into flames; after part of the crew bailed out, it crashed near one of the St. Omer airfields. It was then 1232, eight minutes after takeoff.

The rest of the Fuehrungsverband was occupied with the escort. Galland once more penetrated the screen and attacked a bomber, this one in the lead vee. It broke away from the formation, its right engine in flames. Galland saw two parachutes and noted the time; it was 1236. At that moment, tracers flashed past his cockpit from the rear. He escaped his attacker by a quick split-S into a cloud. Trailing coolant, his engine temperature climbing rapidly, he sighted Calais-Marck airfield and made a smooth forced landing. A half hour later, he was returned to Audembert in a courier aircraft.

At about 1600, the second British attack of the day was reported. Again the Geschwader was ordered up; again Galland took off, this time alone. (Obfw. Hegenauer, his regular wingman, had been shot down that morning. He was uninjured, but had not yet returned to Audembert.) Just after joining up with the First Gruppe southeast of Boulogne, Galland sighted a Spitfire formation below them. A quick attack, and one of the rear Spitfires dove away in flames. Flying without a wingman, Galland wanted to witness the crash himself, and committed the cardinal sin of fighter pilots—he kept his eyes on his target for too long. Suddenly, as he recalled in his memoir *Die Ersten und die Letzten,*

> . . . my head and right arm were hit hard. My airplane was in a bad way. The wings were ripped up by cannon shells. I was sitting half in the open—the right side of the fuselage had been torn away by shellfire. Fuel and coolant were streaming out. Instinctively, I

broke away to the north. I noted that my heavily damaged Me, its engine now shut down, was still controllable. I was at 6,000 meters [19,500 feet] and decided to glide home. My arm and head were bleeding, but I felt no pain—no time for that. My vital parts appeared to be all right. My calm deliberations were interrupted by the explosion of the fuel tank. The entire fuselage was enveloped in flames, and burning fuel ran into the cockpit. . . . My only thought now was escape. I pulled the canopy release—no luck! Jammed! I unbuckled my seat harness and pushed on the canopy. Too much wind resistance. There were bright flames all around me. . . . These were the most terrible seconds of my life. In mortal fear, I pressed against the canopy with all my strength. It moved slightly, and the airstream tore it away. I pushed the stick forward, but did not clear the wreckage as I had hoped—my seat pack had caught on the edge of the cockpit. I grabbed the radio mast and pushed with my feed. . . . Suddenly I was falling free . . . in my panic I grabbed the quick-release knob of my harness instead of the chute handle. I caught the near-fatal error in time, opened the chute, and floated softly to earth. . . .

That evening, Galland was patched up at the naval hospital in Hardinghem by his good friend Dr. Heim. Oberst Osterkamp came over from Le Touquet to congratulate him on his survival and on the Geschwader's successes. Then Osterkamp sprang the news that Galland was to be the first recipient of the Wehrmacht's new top decoration for heroism, the Knight's Cross with Oak Leaves and Swords.

Germany's invasion of the Soviet Union on 22 June provided the RAF with a strategic rationale for its daylight offensive—it would reduce the pressure on the Russians by forcing the Luftwaffe to return fighter units to western Europe. As it turned out, this did not happen; the 250 fighters of JG 2 and JG 26 already in France and Belgium proved sufficient. The tactics of both sides would remain unchanged through the summer.

Heinz Gottlob was a typical German pilot of the period. A former enlisted man, he had won a wartime commission and was now an Oberleutnant in Oblt. Josef "Pips" Priller's 1st Staffel. He had five victories to his credit. In the evening of 23 June, a No. 11 Group Rodeo provoked a response from I/JG 26. As Priller prepared to attack a formation of Spitfires, Gottlob, leading the second Rotte of Priller's Schwarm,

. . . saw three Spitfires approaching the rear of the Staffel. My Rotte broke into this attack; the Spitfires evaded my attack by sharp turns. I climbed above them and began turning, waiting for them to break out of their circle and head to sea. However, my Rotte was itself attacked from above, and I had to dive away. After I had shaken off this attack, I saw a lone Spitfire flying in a north-westerly direction. It was still over land, at 6,000 meters [19,500 feet]. I flew after it, approaching to twenty meters without being observed.

I then opened fire with all my weapons from behind and beneath it. The bottom of its fuselage started smoking; pieces then broke off the fuselage and wings. The plane pulled up, stalled, and fell away to the left. . . . I saw the Spitfire hit the water. The pilot had not bailed out.

The preceding quotation is from Heinz Gottlob's combat report. His promising career with JG 26 lasted only two more days. The 25th of June was another two-Circus day; each involved two squadrons of Blenheims and sixteen squadrons of fighters. The First Gruppe engaged both raids, claiming five Spitfires in the morning without loss; they were not as successful in the afternoon, making no claims and suffering one casualty—Oblt. Gottlob. Quoting Heinz Gottlob:

Priller led one Schwarm, and I led the other. We saw about eighteen Spitfires over the Channel. They had apparently already seen us, since they were flying in a defensive circle. We were at about 8,500 meters [28,000 feet]. The Indians were about 500 meters [1,600 feet] below us. Priller banked to the left to reach firing position. My Schwarm cut behind him. Suddenly there was an explosion in my airplane. Holes appeared in the floor of the cockpit, between my legs. I saw the legs of my fur flying boots ripple as several shots passed through them. Then several cannon shells hit the right side of my cockpit. I tried to dive away using my elevators, but got no response. . . . Since I was already in a left bank, I kicked the rudder sharply and entered a wingover toward the ground. I needed to dive to an altitude at which I could bail out without suffocating. During the dive, I noticed that my oxygen cylinder was empty, surrounded by blue fumes. Shot through! Fortunately, I was not prone to altitude sickness. I ripped my mask off at 4,200 meters [14,000 feet], and prepared to bail out. I was then hit again. Since all the fragments came from beneath my instrument panel and flew back above my head, I believe that this was my own ammunition exploding. Everything now happened lightning-fast. . . . Suddenly I was struck on the chin with such force that my head flew back to the right. . . . I felt terrible, piercing pain in my nose, eyes, and skull.

I began to lose my will and my consciousness. I squinted at the release lever, but could not summon the strength to bail out. As everything was turning black, a voice called out, "Get out now!" I actually heard the voice, but have no memory of what came afterward. . . . I do not know whether my parachute opened by itself, or whether I struck the tail and that caused it to open.

Although the battle had begun over mid-Channel, I was now over French soil, fortunately near the Naval hospital at Harding-hem. . . . At 2105 I landed at the feet of a surgeon from the hospital, who was out taking a walk. . . . I regained consciousness eight days later.

Heinz Gottlob never returned to JG 26.

The Geschwader suffered another serious loss on 28 June— Oblt. Gustav "Micky" Sprick, Kapitaen of the 8th Staffel and a holder of the Knight's Cross, was killed while battling Spitfires near St. Omer. Sprick performed a routine split-S maneuver, only to have the right wing of his Bf 109F-2 collapse. Sprick had no chance to escape and died in the crash; his final victory total was thirty-one, gained in 192 combat sorties.

Another Staffelkapitaen, Oblt. Martin Rysavy of the 2nd Staffel, was killed on 2 July—shot down by German 88-mm flak. His loss was the only blemish on JG 26's record for an otherwise successful day. All three Gruppen intercepted Circus No. 29, an abortive raid on Lille by twelve Blenheims, as did parts of JG 2. JG 26 claimed at least eight victories: five fighters and three bombers. Four Blenheims were in fact lost. No. 11 Group claimed 19-4-7 Bf 109s, while losing eight pilots. No German pilots were lost, and only four Bf 109s were lost or seriously damaged in the aerial combat.

The cost of the "nonstop offensive" to the Luftwaffe, while far from negligible, was proving bearable. The two Kanalgeschwader suffered the following losses between 14 June and 4 July:

	Pilots Killed & Prisoner	Pilots Wounded (Combat)	Pilots Injured (Accident)	Aircraft Destroyed	Aircraft Damaged
JG 26	19	3	1	33	25
JG 2	13	2	0	15	8
Total	32	5	1	48	33

Fighter Command lost sixty-two pilots and eighty aircraft during the same period; the score was thus approximately two to one in the Luftwaffe's favor. Fighter Command's victory claims totaled 214-84-95 German fighters. As in the Battle of Britain, these inflated claims were allowed to stand for morale purposes, even though RAF Intelligence kept an accurate Luftwaffe order of battle and monitored the German requests for replacement aircraft by Ultra radio intercepts. Air Marshal Sholto Douglas had to know that his pilots' claims, amounting to 167 percent of German table of organization strength in the theater, were absurdly high.

The first of the RAF's four-engined heavy bombers, the Short Stirling, was entering service, and the decision was made to use it to beef up the bomber strength of the Circuses. During July, the first two Stirling squadrons flew a number of daylight raids. On 10 July, No. 7 Squadron sent three Stirlings to bomb Boulogne. One ran into a salvo of flak over the target and blew up; another was attacked by a Messerschmitt after regaining the English coast. The Stirling's tail section was damaged, but its upper gunner claimed hits in the German fighter's engine.

This German fighter was the Bf 109F-2 of Major Rolf Pingel, Kommandeur of I/JG 26. Pingel had followed the Stirling across the Channel and made a lone attack. The bomber's return fire damaged Pingel's engine, which began to overheat. Pingel descended to low altitude over southern England to evade RAF fighter patrols and found himself too low to bail out. He then made a smooth belly landing in a grain field. His attempt to set his aircraft on fire was interrupted by a British soldier's burst of machine-gun fire. Thus Rolf Pingel's victory string was ended at twenty-two, and the British obtained their first example of a Bf 109F. It was quickly repaired and joined the Air Fighting Development Unit, which flew it extensively in mock combats until it crashed on 20 October. Pingel's successor as Kommandeur of the First Gruppe was Hptm. Johannes Seifert of the 3rd Staffel, at this time the senior commissioned pilot of the Geschwader in length of service, having joined I/JG 234 in Cologne in January 1938.

As Pingel's Bf 109F-2 was being prepared for its first flight under its new ownership, newer models of Messerschmitt's fighter were being taken on strength by JG 26. The DB 601E engine was at last ready for service and made its first appearances in the Bf 109F-3 and F-4. The former had the same armament as the F-2; it was quickly supplanted on the production lines by the F-4, which was armed with two MG 17s and a new engine cannon, the MG 151/20, which was an MG 151 rebored from its original 15-mm to 20-mm. The DB 601E provided the Bf 109F-4 with 1350 horsepower, which gave its pilots a significant speed and full throttle height advantage over the Spitfire V—390 mph at 22,000 feet, versus 370 mph at 20,000 feet. Perhaps the most enthusiastic supporters of the DB 601E were found among the Luftwaffe's supply officers. The new engine burned 87-octane B4 fuel, which was always in more plentiful supply than the 96-octane C3 fuel required by the DB 601N.

Oblt. Pips Priller was enjoying a remarkable run of victories since the Geschwader's return to the Channel. Between 16 June and 11 July he shot down nineteen RAF aircraft, including seventeen Spitfires, to bring his confirmed victory total to thirty-nine. The ground staff of his 1st Staffel had prepared a garland of oak leaves to drape around his neck when he returned after his fortieth—forty victories was the requirement at that time for the award of the Knight's Cross with Oak Leaves. At 0947 on 14 July, Priller's Staffel took off to intercept Spitfires. From Priller's combat report:

> I wanted to attack two Spitfires that were high above us in the vapor trails. But my engine was acting up, and it was impossible to overtake them. The Spitfires turned about and came toward us. I pulled my aircraft's nose up and opened fire from about 100 meters, directly in front of them. I hit one in the cockpit and engine, and its pilot bailed out. I then had to dive away steeply, as I came under attack by the second Spitfire, which was firing at me from very close range.

Priller's fortieth victim was a Spitfire V piloted by Flt. Sgt. W. M. Lamberton of No. 72 Squadron. His flight of three was flying in line astern formation, with Lamberton as No. 2. He states that his entire flight, and indeed most of the squadron, consisted of green youngsters. His wing was at 33,000 feet above St. Omer and had just turned to return home, putting the sun at their backs. Lamberton was watching a Staffel of eleven Bf 109s straining to reach his altitude, when his Spitfire suddenly erupted in flames. Lamberton was able to escape his blazing plane and survived his descent through the cold and thin atmosphere. He landed in a French grainfield, was immediately gathered up by German soldiers, and spent the next five weeks in the hospital at Guines. He did not learn until after the war that Priller's attack had come from dead ahead. Lamberton never saw him, as his view ahead was obstructed by his own fighter's engine cowling—at high altitude, the Spitfire flew at a markedly nose-high angle.

Feldwebel Ernst Jaeckel of the 2nd Staffel put his brand-new Bf 109-4 to good use on 18 July. His combat report states:

> My Schwarm was covering a convoy northwest of Dunkirk. At 1115, several enemy aircraft were reported approaching the convoy at altitudes between zero and 2,000 meters [6,500 feet]. My Schwarm climbed to 2,500 meters [8,000 feet], and circled directly over the convoy. At 1120, I saw four bombers approaching the convoy from the northwest; they were flying in a single row, about three meters [ten feet] off the water. They were covered by about fifteen Spitfires at 2,000 meters. I dove on the Spitfires and opened fire from their rear, which caused their formation to fly apart. I continued the dive with my Schwarm, and overtook the bombers at great speed. The lead bomber, a Bristol Blenheim, had already dropped its bombs on the convoy. As I prepared to attack one of the Blenheims, I saw a large aircraft, type unknown, somewhat farther away. It was flying at three meters altitude, and had an escort of four Spitfires. I immediately turned toward this aircraft, and approached it from the right rear. The Spitfires above me disappeared. I approached the bomber, but did not open fire, as I wanted to identify the type. At about two hundred meters range its rear turret opened fire. . . . At 100 meters I saw the roundels on its fuselage and wings, and opened fire on the turret with my cannon. I passed close by the left side, and saw damage to the turret, the fuselage, and the cockpit. I also saw that the plane had four engines.

. . . my wingman and the second Rotte of my Schwarm also made attacks from the rear. . . . After my second attack, the rear gunner stopped firing (probably dead). . . . The aircraft had reversed course after the first attack, and now flew toward Dover, about two meters above the water. It was losing a lot of oil, which left a slick on the water. . . . I made two more attacks, and my wingman made one, while my second Rotte protected us from the Spitfires. . . . The bomber was less than three miles southeast of Deal when I made my fifth and last attack. I closed to about twenty meters. . . . As I prepared to make yet another attack, I saw its extended landing gear strike the water. The plane bounced once and settled in the water. . . . I saw an English speedboat approaching the crash site. . . . At that I headed home, short of fuel.

Jaeckel's victim was a Stirling from No. 15 Squadron. As the first German pilot to bring down a four-engined bomber, Jaeckel was awarded 500 Reichsmarks and an honor trophy.

Late on the evening of 23 July, a Rodeo by No. 11 Group drew a spirited response from JG 26. Adolf Galland shot down two Spitfires. His brother, Oblt. Wilhelm-Ferdinand "Wutz" Galland, who had just become a fighter pilot after beginning the war as a Luftwaffe officer in the antiaircraft artillery, claimed his first victory, a Spitfire, but it was not confirmed. It is probable that Adolf Galland suffered his second war wound on this mission, although the date given in his memoirs is 2 July. While battling one Spitfire, Galland's Bf 109F-4 was hit from behind by another. A cannon shell hit a piece of armor plating that Galland's crew chief had only recently installed in the rear of the cockpit. Galland escaped, landed safely, and had Dr. Heim sew up his bloodied head once again. Galland was then grounded long enough for him to report to Adolf Hitler in East Prussia for his investiture with the Swords to his Knight's Cross.

German military tradition has always fostered unit pride and loyalty. Transfers between units are rare. The typical Luftwaffe fighter pilot remained with his original combat unit until he was permanently removed from combat—by death, capture, or incapacitating wound. Experienced combat leaders were an exception to this rule; they were in such short supply that they were shuttled among the units with the most pressing immediate needs. Occasionally, however, promising enlisted pilots were made available for transfer, and Galland was quick to claim his share. One such pilot was Unteroffizier Adolf "Addi" Glunz. Glunz completed his training in early 1941 and joined 4/JG 52 on the Channel. He moved east with JG 52 and claimed five victories in the first three weeks of the Russian campaign, an excellent record for a new pilot. He was then transferred to JG 26, and upon his arrival in mid-July was assigned to the 4th Staffel. He flew his first check flight with his new unit on 24 July. Addi Glunz was to become one of the Schlageter Geschwader's most successful pilots.

The results of the air offensive were reviewed by the RAF Command Staff in a meeting at the end of July. The Commander-in-Chief of Bomber Command was not convinced that the Circuses were accomplishing anything useful and proposed to withdraw his few Stirling heavy bombers from the daylight campaign. Sholto Douglas argued that alone, his fighters could not hope to entice the enemy up to do battle. The Chief of the Air Staff's decision was to continue the Circuses, but without the Stirlings. No. 2 Group's Blenheims would continue to provide the strike force until that Group could replace them with more capable aircraft.

ARRIVAL OF THE FW 190

The long association of Jagdgeschwader 26 with Kurt Tank's famous fighter, the Focke-Wulf 190, began in March 1941, when a detachment of thirty men from II/JG 26 arrived at the Luftwaffe's Rechlin test facility for the operational testing of the new fighter. The new unit, the Erprobungsstaffel (Operational Test Squadron) 190, was commanded by Oblt. Otto Behrens and included Oblt. Karl Borris. Both men had originally enlisted in the prewar Luftwaffe as mechanics, and their technical abilities were to be sorely tested in the following months. Behrens's skills and enthusiasm are generally credited with saving the entire FW 190 project from cancellation.

Karl Borris has recorded his early impressions:

> From the first takeoff we were convinced of the robustness and the excellent flying qualities of the new aircraft. However, the BMW 801 engine, a new twin-row, 14-cylinder, air-cooled radial design,

gave us nothing but misery. Whatever could possibly go wrong with it, did. We hardly dared to leave the immediate vicinity of the airfield with our six prototype machines. Oil lines ruptured. The heavily armored oil cooler ring in front of the engine broke often. The bottom cylinder of the rear row seized again and again, since the oil pump and the cooling surfaces were too small. Leaking fuel lines left the pilots in a dazed state from the fumes, unable to climb out of their airplanes unaided. The constant speed propeller often failed to work properly. . . . Professor Tank tried to meet our demands in the most direct manner, avoiding the bureaucracy. The RLM propeller specialists and the Rechlin test pilots could only shake their heads when we soared across the field, smoking and stinking. An RLM commission . . . wanted to scratch the FW 190 from consideration for active service. We protested vehemently, because the airframe itself was truly outstanding.

Although problems with the engines continued to plague the test program, the FW 190 was cleared for service in July. At the end of the month, Erprobungsstaffel 190 moved to the Paris field of Le Bourget to begin training the pilots of II/JG 26 on the first service model, the FW 190A-1. The first Second Gruppe pilot to trade in his obsolescent Bf 109E-7 for factory-new Focke-Wulf was the Gruppenkommandeur, Hptm. Walter Adolph. The 6th Staffel, under Oblt. Walter Schneider, then received their aircraft, followed by the 4th and 5th Staffeln in succession. By 1 September, the entire Gruppe was working up on the new fighter. Behrens and Borris were soon released to return to their combat Staffeln, and the test unit was disbanded. The Second Gruppe moved from Maldeghem to Moorsele, and then to Wevelghem, all in western Belgium. The latter two bases offered better workshop and hangar facilities than Maldeghem; these were undoubtedly needed by the new aircraft and their troublesome engines.

A SUCCESSFUL SUMMER

The JG 26 Geschwaderstab and the six remaining Messerschmitt Staffeln—the 7th Staffel had by now returned from its Mediterranean tour—continued their battles against the RAF. Oblt. Johannes Schmid ran up an outstanding string of successes in August. A new arrival in the Geschwader, he was selected by

Galland to fly in the Stabsschwarm. On 7 August he proved his worth to the Kommodore by shooting a Spitfire off Galland's tail. Ten minutes later, he claimed another, and on his second sortie of the day, a third. All were hit from behind at close range, the method of attack preferred by Galland himself. Schmid shot down at least nine more aircraft in the following two weeks and was awarded the Knight's Cross on 21 August, after 26 victories. He was promoted to Hauptmann, and immediately given command of the 8th Staffel.

In August, the fighters of the Kanalgeschwader increased their victory ratio over Fighter Command. The RAF lost ninety-eight Spitfires and ten Hurricanes during the month, while JG 2 and JG 26 lost a total of eighteen pilots. One important factor was the relative experience level of the two fighter forces. Very few Battle of Britain veterans remained in Fighter Command, which now contained a number of new Commonwealth and Allied squadrons. JG 26, on the other hand, could claim some of the most experienced and skilled fighter pilots in the world. Adolf Galland ended August with eighty-one victories; Joachim Muencheberg, who was still leading the 7th Staffel, had fifty; and Pips Priller had forty-six.

The 9th of August began as another routine day for JG 26. A large formation of approaching RAF bombers and fighters was reported and was intercepted. The five Blenheims jettisoned their bombs, and general combat ensued between the escort and the German fighters, which cost the British five Spitfires and pilots, and the Germans two Bf 109s and one pilot. The day ceased to be routine when the Schlageter pilots returned to base and learned that one of their victims was the celebrated legless pilot, Douglas Bader. The stories of Wing Commander Bader's last combat, and his subsequent escapades while in captivity, have been told so often that they do not bear repeating here. It is worth noting, however, that JG 26 veterans who were not combat pilots, when asked to name one especially memorable event during their military career, almost invariably pick the story of Bader's capture and subsequent entertainment at Geschwader headquarters. The episode touched deep chords in the German psyche—first, there was genuine respect for Bader and his obvious courage (especially after his escape from the local hospital); second, his courteous reception by Galland recalled the long-dead codes of chivalry.

Despite Adolf Galland's personal success with the Bf 109F, he complained constantly to the Armament Staff in Berlin about its armament. He wanted wing armament, arguing that its greater dispersion of fire was necessary to ensure hits by inexperienced pilots, and he also contended that the rifle-caliber MG 17s were obsolete against modern armored combat aircraft. Galland felt strongly enough about the matter to experiment with the armament of his personal aircraft. He scored thirteen victories with three of these "specials." In two of them, the cowl MG 17s were replaced with 12.7-mm MG 131s. His unit metalsmiths succeeded in covering the large breeches of the MG 131s with small bumps rather than the disfiguring "Beulen" (boils) found necessary by Messerschmitt's engineers when the same up-gunning was accomplished much later on the Bf 109G-5. The nose armament of the third "special" was a standard MG 151/20 and two MG 17s—but it also carried two MG FF cannon in the wings. This was the only F-model or later Bf 109 to carry internal wing armament into combat.

The Second Gruppe introduced their FW 190s to combat slowly and cautiously. Their BMW 801C-1 engines were still giving problems. The unit's safety record was excellent, however—no pilots were killed while training on the FW 190, and only one was injured. The first Focke-Wulf fatality, on 29 August, was caused by German flak. The first loss of a FW 190 in aerial combat did not occur until 18 September, when the II/JG 26 Gruppenkommandeur, Hptm. Walter Adolph, failed to return from a mission. Adolph, a Knight's Cross holder with twenty-eight victories, led a flight of eight aircraft on a convoy escort mission off Ostend. They encountered a force of No. 88 Sqd. Blenheims with Spitfire and Hurricane escort. During the sharp battle, the German unit was split up. The Kommandeur did not join up after the action and did not return to Moorsele. Three weeks later, his body washed up on a Belgian beach.

On 19 September, Joachim Muencheberg was promoted to Hauptmann and given command of the Second Gruppe. Oblt. Mietusch took over Muencheberg's 7th Staffel in the Third Gruppe. Oblt. Schneider's 6th Staffel pilots had by now gained confidence in their Focke-Wulfs and began to score with them. On 21 September, they shot down four Spitfires over Boulogne, without loss to themselves. In October and November, Muencheberg and some of his more experienced pilots, such as Karl Borris, bagged a number of Spitfires, as did newcomers Wutz Galland and Addi Glunz. Encounter reports describing a fast radial-engined fighter were at first discounted by British Intelligence. Not until 13 October was the first clear gun-camera evidence obtained and the new fighter properly identified by the RAF.

Circus No. 108A targeted the Arques ship lift on 13 October. The offensive force consisted of six No. 139 Sqd. Blenheims. Adolf Galland found a new way to penetrate the "beehive" and attack the Blenheims—from directly beneath, while still in his climb. His target burst into flames and crashed, and Galland dove away untouched. His wingman, however, was not as fortunate. He was hit by the turret gunner of his target and crashed to his death. Galland's wingman on this occasion was Lt. Peter Goering, a nephew of the Reichsmarschall. Goering had completed his training in the JG 26 Ergaenzungsgruppe, or advanced training group, less than three weeks previously. The Bf 109 and FW 190 pilots of the First and Second Gruppen claimed five Spitfires from the escort, without loss.

On 6 November, one of the rising stars of the Geschwader was killed in a stupid accident. Hptm. Johannes Schmid, Kapitaen of 8/JG 26, was leading the Third Gruppe in the absence of Gerhard Schoepfel, who was on leave. Above the Channel, Schmid led an attack on two dozen Spitfires, diving on them at high speed. His attack brought down one of the Spitfires, for his 45th victory. While Schmid was circling the crash site, admiring his own work, the wing of his Bf 109F-4 struck the water and broke off. The plane hit the water and sank immediately. Karl Borris succeeded Schmid as leader of the 8th Staffel.

The RLM's initial doubts about the FW 190 had been resolved, and new production lines had started up at Arado and AGO. By October, three plants were turning out FW 190A-2s. This new model had a slightly improved engine, the BMW 801C-2 of 1600 hp, and increased armament. The original Focke-Wulf design had called for an armament of only four 7.9-mm MG 17 machine guns. These had been augmented in the FW 190A-1 by two MG FF cannon in the outer wings. In the A-2, the MG 17s in the wing roots were replaced by potent MG 151/20 machine cannon, timed by newly developed interrupter gear. The Third Gruppe moved from Liegescourt to Coquelles and began their conversion training. Rolf Schroedter, Third Gruppe technical officer, recalls that the persistent overheating problem with the lower rear cylinder of the BMW 801 was solved by a simple rerouting of the exhaust, which could be accomplished in the Gruppe's own workshop.

Circus No. 110, which was ordered on 8 November, proved to be the last Circus of 1941. A dozen Blenheims attempted unsuccessfully to bomb the railroad repair facility at Lille. According to the official British history

> . . . errors in navigation and timing, accentuated by a high wind, led to the failure of an elaborately planned complex of operations. . . . Fourteen pilots of Fighter Command were lost in a single day, at no cost to the Germans save two aircraft damaged.

German casualties were slightly greater than this quote indicates. Three JG 26 FW 190A-1s were destroyed in forced landings; one pilot was killed and another suffered severe injuries. The fourteen acknowledged Fighter Command losses match exactly the fourteen Spitfire claims filed by JG 26. Among the victorious pilots were Obstlt. Galland (Nos. 92 and 93), Hptm. Seifert (No. 23), Hptm. Priller (Nos. 57 and 58), Hptm. Muencheberg (Nos. 58 and 59), Oblt. Kurt Ebersberger, the Kapitaen of the 4th Staffel (No. 16), and Fw. Glunz of the 4th Staffel (No. 8). The 1941 hunting season was at an end.

GALLAND TO BERLIN

On 17 November Genobst. Ernst Udet, Generalluftzeugmeister (Chief of Air Equipment) of the Luftwaffe, committed suicide in Berlin. It was reported that he died while testing a new airplane, and he was given a state funeral. Adolf Galland was one of the six fighter pilots forming the guard of honor. Oberst Werner Moelders, the General der Jagdflieger (General of the Fighter Arm), was in Russia on an inspection tour of the Eastern front and missed the funeral because of bad weather. While en route back to France, Galland was summoned from his train and given the news that Moelders's

103

He 111 had crashed, killing him instantly. Galland was to return to Berlin immediately.

At Moelders's funeral, Reichsmarschall Goering gave Adolf Galland the unwelcome news that Galland was to succeed Moelders as General der Jagdflieger, which was a staff position at the RLM in Berlin. On the morning of 5 December, the men of the Geschwader were assembled under cold, gray skies. Reichsmarschall Goering approached, and Gerhard Schoepfel, Galland's successor as Kommodore, gave his report. Galland's promotion to Oberst was announced, and he took his official leave of the Geschwader. With ninety-four victories, he was at that time the most successful German fighter pilot opposing the RAF in the West. Galland's departure meant promotions for several Geschwader officers—Hptm. Priller replaced Major Schoepfel as Kommandeur of the Third Gruppe, and Oblt. Josef Haiboeck took over Priller's 1st Staffel.

Some of the Jagdgruppen transferred to new bases before winter set in. JG 2 shifted farther to the west, better to protect the German battle cruisers at Brest, which were under frequent attack by Bomber Command. Hptm. Muencheberg's Second Gruppe was ordered to move from its fields in Belgium to Abbeville-Drucat, which was being vacated by JG 2. The transfer flight resulted in a tragedy. Oblt. Schneider, leading his 6th Staffel through heavy fog, became disoriented and flew into a hill. Four of his pilots followed him to their deaths. Funerals for the five men were conducted on Christmas Day, at the Gruppe's new base in Abbeville.

At year's end, FW 190A-2s began to arrive for the re-equipment of the First Gruppe and the Geschwaderstab. The JG 26 scoreboard for the war to date was well in the Germans' favor—900 victory claims had been confirmed, in exchange for ninety-five pilots killed in combat, twenty-two killed in flying accidents, and thirty-four taken prisoner.

Across the Channel, the end of 1941 found Fighter Command at a new peak in strength. Sholto Douglas now controlled an even 100 squadrons. But the new war in the Pacific, and the galling fact that the true victory to loss ratio for the previous six months was well in the Luftwaffe's favor, compelled the War Cabinet to warn the Air Marshal that a more defensive policy was now "a disagreeable necessity." The brakes were applied to the nonstop offensive.

The Schlageter fighters, and the Richthofen Geschwader to

their west, had totally disrupted the British daylight air strategy for 1941. Between 14 June and 31 December, the RAF lost 411 fighters over the Channel and the continent, while claiming the destruction of 731 Luftwaffe fighters. The true loss to the Germans was only 103 fighters. In all of 1941, JG 26 lost forty-seven pilots killed in combat, seventeen killed in accidents, and three taken prisoner. These casualties, while serious, were certainly tolerable, and the experienced fighter pilots of the Kanalgeschwader were confident that in the new year their Focke-Wulfs would increase the German margin of superiority still further.

6
ABBEVILLE KIDS AND ST. OMER BOYS
1942

ONE DAY ON THE KANALFRONT

IT WAS CLOUDLESS AND UNSEASONABLY WARM. AFTER A LONG period of inactivity the British had recently resumed their flights over the coast. The day looked favorable for the Tommies to put in an appearance, but the morning passed quietly in the Geschwader command post at Audembert. Not until 1400 did the radio intercept unit at Wissant report test flights over the airfields of southern England, then radio silence. This sequence was often the first indication of a planned attack. At 1500, the Freya units at Wissant and Domburg were ordered to pay particular attention to the Thames Estuary and the area south of London.

At 1545, one of the radiomen let out a shout. Hptm. Langer, the Geschwader communications officer, ran to the master transmitter and switched it to "all locations" while activating the siren for Audembert. He gave the first warning: "Achtung! Achtung! Battle alarm! Many enemy aircraft over the Thames Estuary. Acknowledge." One after another the panel lamps lit up, indicating that the three Gruppen had understood the message.

The Kommodore, Major Schoepfel, stepped in, ready for take-off in his life jacket, and sized up the situation. He was accompanied by Hptm. Philipp, the Geschwader operations officer, who had been ordered by Jafue 2 to control the mission. The pilots of the

106

Stabsschwarm and the Fuehrungsstaffel were already sitting in their cockpits. They were kept informed by loudspeakers on the field. Each pilot had a small map of the operational zone and checked it after each announcement.

The British had now formed up, but their direction of travel was uncertain. The minutes passed, filled with tension. Finally the enemy set course eastward, to Margate. Langer announced, "Enemy formation heading east. Now over the Thames in area Ludwig Dora 6." Schoepfel spoke briefly to Philipp, then told Langer to order the First and Second Gruppen to take off; Third Gruppe would be held on the ground at Coquelles, in case the British approach proved to be a feint. Langer announced, "First and Second Gruppen take off immediately. Assemble over St. Omer. The Kommodore is in command. Acknowledge."

While the Gruppen were acknowledging receipt of the order, Schoepfel ran outside to his Focke-Wulf. Sixteen engines were turning over. The aircraft quickly began to taxi to their takeoff positions, from which they took off in Schwaerme. Activity picked up in the radio room as communication was established with the aircraft. Langer maintained a running account of the British approach over the public address system. The Freya reports now came in more frequently and were plotted on a large chart in the operations room. At 1558, the last German fighter was reported airborne.

By 1603, the RAF formation was about thirty miles northeast of Dunkirk. Langer and his crew put on headsets. The first bearings were transmitted: "Indians [enemy fighters] in Ludwig Emil 6—Caruso [direction] southeast." "Viktor, Viktor" came the reply. Only now was the first altitude information received; this came from a Wuerzburg unit equipped with modified fire-control radar. The new data were passed to the aircraft: "Indians at Hanni 5 to 7 [altitude 5-7,000 meters]—now in Martha Friedrich 1—Caruso south. Inter Viktor?" Again, "Viktor, Viktor" from Schoepfel.

The British formation flew over the coast. The first ground sighting reported them as Bostons, with strong fighter escort. Hptm. Philipp gave the attack order. "Proceed in direction Anton [Dunkirk]. Autos [bombers] and Indians—Caruso south—now in Martha Friedrich 7." Tension built in the operations room. At 1614 came the cry, "Achtung, Spitfeuer!" Then, "Autos, below to the left!" Radio silence was broken for good. The usual shouts and oaths were heard, then the cry of triumph—"Horrido! Horrido!"—signaling the first "kill." Ground observers reported air battles over their positions—aircraft in flames—crashes. Bombs were dropping on the Hazebrouck railroad yards. The observers soon reported that the British had turned back to the north. By 1625, the British had regained the ocean. Activity in the operations room ebbed. Finally, at 1630, one last "Horrido!" was heard from an especially persistent pilot.

At 1635 aircraft engines were heard in the distance. Soon the First Gruppe's Focke-Wulfs and Messerschmitts passed over Audembert en route to St. Omer. Some rocked their wings to signal victories. Schoepfel landed and taxied to his aircraft's service point, the one nearest the command post. He went inside, looked over the situation map, and waited for the telephoned reports of his Kommandeure, Hptm. Seifert and Hptm. Muencheberg. Hptm. Philipp compiled the new aircraft availability data as they were reported by the Gruppen, in order to pass on the Geschwader's state of readiness to the Jafue.

Ground stations telephoned in with crash sightings, which were taken down by the intelligence officer. Late in the evening, a complete report on the mission was transmitted to Jafue 2, which sent it in turn to the headquarters of Luftflotte 3. The Geschwader had sustained no casualties. One First Gruppe Bf 109F-4 had force-landed at Dunkirk after the battle; it was repairable. Spitfires were claimed by the Kommandeur and one pilot of the First Gruppe, and by the Kommandeur and four pilots of the Second. The late victory cry had come from Addi Glunz. He had pursued fifteen Spitfires back toward England, had caught them at mid-Channel, and had attacked from above, entirely alone. He had shot one Spitfire into the sea, and had damaged another, but had broken off the action when his cockpit suddenly became unbearably hot. Back at Abbeville it was found that two of his exhaust pipes had burned through, allowing the exhaust to enter the cockpit; he was lucky that he had not been asphyxiated. As it was now fully dark, the Gruppen were released from duty. The operations room clerk made the last entry in the Geschwader war diary. 13 March 1942 was now history.

WINTER ON THE CHANNEL COAST

The third winter of the war found the Geschwader pressed forward against the Channel. The Royal Air Force's 1941 losses and its other global commitments brought a temporary halt to its daily flights over France. Luftflotte 3 ordered its fighters to move nearer to the coast, improving its ability to monitor events on the other side. The winter weather restricted flying by both opponents. The Germans conducted the closest thing to routine offensive operations. Each morning and evening, weather permitting, JG 26 sent Rotten of two aircraft to reconnoiter the English coast.

The fields of the Stab and the First and Third Gruppen were close to Calais, just across the Straits of Dover from England. They were typical war-built fighter airfields, each with no more than one hard-surfaced runway. Normal procedure called for takeoffs and landings to be made on grass. Grass fields were adequate in good weather and permitted rapid takeoffs by Rotten and Schwaerme. Such non-improved fields became waterlogged in winter, however, limiting operations.

Only one type of built-for-the-purpose building was to be found on most of these fields—the maintenance hangar. The Geschwader and Gruppe command posts and the Staffel ready rooms normally occupied trailers; however, permanent buildings were not passed up if suitable ones were available on-site. The pilots and ground crews were quartered in nearby towns or chateaux. No permanent revetments were available for the aircraft, which were either parked in the open, under netting and the sparse tree cover available on the coast, or in the hangars.

The Second Gruppe was based farther to the southwest, at Abbeville-Drucat near the mouth of the Somme River. Drucat was the best-equipped of the Geschwader's four airfields, boasting three concrete runways. The field lay on the Somme River plateau, near the eastern edge of the city of Abbeville. It too was a war service base with no permanent installations, only camouflaged wooden barracks. Flat-roofed wooden hangars with a capacity of three or four Focke Wulfs had been built to service the aircraft. Each Staffel dispersal contained several of these hangars, which were covered by huge camouflage nets.

THE CHANNEL DASH

During late January and early February, the Geschwader's daily routine was interrupted by unusual orders detailing away a number of staff personnel, especially communications specialists, and calling for supply dumps to be set up at several coastal airfields. Obviously, something out of the ordinary was going on, but no one at the Geschwader level, not even the Kommodore, Major Schoepfel, was let in on the plan. In the afternoon of 11 February, Schoepfel was told that the General der Jagdflieger, Oberst Galland, was en route to the JG 26 command post to conduct a briefing. Schoepfel's Gruppe and Staffel leaders, plus those of JG 2 to the west, and JG 1, which until now had been stationed in northern Germany, were to attend.

Galland soon arrived from Germany in a Ju 52; his news was indeed extraordinary. Since early 1941, a powerful German fleet containing the battle cruisers *Scharnhorst* and *Gneisenau* and the heavy cruiser *Prinz Eugen* had been harbored at Brest. In a few hours, this fleet was to leave harbor and make for Germany; not by way of the open sea to the north of the British Isles, but through the English Channel. Movement of the ships had been ordered by Hitler himself. Galland had argued for a nighttime departure, which would bring the ships into the Straits of Dover in broad daylight. He reasoned that the first part of the voyage could probably be made in secret, and that based on recent experience, the Jagdgeschwader along the Channel could fend off the RAF's attacks during daylight. Galland's plan was approved, and Hitler rewarded the brash young colonel with responsibility for the air aspects of the operation.

Galland accepted his first assignment to high command with his customary energy and enthusiasm. His forces comprised only 252 day fighters—the full operational strength of JG 1, JG 2, JG 26, and the fighter school in Paris—plus a few night fighters. The success of the operation would be possible only if secrecy could be maintained until the last possible moment—that is, until the fleet was in the Channel itself. Galland did all of the planning himself, in his Berlin office. The Luftwaffe personnel necessary to man fighter control staffs on the ships were assembled under various subterfuges and smuggled aboard, along with the necessary communications equipment. For continuous daylight coverage the fighter escorts would need to parallel the ships' course, land on fields to the east of their original takeoff point, refuel, and return to escort duty—some units as many as three times.

Galland's plan was laid out in great precision. It called for continuous escort by four Schwaerme, two at low and two at high altitude. One of each pair of Schwaerme would be on the English side of the formation, and the other would be on the French side. Each Schwarm was to fly in broad figure eights along the length of the formation. All aircraft were to fly at minimum altitude and in complete radio silence until the code words "open visor" were received. The sixteen aircraft were to remain over the ships for thirty minutes. Relief was to take place over the naval formation, so there would be a ten-minute overlap. Ramming was authorized if necessary to prevent enemy aircraft from approaching the ships. A small reserve force was held at cockpit readiness, but any ship damaged severely enough to cause it to fall behind the formation would have to be left unprotected, as the fighter force was insufficient in number to cover two areas simultaneously.

At the briefing, Galland announced that he would command the entire air operation from Schoepfel's own command post; none of the staff of the local fighter organization would be used. Before dawn the next morning, Schoepfel headed to the Third Gruppe's base at Coquelles. Since he had no command function in the forthcoming operation, he would lead his old unit in combat.

Galland's plan worked to perfection, despite a three-hour delay in the ships' departure necessitated by an untimely raid on Brest by Bomber Command. He was aided by equal measures of good luck and British blockheadedness. But for equipment defects and a good German smoke screen, the RAF's routine early morning reconnaissance of Brest would have detected the formation's departure. Several coastal radar units observed unusual activity in the Channel, but in each case either they or the units they attempted to warn lacked the proper codes to bring about action. At about 1125 (German time) two Spitfires were spotted above the naval formation. Since the Germans were enforcing strict radio silence, there was no way to tell Galland. Galland was, in fact, dependent on the efficient German radio intercept service to inform him of the first British contact report. He received no message at this time. The two Spitfires were piloted by a British group captain and his wingman, who were returning from an impromptu Rhubarb over northern France. They spotted the German ships but, following standing orders, did not break radio silence, not even to report the largest formation of enemy ships seen in the Channel since the Spanish Armada.

A later pair of Spitfires, sent up on the pleading of a radar unit commander, broke radio silence to report the sighting in mid-Channel of three large German warships and twenty-plus escort ships, heading in the direction of Dover. The British radio message was intercepted and reported to Galland immediately. He delayed giving the order "open visor," however, believing correctly that the first reaction of the British would be merely to send out another plane to confirm the first report.

The British muddle continued. The coastal defense forces did not begin to react for an hour, and yet another hour had elapsed before the only British air unit in England specifically trained to attack the enemy capital ships received its orders. This was a half-squadron from the Fleet Air Arm, comprising six Fairey Swordfish torpedo bombers. At 1325 Lieutenant Commander Eugene Esmonde signaled his painfully slow biplanes to begin their takeoff rolls from Manston. Only one of the five Spitfire squadrons assigned to escort them made rendezvous. After circling for a few minutes, Esmonde waved his hand resignedly and led his formation out to sea; the ten Spitfires dutifully formed a screen around them.

As the sixteen aircraft making up the first British attack force bore down on the naval formation from the north, Gerhard Schoepfel was approaching it from the south, leading sixteen FW 190s of III/JG 26. There was a thick cloud layer at 1,600 feet, but visibility beneath it was good. Schoepfel found the naval formation easily— two battle cruisers and one heavy cruiser in line astern, surrounded by a screen of seven destroyers, plus numerous torpedo boats. He began searching for the sixteen Bf 109s of JG 2 that he was to relieve. At this moment his radio crackled with a signal from the shipboard fighter controller, vectoring him toward the approaching British aircraft. Only now did Adolf Galland, a few miles away in Audembert, give the order to "open visor."

Some of Schoepfel's Focke-Wulfs engaged the Spitfire squadron, which defended itself with great skill, shooting down three aircraft of 9/JG 26. The rest of this Staffel passed right through the thin Spitfire screen and fell on the Swordfish. Esmonde's was the first to go down; its upper wing was blown off by a burst of cannon fire. Although several Swordfish managed to begin their runs and drop their "fish," all six of the biplanes were soon aflame on the water. No torpedo found a target. Of the eighteen Swordfish crewmen, only five survived to be pulled from the Channel later by the crews of Royal Navy light craft. Commander Esmonde was not among them.

British air attacks continued throughout the daylight hours, despite steadily deteriorating weather. The attacks were small in scale and uncoordinated, and the German fighter screen proved sufficient to fight them off. The Focke-Wulfs and Messerschmitts even had time to strafe the Royal Navy motor torpedo boats and old destroyers that periodically attempted to attack from out of the mist. By midnight the fleet had reached the Elbe River and sanctuary. No British shell, bomb, or torpedo had touched a German ship.

The Schlageter fighters kept up their patrols from dawn until dusk. Seven aerial victories and six probables were awarded to JG 26 pilots. The British lost seventeen fighters, twenty RAF bombers, and the six FAA Swordfish. A total of seventeen German fighters and eleven pilots were lost from the three Jagdgeschwader engaged; JG 26 lost four FW 190s and their pilots. Although the end result of this episode was a strategic defeat for the German Navy, which had by its own action bottled up its capital ships in home waters, the German tactical victory had been complete, and the damage to British prestige, incalculable. After the war, Adolf Galland called the operation the "greatest hour" of his career.

FORMATION OF THE JABOSTAFFELN

The failure of the Wehrmacht to defeat the Soviet Union before winter ensured the continuation of a multifront war well into 1942. To maintain offensive pressure on Britain by day, the German High Command decided to resume the fighter-bomber raids that had met with some success in the final period of the Battle of Britain. This time, the Luftwaffe decided to set up new specialist units for the task, rather than dilute the strength of the pure fighter units then stationed in France. On 10 March 1942, Luftflotte 3 ordered the establishment of two Jagdbomber (or "Jabo") Staffeln, one in each of the two Channel Jagdgeschwader. The new units were designated 10 (Jabo)/JG 2 and 10 (Jabo)/JG 26. Pilots with 1940 fighter-bomber experience were sought out for these Staffeln, which in mid-April became operational in Bf 109F-4/R1s, the latest bomb-carrying model of the Messerschmitt fighter. Missions were usually flown in a strength of one or two Schwaerme against military and industrial installations on the southern coast of England. The Messerschmitts carried one 551-lb bomb apiece and depended on speed, surprise, and extreme low altitude for survival. They normally flew alone, without fighter escort. 10 (Jabo)/JG 26 was subordinated to the First Gruppe for administration and was based with it at St. Omer-Arques. It sustained its first casualty on 24 April, when a pilot was shot down and killed by antiaircraft fire during a two-plane raid on Folkestone.

In June, the JG 26 Jabostaffel moved to Le Bourget airfield outside Paris. Here it received new FW 109A-3/U3s, the first model of the Focke-Wulf fighter equipped to carry bombs. By August, 10 (Jabo)/JG 26 was fully operational in its new aircraft, which could carry one 1,100-lb bomb under the fuselage and four 110-lb bombs on wing racks. The Staffel returned to St. Omer, where it stayed for the rest of 1942, except for a three-week detachment to Marseilles in November.

During its period on operations in 1942, 10 (Jabo)/JG 26 suffered the highest casualties of any JG 26 Staffel. It lost nine pilots killed (including one Kapitaen) and two taken prisoner (including another Kapitaen). Gerhard Schoepfel, their Kommodore during this period, believes that the courage of the fighter-bomber pilots was insufficiently recognized or rewarded, and that each successful Jabo sortie should have counted as much toward medals and promotions as an aerial victory gained by the conventional fighters.

The spring of 1942 found Fighter Command no closer than in 1940 to finding a defense against the Jabo raids. Spitfires were unable to catch the Focke-Wulf at low altitude; the most effective weapon against the low-level raiders remained light antiaircraft fire. The new Hawker Typhoon, which began entering service in late 1942, proved to have excellent speed and acceleration at ground level, and was assigned the anti-Jabo role. By mid-1943, the Typhoon had made low-level daylight operations over England unprofitable for the Germans, and the Jabos were transferred to other, less well-defended theaters.

RENEWAL OF THE BRITISH OFFENSIVE

Early in March, Churchill authorized the resumption of raids over France with the admonition that Fighter Command was expected to destroy German aircraft "plane for plane." No new tactics had been developed in the interim, and Air Marshal Sholto Douglas was thus obliged to order a replay of the previous fall's massive raids and sweeps. Air Vice Marshal Leigh-Mallory's No. 11 Group squadrons flew the Spitfire Vb, the latest variant of the Spitfire V. Their most frequent opponent, Jagdgeschwader 26, was equipped exclusively with FW 190A-1s and A-2s, after the First Gruppe surrendered the last of its Bf 109Fs in early April. The level of combat skill the RAF's Fighter Command had dropped sharply as experienced pilots were ordered away to reinforce the Mediterranean and Pacific theaters. Across the Channel, the combat skills of the average German pilot had never been greater, as the Circuses of 1941 had given the Germans much valuable experience at minimal cost. The qualitative superiority of the Jagdwaffe over its Western enemies was at its zenith.

By the spring of 1942 the German air defense network in France and Belgium rivaled Britain's in effectiveness—a remarkable accomplishment, achieved in just one year. A successful defense of the coastal region required the earliest warning possible; this was the responsibility of the radio intercept service and the Freya early warning radars, which were now thick along the coast. A second chain of Freyas were located 30-50 miles inland. Bearings from the two chains allowed a continuous estimation of the location of enemy formations, once they had crossed the coast. The FW 190s of formation leaders were equipped with FuG 25a IFF (Identification, Friend from Foe) equipment. This device contained a receiver that detected the Freya beams and a transmitter which then responded with a timed signal. This signal altered the shape of the pulse displayed by the Freya receiver, permitting the fighter control unit to distinguish friendly formations from enemy. Interceptions could be controlled by Jafue 2, but often in this period the responsibility was delegated to the operations room of JG 26 itself. A command network ensured the rapid, simultaneous transmission of orders. All messages from the Geschwader operations room were sent via land line to radio equipment that was located in each Gruppe command post and remained turned on during all periods of readiness. All incoming messages were rebroadcast over an extensive network of loudspeakers located in the Gruppe command post, in the Staffel ready rooms, and around the airfields. Thus every pilot could hear the assembly point and altitude, and the latest estimate of the tactical situation, while awaiting his order to take off.

The air war on the Kanalfront picked up where it had left off the previous autumn. The Germans retained their superiority in equipment and tactics. The first Circus of 1942 was flown on 8 March. It led to a massive air battle over Dunkirk that cost JG 26 two fighters and their pilots, while the RAF lost one Douglas Boston lightbomber and three Spitfires. In March, RAF Fighter Command lost thirty-two Spitfires with their pilots. JG 26 lost five pilots killed; the losses of JG 2 were equally low. Churchill's "plane for plane" requirement was not being met, but Sholto Douglas and Leigh-Mallory saw no option but to continue the offensive much as before. Mission plans grew ever more complex, with the addition of feints and diversions. The skill of German controllers grew proportionately, and the tactical initiative remained firmly in the hands of the defenders.

British fighter losses increased in April to 103 Spitfires and one Hurricane; RAF pilot losses included one group captain and two wing leaders. German losses remained low. Twelve JG 26 pilots lost their lives in April's combats; another five were killed in accidents. III/JG 26 was pulled back from the coast in early April, moving to Wevelghem in western Belgium. The Belgian Air Force had built the field in 1922, and it was relatively well equipped. By 1 June, the Geschwaderstab had left its familiar surroundings at Audembert for Wizernes, near the First Gruppe's base at Arques. The two fields were part of the complex of bases that had been developed around St. Omer. The new base alignment gave Jafue 2 more flexibility, and it better protected the important Lille area, but it reduced the strength available for forward interceptions over the Channel.

FOCKE-WULF SUMMER

JG 2, based to the west of JG 26, had replaced almost all of its own Bf 109Fs with FW 190As by the end of April, increasing the German qualitative superiority even more. Fighter Command's high losses continued through May. Its pleas for improved equipment would be answered by the Supermarine Spitfire IX and its Merlin 61, an outstanding new engine from Rolls-Royce. Production lines were beginning to roll, but introduction of the new Spitfire into the service units was still some time away. Fighter Command and No. 2 Group of Bomber Command adopted a new method of rendezvous to delay detection by German radar. The aircraft now met below 500 feet altitude, in complete radio silence, and remained at sea level until just before the coast was reached. All aircraft then pulled up in a steep climb to evade the coastal flak belt. Frequently, this tactic left the Focke-Wulfs with insufficient time to climb above the RAF formations. However, the German pilots were so skilled that many formation leaders were willing to dogfight with the Spitfires at low altitude.

On 1 June, the fighter duel on the Channel began with a massive sweep of Calais by the Spitfires of the Biggin Hill and North Weald wings. The German fighter controller recognized it as an innocuous Rodeo and did not order his fighters up. Circus No. 178 then took to the air. Its composition and complexity was typical of the period. The punch was supplied by eight bomb-carrying Hurricane IIbs, which were escorted by thirty-six Spitfires from the Hornchurch Wing. High cover was the responsibility of forty-eight Biggin Hill Spitfires. Target cover was supplied by forty-eight Spitfires from the Debden Wing, while another thirty-six Spitfires flew a diversion to Gravelines.

The German Freya radars tracked the 176 fighters from 1300 hours, but as the ground spotters could see no bombers, the controller continued to hold the Focke-Wulfs at readiness. The Hurricanes bombed targets in Bruges without fighter interference. At 1320, Hptm. Priller's III/JG 26 was finally ordered up from Wevelghem, at about the same time as Hptm. Seifert's I/JG 26 left St. Omer–Arques. The two Gruppen met up over Ostend, both climbing at their maximum rates. A Spitfire formation was clearly visible in the cloudless skies ahead. The Focke-Wulfs continued climbing and reached 30,000 feet off Blankenberge, 5-10,000 feet above the British formation, which contained the four Spitfire squadrons of the Debden Wing. Priller ordered one Staffel to feint at the large formation. Twelve Focke-Wulfs promptly dove on the Spitfires and broke away. The Debden Wing's commander ordered his pilots to break into the presumed attack. One squadron fell behind on the turn, destroying the cohesion of the formation. At this, Priller led his remaining fighters into the middle of the straggling squadron, while Seifert, whose First Gruppe had remained up-sun, bounced the high-cover squadron. Within seconds, several Spitfires were spiraling toward the Channel. Individual combats continued for several minutes before the surviving pilots extricated themselves and headed for their respective bases.

The Debden Wing lost its commander and eight Spitfires in this combat; only one British pilot was rescued from the Channel. Five more fighters made it back to England with serious damage. The known claims of the Schlageter fighters match the RAF's losses exactly. The Debden pilots claimed 3-0-3 Focke-Wulfs. In reality, no German fighter was lost; no Focke-Wulf even suffered any reportable damage.

The next day, 2 June, was the blackest in the career of Sqd. Ldr. Al Deere, one of the Battle of Britain's most famous pilots. After a six months tour in the USA, the New Zealander had taken over No. 403 Squadron (RCAF). The squadron was being rebuilt after its losses that spring, and most of the pilots were new to combat. Deere had been warned by his friends about Fighter Command that it was "bloody tough going over the other side now," but the FW 190 and its superb combat abilities was not a major topic of conversation in his green squadron's mess. Two weeks' operations had resulted in little combat, and confidence remained high.

No. 403 Squadron took part in the second Rodeo of the morning, which was a two-wing sweep of the St. Omer area. Deere's pilots flew at 27,000 feet, as top cover for the North Weald Wing, which flew above the Hornchurch Wing. Again, the German controller waited until the British were overland before ordering up the defenders—today these comprised Hptm. Muencheberg's II/JG 26 from Abbeville-Drucat, along with Seifert's I/JG 26 from St. Omer-Arques. As the Spitfire formation headed back out to sea, a Staffel of Focke-Wulfs was spotted behind No. 403 Squadron, closing fast. When they had reached the proper distance, Deere ordered a prearranged three-way break. Halfway through this complicated maneuver, Deere's Spitfires were hit from the clouds above one flank by the other two Staffeln of the pursuing Gruppe. After passing through the first formation, the Spitfires were struck from the clouds yet again, by the second JG 26 Gruppe. Deere's dozen pilots fought for their lives while their comrades in the other Spitfire squadrons, mindful of their orders to avoid combat in tactically unfavorable conditions, left them to their fate and returned to England.

The Canadian pilots had to evade the German attacks and break for home as best they could. Three Spitfires made it back to their field at Rochford. Two more force-landed at Manston; one of these was a complete writeoff. The other seven planes came down in the Channel. Only one of their pilots was rescued. The survivors claimed no victories over the Focke-Wulfs. This battle, which lasted only seven minutes, resulted in eight confirmed JG 26 claims. Hptm. Muencheberg tallied his eightieth and eighty-first victories, while two of his Second Gruppe pilots scored singles. Hptm. Seifert scored his thirty-fifth victory, and three other First Gruppe pilots scored.

The cumulative effect of encounters such as these was the demoralization of all levels of Fighter Command, from top to bottom. The Air Ministry was slow to react, apparently lulled into complacency by its own government's constant claims of aerial success. On 17 July, Sholto Douglas put the matter bluntly in a letter to his superiors:

> We are now in a position of inferiority. . . . There is no doubt in my mind, nor in the minds of my fighter pilots, that the FW 190 is the best all-round fighter in the world today.

The Allied pilots attempted to console themselves with the belief that they were opposed by the best of Germany's pilots, a hand-picked Geschwader known variously as "Goering's yellow-nosed elite," the "Abbeville Boys" (later Americanized to "Abbeville Kids"), and the "St. Omer Boys." The men of JG 26 were flattered and somewhat amused by these appellations when they heard them from captured Allied airmen. It was well-known in the Luftwaffe that the Jagdwaffe got the cream of the pilots graduating from the training schools, and there was evidence that the best of these were sent west rather than east, but the most important process leading to the Geschwader's lofty position was Darwinian—only the naturally gifted pilots survived their first few missions; they then had daily opportunities to increase their skills against high-quality op-

119

position Until bad luck or fatigue ended their careers, they could objectively be considered members of a very elite fraternity, that of the world's best fighter pilots.

On 23 June, the adjutant of III/JG 2 presented the British with a brand-new FW 190A-3. This pilot became disoriented during combat over England, mistook the Bristol Channel for the English Channel, and landed at the Royal Air Force airbase at Pembrey, thinking he was in France. At last the mystique surrounding the Focke-Wulf fighter could be dispelled, and tactics developed to defeat it. Mock combats with a Spitfire Vb rapidly proved what Fighter Command's pilots had been claiming for some time—the German fighter was superior in all flight parameters except turning radius. The seemingly magical ability of the Focke-Wulf fighter to disappear in the blink of an eye was attributable primarily to its well-balanced aileron controls, which gave the aircraft the highest rate of roll of any World War II fighter, Allied or Axis. The split-S maneuver, a half-roll followed by a dive, would leave any pursuing Spitfire hopelessly behind. The FW 190 was found to be 25-30 mph faster than the Spitfire Vb at all altitudes up to 25,000 feet. The Air Fighting Development Unit's main recommendation for Fighter Command's Spitfire Vb pilots did nothing to boost their offensive spirit. The Spitfire pilots were instructed to draw the Germans as close to England as possible, and then circle, until the Focke-Wulfs ran low on fuel and were forced to break off combat.

The Spitfire IX was only now starting to reach the squadrons. In July, Hornchurch's No. 64 Squadron was the first to begin operations with the new fighter. The Spitfire IX was an even match for the FW 190. The climb rates and top speeds of the two fighters were nearly the same at low and medium altitudes; the two-stage supercharger of the Merlin 61 gave the advantage to the Spitfire at altitudes above 25,000 feet. The usual generality concerning relative maneuverabilities still held—the British fighter was better in turns on the horizontal plane, while the German excelled in zoom climbs and dives, and aileron rolls.

Although the FW 190 was superior to the other single-engined German fighter, the Bf 109, in most combat parameters, the Messerschmitt fighter remained numerically predominant in the Jagdwaffe, and its development continued. The Bf 109G began coming off the Augsburg production lines in the spring of 1942. The first variant of this model to be released for operational service, the Bf 109G-1, was intended for high-altitude service, and possessed a rudimentary pressurized cabin. The first Luftwaffe units to receive the new fighter were the two Kanalgeschwader. 1/JG 2 was re-equipped in late May and was then redesignated as a high-altitude Staffel, 11 (Hoehen)/JG 2. 11 (Hoehen)/JG 26 was formed in July, around a nucleus from I/JG 26. The two Messerschmitt Staffeln were assigned the dual missions of high-altitude interceptions and cover for their brethren flying altitude-limited Focke-Wulfs. The first Kapitaen of 11 (Hoehen)/JG 26 was Oblt. Johannes Schmidt, who brought with him from I/JG 26 a cadre of experienced pilots. 11 (Hoehen)/JG 2 was commanded by Oblt. Rudi Pflanz, one of the Richthofen Geschwader's most successful pilots. His Staffel was placed under JG 26 for the summer hunting season and began operations from Liegescourt, northeast of Abbeville.

The early summer was remarkable, however, for its lack of aerial activity. Uffz. Peter Crump arrived at the Geschwader in mid-June as a new pilot and was assigned to the 5th Staffel at Abbeville. He moved into the Staffel's lodgings in a well-landscaped chateau three miles east of Drucat and, after making a few familiarization flights, was put on the duty roster. Peter Crump describes life as a new member of the Abbeville Kids:

> Almost six weeks passed before I saw my first Spitfire. We pilots whiled away the time in all sorts of ways. Many played chess or skat. If one wanted fresh air and sun, he could doze or read a book on the lawn in front of the pilots' readiness barracks. An occasional swim in a large water tank next to the dispersal was a welcome diversion. Now and then we had informal classes in aircraft recognition, air combat tactics, new intelligence about the enemy—especially conditions in their countries—and general discussions on the course of the war. Movies were also shown in the command post.
>
> The flying routine varied. Today a repaired aircraft might be test-flown; tomorrow a Focke-Wulf might have to be fetched from somewhere. Firing exercises might be conducted against ground targets, or against phantom targets over the ocean. We finally began to train on modern tactics against bombers, using He 111s or Do 217s on detachment. At times we escorted ships. From time to time, at irregular intervals and at various times of day, we were required to scramble against approaching enemy aircraft formations.

121

As martial activities remained in the doldrums, the readiness routine was altered. Only one Staffel had to remain at the field until "lanternlight," while the other two Staffeln were released to seek out entertainment in Abbeville. And if the weather was bad, only one Staffel might remain at the field for the entire day, or even one Schwarm.

On 24 July, a new phase of our life at the front began. Almost every evening, the Gruppe's aircraft would fly inland from Abbeville to Cambrai, or to another of several dispersal fields. This was a security precaution against sudden attacks on the Somme lowlands by commando units form the nearby coast. These transfer flights were well-liked by the pilots, because there was a school for Luftnachrichten-helferinnen [Luftwaffe airwomen] in Cambrai. The flights continued until October, when they were stopped because of the increasingly unfavorable autumn weather conditions.

At noon on 26 July, Uffz. Crump's Alarmstart (scramble) resulted in his first encounter with the enemy, and his first credited combat sortie. Two Schwaerme from the Second Gruppe were ordered to intercept a formation of enemy fighters reported circling over the Channel, north of Calais. The eight Focke-Wulf pilots were all enlisted men and were led by an experienced Oberfeldwebel, Walter Meyer. Crump flew as Meyer's wingman. Meyer led his fighters up from Abbeville and then directly westward, away from the Spitfires. He circled back and hit them from the direction of the English coast, out of the early-afternoon sun. The bounce was completely successful; Meyer's first burst hit a Spitfire which immediately gave off black smoke, tipped over one wing, and struck the water. Within minutes, two more British fighters had hit the Channel. Crump took little part in the action. It was all he could do to keep Meyer in sight. Just as he began to comprehend what was happening around him, the battle was over.

After returning unharmed to Drucat, the jubilant German pilots were sobered at their debriefing by the news that the Spitfires had been searching for a downed pilot and had committed the fatal error of climbing into the range of the German coastal radar. The episode was the topic of heated conversations in the Staffel ready room for the next several days. Since 1940, the policy of both combatants had been to treat naval and air forces engaged on "missions of mercy" in the Channel as legitimate targets. The victims of this policy were the pilots themselves, any of whom could find themselves one day floating in the icy waters and despairing of salvation. What remained of the unwritten code of aerial chivalry? "Who started this swinish business?" Crump and the others asked themselves.

On 23 July, the Second Gruppe said farewell to its popular Kommandeur Hptm. Joachim Muencheberg. The uniquely talented 23-year-old pilot was being sent to the Eastern Front, as an "apprentice Kommodore," as he casually put it. His actual assignment was an indication of the high esteem in which he was held in the Luftwaffe. He was under orders to tour all of the Jagdgeschwader in the east, as a novel form of training before taking up a post as a Geschwaderkommodore. Muencheberg was the highest-scoring pilot in the JG 26 at the time he left, with eighty-three victories. He was to score another fifty-two victories before losing his life in North Africa while Kommodore of JG 77.

On 30 July, Fighter Command directed Circus No. 200 at their tormentors on Abbeville-Drucat airfield. The bombers, six Bostons, were shielded by the usual massive force of Spitfires. No. 64 Squadron's Spitfire IXs encountered FW 190s for the first time and claimed 5-0-1 of them for the day, without loss to themselves. Despite No. 64 Squadron's claims, only one FW 190 and pilot were lost. The older Spitfire Vbs did not fare well; fourteen failed to return. At least ten were claimed by JG 26 pilots from the First and Third Gruppen.

A repeat of the operation the following day brought almost the same results. This time the Abbeville Kids of II/JG 26 rose to defend their own field and claimed the destruction of fifteen Spitfires. Fighter Command claimed 11-1-5 fighters while losing eleven pilots. JG 26 suffered one casualty, an injured pilot. There was at least one fatality from JG 2; Oblt. Rudi Pflanz, Kapitaen of 11 (Hoehen)/JG 2 at Liegescourt, was killed over Abbeville by Spitfires. After this raid, Allied air activity over the Continent decreased sharply and remained at a very low level of the next two weeks.

Throughout the summer, the German Kanaljaeger (Channel fighters) continued their successful defensive tactics against the Circuses and Rodeos. The German controllers never lost the tactical initiative, and the victory ratio favored their pilots by a wide margin.

German casualties were light. In the three months preceding mid-August, JG 26 lost only six pilots killed and one taken prisoner, while its companion Kanalgeschwader, JG 2, lost twenty-seven killed and five taken prisoners.

THE DIEPPE RAID

For 5/JG 26 at Abbeville, 19 August began as another normal day of operations. The duty pilots arose as usual and rode the Staffel vehicle to the airfield in the dim light of early dawn. They arrived at the dispersal shortly after 0600 and were greeted with impatience by the line chief. An order had already been received from the Gruppe command post—two aircraft were to take off immediately, fly to the Somme Estuary, make a brief reconnaissance, and return. No further details were available from the Gruppe.

Oblt. Horst Sternberg, the vehicle's driver and the only officer among the duty pilots, detailed Uffz. Peter Crump to be his wingman. Since Crump was a novice without a permanently assigned aircraft, Sternberg ordered him to fly "Black 8," the Focke-Wulf of the Staffelkapitaen, Oblt. Wutz Galland. They took off in the weak dawn light. While underway, the Jafue ordered them to fly to Dieppe. The pair remained at minimum altitude. A short time later, while paralleling the coast, the pilots spotted a continuous stream of sparks, as from a fireworks display. Shells burst in ghostly silence; mounds of earth flew into the air. Then the German pilots saw the cause—the explosions on shore were the result of salvos fired by ships half-hidden in the bluish gray of the nearby sea. As the pair overflew Dieppe, they could see landing craft approaching the beach in front of the town. Since Sternberg's orders were to gain a rapid, general impression of the course of events, he avoided the beach area, as well as several Spitfires that Crump called out. As the Focke-Wulfs crossed the southern edge of the town, they were taken under fire by German light flak. The string of pearls reached out to Crump's aircraft and passed cleanly through it. At this, Sternberg ordered a return to Abbeville.

When Sternberg reported back, he was chewed out by Galland for letting Crump fly his aircraft. It was now damaged, unavailable for further operations—and it was already obvious that the day ahead would require a maximum effort from the Geschwader. Sternberg and Crump had been the Luftwaffe's first witnesses to Operation Jubilee, the Allied raid on Dieppe.

The Dieppe operation was the first major Allied amphibious assault of the war. Its motivation, planning, and execution have remained the subjects of dispute. Its aerial side, the only one of concern here, is no less controversial than its naval and ground aspects. Sholto Douglas saw the raid as an opportunity to force the elusive Jagdwaffe to do battle on the RAF's own terms. He assigned command responsibility to No. 11 Group's Leigh-Mallory, who was given control of fifty-six fighter squadrons—750 aircraft—for the operation. There were only four Spitfire IX squadrons; the rest were equipped with earlier Spitfire models and obsolete Hurricanes. Leigh-Mallory also had four squadrons of reconnaissance Mustangs, which were just entering service with the RAF. His bomber component comprised a paltry five squadrons of Blenheims and Bostons.

The German fighter units opposing this large force were the well-tried Kanalgeschwader JG 2 and JG 26, each with about 110 operational fighters. The struggle for air supremacy over the beach-head would thus find the German fighters outnumbered by more than three to one. The only German "day bombers" in the West were the twenty FW 190s of the two Jabostaffeln. Around 220 night bombers, Do 217s and Ju 88s, were scattered on various bases in the Netherlands and northern France.

The Allied fleet reached the French coast without discovery by the Luftwaffe. The German controllers were not quite sure what they were dealing with, but at 0618, just as Sternberg's patrol Rotte was taking off, the first attack force was ordered up—ten FW 190s of 1/JG 26. Sixteen Focke-Wulfs from 2/JG 26 and 3/JG 26 soon followed them away from St. Omer-Arques, as did some Bf 109Gs from the newly operational 11th Staffel. The four Staffel formations soon broke up in individual combats with the Spitfire umbrella above Dieppe. Oblt. Schmidt's Messerschmitts were vectored over the sea six miles north of Dieppe. During a low-level dogfight, Schmidt attempted a split-S without sufficient recovery altitude and crashed into the Channel.

The next Luftwaffe formation to reach the beachhead was sent from Wevelghem by III/JG 26 at 0700. Its size and effect have not been determined. II/JG 26 at Abbeville and Amiens apparently supplied the first truly large-scale defensive reaction. The Gruppe took off at about 0750, reached Dieppe at altitude and in good formation, and hit the Spitfire formations hard. According to British radio intercepts, the average number of German fighters over the beachhead increased from twenty to thirty at 0830, and reached an estimated one hundred by 0930. All of these aircraft were from JG 26. Twenty-seven Spitfires were shot down by the Schlageter Geschwader prior to 1040, when the first formation from the Richthofen Geschwader reached the combat zone from Le Havre.

The first major German bomber raid reached Dieppe at 1100. It consisted of Do 217s, flying from their bases in the Netherlands. The formation picked up an escort of Focke-Wulfs from I/JG 26 and III/JG 26 while en route. The escort was of spotty quality, as the day fighters had never before operated with night bombers. The bombers had been briefed to attack ships, which were the easiest targets to locate. They made their bomb runs at moderate altitude—5-6,000 feet—in small formations of from three to fifteen aircraft. The Dorniers continued to make small-scale attacks throughout the afternoon and lost sixteen of their number. An estimated total of 145 sorties were flown on 19 August by the German medium-bomber force.

At 1130, the closest major airfield to Dieppe, Abbeville-Drucat, was bombed by twenty-four Boeing B-17 Flying Fortresses of the American Eighth Bomber Command's 97th Bomb Group. The raid coincided with the scheduled time of the British withdrawal from the beachhead. The B-17s made their bombing run from 23,000 feet. The flak defenses were alert and scored several hits, but no interceptions were made by German fighters, which were fully occupied elsewhere. The British radio intercept service reported that the airfield was put out of action for several hours—or at least it went off the air, which might have been simply the result of an emergency plan. Whatever the temporary condition of the airfield, the German defense effort was not appreciably affected. II/JG 26 continued normal operations from its satellite airfields at Cambrai-Epinoy, Liegescourt, and Amiens. The Allies' first attempt at battlefield interdiction by heavy bombers was not a success. A bombing force many times larger than the infant Eighth Bomber Command would have been necessary to take out the dozen German airfields within striking range of Dieppe.

By noon, the withdrawal from the beachhead was well underway. The Spitfire umbrella was unbroken, so by British reckoning, "air superiority" had been achieved and maintained. However, the Germans were playing by different rules. The British bombers were so few in numbers that they were impossible to locate and intercept in the general melee over Dieppe; the German fighter pilots, when released from escort duty, reverted to their well-practiced tactics of attrition against the numerically superior Spitfires. It was business as usual for the German controllers; the British radio monitors were impressed by their calmness and obvious command of the situation. The Luftwaffe saw no need to alert any units other than those in the immediate area of Dieppe; the only reserves drawn upon were the repaired aircraft in the rear workshops.

Uffz. Crump of 5/JG 26 was one pilot who carried on with his usual routine. He was ordered to take the train to Amiens, in order to ferry back a newly repaired Focke-Wulf from the workshop there. At around noon, he arrived back at Abbeville in "Black 2" and landed on the ostensibly unserviceable airfield without incident. The early-morning tension had already been relieved, and for the balance of the day, the Second Gruppe's missions were flown in Staffel strength, or less, and were of the nature of patrols and reconnaissance flights.

The two Jabostaffeln were employed throughout the day against naval targets. At about 1400, two FW 190s from 10 (Jabo)/JG 2 dove on the destroyer *Berkeley;* one scored a direct hit on the ship's stern with a 1,100-lb bomb. The destroyer was sunk later in the day by British forces and proved the only major warship lost on 19 August by the Royal Navy. 10 (Jabo)/JG 26 reported attacking warships, transports, torpedo boats, and landing craft.

One of 5/JG 26's missions typifies the activity of late afternoon. A Schwarm was ordered to fly a freie Jagd to Dieppe. Oblt. Wutz Galland led it himself, choosing Uffz. Crump to be his wingman. The four Focke-Wulfs took off from Abbeville at 1724 and were soon over the former combat zone. It was deserted; the only signs of the morning's combat were the destroyed houses along the beach, the abandoned military equipment, and the corpses floating in the water. Galland finally spotted a target—a small, twin-stacked steamer, lying abandoned about 500 yards offshore. Galland led his four Focke-Wulfs in a strafing run on the derelict. To the amazement of the German pilots, their fire resulted in a large explosion amidships, which tore the steamer apart. It sank a few minutes later in the rising tide, bow and stern upraised.

The Focke-Wulf pilots next spotted a vessel disappearing northward behind a large bow plume. It was a British speedboat, recognizable by its black-and-white checkered bow. The fighters made a coordinated strafing attack in pairs. The boat defended itself with cannon fire, while zigzagging at top speed. The battle ended after the second strafing run. The ship's wedge-shaped bow plume suddenly vanished. It was followed into oblivion by the boat itself, which quickly disappeared beneath the waves. Elated, the German pilots returned to Abbeville, from which they were to be ordered to fly one more patrol before nightfall.

When the last Focke-Wulf touched down at 2121, the Geschwader's effort had totaled 377 sorties in thirty-six missions. Most pilots flew either three or four sorties. Their claims over RAF fighters totaled forty that were later confirmed, plus eleven probables.

The Allied fighter pilots touching down in England after their last sorties of the day were, of course, exhausted, but most were also exhilarated by their apparent success. No. 11 Group had maintained an apparently overwhelming number of fighters over the battlefield at all times. The German fighters had been forced away from the beachhead, to spend the day nibbling away at the periphery of the armada. The RAF's victory claims totaled 47-27-76 FW 190s; 3-1-2 Bf 109s; 33-8-46 Do 217s; 8-3-11 Ju 88s; and 5-0-0 He 111s. The British losses, when totaled at the end of the day, were sobering—seventy-one pilots and ten aircrew were killed or missing, and 106 aircraft had not returned, including eighty-eight fighters. The total number of Luftwaffe aircraft claimed destroyed, ninety-six, was close enough to the RAF's losses to justify claims of a modest air success. However, when an intelligence report was received from France claiming that German losses had totaled 160 aircraft, Leigh-Mallory accepted the larger number as factual and trumpeted his supposed great victory to the press.

Actual Luftwaffe losses totaled no more than forty-eight aircraft, a number confirmed from the German aircraft loss records. A recent study can find no more than twenty fighter losses, fourteen from JG 2 and six from JG 26. Fourteen fighter pilots lost their lives, eight from JG 2 and six from JG 26. JG 2 pilots claimed fifty-nine aerial victories, while JG 26 claimed forty. Even considering that not all the British losses were to German fighters, the German total of ninety-nine victory claims is a very close match with the actual RAF loss total of 106.

The Allied claims of an overall aerial victory cannot be justified in any sense today. The ratio of aerial victories favored the Germans by a wide margin. Furthermore, the local aerial superiority "won" over Dieppe was a chimera. Temporary occupation of a section of airspace is pointless in itself—it is only of value as a means to an end. At Dieppe, the RAF aerial umbrella aided the endeavors of neither the ground forces nor the pathetically few tactical aircraft. Claims of a successful battle of attrition were bolstered by Ultra intercepts of the daily Luftwaffe serviceability returns—the 230 single-engined fighters available to the two Kanalgeschwader at dawn on 19 August had been reduced to seventy by sunset. However, the next piece of data in this set was conveniently ignored. At dawn on 20 August, JG 2 and JG 26 had 194 fighters available for duty; the fighters reported as unserviceable the previous evening included, as usual, all aircraft with armament, engine, or airframe defects of any magnitude. Most were repaired overnight in the Geschwader's own workshops. The battle of attrition thus resulted in a one day shortfall of thirty-six fighters, or 16 percent.

Operation Torch, the Allied invasion of North Africa, would soon begin siphoning off fighter squadrons from the United Kingdom. Operation Jubilee thus marked the apogee of Fighter Command's numerical strength. Gen. Alan Brooke, Chief of the Imperial General Staff, summarized the end result of the Dieppe operation as follows:

> This bloody affair, though productive of many valuable lessons, ended the summer's attempt to draw off planes from Russia by trailing Fighter Command's coat over northern France—a gesture that had cost Britain nearly a thousand pilots and aircraft.

A NEW ENEMY

Although the period of massive Circuses had passed, Fighter Command sent flights of Spitfires across the Channel from time to time to test the German defenses and to furnish diversions and escort for their new partners in the daylight offensive—the American Eighth Air Force. On 27 August, a Spitfire formation was reported very near the French coast. The fighters had crossed the Somme Estuary at low altitude and were only detected by radar as they climbed to avoid the coastal flak emplacements. The 5th Staffel, which had the duty at Abbeville, was scrambled to intercept them. Oblt. Wutz Galland led his Staffel in a head-on attack just north of Drucat village, which adjoined the airfield. The Spitfire formation broke up and the pursuit began. Uffz. Crump caught up to one of the British fighters at the coast. He prepared to open fire from a climbing right turn at 100 yards altitude. This was the first time since arriving on the Channel that he had attained a favorable attack position. His training, and the advice of his battle-tested Staffel comrades, flashed through his mind—"In a turning battle, keep the longitudinal axis of the enemy aircraft out of your own line of vision; the tighter the bank, the greater the lead angle." His first burst of cannon fire struck the engine of the Spitfire, which erupted into flames. The British pilot saved himself by bailing out and "going for a swim"—German pilot slang for landing in the water.

Peter Crump's victory was one of five for the Staffel, which suffered no damage or loss. Back on the ground at Abbeville, he basked in the special recognition awarded a pilot after his first aerial victory. It had been a long time in coming. Crump had enlisted in the Luftwaffe in 1937 with the goal of becoming a fighter pilot. He was selected for flight school and completed his training in June 1940. He was ordered to JG 53, reaching it just as the Battle of Britain began. Always a man of independent mind and speech, Crump fell out with his Staffelkapitaen, who took him off flight duty for "defects of character" and had him returned to Germany for general military service. After a year's struggle with the "Moloch of the military bureaucracy" (in Crump's words), he was rehabilitated and allowed to begin anew his career as a combat pilot. Peter Crump was blessed with the good reflexes and vision needed to survive in the air over western Europe, and he flew in combat of the next three years, ending the war as a Staffelkapitaen in I/JG 26.

The American Eighth Air Force, which would ultimately end the Luftwaffe's dominance of the skies over western Europe, began small overflights of the French and Belgian coastal regions in August. Weak in strength and lacking combat experience, the Eighth Bomber Command's first raids barely crossed the coast and were directed at airfields, railroad yards, and the few industrial targets unfortunate enough to be located within range of the B-17s' Spitfire escort. The air marshals of the RAF disagreed with the air doctrine of the Americans, who were planning the unescorted daylight bombing of German industrial targets. However, the British were perfectly willing to share with the Americans the task of harassing the Luftwaffe in the occupied countries.

The first months of the Eighth Air Force's offensive thus found the American heavy bombers taking the role formerly played by the weak RAF Blenheim and Boston formations. The B-17s and Consolidated B-24 Liberators were the bait that would entice the Jagdwaffe to battle. There was one major difference from the days of the Circuses. The American bombers, however small their numbers, carried a bomb load of sufficient size to punish their targets. Thus the Germans no longer could decline to attack the bombers when circumstances were unfavorable—they were forced to defend against every raid and therefore lost the tactical initiative that they had maintained for more than a year.

American strength was slow to develop, which was fortunate for the Luftwaffe, which had made no plans to deal with the threat of the heavy bombers. It was lacking the proper equipment, tactics, and numbers of fighters. The performance of the Kanaljaegers' beloved Focke-Wulf fighters dropped off markedly above 25,000 feet, which happened to be the altitude preferred by the B-17 formations. The fighter units on the coast needed more warning than their controllers had been accustomed to providing if they were even to reach the bombers' altitude. Several of the early raids were not intercepted at all, arousing the wrath of both Hermann Goering and Adolf Galland. Galland was promoted to Generalmajor on 19 November, giving him a rank equal to his position as General der Jagdflieger. At age thirty he was the youngest general in the Luftwaffe. Concerned about the apparent decline in performance of his favorite fighter unit, General Galland made a personal visit to the coast to assure himself that Major Schoepfel had the situation under control.

A typical interception in the fall of 1942 has been described by Johannes Naumann, at that time an Oberleutnant in II/JG 26.

The Gruppe was ordered to attack the bombers on their return flight, as there was no chance of reaching them before the bomb run. The B-17s were flying in a staggered formation at about 26,000 feet. The Focke-Wulfs finally struggled up to 27,000 feet, only to see the American formation receding into the distance. The speed of the FW 190s at that altitude was little greater than that of the bombers, and a stern chase closed the range only very slowly. Frustrated, Naumann opened fire with his MG 151/20 cannon at the extreme range of 750 yards, to no effect. By this time, half of the original formation of twenty-four Focke-Wulfs had dropped out of the chase for one reason or another. Suddenly there was a loud noise from in front of Naumann's feet—his engine had exploded, bringing his combat sortie to a sudden end. No bombers were downed; none had even suffered visible damage.

Karl Borris, in 1942 the Kapitaen of the 8th Staffel, has discussed the emotional impact of the enemy bombers on the German pilots, who were now facing the most formidable challenge of their lives. The size of the heavy bombers and their formations, and their unprecedented defensive firepower, could not be described adequately to a green pilot; they had to be experienced firsthand. The classical stern attack, which at that time was the only approved method, was frequently initiated and broken off too soon to cause damage. Range estimation proved difficult. The Revi gunsight was sized for attacks on fighters; the wings of a typical fighter filled its sighting circle at 100 yards range. The bombers loomed huge in the Revi long before the German fighters reached effective range. The bomber gunners opened fire as soon as a target was seen, in order to disrupt or ward off attacks. The Americans' Browning .50-inch machine guns had a high muzzle velocity and a greater range than the Germans' MG 17s, whose tracers were used to help sight their MG 151 cannon. So the fighter pilots' cockpits were surrounded by red tracers, "swarming like wasps" in Borris's words, long before they themselves could open fire effectively; and because of the low closing speeds, this extremely uncomfortable situation could continue for several minutes. German formation attacks were rarely carried out exactly as planned. Some pilots would invariably break away prematurely, and the rest would pass through the bomber formation at whatever angle and orientation promised the best chance for survival. The formation leaders found it difficult to reassemble the scattered fighters, and each successive attack could be counted on for no greater than half the strength of the one preceding it.

The Eighth Bomber Command's first nine missions were carried out without the loss of a single bomber. On 6 September, an attack on the Potez aircraft factory on Meaulte cost them two B-17s, both victims of the Abbeville Kids of II/JG 26. They attacked the thirty Flying Fortresses continuously from the French coast in to the target. The escort, four squadrons of Spitfire IXs, did not catch up to the bomber force until the coast was reached, and apparently never reached proper position. The high cover, No. 133 "Eagle" Squadron, was flying at 28,000 feet when it was bounced and dispersed by JG 26 Focke-Wulfs attacking from above and behind. Three Spitfires failed to return. The bombers sustained repeated attacks by 45-50 FW 190s and a few Bf 109s. Attacks came from all directions, and nearly all of the B-17s sustained damage. The honor of the Luftwaffe's first "kill" of an American heavy bomber went to Hptm. Conny Meyer, the Second Gruppe's Kommandeur. His target, a B-17 of the 97th Bomb Group, went down near Amiens at 1855. The Focke-Wulfs pursued the bombers back across the French coast. A B-17 of the 92nd Bomb Group succumbed to attacks by at least five 4th Staffel fighters and crashed into the sea near Le Treport.

The credit for this interception belonged to the German radar and radio intercept services and to the fighter control organization, which were rapidly rising to the new challenge. Any major increase in activity on the American radio frequencies foretold a genuine raid; American strength was insufficient for diversions. German radar could pick up the formations before they crossed the English coast, which had not been the case with the Channel-hugging Circuses. Morale in the Jagdgeschwader picked up, although the apparent low destructive capacity of their weapons was frustrating. More effective ammunition was promised shortly. In the meantime, the ability of the B-17s to absorb damage and keep flying was becoming legendary. On one early raid, Oblt. Kurt Ruppert of the 9th Staffel repeatedly attacked an isolated B-17. Three engines were shot up; one fell off the plane and crashed into the Channel. Out of ammunition, Ruppert watched in amazement as the plane continued to fly on one engine, its crew throwing out equipment, guns, and ammunition. The bomber succeeded in making it back across the Channel, force-landing on the beach at Ramsgate.

The bomber gunners did not down their first JG 26 Focke-Wulf until 2 October, when an aircraft of the 4th Staffel was hit during a stern attack on a formation of thirty-two B-17s making another raid on Meaulte. The pilot succeeded in force-landing his damaged aircraft but died in the hospital.

The next raid, on 9 October, was the strongest American effort to date. One hundred and eight bombers were dispatched to attack the Lille-Courtrai area. III/JG 26's airfield at Wevelghem was among the targets, and its Kommandeur, Hptm. Priller, led the German defensive effort. His three Staffeln had dispersed inland for the night and had just landed back at Wevelghem at 0900 when the order was given to scramble. The Gruppe flew northward, straining for altitude. This was Priller's first sight of B-17s from the air; he misjudged their size and thus underestimated the altitude of the bombers. He had to repeat his attack orders three times, as he reached what he thought was the bombers' altitude only to see them still above him. The bombers flew in vees of three, but in no apparent overall formation; they reminded Lt. Otto "Stotto" Stammberger, who was leading the 9th Staffel, of a large cloud of bumblebees. The bombers passed by the fighters, which were still climbing through 26,000 feet. The bomber formation then made a sharp left turn south of Lille, and the Focke-Wulf pilots were able to reach attack position. Pairs of fighters attacked the individual vees from the rear. Hptm. Priller saw his target, a B-17 of the 306th Bomber Group, crash south of Lille.

Lt. Stammberger led his Staffel against another formation of bombers. He saw the contrails of the fighter escort, but they remained far above the fight. His pilots attacked the "barn doors" like wild men, approaching from behind at full throttle and diving away. Stammberger saw that his fire was having no effect; he suddenly realized that he was firing from much too far away. Approaching closer, he saw strikes on the bomber's left wing. Still unmolested by the Allied fighters, he attacked the bomber repeatedly. By the third pass, both left engines were blazing; he then fired at the right outboard engine as the bomber spiraled downward in broad left turns. Four or five men bailed out at 6,000 feet; the Fortress then hit the ground east of Vendeville. Stammberger gave his full attention to the crash of the bomber. When he again looked up, the sky was empty. Out of ammunition, he headed back to Wevelghem.

The 7th Staffel made an effective attack, led by its Kapitaen, Hptm. Klaus Mietusch, who had overcome his earlier hesitation in the air and who now had to guard against pressing his attacks too closely. Mietusch's first target was identified as an RAF Stirling; it was actually a B-24 Liberator of the 93rd Bomb Group. The bomber crashed near Lille. Mietusch made a second pass through the formation and damaged a B-17, which later ditched in the Channel. Mietusch's wingman was hit by defensive fire in the first attack. He jumped from his plane, but he was unable to open his parachute because of his wounds and fell to his death.

The Third Gruppe's toll of four bombers was the heaviest single-mission loss yet suffered by the Eighth Air Force. Many of the returning bombers had been damaged, and bombing accuracy was poor, but the Americans proclaimed a decisive victory over the Luftwaffe. The gunners claimed fifty-six fighters destroyed, twenty-six probably destroyed, and twenty damaged. Although Allied intelligence knew full well that the claims were greater than the strength of the entire German defensive force, and the total was subsequently lowered sharply, the original numbers were quoted in a radio broadcast by President Roosevelt himself, to the great amusement of the German pilots, who had suffered only one casualty.

This raid on Lille marked the high point of the American effort in 1942. The two most experienced heavy bomb groups were withdrawn from combat in preparation for a move to North Africa. The groups left in England were inadequately trained and had to be introduced to combat slowly. The first raid to exceed that of 9 October in strength was not mounted until 17 April 1943.

A TIME OF TRIALS

The Allied bombing offensive evoked a typical reaction from Adolf Hitler. As always when attacked, his mind turned to retaliation. A "vengeance attack" on Canterbury was ordered for 31 October. It developed into the largest daylight raid on England since 1940. The only day bombers available were the FW 190A-4/U4s of the two Jabostaffeln. They had only nineteen serviceable aircraft between them, so bomb racks were hung from forty-nine FW 190A fighters of JG 26's First and Second Gruppen. The attack was timed for dusk. II/JG 2 joined III/JG 26 at St. Omer-Fort Rouge, making up an escort force of sixty-two FW 190s under the command of Hptm. Priller. Six more fighters were detailed to fly a diversionary sweep.

The large fighter force roared across the Channel five feet above the waves, well below a cloud deck at 600 feet. Complete surprise was attained. The barrage balloons were raised swiftly and caused some fighters to drop their bombs prematurely. However, thirty-one bombs exploded in Canterbury, causing considerable damage. The fighters wheeled about and returned to the coast as rapidly as they had arrived. The British fighter defenses, hampered by the low cloud cover, caught only one fighter over England; this FW 190, from JG 2, was shot down and its pilot was captured.

The only other German loss that day was a sobering one for the pilots of JG 26. Lt. Paul Galland was the youngest of three brothers to serve in the Schlageter Geschwader. He had joined 8/JG 26 on 28 February 1941, and he soon proved himself a competent combat pilot. In the early afternoon of 31 October, he shot down a Boston that had attacked the power station at Comines, for his seventeenth combat victory. During the mission to Canterbury that same evening, he lost his unit among the many Focke-Wulfs in the low clouds. On his return flight, while nine miles from Calais, he heard a German pilot calling for assistance. After flying two search curves, he saw in the distance an FW 190 close above the water, pursued by a Spitfire. He went to the German pilot's aid, but the Spitfire pilot spotted him and pulled up sharply into the cloud deck. Galland entered a tight climbing turn, but stalled out and had to dive away to regain flying speed. At this instant, the Spitfire broke from the clouds in firing position and shot him down in flames. Galland's wingman then shot down the Spitfire, but this was no consolation to the members of the Geschwader.

The Luftwaffe's raid on Canterbury, while successful, was not immediately repeated. On 8 November, the Allies landed in north-western Africa. The Germans were forced to defend this new front with fighter units taken from western Europe—an early example of the fire-fighting tactics that would become routine in the over-stretched Jagdwaffe. The two Bf 109G-equipped Staffeln, 11 (Hoehen)/JG 2 and 11 (Hoehen)/JG 26, were ordered to Tunisia,

A 2nd Staffel Bf 109E-1 photographed during a live firing exercise on the island of Sylt in the summer of 1939. (Buchmann)

"In the field" at Odendorf, 1 September 1939. Pilots of the 2nd Staffel listen to Hitler's declaration of war on Poland. From left: Lt. Blume (POW 18 August 1940), Lt. Regenauer (POW 12 August 1940), Hptm. Kienitz, Lt. Mueller-Duehe (KIA 18 August 1940). Standing: Oblt. Losigkeit, Lt. Buerschgens (POW 1 September 1940). (Buerschgens)

Dispersed Bf 109E-1s of the 4th Staffel, photographed at Boenninghardt just before the beginning of the war. (Balloff via Eickhoff)

Lt. Buerschgens's Bf 109E "Red 5" of the 2nd Staffel, after he had claimed the Geschwader's first victory—Merzig, 28 September 1939. (Buerschgens)

Hptm. Karl Ebbighausen, Kommandeur of the Second Gruppe from May 1940 until his death in August, in his Bf 109E. The personal emblems are symbolic of his days with J/88 in Spain. (Lorant via Crow)

A partially tarped 8th Staffel Bf 109E, photographed in late 1939. The squadron emblem, the cartoon character Adamson, shows up well. (Sundermann)

The 1st Staffel at readiness at Werl in February 1940. The first Rotte is just taking off. (Backhaus via Meyer)

Oblt. Schoepfel, Major Galland, and Oblt. Muencheberg, the first three Knight's Cross winners from the Third Gruppe—Audembert, 24 September 1940. (Bundesarchiv)

Josef Buerschgens as a prisoner of war, as seen in the New York *Herald Tribune* on 16 September 1940. The headline read, "Nazi with a sense of humor captured by the British." When approached by the ticket taker, Buerschgens had smiled and said, "Season pass!" (Buerschgens)

A Bf 109F of the 8th Staffel, photographed after the Geschwader's return to the Channel coast in mid-1941. Soon afterward JG 26 painted out all Geschwader and Staffel emblems on its aircraft. (Schmidt via Meyer)

Major Galland debriefs his Third Gruppe in early August 1940. Those visible, from left: Hptm. Schoepfel, Oblt. Beyer (POW 28 August 1940), Lt. Mueller-Duehe (KIA 18 August 1940), Lt. Buerschgens (POW 1 September 1940), Lt. Christinnecke (KIA 6 September 1940), Maj. Galland, Lt. Sprick (KIA 28 June 1941), Lt. Muencheberg (KIA 23 March 1943), unknown, Hptm. Dr. Schroedter. (Buerschgens)

7th Staffel radio technicians check out the communications gear in Oblt. Mietusch's Bf 109E-7 "White 13"—Gela, Sicily, spring 1941. (Bundesarchiv)

Oblt. Mietusch conducts an informal briefing of 7th Staffel pilots on Sicily. From left: Mietusch (KIA 17 September 1944), Uffz. Kuehdorf, unknown, Obfw. Laube, Lt. Johannsen (KIA 28 March 1942), Uffz. Mondry (KIA 31 May 1943). (Bundesarchiv)

Lt. Heinz Ebeling. (Meyer)

Oblt. Klaus Mietusch. (Meyer)

Maj. Wilhelm-Ferdinand Galland. (Bundesarchiv)

Hptm. Karl Borris. (Meyer)

A FW 190A-1 of the first service unit to employ the Focke-Wulf fighter, 6/JG 26—Moorsele, Belgium, autumn 1941. (Bundesarchiv)

The FW 190A-1 of Oblt. Schneider, Kapitaen of the 6th Staffel, photographed at Wevelghem in November 1941. (Barbas)

along with the FW 190-equipped II/JG 2. On 9 November, another fighter Gruppe, I/JG 2, and the two Jabostaffeln, 10 (Jabo)/JG 2 and 10 (Jabo)/JG 26, flew to Marseilles to support the German occupation of Vichy France, and to guard against the possible invasion of Southern France by the Allies. 10 (Jabo)/JG 26 returned to its Channel base at St. Omer-Wizernes a few days later, but the other units remained in the south. The aerial defense of the Channel coast was thus left to four Jagdgruppen: I/JG 26, II/JG 26, III/JG 26, and III/JG 2. To bolster the defenses of the Paris area, 9/JG 26 was subordinated to III/JG 2. Lt. Stammberger led his Staffel to Beaumont le Roger, south of Le Havre, on 27 November.

The story of 11 (Hoehen)/JG 26 is a tragic one. Three of the four Ju 52s carrying the Staffel's ground crews to Africa were shot down on the flight from Sicily. On 3 December, B-17s of the American Twelfth Air Force bombed the Staffel's airfield outside Tunis. The entire unit was caught on the ground; six pilots—half the Staffel's strength—were killed. The Staffel had to be disbanded. Its surviving members were used to reinforce the three Staffeln of II/JG 51.

A new 11th Staffel was established in the Third Gruppe at the end of the year. There is some evidence that Major Schoepfel intended the unit to function as an Endausbildungsstaffel, or operational training squadron, since the pilots reaching the Channel front directly from the Luftwaffe training schools did not have the skills necessary to survive in the demanding Western theater. Whatever Schoepfel's plan may have been, the Staffel was thrown into battle in early 1943, and soon lost whatever distinct character it may have had as a training unit.

The monotonous winter routine followed by the German fighter pilots in France and Belgium was enlivened by reconnaissance flights to the English coast, which were flown by single Rotten drawn from the various Staffeln on a rotating schedule. A new, very unpopular task was added after the receipt of a verbal Fuehrerbefehl (Hitler order) that vengeance attacks on southern England were now to be carried out by the conventional fighter units. Purely civilian targets were to be attacked. On 27 November, one 5th Staffel Rotte was ordered to carry out the first of these missions. The two aircraft attacked a railroad train on the Dungeness peninsula. Their cannon fire caused the locomotive to explode; one Focke-Wulf was struck by the debris and crashed, killing its pilot. On 16 December, Uffz. Crump participated in one of these vengeance missions as a member of a 5th Staffel Schwarm. He recalls strafing the hotels on the beach front, crossing the coast, and firing on anything that he saw moving—men, farm animals, and vehicles.

This period of reduced aerial activity was used to develop tactics and to introduce part of the Geschwader to new equipment— the Bf 109G. Having overcome most of its original problems, the FW 190 was now in great demand on all of the Luftwaffe's widespread combat fronts, for reconnaissance and ground attack duties as well as in its original air superiority role. Kurt Tank's fighter was in chronic short supply. If someone had to give them up, the two Kanalgeschwader were the most logical choices, since they could most readily utilize the latest model Bf 109, which was in its element above 30,000 feet. The Second Gruppe was scheduled to re-equip with the Bf 109G before the Third, but apparently Hptm. Meyer and his successor as II/JG 26 Kommandeur, Hptm. Wutz Galland, succeeded in stalling until the order was rescinded. By the spring of 1943, the Third Gruppe was equipped exclusively with Messerschmitts, while the Second Gruppe exchanged the few that they had received for more of their beloved Focke-Wulfs.

The production variants of the Bf 109 and FW 190 reaching the Geschwader at the end of the year differed only in detail from 1941's models. Both fighter designs showed unmistakable signs of reaching maturity. Weights continued to rise, and engine power had to be increased to keep pace. Barred from major increases in engine compression ratios by Germany's chronic shortage of high-strength, high-temperature metal alloys and high-octane aviation fuel, engineers sought chemical additives to increase the energy of the detonations within the existing engines' cylinders. Thus the Bf 109G-1's DB 605A engine used nitrous oxide (GM1) injection as a means of temporarily boosting engine power at altitude. The Bf 109G-4 was based on the G-1, but lacked the earlier fighter's complicated pressurization system, and was equipped with a new radio, the FuG 16Z, which had multiple channels and homing capabilities. The FW 190A-3 had a new BMW 801D-2 engine with greater power than its predecessor. Cooling louvers, cut into the cowling, finally solved the Focke-Wulf fighter's overheating problem. The FW 190A-3 was succeeded in late 1942 by the A-4, which had the

FuG 16Z radio and a methanol-water power boost system (MW 50) to increase engine output *below* 16,000 feet. The natural limitations of the BMW 801 radial engine could not be overcome; the FW 190A would remain a low- to medium-altitude fighter.

The Bf 109G-4 was an excellent dogfighter, especially at high altitudes, and could have played a useful role as high cover, taking on the Allied escort fighters. However, the Luftwaffe had too few fighters to employ them in such limited specialist roles and was thus forced to use the Bf 109 and FW 190 units interchangeably. The Bf 109G-4's standard armament of two MG 17 machine guns and one MG 151/20 machine cannon was too light to do much damage to B-17s and B-24s. The Bf 109 was also notorious for its light construction. All in all, the FW 190 was a much more survivable aircraft, and it was the mount preferred by most of the experienced western Jagdflieger in 1942–1943.

In late 1942, the German fighter commanders spent hours discussing the best tactics to use against the heavies. Aircraft models were built, and attack angles were studied. It was concluded that an attack from the front offered the best chance of destroying a bomber, or at least of killing its cockpit crew. It also appeared that the defensive armament of the bombers was weakest in the nose. On 23 November, Hptm. Egon Mayer of III/JG 2 had the first opportunity to test these new ideas. His Gruppe had the sole responsibility for the aerial defense of the U-boat bases in western France. Bad weather on that day caused most of the bombers to turn back before reaching their target, St. Nazaire. The nine B-17s remaining were greeted on their bomb run by Mayer's Focke-Wulfs, which attacked from dead ahead in Ketten of three. Four B-17s tumbled from the formation, victims of the Luftwaffe's most successful single pass through the heavies to date.

On 20 December the Americans staged their largest raid since Lille. One hundred and one B-17s and B-24s were dispatched to bomb the important Luftwaffe servicing base at Romilly-sur-Seine, sixty miles southeast of Paris, and 100 miles farther inland than any target previously attacked by the Eighth. Twelve squadrons of RAF and USAAF Spitfires escorted the bombers across the Channel but had to turn back near Rouen. This was the opportunity for which Major Schoepfel had been waiting. II/JG 26, which was paralleling the formation, immediately hit the 91st Bomb Group from dead ahead. Two B-17s went down. The 91st Group then endured one hour of continuous combat, without further loss. The three Gruppen of JG 26 and Mayer's III/JG 2, with 9/JG 26 attached, attacked in relays; the last German fighters did not break off until the return escort was spotted over the Channel. Lt. Stammberger's 9th Staffel flew a very successful mission. One B-17 was seen by Stammberger to flip end-for-end before its tail section broke off and the bomber began its last dive. Stammberger's own target began shaking and shuddering under the fire of his guns. As he started a second head-on pass, its crew began bailing out at short intervals. Eventually there were nine parachutes hanging in the bright blue sky. The bomber turned around them in flat spirals, before exploding on the ground.

Five B-17s went down over France, and thirty-one sustained combat damage. Initial American claims of fifty-three German fighters destroyed were later reduced to twenty-one. JG 26 claimed at least four B-17s and lost one plane and pilot. III/JG 2 lost two pilots killed. Many German fighters ran out of fuel in the prolonged engagement. Their pilot's radioed reports of forced landings were interpreted by Allied intelligence as evidence of widespread combat damage to the German formations, corroborating the bomber crews' claims; most of these reports referred instead to routine dead-stick landings, and only four fighters are believed to have been damaged beyond repair.

As winter set in, both sides worked feverishly on equipment and tactics. Armorers on every American bomber base in England improvised fittings in the noses of their B-17s and B-24s to accommodate additional machine guns. New formations and tactical doctrine were established throughout the Eighth Air Force. On the German side, commanders and pilots alike were disappointed in the small number of bombers being brought down. Attack formations were to be increased in size, and tactics were to be modified. On 20 December, most attacks had been made from dead ahead—twelve o'clock level, as viewed from the bombers. The bombers were in effective firing range for only a fraction of a second at the closing speed of 550 mph, and the flat angle of attack and the high altitude made range estimation extremely difficult. Pilots could not keep the possibility of collision from their minds, and many broke off their attacks far too soon. Karl Borris has stated that after experimentation, the optimum attack angle was found to be from dead ahead as before, but from ten degrees above the horizontal. A constant angle of fire could be maintained, similar to that practiced often against ground targets. The proper lead was attained by keeping the Revi's crosshairs on the nose of the bomber. Distance estimation was simplified, and even the less experienced pilots could score hits. Thus was born the form of attack most feared by bomber crews—from twelve o'clock high.

By year's end, General Galland was ready to publish a new set of tactical regulations prescribing the methods of attack on heavy bombers. The preferred method was now to be from the front. Fighter units were to fly on a course parallel to and on one side of the bombers until about three miles ahead of them. They were then to turn in by Schwaerme and attack head-on. They were to aim at the bombers' cockpits, open fire at 900 yards, and maintain a near-level course, passing above their target after ceasing fire. The second approved attack method was from the rear. Concentrated attacks were specified; the fighters were to attack by Schwaerme in rapid succession, at high speed, and pass over the bombers after ceasing fire.

In Galland's mind, one key to success with these tactics was for the fighters to maintain formation, or at least visual contact, in order to permit repeated concentrated attacks. Keeping position above the bombers was essential—and yet, from now until the end of the war, the German pilot's favorite method of ending an attack from either front or rear was with a split-S, which left him far beneath the attacked formation, and alone. Many pilots facing the hailstorm of defensive fire felt an irresistible urge to break off their attacks too soon. Although the bombers' guns did not bring down many German fighters, their streams of .50-inch tracers did in fact form an extremely effective defensive shield.

7

SCHLAGETER FIGHTERS ON THE EASTERN FRONT

January–July 1943

THE FIRST GRUPPE LEAVES THE KANALFRONT

DURING THE FIRST WEEK OF JANUARY 1943, MAJOR SCHOEPFEL and Major Priller were summoned by General Galland to a meeting of fighter leaders in Berlin. Two announcements were made which were of great significance to the pair. First, Gerhard Schoepfel was to leave JG 26 and become operations officer of Jafue (Fighter Command) Brittany in Rennes; Pips Priller was named Schoepfel's replacement as Kommodore of JG 26. Second, the long-standing rumors of Jagdgeschwader 26's transfer to the Russian front were confirmed. JG 26 was to trade places with the Green Hearts Geschwader, JG 54. The exchange was to take place by Gruppen and Staffeln, staged to permit continuity of defensive coverage. Only the pilots, key staff members, and certain items of critical equipment were to move. Maintenance crews, aircraft, and all other equipment were to remain on their original bases.

Once back at the Geschwader's new headquarters at Lille-Vendeville, the newly appointed Kommodore made plans to move his unit to the Soviet Union. His pilots were enthusiastic about the idea—the quality of the Soviet opposition remained low, and aerial victories, the prerequisite for honors and promotions in the Jagdwaffe, were still easy to obtain. Priller selected Major Johannes Seifert's First Gruppe to move first. It was to trade places with III/

JG 54. Klaus Mietusch's 7th Staffel would follow, in exchange for 4/JG 54. Seifert's Gruppe contained several pilots with experience against the Red Air Force, including two Staffelkapitaene, Hptm. Walter Hoeckner of the 1st Staffel and Hptm. Rolf Hermichen of the 3rd. Obfw. Alfred "Fred" Heckmann, a Knight's Cross recipient with more than fifty victories on the Eastern front, was a welcome recent addition to the 1st Staffel.

In late January, the pilots of the First Gruppe moved by train to Heiligenbeil, a major Luftwaffe servicing base in East Prussia. Here they obtained brand-new FW 190A-5 fighters. The next few days were spent installing and testing the planes' radios and armament. Hptm. Hermichen, who knew the area well from a tour as a Bf 110 pilot in 1941, led the Gruppe to their new base at Rielbitzi, west of Lake Ilmen in northern Russia.

The Schlageter pilots' host unit, Jagdgeschwader 54, was the sole single-engined fighter Geschwader in Luftflotte 1, which was responsible for supporting Army Group North. Rielbitzi covered the southern end of Luftflotte 1's area of responsibility. It was a typical Feldflugplatz, or front-line airfield, and had first been occupied by the Green Hearts in September 1941.

The pilots moved into their quarters in the village adjacent to the field and were briefed on their new assignments. Combat in Russia was far different from anything they had experienced on the Channel front. Aircraft seldom flew above 10,000 feet, and most combats took place well below that altitude. Luftwaffe fighters never flew in greater than Staffel strength; the Schwarm was the most common tactical formation, and many patrols were flown by Rotten of two aircraft. Dead reckoning navigation, or pilotage, was extremely important. German pilots tried to keep a sense of the location of their own lines from the moment of takeoff, and if possible remained within gliding distance of friendly territory. Few pilots survived a crash landing behind the Russian lines. Finally, whenever beyond the lines, they had to be concerned with Soviet anti-aircraft fire, which was usually far more dangerous than Soviet fighters.

The freie Jagd was the preferred mission. On the Eastern Front, these were most often flown by Schwaerme against reported formations of Soviet bombers and attack aircraft. The German patrols usually remained well behind their own lines, and their losses were very light. The Luftwaffe had originated the tactics of the Schwarm, and the skilled teamwork of the German pilots made them almost invulnerable to Soviet fighters at this stage of the war.

The newcomers sat through their lessons impatiently, while their aircraft were made ready for combat. FW 190s were new to JG 54's holdover ground crews, who took a few days to adapt the fighter's maintenance procedures for the minus-40-degree temperatures. The pilots studied their maps, compared them against the frozen wasteland surrounding them, and waited to be declared operational.

THE SITUATION IN THE NORTH IS STABILIZED

The Gruppe's first assignment was ground attack, a new task for the Schlageter pilots. The Demyansk salient, a German-occupied bulge in the Soviet lines that had been formed during the Soviet winter offensive of 1941, was just south of I/JG 26's base on Lake Ilmen. In November 1942, the Russians had begun an offensive to eliminate the salient. Their attacks had persisted, in decreasing strength. Seifert's men were ordered to strafe the hordes of Russian infantry that were massed along the shores of the lake and attack the motorized sleds and horse-drawn supply trains in the Russians' rear. After several hard days, on each of which the pilots flew between eight and ten missions, the Russians pulled back.

The commander of Army Group North now requested permission to begin a staged withdrawal from the salient, which lengthened his lines to no strategic or tactical purpose. Sobered by the ongoing catastrophe at Stalingrad, Hitler uncharacteristically gave his permission. I/JG 26's new assignment was to cover II Corps as it prepared to withdraw from the salient. The Gruppe's first encounters with the Red Air Force took place on 16 February. The Gruppenstab and the 1st Staffel attacked a large gaggle of Il-2 *Shturmoviki* and downed eleven of the massively armored attack planes without loss to themselves. The heavily armed Focke-Wulf fighter gave promise of solving the vexing problem of the *Shturmovik*, which had proved nearly invulnerable to the attacks of three-gunned Bf 109Fs and Bf 109Gs.

The 17th brought more combat, in which three Lend-Lease P-40C Tomahawks were downed; the day also brought the

Gruppe's first eastern casualties. One pilot was killed by Russian flak near Demyansk; another struck the ground while maneuvering to attack Il-2s and crashed to his death. A third was shot down by Yak fighters, and survived a crash landing within the German lines.

For the next month, II Corps fought to withdraw from Demyansk in an orderly fashion, while the Soviets attempted to catch them on open ground and destroy them from the air. Major General F. A. Kostenko, the local Soviet fighter commander, has written that this campaign saw the first serious Soviet challenge to German fighter supremacy. In his view, the Soviet pilots, many in new Yak-7bs and La-5s, were successful in both offensive and defensive roles. They frequently fought through the fighter sweeps that preceded German bomber attacks—the Germans lacked sufficient fighters for orthodox escort formations—in order to fall on the bombers. The Soviet fighters were so successful in their own escort role that Kostenko began calling upon the Il-2s to bait the Focke-Wulfs and Messerschmitts into combat. The performance of General Kostenko's command was so impressive that it was awarded the coveted Guards designation, becoming the 1st Guards Fighter Air Corps.

The German fighter units on the scene, I/JG 26 in its FW 190s and II/JG 54 in Bf 109Gs, were unaware that their supremacy was under serious challenge. Between 18 February and 18 March, Seifert's pilots claimed seventy-five aerial victories, while suffering only three combat casualties. The most common targets were Il-2 and Pe-2 attack planes; fighter types shot down included P-39s, P-40s, MiG-3s, and LaGG-3s, in addition to a few of the new Yakovlev and Lavochkin models. The most successful day was 5 March, which saw fourteen victory claims filed. The largest bag by a pilot on a single day came on 7 March, when Hptm. Hoeckner shot down four Il-2s and two P-40Cs. The Gruppe suffered three combat losses during this period; the pilots simply failed to return from combat sorties and were never heard from again. A noncombat fatality occurred on 7 March; a pilot was trapped in his cockpit and burned to death when his FW 190 crashed while taking off from Rielbitzi.

THE SEVENTH STAFFEL ON THE LENINGRAD FRONT

The second stage of the Geschwader exchange saw Hptm. Klaus Mietusch's nomadic 7/JG 26 leave Courtrai by rail, beginning in late January. The Staffel was ordered to Gatschina in the Leningrad area, where it was subordinated to Hptm. Philipp's I/JG 54. Philipp's Gruppe had recently returned to Russia from East Prussia, where they had exchanged their Messerschmitts for Focke-Wulfs. Mietusch's pilots did not see combat for some time, but flew training missions with I/JG 54 as the Green Hearts broke in their own Focke-Wulfs.

After a mostly uneventful 1942, the northern sector of Army Group North's front had erupted in early January 1943, when the Red Army began an offensive to relieve besieged Leningrad. Two army groups succeeded in linking up at the town of Schluesselburg, on the southern shore of Lake Ladoga, thus relieving the siege. The Germans sealed off the penetration by 18 January, but they could not throw the Russians out of the corridor they had won. Only six miles wide, every square foot of it was within range of German field artillery. Soviet attempts to widen the corridor continued until 1 April, without further success.

According to his logbook, the 7th Staffel's Fw. Xaver Ellenrieder flew over this front for the first time on 12 March. He then began flying combat sorties almost daily. Apart from a few weather reconnaissance flights and freie Jagden, most of his missions were escort flights for Hs 126 tactical reconnaissance aircraft and Bf 110, Ju 87, and Ju 88 bombers. Encounters with the Red Air Force were few. Ellenrieder battled LaGG-3s for the first time on 19 March. On 26 March he met them again and shot one down, for his first victory.

The 7th Staffel remained outside Leningrad for its entire time in the Soviet Union, flying a daily routine of front-line patrols. Hptm. Mietusch was injured on 20 March when his Focke-Wulf overturned on takeoff. While Mietusch was out of action Obfw. Heinz Kemethmueller was transferred into the Staffel to give it the benefit of his experience—Kemethmueller had won a Knight's Cross on the Eastern front in 1942, before joining 9/JG 26 in Belgium. This tour's first known aerial combats by these two Experten did not take place until 21 May, when Hptm. Mietusch shot down two LaGG-3s, one I-153, and one Pe-2, for his thirtieth to thirty-third victories, while Obfw. Kemethmueller claimed one LaGG-3, one I-16, and one Pe-2; these were his sixty-third to sixty-fifth victories.

The Staffel's last major air battle over the Soviet Union took place early in the morning of 18 June. At least part of the unit took off from Siverskaya at 0600, and was soon engaged in combat over the front. Hptm. Mietusch shot down two LaGG-3 fighters, while Obfw. Kemethmueller downed a Yak-1. Fw. Erich Jauer and his wingman engaged P-40s, and Jauer shot down two; his wingman then lost contact and returned to base alone. Jauer was shot down behind the Soviet lines and taken prisoner, but he had the good fortune to survive the war. The Staffel's last known victories in the East were gained four days later. Hptm. Mietusch claimed two LaGG-3s, while Obfw. Kemethmueller downed an Il-2. On 29 June, the 7th Staffel suffered its last casualty in the East, when a pilot failed to return from a mission over Schluesselburg.

SPRINGTIME LULL

At the conclusion of the Demyansk withdrawal, I/JG 26 flew south to Smolensk, to cover the final stages of Operation Bueffel (Buffalo). This was yet another line-straightening move, this one by Army Group Center. At its successful conclusion, the Russian spring rains imposed a truce of several weeks' duration. The usual freie Jagden, weather flights, and bomber escort missions then began again, but opportunities for aerial combat were few. During May, the 3rd Staffel was detached for antipartisan duty. The Gruppe claimed only thirty-eight aerial victories between 19 March and 6 June, when it began returning to the West. The most unusual claim was filed by a 3rd Staffel pilot, who shot down a Curtiss O-52 Owl, one of only nineteen of the tubby observation planes to reach the Soviet Union via Lend-Lease. Fw. Karl "Charlie" Willius of the 2nd Staffel was the most successful pilot during this period, claiming nine victories. His best day was 13 May, when he shot down three Pe-2s and one MiG-3, for his twenty-fourth to twenty-seventh victories.

Casualties remained light during the spring. Lt. Arno Staschen of the 2nd Staffel died under tragic circumstances. On 13 May he became lost while flying near Yelnya, east of Smolensk. At 2130, out of fuel, he made a forced landing in a field. He hid himself overnight in some nearby woods, as the area was known to contain partisans. The next day, nearby villagers reported a suspicious person in the woods. The German army sent Hilfswilligen (Russian volunteers) to flush out the suspected Russian agent. Staschen, hearing the troops call out in Russian, assumed that he was under attack by partisans and opened fire with his pistol. At this, he was shot and killed by the Hilfswilligen.

On 1 June, Major Johannes Seifert received word that he was to give up command of the First Gruppe and take a position on the staff of the German mission to Bulgaria. Unknown to Seifert, his mother had invoked a little-used law and requested his removal from combat duty. His younger brother Gerhard had been a pilot in III/JG 26 until his death on the Kanalfront in February. Johannes was now the sole remaining male in the family and was thus exempted by law from front-line service. When I/JG 26 returned to France, it was temporarily without a Kommandeur.

THE RETURN

During the spring of 1943, the growing American Eighth Air Force brought increasing pressure on the German defenses in the West. It was obvious to General Galland that the unique skills of JG 26 could best be employed in the area of greatest danger; that is, on the Kanalfront. The move of the rest of the Geschwader to the Eastern front was first postponed and then canceled. Finally, in early June, the First Gruppe was ordered to return to France.

The 10th of June found them at Poix airfield on the Somme, available once again for combat duty in the West. Their Eastern score totaled 126 Russian aircraft shot down, in exchange for nine German pilots and three ground personnel killed.

The 7th Staffel remained in the Soviet Union until July. Its final score was sixty-three aircraft shot down, for the loss of two pilots killed and one taken prisoner. It too lost its commander before leaving the East. On 29 June, Klaus Mietusch received word of his appointment as Kommandeur of III/JG 26 and left for the West. He was replaced as Staffelkapitaen by his deputy, Hptm. Kelch. Upon its return, 7/JG 26 rejoined Mietusch and the Third Gruppe.

The Schlageter fighters had compiled an excellent record in the East, but had had no effect whatsoever on the course of events in that theater. Galland and the Luftwaffe High Command had hopes that the return of the experienced Kanaljaeger to the West just might provide enough additional strength to tip the balance, at least temporarily, against the air forces of the western Allies.

8
HOLDING IN THE WEST
January–June 1943

THE JABO EFFORT PEAKS

It was noon. Visibility along the channel coast was only fair at sea level, with continuous cloud cover at 2,000 feet; perfect conditions for the audacious operation just underway. The propeller wash of thirty-eight FW 190s raised plumes of spray as the fighters crossed the French coast and spread out in loose line abreast formation, less than ten feet above the water. Two dozen of the aircraft carried bombs; they represented the full strength of the two Jabostaffeln, 10 (Jabo)/JG 2 and 10 (Jabo)/JG 26, which were flying a rare combined mission. The other aircraft were from I/JG 2, assigned as escort. At 1220, the formation crossed the English coast, at Eastbourne, and raced for London. The British defenses were caught completely by surprise. The barrage balloons were down; some were hastily raised, but at least ten came back to earth even more quickly, flamed by the Focke-Wulfs of the Richthofen Geschwader. Londoners south of the Thames looked up as the fighters roared past at rooftop height. Some dropped their bombs onto the dock area, causing one large warehouse to go up in flames; others bombed the crowded streets of Greenwich, resulting in a number of civilian casualties. The aircraft banked up and to the right and made their escape. Some followed the Thames southeast to the coast, while the rest retraced their course across the counties of Surrey and Sussex.

As the Jabos reached the southern coast, the FW 190A-4/U3

150

piloted by Lt. Hermann Hoch of 10 (Jabo)/JG 26 was hit in the engine by light antiaircraft fire. Hoch headed out to sea, but he turned back when it became apparent that he would not make the French coast. His belly landing was intentionally rough; his plane hit near the top of a small hill, crested it, and bounced and skidded two hundred yards into a grove of saplings. Hoch jumped from his aircraft, fitted the detonator and fuse into the demolition charge, and pulled the ring, in full view of a growing crowd of onlookers. He calmly warned two soldiers who were approaching the scene to keep their distance. They clambered onto the wreckage anyway, but thought better of it when Hoch hit the ground, and jumped from the plane just as it blew up. Hoch was then marched off into captivity, the only casualty from the first wave of this attack, the Great London Raid of 20 January 1943.

The second wave, containing the three dozen Bf 109Gs and FW 190As of II/JG 26, reached Eastbourne ten minutes after the first formation. They flew at 10,000 feet, well above the cloud deck. Some carried bombs. A few of these planes may have reached London, but most scattered their loads near Brighton. Fighter Command was by now fully alerted, and fighters from all of No. 11 Group's airfields had scrambled and headed for the southern coast. One 5th Staffel Focke-Wulf pilot bailed out into captivity after he was hit by a No. 340 (Free French) Sqd. Spitfire. Two Typhoons from No. 609 Squadron attacked two Schwaerme of 6th Staffel Bf 109s. The two Schwaerme attempted a crisscross maneuver which went awry in the clouds. Two of the Messerschmitts collided, and a third was shot down. One German pilot was killed, and two bailed out into the Channel, from which they were pulled by the British air-sea rescue service. A fourth pilot suffered eye injuries from the explosion of his leader's aircraft but brought his Messerschmitt back to Abbeville-Drucat, where it was further damaged in his forced landing. According to the post-mission report written by Adolf Galland, the second wave's failure was the result of "operational mistakes" and poor leadership.

Spitfires and Typhoons pursued the German fighters across the Channel and shot down another 6th Staffel Messerschmitt over Cap Gris Nez. 2/JG 26, which was defending the Geschwader's coastal bases, shot down one Spitfire, for the loss of one Focke-Wulf and pilot.

The Third Gruppe of JG 26 had the task of high cover for the withdrawal. Major Priller, JG 26's brand-new Kommodore, took off from Wevelghem at 1211 at the head of his former Gruppe. The Focke-Wulfs climbed to 18,000 feet and swept along the Dover coast. The Kommodore shot down one Spitfire north of Canterbury; Hptm. Mietusch of the 7th Staffel forced two Spitfire pilots to bail out of their aircraft.

By mid-afternoon, the action had died down. All that remained was to sweep the Channel looking for survivors. London had been hit by six tons of bombs, but JG 26 had suffered its heaviest single-day casualties to date—eight pilots were missing, and two had returned with serious injuries. The Geschwader's victories totaled only four. The 6th Staffel had lost most of its Bf 109s in the battle, and shortly thereafter turned in the remainder in exchange for FW 190s. The Third Gruppe re-equipped with Messerschmitts over the next few months, according to plan, but the Second Gruppe was permitted to continue flying Focke-Wulfs, which was a popular decision with most of its pilots.

The Great London Raid was not repeated. The Germans were too few in numbers, and the British defenders were too strong—Fighter Command flew 214 sorties on 20 January against the ninety attackers. Never again would the fighter Staffeln of the Schlageter Geschwader appear in strength over England.

On 17 February, the JG 26 Jabostaffel was redesignated 10 (Jabo)/JG 54, as it was planned to leave the Staffel in France when the rest of JG 26 moved to the Eastern front. A change-of-command ceremony was held at St. Omer-Wizernes. It was attended by the Kommodore of the Green Hearts, Obstlt. Hannes Trautloft, who flew over from his command in the East. The Jabo pilots removed their Schlageter armbands, but little else changed; they remained under JG 26 for administration, while tactically they operated independently, as before.

The two Jabostaffeln, 10 (Jabo)/JG 2 and 10 (Jabo)/JG 54, flew several more full-strength missions that spring. Casualties were high, and results were negligible. On 24 March, the Kapitaen of 10 (Jabo)/JG 54, Oblt. Paul Keller, led fifteen FW 190s on a low-altitude approach to Ashford. The formation split up near the town; one flight bombed the railroad station with good results, while most of the remaining aircraft scattered their bombs in the town. Keller himself strafed a gasoline truck standing in a factory yard and blew it up. Keller's aircraft, which was still carrying its bomb, then exploded. Its bomb had been hit, either by fragments from the truck or by a light antiaircraft shell. The double explosion caused serious damage to the factory.

The popular Oblt. Keller, known as "Bombenkeller" (Bomb Shelter), was succeeded by Oblt. Erwin Busch, who retained command of the fighter-bomber unit for the rest of the war. Busch's personal survival was a matter of phenomenal luck; during its year in combat on the Channel, the Staffel lost twenty pilots, well over 100 percent of its assigned strength. In late March, the two Jabostaffeln became part of a new Schnellkampfgeschwader, or fast bomber wing. The former 10 (Jabo)/JG 26 was redesignated 14/ SKG 10. It soon moved to Italy, and from there to the Eastern front, where it served until the end of the war.

CHANGE OF COMMAND

On 10 January, Major Schoepfel had turned command of the Geschwader over to Major Josef "Pips" Priller. Schoepfel then left to take up his new position as operations officer at Jafue Brittany, which was responsible for the defense of the U-boat bases in western France. Schoepfel, a member of the Luftwaffe since 1936 and an officer in JG 26 since June of 1938, was to hold a variety of positions during the remainder of the war. The overextended Luftwaffe was forced to shuffle its few battle-tested field-grade commanders just as it moved its combat units—from one crisis point to another. Schoepfel left Brittany to become fighter commander of first Sicily, and next, Norway. He became Kommodore of JG 4 in Germany and was wounded; he then commanded the fighter defenses of Hungary, attended the last course of the War Academy at Gatow, commanded yet another Jagdgeschwader, JG 6, for a few weeks, and finished the war as fighter commander in Czechoslovakia. He was released by his American captors, only to be arrested and imprisoned by the Russians. Schoepfel finally returned to Germany at the end of 1949.

Pips Priller was twenty-seven years old when he was named Kommodore; he too had been a member of the Luftwaffe since 1936. During the Battle of Britain he had been a successful pilot and Staffelkapitaen in Moelders's JG 51, and had been awarded the Knight's Cross in October 1940. Soon thereafter, he was transferred to JG 26, where he took over its 1st Staffel. He had replaced Gerhard Schoepfel as Kommandeur of the Third Gruppe when the latter took command of the Geschwader, and he now succeeded Schoepfel once again.

Priller was the top-scoring pilot then in the Geschwader and had thus proven himself by combat, the main requirement for promotion in the Jagdwaffe. He was also an excellent formation leader and tactician. He was a notable bon vivant, displaying an outgoing, effervescent personality in public. However, he took the responsibilities of command seriously. He was always concerned for the welfare of his men, who responded by holding him in great respect and affection. In the words of a war correspondent who visited the Geschwader frequently, Priller "combined great ambition, a high sense of duty, and an iron-hard will with social consciousness."

The combat strengths of both the Allied attackers and the German defenders along the Kanalfront waned during the winter of 1942–1943. The Allies moved a number of units to their new theater in northwest Africa; the Germans made countermoves to the Mediterranean and, in addition, initiated the planned exchange of JG 26 with JG 54. Gen. Junck of Jagddivision 3, who commanded the German fighters in the West, ordered some of his units to move to new bases. The headquarters of JG 26 transferred from St. Omer southeast to Lille-Vendeville, while the Abbeville Kids of the Second Gruppe bade farewell to Abbeville-Drucat, the site of their greatest fame, and moved east to Vitry, near the industrial city of Douai. Both new fields were prewar French airbases with concrete runways, well suited to winter operations. The Third Gruppe stayed at Wevelghem, in western Belgium near the French border. When the First Gruppe and the 7th Staffel departed for the Soviet Union, the six JG 26 fighter Staffeln left in the West were concentrated in a small triangle in the industrial region along the French-Belgian border, across the most direct aerial route from England to the Ruhr. The prime responsibility for the defense of central and western France was left to JG 2, which, like JG 26, was presently operating the only two Gruppen. In January, 9/JG 26 was loaned to III/JG 2 in Vannes, in order to bolster the defenses of the U-boat bases in Brittany. This Staffel returned to its parent III/JG 26 in mid-February.

The two JG 26 Jagdgruppen in the West received new Kommandeure. Hptm. Fritz Geisshardt transferred in from I/JG 77 in North Africa to take command of Priller's old Third Gruppe. Geisshardt was a 100-victory Experte and wore the Knight's Cross with Oak Leaves; nearly all of his successes had been gained in the East. The Second Gruppe's new Kommandeur was Hptm. Wilhelm-Ferdinand "Wutz" Galland; his predecessor Hptm. "Conny" Meyer transferred from the Geschwader. Wutz Galland did not begin flight training until late 1940. In mid-1941 he joined his brothers Adolf and Paul in the Schlageter Geschwader. He was successful from the start; he was soon given command of a Staffel, and now, at age 28, a Gruppe. By all indications, his promotions were based on merit and not nepotism. He had a warm and open personality, and he became a very popular as well as a highly successful Gruppenkommandeur. The surviving pilots of his Gruppe have fond memories of his late-night drinking parties with them in the pilots' mess. Many Geschwader veterans consider Wutz to have been the best fighter pilot in the Galland family, although no one equaled the cold-eyed and steel-hearted Adolf as a combat leader.

In early February, Major "Seppl" Seiler's III/JG 54, containing the Green Heart Geschwader's 7th, 8th, and 9th Staffeln, boarded trains in Smolensk and headed for the Kanalfront. They were followed soon afterward by Oblt. Graf Matuschka and his 4/JG 54. The pilots picked up new Bf 109Gs in Germany and flew them to Vendeville. Graf Matuschka's Staffel was subordinated to III/JG 26 in Wevelghem, where Hptm. Geisshardt made the newcomers at home. 4/JG 54 replaced 7/JG 26, which was now in the Soviet Union, smoothly and without incident.

Amalgamation of the Third Gruppe of JG 54 into the Western order of battle was another matter, however. Too large to incorporate in the flying organizations already present, the unit had to undergo a crash course in the rigorous conditions of the Western front. Everything was more difficult than in the East, beginning with the burdensome personal equipment—oxygen mask, life jacket, flare gun, et cetera—and continuing with the need to maintain close formation in high altitude flight. All of this had to be mastered before the pilots could be pitted against the western Allies. The Gruppe trained for a month, closely watched by Major Priller, who took his responsibility for the new unit very seriously. He monitored their formation flights from the air, and several times bounced them from behind without being spotted by a single pilot. Disgusted, Priller stubbornly refused to declare the Gruppe operational. In late March, III/JG 54 was detached from JG 26 and ordered to Oldenburg, near Bremen. From this location, it could assist JG 1 in defending northern Germany against the infrequent raids of the American Eighth Bomber Command, while remaining outside the range of Allied fighters.

Priller's low-strength Geschwader spent much of the flying time available in early 1943 evaluating new weapons and tactics. Head-on attacks were now preferred for breaking up heavy bomber formations. The German fighter formations had to be increased in size and cohesiveness in order to maintain their effectiveness against the ever-growing bomber formations. Thus the experienced Schlageter pilots were required to practice high-altitude formation flying under the scrutiny of their Kommodore. The new weapons tested included 21-cm mortar shells, fired from underwing tubes; aerial mines with barometric or acoustic fuses; and bombs trailed from cables. All were rejected at this time by the Kanaljaeger as too detrimental to the maneuverability of their aircraft. Necessity forced the adoption of some of these weapons later in the year.

According to Ernst Battmer, the Geschwader technical officer, Priller himself was called on to evaluate a new gyroscopic gunsight. This too was rejected and did not reappear in the operational units until the last weeks of the war. Had the gunsight been adopted in 1943, it could have compensated to a great extent for the low standards of marksmanship exhibited by the pilots of the Jagdwaffe in 1944 and 1945.

BATTLES WITH THE RAF

At the beginning of 1943, the American Eighth Bomber Command could muster only four groups of B-17s and two low-strength groups of B-24s. The Eighth Fighter Command had only one unit on strength—the Spitfire-equipped 4th Fighter Group, which had been formed from the RAF's three Eagle Squadrons. Once again the task of maintaining pressure on the German defenses in France and the Low Countries fell to the Royal Air Force. The RAF's tactical bomber command, No. 2 Group, had replaced its dreadful Blenheims with more modern Bostons, Venturas, and Mosquitoes, and was prepared to resume flying missions to the Continent. The RAF's Fighter Command was available to escort both American and British bombers but was limited to the coastal regions by the short range of its Spitfires. The newest British fighter, the Hawker Typhoon, was unsuitable for escort work, but it proved valuable at low level, once cured of its propensity for falling apart in flight. And the RAF's Army Co-operation Command now had a few of the fastest low-altitude fighters in the world on strength, in the form of Allison-engined North American Mustang Is, and could finally venture into the skies over the Continent with some assurance of survival. Rhubarbs were flown frequently by flights of Typhoons or Mustangs. The German fighter defense organization was not allowed to relax, even during the dreary coastal winter.

The weather on 23 January appeared to favor RAF raids. There was high cloud cover, with scattered clouds at low altitude; visibility otherwise was good. The German countermeasures against Rhubarbs called for overlapping coastal patrols by pairs of fighters. The Second Gruppe was still flying from Abbeville; the sector assigned to it was Boulogne-Dieppe. At about noon, Galland's successor as Kapitaen of the 5th Staffel, Oblt. Horst Sternberg, walked into the pilots' ready room, nodded to a pair of Unteroffiziere, and grunted, "Your turn." Peter Crump was picked as Rottenfuehrer (element leader); the equally inexperienced Hans Meyer would be his wingman. Sternberg looked out the window and waved toward a pair of fighters, saying, "Why don't you take the 109s." This was not a popular choice with Crump, but it would be a good opportunity to gain experience in the Staffel's new equipment. After a short period at cockpit readiness, they were ordered to relieve a pair of 6th Staffel aircraft in the air. While preparing to take off, the pilots heard the Jafue report a flight of four Indians south of Boulogne. Since they were taking off in a northwesterly direction, Crump ordered his wingman to head for the stated area at minimum altitude, and without any appreciable change in course. Shortly after takeoff, Crump spotted two dots at ten o'clock; these quickly became visible as two Mustangs, coming directly at him. Crump had already grasped his firing lever and had the enemy leader in his sights before he was seen in turn. Startled, the leader broke away, presenting his underside as a target. After taking a short burst of fire, the Mustang fell away over its left wing.

Crump next turned his attention to the other Mustang. It had banked toward his fighter and was firing behind him. Crump pulled his aircraft into a tighter bank. After several turns, the Messerschmitt gained on the Mustang, and Crump put some short bursts of fire into its left rear fuselage and tail. At this, the Allied pilot gave up, and turned toward a large field in order to make a forced landing. Crump saw Meyer preparing to make a firing pass at the Mustang. "Stop that, Meyer! He's landing!" Crump shouted over the radio.

After this engagement, Crump resumed his surveillance flight, since four Mustangs had been reported. Toward the end of the patrol, Crump spotted another Mustang over the Somme Estuary, coming from the direction of Dieppe. Its pilot saw the Germans, which were at a higher altitude over the coastal region near the river's mouth; he banked toward the northwest and flew off. Crump ordered Meyer to make the attack, but the latter pilot and his airplane had disappeared. Crump chased after the Mustang at full throttle but could not close to less than 500 yards. He cursed not being in his Focke-Wulf, while peppering the enemy fighter with short bursts of cannon fire. The Mustang rocked back and forth at each burst and then barreled away, right on the water. Crump gave up the chase when his Messerschmitt's cannon ran out of ammunition.

Back at Abbeville, Peter Crump reported his double victory to his Kapitaen, only to be greeted with scorn—the victories had already been credited to Uffz. Gerhard Vogt of the 6th Staffel, the leader of the earlier patrol. Crump's wingman had not yet reported in. When the young Unteroffizier Meyer finally came through the door, he was covered in blood and feathers. Meyer stated that shortly after sighting the third Mustang, a bird had hit the front of his canopy and had knocked the armored glass loose from one side of its frame, filling the cockpit with "bird soup." After Meyer had attested to Crump's victories, the three men climbed into the Staffel automobile and headed to the Gruppe command post to sort out the stories.

The confusion was quickly cleared up. Vogt had heard the Jafue's report of the enemy, but he had been at the far end of the patrol area; he and his wingman, who was also named Meyer, had had to land at another base when their fuel ran low. The first contact report heard in the command post had been Crump's shouted order to *his* wingman Meyer to hold his fire. A request by the command post to report the location of the enemy had brought only the unedifying reply, "All of the Indians have been shot down!" As the puzzled men on the ground could not tell who was shouting, and Vogt was an experienced pilot with eleven victories, they had jumped to the conclusion that it was Vogt.

On rare occasions, the RAF fighters sweeping occupied Europe dealt out punishment as severe as that which they typically received. On 27 February, the Second Gruppe took off from Vitry to intercept a large Spitfire formation over the French-Belgian coast. As the Germans approached, the British turned away. Hptm. Galland saw an opportunity to cut off part of the formation and flew out to sea. Oblt. Sternberg's 5th Staffel was at the right rear of the formation, with Uffz. Crump and his wingman flying at the extreme right. A report of four Spitfires above and to the right of the Gruppe was ignored by Sternberg, who maintained his Staffel's position in the Gruppe formation. The Spitfires' bounce downed two Focke-Wulfs. The remainder of the 5th Staffel broke into the attack. Crump followed his formation leader in a climbing turn toward the Spitfires. The fighter closest to Crump presented him with a target at a deflection of 40-50 degrees. At 300 yards range, Crump fired a short burst from all six guns. The Spitfire tipped over its left wing, leveled off, and toppled over again, its controls obviously damaged. A fascinated Peter Crump watched the enemy pilot repeat this falling-leaf maneuver until he had used up most of his altitude of 25,000 feet; at this point the Allied pilot gave up and bailed out.

Late in the afternoon of 20 April, an unfortunate series of conflicting orders from the Jafue left six aircraft of the 5th Staffel facing a head-on attack by a large formation of Spitfires out of the setting sun. After the first attack, one Focke-Wulf spun out and hit the water. The Germans scattered in all directions. Peter Crump, newly promoted to Feldwebel, tried a favorite escape maneuver—he spun out of a tight turn and dove, apparently out of control, until just enough altitude remained for recovery. He then pulled out and headed for the coast, skimming the Channel. He rejoined his four surviving comrades at Vitry.

The next day, the Second Gruppe's pilots were paraded at their Vitry base for an inspection by Generalfeldmarschall Sperrle.

Sperrle's speech was interrupted by the loudspeaker's urgent squawk—a large enemy force was approaching the Somme Estuary at an altitude of only 9,000 feet. The Gruppe's pilots broke ranks and ran for their aircraft, leaving Sperrle standing in the square. Galland's three Staffeln caught up to the Allied formation as it wheeled north after bombing the Abbeville railroad yards. Galland ordered his Stab flight and one Staffel to attack the bombers, eleven Venturas of No. 21 Squadron, while the other fighters took on the Spitfire escort. The FW 190s made simultaneous passes from the front, the front quarter, and beneath the bombers, slashing through the fighter screen and breaking off their attacks only fifty yards from the Venturas. Three bombers burst into flames and crashed, two from the attacks of the Kommandeur himself; the third was credited to Oblt. Sternberg.

Both fighter formations broke apart, Spitfire and Focke-Wulf tumbling in and out of towering clouds in a deadly game of cat-and-mouse. After the furious action had nearly spent itself, Fw. Crump spotted a lone Spitfire flying away from him, silhouetted against a cloud. After a quick look in all directions—more Spitfires could break out of the clouds at any time—he attacked, damaging it in the engine and the underside of the fuselage. Emitting a cloud of black smoke, the Spitfire broke to the left, dove away in a flat curve, and crashed south of Boismont. Crump was the last pilot to land; he learned that his Gruppe had suffered no casualties or damage. An unperturbed Sperrle had already resumed his inspection.

A SLOW BUILDUP

The year's first heavy bomber raid on the territory defended by JG 26 took place on 13 January. Seventy-two B-17s of the Eighth Bomber Command's 1st Bomb Wing attacked the Fives locomotive works in Lille. While on the bomb run at 22,000 feet, the leading 305th Bomb Group was greeted by twenty to twenty-five Focke-Wulfs from the First and Second Gruppen. The fighters flew in line astern; each flight contained five or six aircraft. All attacks were made from dead ahead and on the same level as the bombers. Most fighters attacked singly, half-rolling into a split-S upon reaching the bomber formation. Only the 305th Group was attacked. Ten of its twenty-two Fortresses were damaged, some severely, but only one bomber failed to return to its base at Chelveston. That evening Pips Priller and his Kommandeur critiqued the day's mission. Destruction of a higher percentage of the bombers was going to require improved tactics—and the debate as to just what these should be went on into the night.

The logical next step for the German fighter pilots was to attack the bombers simultaneously, rather than in trail. On 23 January, an attack on Lorient was met by JG 2, which attacked in flights of six aircraft. Five B-17s were shot down out of thirty-five, and a new round in the battle was underway. The next raid on the U-boat bases took place on 16 February. Aggressive head-on attacks by III/JG 2 and 9/JG 26 brought down six of the sixty-eight attacking B-17s; the bombers' target, the U-boat basin locks at St. Nazaire, was missed completely. Lt. Otto "Stotto" Stammberger, leading 9/JG 26 in the absence of its Kapitaen, hit one Fortress in the cockpit, and saw it fall out of formation, but was himself hit in the hand and had to dive away, so was unable to file a claim. The B-17 was then shot down by another Staffel pilot, who was given credit for the final destruction of the bomber. The next day, the 9th Staffel was ordered to rejoin its parent Gruppe in Belgium. Stammberger led the Staffel to III/JG 26's base at Wevelghem. One week later, he was promoted to Oberleutnant and ordered to Vitry to take command of the Second Gruppe's 4th Staffel.

On 8 March, sixteen B-24s headed across the Channel to bomb Rouen, escorted by three squadrons of RAF Spitfires. This small force was an ideal target for a coordinated attack by the understrength Schlageter fighters. Pips Priller led the Third Gruppe in an attack on the Spitfire escort, while the Second Gruppe took on the Liberators. Wutz Galland led his Focke-Wulfs in a tight right bank into a head-on attack "von Schnauze auf Schnauze" (snout to snout). Their attack was devastating. The lead bomber burst into flames, followed by the Number 2 aircraft in the lead vee. The bomber formation fell apart completely; bombs were scattered over the French countryside as the aircraft sought to evade the German fighters. Peter Crump fired a long burst at his target, from long range, and could clearly see a number of hits in the cockpit area. As he dove away in a split-S, he saw to his horror that he was in the path of the Liberator's jettisoned bombs. He evaded them by a tight turn, but lost sight of his target, and could no longer say with

certainty which of the enemy aircraft now falling from the sky was
his. He saw his presumed victim crash in a patch of trees north of
the Seine; however, without a witness, Crump was not awarded the
victory. The B-24 claims of three Second Gruppe pilots were confirmed. The two lead B-24s, from the 44th Bomb Group, crashed in
France, while a 93rd Bomb Group aircraft crashed after reaching
England. The Schlageter fighters also claimed at least two Spitfires
shot down, while suffering no damage or loss to themselves. They
were proudest, however, of having forced the bombers to turn back
before reaching their target. This proved to be the only such triumph ever gained over the Eighth Air Force.

For the next few weeks, the Americans flew very few bombing
missions, awaiting the buildup of their own escort fighter force. In
the interim, the Allies were forced to rely on feints and diversions to
confuse and wear down the German defenders. Peter Crump has
vivid memories of one intercept mission during this period:

A new tactic of the heavy formations made its first appearance.
The direction of attack appeared to be over Holland into the Ruhr,
and so we of the opposing defenses were disposed accordingly. During their approach they turned, and left England on a southerly
course, as if to attack a target in France. But the entire maneuver was
then reversed; after flying south they then turned back east. In the
meantime, we were being led this way and that, and would soon be
unable to attack the enemy formation due to low fuel. Auxiliary fuel
tanks were available, but we were flying this mission without them.
Which day this was I do not know, since there is no such entry in my
logbook.

As our Gruppe formation flew north, almost to the coast and
almost out of fuel, I spotted the bomber stream in the dusk at eleven
o'clock, on a northwesterly course somewhat below us. My report to
the formation leader Galland brought the reply, "Where are they? I
see nothing!" A second, more detailed report brought the same reply.
Apparently no one else saw the formation—or else the Kommandeur
did not want to see it, having in mind our almost-empty tanks. At
any rate, after a short delay he turned about to a course for home,
with the comment "Ich habe Durst" [I am thirsty], which was code
for low fuel. However, the rest of us were given a free hand to do
what we wanted. A glance at my fuel gauge showed me that an attack
was possible; my wingman agreed with me. In a gentle climb, I
turned my Rotte on a course to the northwest; as we approached the

bomber stream I swung to the right, toward the last Pulk [combat box] of B-17s. I glanced around, and found to my relief that the bombers were without fighter escort. I attacked the nearest B-17, which was at the left of the leading vee, from the front and slightly above. It began to smoke immediately. Flames erupted between its two left engines. The bomber sheered away to the left, trailing a long stream of fire. As long as I watched, it remained on course in a shallow dive. I quickly turned my eyes away from it and the rest of the enemy formation, as it was high time we got away. My wingman had been hit in an aileron and had control problems. But thanks to our altitude, and with some luck, we made smooth landings at Coxyde, a nearby coastal airfield. I do not know to this day what happened to "my" B-17. I know only that from that day onward I was considered to have the best eyes in the Second Gruppe.

Peter Crump's comment about his logbook is a reminder that the German pilots' logs were not maintained by the pilots themselves, but by the Staffel clerks. Errors occur with some frequency in these documents. In this case, as in others, Crump's memory is more accurate than his written records. This combat took place on 31 March 1943, and the American mission reports confirm his statement in every detail. The day's target was Rotterdam, but the entire formation was blown off course by unanticipated high winds, resulting in numerous course changes above the Channel. Four of the six bomber groups aborted the mission, and Galland's formation caught up to the other units when they were halfway back across the Channel. Wutz Galland's radioed concerns over his fuel state, and his final order to make one pass from the rear, were picked up by the British radio intercept service and interpreted correctly. The British knew Galland well—the German formation leaders preferred to use nicknames rather than code names while in the air, and Wutz's "handle" (pronounced "Vootz") was one of the most distinctive on the Channel coast. Peter Crump's target was the 305th Bomb Group's *Southern Comfort*. It caught fire between its No. 1 and No. 2 engines (the left two), and its pilot pulled it from formation, streaming flames and black, oil-fed smoke. He headed west in solid cloud, and when the navigator estimated that they were over England the pilot, prompted by his left wing's buckling metal and solid flames, gave the order to bail out.

The only other German formation to reach the bombers was

Oblt. Stammberger's 4th Staffel, which was split from the Second Gruppe and sent after what proved to be a diversionary formation of B-24s. Stammberger made one attack from the front and a second from the rear, after which one B-24 dropped from the formation in flames. Stammberger saw it crash into the Channel, but the rest of his Staffel were on their way home, and he could find no witness to the crash. That evening, the Wissant listening service reported that a B-24 had radioed at 1245 that it was no longer controllable due to enemy action, and that its crew was going to bail out. The time and the bomber's location, sixty miles north of Ostend, matched Stammberger's encounter report perfectly, giving him the basis to file a claim, which was, however, rejected by the RLM. The B-24 was from the 93rd Bomb Group; no one survived its crash. Crump's and Stammberger's victims were the only two bombers lost on 31 March. Ironically, neither loss resulted in a victory credit on the German books.

At that time, Stotto Stammberger had one of the best records against the heavy bombers of any German pilot. After joining 9/ JG 26 in February 1941, he had gotten off to an extremely slow start; his first air victory, a Spitfire, did not come until the Dieppe raid in August 1942. However, his first encounter with B-17s that October was successful, and he had now brought down four heavy bombers. A war correspondent quoted Stotto's self-analysis: ". . . I simply couldn't handle the Spitfires. It might be that I wasn't cut out for turning around, but I am built more for boring straight in!"

The target for the Eighth on 4 April was the Renault plant in Paris. Three diversions drew the German defenders away and permitted the lead 305th Bomb Group to destroy the complex; 498 out of 500 bombs fell within the target area. JG 2, in whose territory the target lay, never did make an interception, but when the homeward bound B-17s reached Rouen, they were savaged by JG 26. Some seventy-five Schlageter fighters flew a maximum-strength mission. The yellow-nosed FW 190s and Bf 109s circled up sun, turned, and dove on the bombers. Most attacks were made from eleven, twelve, and one o'clock high, by one or two Schwaerme simultaneously. Spacing between the German attacking units was much closer than previously, only 1,000-1,500 yards, catching bombers out of position when they jinked to evade the previous fighters. Most attacks hit the low squadron of the leading 305th Bomb Group, in "coffin corner"; it lost three aircraft. One more B-17 went down before the Spitfire escort arrived. Galland's Second Gruppe then took on the Spitfires in a wild, massive battle that extended over the Channel. The Focke-Wulf pilots claimed five Spitfires, without loss to themselves. Two of the B-17s were credited to Galland; the others went to Third Gruppe pilots. German losses to the bomber gunners were heavier than usual; two pilots died, and a third was injured.

A quote from the intelligence summary included with that evening's Eighth Bomber Command mission report illustrates the close watch that the Allies kept on the former Abbeville Kids of II/JG 26:

> Of the two Pas de Calais wings, it was the one from Vitry which made the more purposeful attempt to get into contact with the enemy. Under their wing leader, Wutz Galland, they went in to attack from 1426. The intersquad [radio] reflects the fierceness of the attacks, pressed home again and again. . . . The tactics of this wing appeared to be to mass together in groups and attack as a tight formation. The Spitfire rear cover was spotted at 1433, and very rapid excited intersquad continued until 1440, reflecting the combats with the Allied fighters. . . .

During this period, the nine Staffeln attached to the Geschwader were deployed as follows. Oblt. Borris's FW 190-equipped 8th Staffel flew from the Geschwader headquarters at Lille-Vendeville, as part of Major Priller's Fuehrungsverband. Hptm. Galland's Second Gruppe, containing the 4th, 5th, 6th, and a newly formed 10th Staffel, flew FW 190s from Vitry. The Bf 109s of the Third Gruppe were at Wevelghem; this unit, commanded by Hptm. Fritz Geisshardt and later Hptm. Kurt Ruppert, contained the 9th, 11th, and a new 12th Staffel, and 4/JG 54. When 7/JG 26 returned from the Soviet Union in July, 4/JG 54 retired to Germany, where it served as the nucleus for a new Gruppe, IV/JG 54, which ultimately went to the Eastern front to provide JG 54 with a third Gruppe. III/JG 54 remained in Germany, as an independent Gruppe in the Reich defense force.

On 5 April, 101 B-17s and B-24s headed for the ERLA aircraft repair facility at Antwerp, escorted by nine squadrons of RAF Spitfires. Again JG 26 was able to put up a large force of fighters. The

Fuehrungsverband and the Third Gruppe began to form up for head-on attacks before the escort turned back at Ghent; the British fighters were too far above and behind the formation to intervene. The first concentrated attack broke up the cohesiveness of the bomber formation. Only eighty-two B-17s managed to bomb their target, and the large number of bombs scattered on civilian targets brought the Americans a rebuke from the Belgian ambassador. The 306th Bomb Group was split up by the Germans' initial pass, and thus bore the brunt of the remainder of the attacks. Hptm. Galland's Second Gruppe made its first attack just as the 306th turned off the target. Stotto Stammberger describes this Gruppe's mission:

> At about 1430, a report was received at Vitry that many bombers were assembling over southeastern England. Neither the direction of the attack nor its target could yet be determined. Our Gruppe was called to cockpit readiness; at this command, thirty pilots climbed into their aircraft and made ready to take off. We received running reports over the loudspeakers of the movements of the aircraft, which were now identified as heavy bombers—about one hundred of them. They were still circling while assembling. At 1445 we were sent off into the air; first to wait over Amiens and then over Bethune. The bomber stream took a southeastern course toward Dunkirk, and we were sent to Dunkirk. The heavies had now reached the coast near Ostend and flew in the direction Ghent-Brussels. We turned and rushed toward Brussels. Past Ghent, the stream suddenly turned east toward Antwerp. We had already been in the air more than a half hour, and had used up over half our fuel, as we had been flying at high speed trying to catch up to the bombers.
>
> After about forty-five minutes, we saw the bombers far ahead on an easterly course; we were to their north. Now we took out after them at full throttle, climbing at a slight angle in order to be able to storm through the formation from the front. Suddenly, we saw the bomb carpet of the first formation strike on the southern edge of Antwerp, with large explosions and clouds of smoke. We had just reached a good attack position, and broke to the right, diving on the first Pulk, which made a left turn away from us. But the Pulk following it was in just the right position for our attack. Just as this formation dropped its bombs, I found a Boeing squarely in my sights. Everything now took place in fractions of a second. The salvo from my four cannon and two machine guns hit squarely in the bomber's cockpit; I had to pull up quickly, as the bomber suddenly tipped

forward—the pilot had probably been hit. The aircraft entered a spin to the left. Most of the crew bailed out. The B-17 continued flying, pilotless, for some distance; it finally crashed at about 1535. After my victory, I still had enough fuel for ten or fifteen minutes of flight, and returned to base with as many of my companions as were still with me.

Stotto Stammberger's victory was his fifth. Major Priller stayed with the bomber formation during the bomb run, and at 1528 brought down another B-17; it was the Kommodore's eighty-fourth victory. Hptm. Galland's target crashed at about the same time, for his thirty-eighth victory. The fourth bomber to go down was a straggler, which was chased by Obfw. Addi Glunz, now a Schwarm-fuehrer in Stammberger's 4th Staffel, and was finally brought down at 1538; it was Glunz's thirty-second victory. This B-17's pilot, Robert Seelos, writes:

> Normally, we did not encounter heavy fighter attacks until coming off a target and those that had been hit by flak over the target were falling out of formation. But today the fighters seemed to be waiting for us as soon as we reached the Continent. I took a hit dead center in the prop dome of my number one engine and was unable to feather it and had to let it run wild. . . . Eventually the squadron was all over the sky and four B-17s were lost, including mine. . . . The main portion of the Group overshot the target and hit the small city of Mortsel, killing many women and children—a very bleak day in Belgian history! I had fallen behind, and my bombardier said our bombs were right on target!
>
> By this time my only thoughts were to try to hold off the German fighters and if possible make it to the English Channel and try to crash-land in the water. . . . But the German fighters were peppering the hell out of me, as I could see the tracers going by the windows. Eventually I took a direct hit in the No. 4 engine, which left me with just the two inboards. We were still holding our own at about 20,000 feet, and still had hopes—until the right outboard burst into flames and the controls became almost useless. It was then that I gave the order to abandon the airplane. I held it as level as I could, until I was sure my crew had time to get out, and I then crawled down to the escape hatch in the nose and bailed out. At approximately 10,000 feet I saw two German fighters coming straight at me! If anyone ever "puckered up," it was me! At about fifty yards they banked, in formation—they both saluted me and took off!

All four of the bombers shot down by JG 26 came from the 306th Bomb Group. The Geschwader lost only one pilot in this battle, but it was a serious blow to the unit. Hptm. Fritz Geisshardt, Kommandeur of the Third Gruppe, was hit by return fire on his unit's first pass through the bombers. Bleeding profusely from a wound in the abdomen, Geisshardt dove away from the battle and made a smooth landing on the airfield at Ghent. His blood loss proved fatal; the medical personnel at the Ghent hospital could not save him, and he died early the next morning.

In his report, the commanding general of Eighth Bomber Command's 1st Bomb Wing, Brig. Gen. Frank Armstrong, summed up the mission of 5 April as follows:

> This was the strongest and most aggressive force of fighters that the 1st Bombardment Wing has ever faced. The enemy, with his tactics of attacking in formation, picking out the low aircraft, boring in to make the attack and then breaking away downward as the next wave came in, was successful in destroying four aircraft and acting as a definite deterrent on the bombing run.

ARRIVAL OF THE THUNDERBOLTS

The Eighth Air Force brass waited impatiently for their own Fighter Command to become operational on American equipment, Republic P-47 Thunderbolts. The Spitfire escort provided by RAF Fighter Command was felt to be lacking in two respects. First, the Spitfire's short range limited it to the coastal regions of northern France and Belgium. Second, Royal Air Force tactical doctrine called for "escort" to be flown high above the bombers, rather than within immediate supporting range. In part, this was nothing but the typical fighter pilot/bomber pilot controversy as to what constituted effective escort, but the Americans suspected that their Allies preferred flying in the stratosphere because that is where their aircraft were most superior to those of the enemy. The German fighter controllers soon learned to recognize the Spitfire escort formations, which typically flew at 30,000 feet, at least 5,000 feet above the bombers. The Luftwaffe fighter leaders thus had the option to attack the escort, wait until it turned back, or even sneak in a quick attack on the bombers, diving away before the escort could react.

Three American fighter groups were working up on the P-47, which had the distinction of being the heaviest single-engined fighter in the world. The 4th Fighter Group had been formed from the three RAF Eagle Squadrons, had absorbed RAF doctrine and slang, and were initially dubious about replacing their beloved Spitfires with these "bloody great milk bottles." The 78th Group also had shakedown problems with their new P-47s—the aircraft that they had trained on and brought to Europe, Lockheed P-38 Lightnings, had been taken away from them to replace losses in North Africa. Only the 56th Group was entirely comfortable with their "Jugs"; they had been the first unit to receive them, while still in the US. For now they had to listen in silence as their RAF liaison officers heaped scorn on their aircraft. The P-47 had excellent firepower in its eight .50-caliber machine guns. Its supercharger gave it excellent high-altitude performance, and it was certainly expected to dive well, but the experienced RAF pilots gave it no chance at all as a dogfighter at medium or low altitudes.

By early April, all three American units were ready to test their mounts in combat. Until auxiliary fuel tanks of acceptable design and quality were available, the range of their Thunderbolts was little greater than that of the Spitfires. The American fighter efforts were thus limited to coastal sweeps similar to those flown by their British counterparts. Their first encounter with the Jagdwaffe took place on 15 April. The 4th Group drew first blood over Ostend, claiming three FW 190s destroyed, for the loss of two P-47s and their pilots. This engagement was with II/JG 1, flying somewhat to the west of its usual territory over the Netherlands; the German unit claimed two P-47s and suffered no losses.

Eighth Fighter Command ordered a Rodeo, a fighter sweep of the enemy coast, on 29 April. All three groups were employed, but the 56th Group saw all of the combat. Its sweep of the Dutch coast stirred up a hornet's nest. The low squadron, flying at 28,000 feet, was hit by pairs of JG 26 Focke-Wulfs that swept in from dead ahead, fired short, well-aimed bursts, and dove away. Two Thunderbolts and pilots were lost. No German fighter was hit in the brief encounter.

For the next two weeks, the American fighter sweeps provoked no German reaction. American bomber raids, of course, were a different story. Not only were they the German defenders' top priority, they were the only priority—Goering had issued an order forbidding his fighters to attack enemy fighters, not even to clear away the escort to permit more effective attacks on the bombers. On 4 May, the P-47s and Spitfires combined to keep the German fighters from approaching a formation of seventy-nine B-17s, which bombed Antwerp without losing a single plane. A disgusted JG 26 pilot wrote that evening that the Geschwader's failure had brought "a great salvo from Reichsmarschall Hermann Goering. We should be disbanded—our formation leaders should be arrested—we are all cowardly dogs!"

At noon on 13 May, the Second Gruppe was ordered to scramble from Vitry to oppose a large formation approaching the Belgian coast. Suddenly the Allied formation turned to the south—toward northern France, perhaps to Lille or the industrial region around Bethune. The Focke-Wulf pilots were therefore summoned back to Lille and could then see above them, to the north toward Dunkirk, condensation trails on a southerly course. These proved to belong to a tight formation of Spitfires. Just then the Jafue ordered its pilots to land immediately. Most of the Focke-Wulfs dove away; the only exception was Stotto Stammberger's flight. His radio was defective, and he was concentrating so hard on the Spitfires that he failed to notice the departure of the rest of his own 4th Staffel. He waited for the Spitfires to attack, as called for by the standard German tactics. The other Staffeln should have been to one side and above him, in order to fall on the attackers from above, while Stotto let the Spitfires approach to firing distance before breaking into the attack and commencing the dogfight. But his Schwarm was alone. His second element disappeared on the break, leaving only his wingman, who left the scene when Stammberger's plane was hit and caught fire. Stammberger was at 25,000 feet when his fuel tank exploded; he bailed out, but his chute didn't open fully. A third of it was burned through, and his fall was slowed only by a bubble of trapped air. He was whirled in circles and was knocked out when he landed. He regained consciousness ten days later in the St. Omer hospital, having suffered, in his words, "a severe brain concussion, and second and third degree burns, but fortunately, nothing broken!" Stammberger returned to the front in October but was not restored to combat status.

That afternoon, the B-17 strength of Eighth Bomber Command doubled to eight groups, as four groups flew their first mission. Meaulte and two airfields in the St. Omer region were to be the targets, and the well-practiced Schlageter fighters were the defenders. The Second Gruppe avoided the thirteen squadrons of Spitfires and fell on the B-17s. The 91st Bomb Group, in the low box, caught much of the attack, which was so vicious that the American crewmen assumed, correctly, that it had been made by the Abbeville Kids. The yellow-nosed Focke-Wulfs attacked in Rotten or Schwaerme from twelve o'clock low, thus avoiding the supporting fire of the higher bomber boxes. The first attack came as the lead group crossed the French coast, and the frontal attacks continued until the formation reached the coast on its way back to England. The German fighter pilots contemptuously ignored the supporting Spitfires, which maintained their formation high above the battle.

Major Priller led the Fuehrungsverband and the Third Gruppe against the high boxes and their Spitfire cover. The 305th Bomb Group reported that the Messerschmitts and Focke-Wulfs attacked from the rear, from five to eight o'clock; usually several aircraft flew in trail. Attacks were pressed home, and many attackers flew right through the bomber formation. American losses totaled three B-17s, which matched JG 26's claims; at least three RAF Spitfires were also claimed. One B-17 was severely damaged by a bomb dropped by a FW 190, but reached its home base. German losses for the day were limited to one young Unteroffizier, who was shot down in flames by a Spitfire, and Oblt. Stammberger, whose combat has already been described.

On 14 May, Eighth Bomber Command struck at one of their tormentors' bases. The new 4th Bomb Wing attacked Wevelghem airfield, as well as Antwerp, in a powerful diversion in support of the major raid of the day, an attack on Kiel by the more experienced 1st Bomb Wing. The two bomb groups assigned to take out Wevelghem did an effective job, killing and wounding a number of ground personnel and pilots, destroying and damaging aircraft, and carpeting the landing ground with craters. For the first time, a JG 26 airfield was left unserviceable by an air raid. The Third Gruppe was forced to move to Lille-Nord. Oblt. Erwin Leykauf, Kapitaen of the 12th Staffel and a newcomer to the Western theater, unwisely decided to take off during the raid; he promptly wrecked his Messerschmitt by shearing its landing gear off in a bomb crater.

The air combats associated with this raid were widespread and

171

bitterly fought. Pilots from the Second Gruppe shot down two 351st Bomb Group B-17s, one 78th Fighter Group P-47, and one Spitfire from the supporting force. German fighter losses to the new B-17 groups were unusually high. Two 5th Staffel pilots were killed by bomber fire, and Hptm. Karl Borris, Kapitaen of the 8th Staffel, was forced to bail out from his damaged Focke-Wulf. He opened his parachute too soon, and it practically collapsed. Borris was extremely fortunate to survive his fall from 22,000 feet. He suffered numerous broken bones and required a long stay in the hospital. Another pilot of his Staffel was seriously injured by B-17 fire, while a 6th Staffel aircraft became the 78th Fighter Group's first victory claim; its pilot bailed out and survived. Lt. Paul Schauder's 9th Staffel Bf 109G collided with a Spitfire immediately after taking off from Wevelghem, causing the crash of both planes. Schauder bailed out successfully, suffering an eye injury.

That afternoon, as the 5th Staffel's Fw. Peter Crump approached the field at Vlissingen on his return from an unsuccessful interception, he spotted a B-17 over the coast, about five miles away and at an altitude of only 2,500 feet. It was coming right at Crump. Although flying on empty, Crump took up a pursuit curve. He could not tell if the bomber was already in trouble. He attacked from the low left rear. A thin flame shot from the bomber's left wing tanks, at the same time as something hit Crump's cockpit. Trash whirled around and he tasted gunpowder on his tongue. Crump concluded that he had been hit by fire from the B-17—but where? After a last glance at the Fortress, which was descending in a steep left bank, trailing flames, Crump made a beeline for Vlissingen. During his landing attempt, it became apparent that his entire electrical system had gone out. The landing gear could be lowered mechanically, but Crump had to land without his flaps and trim tabs. It was a tight fit into a "damned short" landing ground.

The search for the damaging hit brought a surprise. Crump discovered an entrance hole of less than a half-inch diameter in the right side of the fuselage. The shell had then turned at an acute angle and had torn up the cable harness behind the instrument bank on the right side of the cockpit before it exploded. A hands-width higher and the shell would have hit Crump in the abdomen, probably killing him. In Peter Crump's words, "A matter of luck!"

The increasing strength of the Eighth Bomber Command allowed it more flexibility in its choice of targets. It began hitting cities along the north German coast with some frequency. On 23 May, the Third Gruppe moved to Cuxhaven-Nordholz in north Germany, to lend support to JG 1, III/JG 54, and the newly formed JG 11, the only day fighter units within the borders of Germany. The Allied daylight offensive gained momentum the following month. JG 26 claimed the destruction of eleven B-17s and at least twenty-eight Allied fighters during June. The cost to the Geschwader was nine pilots killed and nine injured in combat and flying accidents.

During a sweep of Ostend on 12 June, the 56th Fighter Group claimed its first victory, an FW 190. On the following day, the 56th and 78th Groups saw enough combat to consider themselves fully blooded. On a morning sweep of the coast at 27,000 feet, the 56th Group spotted a Staffel of FW 190s climbing in their direction. Col. Hubert "Hub" Zemke, the Group commander, led two flights of Thunderbolts down on the German fighters. The Focke-Wulf pilots, from 10/JG 26, were taken by surprise. Zemke shot down two, while Lt. Robert Johnson exploded a third. The 10th Staffel lost one pilot killed and a second wounded in this combat.

The Thunderbolt sweep was in support of unescorted Eighth Bomber Command raids on Kiel and Bremen. Hptm. Kurt Ruppert led thirty-two Third Gruppe Bf 109Gs up from their new base at Nordholz to intercept the Kiel attackers. As the Messerschmitts made a rear pass on the lead group, Ruppert was hit and bailed out. He attempted to open his parachute before his speed had dropped sufficiently in free-fall, and the harness ripped, throwing Ruppert free and to his death. German parachutes had caused the death of many pilots; within a year, the old hemp harnesses would be replaced by a synthetic material similar to nylon. Ruppert was the only JG 26 casualty in this battle, which cost the lead group eight Flying Fortresses. The 4th Bomb Wing lost a total of twenty-two B-17s out of seventy-six dispatched.

The day's activities were not yet over. In the late afternoon, forty-four P-47s of the 78th Group flew a sweep over Ypres and St. Pol. The Second Gruppe was up in good time. They were not spotted by the Thunderbolt formation until they were diving to the attack from ten o'clock high. Two P-47s went down in the resulting dogfight. No German fighters were lost, although three "probables" were awarded to American pilots. Three German pilots were awarded victory credits.

June 22 brought a major Eighth Air Force attack on Huels. Two new B-17 groups were ordered to fly a diversionary raid into the hornet's nest around Antwerp. The green units missed the rendezvous with their fighter escort and proceeded across the Channel alone, assuming that the Allied fighters had gone on ahead. Instead, the first fighters seen by the American bomber crews were the FW 190s of JG 26's Fuehrungsverband and Second Gruppe, coming out of a slight haze at a closing speed of 500 miles per hour. The first signs of their presence were the gun flashes from their wing cannon. The first flight of six flashed through the bomber formation, untouched by defensive fire; there had been no defensive fire. By the time the fourth and last Schwarm attacked, the defenders were firing at them with all guns. After the Focke-Wulfs passed through the two bomber boxes, they broke to the left, climbing back to attack again from the rear and rear quarter. They expertly kept the morning sun at their backs to blind the bomber gunners. The German fighters broke off their attacks only when the bombers began their bomb runs and came under fire from the Antwerp flak. By now, four B-17s were falling from the sky. Three FW 190s weré damaged sufficiently by the bombers to require forced landings. As the B-17 boxes turned off target, the withdrawal escort, the 4th and 78th Fighter Groups, arrived and waded into the Focke-Wulfs. The battle must have been more than normally chaotic; the Thunderbolt pilots claimed the destruction of seven German fighters, when in fact none were lost. The Schlageter fighters claimed one P-47, but all returned safely to England. The four B-17 losses resulted in five confirmed claims for victories, one "shot from formation," and one "final destruction."

On 23 June, Major Priller received the welcome news that his First Gruppe had returned from the Eastern front. It was without a Kommandeur; Priller called Hptm. Borris in the hospital and awarded the position to him. I/JG 26 was not to be assigned to Priller's command immediately, however; instead, it went to Rheine in northwestern Germany, to bolster the defense of the Reich's northern approaches.

The 26th of June brought another triumph for the Abbeville Kids of the Second Gruppe—their most one-sided victory over the

Thunderbolts. The Eighth Bomber Command's targets were air-fields in the Paris area. The 56th Fighter Group was to provide the withdrawal escort and dispatched forty-eight P-47s. Before rendez-vous could be made with the bombers near Forges, France, the American fighters were attacked from the rear by II/JG 26. Instantly, the formation split apart, as the American pilots sought to save themselves. Lt. Robert Johnson's aircraft, flying in the "ass-end Charlie" slot, was hit badly in the initial bounce. A 20-mm cannon shell exploded in the left side of the cockpit and ruptured the hydraulic system. Blinded and burned by the fluid, Johnson attempted to bail out but found his canopy jammed. He then dove for the Channel. He was spotted by a JG 26 pilot, who followed him halfway back, peppering Johnson's plane with light machine-gun fire until he apparently ran out of ammunition. The Focke-Wulf then pulled alongside Johnson's plane, by now a sieve; the German shook his head in amazement, rocked his wings in salute, peeled away, and returned to the Continent.

Johnson made it back for an emergency landing at Manston. Four of his fellow pilots were killed, and a fifth was forced to abandon his plane over the Channel. Five more P-47s returned with damage. The Americans claimed the destruction of two Focke-Wulfs, but none were lost. The German pilots were awarded six victory credits for the downed Thunderbolts. In addition, Major Priller shot down a B-17 on its return flight over Dieppe. The Germans suffered no casualties or damage. The first half of 1943 thus ended on a successful note for the Geschwader.

9
TEMPORARY
ASCENDANCY
July–December 1943

THE BATTLES ESCALATE

THE PILOTS OF THE 2ND STAFFEL HAD ARRIVED AT THEIR AIR-craft before dawn. The skies promised to be clear, and the level of radio traffic coming from England indicated that the day would be a busy one; as the First Gruppe's readiness Staffel they would be the first to respond. Shortly after 0730, their orders were received—a small Allied formation had left the English coast headed toward the Netherlands. Lt. Karl "Charlie" Willius led two Schwaerme, eight FW 190s, up from Grimberghen to intercept it.

The Allied formation contained medium bombers—twenty-three Martin B-26 Marauders from the 386th Bomb Group, which was flying its first combat mission. Their target was the fighter airfield at Woensdrecht, in the Netherlands. Since German fighter opposition was expected, they were given an escort of eight RAF Spitfire squadrons. Rendezvous was made over Orfordness at 0727, and the bombers set course for the continent. They flew at 11,000 feet; the Spitfires were some 5,000 feet above them.

In the meantime, Lt. Willius's eight Focke-Wulfs were straining for altitude as they headed northeast, to put themselves up sun of the incoming raiders. The bombers' location was easily followed by observing the bursts of the coastal flak batteries. The B-26s quickly reached Woensdrecht, but because of the morning haze and

176

the sun's glare, the Group's inexperienced lead bombardier could not line up his bombsight in time, and the first two boxes failed to drop. The last two boxes released their bombs, and the formation turned right, according to plan.

Just at this moment, the tail gunners called out enemy fighters. Willius had gotten his Focke-Wulfs to the eastern side of the Allied formation, where they would be shielded from the escort by the bombers, and ordered an immediate attack. Willius pulled up beneath a straggling bomber and gave it a quick burst of cannon fire. One engine erupted into flames. The B-26 entered a spin and crashed into the water below; there were no survivors. The gunners of the other bombers let fly into the glare of the sun. More than 9,000 rounds of .50-caliber ammunition were fired in opposing the lightning-swift attack.

It was all over in less than a minute. The German fighters broke for the deck before the Spitfires could arrive. The remaining Marauders reached their Boxted base at 0853, having survived a typical ETO baptism of fire. The Group's excited gunners claimed to have downed more enemy fighters than had actually been present. They were ultimately given credit for six destroyed and five probables. The Schlageter fighters in fact suffered one fatality. The leader of Willius's second Schwarm escaped his burning aircraft but was unable to open his parachute, apparently because of his serious wounds. The Spitfires were fended off by some Focke-Wulfs from the 3rd Staffel, which shot down one Spitfire while losing one of their own. The German pilot bailed out without difficulty, but he was injured on landing.

The Luftwaffe gave Charlie Willius credit for the destruction of one "Boston"; it was his thirty-second victory. This had been the Schlageter pilots' first encounter with Marauders. No time was available for the niceties of enemy aircraft identification; this was only the first combat on the very busy morning of 30 July 1943.

The return of JG 26's First Gruppe from the Soviet Union in June had provided a welcome reinforcement for the hard-working Jagdwaffe units in northwestern Europe. I/JG 26 was first ordered to Rheine, but when the newly organized JG 11 became fully operational in the same region, the Gruppe was sent back to Belgium, where it returned to the control of Major Priller and its home Geschwader. III/JG 26 was at Cuxhaven-Nordholz throughout July, under the direct operational control of the Jafue defending the north German coast. The Gruppe moved to Amsterdam's Schipol airport, and back to JG 26's control, in early August.

Pips Priller now had as many as twelve Staffeln at his disposal. However, he had little opportunity to lead them personally. In July he was ordered to fill in for Oberst Vieck as commander of Jafue 2, which was headquartered in St. Pol. Priller remained Kommodore of JG 26, thus occupying two full-time posts. The Luftwaffe's extreme shortage of talent in the upper ranks forced him to commute between Lille and St. Pol almost daily and brought a temporary end to his combat flying. When Obst. Vieck returned to his duties in late August, Priller moved his Geschwaderstab and his Fuehrungs-staffel, the 8th, from Lille-Vendeville to Schipol. Karl Borris brought the First Gruppe and its 1st, 2nd, and 3rd Staffeln to Brussels' Grimbergen field in mid-July. Wutz Galland's Second Gruppe, with the 4th, 5th, 6th, and 10th Staffeln, occupied a number of bases in this period—more than can be listed in detail. When the 7th Staffel returned from the Soviet Union in July, it rejoined Klaus Mietusch's Third Gruppe, giving it four Staffeln; the others were the 9th, 11th, and 12th.

The frequency with which the Geschwader's constituent Gruppen and Staffeln were shuffled around the airfields of northern France, the Low Countries, and northwestern Germany is a testimony to the efficiency and skill of the unit's experienced ground organization. In 1943 the Gruppen of the other western Geschwader had more or less permanent bases; the Schlageter fighters, however, were invariably moved near the currently favored course of the Eighth Air Force bomber stream.

Although after the attrition of almost four years' combat the level of training of the average JG 26 pilot had decreased, the combat efficiency of the Geschwader as a whole had never been greater. Major Priller led the Geschwader victory list with ninety claims. Hptm. Borris, with twenty-six victories, and Hptm. Mietusch, with forty-five, were among the few JG 26 pilots from 1939 still flying combat in the unit; most of the rest had been lost, either as casualties or transfers. Only two Staffelkapitaene, Beese and Ebersberger, had served in JG 26 as far back as the Battle of Britain. The combat strength of the Geschwader resided in the surviving replacement pilots of 1941–1942, who were now at the peaks of their skills. The victory totals of the best of them were in the twenty to fifty range. These were low by the inflated standards set on the Eastern front, but the ability of men such as Galland, Glunz, and Willius to score steadily while staying alive in the dangerous western skies marked them as some of the very best fighter pilots in the world.

The pilots of the western Geschwader were convinced that their eastern brethren received more than their fair share of battle honors. Promotions and awards in the German Air Force were based on success in combat. This basic principle could not be changed, but in recognition of the difficulty of the struggle against the heavy bombers, the Luftwaffe instituted a point system for decorations. Points were awarded to fighter pilots as follows:

	POINTS AWARDED PER		
Aircraft Type:	Abschuss (Destroyed)	Herausschuss (Separation)	Endgueltige Vernichtung (Final Destruction)
Single-engined fighter	1	0	0
Twin-engined bomber	2	1	½
Four-engined bomber	3	2	1

The system recognized the fact that achieving a Herausschuss, that is, damaging a bomber enough to force it from its combat box, was a more difficult task than the final destruction of a damaged straggler. Decorations were awarded after the following point totals had been reached:

Award	Points
Iron Cross 2nd Class	1
Iron Cross 1st Class	3
Honor Cup	10
German Cross	20
Knight's Cross	40

The Knight's Cross, which was worn on a ribbon around the neck, even in combat, was recognized in the Jagdwaffe as a sign of a true Experte. Glory-hungry pilots were said to have a "neck rash." If it was their luck to be assigned to JG 26, their necks in all likelihood continued to itch until their deaths. Only one Knight's Cross was awarded to a JG 26 pilot in each of the years 1941 and 1942, while two pilots, Wutz Galland and Addi Glunz, were so rewarded in 1943. The higher grades of the Knight's Cross, which in ascending order were the Oak Leaves, Swords, and Diamonds, were awarded in some number in the East but were very uncommon in JG 26. During the entire war, only five pilots received any of the higher decorations while with JG 26.

It has been pointed out in many postwar references that the point system existed for the purpose of award qualification only. "Victory claims" and "points" were two distinct statistics. The requirements for the verification of victory claims remained unchanged; only the RLM in Berlin could confirm a claim, and this procedure could take more than a year. The practice of claiming "separations" died out in JG 26 in 1944, but it was quite common during the savage combats of 1943. Research for this book revealed that many pilots' "separation" claims were ultimately awarded as "victories"; occasionally claims by other pilots were allowed for the "final destruction" of the same aircraft. It is easy to see that the system led to claims duplication by a factor of as much as two. Perhaps not coincidentally, the daily Wehrmacht communiqués of this period habitually overclaimed American bomber losses by a factor of roughly two. German claims for the destruction of heavy bombers (even when confirmed) are more difficult to reconcile with Allied losses than claims for any other aircraft type; it is probable that part of the explanation lies with the point system.

The Schlageter fighters saw little combat during the first two weeks of July. Bad weather canceled many American bomber missions. The routine Spitfire and P-47 sweeps were for the most part ignored. A number of new pilots reported to the Geschwader from the training Gruppen and began their familiarization training. On the 5th, Klaus Mietusch returned from the Soviet Union to take command of the Third Gruppe in Nordholz, bumping Rolf Hermichen to the command of the First Gruppe's 3rd Staffel. The 12th Staffel's Oblt. Erwin Leykauf transferred out and was replaced as

Kapitaen by Hptm. Herman Staiger, who transferred in from JG 51 "Moelders."

On 24 July, the Eighth Bomber Command, buoyed by forecasts of good weather, began a campaign called Blitz Week with an ambitious and completely successful attack on magnesium and aluminum plants under construction at Heroya, Norway. The Command had grown to the point that it could now put 300 bombers over a target. On the first six days of Blitz Week, JG 26's First and Second Gruppen were employed primarily against Allied sweeps and diversions, and claimed six RAF fighters, one Boston, and one straggling B-17, while losing two pilots in accidents. The American 4th Fighter Group flew the ETO's first belly tank show on the 28th, meeting the bombers at Emmerich, Germany, just over the Dutch border. The Thunderbolt pilots broke up an attack by forty-five German fighters, claiming nine destroyed. One of the units chased off by the P-47s was I/JG 26, in its first battle with the heavy bombers since its return to the west. Prior to the Thunderbolts' arrival, Borris's men downed one B-17. The Thunderbolts shot down one First Gruppe FW 190, whose pilot bailed out with light injuries. The bombers shot down two more Gruppe aircraft. One of these pilots bailed out safely. The second, Obfw. Waldemar "Vladimir" Soeffing, elected to ride his aircraft down; it hit one of the many water-filled ditches around Dordrecht and overturned, breaking Soeffing's neck. The pilot, who was as rugged as his Slavic nickname implied, survived, and resumed his combat career with the First Gruppe in 1944.

Late on the 28th, the Second Gruppe moved from Vitry to Deelen, in the Netherlands. They saw no action on the 29th, but they were perfectly positioned the next day to intercept the final raid of Blitz Week, an attack on Kassel in deep central Germany. Aerial activity began early on 30 July, with attacks on the coastal airfields. A force of nearly two hundred B-17s was crossing the English coast by 0830. Surprisingly, the outbound escort consisted only of Spitfires, which turned back at the Dutch coast. The bombers' course took them directly over Woensdrecht airfield, by now fully recovered from the early-morning B-26 raid described at the beginning of this chapter. The fighters from Woensdrecht, part of II/JG 1, were the first to hit the bombers, followed by 8/JG 26 from Lille, which made stern attacks that downed two B-17s. Uffz. Gerd Wiegand of the 8th Staffel was shot down by the defenders' fire, but he bailed out without injury.

The First and Second Gruppen were held on the ground to await the bombers' return. They were then made part of a concentrated attack force containing fighters from all four of the German defensive zones—the first time this tactic had been used. The Second Gruppe attacked the bomber stream near Appeldoorn. They downed two B-17s, but lost three FW 190s. One pilot crash-landed his aircraft, but died of his injuries in the hospital. The other two pilots, Fw. Wilhelm Mayer and Fw. Gerhard Vogt, were inseparable companions on the ground, and the gossips in their Staffel took malicious delight in the fact that both were shot down on the same mission. Mayer made a successful crash landing, suffering only light injuries. When Vogt's fighter was hit, he first attempted to ram his target, then bailed out, seriously wounded.

The First Gruppe also made a successful attack on the homeward-bound bomber force, claiming two B-17s destroyed, in return for one plane and pilot. The day's battles with the B-17s were brought to an end by the arrival of the American escort. The American fighters—107 P-47s from all three operational groups, the 4th, 56th, and 78th—found the bombers under attack by "150-200 German fighters," many of which turned their attention to the Thunderbolts after evading the Americans' initial attack. Three P-47s were claimed by pilots of the First and Second Gruppen. No JG 26 aircraft were shot down by the P-47s, which nevertheless emerged the clear victors overall after their heaviest combat to date. The 335th Squadron of the 4th Group claimed 5-0-2 FW 190s, while losing one pilot. The 56th Group claimed 3-1-1 Bf 109s and 0-0-1 FW 190s, while losing two pilots. The 78th Group, at this time the most successful American fighter unit, claimed 10-0-3 FW 190s and 6-0-1 Bf 109s, but lost three pilots, including their commanding officer. On this mission Maj. Eugene Roberts of the 78th scored the fist triple victory in the ETO, while Capt. Charles London of the same unit downed two fighters, and returned to Duxford as the Eighth Air Force's first ace. The total score clearly favored the Americans; their victims probably belonged to the two north German Jagdgeschwader, JG 1 and JG 11.

The Germans flew nearly 300 defensive sorties on the 30th; of these about forty were second sorties. Although a large concentration of fighters was achieved in time to attack the homeward-bound bombers, and arrangements for the replenishment and control of the force proved satisfactory, the results were disappointing. Only twelve bombers were brought down. The Schlageter fighters were awarded four victory credits for B-17s; several more of their claims were rejected by the RLM or were never filed by the Geschwader.

Some Blitz Week targets were in north Germany. The Third Gruppe in Nordholz scored heavily against the unescorted bomber formations. The newest member of this Gruppe, Hptm. Staiger of the 12th Staffel, shot down no fewer than five heavy bombers during the week. Other successful pilots were Hptm. Mietusch and Obfw. Kemethmueller. Only two of the Gruppe's Bf 109s were lost; one pilot was killed and the other injured.

The months of July and August saw the first evidence of a new Luftwaffe commitment to a defense in depth against the American air offensive. Thirteen Jagdgruppen and Zerostoerergruppen were added to the home defenses; some were newly formed, and others transferred from other fronts. However, for nearly two weeks following Blitz Week the skies over the Channel coast were free of combat. On 12 August, 330 B-17s from sixteen bomb groups were sent to attack industrial targets in the Ruhr. The 1st Bomb Wing lost cohesion and was forced to bomb targets of opportunity. The P-47 escort was unable to provide effective cover for the scattered bombers. Only one group, the 4th, made contact with German fighters, claiming 1-0-1 FW 190s and 3-1-0 Bf 109s. The FW 190 belonged to 8/JG 26, and its pilot was killed; he was the Geschwader's only casualty. The First and Second Gruppen made numerous attacks on the unescorted bombers and claimed eleven B-17s destroyed, although the RLM ultimately rejected four of the claims. The Americans' bomber losses totaled twenty-five B-17s.

One of the victors on the morning of the 12th was Uffz. Jan Schild, who was flying his 115th combat sortie with the 2nd Staffel. His First Gruppe took off from Woensdrecht shortly after 0800 and formed up for an attack on the bomber stream, which was flying southeast up the Scheldt Estuary at 16,000 feet. Schild had never seen so many aircraft in the air at one time. The bomber formations appeared to be putting on a fireworks exhibition. Each bomber was wreathed in smoke from its own gunfire, while tracers sprayed in all directions. The bombers grew in the fighters' sights with unbelievable speed. The German pilots had all been taught that they had only two seconds to get off an effective burst of cannon fire. Schild's attack forced one B-17 to drop behind its formation. He lost sight of it after he dove away, but he was credited with a separation. Although this appears to have been a rather routine interception, Schild considers it to have been one of his most memorable missions—and with good reason. Since his return from the Soviet Union, he had claimed four B-17s shot down, but this one was the first to be confirmed. In fact, this was his first confirmed victory of any kind, after a year in France, the Low Countries, and the Soviet Union with 2/JG 26.

THE SCHWEINFURT-REGENSBURG RAID

As dawn broke on 17 August, the clear skies over German-occupied western Europe presaged a major Allied operation. The efficient German radio intercept service on the coast had been picking up test signals for hours; this was an infallible warning of a major raid. The radio chatter continued as the bombers taxied, took off, and assembled. Radio silence was the rule once the combat boxes crossed the English coast, but by then the defenses had had at least six hours to prepare for the coming attack.

The regular occupants of Woensdrecht airfield, II/JG 1, had recently been reinforced by a second Gruppe, Hptm. Borris's I/JG 26. Several recent raids had passed directly over the field, which was on a direct line between the American bomber bases and the Ruhr. Oberst Grabmann, the commander of the local Jafue and a prewar Schlageter Gruppenkommandeur, was quick to get Woensdrecht's Focke-Wulfs airborne; in fact, they took off before the American armada began crossing the English coast at 1035. The force headed in the predicted direction, and the fighters had only to climb in circles above their own field and await the enemy's arrival.

The enemy force consisted of 146 B-17s of the 4th Bomb Wing, escorted by P-47s of the 353rd Fighter Group, which was flying its first combat mission. The bombers were en route to bomb the Messerschmitt factory at Regensburg, following which they were to proceed to North Africa. At this time the Germans did not know the bombers' target or final destination, but they were quick to observe and profit from the straight course necessitated by the distances involved. The four Bf 109 Staffeln of the Third Gruppe were ordered at 1055 to take off from Amsterdam's Schipol airport and head due south to intercept the bombers. This force was in all probability led by Obstlt. Priller and accompanied by the Stabs-schwarm and the 8th Staffel.

The first fighters to approach the American force were the FW 190s of II/JG 1; these drew off the entire P-47 group, leaving the bombers unprotected. Karl Borris took advantage of the opportunity to lead his formation in a classical head-on attack. He was up sun and slightly above the bombers, in perfect position. The Focke-Wulfs swept around in a left turn and raced through the Fortresses. The fighters traversed the second combat wing in the strung-out formation and then hit the trailing wing. Borris's own target, the last aircraft in the middle formation, burst into flames, sheered from the formation, and dove to earth—the first loss of the day for either side. Several B-17s in the rear combat wing began to smoke from dam-aged engines. As was their custom, the Focke-Wulfs broke in all directions after their firing pass, some flashing between the bombers in the individual boxes. None of the German fighters were seriously damaged during their attack.

Karl Borris had a well-founded reputation as a martinet. He believed in strict adherence to orders and regulations both on the ground and in the air. Such discipline was a requirement for sur-vival in western skies, and it gained him the respect of his pilots. His attack had been successful; several B-17s, and no Focke-Wulfs, had suffered fatal damage. His orders thus satisfied, Borris did not at-tempt to re-form his Gruppe for a second attack but was content to let his pilots search for stragglers while remaining in the general area of their base at Woensdrecht; there would be plenty of time to land and refuel before the expected return of the bomber force.

The next major attack was made by the Third Gruppe. Upon its arrival it bored in on the rear of the bomber stream, which was totally unprotected by fighters. The Messerschmitts formed up, turned, and attacked the rear wing head-on. Only one bomber, the target of Obfw. Heinz Kemethmueller, was forced from the forma-tion by this initial attack, but the German pilots came back in repeatedly over the next fifteen minutes. Their Kommandeur, Klaus Mietusch, shared some of Borris's aloofness on the ground, but presented an altogether different personality in the air. A true "death or glory" pilot when targets were in sight, Mietusch paid no apparent heed to his own personal safety or that of his pilots, who were under his orders to keep up the attack until forced by damage, low fuel, or low ammunition to break off. They concentrated on the rear two combat wings. At 1141, the Messerschmitts, accompanied by a few FW 190s, which were probably from Priller's Stabsschwarm, were seen by the Americans to approach the rear wing from six o'clock low, pull ahead and, after a climbing turn, attack head-on. Three damaged Fortresses dropped back after this firing pass. One was the 95th Group's *Bay-Be*. Its right waist gunner, William Binnebose, describes the events of the next few minutes, and their ironic dénouement:

> After we could no longer keep up with the rest of the group, Lieutenant Baker turned around, and we headed back toward England. As soon as the fighters saw this, they knew we were theirs. They made a pass at us from the front, eleven o'clock, at the same altitude, so that neither our top turret nor our ball gunner could get a good shot at them. They knocked out the inboard engine on the left, and as the inboard engine on the right had been knocked out by flak, we were in very bad shape. I was wounded on this last attack.
>
> The next attack came from just one plane; it came in on my side of the plane, at four o'clock high. We were hit by this plane and got the order to bail out. . . . I was taken to a hospital and had my foot taken care of by a Belgian doctor. I was then taken to a German naval hospital in nearby Beverloo. Shortly after I was put in a bed, they brought in a German pilot, Fw. Werner Kraft of the 9th Staffel of JG 26, and put him in a bed in the same room. With the help of a Luftwaffe boy we talked to each other. Kraft was the pilot of the lone last Messerschmitt that had come in at us. From our discussion and his sketches, it became clear that it was my gun that had shot him down.

The other two B-17s that pulled away from the rear box were shot down by the lurking Focke-Wulfs of the First Gruppe. A Messerschmitt pilot from the 12th Staffel was shot down and killed on his pass through the rear B-17 wing; he was JG 26's first fatality for the day. Another of Mietusch's pilots, Oblt. Hans-Georg Dippel, Kapitaen of the 9th Staffel, bailed out uninjured after cartwheeling through the bomber formation in a scene spectacular enough to stand out on a day filled with mind-numbing horrors. Dippel had made a basic error by attempting a rear attack on the lead group of the lead wing; this subjected his Messerschmitt to the fire of at least sixty bomber gunners. The Third Gruppe suffered one further loss before the end of its mission. After the 353rd Fighter Group had turned about to return to England, its commander, Major Loren McCollom, saw a formation of Bf 109s 2,000 feet below him, at 24,000 feet. He dove on them undetected and loosed a burst from his eight .50s at the tail-end aircraft, observing "many strikes and sheets of flame." The plane fell away out of control, and McCollom had scored his group's first victory. The Messerschmitt pilot, Heinz Kemethmueller, was saved by his armor plate; his only injuries were to his hands, when the control column was shot from them. He stayed with his disintegrating plane and bailed out at the approved low altitude, destined for a short hospital stay.

So far that morning, Oberst Grabmann's job had been unusually easy. First, the heavy bombers had made a direct flight across Holland, with none of the usual feints and turns. Second, the diversionary attacks on coastal targets that normally preceded the main force were uncustomarily absent. Not until the heavy bombers were well across the coast did the German radars begin picking up new activity over the Channel. Five small-scale raids were ultimately plotted. They could be countered with the forces already available near the coast, without hindering the German concentration against the expected return of the heavy bombers. The overall Allied plan had obviously gone seriously awry.

The four Staffeln of II/JG 26 had spent the previous night at separate dispersal fields, as was their custom. They had not been assembled in time to meet the first wave of B-17s, but they were available in Staffel strength to counter air raids on coastal targets. The Spitfires escorting the first such raid, a B-26 attack on the dispersal field at Bryas, successfully fended off the German defenders. One shot down a Focke-Wulf from 10/JG 26, killing its pilot. The FW 190s, heavily outnumbered by the Spitfires, quickly broke off their attack.

Meanwhile, the Spitfire high cover took on a Staffel of Bf 109s. This was 11/JG 26, which had apparently not taken part in the attack on the bomber stream. This Staffel, which according to some records had been employed until recently as an operational training unit, was usually detailed to subsidiary tasks such as this one. It was led today by an enlisted pilot who had just returned to combat duty after a long tour as an instructor. He was surprised by the high cover before he could lead his attack on the B-26s and responded with the maneuver used to escape from Spitfires for the past three years—he broke for the deck. The Spitfires were new Mk IXBs, and one was able to catch the Staffel leader after a long chase and shoot him down. The surviving Messerschmitts did not re-form, and they were never seen by the Marauder formation.

Only one more of the coastal attacks was opposed by German fighters, this time with somewhat greater success. Twenty Typhoons were sent to attack the JG 26 base at Lille-Vendeville. They raced across the Channel at minimum altitude, to avoid radar detection. This type of attack had proven as difficult for the Germans to defend against from the air as the Jabo attacks on southern England had been for the RAF. However, this time a pair of 8th Staffel FW 190s found themselves in position to make a single, long-range pass on one of the escorting squadrons. One No. 182 Sqd. Typhoon was hit and fell away in a spin. Its pilot regained control, but it crashed into the sea on its return flight.

At 1307, the surviving bombers of the 4th Bomb Wing completed their bomb run at Regensburg and made a hard right turn, heading for the Austrian Alps and, ultimately, North Africa. The German defenses were caught by surprise. Thirteen Gruppen of single-engined fighters had been assembled along the bombers' assumed return route; this was the largest defensive force yet seen over Europe. It was not to be wasted, however—it was perfectly positioned to oppose the second B-17 raid of the day, the 1st Bomb Wing's attack on the ball-bearing factories of Schweinfurt.

The Allied disaster in the making was the result of the blind adherence to a plan long after external circumstances—the English weather—had destroyed its underlying rationale. The original intention was to surprise the defenders by passing a second force close along the track of the first, timed to catch the German fighters on the ground for refueling. But fog at the 1st Bomb Wing's inland airfields prevented the B-17s from taking off on time. The delay was prolonged by the decision to wait for the return and refueling of the Regensburg force's fighter escort. Not until 1426 did the 230 B-17s of the Schweinfurt force begin crossing the English coast. At 1439, the Third Gruppe was ordered to take off from Schipol; at 1443 the fighters at Woensdrecht, once again in the bombers' path, began taking to the air. The only component of JG 26 not included in this initial response to the second raid was the Second Gruppe. The Gruppe's aircraft were instead ordered to concentrate at the small field of Lille-Nord. The RAF radio intercept service took note of the lack of radio activity from the Second Gruppe's usual airfields. The Eighth Bomber Command saw in the Gruppe's absence from the battle a rare example of a positive, demonstrated benefit from the coastal raids flown in conjunction with every major mission. Its post-mission report stated:

> The elimination of the formidable Vitry-Lille wings, considered the elite fighter wings of the GAF, during the inward flight by diversionary attacks is worthy of note. These units have consistently provided our forces with the stiffest opposition encountered in this theater.

The revised American plan allotted the Schweinfurt force a much larger fighter escort than its predecessor. Eight squadrons of Spitfires accompanied the B-17s as far as Antwerp. There they were to be relieved by two groups of P-47s, which could stay with the bombers as far as Eupen, on the Belgian side of the German border.

The Spitfires fended off the early attacks by the Woensdrecht fighters and shot down one 3rd Staffel FW 190, whose pilot bailed out. One of the two P-47 groups, the 4th, missed rendezvous, and never reached its assigned position over the leading wings. The other unit, the 78th Fighter Group, carried out its escort of the rear B-17 wings exactly as ordered. It saw little combat, as the German fighters sheered off upon sighting the Thunderbolts and headed for the less well-defended van of the bomber stream. At this time, one B-17 of the leading group spun out and broke up after a head-on attack by the Focke-Wulfs of I/JG 26.

Oberst Grabmann timed the approach of most of his defenders so that they contacted the bombers immediately after the escort turned back, as expected, at Eupen. For the next two hours, the bombers were battered by as many as nine Jagdgruppen at one time—an intensity of attack far in excess of anything previously

189

experienced. Klaus Mietusch's Third Gruppe was among these attackers, which shot down twenty-nine B-17s. The leading wing
suffered by far the heaviest losses; the absence of an escort had
permitted the first German defenders to prepare well-coordinated
attacks in the undisturbed air ahead of the formation. Once the
cohesiveness of the leading wing had been broken, successful attacks
sought them out as the least well-defended part of the formation, in
accord with the usual German pattern.

The German attacks slacked off when the B-17s began their
bomb run on Schweinfurt. On the bombers' return flight over Germany, the bombers were struck by only the occasional fighter. The
Germans were as exhausted as the Americans; their controllers were
counting heavily on the attack of the only fresh Gruppe left in the
area—Wutz Galland's II/JG 26. Prior to takeoff, Galland had lec-
tured his pilots on the importance of their mission to the Father-
land, reminding them of Goering's admonition that the bombers
were to be attacked "at any cost." Galland now led three Staffeln
southeast, along the reciprocal of the bombers' course, and met the
bomber stream head-on, just east of the German border with Belgium. His attack caught the lead wing of the rear half of the formation and cost it two B-17s. Galland then re-formed his
Stabsschwarm and led it toward the front of this half of the formation, for a second head-on attack.

At this moment the Germans were stunned by fighters attacking from their rear—from the direction of Germany. Colonel Hub
Zemke had led his "Wolfpack," the P-47s of the 56th Fighter
Group, farther east than they had ever flown before. He had reached
the rendezvous point, exactly on time and course, and had then
overflown the B-17 formation unobserved by the German attackers,
who were thus set up to be struck a severe blow. Wutz Galland
disappeared after the initial bounce by the Thunderbolts, apparently
the victim of Capt. Walker "Bud" Mahurin, whose target blew up
under the fire of his eight machine guns, leaving only a smoke ring
in the sky to mark its former location. Galland's remains were
discovered two months later, buried with the wreckage of his aircraft
twelve feet deep in the soft soil near Maastricht.

In the prolonged melee that followed, the Thunderbolt pilots
claimed the destruction of 7-0-1 FW 190s; 4-1-1 Bf 109s; and 5-0-7
twin-engined fighters. The total German losses in this action appear

to have been five FW 190s, one Bf 109, and four Bf 110s. II/JG 26 lost a second FW 190, whose pilot bailed out with light injuries.

Zemke's tactics broke up the attack formations of the German pilots, who were forced to turn on the Thunderbolts. The 56th Group lost three P-47s; claims for these P-47s were filed by five German pilots. When the 56th Group was relieved by the 353rd, there were no large Luftwaffe formations in the area; the remaining German fighters were scattered far and wide, searching for stragglers. Obfw. Glunz was the only German pilot to make a successful attack on the bomber stream after the arrival of the escort. Calmly sticking to his orders despite the chaos around him, he maintained contact with the bombers and finally shot down a 305th Bomb Group B-17 northwest of Diest.

The final leg of the bombers' homeward-bound flight was covered by Spitfires. It was uneventful, with one exception. Lt. Helmut Hoppe, Kapitaen of 4/JG 26, attempted to join a formation of No. 403 Sqd. Spitfires—it is not known whether this was by accident or design. In the wild scramble that followed, the propeller of one Spitfire cut the fuselage of another in two. Hoppe claimed the victory, since he was the German pilot responsible for the destruction of the Spitfire; in the absence of a confirming witness, the claim was, however, denied.

When the day finally ended and the scores were totaled, the Schlageter fighters had claimed the destruction of seventeen B-17s, one of their greatest successes against the "dicke Autos" (fat cars, the code name for enemy heavy bombers) for any day of the war. The pilots of JG 26 also claimed one Typhoon, one Spitfire, and one Thunderbolt. Their losses totaled five pilots killed and five wounded. The event that made the deepest impression on the pilots was the disappearance of the popular and gifted Wutz Galland, a stark reminder to even the most self-confident among them of the fragile threads on which their lives were suspended.

STEADY PRESSURE

The Schweinfurt-Regensburg mission cost the Eighth Air Force sixty B-17s destroyed, 16 percent of the 376 dispatched. For nearly three weeks thereafter, the American bombers limited their attentions to coastal French targets. The massive escorts employed over these short ranges made interception of the heavy bombers unprofitable for the Luftwaffe. JG 26 was airborne daily, however, seeking out opportunities to strike the enemy. On 19 August, the 4th Staffel caught six No. 182 Sqd. Typhoons flying a Ramrod to Amiens and shot down three without loss to themselves. Later in the day, a B-17 raid on airfields in the Netherlands was met head-on by the Stab and the First and Third Gruppen. One Bf 109 and one FW 190 of JG 26 were shot down by the B-17 gunners; both pilots survived. Only two B-17s were lost to German fighters. The P-47 pilots of the 56th and 78th Groups claimed 9-0-3 and 1-0-1 single-engined fighters. Among these losses were three JG 26 aircraft; one Geschwader pilot was killed, and the other two were injured. No American fighters were lost in combat.

The 56th Group's Col. Hub Zemke was the most analytical of the American fighter commanders and had by this time developed a very effective escort formation—which he was not yet advertising, as it did not meet the Eighth Bomber Command's requirements for close escort. Two of his Group's three squadrons flew on the flanks of their assigned bomber wing, their flights flying in loose finger-fours at staggered altitudes. The third squadron free-lanced; it either positioned itself above the bombers, ready to answer calls for assistance, or, if the Group was assigned to the leading wing of the formation, ranged far ahead to break up head-on attacks. Zemke insisted that his men adhere to the tactics best suited to his unit's heavy P-47Cs and early P-47Ds—dive, attack, zoom, and recover. He obviously had the right idea; his unit would end the war with the largest number of aerial victory claims, and the highest claim-to-loss ratio, of any American fighter group in the Eighth Air Force.

The penetration of a well-disciplined fighter screen such as Zemke's would require larger German fighter formations, flying under closer ground control. Surprisingly, there was as yet no centralized command for the German fighter defenses, which were still the responsibility of the local Luftflotten and their control organizations, the Jafue. In early August, JG 26 was under the control of the Jafue for Holland and the Lower Rhine, but the growing strength of the forces behind it soon permitted JG 26 to redeploy on its old fields near the Franco-Belgian coast, where it became part of the 4th Jagddivision in Metz, a unit of Luftflotte 3's Jagdkorps II. Late in the month, the Stab and the Third Gruppe moved to Lille-Vendeville from Schipol; the First Gruppe transferred to Florennes from Grimbergen and Woensdrecht; and the Second Gruppe moved to its old field at Cambrai-Epinoy from Deelen and Volkel.

On 29 August, Obfw. Addi Glunz of the 4th Staffel was awarded the Knight's Cross—the only JG 26 noncommissioned officer ever to be so honored. The 25-year-old Glunz was the son of a North German railroad official. His only ambition from the time he first flew a glider was to become a fighter pilot. He began flight training in the Luftwaffe in the spring of 1939. He was chosen for fighter training and began that phase of his career in July 1940. He received the full peacetime-paced training course and reported to JG 52 in April 1941. By mid-July, he had scored five victories on the Eastern front. Adolf Galland pulled some strings and had him reassigned to JG 26. Glunz quickly became acclimated to life on the Kanalfront. His victory total climbed steadily; at forty it brought him the Knight's Cross.

Addi Glunz was to remain a combat pilot with the Second Gruppe until he transferred to jets in early 1945. His victory total is impressive, but he is prouder today of another record—he was never shot down or wounded in his entire career. He has yet to meet any other German veteran of the Western front who can make that claim. Glunz sums up the reasons for his success as follows:

> I must say that, first, I had a talent for flying small and maneuverable aircraft. I began flying at age sixteen and won my aerobatic license at age eighteen; I enjoyed frequent aerobatic flying, including heavy fighter aircraft later on. That led naturally to an exact control of the airplane. Second, my vision was especially good at great distances, so that I could usually sight the enemy very early and then had plenty of time to obtain a superior position for the attack. Third, I had the ability to fire accurately from any orientation. Finally, I took to heart Adolf Galland's principle—never abandon the possibility of attack. Attack even from a position of inferiority, to disrupt the enemy's plans. This often results in improving one's own position.
>
> Naturally, I was also very lucky.

Colonel Zemke's 56th Group had begun its climb to preeminence among the fighter units of Eighth Fighter Command. It had a worthy opponent in II/JG 26, which was taken over after Wutz

Galland's death by Hptm. Johannes Naumann. Every encounter between these two units appears to have resulted in vicious, all-out combat; battle honors at this time were about even. On 2 September, II/JG 26 moved up a notch in the standings. The 56th Group's thirty-six P-47s were escorting a force of B-17s that had aborted an attack on Brussels because of cloud cover. Naumann led his thirty FW 190s down through the dense clouds at 24,000 feet and zoomed up beneath the P-47s, entirely unseen. Two of the Thunderbolts in Colonel Zemke's own flight were shot down on the initial bounce. Colonel Zemke's plane was also hit, as was that of Lt. John Vogt, who continued to break into the attacks until he saw a chance to dive away. He then split-S'd for the deck, followed closely by Lt. Dietrich Kehl of the Second Gruppe Stabsschwarm. Vogt's aircraft could not pull full manifold pressure because of a punctured air duct, and Kehl's Focke-Wulf kept up with it easily. Vogt kept kicking his rudder pedals to disrupt Kehl's aim until the German had exhausted his 20-mm ammunition. Kehl then continued to pepper the Thunderbolt with machine-gun fire until the French coast was reached, at which time Kehl turned back in disgust. Vogt crash-landed his flying colander at Eastchurch. Kehl filed a claim for its destruction, which was rejected, as its crash had not been seen. No German plane was hit or even claimed hit in this engagement.

Zemke's Thunderbolts exacted a partial revenge the very next day, when they arrived at Romilly while the FW 190s of II/JG 26 and 8/JG 26 were making head-on passes on the B-17s of the 1st Bomb Wing. The bombers were putting up a stiff defense and had succeeded in shooting down three Focke-Wulfs. One pilot was killed, and two were injured; one of the latter was Fw. Gerhard Vogt, who was already back in combat after his injury on 30 July. Three B-17s were shot down before the P-47s successfully disrupted the attack, killing two JG 26 pilots. In return, one P-47 was shot down by a Second Gruppe pilot.

One of the 8th Staffel pilots on this mission was Uffz. Gerd Wiegand, whose single firing pass on a B-17 missed to one side. After refueling at Paris and returning to Lille-Nord he headed for his quarters and pulled out a battered copybook that he used as a diary. The events of the morning replayed themselves in his mind; he refused to speak to anyone until he had written everything down. He had missed his target once again. This had happened all too often during his thirty-eight combat sorties. His diary was filled with sketches of gunsights, lead angles, and calculations. None of the other replacement pilots showed such single-minded devotion to improving his combat skills. Wiegand had concluded that his long-range eyesight was inadequate and devised exercises to strengthen his eyes, which included staring into the sky and the sun for one hour each day. Such dedication could not help but ultimately bring success in combat, or so Wiegand told himself. He probably would not get another opportunity on that day, however; his FW 190 had sustained some minor damage and was undergoing repairs. It would have to be flight-tested before flying another combat mission. Shortly after the noon meal, Wiegand was summoned to check out his aircraft. We read in his diary:

> Takeoff from Lille at 1400—a test flight in my crate, "Black 10"—am over Merville at 6,000 meters [19,500 feet], when the Jafue reports: "Incoming dicke Ottos [sic] and Indians near Dunkirk." I climb to 7,000 meters [23,000 feet] and fly in that direction—perfect visibility, I can see the whole Valhalla approaching. I approach them in the sun and observe them closely—the bombers turn left—the fighter escort is thrown into disarray and also turns left, hanging beneath me like a cluster of grapes. I cut across their turn and dive beneath them—I approach the Ventura formation hidden by the light bellies of ten Spitfires. No one sees me. Fifty meters behind a Ventura, I open fire—I have to cut back on the gas—I almost ram the Ventura, which now blows apart. I dive away at full throttle. At ground level, the air is clear—the cigar-like fuselage of the Ventura lands on the Gravelines mole. The Gruppe had in the meantime taken off, but landed without making contact—the enemy formation had been reported too late.

A jubilant Gerd Wiegand rocked his wings vigorously as he swept across his landing field. The curse was broken. In his next fifty-one missions, Wiegand would bring down twenty-four more aircraft—a rate approaching one victory for each two combat sorties.

On 11 September, the Second Gruppe had another opportunity to counter a Typhoon raid. In late afternoon, thirty Focke-Wulfs took off from Beauvais to intercept a formation flying below radar altitude west of Dieppe. About halfway to the coast, they reached the enemy formation, which consisted of three squadrons of Typhoons, and dove on them from an altitude of 8,000 feet. Fw. Peter Crump fired at one from the left rear, causing it to trail a thick light-gray plume of smoke and dive away steeply. He soon found a second opponent in the by now general dogfight and, after a quick glance around, attacked from the right rear. It also smoked immediately. The pilot of the Typhoon, now down to ground level, steered toward a meadow directly beneath him; to Crump's astonishment, his landing gear was extended. The plane touched down smoothly, but while still at high speed hit a small group of trees that stood in the meadow and exploded in a fireball.

No Focke-Wulfs were hit in this encounter. The two Typhoons shot down were credited to Crump and Lt. Hoppe. Hptm. Naumann filed a third claim, but this was rejected. Naumann was again serving as Kapitaen of the 6th Staffel, having lost his job as II/JG 26 Gruppenkommandeur to Johannes Seifert. Major Seifert had been reprieved from his exile to Bulgaria after an appeal to General Galland. Since Seifert's old command at First Gruppe was now held by Hptm. Borris, Hptm. Naumann, the junior Gruppenkommandeur in the Geschwader, was bumped from his job to make room for Seifert.

DEFENSIVE REORGANIZATION

On 1 October, the designations of some of the Geschwader's twelve Staffeln were changed, in order to provide each Gruppe with four sequentially numbered Staffeln. To achieve this, one Staffel had to move to another Gruppe. The logical choice was the 8th, which had been separated from its nominal parent Third Gruppe for many months, and had never relinquished its FW 190s for Bf 109s. It became the 4th Staffel, joining the 1st, 2nd, and 3rd in the First Gruppe. The 8th had originated as the 4th Staffel of the Second Gruppe, but it had been renumbered and moved to the Third Gruppe in September 1939. Through all of these moves it kept its own unofficial identity as the Adamsonstaffel, after the cartoon character that had adorned its aircraft from 1939 to 1941.

The 10th Staffel remained in the Second Gruppe but became the 8th Staffel. The other redesignations were as follows: the 4th, 5th, and 6th became the 5th, 6th, and 7th Staffeln, all within the

Second Gruppe. In the Third Gruppe, the 7th became the 9th and the 9th became the 10th, while the 11th and 12th Staffeln retained their designations.

At this time the Luftwaffe tables of organization were revised to reflect the new standard, the four-Staffel Gruppe. The establishment strength of each JG 26 Gruppe was increased to sixty-eight airplanes and pilots. After adding in the four planes of the Geschwader Stabsschwarm, the total Geschwader establishment was 208 aircraft. The true strength was much less than this, however. On a typical day in late 1943, each Gruppe had in reality only forty-five airplanes, and of these only thirty were operational. Gruppe formations rarely contained more than thirty aircraft, and frequently they had only twenty.

In October, the Stab and the Third Gruppe were still at Lille; the Second Gruppe, at Cambrai. The First Gruppe moved to Wevelghem in October, and to Florennes in November. The flying units of the Geschwader were now based closer to one another than for some time previously, presenting opportunities for better coordination and control in the air. Their position in the front line gave them so little time for assembly, however, that JG 26 was never able to fly an intercept mission in Geschwader strength, although this became standard practice among the Jagdgeschwader based in Germany.

The German fighter defenses underwent their most significant reorganization of the war in October. RAF Bomber Command's successes at Hamburg and Peenemunde in July and August, along with the Americans' obvious determination to contest the daytime skies over Germany, had enraged Hitler. Goering in turn had dressed down Luftwaffe Chief of Staff Jeschonnek, who responded by committing suicide. Only then did a shocked and chastened High Command make a serious effort to strengthen the fighter organization, in the face of the Fuehrer's frequently expressed opposition to defensive measures. Genobst. Stumpf was given a new command, the Luftflotte Reich, with total responsibility for the aerial defense of Germany, including command of the antiaircraft regiments as well as both the day and the night fighters. These fighters came under "Beppo" Schmid's First Jagdkorps, which contained four Jagddivisionen. Feldmarschall Sperrle's Luftflotte 3 retained its responsibility for the defense of France, commanding for this purpose the Second Jagdkorps with its 4th Jagddivision. Jagd-geschwader 26 was positioned near the boundary between Stumpf's and Sperrle's Luftflotten and thus had occasion to come under the command of each.

THE MUENSTER RAID

As the sun rose on Sunday, 10 October, the crisp, clear skies over western Europe and a heavy flow of radio traffic from England foretold a large American air attack. As the morning wore on with no indication that the bombers had taken off, Oberst Grabmann, still Jafue in Holland, deduced that the target would be in the Low Countries or northwestern Germany and began concentrating his defenses accordingly. At 1130, the First Gruppe took off from Lille-Nord, heading for the I/JG 1 base at Deelen. Shortly thereafter, the Second Gruppe left its bases and flew to the large permanent Luft-waffe base at Rheine. By luck or good intelligence, the latter Gruppe had been placed within twenty-five miles of Eighth Bomber Com-mand's target for the day, Muenster.

At 1348, the leading 3rd Bomb Division (the former 4th Bomb Wing) began crossing the English coast at Felixstowe. It was fol-lowed fifteen minutes later by the 1st Bomb Division (formerly Wing); a total of 274 B-17s was dispatched. At 1408, a Gruppe of Bf 109s became the first German defenders to leave the ground, eight minutes before the 3rd Bomb Division reached the Dutch coast. The direction of the attackers having been well established, the FW 190s of I/JG 26 and I/JG 1 were ordered to take off from Deelen; a few minutes later II/JG 26 flew their Focke-Wulfs off the runway at Rheine.

The German fighters continued to concentrate along the track of the bombers, which was tracing a line due east across the Neth-erlands. At 1440, the 2nd Bomb Division's diversionary flight over the North Sea aborted, freeing up all the remaining defenders. At least thirteen Jagdgruppen and Zerstoerergruppen, approximately 350 fighters, would ultimately engage the Americans.

A direct course to Muenster had been ordered so that the escorting P-47s could stay with the bombers all the way to the target. A rookie group, the 352nd, kept the leading 3rd Bomb Division well covered until 1448, when its Thunderbolts turned back over Dorsten, Germany. Its relief, the equally new 355th Fighter Group, was still fogbound in England. A careful American plan had once again been spoiled by the English weather. The patient Germans saw their opportunity, and they instantly took advantage of it. The onslaught began.

The crewmen in the leading bomb wing saw an estimated 200 German fighters forming up in front of their combat boxes. At 1453, nine minutes away from Muenster, Schwaerme of FW 190s began level attacks on the low 100th Bomb Group from dead ahead. The Americans estimated that the Focke-Wulfs closed to fifty to seventy-five yards before flicking over and diving away. Within seven minutes, the formation of the "Bloody Hundredth" group had vanished. Six Fortresses had been destroyed; six others were turning back with smoking engines. All were doomed; only one of the thirteen B-17s dispatched by the group returned to England.

Attacks alternated between head-on passes by FW 190s and Bf 109s from a number of Jagdgruppen and rocket barrages from Me 410s positioned behind the leading wing. The fighters broke away briefly when the bombers came within range of the Muenster flak defenses. After the bomb run, the German fighters resumed their attacks, threatening to wipe out the leading wing completely. The high group was singled out after the destruction of the 100th, and lost eight of its eighteen bombers. Rocket attacks by Bf 110s and Me 410s resumed, followed by more head-on attacks by single-engined fighters. Four more B-17s were lost. Finally, as it appeared that the entire wing would be annihilated, the P-47s of the 56th Group arrived to begin their withdrawal escort. They sailed into the middle of the melee, splitting up into flights of four to reach as many German attackers as possible. Lt. Robert Johnson's Thunderbolt was badly damaged by a FW 190, but not until he had shot down two planes to become an ace. Maj. David Schilling of the 56th also downed his fifth German fighter on this mission, as did Capt. Walter Beckham of the 353rd Fighter Group. A number of Second Gruppe fighters continued to attack the bombers in the trailing wings, despite being low on fuel. All but one managed to avoid the attentions of the Thunderbolts; one 8th Staffel pilot was hit by a P-47 and survived a spectacular, cartwheeling attempt at a crash landing at Twente.

Most of the Geschwader's successes came after the bombers

had turned for home. At least six B-17s were claimed destroyed during this period; in return, the bomber gunners were able to shoot down and injure two Third Gruppe Bf 109 pilots. By evening, the Schlageter Geschwader could chalk up another one-sided victory—at least seven B-17s were confirmed destroyed, at a cost of three injured pilots. The other German defenders also did well; for a total loss of twenty-five fighters and twelve crewmen, they had destroyed thirty B-17s and one P-47. Nine of the German losses were twin-engined Bf 110s and Me 410s; it was obvious that these effective bomber destroyers would have to be shielded from the attentions of the American escorts if they were to remain a viable defensive weapon.

THE SECOND SCHWEINFURT RAID

The most successful daylight operation for the twin-engined fighters came only four days later, on the Eighth Air Force's "Black Thursday," 14 October. There were loud groans in the briefing rooms of the B-17 groups as the drapes were drawn back on the target maps and the men learned that their target was to be Schweinfurt. Their fields were blanketed in chilly autumn fog, but when the morning weather reconnaissance reported clear air over the continent, the crews were ordered to their planes. The first of 291 B-17s took off at 1012.

Once again the Americans were sabotaged by the English weather. Two escort groups of P-47s were never able to take off, and a third never found the bombers. Once more the bombers' course traced a straight line across the Low Countries, to maximize the distance over which they could be escorted. Once it was established that a deep penetration raid was in the offing, the German controller tried a new tactic. The first Gruppe of fighters to reach the bomber stream was ordered to attack the escorting fighters rather than the bombers. Over Walcheren Island, twenty Bf 109s, probably from III/JG 1, bounced part of the 353rd Fighter Group, which was covering the van of the bomber force. The attack was fended off by one of the three American squadrons, while the rest maintained their coverage of the bombers. Of the other German fighters that had taken off from Belgium and the southern Netherlands, some attacked the bomber wings farthest from the few American fighters, but most were content to parallel the bomber stream and await the inevitable departure of the P-47s.

The moment the escort turned back near Aachen, the FW 190s and Bf 109s began closing in. The Focke-Wulfs made their attack first—at twelve o'clock high, by Schwaerme. The memoirs of several bomber crewmen refer to these fighters as the Abbeville Kids, by this time a semi-mythical unit well known throughout the Allied air forces for their yellow cowlings and the viciousness of their attacks. Yellow theater markings were carried by many German units, but it is known that II/JG 26 was among the first formations to attack; thus the Americans' identification of the German unit was literally, if unwittingly, correct.

There is no evidence that the Gruppen of JG 26 flew more than one mission apiece against the raiders, and there is no information at all on the activities of the Third Gruppe. Three Second Gruppe pilots claimed to have shot down B-17s between 1330 and 1400 hours. Addi Glunz's logbook entry matches up with the circumstances of the day's only P-47 loss, and he was probably responsible for shooting down this 353rd Group aircraft, although his claim was not filed.

The First Gruppe's attack was made at about 1400. The unit took off from Deelen at 1255 and headed south to intercept the large enemy formation, which was reported to be over Antwerp with an escort of Thunderbolts and Spitfires. The fighters' course placed them in a favorable position for a head-on attack, which brought down two bombers. A 3rd Staffel pilot was hit by the bombers' fire and bailed out, but he died soon after reaching the ground.

Although the role of the Schlageter Geschwader in "Black Thursday" proved to be a minor one, sixty B-17s were destroyed by the Luftwaffe in three hours and fourteen minutes of continuous attacks. The tactics found successful over Muenster were repeated again and again. The twin-engined fighters first fired rockets from outside the range of the defensive gunners. The explosions of the rockets disrupted the bomber formations and facilitated the head-on attacks of the single-engined fighters. Every German fighter unit in western Europe was ultimately employed—833 combat sorties were flown. The Germans lost only thirty-eight fighters. The Wehrmacht communiqué claimed that 121 American aircraft had been brought down. The true losses were only half that, but it was obvious to both sides that the defenders had won a stunning victory. The American doctrine of unescorted daylight bombing was dead. No more deep penetration raids would be made into Germany until the bombers could be escorted all the way to the target. The operational training of the first two groups of truly long-ranged American fighters, Lockheed P-38 Lightnings, was rushed to completion.

THE DUEREN RAID

The next penetration of German airspace was ordered for 20 October. It was to be an attack on Dueren, near the western German border. The mission was to be flown despite reports of heavy cloud cover over the continent, and it was to be the first American use of the British Oboe blind-bombing aid. Once airborne, the bombers found cirrus clouds as high as 30,000 feet, and their formations were quickly split up. Only 114 of the 212 bombers dispatched were able to drop their bombs, with little success. Nine B-17s were lost.

The day proved to be a minor disaster for both sides. II/JG 26 was ordered to take off from Cambrai, through low-lying rain clouds. Nothing went right, beginning with the assembly of the unit. The Gruppe formation broke up completely while penetrating the cloud deck. Because the cloud tops were at widely different altitudes, the emerging pilots could see only a few of their own planes. Fw. Crump found himself flying with only his wingman. This Rotte came face to face with the bomber formation over Brussels. They then flew to one side of it, while trying to climb as high as possible. Crump remembers the magnificent sight—the sun beaming down; the deep blue sky above; the clouds below like cotton. And in between, the bomber formation pressed on to the southeast at 18,000 feet. There was not another German plane in sight. It was two lonely fighter pilots against an armada. Crump's plan was to surprise the formation and its fighter escort from the greatest possible altitude, attacking its lead aircraft from the sun. However, their climb was cut short by the intervention of two Thunderbolts. At this altitude, about 34,000 feet, and in this combat situation, the two Germans had to concede the superiority of the "Donnerbolzen" (Thunderbolts) and their turbo-superchargers. In Crump's words, the short-winded Focke-Wulfs "hung limp and bloated in the sky, like two little sausages." The sharp-eyed Crump spotted the P-47s in time to break into their attack, firing off all six of his guns. He and his wingman avoided further attacks by using their "emergency brakes"; that is, by spinning out. This maneuver was only used in desperate situations; in this case it was successful.

Peter Crump's Focke-Wulf came out of its spin in a vertical dive. It began to shudder. The entire surface of the wings was covered in condensation. He did not dare load the wings further by pulling back on the stick to end the dive. Past the vertical, the aircraft began slowly to pull out by itself, and at 1,000 feet Crump had it back in level flight. Today he is still curious as to his speed in the dive; a glance at the airspeed indicator showed the needle pegged out at 660 miles per hour.

Crump's next problem was right beneath him—the continuous cloud deck. No gap in the clouds was to be seen, and he had no idea where he was. Recalling his scanty training in blind flying, he carefully leveled his aircraft and dove. He caught sight of the ground—a patch of woods. That was just enough to get his bearings; he was over the Ardennes, near the German border. Crump landed at an emergency field. While taxiing in, he damaged his elevator on a piece of wood lying in the grass, bringing the mission to an appropriately miserable end. One bit of good news awaited him, however; his wingman had landed safely at Bonn-Hangelar.

Four JG 26 pilots are known to have claimed victories over B-17s and P-47s, but German losses to the Americans were heavy. JG 26 lost six pilots killed and two wounded, while nine of its aircraft were destroyed. All of the JG 26 casualties were newly arrived replacements. It is certain that none of the four pilots shot down by P-47s had the skill or experience Peter Crump needed to survive after being bounced at 34,000 feet.

The Geschwader's major success of the day was gained by Fw. Gerd Wiegand's Schwarm. The Adamsonstaffel was still operating independently from Lille-Nord. Wiegand's Focke-Wulfs scrambled at 0925 on the report of a large formation crossing the coast, which proved to consist of Spitfires. Wiegand led his small force in an attack, from behind and below an isolated section. The surprise attack was completely successful. According to Gerd Wiegand's records, each of the four members of the Schwarm downed a Spitfire. In reality, two No. 485 Sqd. Spitfires crashed immediately, and a third made it back to England before its engine seized; its pilot then bailed out safely. Surprisingly, the First Gruppe never filed claims for these victories.

Throughout 1943, the Geschwader's pilots engaged in frequent battles with RAF fighters over the coastal regions. Few of these combats have been described in this book, as they were small in scale and had little effect on the overall course of the air war. Occasionally, the Geschwader would suffer a serious casualty. Such was the case on 24 October, when Hptm. Kurt Ebersberger, Kapitaen of the 4th Staffel, was hit by Spitfires after intercepting a B-26 formation. Ebersberger jumped from his plane, but he was too low for his parachute to open. His victory total at the time of his death was twenty-eight. Oblt. Wolfgang Neu was named as Ebersberger's successor. At 35 years of age, Neu was the oldest pilot in the Geschwader. A reservist, Neu realized that he was not a very proficient pilot. He soon voluntarily began flying missions as Fw. Gerd Wiegand's wingman. Wiegand, who now had the highest score in his Staffel, was permitted to lead the entire unit in the air.

The hard-driving Wiegand soon had the 4th Staffel performing up to his own standards of excellence. On 13 November, the Adamsonstaffel was the only unit of JG 26 to make a successful attack on the heavy bombers. The target was Bremen, and Wiegand led the Staffel toward a gaggle of returning bombers over Zwolle. The P-47s had just made rendezvous and had taken up position in front of and above the bombers. Wiegand dove on the bombers, zoomed up, and shot down a P-47, for his eighth victory. Two bombers were downed by his Staffel, which suffered the loss of one FW 190, whose pilot bailed out uninjured.

At 0939 the next morning, Obfw. Addi Glunz took off from Cambrai on a rare lone mission, for which he neither wanted nor needed a wingman. His orders were to shoot down an RAF Mosquito that was returning from its morning reconnaissance mission to the Ruhr. This was a most unusual assignment, but the controllers had been plotting the Mosquito's course for some time and felt that they could lead a pilot to an interception. Addi Glunz, the most proficient pilot in the Second Gruppe, was the man for the job. He climbed steadily through thick gray rain clouds. He leveled out at 28,000 feet, 2,000 feet above the clouds. Here the sky was clear and blue; the sun's glare off the cloud tops gave Glunz the feeling that he was sledding across a blinding white field of snow.

The controller's calculations proved correct. Glunz caught sight of a shadow—and there was the Mosquito, hurtling along just above the fluffy white cloud tops. The Focke-Wulf was 1,600 feet above it. The German pilot pushed his stick gently forward and dove beneath the Mosquito, which maintained its course, streaming a thin white condensation trail. Glunz climbed, very slowly, squinting through his Revi gunsight until the Mosquito filled the circle. One press on the firing knob; a brief salvo of fifty rounds; and the Mosquito and its crew exploded into a million fragments of wood, metal, and flesh. The debris floated slowly earthward, to litter the rain-soaked soil of northern France. Shortly after 1000 hours, Addi Glunz's Focke-Wulf roared across its home field, its wings rocking to announce its pilot's 45th victory.

HARDER BATTLES

As the autumn weather along JG 26's portion of the Kanalfront was settling into its usual dreary routine, the Eighth Air Force shifted its attention to targets in northern Germany. The first P-38 group to reach operational status, the 55th, would shortly provide the bomber with their first escorts to such distant targets as Wilhelmshaven and Bremen. The Lightnings' first penetration of JG 26's defensive territory along the French coast came on 25 November. Bad weather had canceled the planned heavy bomber raid. While Thunderbolts of the 56th and 353rd Fighter Groups were flying the first P-47 dive bombing mission, an attack on the airfield at St. Omer, the 55th Group's P-38s flew a supporting sweep over Lille. It was the latter fighter formation that the Germans chose to contest.

Major Seifert led the 6th and 8th Staffeln of his Second Gruppe up from Cambrai shortly after 1300. Fw. Crump was leading the second element in the Kommandeur's Stabsschwarm. The Gruppe's twenty FW 190s climbed to the northwest toward the approaching P-38 formation, which was sighted at the expected coordinates. The Focke-Wulfs had not yet reached the Lightnings' altitude, and it would have been good tactics, in Peter Crump's opinion, to have turned to one side to obtain a more favorable position for an attack.

But Seifert would have no part of that. To the surprise and discomfort of his pilots, he continued climbing directly toward the Lightnings, which were about 1,500 feet above them. The P-38s overflew the German formation without making an attack; apparently the Focke-Wulfs had not been seen. The Kommandeur then pulled up suddenly and attacked the last plane in the formation. The Lightning pilot, Lt. Manual Aldecoa, saw Seifert's plane and banked into a dive toward his attacker. They went at each other "snout to snout." Crump saw both aircraft take hits, ram each other's right wing, dive away out of control, and crash. Aldecoa bailed out, but his chute streamed, and he was killed; Seifert's body was found still strapped in the wreckage of his plane. Johannes Seifert was a prewar member of JG 26, and in May 1940 had scored the First Gruppe's first victory of the Western campaign. His 439 combat flights had resulted in fifty-four aerial victories; he had been the Geschwader's only pilot to win the Knight's Cross in 1942.

According to Peter Crump, after this brief encounter the P-38 formation reversed course to the north in a broad curve and flew away. This puzzled the German pilots, but since the P-38s were new to the Kanalfront it was concluded that the Lightnings were on a familiarization flight and were not looking for combat. In reality, the P-38s had been vectored toward another German formation by their controller in England. It is not known why Aldecoa did not warn his unit of the planes below them; however, the Americans were now searching elsewhere. The reported aircraft were above the Lightnings in the sun, and difficult to spot. The bogies proved to be Bf 109s. When the American pilots finally saw them, they climbed to the attack and were credited after the resulting combats with the destruction of two Bf 109s (from JG 3) and two FW 190s (from JG 2).

Although one P-38 pilot reported having seen Aldecoa's aircraft in a vertical dive, followed by an (apparently) pursuing FW 190, the destruction of Seifert's aircraft had not been observed by any of the returning American pilots, and no victory claim was filed. The Americans, looking for the enemy in the sun, never suspected that there were a number of Focke-Wulfs beneath them; the JG 26 pilots, for their part, knew nothing of the presence of other German planes in the area. The encounter reports of the two sides seem to be referring to different battles. The sequence of events as related above is confirmed, however, by a close comparison of the official records of the two unit commanders involved. The report of the 55th Group's Lt. Col. Jack Jenkins noted that he changed course (the "broad curve" seen by the JG 26 pilots) shortly before sighting fighters above him at 1316. The victory claim filed in Seifert's behalf after his Gruppe's return noted that his victory (by collision) occurred at—1316 hours.

The next morning, the Focke-Wulfs of the First and Second Gruppen were scrambled to oppose a B-17 raid. The 5th Staffel's 190s had not cleared their Cambrai field when it was swept by Spitfires from the Canadian Biggin Hill Wing, which shot down two FW 190s, killing both pilots. The surviving German pilots headed south and caught the B-17s of the 3rd Bomb Division as they approached Paris over a solid cloud cover. Some of the Focke-Wulfs made an immediate attack from six o'clock low, quickly knocking one Fortress of the low group out of formation. Other FW 190s lined up ahead of a neighboring group, peeled off, and made single passes from about two o'clock.

The escorting 78th Group had to battle not only the Focke-Wulfs, but Bf 190s from JG 2. The P-47s wounded one 6th Staffel pilot, but lost two aircraft to JG 26 FW 190s. JG 26 pilots were credited with two of the four B-17s that were shot down; bomber gunners killed one 8th Staffel pilot.

Klaus Mietusch's Third Gruppe had been separated once more from the rest of the Geschwader. In response to the American attacks on north Germany, it had been ordered to Muenchen-Gladbach, where it became part of the First Jagdkorps. On 30 November, a Lightning pilot from the 20th Fighter Group, which was nearing full operational status, was forced to abort a mission and turn back alone. He failed to reach England, and was recorded as having vanished without a trace in the North Sea. He was the fiftieth victim of Hptm. Mietusch, who shot down the P-38 while on patrol over the Dutch coast.

Mietusch's war with the Lightnings continued the next day. The 20th Group's 77th Squadron was escorting the 2nd Bomb Division's B-24s en route to Solingen when the Third Gruppe Kommandeur made a solo bounce on its rear aircraft, which fell into a spin. A P-38 from the adjacent flight turned toward the Bf 109 and opened fire, but Mietusch evaded easily by breaking right and zooming up about one thousand feet. He then did a wingover and came back through the formation, guns blazing. Honor satisfied, he flicked over and dove away, untouched by American fire.

The 1st of December was a busy day for the entire Geschwader. Heavy activity over England brought all Gruppen to readiness early in the morning. Takeoff was ordered when the heavy bombers crossed the English coast, but once again the 5th Staffel was caught taking off from Cambrai by Canadian Spitfires, which downed the Staffelkapitaen, Hptm. Hoppe, and his wingman, killing both. Obfw. Glunz immediately avenged their deaths. He caught up to the Spitfires southwest of Arras and shot down two of them, including the aircraft that had just shot down his Kapitaen.

Cloud cover forced the 3rd Bomb Division to abandon their mission, while the 1st Division bombed their secondary target, Solingen, and targets of opportunity. The bomber formations became strung out, stretching the available escort past their limit. All eight P-47 and P-38 groups filed claims, but the 56th had the hardest time, running into "absolute hell" in the shape of "some awfully rough boys in Focke-Wulfs," in Robert Johnson's words. In the course of driving numerous FW 190s and Bf 109s away from the bombers, three P-47s were shot down. Two of them were claimed by JG 26 pilots. Four more 56th Group Thunderbolts made it back to England with heavy damage. Zemke's pilots claimed to have shot down three fighters. Four JG 26 pilots were shot down in the vicinity of the bomber stream, but all bailed out successfully. A number of effective attacks were made on the lumbering Fortresses, and B-17s were credited to at least six JG 26 pilots.

Two squadrons of Typhoons from the Second Tactical Air Force were ordered to fly to the Arnhem area in support of the bombers. They encountered several German fighters returning to their bases, and they claimed two destroyed, while losing one of their number to a Second Gruppe pilot. This skirmish proved to be the last of the day for the Geschwader, which claimed twelve Allied aircraft out of the thirty-four that were lost to fighters and flak. Two JG 26 pilots were killed, and five were wounded; seven of the total of nineteen German fighters lost were from JG 26.

For the rest of 1943, the Eighth Bomber Command ordered up its heavy bombers whenever permitted by the weather. The Third Gruppe was based near enough to the North Sea to catch the bomber stream on its flights due east to targets in northernmost Germany. On 20 December, the Gruppe claimed five B-17s shot down out of a force sent to Bremen. JG 26's First and Second Gruppen were fully occupied by the diversions flown by the 9th USAAF and the RAF's second TAF. On this same day, the Allies overwhelmed the defenders along the French and Belgian coasts with raids by 211 B-26s, sixty Mitchells, thirty-seven Bostons, 415 Spitfires, 155 Typhoons, and twenty Hurricanes. JG 26 brought down only one airplane out of this fleet—Fw. Wiegand was credited with his 9th victory, a Spitfire. His 4th Staffel lost one pilot to the Spitfires; the Second Gruppe lost one pilot killed, one injured, and three Focke-Wulfs destroyed.

A new long-ranged fighter entered combat in mid-December. This was the Merlin-engined North American P-51B Mustang, which when available in strength the following spring would initiate the final decline of the German Air Force. For now, however, only a single P-51 unit, the 354th "Pioneer Mustang" Group, was on hand, and the pilots of JG 26 did not encounter it during the month. The Geschwader had all it could handle in the shorter-ranged Thunderbolts. On 22 December, the P-47s were completely successful in keeping the Third Gruppe from the bomber stream. Five Messerschmitts from the Gruppe were shot down in the Rheine-Enschede area between 1410 and 1420 hours, victims of the three senior P-47 groups, the 4th, 56th, and 78th. All five of the Schlageter pilots were killed. The day ended without a single success for the Geschwader.

The last attack of the year on a German target came on 30 December, when Eighth Bomber Command sent 710 B-17s and B-24s to Ludwigshaven. The two Focke-Wulf Gruppen of JG 26 more than made up for the Messerschmitt Gruppe's failure eight days previously. Without suffering a single fatality, the pilots of the First and Second Gruppen shot down five B-17s, one B-24, and four P-47s. The day's outstanding performances belonged to the 7th Staffel, which downed two B-17s and two P-47s, and the 4th Staffel. The latter unit flew two missions from Wevelghem under the leadership of Fw. Wiegand. While stalking the outbound bomber stream, Wiegand inadvertently led his unit into the middle of the 353rd Fighter Group and shot down one P-47. The Americans did not down any Focke-Wulfs, but they effectively broke up the Staffel's formation. Wiegand and his wingman then attacked a straggling B-17 and shot it down; Wiegand gave the victory to the other pilot. That afternoon, Wiegand went after the homeward-bound B-17s and again wound up in combat with P-47s, this time from the 352nd Group. Wiegand shot down another Thunderbolt, for his 11th victory; once again his Staffel came through the battle unscathed.

The year thus ended on a relatively high note for the Geschwader. Its claim-to-loss ratio in 1943 was about four to one. Approximately 575 victory credits were awarded the pilots during the year, 190 of them for combats on the Eastern front. But the number of pilots killed, 158, was more than double that of the previous year. It was equivalent to an annual loss rate of greater than 100 percent, based on the Geschwader's true average strength in pilots. The Allied fighter force in England already exceeded in numbers Germany's total fighter strength on all fronts, and it was growing rapidly. The Americans were now deploying fighters with the range to accompany the bombers to any target in Germany. With the coming of better weather in the spring, the stage would be set for the total defeat of Germany's aerial defenders.

10
THE ALLIES COMMAND
THE SKIES
January–May 1944

THE WAR OF ATTRITION

The four Thunderbolts spread out into search formation. Low on fuel, the pilots reduced power settings to their most economical levels and scudded along above the roiling gray clouds. They were returning from their first-ever escort mission, which had been carried out as ordered, and without incident. The ground had not been sighted since takeoff; clouds extended up to 18,000 feet. At the time scheduled for landfall, they dropped down through the overcast and sighted a grass field, which looked to the exhausted pilots like one of the many Spitfire fields along the southern coast of England. As they circled the field, they were hit by eight I/JG 26 Focke-Wulfs. The Americans' Number 4 pulled back up into the overcast and finally succeeded in reaching England. The other three Thunderbolts were shot down immediately. The Schlageter fighters had just extended a typical Luftwaffe welcome to another new American unit. The Focke-Wulfs had been led by Hptm. Karl Borris in a careful, low-risk bounce of the lost P-47 flight near Cambrai, after it had been tracked across northern Europe for the previous hour by German radar.

The Thunderbolts were the squadron commander's flight from the 358th Fighter Group's 367th Squadron. That 7 January morning the 358th Group pilots had provided penetration support for heavy bombers en route to Ludwigshaven. Successful interceptions in the thick weather were a matter of luck. Three B-17s were claimed by pilots of II/JG 26. That Gruppe then fell afoul of Spitfires of the withdrawal escort and lost three FW 190s and two pilots. It was apparent that the winter of 1943–1944 would not bring any respite in the Allied air offensive.

The new year found the Geschwader occupying familiar territory in the industrial region along the border between northern France and Belgium. The Stab was at Lille-Nord, France, a small airfield with limited facilities. On 30 December, Obstlt. Priller had been ordered to fill in once again for Oberst Vieck at the St. Pol Jafue and had to commute daily between the two headquarters. Hptm. Borris's First Gruppe was at Florennes in Belgium, on a field built by the Germans in 1942. This was a fully equipped base with concrete runways, which were greatly appreciated in the wet winter weather. The Second Gruppe, under Hptm. Gaeth, was at Epinoy, near Cambrai, France. Epinoy was a much improved field that had recently obtained its own hard-surfaced runways. Hptm. Mietusch's Third Gruppe was at Dinant, Belgium, on a field that had only recently been upgraded from an emergency landing ground. JG 26 and its longtime rival Kanalgeschwader, JG 2 "Richthofen," made up the day fighter strength of Jagdkorps II, which was headquartered in Metz. Jagdkorps II belonged to Generalfeldmarschall Sperrle's Luftflotte 3, based in Paris. At this time JG 26 was not part of Luftflotte Reich, the organization charged specifically with the air defense of Germany. The individual Gruppen of the Geschwader, especially the Third, were detailed to Luftflotte Reich from time to time for specific emergencies. The details of the Luftwaffe organization chart scarcely mattered to the pilots of the Geschwader, of course. Their responsibility remained the front-line defense of the greater German Reich.

The Third Gruppe was now equipped with Messerschmitt Bf 109G-6s. Their 1475 horsepower DB 605A in-line engines provided a top speed of 386 mph at 22,600 feet. The Messerschmitt's standard armament of one MG 151/20 cannon and two MG 131 heavy machine guns was adequate against Allied fighters, but it was too light to pose much of a threat to B-17s or B-24s. German records frequently refer to the unit as a "light" Gruppe, which implies that their mission was high-altitude cover for the more heavily armed and armored FW 190 Gruppen. This task was well within the capabilities of the Bf 109G, which had excellent high-altitude performance. The Gruppe's pilots were rarely allowed to ply this specialized trade, however. The Luftwaffe High Command's policy with regard to attacking escort fighters vacillated between grudging permission and prohibition. Also, as mentioned previously, JG 26's position in the "front line" did not allow time to form up the Geschwader as a unit. The Third Gruppe was employed most frequently as a bomber-interception unit, as were all of the Gruppen based along the coast. The Messerschmitts were given the punch to knock down heavy bombers in the form of rocket mortar tubes or MG 151/20 cannons in underwing gondolas. Thus laden, their maneuverability and speed were drastically reduced, making them easy prey for the escort fighters.

The rest of the Geschwader flew FW 190As. The standard production model of Kurt Tank's robust little fighter was now the FW 190A-6. The A-6 featured a strengthened wing and heavier armor and armament than earlier models. It was originally intended for the Eastern front, but since its greater weight imposed no noticeable performance penalty, it became a very popular mount with the pilots defending the West. The FW 190A-6's 1700 horsepower BMW 801D radial engine gave the plane a top speed of 405 mph at 20,700 feet, but the fighter's performance decreased sharply above that altitude. The fighter's armament of four MG 151/20 wing cannon and two MG 17 machine guns provided ample destructive power against Allied aircraft.

In early 1944, the Schlageter pilots found themselves opposing five Allied fighter types. The Supermarine Spitfire was still the most common fighter in the United Kingdom. At this time, Spitfires of RAF Fighter Command provided the short-range escort and cover for the American heavy bomber formations. The German pilots never lost their high regard for the Spitfire's capabilities but had generally found the large and normally unaggressive formations flown by Fighter Command easy to avoid. Changes in Allied commanders and doctrine in early 1944 would restore the Spitfire as a potent threat. The other important RAF day fighter, the Hawker Typhoon, had excellent speed near the ground and was being used effectively on Rhubarbs. Single flights of Focke-Wulfs were scrambled frequently by JG 26's First or Second Gruppen to oppose these intruders. The victor in these small-scale encounters was usually the pilot with the better luck—or the better eyesight.

Of the three American fighters, the P-51 Mustang was still very much an unknown quantity to the Germans; at year's beginning it equipped only a single group. The P-38 Lightning was flown by two groups. Its size and unique appearance made it easy to spot, and to stalk or avoid, as appropriate. The only feature of the Lightning that impressed the Germans was its heavy, concentrated armament. The most numerous American escort fighter was the P-47D Thunderbolt, which equipped ten groups. When flown by an experienced pilot, the "Jug" had proved able to hold its own at high altitude against any German fighter. New models had engines equipped with water injection, which boosted combat performance at all operational altitudes. Another modification, the paddle-blade propeller, markedly improved low-altitude climb rate. The new props were retrofitted to all P-47s in the United Kingdom as rapidly as possible. In the P-47D, the Americans had an airplane capable of driving the Luftwaffe from the skies. Thunderbolt pilots could chase their targets from the vicinity of the bomber stream all the way to the deck, confident of their mount's ability to return them, if necessary, to the security of high altitude. The only barrier to more aggressive tactics by the American fighter pilots was the Eighth Air Force policy requiring close escort—and that was now about to change.

In early January, Gen. Dwight D. Eisenhower came to England from the Mediterranean theater to assume his new position as Supreme Commander for the invasion of western Europe. He brought with him his air team, which consisted of several commanders with whom the general had worked and felt comfortable. Two of them had an important impact on JG 26 and the Jagdwaffe. One, Air Vice-Marshal Harry Broadhurst, took command of the fighter component of the new Second Tactical Air Force, which contained many squadrons formerly belonging to Fighter Command. The British fighters were relieved of much of their escort responsibility as they took up their new task, which was to help soften up the invasion coast. The old warning "Achtung Spitfeuer" once again chilled the German fighter pilots along the Channel coast, as the Spitfire formations dropped to the deck in their search for aerial targets.

Another important member of Eisenhower's air team was Lt.

Gen. James Doolittle, who took over the Eighth Air Force from Lt. Gen. Ira Eaker. Eisenhower's arrival imbued the strategic air campaign with a new sense of urgency. He made it plain that Allied air superiority was a prerequisite for the successful invasion of the Continent. Since the invasion was scheduled for late spring, the air commanders would have to reorder their priorities—and fast. The Allies could wait no longer for the bomber generals to fulfill their dream of defeating Germany by strategic bombing alone. In Jimmy Doolittle, Eisenhower had the perfect airman for the task ahead. Doolittle, a reservist, had no particular loyalty to the theories of strategic bombing. Always a pragmatist, he was quick to throw out policies that did not contribute to his immediate goal of defeating the German Air Force. The bombers were ordered to fly in weather that would previously have grounded them. Bombing accuracy suffered, but this was no longer considered as important as keeping pressure on the Luftwaffe. American escort doctrine soon changed; the fighters were ordered to patrol fixed zones along the bombers' track instead of escorting specific bomber wings. This subtle change in tactics permitted the escort formation leaders to concentrate on finding enemy fighters, rather than the "correct" bomber formation—bomber units that missed rendezvous were left to fend for themselves.

It was Doolittle's final innovation that sealed the fate of the German Air Force. At the urging of Maj. Gen. William Kepner of Eighth Fighter Command, Doolittle ordered that the escort fighters, once their patrol shift was over, were to drop to low altitude, seeking out and destroying German fighters wherever they could be found. This aggressive attitude by the high command, added to further improvements in equipment and total domination in numbers— there were ultimately thirty-three American fighter groups in England—permitted Eisenhower's demand to be fully satisfied by D-Day, 6 June.

General Doolittle could do nothing about the miserable winter weather over northern Europe. Despite his desires and exhortations, only nine raids could be mounted against German targets in January. The weather conditions and the small size of the escort force permitted the experienced German defenders to punish several of the raids severely. On 11 January, all three bomb divisions of the Eighth Air Force took off and assembled, but worsening conditions over the continent forced the recall of all of the 2nd and most of the 3rd Division, as well as much of the escort. The B-17s of the 1st Division made a successful attack on the FW 190 factory at Oschersleben but suffered heavily from continuous fighter attacks. The two Focke-Wulf Gruppen of JG 26 were ordered up to intercept the formation on its return flight. This description of the First Gruppe's battle is quoted from the diary of Fw. Gerd Wiegand:

> 11 January 1944—79th combat sortie (two B-17s downed):
> We move back to Florennes at 0900—Many "dicke Ottos" assembling over London—Takeoff at 1222 in Gruppe formation—Belly tanks carried—My Staffel assigned high-altitude escort—Borris leads the Gruppe—From Brussels on, solid cloud deck at 2,000 meters [6,500 feet]—West of Nordhorn, nineteen B-17s sighted without escort! We haven't seen this in quite a while. I hover above the Gruppe, beneath the condensation trails—Report the air clear—Borris overtakes the B-17 formation at their altitude—The formation appears nervous, but presses tightly together—It seems an eternity before all is ready—Borris banks toward the right flank of the formation—I press forward and line up with Borris, preparing to attack the left flank simultaneously. Fire at 20 degrees deflection, 10 degrees elevation, 1½ sight radii—The B-17's left wing falls off and strikes the next B-17—I split-S—Attack a B-17 from the rear—Shoot off the third B-17's elevator, am almost struck by it—I am hit in the oil tank—Canopy open—It jams—I dive away to the south, into an isolated cloud bank—I see the ground, but where am I? Set course to the southwest—Finally see the Waal—Five minutes from Deelen—Ready to bail out, since Arnhem is to one side—I buckle up—Deelen beneath me. Canopy washer does no good; as soon as I stop it clouds up again—Prop stops—I feather it—Blind approach curve—Sideslip—I break through the cloud bank at 200 meters [650 feet]—Gear down—Land—My "oil sardine" sits in the middle of the field—A record is playing over the loudspeaker: "Sing, nightingale, sing."

The German onslaught left the bomber formation in shreds. When the one-sided combat was over, eight B-17s had fallen under the fire of the First Gruppe's cannon. The Second Gruppe claimed three more B-17s in the same area. The battle cost the two Gruppen four Focke-Wulfs, but no pilots.

The FW 190 pilots recorded another solid triumph over the heavy bombers on the 21st. Nearly 800 bombers were dispatched to bomb the newly identified V-weapon launch sites in the Pas de Calais area of France. The weather closed in, and some formations spent so much time over France attempting to make clear target identifications that the escort plan broke down. The First Gruppe located an unprotected Pulk of B-24s. Since the bombers were already near the coast on their return flight, Hptm. Borris ordered his fifteen pilots to attack from the rear of the formation. The fighters made repeated stern attacks and succeeded in shooting down five 44th Bomb Group Liberators. The bomber gunners claimed four Focke-Wulfs, but none in fact were lost.

The Geschwader did not pass the day unscathed, however; the Third Gruppe lost two Messerschmitts and one pilot. A flight of P-47s from the 353rd Fighter Group, flying near St. Quentin, came across a Schwarm of four 12th Staffel Bf 109s beneath them. The Thunderbolt pilots made an undetected bounce from out of the sun. Their leader, Maj. Walter Beckham, hit the trailing fighter with a short burst of machine-gun fire. The Messerschmitt burst into flames. Its pilot bailed out quickly, suffering only light injuries. Beckham shifted his sights to the lead fighter, which exploded under the fire of his eight .50s. The pilot of this Messerschmitt was killed instantly.

The next major Eighth Air Force mission took place on 29 January. The bombers' target was Frankfurt. The First and Second Gruppen claimed seven B-17s destroyed, one separated from its formation, and one straggling bomber shot down; two B-24s destroyed plus two separated; and two P-47s and two P-38s destroyed. Bad weather split up many formations, and most German attacks were made by individual Staffeln. The Geschwader fought the Americans from central Germany to the English Channel. Three JG 26 pilots were killed, and another wounded.

The 7th Staffel encountered a small Pulk of B-24s near Trier. Their first pass damaged several bombers. As the Staffel continued to stalk the Liberators through the clouds, it was overtaken by the P-38s of the 20th Fighter Group's 79th Squadron. The Germans broke formation and sought cover. One Focke-Wulf was hit by a Lightning's fire and pulled up toward the sun, smoking heavily; its pilot later had to bail out. All but one of the other German pilots succeeded in evading the attack. The inexperienced Gefr. Alfred Teichmann was caught flying straight and level by a P-38 pilot who opened fire from dead astern, quickly closing to seventy-five yards range. The FW 190 spun out in flames, and it was still spinning when it entered the overcast at 4,000 feet. Teichmann and his aircraft disappeared without a trace. Not until 1974 was the wreckage discovered. Aviation historian Werner Girbig was called upon to assist in the excavation and succeeded in identifying Teichmann's remains. The bodies of many other airmen remain buried with their aircraft in the soft soil of northwestern Germany and the Low Countries.

The vulnerability of men such as Teichmann was yet another burden to be borne by the hard-pressed German formation leaders. The Jagdwaffe had by now abandoned the finger-four Schwarm formation developed in Spain. The finger-four was effective only if all its members carried out their well-defined roles. In order to give some protection to their inexperienced wingmen, the Germans found it necessary to pull them up even with their element leaders into a line-abreast formation, consequently reducing the angles of clear sight and the overall efficiency of the Schwarm.

Gefr. Teichmann's death was swiftly avenged. The next day, the bombers set out for Brunswick. The 20th Fighter Group had responsibility for penetration, target, and withdrawal support of the 3rd Division's B-17s. After an hour of intermittent combat, the Group's 79th Squadron split up to return in separate flights. One of these flights was bounced east of Arnhem by Lt. Charlie Willius and the eight FW 190s of his 2nd Staffel. After one swift pass, the Focke-Wulfs disappeared. Two P-38s, including that of the squadron commander, were last seen spinning into the overcast at 5,000 feet.

Despite what Doolittle considered a less than full-scale effort on the part of his forces, the fighter force defending the Reich lost 160 pilots and 233 aircraft in January. Germany lost a total of 391 single-engined fighters during the month, one-quarter of its strength. JG 26 lost fourteen pilots killed in combat and a further six in accidents, amounting to 11 percent of the pilots on its roster at the start of the month. Other pilots were removed from combat because of wounds; the most prominent of these was Major Wilhelm Gaeth, the Second Gruppe Kommandeur, who was shot down by

Spitfires on 14 January. Gaeth never returned to duty with JG 26, and in early February he was replaced as Kommandeur by Hptm. Johannes Naumann of the 7th Staffel. Two JG 26 Staffelkapitaene were lost in January. After the Kapitaen of the 5th Staffel was killed by Spitfires on the 14th, he was replaced as Staffelfuehrer (a probationary Staffelkapitaen) by Obfw. Addi Glunz. The appointment of Glunz to a position of such responsibility while still a noncommissioned officer was indicative of the Jagdwaffe's desperate shortage of leaders. From this time forward, Staffelkapitaen openings would be filled by the direct commissioning of successful enlisted pilots. These men received no type of officers' training; successful command at the Staffel level was apparently considered a matter of instinct. Some of these pilots, such as Charlie Willius and Addi Glunz, would rise to their responsibilities and become outstanding combat leaders; others would not.

In February, the pressure was kept on the Schlageter pilots, who found themselves being scrambled against Allied formations in weather conditions that would have grounded the heavy bombers the previous year. Invaluable formation leaders continued to be lost. Oblt. Artur Beese, Kapitaen of the 1st Staffel, was killed by P-47s on 6 February, while intercepting B-17s near Paris. Beese, who had scored twenty-two victories in 285 combat sorties, was one of the last of the prewar Geschwader pilots still flying with the unit.

BIG WEEK

Time was passing too swiftly to suit the headquarters staff of the Eighth Air Force. They needed a week of good weather to carry out Operation Argument, their long-planned knockout blow to the German aircraft industry. On 19 February, the meteorologists detected an extensive high-pressure area moving across Germany and predicted several consecutive days of good weather. The next six days, soon dubbed Big Week, saw the strategic bombing campaign reach a new peak of intensity.

On 20 February, the Eighth Air Force dispatched sixteen combat wings, 1,003 B-17s and B-24s, against twelve German aircraft factories in central and eastern Germany and western Poland. Two widely separated forces were employed. The American planners succeeded in disguising the points and times of attack. JG 26's First

219

and Third Gruppen were apparently kept on the ground for the entire day. The Second Gruppe's thirty Focke-Wulfs flew from Cambrai to Athies in the morning and took off to oppose the returning bombers in mid-afternoon. The Gruppe filed only two victory claims, and neither were confirmed. The Americans lost only twenty-one bombers and four fighters; the German defenders lost a total of fifty-three single-engined, and twenty-five twin-engined fighters. The day had been a brilliant success for the Allies. Several targets had been severely damaged. Radio intercepts indicated an unprecedented degree of disorganization and confusion on the part of the German fighter controllers. Only 362 defensive sorties had been flown, about half the number the Allies had expected.

Worsening weather on the next day brought a reduced scale of operations. Only 282 defensive sorties were flown, resulting in the destruction of sixteen bombers and six fighters. Thirty-five German fighters were lost. JG 26's effort was minimal. Obfw. Glunz claimed the only victory, a B-17. No losses were sustained by the Geschwader.

The German defenders tried new tactics on 22 February, with some degree of success. Fighters were concentrated early against the penetration leg of the mission, which typically was defended by fewer escorts than the target or withdrawal legs. JG 26's First Gruppe flew two missions, without result. The Third Gruppe claimed at least one victory, a P-47. The Second Gruppe was active for the entire afternoon against both the outbound and the returning bomber formations. On their first mission, the Gruppe's pilots repeated their tactics of the previous fall, attacking as many times as possible and maintaining contact with the bomber stream until the state of their fuel forced them to break off. Obfw. Glunz, at the head of his 5th Staffel, had his most successful day of the war. After taking off from Athies at 1125, he shot down two B-17s and separated a third from its formation, before landing at Muenchen-Gladbach at 1304. Two more B-17s were shot down by the Gruppe on this mission, which cost it only one FW 190, and no pilots. Returning to combat later in the afternoon, Glunz claimed two more B-17s and one P-47 destroyed. Another Gruppe pilot claimed a P-47, and one FW 190 was lost to the bombers' gunners. Glunz's claims on the 22nd ultimately resulted in four victory credits, his fifty-fifth to fifty-eighth.

The 22nd of February was a rough day for the 6th Staffel's Fw.

Peter Crump. His first sortie brought no success. After taking off from Athies, he followed the bombers for ninety minutes, but could not penetrate the escort screen. He finally broke contact and landed with his last fuel on the Duisberg "Miniplatz" (emergency field). He had to refuel his Focke-Wulf by himself, using a hand pump and some fifty-gallon drums. He then took off for Duesseldorf, where all the Gruppe pilots who had participated in the morning mission had been ordered to assemble. However, besides Crump, the only Second Gruppe pilots who turned up were his Staffelkapitaen, Hptm. Horst Sternberg, and the young Uffz. Paul Gross of the 5th Staffel.

New orders were received—the FW 190s and Bf 109s on hand from the first mission, belonging to a number of Gruppen and Geschwader, would fly to reinforce the fighter force still available at Venlo, in the Netherlands. Before takeoff, Sternberg pulled Gross and Crump aside and told them that the three pilots would fly together as a Kette. He then gave Crump a direct order to remain beside him at all times—a stinging insult to the independent-minded and highly experienced Peter Crump.

When the dozen aircraft from Duesseldorf arrived at Venlo, they found between thirty and forty FW 190s and Bf 109s ready to take off. After a broad circuit of the field, the hodge-podge formation took up a course to the east, under the command of a major, and climbed to attack the homeward-bound bomber formations. They had reached 11,000 feet when the lead Fortress was sighted at 20,000 feet, on the opposite course. The formation leader turned immediately to a parallel course, until the German fighters could reach attack altitude.

To Crump's great astonishment, Sternberg did not follow this maneuver but continued flying straight ahead. Far ahead of them, a badly damaged B-17 spiraled away from the bomber stream in a broad left turn, trailing thick smoke. Seeing the possibility of an easy kill, Sternberg had abandoned his formation. He began his attack on the crippled bomber from beneath. Peter Crump, shocked by his Kapitaen's open breach of Luftwaffe discipline, turned to search the cloudless sky behind them—and saw a dozen Thunderbolts streaming down. Their leader immediately attacked Sternberg's aircraft. Crump raked the P-47 with a quick burst, then dove for his life.

The Thunderbolts were the 4th Fighter Group's 335th Squadron, led by Major George Carpenter. Carpenter opened fire on Sternberg's aircraft from 300 yards. When alerted by the tracers, the German pilot broke violently but could not elude the P-47. After two turns, the Focke-Wulf entered a shallow dive. Carpenter stayed behind it, scoring hits that caused pieces to fly off. The American pilot pulled off to the right at an altitude of 500 feet and watched Sternberg's aircraft fly into the ground and explode.

Major Carpenter's wingman attacked the aircraft of Uffz. Gross. His first pass overshot his target, but Gross made only gentle maneuvers, permitting the P-47 to regain firing position. Only now did Gross attempt a sharp turn, but the Thunderbolt overtook him once more, firing down to a distance of thirty to fifty yards. As the P-47 went past the German plane, its pilot was observed jumping out. Gross's chute opened, but he had been hit by machine-gun fire, and he died before reaching the ground.

The second element in Carpenter's flight made a quick turn with Crump and then followed him in his dive. They chased him to the deck, but could not close to effective firing range, and broke off the attack. The pursuit was then taken up by three P-47s of the 78th Fighter Group's 83rd Squadron, which had reached the bomber stream a few minutes after the 4th Group. Up to this point, Peter Crump's aircraft had not been hit, and he decided that his best means of escape was to out-climb the heavier Thunderbolts. However, Crump's maneuver allowed two P-47s to close the range. The three aircraft entered a tight circle; then, in Peter Crump's words:

> My own initial thoughts of reversing my turn were stopped suddenly by an inferno of sound and light. My stick was ripped from my hands, trash whirled around, and a rush of flames shot past my face. So this is what it is like to be shot down! Another, unobserved, Thunderbolt had blown his nose on me with a full charge, as we pilots say. With a single reflexive motion I threw off the canopy, drew up my legs, and climbed out.
>
> Knowing that I was at low altitude, I pulled my ripcord immediately. The chute opened smoothly; after one pendulum swing I contacted Mother Earth. Apart from tearing ligaments in my right knee when I contacted the frozen bare ground—it was winter, after all—and a minor flesh wound, I had survived the disaster in good health.
>
> The action had taken place near a village. I landed in a field

near a house. I was in Germany, about twenty-four miles north of Aachen; I learned this after awakening from a half-hour's loss of consciousness. In the residents' words, the devil had gotten loose over their village that afternoon. Five aircraft lay strewn in pieces—two of the enemy's and three German fighters. One was a crash-landed B-17, which ground-looped barely one hundred yards from a house. My Focke-Wulf had dug a deep crater in the embankment of a small stream that flowed past the village.

I was told the locations of the other two German crash sites. Since I could scarcely move on account of my injured knee, I was taken there in an automobile. My fears were confirmed; they were the other two members of my flight, both dead.

I learned one more thing on my return to military authority—the Thunderbolt pilot who added me to his victory list was not pleased at his success. My jettisoned canopy flew into his propeller and ripped it off. He wound up a prisoner of war.

This last statement is the only part of Peter Crump's account that cannot be reconciled with the American records. It was the third member of the 78th Group flight who shot Crump down. Arriving late, he decided not to join the Lufbery, but instead cut across the circle, striking Crump's aircraft squarely with a high-deflection burst of machine-gun fire. The German pilot immediately jettisoned his canopy and bailed out; the canopy *almost* struck the flight leader's P-47, but he avoided it by pulling up sharply.

Bombing results on the 22nd were mediocre, and the Americans considered the bomber losses to be excessively high, at forty-one. Eight hundred bombers had been dispatched, but only 430 were credited with combat sorties. However, the war of attrition against the Jagdwaffe reached new levels of success. Forty-eight single-engined, and sixteen twin-engined fighters were lost by the Germans on their 332 defensive sorties.

After standing down for one day, the Eighth Air Force resumed its offensive. JG 26 was fully engaged on the 24th. All three Gruppen sustained casualties. The Third Gruppe suffered the worst; four of its pilots were lost to the heavy bombers and P-47s. A pilot of the Second Gruppe disappeared, probably crashing in the Ems moors. At least three B-17s, one P-38, and one P-47 were claimed by the Geschwader's pilots during the day.

The rendezvous field on the 24th was Rheine. Eleven Schlageter pilots turned up; their senior officer present, Hptm. Borris, took command. After refueling, Borris and his wingman had just begun their takeoff rolls when two Thunderbolts roared across the field. Within seconds the trailing Focke-Wulf was reduced to a crumpled, flaming heap, its pilot dead. Seconds later, Borris reported the destruction of one of the Thunderbolts north of Rheine, hit as it banked away following its victory. The other P-47 escaped.

The ten remaining 190s circled the field once while forming up. After assuming course, Borris and his improvised Staffel soon saw a formation of B-24s near Wetzlar. Oblt. Matoni (5th Staffel) took on the rear Liberator, while Obfw. Heckmann (3rd) and Lt. Radener (7th) attacked the two on the outside of the formation from the rear, firing long bursts. Matoni's Liberator was the first to fall, striking the ground near Rastorf. A few minutes later, Radener's B-24 crashed northwest of Wetzlar. Any pilot who still had ammunition attempted a second approach. Oblt. Hartigs and Lt. Willius, both of the 2nd Staffel, each downed a B-24. When Waldi Radener pressed his firing button on the second attack, he reported himself "impotent." Just then he was jumped by two P-51s. He broke sharply and soon found himself alone with one of them above a broad plain. No clouds—no cover at all. Since his "jam-squirter" was empty, he had only one option—force his opponent into ever tighter turns, nose to nose; to continue the battle until the Mustang ran low on fuel.

The American pilot sought after each turn to head west, but without success. Radener forced the turning battle, until then primarily horizontal, onto the vertical plane. For seven long minutes he shouted over the radio for anyone with ammunition to meet him over the Westerwald. But then the unexpected happened—the Mustang's engine coughed and began spewing clouds of white smoke. The American pilot immediately broke out of the turn and set a straight course for the northwest. When Radener took position on the wing of the stricken bird, the American pilot half-rolled and jumped out. Radener reported seeing the crash of the machine on the autobahn near Bonn but did not wait for the parachutist to land, since he himself had been flying for ten minutes with his red fuel lamp burning. The Mustang belonged to the 357th Fighter Group, and it did indeed fail to return, but Radener, lacking witnesses, did not file a victory claim.

When the day's scores were tallied, Walter Matoni's victory, his thirteenth, was judged to be the Geschwader's 2,000th. Such round-number milestones were always cause for recognition in the Wehrmacht. Oblt. Matoni was the next day awarded command of Obfw. Glunz's 5th Staffel. Glunz transferred to Matoni's old Staffel, the 6th, as a Schwarmfuehrer (flight leader).

The victory totals for the Geschwader's Gruppen as of 24 February 1944 were reported as part of the commemoration. Since the detailed victory lists of the Stab and the Third Gruppe failed to survive the war, these totals are of interest here:

Stab/JG 26	117 victory claims
I/JG 26	625
II/JG 26	649
III/JG 26	609
JG 26	2,000 victory claims

As noted previously, the Geschwader's figures represent claims filed with the RLM, not victory credits finally awarded, which were lower by 10 to 20 percent.

The Germans lost thirty-nine single-engined and fourteen twin-engined fighters on the 24th, a 15.7 percent loss rate based on the 336 sorties flown. The Americans lost forty-four heavy bombers, 5.4 percent of those dispatched, and only ten, or 1.3 percent, of the fighters. The war of attrition was clearly going in the Allies' favor.

The 25th of February was another day of hectic activity for the Schlageter fighters. The bombers passed right over the Geschwader's bases in a seemingly unending stream, and the Second and Third Gruppen were able to fly two missions against them. The Second Gruppe claimed two B-17s from the outbound, and two from the returning formations, but lost two experienced pilots to the P-47s. The Third Gruppe successfully penetrated the escort screen on both its missions. Mietusch downed an outbound B-17 and shot a B-17 of the returning force out of its formation, and three of his Staffelkapitaene claimed B-17s. Much to the surprise of the First Gruppe's pilots, Borris's unit was scrambled, not to intercept the heavy bomber stream, but to attack a formation of medium bombers that was en route to bomb airfields in the Netherlands. Lt. Willius, with a history of success against the Marauders, shot down two of them. A total of four B-26s from this formation failed to return to England.

The 25th proved to be the last day of Big Week, as the weather then turned sour. The two strategic Air Forces, the Eighth in England and the Fifteenth in Italy, mounted maximum-strength raids on those airplane factories in southern Germany that had not yet been crossed off the target list. Because of the close spacing of its targets, the Eighth was able to form its 754 bombers into a single, well-protected stream, and as a result it lost only thirty-one bombers. JG 26 flew about ninety combat sorties against the England-based raiders, out of a total of 200 flown by the entire Jagdwaffe. JG 26's casualties were disproportionately light; only three of the twenty-eight German fighters lost were from the Geschwader.

Contrary to the general American belief at the time, their bombing attacks during Big Week did not cripple the German aviation industry. Another, very real, victory had been won that week, however, even though no single battle with the drama of a Schweinfurt had been fought. Aerial superiority had passed irrevocably to the Allies. The message of 25 February was crystal-clear to the American planners—Allied fighters could dominate the air over any part of Europe by their mere appearance. The German fighter force suffered no net decrease in numerical strength during Big Week, and it remained a formidable foe. But the era of maximum defensive effort against every American bombing raid was over. The hit-and-run tactics that the Schlageter pilots had found necessary for their personal survival now became the unofficial policy of the entire Jagdwaffe.

During February the German fighter force lost 17.9 percent of its pilot strength. The Reich defense force lost 225 pilots killed and missing, and 141 wounded. JG 26 lost fifteen pilots killed in action, and a further three in accidents; among the dead were three of the Geschwader's twelve Staffelkapitaene.

THE BERLIN RAIDS

The weather closed in after 25 February, ending combat flying for the month. March brought a continuation of the poor winter weather. The Eighth Air Force flew raids on every day the weather over its English bases permitted takeoff and assembly, even if its targets had to be bombed through cloud. On 2 March the target was Frankfurt. JG 26's First and Second Gruppen were sent up against the outbound bombers, reaching the bomber stream near Trier. Fourteen Second Gruppe FW 190s dove from 27,000 feet through the rear box of B-17s, 2,000 feet below. They were then driven off by two squadrons of P-47s from the 365th Fighter Group, a new unit belonging to the tactical Ninth Air Force. Most of the German pilots continued their dives, heading for breaks in the clouds below. The Thunderbolt pilots, confident of their abilities in this, their first air combat, followed the Focke-Wulfs down, and shot down three aircraft of the 6th Staffel without loss to themselves. Two pilots, including the Staffelkapitaen, were killed, and the third was injured. Obfw. Glunz was named the new leader of the 6th Staffel. The First Gruppe lost no aircraft to American fighters, but two of its FW 190s collided in the clouds, killing both pilots. The First and Second Gruppen claimed the destruction of three B-17s, a poor return for the loss of five pilots. The Third Gruppe was also active, shooting down at least one B-17, and losing one Bf 109 to a P-38.

During March the American air planners deliberately chose targets that would provoke the strongest possible reaction by the German fighter defenses. On 4 March the target was Berlin. Because of the extremely poor weather the mission was recalled. The 20th Fighter Group attempted to provide withdrawal support, but it was unable to find the bombers. A number of the Lightnings had engine problems, and some pilots had to cross the Channel on one engine. Fw. Gerd Wiegand was sitting in the cockpit of his FW 190 at Wevelghem—despite the bad weather, a Rotte of fighters had been ordered to remain at readiness—when a crippled P-38 whistled overhead on one engine. Wiegand took off immediately and gave chase. The two planes flew in and out of the clouds for several minutes. The Lightning suddenly emerged from the mist, right in front of Wiegand. The German pilot wanted to force the American fighter down in one piece, and so he deliberately fired to one side. But the Lightning broke into the attack, and Wiegand shot it down, taking care not to hit the pilot. The American bailed out at 6,000 feet, and Wiegand returned to Wevelghem, landed, and hurried to the crash site. A parachute was floating in the Lys River; Wiegand was told that the pilot had drowned. He had in fact been whisked under cover by Belgian civilians, and he eventually made his way back to England via the Resistance.

On 6 March, General Doolittle finally succeeded in putting his bomber force over Berlin. Seven hundred and thirty bombers were escorted by 644 fighters from the Eighth and Ninth US Air Forces and the RAF. A total of 943 escort sorties were flown, since many units flew two missions. As expected, the defenses countered with their full strength, putting up a total of 528 sorties. The course of the bomber stream led them across the Netherlands, to the north of JG 26's normal defensive territory. Individual Staffeln from the First and Second Gruppen were scrambled from Wevelghem, Beauvais, and Cambrai and ordered to patrol the Reims area, ready to attack in case the bomber stream turned toward the south. The bombers maintained a due easterly course toward Berlin, however, and the Focke-Wulfs were ordered to land at airfields in Germany to refuel and await the Americans' return flight. This force, plus the remainder of I/JG 26, which took off from Florennes, met the returning bombers over Lingen at 1450, and made a successful attack. Pilots of the First Gruppe claimed two B-17s, two B-24s, and one P-47 destroyed, while the Second Gruppe claimed one B-17. Only one Focke-Wulf was lost to the escort; its pilot bailed out successfully. In the meantime, the Third Gruppe was sent after an obvious diversion—a B-26 raid on Poix. Hptm. Mietusch led an attack on the escort and shot down one No. 3 Sqd. Typhoon.

The Eighth Air Force lost sixty-nine bombers on 6 March, its greatest loss on any raid of the war. The Germans lost sixty-six fighters, or 12.5 percent of those scrambled. The bomber loss rate of 10 percent, while high, was no hindrance to further operations of the same magnitude. Berlin was the target again on 8 March. All of JG 26 was ordered to attack the outbound bomber stream. The First Gruppe had no luck against the bombers. The 4th Staffel's Gerd Wiegand, by now a Faehnrich-Feldwebel, or officer candidate, shot down a P-47, but he was shot down in turn by another and suffered injuries that kept him out of combat for three months. The Second Gruppe was more successful; its pilots claimed four B-17s destroyed and two more separated from formation, plus one P-51 destroyed. Hptm. Mietusch shot a B-17 from its formation; his Third Gruppe suffered no losses.

The three Gruppen were ordered up again in late afternoon, in greatly reduced strength, against the returning bombers. Only the Third Gruppe had any success. Its first attempt to close with the bombers was fended off by the escort, which shot down one Bf 109, killing its pilot. Klaus Mietusch, leading only two fighters, made a beam attack on the rear bombers of a combat wing and then rolled away. A flight of P-47s from the 352nd Fighter Group went after the three Messerschmitts. Two got on the tail of Mietusch's wingman. When Mietusch went to his aid, the leader of the P-47 flight was able to damage the German plane with a burst of fire at high deflection. Mietusch broke for the deck, and the Thunderbolt pilot was able to close on him easily, firing down to a range of 100 yards. Large pieces flew off the 109, which was a mass of flames. Mietusch jettisoned his canopy, preparing to bail out. The American pilot pulled alongside the Messerschmitt and noted its fuselage marking for his encounter report—the twin chevrons and bar of a Gruppen-kommandeur. As the P-47 skidded beneath the blazing fighter to give it another burst of fire, Mietusch jumped out. His chute opened immediately, and he landed safely, but with injuries severe enough to keep him in the hospital for the next few weeks. Hptm. Staiger of the 12th Staffel, who shot down two B-17s on this day, took command of the Gruppe until Mietusch's return.

The heavy bombers' losses on 8 March were only thirty-seven out of 623 dispatched. American fighter pilots claimed 77-9-33 German fighters. The Eighth Fighter Command summary of the mission noted that "the enemy effort was decidedly smaller than the last Berlin attack." Allied Intelligence estimated that the Luftwaffe single-engined fighters had flown only 120 sorties; the Zerstoerer, thirty. The next day the bombers were sent to Berlin once more, despite continuous cloud cover over the continent. JG 26 was kept on the ground, along with the rest of the defensive fighter force. For the first time, the Germans permitted the bombers to attack a key target without even a token interception by their fighters. Only eight bombers failed to return; all of them were lost to antiaircraft fire.

Bad weather limited the Geschwader's operations for the rest of March. On the 16th, the weather was good enough to permit a bombing mission by the Eighth Air Force to Augsburg, in southern Germany. JG 26 was to assemble at Reims to intercept returning bombers. One 11th Staffel replacement pilot, Uffz. Heinz Gehrke, was scheduled to fly his first combat mission. His Third Gruppe first took off from Lille-Vendeville for Reims. Heinz Gehrke recalls:

I was very excited. Wherever I looked, the sky was full of airplanes. That was very reassuring. We landed in Reims, and were refueled and made ready for a combat mission. I overheard from the conversations of the other pilots that they were glad they had all landed in one piece. I then realized that the planes that I had thought to be ours had been Allied! They were flying above us, at their escort altitudes. I had thought that I was covered, which was a great mistake. But the first sortie of all "beginners without spurs" such as myself was probably the same, even in a distinguished mob like JG 26.

That afternoon we received orders to take off against the returning heavy bombers. My simple mission as a Rottenflieger was to stay with Fw. Laub. It wasn't long until heavy bombers were reported over the radio. And sure enough, there they were. I felt uncomfortable, but it was true—and there were no escort fighters with them. Our Staffel made an attack on a group of Liberators on the far right edge of the formation. One 109 after another attacked. I was the last. All of my fighter school training came flooding back into my mind— the best position, et cetera. Suddenly, I was behind one of the Liberators—apparently hit, it had sheered away from the formation at a sharp angle. I thought to myself that I would shoot it down. After I had made three attacks, scoring effective strikes, the bomber dropped away. I wanted to rejoin my Staffel, but they were gone. In my excitement I had forgotten everything, losing my Rottenfuehrer and my unit.

I then saw several fighters circling in the distance. In the belief that they were my unit, I approached them, happy to have rejoined my comrades. But they turned out to be Thunderbolts rather than Messerschmitts. They saw me, and the jig was up. Four of them came after me. I stood my bird on its head, and dropped away from 6,000 meters [19,500 feet]. To err is human—in war, fatal. Diving after me, the Thunderbolts filled my crate full of lead, but I dove on. After a short time, my machine suddenly leveled off and began to fly straight ahead, although I pushed on the stick like a madman, trying to dive. The stick moved beneath my hand, but I had no control. What is the last resort of a fighter pilot? Bail out. I jettisoned the canopy, unbuckled myself, and jumped out. I counted—21, 22, 23, 24, 25—and pulled the handle. Thank God, the chute opened, and soon I was sitting on the ground, more a wretched heap than a hero.

I could move only with difficulty because of a severe back pain—I then realized that I had struck my aircraft's tail when I bailed out.

The four Thunderbolt pilots could scarcely believe their good fortune when Gehrke's plane was spotted barreling toward them. The Americans belonged to the 356th Fighter Group, which was known as the "hard luck group" of Eighth Fighter Command for its seeming inability to come into contact with the enemy. Their report stated that they had been bounced by a lone Messerschmitt out of a clear sky; they undoubtedly assumed that it had been piloted by a fanatic Nazi rather than a confused, grass-green pilot. Two pilots filed a joint claim for the destruction of the 109.

Heinz Gehrke was ultimately credited with the final destruction of his B-24. Hptm. Staiger downed another B-24. The First and Second Gruppen filed no claims. The two Focke-Wulf Gruppen each lost two pilots killed; the Third Gruppe lost one killed and three wounded.

Also on the 16th, Obstlt. Priller was finally relieved as Jafue at St. Pol and returned to Lille to command his Geschwader full time. Hptm. Mietusch received a hard-earned Knight's Cross on the 26th, after his 60th victory. Despite continued bad weather, Eighth Bomber Command managed to fly twenty-three missions during the month; these cost them 349 bombers. During March the German fighter force lost 22 percent of its total pilot strength. The Reich defense force lost 229 pilots killed and missing, and 103 wounded. JG 26 lost twenty pilots killed in action, plus seven in accidents; the dead included two Staffelkapitaene. The Jagdwaffe was incapable of replacing its losses of the previous two months during the late-March lull. On 31 March, JG 26, which had an establishment strength of 208 airplanes and pilots, reported fifty-seven aircraft operational out of seventy-three on strength. Of 175 pilots "on the books" of the Geschwader, only seventy-six were fit for duty.

JAEGERSCHRECK—FEAR OF FIGHTERS

The weather continued unsuitable for flying through the first week of April. Several promotions came through. Karl Borris and Klaus Mietusch were promoted to Major, and Addi Glunz and Jan Schild were commissioned as Leutnants. On 8 April a large bomber force was detected forming up over England. I/JG 26 was ordered to assemble at Wevelghem. Its 2nd Staffel, led by Oblt. Charlie Willius, took off from Florennes at 1415 to make the transfer. Ten aircraft took off, but several turned back because of engine problems. Near Brussels, the Staffel received a radioed order from the Jafue to attack a heavy bomber formation over the Netherlands. The lead bomber box, about thirty-six B-24s with heavy fighter escort, was spotted at 1540, above the Zuider Zee. Willius ordered a frontal attack. The little band of Focke-Wulfs tore through the bombers and climbed back into the sun. Willius's target dropped away from the formation in flames. While re-forming, the Staffel was hit by a flight of four Thunderbolts from the 361st Fighter Group. Willius and his wingman, Lt. Jan Schild, split-S'd and headed for the deck. Schild saw a Thunderbolt 150 yards behind Willius's aircraft, firing; pieces were already flying off the Focke-Wulf. Schild evaded the Thunderbolt attacking him and banked toward the one on Willius' tail, giving it a high-deflection burst from the side. The American fighter broke off its attack, trailing smoke. Schild claimed its probable destruction, but the fighter was apparently not severely damaged. Willius's Focke-Wulf was then seen by the Americans to spin into the ground and explode. Schild dove away again, evading another flight of P-47s by flying at low level between the smokestacks and towers of the Ruhr. No German witnessed Willius's crash. His body was not recovered until 1967, buried in his FW 190 fifteen feet deep in a Dutch polder. Oblt. Willius received a posthumous award of the Knight's Cross for his forty-eight victories, obtained on 371 combat flights. Lt. Schild replaced him as leader of the 2nd Staffel.

The second pair of Thunderbolts in the flight dove through these combatants in search of their own targets. One pilot put a burst of .50-caliber machine-gun fire into a Focke-Wulf from 100 yards range, at which the 190 took violent evasive action, split-S'd, and dove vertically away. The American pilot lost sight of it but claimed its probable destruction. The German fighter did, in fact, continue its terminal dive into the ground, taking Faehnenjunker-Oberfeldwebel (Senior Officer Candidate) Emil Babenz of the 2nd Staffel to his death. Babenz was one of the most experienced pilots in the Geschwader. He had been an original member of the 11th Hoehen (high-altitude) Staffel in 1942, and had survived its destruction in Tunisia, ultimately returning to JG 26 after serving in the Mediterranean theater with JG 53. He had been credited with twenty-four victories in 335 combat flights. The loss of two such senior pilots as Willius and Babenz in a single combat was a severe blow to the First Gruppe.

On 12 April, 455 heavy bombers took off from England to bomb targets in southern Germany. Clouds and dense contrails caused severe problems in assembly and rendezvous and ultimately forced the cancellation of the mission. The B-24s of the 2nd Bomb Division did not turn back until they had reached the German border. Over Luettich they encountered the FW 190s of II/JG 26. When a thin layer of stratus cloud interposed itself between the 445th Bomb Group and its fighter escort, the German fighters attacked from beneath, pumping 20-mm cannon shells into the Liberators' thin bellies. Five bombers went down before the Thunderbolt escorts regained sight of their charges and dove to their defense. The German pilots were credited with two outright victories, seven bombers separated from formation, and one destroyed after separation. Many damaged bombers were able to reach the clouds and thus escape destruction. The P-47s shot down and killed three new Gruppe pilots. Another Geschwader casualty was Major Mietusch, whose Bf 109 overturned after it hit a rut landing at Etain. Mietusch suffered a concussion and was sent back to the hospital for another three weeks.

The next day, the bombers again tried to reach their targets in southern Germany. JG 26's Second and Third Gruppen successfully penetrated the bomber stream, as did their Kommodore. Obstlt. Priller shot down a B-17 near Poperinghe, southeast of Dunkirk. This was his ninety-sixth victory, the first since the Muenster raid the previous October. His numerous responsibilities on the ground had kept him from the job he preferred, that of leading his men in combat. The Second Gruppe claimed two P-47s destroyed and two B-17s separated from formation; known Third Gruppe claims include one B-17, one P-47, and one P-38.

The next bomber interception did not come until the 22nd. This time it was the turn of the First Gruppe to score; its pilots claimed two B-24s and two P-47s. One of the successful pilots was Obfw. Waldemar "Vladimir" Soeffing, who had recently returned to the Gruppe after recovering from a broken neck suffered the previous July. The Gruppe's only combat loss of the day was another one of its few experienced formation leaders. Hptm. Wolfgang Neu, Kapitaen of the 4th Staffel, was killed in combat over the Eifel. Neu's final record was twelve air victories, including seven heavy bombers, gained in 111 combat sorties.

Hptm. Hermann Staiger, temporarily in command of Mietusch's Third Gruppe, had been ordered on the 18th to lead the unit to Munich, in anticipation of an American attack on the Nazi movement's birthplace on Hitler's birthday, 20 April. According to Staiger, the first few days on the field at Neubiberg were spent playing skat in the ready rooms. After an ineffective interception on 23 April, which cost the life of one pilot, Staiger and a number of his men spent the evening in the bar of a Munich hotel. They left the bar during an air raid alert and returned to their base, where the drinking continued. Arising the next morning after only a few hours sleep, a number of Staiger's pilots, and the Hauptmann himself, were suffering from severe headaches.

The pilots spent several hours at readiness. The order to take off was finally received in late morning. An ungodly chorus of voices came over the radio from the fighter units in the area—heavy bombers were coming. Amid all the confusion, one clear female voice was heard, coming from the Jafue control center somewhere in the Munich area. A female controller was a novelty to the men of the Kanalgeschwader. Generalfeldmarschall Sperrle barely tolerated the presence of servicewomen in his Luftflotte 3 and did not allow them to fill positions of such responsibility. The calm soprano voice guided Staiger's men directly to the bomber stream. Staiger noted the presence of an extremely large fighter escort. Staiger's Gruppe of thirty Messerschmitts was opposed by several hundred aircraft. He thus decided to shadow the formation until he saw a more favorable opportunity to attack. Since they were flying barely within sight of the bombers, and up sun, they remained undetected. The bombers overflew Munich and bombed airfields in eastern Bavaria. On the return flight, the American fighters' relief failed to make contact with the bombers. Staiger watched the target-support escort force depart and only then ordered his pilots to attack the bombers.

The German pilots hadn't seen this in a long time—a Pulk of twenty-five to thirty heavy bombers, without fighter escort. Staiger's men carried out a textbook attack from twelve o'clock high. Staiger's own Messerschmitt carried a 30-mm MK 108 cannon in its nose, and he used it to good effect, shooting down two B-17s and forcing two more from their formations, to be shot down by Staiger's wingman. The German fighters attacked repeatedly, retiring only when they had exhausted their ammunition. Their final score totaled seventeen victories, which were gained without a single loss. Their repeated head-on attacks succeeded in breaking up the enemy combat box; thus separated, the B-17s were fairly easy prey. Staiger's headache returned as soon as he landed at Holzkirchen. Flying on pure oxygen, a well-known hangover cure, he had "driven off the tomcat," but for only one and one-half hours.

The mission of the 11th Staffel's Uffz. Gehrke was no less memorable than that of his chief. Heinz Gehrke recalls:

> Staiger gave the order over the radio—we attack from the front and reassemble afterward at altitude so-and-so. My heart dropped into my boots. Never before had I attacked heavy bombers from the front, but my Staffel comrades were around me, and it would be all right. How can I describe the sensations of such an attack, straight through the enemy formation? It literally took my breath away. We went hell-for-leather, thrown about like leaves in the wind by the prop wash. I was so nervous that I forgot everything. I just flew straight ahead, firing. Everything happened lightning-quick, and I suddenly found myself alone. In my excitement I had forgotten the assembly altitude and coordinates. What to do now? While looking for my unit, I spotted another 109 nearby, doing likewise. We joined up for mutual support. And as the devil would have it, a lone Fortress appeared 1,000 meters [3,250 feet] beneath us, glistening in the sun. We attacked, and I had the good fortune to hit its right inboard engine with my cannon. The right wing broke out in flames, and the aircraft went into a spin, crashing near Donauwoerth. I was able to observe the crash. Now I had to get down, as my fuel was running out. We two 109s sought to land in Neuburg. I made a steep bank to advertise my success to the field below, and then landed. I waited in vain for my companion to land, for just as I entered my turn he was shot down. Several Mustangs had appeared just behind us; they not only shot down my unknown companion, but proceeded to strafe the airfield. It was with weak knees, pounding heart, and increased blood pressure that I realized that I had just escaped being shot down myself. That evening I flew back to Neubiberg and reported my victory and the other details of the mission.

I remember that Hptm. Staiger sent the Frau or Fraulein in the command post a bouquet of roses.

The Third Gruppe's successes over southern Germany on the 24th were counterbalanced by a poor performance by the Second Gruppe back on the Kanalfront. Three Staffeln of II/JG 26 took to the air, under the command of the 7th Staffel's Oblt. Waldi Radener, and joined two Staffeln of JG 2 in an attack on the outbound bomber stream. The Allied radio intercept service observed that Waldi's transmissions to his men were filled with cautious instructions to "close up" and "look out." Noticeably absent were the Abbeville Kids' usual shouts of "Sieg Heil!" and "Horrido!" No Second Gruppe aircraft was lost in this encounter, but only one Gruppe pilot, Radener himself, filed a victory claim, and it was rejected. Late in the afternoon a small Second Gruppe formation was vectored toward the bombers' return route, but the German pilots' radio transmissions indicated that they were more interested in avoiding the escort fighters than in locating the bombers. No contact was made with the American formations. The lack of aggressiveness shown by the once-fearsome Kanalgeschwader was duly noted in the Eighth Air Force after-mission report.

The German fighter pilots' failures were equally apparent in Berlin. Someone in the RLM coined the word "Jaegerschreck," meaning fear of fighters, to describe the pilots' excessive caution. Hermann Goering used the term to excoriate the Jagdwaffe in several speeches; the caustically outspoken Adolf Galland was known to use it himself. The hapless pilots felt the insults of their leaders in Berlin to be totally unjustified. When intercepting a bomber formation, their orders were to attack only the bombers. When the fighter screen was too thick to penetrate, their only course of action was to avoid combat. After running before the enemy a few times, the young German pilots lost their natural aggressiveness. This was exactly the result General Galland had predicted when the RLM had refused his earlier pleas to allow the Kanalgeschwader to attack the escort fighters, thinning the screen for the benefit of the fighters based in the Reich. As the Allied fighters became more numerous and experienced, the gaps in their escort coverage disappeared. The Jagdwaffe's orders were now impossible to execute; the German defensive strategy was bankrupt. Berlin's response was to exhort its fighter pilots to fight more bravely, compensating for their qualitative and quantitative inferiority with superior strength of character.

Someone in authority had the common sense to realize that mental toughness could not overcome physical exhaustion and ordered the Gruppen of the Kanalgeschwader to be rested. On the very day just described, 24 April, the pilots of I/JG 26 flew to Cazaux in southern France for a short rest period. II/JG 26 was involved in two more battles before the end of April. On the 27th, a vicious engagement with Thunderbolts took place near Reims. The Gruppe's fifteen FW 190s took on two squadrons of the 356th Fighter Group. At some point in the prolonged battle, Focke-Wulfs from JG 2 became involved. The "luckless" 356th acquitted itself fairly well. The Thunderbolt pilots claimed 4-0-1 FW 190s and killed one Second Gruppe pilot, plus the Kommodore of JG 2, Major Kurt Ubben. Other JG 2 aircraft were probably lost in this battle as well. Three P-47s were shot down. On the 29th, the Second Gruppe intercepted a bomber formation en route to Berlin and downed two B-17s, without loss.

At a May conference, Galland reported to Goering that Luftflotte Reich had lost 38 percent of its fighter pilots in April, while the neighboring Luftflotte 3 (JG 26's parent organization) had lost 24 percent of its pilots. This casualty rate was ruinous, considering the low state of Germany's manpower reserves and the length of time needed to train pilots, even under Germany's accelerated program. The entire Luftwaffe lost 489 fighter pilots in April, while completing the training of only 396. JG 26 lost sixteen pilots in combat, and a further six in accidents; the dead included two more Staffelkapitaene. Eighth Bomber Command lost 409 bombers in April. This was 25 percent of its average strength, and its highest single-month loss of the war. However, the Americans could easily replace their losses. The Germans could not.

Early on the morning of 5 May, ten FW 190s of the Second Gruppe took off from Cambrai-Sud to fly to another airfield in the area. While flying at low altitude through the ground haze, they were spotted briefly by Wing Leader Johnnie Johnson, who was leading the two Spitfire squadrons of his new No. 144 Wing (RCAF) on a sweep of the Lille area in advance of a B-26 bombing raid. Johnson ordered two flights of his fighters to drop into the mist and look for the German planes. The Focke-Wulfs suddenly whipped around and came at the stalking Spitfires head-on. A general dog-fight ensued in which two Second Gruppe pilots were shot down and killed; one Canadian pilot disappeared during the fight and did not return from the mission.

Peter Crump was one of the ten Focke-Wulf pilots, but he did not take part in the head-on attack. His belly tank would not drop, and he sought cover in the low-lying clouds. Repeated attempts to drop the tank were unsuccessful, but he was flushed from cover by a fellow pilot's urgent call for help. Crump shot from the cloud layer, heading for the deck. Only two aircraft were in sight—the threatened Focke-Wulf and a single Spitfire. Crump opened his throttle wide and engaged his methanol-water emergency boost. He ordered the Focke-Wulf pilot to bank sharply to the right, to close the distance and allow Crump to open fire on the Spitfire, but the German fighter continued flying straight and level. The Spitfire's gunfire soon struck home, and the FW 190 disappeared below the horizon, trailing a black smoke plume. In the meantime, Crump had been seen by the Spitfire pilot, who banked left toward the cloud bank and took up a northwest course for England, covering his blind angle underneath by rocking to and fro. He looked for Crump but could not see him, since as soon as he turned, Crump followed him, remaining in his dead angle. The Focke-Wulf matched the Spitfire's every movement—all the time at minimum altitude. The Spitfire soon stopped rocking. Its pilot had concluded that he was alone, and flew on calmly in the direction of the coast, about 600 feet below the stratus deck. Crump drew ever nearer, until he was directly beneath the Spitfire. After a last glance to his rear, Crump zoomed up and opened fire. The Spitfire immediately flipped onto its back and headed straight for a sloping field. The fighter crashed into a line of poplar trees, splintering them into a neat row of logs that led up to the single building nearby. Peter Crump retains a vivid mental picture of the site, which reminded him of a sawmill.

Two days later, the First Gruppe lost yet another of its most experienced pilots. The unit had returned to the combat zone on 1 May, basing at Denain. On the morning of the 9th, they had flown to Laon-Athies and had just taken off to intercept a B-24 formation when the 3rd Staffel was attacked by a flight of No. 411 Sqd. Spitfires, which quickly shot down two FW 190s. Oberfaehnrich (Senior Officer Cadet) Erich Scheyda and his wingman both died in their aircraft. Scheyda had been with JG 26 since August 1941 and had been credited with twenty victories in 188 combat missions.

The next day it was the Third Gruppe's turn to lose one of its best men. Hptm. Hans-Georg Dippel, Kapitaen of the 9th Staffel, was a highly competent acrobatic pilot, with perhaps an excess of self-confidence. While on a training flight, he pulled up sharply while flying at low speed. His Bf 109 stalled, and he crashed before he could regain control. Dippel had gained nineteen victories in his 272 missions with the Geschwader. He was replaced as leader of the 9th Staffel by Oblt. Viktor Hilgendorff, a 29-year-old prewar pilot who had recently returned to duty after a crash in 1942 that had cost him his right leg. Hilgendorff was noted for his courage, and for the vigor with which he expressed his political convictions; he was one of the few outspoken National Socialists in the Geschwader.

THE FIRST ATTACKS ON THE OIL INDUSTRY

The Combined Bomber Offensive, which was the strategic campaign conducted by the American and British heavy bomber forces, had ended on 1 April. Control of the heavy bombers had then passed to General Eisenhower's headquarters. The senior American air officer, General Spaatz, obtained permission to continue attacking targets in Germany whenever permitted by the weather. He argued successfully that this would not prevent his bombers from fulfilling their duties in support of the invasion. On 12 May, Spaatz ordered Doolittle to begin their long-planned campaign against the German petroleum industry. Eight hundred and eighty-six bombers and 735 escorts were dispatched against six German oil refineries. Only one JG 26 Gruppe was employed against this raid, the Third. It flew two missions, attacking both the outbound and inbound bomber streams over the Ardennes. The Messerschmitts forced three B-17s from their formations and lost one plane and pilot to the escorts.

The next day, the Second Gruppe flew to Mont de Marsan, south of Bordeaux near the Spanish border. Although this was intended to be a rest period, the Gruppe was placed under the tactical command of Jafue Brittany, which was part of Genlt. Werner

239

Junck's 5th Jagddivision. This command had been established in France for the purpose of controlling the Luftwaffe fighters that would be sent there to oppose the Allied invasion. While the pilots of the Second Gruppe enjoyed their light duties, the rest of the Geschwader continued its war against the Allied air forces, using hit-and-run tactics. On 20 May, FW 190s of the First Gruppe lured one flight of 355th Fighter Group P-51s away from its squadron. While climbing, the Mustangs were bounced from above and behind by six fighters from the 1st Staffel. Two Mustangs fell in flames; the German fighters continued their dive through the American formation to safety.

Not all air combats resulted in entries in the victory and casualty lists. On 23 May, the Third Gruppe was ordered to intercept a heavy bomber formation over Colmar. A frontal attack was planned, but it was broken off with the approach of the Mustang escort. Fw. Erhard Tippe was a new pilot in the 11th Staffel. He recalls:

I was flying as Karlchen Laub's wingman. We had just taken our sights off the heavy bombers when eight Mustangs crossed beneath my wing, passing in front of my crosshairs. Laub broke away in a dive; he told me later that he wouldn't have given a pfennig for my chances. I decided to test-fire my weapons. The tracers so startled our pursuers that six of them broke away. Wonderful! We were prepared to take on the other two. We fought from the clouds down to the treetops of the Vosges, each seeking to get a Mustang in our sights. Five hundred feet over Colmar, Laub, who was in front of me with his Mustang, suddenly broke around sharply with his quarry. We then went around nose to nose. On each pass we fired at our persecutors. Laub suddenly disappeared. His opponent had probably taken a hit and vanished into a cloud. I had mine in my crosshairs repeatedly. My "Yellow 13" had to give its utmost. After a dogfight ranging from fifty to 1,000 meters altitude, I finally got the upper hand. I reached the best firing position possible. Soon I would score my first victory! Calmly I took aim—pressed on the firing knob— Christ! Nothing! I flew close by my opponent, waved a short greeting, and broke away in a steep dive. He did not follow me. Now I had only to find my way to my home field. A feeling of contentment came over me; I had come through the test in good shape. That my weapons would not fire was a matter of fate. It turned out that my cannon's ammunition belt was torn, disabling it, and my machine gun rounds had somehow turned ninety degrees in their chutes. Thus I had lost my certain victory.

As the date for the invasion approached, the heavy bombers intensified their attacks on rail installations and airfields in France and Belgium. More than 400 bombers were sent out on 25 May, escorted by 600 fighters. Mietusch's Gruppe was ordered up in maximum strength to seek out a break in the escort cover. The 356th Fighter Group finished its close escort assignment near Neufchateau, noted that the bombers were well covered by other fighter units, and headed toward the Messerschmitts, which had been reported by the Allied controller, and which had been sighted by the Thunderbolt pilots themselves, coming in from the north about 5,000 feet above the bombers. A headlong attack by two of the three P-47 squadrons scattered the German fighters to the four winds. Three Bf 109s went down; only one pilot was able to save himself by taking to his parachute. The Thunderbolts climbed back to rejoin their group at 18,000 feet; the surviving Messerschmitt pilots made their way back to their field at Nancy singly or in pairs, having long since given up any hope of making a successful attack that day.

The continuing struggle against ever-increasing odds cost the German home defenses 276 fighter pilots and 487 fighters in May. The German fighter arm lost 25 percent of its pilots and 50 percent of its aircraft during the month. Despite strenuous efforts to build up the Jagdwaffe, the number of fighter pilots on duty had dropped since the start of the year, from 2,395 to 2,283. Losses totaled 2,262 pilots, or about 100 percent of average strength. JG 26's own mission count decreased in May, probably in anticipation of its projected role as a front-line defender against the forthcoming invasion. From 1 May through 5 June, the Geschwader lost fourteen pilots killed in combat and six in accidents. It had lost 106 pilots since the beginning of 1944, which was 50 percent of establishment strength, but 140 percent of the average number of pilots actually available for combat duty with the unit. The members of JG 26 killed so far in 1944 included eleven Staffel leaders; the experience lost with these men was, of course, irreplaceable.

11
THE INVASION FRONT
6 June–3 September 1944

D-DAY

Pips Priller slammed down the telephone in his Lille command post and shouted for Hptm. Philipp, his operations officer. The 5th Jagddivision had just called with orders to move the Geschwader headquarters to Poix immediately. The reason? The long-awaited Allied invasion had apparently begun. Large forces were reported coming ashore on the coast of Normandy. Priller's headquarters, which had been placed behind the Pas de Calais in anticipation of a landing in that area, would have to move closer to the actual combat zone. None of his three Gruppen were immediately available for combat duty. Two had been ordered to move inland the previous evening, over Priller's vehement protests. The ground column of the First Gruppe was on the road, en route to Reims; the Third Gruppe was heading toward Nancy. The Second Gruppe was still resting at Mont de Marsan, near Biarritz in far southern France. It took an hour for the Kommodore to set his forces properly in motion. Then, at 0800 on that gray morning of 6 June, Priller and his wingman, Uffz. Heinz Wodarczyk, headed for their Focke-Wulfs, which as usual were parked just outside the command post. The Luftwaffe's initial response to the invasion was under way.

Priller's only orders to his longtime wingman were to stick

close. They headed west at low altitude, spotting Spitfires above them as far east as Abbeville. Near Le Havre the duo climbed into the solid cloud bank. When they emerged, the ships of the largest assault landing in history were spread before their eyes. After a shouted "Good luck!" to Wodarczyk, Priller dove for the beach at 400 miles per hour. The British soldiers on Sword, the easternmost of the five landing beaches, jumped for cover as the two fighters roared fifty feet overhead, their machine guns and cannon clattering. The fleet's antiaircraft guns opened fire with every gun that could track them, but the Focke-Wulfs flew through the barrage unscathed. After traversing the beach, the two pilots climbed for the clouds, honor satisfied.

THE DEFENSIVE PLAN AND ITS EXECUTION

The preceding vignette depicts the German Air Force's only appearance over the beachhead on D-Day morning. It is the best-known single episode in the Geschwader's history, thanks to its inclusion in Cornelius Ryan's popular history *The Longest Day*. It is commonly believed today that it accurately represents the entire period of the invasion; that the Luftwaffe was so depleted that it never made an appearance in strength over Normandy. There is some truth to this, in that the Allies' aerial supremacy over the landing grounds was never seriously challenged. This is not because no such effort was made, however. The Luftwaffe had a longstanding plan to reinforce the fighter force in France with units from the home defense forces, and the plan was in fact carried out. By the evening of 7 June, there were only six Gruppen of single-engined fighters left in Germany; seventeen Gruppen were in France. At full strength this would have amounted to a force of 1,100 aircraft. However, most units were at half strength or less, and owing to the disorganization resulting from the rapid move and the chaotic state of most French airfields, only 289 were reported operational in the strength return radioed to the RLM on the night of 7 June.

Had the reinforcements arrived on D-Day morning, instead of the next day, they would possibly have had an impact on the course of the invasion. As it was, they could never concentrate in sufficient strength to have an appreciable effect on events on the ground. About half of the new fighter units were assigned to Fliegerkorps II, a ground attack command that had established a fully staffed head-quarters in France in advance of the invasion. The experience of most of the pilots arriving from Germany was limited to bomber interception, and they proved totally ineffective in their new role as fighter-bomber pilots. On 12 June, the Ultra organization decoded an order calling on all Jagdgruppen in France to remove their bomb racks and keep them off until further notice. This was clear evidence that the Luftwaffe's plan of defense had collapsed, and that in the future the Allied ground forces would have to contend with nothing more dangerous from the German fighters than rocket and cannon fire. Fliegerkorps II was soon disbanded, and its commanding general and staff were sent back to Germany. Its Jagdgruppen were given to the 5th Jagddivision, which already commanded the other fighter units nearest the invasion zone. The twenty Jagdgruppen ultimately under the 5th Jagddivision's direction overstrained its control apparatus, and most fighter missions during the invasion period had to be conducted as freie Jagden, uncontrolled sweeps, which was an inefficient utilization of already insufficient resources.

The three Gruppen of Jagdgeschwader 26 reached the battle zone on the afternoon of 6 June and they accounted for a fair portion of the 172 combat sorties flown on D-Day by Fliegerkorps II and the 5th Jagddivision in opposition to the 14,000 sorties of the Allied Expeditionary Air Force. Few details of the Geschwader's activities on the 6th have survived. At least one Allied plane, a P-51, was claimed destroyed, and one FW 190 pilot was lost. The combat units settled into fields in the Paris-Reims region. The Stab flew from Chaumont for several weeks; the First Gruppe, from nearby Cormeilles and Boissy le Bois. The Second Gruppe reached Guyancourt, in the greater Paris area, on 6 June and remained there. The Third Gruppe moved to Paris on 7 June, the 9th and 11th Staffeln to Villacoublay Nord, and the 10th and 12th to nearby Villacoublay Sud. The ground staffs, forced to come by road, straggled in over the next few days.

The Third Gruppe was still flying its old Bf 109G-6 Beulen, or "boils," so named for the bulbous fairings covering the breeches of their cowling-mounted MG 131 machine guns. The rest of the Geschwader was equipped with the FW 190A-7 and the more common FW 190A-8. The latter was to become the FW 190 model built in the greatest numbers, 1,334 eventually rolling off the production lines. Both the A-7 and the A-8 retained the four wing-mounted MG 151 machine cannons of the A-6, but 12.7-mm MG 131s now replaced the rifle-caliber MG 17 machine guns above the engine. One common variant, the FW 190A-8/R4, had GM1 (nitrous oxide) boost, which increased top speed by as much as 36 mph, depending on altitude.

The Geschwader flew mainly fighter sweeps and patrols against the ubiquitous Allied fighter-bombers. On 7 June, Obstlt. Priller claimed his 97th and 98th victories, a P-47 and a P-51. Pilots of the First and Second Gruppen claimed eight American fighters that day, against two losses. On the 8th, the Second Gruppe downed four American fighters, and the Third Gruppe shot down at least two more, for a loss to the Geschwader of one pilot.

The morning of 9 June passed peacefully at the Geschwader's temporary headquarters in Chaumont. Low-lying clouds, haze, and drizzling rain made operational flying impossible. Most of the pilots lay tightly packed on straw in their tents, trying to grab some sleep. Obstlt. Priller had set up his command post in a still undamaged barracks, in a bare room containing two chairs, two tables, a telephone, and a wall map. As his staff had not yet arrived, he functioned as telephonist, clerk, and pilot. His sole vice at this time was cigars; his mouth was seldom without one.

The rain let up in early afternoon. A mission was ordered for 1530. Two hours later the aircraft returned. No contact had been made with enemy aircraft; the weather over southeastern England was obviously too bad for them to take off. Since the local weather remained flyable, Priller ordered a ground strafing mission. Shortly before sunset, eleven Focke-Wulfs from the First Gruppe flew their second mission of the day, led by the Kommodore. For unknown reasons they were unable to reach the beachhead. Instead, they headed for the Allied airborne forces' D-Day landing grounds and destroyed fifteen gliders by gunfire. The gliders had been left undefended, as they were in fact utterly worthless targets. This attack, and the pilots' consequent "victory" claims, are a sad commentary on the relevance and effectiveness of the German fighter force at this stage of the war.

The weather improved on the 10th, with only intermittent rain showers. Pilots of the Second Gruppe caught Allied fighters on two separate missions, downing a P-47 in mid-afternoon, while later in the evening Lt. Addi Glunz, Kapitaen of the 6th Staffel, shot down three American fighters in two minutes, for his sixty-second, sixty-third, and sixty-fourth victories. Although these were identified in Glunz's logbook and in the Gruppe victory list as P-47s, they were described in the official communiqué as P-51s. A war correspondent sought out the taciturn Addi Glunz a few days after this sortie, and recorded this interview:

> Finally Glunz began to speak of the missions of the past few days. Yes, he had shot down three Mustangs in two minutes. He reported dispassionately and clearly of the dance around the cloud banks after he had shot the first one down in flames. How he emerged from the cumulus cloud to find himself almost at ramming distance from two more. The tail of one Mustang loomed up ghost-like in front of the nose of his aircraft. Only a few feet more, and both of them would have had it. At this moment the two planes shot out of the cloud. A press on the firing button and the Mustang was burning. But there was another one, flying ten meters to one side. So Glunz skidded his plane to the right and, continuing to fire, hosed the last enemy aircraft with shells. It also fell away. How simple it is to write down! Only his fellow pilots know how difficult it is to pull off these "typical Glunzisch stunts."

On the 11th, the American Lightning groups were released from their patrol duties over the shipping lanes and headed inland to join in the general attacks on the German defenses. The 55th Group bombed railroad trains and marshaling yards in the Compiegne area. After turning for England, one of the Group's squadrons received word from their controller of air activity at Beauvais. They turned on to the new course, but as they reached the airfield they were struck by ten FW 190s, piloted by Priller, Wodarczyk, and the 4th Staffel. The resulting action is best described in the words of the 4th Staffel's Gerd Wiegand, now a commissioned officer. From Lt. Wiegand's combat diary:

> 11 June 1944—106th combat sortie (two P-38s downed):
> Takeoff is at 1430—Priller leads—We climb inland; our orders are to protect our roads—Radio message: "Lightnings over the field"—Our reply: "We're coming!"—There is four-tenths cloud cover. We see ten Lightnings at 2,000 meters

[6,500 feet], our own altitude—We climb at full throttle, fly above them, and attack one flight—Priller shoots one Lightning down—The right element dives to the left—I hang on to them—There's a confusing whirl of planes. I fire; a Lightning burns—I fly after the other, a mile ahead, all alone—Back and forth—Suddenly it turns left on a reciprocal course—I open fire immediately—I see tracers, then my canopy blackens—My oil tank is hit!—There's a horrible noise—I'm hanging with my legs in the air—I disconnect my microphone and open my parachute—My right leg swings to and fro—Six Lightnings circle my parachute—I strike the ground with a painful smack, in a field 3 km north of Compiegne—My thigh is shattered— Four hours later it's into the hospital and under anesthesia— Good night!

Gerd Wiegand recovered from his injury, but he never returned to JG 26. His American opponent took a 70-degree deflection shot and saw strikes in front of the Focke-Wulf's cockpit, and smoke from its engine, before he was taken under attack himself and snap-rolled into a cloud. His victory was confirmed by his squadron commander, who circled the descending Wiegand. A total of four victory credits for P-38s were awarded to the German pilots in this battle; only two P-38s were in fact lost.

Two days later, III/JG 26 formed the escort for other Bf 109s that made rocket mortar attacks on armor in the British sector of the beachhead. On the return flight, contact was made with American fighters, and the Gruppe formation was split up. Suddenly, the 11th Staffel's Uffz. Gehrke found himself entirely alone—a sensation he was getting used to. With little ammunition and even less fuel, he had to make an intermediate landing in Orleans. After refueling, he received clearance to return to Paris and took off again. Heinz Gehrke continues the story:

After scarcely ten minutes flying time, a huge cloud of dust loomed up in my path. I thought at first, my God, could farmers make such a mess with threshing machines? These weren't farm implements, however, but Thunderbolts, attacking ground targets. Shortly thereafter I made them out, circling—and they in turn saw me. A fateful question—what to do? One against twelve? I turned east and flew balls-out at minimum altitude. They came after me, ignoring the fact that I was flying only two to three meters [six to ten feet] above the ground, pulling up for each hedgerow and tree. With beautiful precision the Thunderbolts made one attack after another. As I pulled up to miss a power line, my crate cracked open. My engine was hit, and began to smoke heavily. I climbed out. My chute opened, and I found myself sitting stupefied on the ground. My 109 landed in a village and not only burned itself up, but also ignited a French farmhouse. Due to shock and my injuries—shell splinters in both legs—I remained numbly on the ground for a while, until some Frenchmen approached me from the village, their purpose clear. With scythes, sticks, and possibly even guns—I'm not 100 percent sure—they wanted to know if I was guilty of burning down the house. By sheer luck a Wehrmacht truck full of soldiers came by just then, and took me away from the Frenchmen to the security of a hospital in Orleans. Ten days in hospital and then back to my Staffel. They were glad to have another pilot back on duty; we had suffered a number of pilot casualties in my absence.

Heinz Gehrke had encountered a squadron from the 78th Fighter Group, on a train-busting mission near Orleans. According to the American records, one pilot called out a 109, which he spotted "stooging along on the deck." He took an awkward deflection shot and at first thought the Messerschmitt had crashed. He then saw it again, and the chase was on. Firing from 800 yards, he closed the range somewhat, but he ran out of ammunition. His squadron commander then closed to 150 yards, firing short bursts that caused pieces to fly off the 109. As it caught fire, Gehrke jumped. The airplane then hit the ground and exploded.

The airfields around Paris, which were now home to the three Gruppen of JG 26, plus III/JG 54 and several other fighter units, were high priority bombing targets for the Allies. At 0645 on 14 June, III/JG 26 took off from Villacoublay to intercept a formation of B-17s headed for Le Bourget. The Gruppe fought its way through the escort, the 55th Fighter Group's P-38s, and Major Mietusch brought down one of the eleven B-17s that failed to return from the mission. Three Lightnings were lost to the Messerschmitts, while two of Mietusch's young pilots were killed. The 11th Staffel's Uffz. Erhard Tippe has recorded his impressions of this mission, which was the Third Gruppe's most successful of the period:

Today I was to be Wolfgang "Poldi" Polster's wingman; we flew right up front, in the Kommandeur's Schwarm. We immediately climbed to about 8,000 meters [26,000 feet] altitude, north of Paris. Our eighteen Bf 109s flew in a single battle line. Suddenly we saw sixty Lightnings 2,000 meters [6,500 feet] beneath us, flying in a formation identical to ours. Kommandeur Mietusch lifted his wing and dove; we immediately followed. Like birds of prey we fell from the sky, picking our victims with precision. The first Lightning exploded immediately, hit by the Kommandeur. The second went in the same way. The third turned to the right. I had it by the neck; it altered its bank, but I tightened my turn and opened fire. The Lightning fell away below, out of control. Poldi had a similar battle with his, and had the same success. Now we had to get away as quickly as possible, as sixty Thunderbolts had suddenly turned up. I dove away steeply, but now four Lightnings had me in their sights, right over Paris. There was a cloud, if I could only reach it! Just as I disappeared in it, one pursuer let off a burst of fire. My 109 showed a white plume. A coolant line hit! The temperature climbed immediately. I closed the throttle and glided in an easterly direction. When I left the cloud my pursuers were nowhere to be seen. I landed my good old "Yellow 13" on its belly just outside Paris. We had scored seven victories—a great success. We had also lost seven aircraft, but most were not total losses. It had again been eighteen against 120, the same odds we faced daily.

The next morning Obstlt. Priller received his orders very early. He was to take off from Guyancourt at 0625 as formation leader of II/JG 26, III/JG 26, and III/JG 54; their mission was to sweep an area northwest of Caen. It promised to be a sunny, cloudless day, and soon the German fighters had assembled and were barreling along above the Normandy countryside. Before reaching the beachhead, however, they were ordered to change course. Five Pulks of heavy enemy bombers were just then crossing the French coast, flying in the direction of Paris. The Kommodore, at the head of the formation, spotted them first—small, twinkling points of light at about 16,000 feet altitude. He also saw the escort fighters swarming above them, and decided on a swift attack. Quoting his combat report:

> I made an oblique attack on the first box from the side, at the same altitude, and obtained several strikes on one of the Boeings

flying on the left side of the formation. After a battle at close range with the very strong escort, I attacked a formation of about twenty Liberators from the front. I fired at the Liberator flying the left outboard position in the first vee, and saw strikes in the cockpit and on the two left engines. After I dove away I saw the Liberator sheer away from the formation, bright flames coming from three engines, and dive. I could not see it hit the ground because of the continuing air battle.

Priller's Liberator belonged to the 492nd Bomb Group. It headed for the beachhead on two engines. When the propeller governor on a third engine quit, the pilot told the crew to stand by. They were at 7,000 feet, and the coast was visible thirty miles away. The navigator signaled, mistakenly, that they were over Allied territory and bailed out. A moment later the fourth engine quit, prompting all the remaining crew but the pilot to bail out within fifteen seconds. The pilot then trimmed the plane and jumped out himself. The navigator was captured, but the other nine men landed safely within the Allied lines. Ironically, the navigator's error saved his life; the rest of his crew were killed in the crash of another B-24 less than three weeks later.

Pips Priller's victory was his 100th. All had been obtained on the Channel front. Only a handful of pilots had scored a hundred victories in the West; such a milestone gave the Geschwader cause for genuine celebration. After Priller landed, he was presented with a gift from his officers, a bouquet of flowers, and a letter from his wife, who was expecting their first child in a few weeks. He tore first into the latter, scanned it briefly, and muttered, "Thank God, all goes well at home!" The festivities could begin. Messages congratulating Priller on his extraordinary achievement continued to arrive at Chaumont for the next several weeks. At the end of June, he was summoned to Adolf Hitler's headquarters to receive the Swords to his Knight's Cross. He was the second (and last) pilot to be awarded this decoration while a member of JG 26.

Mietusch's Gruppe also found a Liberator Pulk that morning. His Bf 109s were able to make three attacks on the 392nd Bomb Group's formation. The bomber gunners claimed two victories; one Messerschmitt was in fact downed. Uffz. Tippe's performance on the 14th had indicated that he was fast becoming a reliable, competent fighter pilot. Klaus Mietusch had noticed the young Unteroffizier and had plans for him, as noted in Erhard Tippe's continuing narrative:

> Today I flew as my Gruppenkommandeur's wingman. It was a real honor to fly with the Kommandeur at the head of the formation. As usual, we climbed to 8,000 meters [26,000 feet]. Southwest of Chartres we spotted a Pulk of Liberators with strong fighter escort. Before the latter could see us, we made an immediate attack on the bombers. Rushing upon them at great speed, we totally surprised the formation. One Liberator quickly exploded, the victim of the Kommandeur. He had a remarkably good aim. My victim did not explode, but rather dove away to the right, trailing two plumes of smoke. After landing, I got three comrades to confirm my success as a certain Herausschuss [separation]. Major Mietusch was still at the dispersal with my Staffelkapitaen when I reported back from the mission. He congratulated me on my second victory, and continued, "Now, I want to give a little advice to Tippe. First, don't take off so close to me; that is always risky with the Bf 109. Second, you must remain with me after the attack. Now, before the next mission, pick out an airplane from the Stab flight. We shall then fly together, understand?" "Jawohl, Herr Major!" After these words I was graciously dismissed.

The claims of Mietusch and Tippe matched the actual losses of the 392nd Bomb Group. One B-24 was shot down immediately, while a second badly damaged bomber made it back across the Channel and crashed at an English emergency field.

Over the next week, the Schlageter pilots began to encounter the aircraft of the British Second Tactical Air Force with greater frequency. An early morning mission on the 16th brought Uffz. Tippe's promising combat career to an end. Erhard Tippe concludes his story:

> I spent an almost sleepless night, bothered by the frequent alarms and subsequent warnings. When the orderly awakened us at 0410, I leapt immediately for the bathroom and took an ice-cold bath to shake off the night. At the pilots' mess during breakfast, the Old Man [Lt. Peter Reischer] told me that I was again to be the Kommandeur's wingman, and that I needed to go to the Gruppe command post. Then we went to the field to get ready for the early scramble. My aircraft from the previous day was not operational, and

251

so I had to select another from several which were standing some distance away in a hangar. I thus had to take off last, and alone. Three Gruppen of Bf 109s were flying in front of me. I checked them out one by one. The one flying on the right was not mine. Neither was the one in the middle. I was still flying with that one, however, when it dropped through the cloud deck.

There was a gigantic array of ships. Barrage balloons with steel wires hanging from one to the other. Further progress was impossible. Course change of 180 degrees. I was in the middle of an undisciplined mob. To avoid being rammed, I pulled up sharply, disappeared into a cloud, and lost my connection with this unknown Gruppe. When I came out of the cloud, there were two aircraft in front of me. For a moment I thought they were Bf 109s, but I soon made them out to be Spitfires. Right beside me were six more Spitfires. Escape at low altitude was unfortunately not possible, since I was surrounded by the enemy. I tried to reach a protective cloud by climbing in a tight bank. All went well for a while, as they could not draw lead in the spiral. But the Spitfires drew closer, and I could do nothing in the face of their superior performance. One after the other took the lead and opened fire with all barrels. The fourth or fifth hit my good bird, which immediately showed the white plume indicating radiator damage. The temperature quickly climbed out of the permitted range.

I was flying at 1,300 meters [4,200 feet]; the cloud deck was at about 2,000 meters [6,500 feet], and my aircraft was no longer airworthy. So what to do? Canopy off and climb out. I free-fell until I was about 300 meters [1,000 feet] above the ground, delaying opening my chute until the last moment, since there had been several recent cases of pilots being shot hanging in their parachutes. I landed in a bramble bush. . . .

Suddenly three Canadian soldiers with machine pistols appeared in front of me. "Come on, boy!" was how they put it to me, just that simply. As I took off my parachute, I realized that my right shoulder was injured. I could no longer bend my right arm. I crept painfully out of the bushes. . . .

Erhard Tippe's opponents were from No. 443 Squadron (RCAF), six of whose Spitfires scrambled from their French airstrip at 0500 to intercept twenty Bf 109s. Tippe's was the only one shot down. He was the only Geschwader pilot taken prisoner in June; that this was a rare occurrence is indicative of the small percentage of the unit's sorties that succeeded in crossing the battle lines.

The next day, the Second Gruppe was involved in a number of combats with American and British fighters over the battlefield. Four young Unteroffiziere from the Gruppe failed to return. The surviving Focke-Wulf pilots claimed the destruction of two P-47s and two P-51s. On the 18th, Addi Glunz took a young pilot of the 7th Staffel with him on a two-plane evening sweep. They encountered a pair of tactical reconnaissance Mustangs, from No. 414 Squadron (RCAF), and shot them both down. The more experienced of the Geschwader's pilots could best most Allied pilots in single combat, but such opportunities came rarely.

HOPELESS INFERIORITY

Despite their isolated successes, the fighters of Jagdkorps II were totally incapable of any effective challenge to Allied air supremacy. The Allies followed the consequent intramural squabbles with interest, thanks to their Ultra intercepts. At a conference of fighter commanders on 20 June, Major Mietusch and Hptm. Weiss, the Kommandeur of III/JG 54, expressed their opinion that severe losses over the beachhead could only be minimized by flying in large formations, because of the shortage of leaders and the poor state of training of the replacement pilots. On the same day, the commanding general of Flakkorps III complained to Generalfeldmarschall Sperrle about the absence of German fighters over the front. In the words of the chief of staff of Jagdkorps II, "Destructive criticism of the day fighters became increasingly prevalent."

Early in the afternoon of 22 June, the Third Gruppe took off from Villacoublay in full strength. Their mission was to seek out Allied fighter-bombers near Cherbourg. Before reaching their patrol zone, however, they became embroiled with more Jabos than they could handle. Southwest of Caen, Lt. Peter Reischer led the eight Bf 109s of his 11th Staffel in a bounce of four 365th Fighter Group P-47s. They were spotted, and as the P-47s broke into them the American cover flight dove on the Messerschmitts from above. The leader of this flight picked out Reischer's Bf 109, which led the P-47 toward the ground in a series of violent maneuvers. The American pilot blacked out in a low-altitude split-S and lost Reischer, who had to crash-land his damaged aircraft a few minutes later.

The rest of Reischer's Staffel, sandwiched between the two

flights of P-47s, fought for their lives. Two German pilots were killed, and a third bailed out, while one P-47 was shot down. Two more flights of P-47s fell on two 109s leaving the area and engaged them in a turning combat in which the German fighters had the advantage. One P-47 was shot down before one of their number managed to cut across the Lufbery and shoot down one of the Messerschmitts.

In the meantime, two squadrons from another Ninth Air Force P-47 group, the 368th, had encountered formations of Messerschmitts west of Vire and shot down several in small-scale dogfights. One III/JG 26 pilot was killed and three bailed out wounded after these combats. Claims by the two P-47 units totaled 9-1-4 Bf 109s. According to the 5th Jagddivision war diary, twelve III/JG 26 pilots had failed to return to base or make their whereabouts known by nightfall. Eight of these pilots can be accounted for in the casualty list; the other four had either made emergency landings or had bailed out unwounded.

The results of the mission of 22 June lent further credence to Major Mietusch's complaints. The highly proficient Hptm. Staiger had been ordered from the Third Gruppe to the First in mid-May, to fill in for Major Borris during a lengthy absence by the latter. Mietusch's Gruppe now contained only three officers with experience as combat leaders—himself, Lt. Reischer, and Oblt. Paul Schauder of the 10th Staffel. The unit was proving unable to best even the enemy's fighter-bombers, which were piloted, it was to be assumed, by young men with as little experience in air-to-air combat as Mietusch's average enlisted pilot. His Bf 109s were slower than every Allied fighter type at low altitude, severely limiting his pilots' chances of escaping from an unfavorable combat situation. Whenever possible, the Messerschmitts were employed as high cover, leaving the job of ground attack to the faster and more heavily armored FW 190s. But Mietusch's aircraft proved vulnerable even as pure fighters. Morale in the Gruppe began to drop.

The two Focke-Wulf Gruppen were in better shape. Most of their Staffeln contained at least two experienced officers, and the pilots had a high degree of confidence in their aircraft. Many surviving German pilots claim today that the FW 190A could outrun any Allied fighter on the deck, regardless of the official performance figures. The fighter's superb rate of roll gave it a useful maneuver for both attack and escape. And the weight and dispersion of fire of its wing-mounted cannon gave even the most inexperienced pilot a chance to knock down enemy aircraft. The claim-to-loss ratio of both the First and Second Gruppen remained well over two to one throughout the summer; this was a far better performance than that of the Jagdwaffe as a whole.

While the Third Gruppe was struggling against the Jabos on 22 June, the young Kapitaene of the 7th and 8th Staffeln, Lts. Vogt and Hofmann, were each shooting down a heavy bomber east of Paris. Their Gruppe suffered no losses to the heavy bombers or their escort. Formation leaders dominated JG 26's win and loss column on the 23rd. Vogt and Hofmann teamed up on an afternoon patrol northeast of Caen and shot down two No. 414 Squadron (RCAF) Mustangs that were scouting the battle lines. Hptm. Staiger, in temporary command of the First Gruppe, shot down a Spitfire, while Major Mietusch returned to his private war against the Lightnings and shot down two 55th Fighter Group P-38s. He and his wingman caught the American squadron circling in the vicinity of Villacoublay and made an immediate attack, in order to distract the American pilots and permit his own men to land. The Geschwader's only casualty for the day was the Second Gruppe's Kommandeur, Hptm. Johannes Naumann, who chased a Mustang back across no-man's-land and was then hit by British flak. Naumann bailed out, injuring both legs when they struck the tail of his aircraft. Fortunately, he landed within the German lines.

The Schlageter pilots' wearying routine continued for the rest of June. Whenever the weather was flyable, they were either on readiness or in the air, from dawn at 0400 to full darkness at 2300. Their main meal was at noon, and it was brought to them by truck. A typical meal consisted of potatoes, goulash, and mashed peas, "as much as they wanted," in the words of an enlisted pilot. Weather and flight duties permitting, they would then nap under the neighboring trees. They spent the brief nights in tents near their dispersals; the few buildings as yet undamaged by bombs were needed by the ground staff. Both Guyancourt and Villacoublay had been major air bases of the French Air Force. Their grass strips had well-engineered drainage, and few aircraft were lost in takeoff or landing accidents. Both bases were almost surrounded by woods, providing excellent camouflage for the aircraft dispersals. The maintenance crews worked around the clock to keep their aircraft serviceable. Fuel and spare parts were in good supply. The major deficiencies were simply in the numbers of planes and pilots.

Two events of note took place near the end of the month. On the 24th, Addi Glunz was awarded the Oak Leaves to his Knight's Cross, after his 65th victory. On the 28th, a new Kommandeur arrived for the Second Gruppe. Hptm. Naumann required hospitalization for his injuries, and Priller succeeded in obtaining as his replacement an experienced pilot from the Green Hearts, a man with an outstanding reputation as an aggressive combat leader— Hptm. Emil Lang. The 35-year-old Lang was a former Lufthansa pilot and a noted athlete. He had gained 159 victories with JG 54, mostly on the Eastern Front, and wore the Oak Leaves to the Knight's Cross. Priller had to give up an officer in exchange for Lang. He selected the newest officer in the Second Gruppe, Lt. Peter Crump, who had only received his commission on the 17th of June. Crump moved to the Green Hearts' side of Villacoublay on 15 July. Lang, a long-time Staffelkapitaen in JG 54, was overdue for promotion to Gruppenkommandeur, and was prepared to make the most of his opportunity. His long combat tour had done nothing to sap his energy, and he swiftly made his mark on the Second Gruppe, which already led the Geschwader in victories and victory-to-loss ratio.

By the end of June, the Geschwader's service on the invasion front had cost it twenty-eight pilots killed in combat and another three in accidents. One pilot had been taken prisoner, and at least twenty-four had been injured. The wounded included one Gruppenkommandeur and four Staffelkapitaene. Based on the Luftwaffe strength returns, the Geschwader's three Gruppen represented 15 percent of the 5th Jagddivision's fighter strength on this day. The pilots of JG 26 claimed at least seventy-seven victories during June; this was about one-quarter of all the 5th Jagddivision's victory claims.

A document prepared by an OKL staff officer after a visit to Luftflotte 3 has preserved some telling statistics for the period 6–30 June. Luftflotte 3's fighter organization, Jagdkorps II, commanded twenty single-engined fighter Gruppen in its two Jagddivisionen, the 4th and the 5th. Its table of organization strength was 1,300 fighters and pilots; actual strength on the evening of 30 June was 233 airplanes and 419 pilots. Victory claims by pilots of single-engined fighters over occupied France and the Low Countries totaled 414, against 458 losses. A total of 998 fighters had reached the invasion front as reinforcements, but almost half had already been destroyed. Single-engined fighters had flown 10,061 sorties on the invasion front, counting pure fighter, fighter-bomber, and reconnaissance missions, against an estimated 120,000–140,000 sorties flown by the Allies. It was the opinion of the Jagdkorps II staff that it was pointless to attack heavy bomber formations, since there was no possibility of destroying enough aircraft to lessen the effect of their bombing attacks. Fighter attacks were to be directed instead at enemy fighter-bombers and artillery spotters, as these presented the greatest threat to the army. The loss rate on combat missions was running 20 to 30 percent. Three German fighters were being lost for every Allied fighter loss. Pilots were being lost at the rate of two for one.

On 5 July, Ultra intercepted an order by Reichsmarschall Goering stating that because of the recent high rate of loss of indispensable combat leaders, these men could no longer fly combat missions unless at least the following numbers of aircraft were available in support: Staffelkapitaene required six aircraft; Gruppenkommandeure, fifteen; and Geschwaderkommodoren, forty-five. Some units were severely constrained by this order. II/JG 26, by pushing its "black men" (ground crews) to the limit, was barely able to report enough Focke-Wulfs operational to permit its new Kommandeur to fly. Hptm. Lang had brought with him from III/JG 54 an experienced Staffel leader, Lt. Alfred Gross, as his wingman. Thus supported, he took to the air on 9 July, and upon his return reported the destruction of three Spitfires within six minutes over Caen. He was then effectively grounded by the low strength of his Gruppe.

Major Borris returned to the Geschwader but did not immediately reclaim the command of the First Gruppe from Hptm. Staiger. He did fly missions, however, and on 14 July he led the First Gruppe west from Paris on a hunt for American fighter-bombers. Near Alencon they encountered two squadrons of the 358th Fighter Group. Splitting into Schwaerme, the Focke-Wulfs dove from the clouds, made brief firing passes, and zoomed back to safety, carrying out their longtime leader's careful tactics to perfection. They returned to Guyancourt to claim the destruction of five

Thunderbolts; one claim was later disallowed. Four Thunderbolts were in fact shot down. The surviving American pilots claimed six German fighters and were ultimately credited with two. Only one of Borris's men was shot down; he bailed out and survived.

In mid-July, Uffz. Heinz Gehrke of 11th Staffel claimed a most unusual victory. Several Gruppen took off from their Paris fields to intercept a formation of heavy bombers, which were reportedly unescorted. When the Third Gruppe reached the bombers, they were seen to be flying in a most peculiar formation—scarcely a formation at all. Coming closer, they were recognized as British Lancasters—night bombers, which with the decline of the Jagdwaffe were now being used occasionally by day. However, something had gone wrong with the Allied escort plan, and the Lancasters had already been punished by German fighters before the arrival of the Third Gruppe. Gehrke's element leader, Fw. Karl Laub, selected a straggling Lancaster that was flying at 10,000 feet. The two pilots could see the tail gunner slumped over, dead; the turret was totally destroyed. The Messerschmitts were able to attack from the rear, entirely unmolested. During the attack the bomber crewmen, who had no weapons that could bear on the fighters, threw bundles of window (radar-reflecting aluminum foil) out of their aircraft, in an apparent attempt to distract or defy the German pilots. Gehrke's fire hit the left outboard engine, and the bomber dove away, smoking. As the bomber had previously been damaged, Gehrke was not awarded a full victory credit, but rather one for a "final destruction." Heinz Gehrke is uncertain of the exact date of this combat, but five Lancasters were lost on 15 July in a raid on Nevers, sixty miles south of Paris. It is possible that some of these Lancasters fell victim to the guns of III/JG 26.

That Gruppe was hammered once again, however, on 17 July. Its sweep of the Caen area in mid-afternoon ended in a large battle with Allied fighters. Major Mietusch claimed one Spitfire, but two of his pilots were shot down and killed, and two more were injured. This was Heinz Gehrke's first time to fly as Mietusch's wingman. His sole job was to protect his Kommandeur, and he remembers that his head was rotating constantly from side to side as though on a swivel, checking to his rear. En route back to Villacoublay, he sighted an aircraft, and immediately cried over the radio, "Otter Mietusch from Otter Gehrke, question mark behind us!" (The Jagdwaffe had at last begun using identity codes in the air; III/JG 26 were the "Otters.") Mietusch replied, "Victor, victor, I see," but held course. Disaster struck a minute later, in the form of an Allied fighter. Gehrke yelled into the radio, "Mietusch, Spitfires behind us!", turned into the enemy aircraft, and opened fire. A wild dogfight ensued, with the result that Mietusch was shot down and did not return to the Gruppe until the next day. Gehrke, having lost his chief, dreaded his own return to base. Fortunately for him, his radio transmissions had been received in the Gruppe command post and overheard by Oberst Hannes Trautloft, who was visiting the unit in his role as inspector of the day fighters. Trautloft, for years the Green Hearts' Kommodore, was a tolerant and understanding officer and absolved Heinz Gehrke of any responsibility for Mietusch's downing. Klaus Mietusch was a high-strung man who from all indications had almost reached his breaking point from the strain of his many responsibilities—he was not only the Gruppe's administrative and combat leader, but also its only consistent scorer. He rarely spoke to his enlisted pilots and, after returning from hospitalization in Germany, did not seek out Gehrke, either to rebuke him or to thank him for his actions on the 17th.

Later that evening, the Third Gruppe again encountered Allied fighters. The unit was flying near Evreux, as part of a large mixed formation of fighters that was attacked from below by seven P-51s of the 354th "Pioneer Mustang" Group. III/JG 26 lost two more pilots killed, but in return shot down two of the Mustangs. The next day, a flight of Thunderbolts from the 373rd Fighter Group encountered "twenty FW 190s and Bf 109s" at 14,000 feet north of Dreux, dove on six of them from 4,000 feet above, and shot down two without loss. The survivors were chased back toward Paris but were let go when the American flight leader ran out of ammunition. The German victims were the 9th Staffel's one-legged Kapitaen, Oblt. Viktor Hilgendorff, and his wingman, Lt. Voelmle, who filed this report:

> On 18 July 1944, I took off at 0910 as Oblt. Hilgendorff's wingman for a freie Jagd around Caen. Our Gruppe was dispersed by Lightnings, which attacked us from above soon after takeoff. Oblt. Hilgendorff sought to gain altitude toward the southwest. We fired at six Thunderbolts which we approached head-on at our altitude. . . .

The Thunderbolts banked around and followed us, but could not catch us in our climb.

Over Dreux at 0945, at about 4,500 meters [15,000 feet], we sighted 10–12 Thunderbolts. They approached from the sun, split up, and attacked us from several directions. While the battle was still developing, I kept Oblt. Hilgendorff in sight. I lost him when a Thunderbolt, approaching in a right bank from the side, hit my fuselage and cockpit. Since my aircraft had become uncontrollable, I climbed out. While hanging in my parachute, I heard gunfire in my vicinity, and now and then shots went past me, but due to light shrapnel wounds to my face I could see almost nothing.

The statement from ground witnesses that Oblt. Hilgendorff was shot while hanging in his parachute appears believable. . . . The gunfire I heard while in my parachute could only have been meant for Oblt. Hilgendorff. I myself was not fired at, and there were no German aircraft in the vicinity.

A "new" Luftwaffe weapon was reintroduced to I/JG 26 on 15 July. The 21-cm rocket mortar shells used in 1943 to break up bomber formations were now slung once more beneath the wings of their FW 190s; this time they were to be employed against Allied armor. The rockets were spectacular but highly inaccurate weapons; the First Gruppe's pilots heartily disliked both the rockets and their heavy launch tubes.

On 20 July, the Second Gruppe received the good news that it was to be withdrawn—all the way back to Germany. The Gruppe's remaining pilots flew to Reinsehlen that same day. On 25 July, Eisenhower's armies began Operation Cobra and succeeded in breaking out of their Normandy beachhead. The Luftwaffe was helpless to intervene. Jagdkorps II reported a total of thirty operational fighters on 29 July. This total included the remnants of III/JG 26, still at Villacoublay, as well as the Stab and the First Gruppe, which moved from the shattered fields around Chaumont on the 29th, but only as far as Rambouillet. This new field was also in the greater Paris area. At this time, Major Borris resumed command of the First Gruppe; Hptm. Staiger left that unit to take over a Gruppe in JG 1. JG 26 claimed at least thirty aerial victories in July, at the cost of twenty pilots killed in combat (including two Staffelkapitaene), one killed in a flying accident, and at least sixteen injured, including two more Kapitaene. Their ratio of victories to losses had dropped sharply from June, in large part because their losses had not been replaced, and they had been forced to fly in ever-smaller formations.

SUCCESSES AND FAILURES

Once back in Germany, Emil Lang set about rebuilding his Gruppe in his typically energetic and unconventional manner. As August began, Lt. Gerhard Vogt was sent on a recruiting trip to the Ergaenzungsgruppen (advanced training groups). He landed first at Hohensalza in eastern Germany, and told the assembled FW 190 pilot trainees that they would be given the opportunity to volunteer for service in the famous Schlageter Geschwader, in the Gruppe commanded by the renowned Hptm. Emil Lang, who was quoted as saying, "Give me several experienced Staffelkapitaene and Schwarmfuehrer, and I will seek out the rest from among the Nach-wuchs and get results." (Nachwuchs, or "new growth," was the term commonly used in Germany for the late-war crop of poorly trained replacement pilots.) A number of the Nachwuchs stepped forward, including Ottomar Kruse and Walter Stumpf. Vogt's task was to evaluate the volunteers' flying skills and take only the best back to Reinsehlen. The first test flight brought disaster. Vogt banked away from the rest of his Schwarm, which, in order not to lose him, had to make a steeper turn. The fourth pilot attempted to shorten the curve still further with a half roll. He knew that he was near the ground and pulled up too sharply, stalled out, and hit the ground not far from the command post. The FW 190 smashed itself to pieces; the unfortunate pilot was thrown a good fifty yards, and he died instantly. Back on the ground, Lt. Vogt expressed his regrets at the man's death, while commenting on how well he had main-tained position during the test flight. Vogt was obviously unnerved, however, and called off the remaining evaluation flights. All of the surviving volunteers, a total of eight to ten men, were selected, and their orders to join II/JG 26 at Reinsehlen were soon in hand. Walter Stumpf's logbook indicates that he joined the combat unit after a total of 180 hours of flight training. He had spent fewer than twenty hours at the controls of a fighter aircraft. A typical RAF fighter pilot had 450 hours of flight training before receiving his first operational posting; the average American pilot, 600 hours.

261

From their fields around Paris, the rest of the Geschwader continued the struggle, against ever-increasing odds. The Luftwaffe attempted to support the German Army's attack on Mortain, which was Hitler's response to the American breakout at Avranches. But Jagdkorps II was hard pressed to mount even one hundred combat sorties per day. Full-strength Gruppe missions were flown by eight to ten aircraft; to put as many as twenty fighters in the air frequently required the combined efforts of four or five Gruppen.

Several Schlageter pilots were lost to Allied antiaircraft fire. Two 2nd Staffel pilots were shot down and taken prisoner while strafing road convoys. However, most German fighter formations were intercepted by Allied fighters before they reached the battle lines. At 1400 on 7 August, six rocket-carrying First Gruppe FW 190s and eighteen Third Gruppe Bf 109s flew a combined mission with III/JG 1, III/JG 3, I/JG 5, and III/JG 54. Their orders called for an attack on an American ground column, but the German fighters were set upon and dispersed by several squadrons of Ninth Air Force P-47s and P-51s, which claimed a total of 12-0-2 victories. The first sighting was apparently made by eight P-47s of the 368th Fighter Group, who reported the approach of "35+" Messerschmitts carrying bombs (probably drop tanks) and heading toward the American lines. When the P-47s were spotted, the German fighters jettisoned their loads and began to orbit a large cumulus cloud. The American squadron commander radioed for help, which soon arrived. The P-47s then fell on the Messerschmitts, which in the words of the Americans "did not want to fight. Some hit the deck and started for home; others just milled around as though they didn't know what had happened." Two pilots from III/JG 26 were killed in this engagement. Gefr. Hans Thran bailed out successfully but, according to ground witnesses, was shot in his parachute by a P-47 pilot while only sixty feet above the ground. German pilots had a fear of being killed while hanging helpless in their parachutes, and every such report was investigated and carefully documented. These incidents were especially common during the summer and autumn of 1944.

Back in Germany, II/JG 26 was absorbing its new pilots and preparing to return to the front. Ogfr. Walter Stumpf had been assigned to Lt. Hans Prager's 7th Staffel; Uffz. Ottomar Kruse, to Lt. Wilhelm Hofmann's 8th. The Gruppe quickly grew from thirty pilots to seventy-eight, a number that still sticks in Ottomar Kruse's mind. Formation and simulated combat flights were flown. While on the ground, the experienced pilots talked flying constantly, while the Nachwuchs listened intently. There was much to be learned from the old hands—how they had attacked, how they had gotten away. Hofmann gave this advice to his pilots: "If you ever have to bail out, remember that the Americans are known to shoot us in our parachutes. Therefore, free-fall to about 200 meters; only that way can you be sure of survival. I have seen one of my best friends torn to bits by enemy cannon fire while still hanging in his chute." Hofmann was a hard man, and he swore that he would kill any enemy pilot he caught in the same situation.

At 1100 on 12 August, the pilots of the Second Gruppe received their orders to leave Reinsehlen. By 1200 the aircraft were loaded, and the pilots went to eat their noon meal. Suddenly the word came—movement canceled. Walter Stumpf delayed his unpacking, since it had taken some time to get everything into his Focke-Wulf's baggage compartment. His kit included a pilot's duffel bag with his clothing, his parachute pack, ground charts, a tool chest, a radio case, spark plugs, and other odds and ends. Some time later, the transfer flight was ordered again. The entire staff of the air base, including many young women, turned out to see them off, and ran alongside the aircraft to the takeoff point. Takeoff was in order of Staffeln—Stabsschwarm, 5th, 6th, 7th, 8th Staffel. All of the aircraft formed up over the field except one, which force-landed with a dead engine. The ground staff waved the large formation off as it headed for Muenchen-Gladbach. Walter Stumpf had no confidence in his own navigational skills and stayed very close to his element leader, Uffz. Heinz Salomon. Upon arrival at Muenchen-Gladbach, they were made to circle the field for some time, until low fuel finally forced them to land in the twilight, which they did without incident.

The pilots saw to the servicing of their planes, reported in, and then headed to the pilots' common room. Hauptmann Lang praised his pilots—"not a single crash." The pilots from the unit stationed on the field greeted them. Supper—fried potatoes, eggs, milk—was brought in and served by the chief paymaster, to the amazement of the Nachwuchs, who were not yet used to the status awarded a German combat pilot.

The pilots were awakened early the next morning, ate breakfast, and headed out to the aircraft. There was an accident on takeoff. One Focke-Wulf lifted off, and then crashed; another bad engine. Its pilot was killed. The remaining pilots were led away by a pilot from the First Gruppe, who promptly got lost. They finally arrived at St. Dizier, low on fuel. Walter Stumpf was uncomfortably hot and sweated profusely. After he landed, a ground crewman pointed out that the cockpit heater had been turned on. Stumpf hadn't even known such a thing existed.

The pilots waited most of the next day for takeoff orders to arrive. Lang finally ordered them to their planes. Just then Lt. Hofmann arrived with twelve more aircraft, which had been unserviceable the previous day. The pilots waited until the newcomers had been refueled, then climbed in their aircraft and taxied out for takeoff. To the new pilots it was a frightening, confusing scene, as aircraft took off from several directions. A Focke-Wulf suffered engine failure and made a forced landing in between those taking off. Miraculously, there were no collisions. The aircraft didn't form up, as the First Gruppe guide had already ordered "Reise-reise" (depart on course).

Uffz. Salomon's landing gear was damaged, and wouldn't retract properly. He and Stumpf were thus the last to leave the field. Salomon landed again, but Stumpf decided to stay with the mob. Stumpf was by himself in the rear, and gave his plane full throttle, as "the last one is bitten by the dogs," in his words. Slowly he caught the others and formed up on Lt. Prager. They remained at low altitude. Soon they spotted the Eiffel Tower—they had reached Paris.

The first report of Indians came from Hofmann; then Lang, then Prager. Kruse and Stumpf saw nothing and thought only of landing. They were now over Guyancourt, which had been the site of Walter Stumpf's basic flight training earlier that year. The airbase now presented a scene of total destruction. Right beside it was a crude landing ground. All of the Gruppe's Staffeln but the 7th landed there. The 7th Staffel flew past it, to an airfield near Rambouillet. Repeatedly there came the report, "Indians at . . ." The Nachwuchs saw nothing; it was all very confusing. Suddenly they banked, on orders over the radio, and prepared to "Lucy-Anton" (land). Walter Stumpf continues:

Where was the airfield? There, a 190 was landing on a plowed field. That had to be it. But there was an overhead power line. Prager and Scharf prepared to land. I was behind them. I now saw a gap in the power line. We landed close behind one another. Ten yards apart, arrayed from left to right. I was on the far right, and oriented myself with the edge of the field. I put on the brakes, and saw nothing in front. Was I heading toward Scharf? I braked sharply, and cleared myself to the left. There was nothing in my path. A ground crewman waved me onward. I needed to clear the field; the next plane was coming in. The man was standing in a patch of woods. I taxied into it; everyone was waving and shaking their fists at me. I switched off the engine and was told that no one was permitted to taxi into the woods; the aircraft were pushed in by hand, tails first. I had been told nothing of this. The plane was pushed back somewhat and covered with camouflage. Heaven be praised, I was back on the ground. The flight had been no fun at all. I had been totally confused about everything. All of our aircraft had now landed, and were being covered with tree limbs. Spitfires and Mustangs had already passed over the field, but had not yet spotted it. However, there were too many of us, perhaps fifty-five aircraft, to stay here for very long.

We all reported our clear status or our deficiencies to Prager. My ship, "Brown 4," was the only one completely operational. I was well pleased with my aircraft. We received help from the First Gruppe's ground crews, since our Staffel support personnel were still in Guyancourt. They were to arrive two days later.

I got my gear from my aircraft. The plane was then covered. We got into a bus that had come up, and left. Three observers on the fenders searched the skies. We traveled most cautiously, since the Tommies kept their eyes on every mousehole. They had a fearsome superiority. There was scarcely a minute in which no enemy aircraft could be seen or heard. So we drove as quickly as possible to our quarters, and went inside. At Rambouillet we lived in a splendid castle with beautiful rooms. We all washed up, ate, and then sat down together. There was doppelkopf—a game popular in the Staffel—music, and cognac, so we were late to bed.

Ottomar Kruse describes his early impressions of Guyancourt:

That's where I had my first taste of being a full fighter pilot, although I hadn't yet seen any action. There were several different types of easy chairs lying about; that's where we stayed when we were on the airfield. The first morning we were there, the Leutnant in charge of the mechanics arrived to report to Lt. Hofmann, my Kapitaen, who was responsible for absolutely everything—we had about 120 men in the Staffel, including the pilots. We younger pilots stood up, which was customary when an officer entered. He didn't bat an eye, but came up to us, greeting each of us as "Herr" [Mister]— "Guten Morgen, Herr Kruse." Somebody told us later to relax; we didn't jump up for officers. We weren't Unteroffiziere or Obergefreite; we were "Herren." This was quite a new experience for me, because discipline was very strict indeed in the German armed forces. You normally had to salute anyone of superior rank.

Combat missions were flown every day. The 8th Staffel's contribution to these was usually four to six planes. Hofmann decided which of his pilots would fly. We had exactly sixteen aircraft and sixteen pilots, of whom eight or nine were Nachwuchs. Each pilot had been assigned his own Focke-Wulf. Mine was the "Blue 6," which I had already determined to be something of a lame pig. Hofmann nearly always chose pilots with previous combat experience. He always looked right past me, to my great disappointment.

While the Second Gruppe was making ready to return to action, the rest of JG 26 continued flying missions from Paris. The First and Third Gruppen had had to absorb their replacement pilots while still engaged in daily combat. Uffz. Hans Kukla was one of these replacements. He had reported to the 4th Staffel on 30 June and flew his third combat sortie on 13 August. Twelve First Gruppe FW 190s took off that morning carrying rocket mortars. Their mission was to attack the eastward flood of Allied armor. They flew at low level, escorted by some JG 3 Bf 109s, which were 6,500 feet above them. Kukla's 4th Staffel had put up one Schwarm for the mission and flew in the rear position. The Schwarmfuehrer was Fw. Robert Hager, an experienced pilot. Kukla flew as Number 4 and was thus the Holzauge—the wooden eye or lookout—for the entire Focke-Wulf formation. After attacking some tanks between Chartres and Le Mans, the formation turned for home. Kukla then made a fatal error; he let his guard drop. The Bf 109 cover had given him a sense of security. When he finally glanced to the rear, the Messerschmitts had turned into Mustangs, which had dispersed the 109s and were bearing down on Kukla's flight. Hans Kukla recalls:

> Since we were at ground level, there was no possibility of defense. I was the first to be hit. My plane took strikes in the engine

and immediately burst into flames. I pulled the nose up and bailed out. My chute opened at sixty feet, and I landed in the garden of a farm. I learned later that my three comrades were all shot down and killed. The farmer's wife told me that I was in no-man's-land. I gave her my parachute, and headed north on foot. . . . During my bail-out I had received a facial burn and severe bruises, which put me out of action until October. . . .

The Mustang that shot downed Kukla was from the Ninth Air Force's 363rd Fighter Group. Eight P-51s took off at around 0700 for a patrol of the Alencon-Le Mans area. The second of the two flights was led by Lt. Lee Webster and flew at about 9,000 feet. Near the end of their patrol, Webster spotted aircraft below, headed east at 4,000 feet. His cover flight did not hear Webster's call, so he led his four Mustangs down alone. He identified the bogies as Bf 109s and saw a dozen more aircraft in front of them, on the deck. The 109s turned into the attack. Webster's first salvo sent one Messer-schmitt pilot over the side. The American pilot broke out of his turn and headed for the formation below with his wingman, Lt. George Brooks, leaving the remaining 109s to his Number 3 and Number 4. He joined the tail end of a formation of about ten FW 190s. He missed the rear plane with his first burst but then corrected and scored hits all over the fuselage. The pilot—Hans Kukla—pulled his nose up and bailed out. The next plane in line took a full salvo from Brook's four .50s and entered a "dead man's turn" to the right. Webster had now opened fire on Hager's wingman and saw his plane burst into flames and crash. Robert Hager succeeded in turn-ing his Focke-Wulf around; someone managed at this point to dam-age Webster's plane, but Hager then fell to his death. The two P-51 pilots had shot down the entire 4th Staffel Schwarm.

Emil Lang still did not consider his Second Gruppe fully op-erational. He scheduled an orientation flight for early 15 August. There were more pilots than serviceable airplanes. Walter Stumpf was not picked to fly, so he watched from the ground as another Nachwuchs took off in Stumpf's "Brown 4." Takeoff was delayed by the tactical situation, but the mission finally got underway. The runway was a field of dry stubble. As the aircraft took off, they disappeared into a huge dust cloud that hung in the air for at least ten minutes. The 7th Staffel formed up over Rambouillet and flew in formation to Guyancourt to join up with the Gruppe. The rest of the Staffel stood on the field, waiting, watching, and smoking.

Eight Thunderbolts then made a firing pass on Rambouillet field. Just as they pulled up and started off, the 7th Staffel returned with the rest of the Second Gruppe, and Stumpf witnessed his first air combat:

It was only a small battle, but nonetheless the howling and shrieking seemed to go on forever. There, a cloud of smoke—a crash. Was it American, British, or one of ours? We couldn't tell; it was too far away. There, another and yet another! Hopefully none of them were ours. Four aircraft came down in a screaming dive. Two Thunderbolts in front, two of ours behind. They disappeared on the deck. Something caught fire nearby. A burst of fire, an engine roar. Suddenly a Thunderbolt hurtled right over our field, followed at some eighty meters [ninety yards] by a Focke-Wulf. Why hadn't he dropped his belly tank? A dogfight right above us. The Focke-Wulf was in perfect position, firing and obtaining strikes. We looked for cover, since it was obvious that the Thunderbolt would soon come crashing down.

"Keep firing, man, the Thunderbolt is done for. It's giving you the slip; keep firing!" What was going on? The Thunderbolt pitched over, righted itself, and flew away to the west. What was the matter with the Focke? Such a good position—keep firing! But it pulled up and flew away. We hit ourselves on our heads. How was such a thing possible? We later learned that it was Lt. Stein. His tank wouldn't release, but he had still scored one victory before he ran out of ammunition over the field.

In the meantime all became quiet. What had happened to the others? Hopefully, all would return. Restlessly, impatiently, we waited. Had they contacted the enemy again? Finally, our aircraft returned. We heard them first. Then they circled the field. Prager rocked his wings—a victory! Now they landed quickly. There, what is that? "Good lord, drop your landing gear, man, drop your gear!" It was crazy to attempt a belly landing carrying an auxiliary tank. "Drop your tank!" Too late, he had already set down—cracking, grinding, sliding. Surely it would catch fire, but no—the tank ripped away.

Prager and his wingman had to pull up to avoid something burning in the field. Good God, another drop tank. Two more arrived wanting to land. One pulled up; the other landed long—he finally set down, braking, braking, to the very edge of the field. Now the last aircraft came in. All landed quite fast and taxied, braking, directly into the woods. No one was missing! Who had smashed his mill in the belly landing? It was the man in my "Brown 4"! Good God, my first-class ship was now a dung heap. What had happened? The engine had puked and quit. Belly landing. Not too much damage—flaps and prop smashed.

Prager filed his victory claim with the command post. The Gruppe claimed a total of eight Thunderbolts. Hopefully my "Brown 4" would soon be operational again. Off duty at 1900, to supper by bus. The Staffel support personnel arrived suddenly with all our vehicles. We all joined in to help them unpack. At 2200 we heard the cry, "Enemy armor approaching." The Staffel had to pack up immediately. The pilots packed only the essentials into their aircraft. Great excitement as the Staffel personnel packed—everyone helped. We pilots loaded the technical services trailer. We could hear the roar of engines—the first armor! By midnight we had everything taken care of. We went to our rooms and tried to sleep. . . .

The Second Gruppe's first successful combat since their return to France resulted in considerable overclaiming. Only three Thunderbolts were in fact shot down. The Gruppe's opponents had been two squadrons of the 373rd Fighter Group, which were bounced after their bombing runs on Rambouillet by twenty FW 190s. The American pilots claimed three FW 190s shot down in return; the Second Gruppe lost two pilots. The 373rd had another run-in with Schlageter fighters before their mission was over. Near Dreux, one of the group's squadrons and a number of P-51s became embroiled with a gaggle of German fighters that had been sent up from Paris. The Thunderbolt pilots suffered no losses and claimed three Bf 109s. One of these was piloted by the 11th Staffel's luckless, but always high-spirited, Uffz. Heinz Gehrke. He recalls:

I went around for a while with a Mustang, who had me by the neck. In such cases we often flew in a corkscrew—we spiraled in the sky in the tightest possible circle, with flaps half or quarter-extended. A good soul in the form of a German fighter pilot helped me by shooting the Mustang off my tail. Its pilot had not noticed that we had become three—tough luck! I had just expressed my thanks over the radio, and begun my flight home with a beautiful split-S, when still more Indians appeared. I was unable to escape, and soon my machine took a number of hits. Whirling through the air, I threw my canopy off. Everything was covered in fuel and oil. Smoke came out of every opening; there was nothing left for me to do but bail out. This time I got out cleanly. My chute opened, and everything became peaceful. However, bad luck soon overtook me—I landed on a train embankment, rolled down the slope, and hit my head on a railroad tie. I lay there numbly and waited for whatever came next. But this time I stayed healthy, except for a throbbing head and neck. A troop of engineers fished me out. "Hurry, hurry!" they yelled at me. It was a demolition squad, which was destroying all power poles, bridges, and tracks. I had come down in no-man's-land. The Americans were in Dreux and were marching on Paris. This squad was the last German unit in front of the onrushing American army, and was attempting to put down obstacles to slow down the advance. So I was picked up by these valiant youths at the last minute and taken to Paris. I could not fly for the next few days because a severe bruise on my neck—probably hit while bailing out—made it too painful. . . .

On 16 August, a mass migration of aircraft and vehicles began from the German airfields west of Paris. Walter Stumpf's day at Rambouillet began early:

At 0300 we were roused to return to the field. Even at night there was continuous enemy activity in the air. We arrived at the field in the breaking dawn. All operational aircraft were to fly to Guyancourt. All the rest were to be blown up—"Brown 4" as well as "Brown 14," which I was to have flown; its oil tank was leaking. Then everything quieted down somewhat. It appeared that the Amis were not moving as rapidly as we had thought. "Brown 14" was repaired and I took it over. Our aircraft slowly disappeared into the sky, by flights and elements. I took off in foul weather—it had started raining. I flew along the road to Trappes, then turned right. Damned rain. I made my approach; flaps down, gear down, speed dropping. Going the right way? Yes, right toward the ground—all right, not too far, there were some scarecrows, now cut the throttle and drop in. I was down, and braked—what was moving over there? Okay, there were the woods, as before. So, now I was off the runway. Where to? There, into a revetment. I jumped out and covered the plane. I was in the 5th Staffel's area. Everything had gone all right, except that I had lost a lot of oil. Salomon landed long, and wrecked his landing gear. One plane landed short, and put down between the scarecrows. Propeller and landing gear were damaged. I headed to the command post. Everything had to remain on the field. We were to move farther east in the afternoon, to Mons en Chausee. "Brown 14" was still not ready, and so I couldn't fly.

At Guyancourt, Ottomar Kruse's "Blue 6" was operational, and he waited eagerly in the ready room. The odds of getting to fly a combat mission were very good. Kruse recalls:

> This time Hofmann had no choice but to take me along, and he assigned me to position Number 4 in his Schwarm. The transfer flight was to be made as a freie Jagd. I had a fantastic feeling as we took off and assumed our positions. I concentrated on keeping formation and looking out behind me, as I had been taught. After we had reached 3,500 meters [11,000 feet] and had flown a short time on a predetermined course, there came the sudden cry, "Indians at ten!" I glanced briefly in direction "ten," but saw nothing but one of our own Schwaerme, which was to the left of us. I tugged once more at my harness. The next moment the enemy were on us. I recognized them as Mustangs. The Old Man banked shallowly to the left, apparently offering himself as a sacrifice. My element leader, who was another beginner, stayed in position with the Kapitaen. I thought to myself, "Shouldn't we now take independent action?" I remained in my Number 4 position, with one eye behind me and the other in front.
>
> I then saw an entire Schwarm of Mustangs curving in on us from the rear, with myself as the first in the line of fire. No one said anything, and Number 3 remained fixed to the Old Man, who kept turning at a constant rate. It didn't occur to me to use the radio; we had had it drummed into our heads to keep our traps shut. The Mustangs banked more tightly. When I could see the leader's gun barrels I had had enough, and pulled up sharply in a half-loop, passing inverted over the enemy aircraft. I could see the pilot of the Number 1 Mustang staring at me. I had lost speed, and now fell in behind the last Mustang. I immediately had yet another Schwarm of Indians on my tail. I turned as before, and when I again saw the guns' mouths, I dove steeply, and the Mustangs passed above me. I zoomed up at high speed, and at that moment a Mustang passed right in front of my nose from my left, at about 300 meters [325 yards] range. I turned right immediately, aimed, and fired. I fired until I almost rammed him, and then passed above him to the right. Flames erupted from the Mustang. It dove away and I saw it crash. I then looked around and could see neither friend nor foe. The mass of fighters fighting around me only seconds before had vanished.

I turned in the direction of Mons en Chausee. In a few minutes I saw an aircraft that I soon recognized as an FW 190. I gave mine the gas in order to overtake it; the other pilot must have seen my plane, and tried to evade me. He said later that he took me to be an enemy. After I had sheered away to the left so that he could see me better, he slowed down, and I closed up on him in my tired "Blue 6." I recognized him as a Schwarmfuehrer in another Staffel. I tried to signal my victory to him in pantomime, but my sign language was not understood.

Arriving at Mons en Chausee, I saw the rest of our aircraft already on the ground. In my mind I recalled victorious fighters in the newsreels, rocking their wings while they roared across the field at low altitude. I made up my mind quickly and shot rocking across the field, banked sharply around, and repeated the scene from the other side before landing. After shutting down my machine, I reported to Hofmann. He gave me a dark look through furrowed eyebrows and wanted to know if I thought I was in the movies. I could not suppress my excitement, and shouted, "I got one!" He looked at me in disbelief, and told me to calm down and tell him everything, in detail. At the end of my story he told me, still in a skeptical tone, that he had seen the crash. He later had the armorer look over my aircraft, without my knowledge. He then called me over to him again, and told me that only my inboard weapons had been fired, and less than 25 percent of my ammunition was gone. I then realized that I had completely forgotten about the knob at the top of the control stick that fired the outer cannon, and had only used the trigger for the inner cannon and the machine guns.

The victory was confirmed, and I still have the leather jacket that Hauptmann Emil Lang, my Gruppenkommandeur, cut through with a borrowed table knife in order to attach my Iron Cross Second Class.

Only eight Mustangs took part in this battle. Their pilots, from the 354th Fighter Group, did not hesitate to attack the "approximately seventy" FW 190s that they encountered over Rambouillet forest. Two P-51s were shot down; one Focke-Wulf pilot bailed out, suffering burns.

The Geschwaderstab and the First Gruppe flew to Chaumont, east of the Seine, on the 16th. The Third Gruppe also headed east, to Rosieres on the Somme. One 9th Staffel Unteroffizier dropped far behind his formation, which contained ten Bf 109s from the 9th and 11th Staffeln. He then turned his aircraft around and headed west. When well past the Allied lines, he half-rolled and bailed out. An anti-Nazi, he had been seeking this opportunity since D-Day, and provided British Air Intelligence with much accurate information about Major Mietusch's Gruppe. The 11th Staffel's Uffz. Heinz Gehrke, who was off operations because of his neck injury, made the trip to Rosieres at night, in a former French armored car. He recalls that a number of Bf 109s had to be blown up on the ground at Villacoublay, as there were not enough pilots to fly them.

Morale in the Third Gruppe remained low, even after it was withdrawn from the Paris cauldron and began to receive replacements. At Rosieres a newly arrived Unteroffizier rapidly lost the enthusiasm with which he had greeted his assignment to this famous combat unit. He told this author:

> In the Ergaenzungsgruppe we young boars were informed only in general about tactics. Special training would have to be provided by the front-line units. My requests in III/JG 26 that I be taught the specific skills I needed fell on deaf ears. The answer to all my questions was the same—"Stick close to your Number 1, your Rotten-fuehrer, for if you lose him, you are as good as dead!" Everything else would come later! This showed an arrogance that was very disillusioning. The optimistic attitude I had had on the evening that my Schwarm landed at Rosieres faded forever, replaced slowly but surely by a sense of reality that urged me to caution. I was bitterly opposed to the officers of this Staffel, who did not believe it their task to give the new pilots all the help possible, but only wanted to survive the last months of this lost war.
>
> I felt rotten. In such a fought-out, war-weary shop, how could I gain the instinctive skills so necessary for my own survival? I can tell you that nothing happened in my adventure to negate this initial impression—my presence as a wingman served only to give my Rottenfuehrer a reasonable chance of survival, through my own sacrifice! Those were my prospects!

Many of the Gruppen of Jagdkorps II had already returned to Germany, totally shattered. The remaining fighters were charged with protecting their army's withdrawal across the Seine. Allied air supremacy made it impossible to give any assistance to the large German force still fighting in the Falaise-Argentan area, far behind the fluid front lines. II/JG 26 was the only fresh, full-strength German fighter unit, and saw continuous action. On 17 August, the Gruppe claimed five Spitfires shot down on two patrols, but four of the unit's pilots were killed by ground fire. That morning the Gruppe made rocket attacks on Allied armor near Dreux, and Hptm. Georg-Peter Eder later received official confirmation of his destruction of three Sherman tanks. Eder had joined the 6th Staffel on 11 August from II/JG 1; the highly experienced career officer was a welcomed reinforcement.

The next morning's dawn mission was flown by I/JG 26; the Second and Third Gruppe bases farther to the east were fogged in. The First Gruppe's early patrol was uneventful. Fog still hung in the valleys separating the hills around Mons en Chausee when the Second Gruppe was ordered to take off. Ottomar Kruse was to be the wingman in the 8th Staffel's covering element. He and his Rottenfuehrer were the last to take off. Just after lift-off they saw above them to the left a dogfight—Focke-Wulfs versus Mustangs. The two FW 190s made a shallow bank to the left, at full throttle and maximum rate of climb. Ottomar Kruse recalls:

> Three Mustangs shot past, 400 meters [1,300 feet] above us to the left. We tore after them, I to the right of my Number 1. However, when I gained firing position, he disappeared beneath my left wing. "Stay here," I thought, "and the Amis will have me." I tipped over my left wing, almost standing on my tail. I felt strikes in my left wing, and saw two holes beside the cannon; the sheet metal protruded up like roses. I had lost speed, and I greased my plane around, almost turning it on its own axis. The ground came up at great speed. Now it was time to stay calm. First I had to bring the plane under control, then check on my surroundings. Fine—now where were the Amis? Still on my tail? I thought about the flak protecting my airfield, now just in front of me. I shot past the control tower, about 300 meters [325 yards] from its 20-mm flak emplacement, and saw its tracers fall behind me. "There may still be one of them back there," I thought, and banked my mill first to the left, and then to the right. No one there. My pals in the flak had done some good shooting.
>
> I then cleared the area at minimum altitude. I passed over the first hill, and saw stretching in front of me a bank of ground fog, miles across. I made a wide turn and hunted for the field. The Mustangs were still hanging about, so there was nothing to do but clear out again. The two holes in my wing were very noticeable.

Damn it, I had no maps. But there was a rail line, and alongside it somewhere would be a city with a landing field. So, along the tracks at low altitude. Sure enough, after 10–15 minutes the desired city appeared. . . . No airfield to be seen, only a track for racing horses. I guessed it to be about 300 meters across. I had to set down, which was only possible with the sun at my back, from the city side. . . . I stopped about twenty meters from the beginning of a plowed field. I turned the plane around and cut the switch. An officer of the Labor Service came up on a bicycle. He answered my question, "Where am I?" with "Arras."

The Mustangs were not American, but belonged to the RAF's No. 315 (Polish) Squadron, flying from England. The Poles claimed sixteen victories, three in behalf of their squadron leader, who failed to return. II/JG 26 claimed five Mustangs and one P-38, but three of the claims were rejected by the RLM. The Gruppe lost eight pilots killed and two wounded; its mission disrupted, the surviving pilots landed as soon as the Polish Mustangs had departed. Kruse's element leader was hit in the legs, bailed out, and was taken to the hospital at Beauvais, where one of his legs had to be amputated.

Despite the morning losses, the Second Gruppe put up another mission at noon, this time accomplished by Borris's First Gruppe and escorted by Mietusch and his Third. Again a large formation of Allied fighters was encountered near the field, but this time the results favored the Schlageter pilots. Four P-47s were claimed by the Second Gruppe, while Klaus Mietusch downed another. One pilot from his Gruppe's 12th Staffel failed to return. Late that evening, Oblt. Jan Schild, a recent transferee from the First Gruppe, led eight Bf 109Gs of his 10th Staffel up from Warvillers, an improvised landing ground on the edge of a small woods, and headed for the action around Beauvais. They caught a squadron of the 4th Fighter Group strafing ground targets and shot down three of its P-51s without loss.

In the meantime, Ottomar Kruse struggled to get back from Arras. Two mechanics from the Gruppe service platoon arrived at the racetrack that afternoon and worked on the Focke-Wulf through the night. Just at dawn, Kruse lifted his machine off the ground, found the right road, and followed it back to Mons-en-Chausee.

Over the next few days, the westernmost units of the

Geschwader withdrew again, closer to the Belgian border. The Stab went to Valenciennes, and the First Gruppe to Vitry. Ground attack missions were attempted daily, but most were broken up by the P-47s and Spitfires. Shortly after noon on 23 August, eighteen II/JG 26 FW 190s met five III/JG 26 Bf 109s and aircraft of four other Jagdgruppen over Montdidier and flew west in search of Allied fighter-bombers. Northeast of Paris, the gaggle of over sixty German fighters was attacked by twenty-four Spitfires of No. 127 Wing (RCAF), led by their wing commander, Johnnie Johnson. Johnson had taken his aircraft southeast of Paris and had then swept northward in hopes of catching some Germans unawares. Johnson's bounce did achieve complete surprise, and his first burst of fire exploded an FW 190's belly tank. The battle then split up into individual dogfights, in which the Spitfires were heavily outnumbered. Johnson downed another 190, but he was then caught up in a Lufbery with six Messerschmitts. For the first time in the war Johnson's aircraft was hit, but he finally outclimbed his pursuers, of whom only the leader was a decent shot, and returned to his base at Crepon. He was the last man back, and found that his wing had claimed twelve German fighters while losing three Spitfires. II/JG 26 claimed the destruction of six Spitfires in this battle, which cost neither the Second nor the Third Gruppe of JG 26 any casualties.

A BLACK DAY FOR THE LIGHTNINGS

On 25 August, the day of Paris's liberation, the fighters of the Ninth Air Force made a concerted effort to knock out the German fighter force remaining in France. The staff of Jagdkorps II apparently had no forewarning and continued to order up the usual missions. Shortly after 1300, sixty-one JG 26 fighters—twelve from the First Gruppe, thirty-two from the Second, and seventeen from the Third—took to the air, along with elements of at least four other Jagdgruppen. The missions of all these units were simply freie Jagden or sweeps, with no coordination among them.

The Second Gruppe formation contained flights from all four of its Staffeln and was led by Hauptmann Lang. They formed up over Mons en Chausee and headed west, climbing for their ordered altitude of 11,000 feet. After a short time, Lt. Hofmann radioed,

"Indians at ten." No one else could see anything. Lang ordered Hofmann to take the lead. After a few seconds, Hofmann said, "I've lost them." A short oath from Lang, then "Reise, reise"—resume course. Before the Gruppe could turn back, Hofmann reported that he again had the enemy planes in sight. Behind Hofmann in the 8th Staffel formation was Uffz. Kruse, who was now an element leader. He had been given a new plane, "Blue 13," which was the only Focke-Wulf in the Staffel without outer wing cannon—Hofmann had told Kruse that he didn't need them. Ottomar Kruse recalls:

> After a few more minutes, I was able to make out in the distance, low to the ground, tiny twinkling objects with twin booms—Lightnings. They were whirling round and round and were apparently concentrating so hard on "making mincemeat" of our ground forces that none of them spotted us. Later we were told that there were sixteen of them. We waited for the order to attack. It came just as we overflew the twirling Lightnings. "From Weasel Anton"—we were the Weasel, Anton was our chief—"I am attacking," and the leading aircraft tipped over, followed by thirty-one 190s. "From Weasel Anton, a victory." The crash of the enemy aircraft could be seen clearly. Now the hunt was on. The Lightnings fell from the sky. I latched on to one, which attempted to evade me by dodging into a small cloud. I dropped below the cloud, passed by it, and was waiting right behind the Ami when he emerged. I was in position to fire, but before I could pull the firing lever, a stream of tracer shot past me. It was coming from two other FW 190s, which were also after my Lightning, but which were firing much too short. I immediately broke to the right. I did not want to be brought down by my own pals. I cursed them both, but all of us beginners were hungry for victories.
>
> I made a large circle and returned, but the battling aircraft seemed to have disappeared from the sky. Only the smoking remains of destroyed airplanes could be seen. So I turned on a homeward course, and after a few minutes met three other Focke-Wulfs, one of which I recognized as that of Lt. Vogt, Kapitaen of the 5th Staffel. Suddenly I saw, 500 meters [1,600 feet] below, three small dots, the rear two with twin booms—Lightnings. The lead aircraft was an FW 190, making frantic turns in an attempt to escape them. I pressed the transmitter button and screamed, "From 'Blue 13'—Indians at 12!" Vogt replied: "Calm down, 'Blue 13.' Repeat." I said it again, this time more quietly. From Vogt, as he dove—"I have

277

them." Meanwhile, the three had turned toward us, and Lt. Vogt had scarcely opened fire on the lead Lightning when he overshot it. The second Lightning saw us in good time, and dove straight down. I banked sharply to the left and gained firing position behind the first one. A short burst of fire, hits in the wings, and the next moment, something shot past to my left. "Engine cowling," I thought, and saw the Lightning, now in a banked dive, crash. I broke around sharply and saw a parachute in front of me. I flew past, not thirty meters from the pilot, and dipped my left wing as a short greeting. I can still see his white face today. He probably thought he was finished. I headed for home once more, thinking to myself that one day it could be my turn.

Two dozen 474th Fighter Group P-38s had formed up over their field at 1250 hours, before heading east to attack airfields in the Laon area. Each carried two 500-pound bombs. The 429th Squadron was above and behind the 428th, at 12,000 feet. The controller called the formation leader and reported "40 + " bandits southeast of Rouen. A few minutes later they were spotted and identified as Bf 109s. The two forces turned toward each other; the Bf 109s dropped their tanks and the P-38s jettisoned their bombs. The head-on pass completely dispersed the 429th Squadron, which split up into flights and elements. The 428th engaged the Messerschmitts, following many of them down to the deck. A small formation of FW 190s also joined the battle at this time. A third force of "20 + " FW 190s— II/JG 26—was then spotted diving on the 428th from above, but the P-38 pilots could do nothing but attempt to evade the attackers individually, or at most, in pairs. Eight of the twelve 428th Lightnings were shot down, as were three from the 429th Squadron. The leader radioed the recall. Capt. James Austin, a 428th flight leader, had lost his flight and was proceeding home with a wingman. Austin saw a lone FW 190 and chased it around a large cumulus cloud to the left. His wingman headed right and never saw Austin again. He did see a "crumpled-wing FW 190" spinning down, on the basis of which Austin was given a victory credit. It is more likely that this was Austin's own aircraft. Austin was trapped in and around the clouds by several FW 190s and shot down. He bailed out with serious injuries, and was captured, but was recovered by American forces in an abandoned German hospital and returned to the United States. Based on a close reading of the American encounter and missing aircrew reports, James Austin was shot down by Ottomar Kruse.

After the Americans tallied their scores, the 429th Squadron was credited with 9-5-2 Bf 109s; the 428th with 9-0-0 Bf 109s and 3-1-0 FW 190s. The 25th of August would go down in the 428th Squadron's history as "Black Friday." In contrast, the pilots of II/JG 26 returned to Mons en Chausee in a jubilant mood. They had suffered no losses and filed claims for twelve Lightnings, eight of which were ultimately confirmed by the RLM. Their high spirits were in no way tempered by knowledge of any Bf 109 losses; Ottomar Kruse, for one, never noticed the presence of the Messerschmitts at all.

Late in the afternoon of the 25th, Jagdkorps II ordered freie Jagden to the area of Amiens by six Jagdgruppen, including II/JG 26 and III/JG 26. Ogfr. Walter Stumpf was picked to fly his first combat sortie and took off in his "Brown 14" at 1838. His aircraft was one of the last to leave the ground and was attacked by P-51s west of the field, before the Gruppe had fully assembled. He escaped from a dogfight with three P-51s and landed again at 1910. His Focke-Wulf had taken fifteen hits. The rest of the Gruppe claimed four P-51s but lost two pilots killed and two others missing. These P-51s belonged to the crack 354th Fighter Group, which lost four Mustangs on this mission but claimed a total of 14-0-3 German fighters.

The weather restricted air operations for the next few days. On the morning of 29 August, JG 26's daily strength return was intercepted by the Allied signal intelligence service. The Stab reported having one aircraft operational and one pilot on duty; the First Gruppe, fourteen aircraft and thirty-four pilots; the Second Gruppe, twenty-eight aircraft and forty-three pilots; and the Third Gruppe, thirteen aircraft and fourteen pilots. That evening, the Geschwader moved to airfields in the Brussels area—the Stab to Brussels-Nord, the First Gruppe to Grimbergen, the Second to Melsbroeck, and the Third to Evere. The only major mission JG 26 was to mount from these fields took place on 31 August. It was flown in full strength—eighteen aircraft took part from I/JG 26, thirty-four from II/JG 26, and seventeen from III/JG 26.

Ottomar Kruse was flying as Number 4 in Hofmann's Schwarm and remembers circling as a total of about 120 aircraft formed up. The Second Gruppe's mission was to be high cover for fighter-bomber attacks on Allied tanks in the Reims area. Kruse became separated from his Schwarm when he had to dodge a flight of 109s passing through the formation. Upon the order "Reise, reise," the mob took up course in a single broad front. Kruse finally spotted Hofmann's Focke-Wulf, distinguishable from the rest by a movie camera that a combat correspondent had hung beneath its wing, and slowly edged back into position. The mission was flown without incident. The first Allied fighters were not seen until the return flight. As the German formation passed beneath a hole in the clouds, there came a cry, "Indians at eleven." The hole quickly closed and the order "Reise, reise" was given. Kruse was thankful, as he was flying the mission with a very thick head from a "boozy-do" the night before.

By the time Melsbroeck was reached, the red fuel warning lights were glowing in all of the Second Gruppe's aircraft. They had to get down as fast as they could. On a normal airfield they could land side-by-side in flights, but Melsbroeck was too small. They dropped into the airfield in a single file, spaced a few hundred yards apart. As soon as a Focke-Wulf's nose was pulled up, its pilot became blind straight ahead, so all hoped that those in front of them would keep their speeds up as they touched down and get out of the way quickly. All thirty-four aircraft landed without incident—something of a minor miracle, in Kruse's opinion. This mission proved to be Kruse's longest of the war—two hours and fifteen minutes in the air.

Forty JG 26 pilots were killed in combat in August, the highest monthly loss so far for the Geschwader. Six were killed in accidents, three were taken prisoner, and more than twenty were injured. At least seventy-five aerial victories were claimed—the total number of Third Gruppe victories is, as usual, unknown.

RETREAT TO THE REICH

By 2 September, British armor was approaching Brussels, and it was time for the Geschwader to retreat once more, this time to German soil. Many of the Allied tactical air units were themselves changing bases, and air activity was light. The transfer began around midday on the 3rd. The Stab and the First Gruppe headed for Krefeld; the Second Gruppe, to Kirchhellen via Duesseldorf; and

The FW 190A-3 assigned to Hptm. Rolf Hermichen of the Geschwader Stab—St. Omer, 1942. (Bundesarchiv)

Oblt. Otto Stammberger.
(Bundesarchiv)

Feldwebel Adolf Glunz.
(Glunz)

Lt. Emil Lang. (Meyer)

Lt. Gerd Wiegand. (Meyer)

The FW 190A-5 of Oblt. Otto Stammberger, Kapitaen of the 4th Staffel in early 1943. The aircraft are parked in the open—clear evidence that Germany still commands the skies over the Continent. (Bundesarchiv)

Hptm. Priller, Kommandeur of the Third Gruppe, describes his seventy-fourth victory to members of his Gruppe. From left: Oblt. Borris (partially masked), Oblt. Philipp (long trousers), Fw. Gruenlinger (KIA 4 September 1943), Priller, Lt. Aistleitner (KIA 14 January 1944), Oblt. Mietusch (partially masked) (KIA 17 September 1944), Oblt. Ruppert (in profile) (KIA 13 June 1943)—Wevelghem, Belgium, 22 June 1942. (Priller)

Oblt. Radener, in "Brown 4," leads a flight of FW 190A-8s of his 7th Staffel from Coesfeld-Stevede in the autumn of 1944. (Sy)

Uffz. Ottomar Kruse of the 8th Staffel, photographed at Coesfeld-Stevede in August 1944. (Kruse)

Uffz. Walter Stumpf of the 7th Staffel, photographed while on leave over Christmas 1944. (Stumpf)

This 7th Staffel FW 190A-8 was abandoned on Melsbroek airfield near Brussels in September 1944, during the Geschwader's retreat to Germany. (Imperial War Museum)

Uffz. Heinz Gehrke of the 11th Staffel in front of his Bf 109G-6 "Yellow 1," photographed at Villacoublay in June 1944. (Gehrke)

Lt. Siegfried Sy, a long-serving pilot in the Second Gruppe. (Sy)

Ogfr. Werner Molge of the 7th Staffel, photographed at Hamburg-Uetersen in March 1945. (Terbeck)

Uffz. Karl-Georg Genth, a late-war replacement pilot in the 12th Staffel. (Genth)

Generalfeldmarschall Sperrle passing out decorations to members of JG 26 in the woods around Guyancourt in June 1944. Inspections no longer took place on parade grounds. (Sy)

Hptm. Walter Krupinski, Kommandeur of the Third Gruppe, discussing local airfield defense with Oberst Priller during the winter of 1944–1945. (Gehrke)

"Brown 10," a 7th Staffel FW 190D-9, taxiing from its dispersal at Nordhorn-Clausheide in January 1945. (Meyer)

The state of the late-war Jagdwaffe is summarized in a single photograph. Pilots of the First Gruppe are shown en route to their dispersal field from Krefeld-Linn in late 1944. Identified pilots are: far left, Ofhr. Schneider; arm in sling, Uffz. Sattler (KIA 26 December 1944); next to Sattler, Uffz. Kukla; in glasses, Hptm. Steindl (KIA 9 January 1945); in lead, Uffz. Kohler (KIA 12 October 1944). (Genth)

"Black 8," a 10th Staffel FW 190D-9. It was jacked up for repairs after a belly landing splintered its wooden propeller, but it was then abandoned to the Allies. (Hildebrandt)

the Third Gruppe, to Muenchen-Gladbach. Most flights were un-eventful. Two were intercepted, however, with disastrous conse-quences.

The First Gruppe's 2nd Staffel was last up from Grimbergen. The ten FW 190s had just taken off and were still flying in trail prior to forming up, when they were hit by P-51s. The Germans were caught defenseless; in less than a minute the burning wreckage of four FW 190s lay strewn about the field below. The leader of the Schwarm, Lt. Karl-Heinz Kempf, was killed instantly. Kempf was a former Green Heart. He had gained sixty-four victories in 445 sorties and had been awarded the Knight's Cross in 1942 while with JG 54 on the Eastern front. Kempf was very popular with his men and was said to consider his primary duty to be the training of young pilots, at which he was very conscientious. Two of his Unteroffiziere died in their aircraft, and a third was able to bail out after being shot in the leg.

The 2nd Staffel was bounced by the Eighth Air Force unit, the 55th Fighter Group's 38th Squadron. The 55th had been the first ETO Lightning group and had fought a number of engagements with JG 26 over the previous months. It had recently re-equipped with P-51 Mustangs. That morning it had escorted heavy bombers to Ludwigshaven. On the return leg, two squadrons broke escort to look for trouble over the Low Countries. Capt. McCauley Clark, a flight leader in the 38th Squadron, spotted activity on the deck from 10,000 feet, called out the bogies, and led his flight down, followed by his squadron commander's flight. The Mustangs' 400-mph dive to the deck caused their windshields to frost up. They made a broad arc to reduce speed and clear their canopies, then came in behind the Focke-Wulfs, whose pilots had still not seen them. Capt. Clark was first across the airfield. He hit his target from dead astern, and its pilot bailed out. Clark's flight members then downed two more FW 190s in flames, and his squadron CO claimed the fourth.

At the Second Gruppe's Melsbroeck base, Hptm. Lang's air-plane had been giving trouble, and his Stabsschwarm thus took off last. His two companions were his longtime wingman, Lt. Alfred Gross, and a promising Nachwuchs, Uffz. Hans-Joachim Borreck. Lang had had problems getting his landing gear up after takeoff, but ten minutes later they were on course at an altitude of 600 feet when Borreck called out fighters to their rear. Lang broke upward, to the left; Gross, straight left. Borreck dove, two fighters on his tail. After taking hits in the wing and engine, he broke hard left and somehow avoided his pursuers. He could see little, as his canopy had oiled over, but did spot Lang's aircraft in a vertical dive toward the ground, its gear extended. Borreck made a forced landing at another Belgian field and caught a ride to Duesseldorf. Gross's report, filed from the hospital, states that he first broke into the attackers and shot one "Spitfire" down; this claim was not confirmed. He saw Lang's 190 diving in flames and then zoomed upward. Gross's plane was hit by an unseen fighter and he bailed out, badly wounded; he never returned to JG 26.

Lang's flight had been hit by the 55th Fighter Group's 338th Squadron. The 338th Squadron was flying two minutes behind the 38th, at 9,000 feet. After the 38th Squadron called out 190s on the deck near Brussels, the commander of the 338th led his own unit down. As he broke out of the cloud layer at 3,000 feet, he saw "three bogies flying a loose formation heading east, balls out on the deck," and started after the Focke-Wulf on the right. Lt. Darrell Cramer, his wingman, took the one on the left. Darrell Cramer continues the story:

> I closed on him very rapidly, because he was not going very fast and I had lots of momentum from our descent. The FW 190 rolled out of a steep left turn and started a turn to his right; just at that time another P-51 cut in between us from my right and descending, but he overshot the 190 because of his speed and the steep turn the FW 190 had executed.
>
> I was closing fast, and because of the FW 190's hard turn to the right the angle off was increasing. I turned a little to the left trying to get farther away from his line of flight and reduce the angle off, and then I turned hard right. Still, as I got within firing range I was about 75 degrees off. . . . I opened fire from about 300 yards. I fired only a short burst as my range decreased very rapidly to less than 200 yards, and the aircraft went out of sight below the nose of my aircraft because of the lead I was pulling. . . .
>
> I broke up and then hard right again. I then saw the FW 190; it was upside down in a steep dive toward the ground. It hit so hard that it generated shock waves along the ground like a rock makes when it is thrown into a pond of water. The airplane skidded a few yards, shedding bits and pieces, and then blew up in a fireball.

Lt. Cramer's victim was undoubtedly Hptm. Lang. All three of the FW 190s were claimed as destroyed. The squadron CO shot down Lt. Gross, while a third pilot's target, which was last seen in a dive at 100 feet but was not observed to crash, was the aircraft piloted by Uffz. Borreck.

Borreck finally reached Duesseldorf, locked in the baggage compartment of an FW 190 from another unit. His dramatic arrival, followed by his announcement of Lang's crash, left the gathered pilots of the Second Gruppe in deep shock. Lang was supposed to be a very lucky pilot. It was said about him that in his entire flying career he had never had an accident. His aircraft had never even been struck by enemy fire. Emil Lang had brought great success to his unit with his superb leadership, and now he was dead, after scoring 173 victories in 403 combat sorties. With this piece of news, the Abbeville Kids' four-year tour of duty in occupied western Europe had come to an end.

12
SUPPORT FOR THE ARMY
September–December 1944

DISORGANIZATION AND RECOVERY

THE END OF THE WEHRMACHT'S WILD RETREAT ACROSS FRANCE and Belgium brought Jagdgeschwader 26 to a temporary refuge behind the German border. On their departure from Brussels, the ground echelons found themselves among endless streams of army trucks, barreling past burning vehicles that had been shot up by the Allied Jabos. Nearer the homeland, the German sense of order quickly reasserted itself—Ernst Battmer recalls being asked to produce his passport by the customs officer on duty at the German border.

The advance of the western Allies came to a halt in early September, stopped not by the Wehrmacht but by their own supply problems. The Germans took full advantage of their unanticipated reprieve to re-form their shattered army units and move them into the much-vaunted West Wall, which in reality had been nothing but a hollow shell prior to September. Starting at the mouth of the Scheldt, the defensive line ran roughly along the Belgian-Dutch, Belgian-German, and Luxembourg-German borders before heading south across France, along the Moselle River to Switzerland. The Luftwaffe High Command assigned the responsibility for the aerial defense of this entire line to Luftflotte 3. Jagdkorps II controlled its day fighter units, which were, from north to south, JG 26,

JG 27, JG 2, and JG 53. For the rest of the year, these four Jagd-geschwader would be solely responsible for the aerial defense of the Western front by day. There was an adequate supply of aircraft, and on 7 September Jagdkorps II reported that it had 337 fighters available. Their effective utilization was not easy, however. The major problem facing Luftflotte 3 in early September was a lack of gasoline; its new bases were not stocked with aviation fuel. Luftflotte 3 thus ordered Jagdkorps II to show "economy and consideration in the use of its fighter units."

The new JG 26 bases were near the Ruhr, in far western Germany. The Geschwaderstab and the First Gruppe settled in at Krefeld and its nearby satellite field, Krefeld-Linn. Krefeld was a prewar Jagdwaffe airbase with a well-drained grass landing ground and a full allotment of hangars, workshops, and barracks. There were no woods nearby to help hide the aircraft, so full use was made of camouflage netting. Krefeld was a mile west of the Rhine River, which made a sharp bend pointing directly at the field. This was a useful navigational aid for the poorly trained German fighter pilots, but it also benefited the Allied reconnaissance aircraft, which kept a close watch on activities at the field.

The Second Gruppe, now commanded by Hptm. Eder, moved east of the Rhine. Its Stab and the 5th and 6th Staffeln occupied the field at Kirchhellen, a typical war-built landing ground with rudimentary facilities. There was only a single hangar, and no barracks, so accommodations were sought in the nearby town. The field was surrounded on all sides by thick woods, which were of great assistance in hiding the Gruppe's Focke-Wulfs from prying Allied eyes. The 7th and 8th Staffeln moved thirty miles north of Kirchhellen, to Coesfeld-Stevede. Construction of the base at Stevede had begun in 1943. It was intended as an intermediate or emergency landing field and, according to residents of the area, saw little activity until 1944. The landing ground was simply a meadow, used normally for grazing cattle. It was a small grassy rectangle, 2,600 feet long and 650 feet wide. The field's length was barely adequate for lightly loaded fighters. When it rained, it became soggy, and the pilots had great difficulty getting their planes off the ground. The dispersals of the two Staffeln were located in the woods. The 7th Staffel was on the north end of the landing ground and ordinarily took off from the northeast to the southwest. Landings were made in the reverse direction when possible, so that the FW 190s could taxi quickly off the field and be hidden from the Allied Jabos. The 8th Staffel was on the south side and used a most unusual takeoff technique—they normally took off from the southwest to the northeast, with the wind to their backs. This enabled them to keep in the cover of the trees until just prior to takeoff. The ground personnel slept in barracks that had been built earlier for antiaircraft troops covering a nearby dummy airfield, while the pilots' quarters were in Coesfeld, in an old training school.

The Third Gruppe was also split between two airfields. The 11th and 12th Staffeln were based at Boenninghardt, one of the Geschwader's original prewar bases, while the Gruppenstab and the 9th and 10th Staffeln moved to Coesfeld-Lette. Lette was originally a dispersal field for Stevede. It is not known why Major Mietusch based his Third Gruppe Stab here instead of at Boenninghardt, which was much better equipped. Lette had a simple 3,900-by-600 foot grass airstrip. Generally takeoffs were made to the east and landings to the west. There were no suitable dispersals or revetments for the aircraft. The Messerschmitts were parked in the surrounding woods or simply under single trees. In the beginning, the pilots slept in the neighboring farmhouses, but shortly after their arrival barracks were completed on the field. In contrast to Stevede, which remained undetected by the Allies, the field at Lette was soon seen by reconnaissance aircraft. Spitfires attacked the field in late October, following which the Gruppe moved on.

One side benefit of the Geschwader's return to the homeland was the opportunity to meet large numbers of young German women. The 7th and 8th Staffeln located a suitable restaurant in Coesfeld and began planning a party to consume some of the alcoholic beverages they had brought with them from Brussels. Lt. Hofmann instructed his pilots to find female companions for the social; they set out in all directions from the field and had little trouble finding dates for the big evening. For a reason he no longer remembers, Ottomar Kruse went to the Coesfeld train station. He spotted his dream maiden there, behind the ticket counter. His first approach was rejected, for the sound reason that "Flyers never keep their appointments." Kruse replied, "The only excuse for me not to make it would be if I were shot down." This line did the trick. She turned a little pale and agreed to meet him at the party, on the night of 16 September.

That same day, 16 September, found all units of the Geschwader in combat for the first time since their return to Germany. All was quiet for most of the day, but at 1740 part of the Third Gruppe at Boenninghardt was sent up after Jabos around Aachen and fought an inconclusive combat with Spitfires. At around this time, Major Borris led his entire First Gruppe to the same area, attacked a formation of P-38s from the 367th Fighter Group, and claimed four without loss to themselves.

The 7th and 8th Staffel duty pilots sat for almost the entire day in the Stevede command post, waiting for mission orders. Eleven machines were made operational from the two Staffeln. Lt. Hofmann chose Uffz. Kruse to be a Rottenfuehrer and ordered him to fly rear cover with Uffz. Erich Klein. They kept looking at their watches. Not much longer and the day would be over, without flying a single mission. Then the phone shrilled. A mission! Gruppe had been trying to reach the post for more than a half hour—there had been a problem with the telephone. It was only ten minutes to takeoff, which was set for 1715. Kruse's mill, "Blue 13," was the farthest away. He sprinted to it. As he was jumping into the cockpit, Hofmann, who was leading the mission, taxied past. Kruse's engine was already warm, so he quickly fell in behind. Klein was waiting at the takeoff point. After giving him the "OK" sign, the pair roared off. The mission was flown at 11,000 feet, the trailing Rotte 600 feet below the rest. Visibility was clear, with broken cumulus clouds. After twenty minutes, "Indians" were called out 1,500 feet below. Eight Thunderbolts. Hofmann signaled, "I am attacking," and dove. Kruse continues:

> The two of us in the high Rotte were in a poor attack position and circled over the pack. Then Lightnings, and more Thunderbolts, emerged from around a large cumulus cloud. Below us was a whirling mass of planes. I didn't quite know what to do. Klein, of course, hung on to me. Then I saw below me a 190 being chased by four Thunderbolts. The 190 was curving away to the left, and the four Thunderbolts followed in a line. "Klein, we are attacking," I shouted. I dove after them at full throttle and fired at the last one from a good 200 meters range. It immediately dove away. Now after the next; it did the same, as did the one in front

of it, the flight's Number 2. I had hit them but had no time to follow them. Number 1 had been warned, and he was a very good fighter pilot. Instead of following his comrades, he laid his aircraft on its right wing, made a hard left climbing turn, and dropped on my tail as I shot past him at high speed. His tracers were all around me, and I broke left from his path. But now I was sitting in the middle of the Amis. A wild dogfight began. Tracers first from one, then from another side. Again and again I was able to slip away. After a short time, my arms and shoulders ached from the constant sharp turns. I had taken several hits. One hole in the canopy, where a shell had gone past my neck. A second shell through the cabin took away my right knee pouch with its contents—I still have my left pouch! Then the engine began to run away as a consequence of further hits; it was time to get out.

First, I had to evade the tracers. The procedure was then automatic—unlatch the canopy, disconnect the radio helmet, off with the harness, jam the stick hard left with my left hand—I squirted out. I felt that I had hit a wall. It became quiet. My hand was on the chute handle. "Don't pull it now—wait until you're only 200 meters up—then open it" went through my head. While falling I turned my head to look down, to better judge my height. Now! There was a sharp jerk and I was dangling, much higher than I had hoped. I grasped the lines with both hands and tugged them, to drop faster. I let go of the lines just above the ground, and hit the release disc. The four harness straps fell away, and I dropped to the ground from a height of two meters. I quickly disappeared into the nearest ditch. Two Thunderbolts circled overhead, but didn't come down to look for me.

I found myself in a hedgerow beside a field. There was a row of poplars not 200 meters away; this meant a road. Coming up on it, I saw roofs through the trees. A village—and with luck, transport back to Coesfeld, perhaps still in time for our evening social. I saw not a soul on my march to the village. At the edge of town I came to a farm with a high wall around the buildings. As I entered through the main gate I saw a man leaning against a side entrance; he appeared to be a foreigner. I asked him where I was. "You are a mile behind the American lines." He could have hit me over the head with a hammer. It was immediately apparent that flight was impossible. It would be light for at least two more hours, and I would surely be seen. I asked him for a glass of water, at which he invited me into the house. After I had taken a few sips, a civilian came into the house and said to me, "The Americans are outside; they would like for you to come out." "Tell the Americans that I will come as soon as I have finished this drink," I replied. He went back out, but reappeared in a few seconds. "The Americans wish you to come out immediately." I stood up and thanked my host. As I left the house, I took in the situation with a quick glance. One Ami threw himself against the wall and took aim at me. Another disappeared behind the entryway; I saw only his helmet and weapon. As I appeared, one soldier was standing across from me, in front of the stone fence, with a Colt in his hand, pointed toward me. He must be the leader, I thought, and marched toward him. When I was ten meters away, he cried, "Stop! Raise your hands!" I laughed, and did as I was told. . . . After three days of various interrogations and having been brought to a large open-air compound, I was finally taken to an airfield. There I was loaded under guard into an American twin-engined plane, and was flown to London.

I would like to find out where I was shot down. The village must be just across the Belgian border. I know we were flying in Aachen's airspace, but where I came down, I just don't know. The battle started above occupied German territory, and must have moved gradually to the west. It was all those little angels, pushing me. . . .

Kruse's last comment was prompted by the fact that none of his 8th Staffel comrades survived the war; landing behind the lines and being taken prisoner probably saved his life. Hofmann's simple bounce proved to be a disaster for the Germans. His intended victims were twelve 50th Fighter Group P-47s. They jettisoned their bombs, turned into the attack, and after the resulting combat claimed 6-0-2 of the eleven attacking Focke-Wulfs. The P-38s reported by several of the surviving Germans were probably from the 370th Fighter Group, returning from a previous engagement in which they claimed five FW 190s without loss. Neither of the American units, both ground attack outfits, lost any aircraft in this engagement with Hofmann's force. It was a very creditable performance for the Americans, none of whom were experienced in air combat. Four 7th Staffel pilots were killed, and a fifth was shot down and taken prisoner, as was the 8th Staffel's Uffz. Kruse. As the final blow, Lt. Hofmann's wingman was shot down on the return flight by German light antiaircraft fire. He bailed out at low altitude, broke both legs, and never returned to the Geschwader.

289

OPERATION MARKET GARDEN

In the early afternoon of 17 September, the Luftflotte 3 head-quarters received word of large-scale Allied paratroop and glider landings in the Netherlands. This was the beginning of Operation Market Garden, the Allies' attempt to outflank the Germans' Rhine defenses by a narrow, deep thrust across Holland. The initial German air response appeared to the Allies to be weak and hesitant, reminiscent of their reaction to the D-Day landings in Normandy. However, the Luftwaffe was doing as much as its permanently weakened state allowed. Luftflotte 3's war diary entry for the date reads:

> In the morning, 145 aircraft of Jagdkorps II provided cover for civilians working on West Wall defenses in the Aachen-Bitburg area. In the afternoon, six formations (about twenty-five aircraft each) were made ready to attack enemy airborne landings in the Arnhem-Nijmegen area, but only three formations carried out operations in the battle area. The remaining aircraft could not take off owing to the approach of bad weather.

The three formations to carry out operations were the three Gruppen of JG 26, the Jagdgeschwader that was based closest to the landing sites. They were not successful, as no German fighter reached the transports. All were fended off by the swarms of Allied escorts. The fighters of the American Eighth and Ninth air forces and RAF Fighter Command flew a total of 1,037 escort and patrol sorties in support of the operation. The First Gruppe claimed three Spitfires near Nijmegen, for the loss of one FW 190 and pilot. The Second Gruppe fought two battles with Mustangs and claimed five of them for the loss of two 8th Staffel Unteroffiziere.

The Third Gruppe also fought a battle with Mustangs, with ruinous consequences for itself. In mid-afternoon, Major Mietusch assembled about fifteen Bf 109s of his scattered command and headed for the landing zones, climbing all the way. The weather had taken a turn for the worse, and there was a continuous layer of thin cloud at 15,000 feet. The Germans climbed through it, and then, while above the Dutch-German border, Mietusch spotted a squadron of P-51s below them. He radioed, "Otter Mietusch, I am attacking!" and dove through the cloud. His first burst of fire destroyed the Number 4 plane of the trailing cover flight.

Oblt. Schild hit the Number 2 Mustang's drop tank, and it dove away trailing a solid sheet of flame. The events of the next few minutes are best stated in the words of the leader of that P-51 flight, Lt. William Beyer of the 361st Fighter Group's 376th Squadron:

> I was the flight leader at the tail end of the squadron. We had flown back and forth between checkpoints for a couple of hours. My wingmen apparently got tired of looking around for enemy aircraft. Only by the grace of God did I happen to look behind us at that particular moment, because in no more than a couple of seconds the enemy would have shot the whole flight down.
>
> I saw about fifteen German fighters closing fast with all their guns firing. I immediately broke 180 degrees and called out the enemy attack. My Number 4 man went down in flames, and my wingman got hit and spun out. I headed straight back into the German fighters and went through the whole group, just about in the center of them. We were separated by only a few feet. . . .
>
> I immediately made another 180-degree turn, picked out one of them, and started to chase it. The rest of the fighters zoomed back up into the clouds and disappeared. We made many violent high-G maneuvers with wide open throttle. When I started to close and fire, I noticed that his plane seemed to have stopped in the air. I had to decide whether to shoot and run, or to try to stop my plane. I cut throttle, lowered flaps, and dropped my wheels—I still kept closing. I had to fishtail and do flat weaves to stay behind him. This maneuver was repeated three times, and on one occasion I almost cut his tail off, we were so close. . . .
>
> Then we started into steep dives. The last one was at around 1,000 feet with flaps down. This last maneuver was deadly and nerve-racking. He went straight down toward the ground, hoping I couldn't pull out. If I pulled out early, he could have come in behind me, so I stayed with him. If we had had our wheels down when we pulled out, we would have been on the ground.
>
> It was after this pullout that I finally was able to get my sights lined up and fire at him. I must have hit him with the first burst, because he kept turning and went into the ground and broke up. Knowing the caliber of this German pilot, I am sure that if I had taken the time to get off some shots when he was slowing down he could have possibly shot me down or made a getaway. My other combat victories were not nearly as spectacular as this one, and it is with this in mind that I can recall it so vividly.

Lt. Beyer's victim was Klaus Mietusch. Mietusch was one of the most fascinating individuals in the Geschwader's history. He was a career officer, had joined the Geschwader in 1938, and was its senior pilot in length of service when he died at age twenty-five. His early combat career was marked by a seemingly endless series of failures and frustrations. A member of the successful 7th Staffel under Muencheberg, he did not come into his own until he succeeded to its command and led it on detached assignment in Russia in 1943. He was the opposite of the typical extroverted, self-confident fighter pilot. He compensated for what he believed to be his lack of ability by an act of will. According to Priller, Mietusch's combat motto was, "Bore in, until the enemy is as large as a barn door in your sights." Again quoting Priller, duty as Mietusch's wingman was an "unforgettable experience." Mietusch was shot down ten times and was wounded at least four times. He was said never to have turned down a mission, and he had logged an incredible 452 combat sorties at the time of his death. His seventy-two victories brought the award of the Oak Leaves to his Knight's Cross, two months after his death.

On 18 September, the weather, that enemy of Allies and Axis alike, took a turn for the worse. This hindered both the Allied efforts to resupply and reinforce the landing zones, and the German attempts to block them. The weather improved slightly on the 19th. Jagdkorps II reported that forty-eight fighter-bomber sorties were flown to the Nijmegen area in the morning. During the afternoon, according to the Luftflotte 3 war diary, 148 German fighters "engaged in dogfights with enemy fighter formations over the target area. By concentrated effort, air superiority was gained over the landing area between 1715 and 1800 hours." This hard-won so-called victory availed nothing to the Germans, as they did not reach their targets, the transport formations themselves. The Allied escort consisted of 127 Spitfires from Fighter Command and 182 P-51s of the Eighth Air Force. Fifty-four of the Mustangs belonged to the 357th Fighter Group, which reached Arnhem in late afternoon to find an eerily lit purplish-blue sky full of milling British, American, and German warplanes; machine-gun strikes on the aircraft flickered like distant fireworks. There was a solid cloud deck at 20,000 feet; another cloud formation walled off the eastern edge of the drop zone, sharply restricting the combat area. The Mustang pilots waded into the cauldron and returned to England claiming 20-1-1 Bf 109s and 5-0-0 FW 190s. The Group lost five pilots, however, including one squadron commander. JG 26 was active over the combat zone all day, and it was probably responsible for all of the 357th Group's losses. One flight of three P-51s, separated from its squadron, was shot down at the same time and location as Lt. Gerhard Vogt's 5th Staffel claimed four mustangs. The missing American squadron commander was last seen by his wingman after a combat with Bf 109s. The fifth P-51 lost was bounced by Bf 109s that dropped out of the clouds. Either or both of these last two P-51s could have been downed by III/JG 26; one suitable claim is known. JG 26 lost only one aircraft during the day, a 6th Staffel FW 190 that failed to return from a strafing attack on the ground troops.

Both sides were grounded by the weather on the 20th. By the next day, the situation of the British 1st Airborne Division in Arnhem was desperate, and the long-delayed drop of the Polish 1st Parachute Brigade was ordered, despite the poor weather. Only ninety American fighters, the Thunderbolts of the 56th and 353rd Fighter Groups, could get off their bases for escort and patrol. The 56th Group engaged a large formation of FW 190s, which fought back aggressively, drawing the combat eastward toward Osnabrueck. The Wolfpack claimed 15-0-1 German fighters for the loss of one P-47, but in their absence the twenty-five FW 190s of I/JG 26 burst from the clouds over s'Hertogenbosch and raked the defenseless transports of the RAF's 38th and 46th Groups. Seventeen "Douglas transports" were claimed shot down by Borris's men, who then escaped unscathed. The most successful pilot was the 3rd Staffel's Oblt. Fred Heckmann, who downed four planes, for his sixty-sixth to sixty-ninth victories.

The 353rd Group's Thunderbolts reached the Nijmegen area in time to break up the attacks by the Second and Third Gruppen on the transports, but not until the Focke-Wulf pilots had downed three. The American pilots claimed 3-1-1 FW 190s and one Bf 109 but lost one P-47 to Lt. Hofmann. JG 26's losses were two FW 190s and one Bf 109; one of the pilots survived.

The British lost thirteen Stirlings and ten Dakotas on this mission, out of 114 transports dispatched. Some were undoubtedly shot down by antiaircraft fire, but the actual losses to JG 26 were very close to the twenty claims submitted. This proved to be the only successful attack by the Luftwaffe on what turned out to be the largest aerial assault and resupply operation of the war.

Far behind the battle lines, the Luftwaffe was preparing for what now appeared to be a lengthy battle at the frontiers to the homeland. In Berlin, Genlt. Adolf Galland, the General of the Fighter Arm, readied plans for a "grosse Schlag" (great blow) against the American Eighth Air Force. The Jagdwaffe was to be conserved and built up for use in one mighty full-strength mission against the heavy bombers. General Galland hoped to shoot down 400–500 bombers. This would force a pause in the American bomber offensive of sufficient length to permit Galland's great hope, the jet-powered Me 262, to reach the operational units in large numbers. Somewhat to Galland's surprise, the Luftwaffe High Command expressed no opposition to his plans at this time, and he proceeded to build up a reserve force of seven Jagdgeschwader. Goering's contribution to the defensive effort was another exhortation to his troops. Its retransmission by Luftflotte 3 was read by the Allies, thanks to Ultra; in it Goering ordered every effort to be made for the aerial defense of the Reich. He empowered local commands to court-martial suspected cowards on the spot and, if convicted, to execute them by firing squad in front of the assembled personnel. Soon after this speech, Luftflotte 3 was downgraded in status and renamed Luftwaffenkommando West (Lkdo West), but its mission remained unchanged—the aerial defense of the Western front.

During the last week of September, JG 26 strained to meet its responsibilities along the newly established front line of its operational zone, which now ran along the lower Maas and Waal rivers in the Netherlands, and then south along the Dutch-German border. The Jagdwaffe would never again command the air over the battle lines. The German fighter pilots fought their battles from ambush, seeking out opportunities to pick off isolated Allied aircraft or unwary formations. However, when prolonged combat was inevitable, the experienced formation leaders of the First and Second Gruppen could often bring the battle to a successful conclusion. On 23 September, Major Borris, on a freie Jagd over the Goch-Wesel area, spotted a large formation of P-51s beneath him and reverted to an old Jagdwaffe trick. One flight of his FW 190s was sent down through the formation as a decoy; the remainder stayed above to fall on the Americans when they dove after the sacrificial flight. The

Mustangs, which belonged to the Eighth Air Force's 339th Fighter Group, split up and went after both German formations. A general battle followed, in which the Americans claimed 7-1-1 Focke-Wulfs while losing four Mustangs. Borris's force claimed four P-51s, while losing three pilots.

Two hours later, it was the Second Gruppe's turn to patrol the same area. Over Goch the German pilots caught sight of four P-51s far below them. The Mustangs, from the 352nd Fighter Group, were returning from their patrol flying straight and level, at an altitude of only 4,000 feet. The rest of their squadron heard only the single radioed word "Break!" from the flight leader. The four P-51s and pilots the simply disappeared, the victims of a perfect bounce. It was led by the 5th Staffel's Lt. Vogt, who claimed his forty-first and forty-second victims. The single German casualty collided with a P-51 that had just been shot down and crashed to his death.

By the 23rd of September, the two Canadian Spitfire wings of Second TAF were operational from new bases in Belgium; they were given the task of protecting the Allies' newly won bridges at Nijmegen and what was left of the British perimeter around Arnhem. The Typhoons of Second TAF also made tentative forays into the area; on 24 September the 4th Staffel's Lt. Xaver Ellenrieder shot down the Typhoon of No. 137 Squadron's CO over Goch.

The 25th brought an improvement in the weather, and Jagdkorps II ordered large missions against the lower Rhine crossings at Oosterbeek and the Nijmegen bridges. One bomb hit the main Nijmegen bridge, which remained in service. The Spitfires of Second TAF's No. 83 Group swarmed over the attackers, claiming 14-0-5. According to the Lkdo West diary, German losses from all causes totaled eighteen aircraft. The Germans claimed ten certain and four probable RAF fighters. The British lost eleven Spitfires, resulting in a much poorer claim-to-loss ratio than usual for the Allies, possibly a reflection of the Spitfire pilots' lack of recent aerial opposition.

JG 26 played a major, and successful, role in these combats. Many pilots flew two sorties. The First and Second Gruppen each claimed four Spitfires, without loss. The pilots also made strafing attacks on ground troops. The Third Gruppe flew a rare ground attack mission to Nijmegen in the morning and the more common anti-Jabo sweep in the afternoon. Its aerial successes are unknown, and the Geschwader's only two casualties of the day were theirs. One was Uffz. Hermann Ayerle of the 12th Staffel, who was shot down by Spitfires, bailed out, and was badly banged up when he hit the ground. Ayerle was awarded the Wound Badge in Silver for this, his fourth wound of the war. The second Third Gruppe casualty likewise survived his bailout.

Lkdo West's diary entries establish a framework that helps put the Geschwader's efforts into perspective. Luftflotte Reich, to which Lkdo West was at this time subordinated, ordered Jagdkorps II to delay the takeoff of its fighters whenever enemy aircraft were known to be in the area. This order greatly reduced the number of cheap victories obtained by Allied fighters over known German airfields but also effected a net reduction in the number of missions that could be flown. The primary mission of Lkdo West's fighters was clarified by Reichsmarschall Goering's order that its fighter formations were to be employed solely against Allied fighter-bombers— that is, on anti-Jabo missions. Ground support operations were to be undertaken only in emergencies, or as an alternative mission if no enemy aircraft were encountered.

On 27 September, the fighters of Jagdkorps II tried all day to penetrate the Spitfire screen to the east of the new Allied line across southern Holland. The First Gruppe of JG 26 claimed one Spitfire, and the Second Gruppe, four. These victories cost the Geschwader much more dearly than those won two days previously. Seven pilots from the two Focke-Wulf Gruppen were killed.

Judged solely by the victory-to-loss ratio, September 1944 was a very successful month for Jagdgeschwader 26. This ratio was well over two to one, based on an incomplete victory total of sixty-six and a complete loss total of thirty-one (twenty-seven pilots killed in combat, one killed in an accident, and three taken prisoner). Of course, given the vast disparity in the sizes of the opposing air forces, the Geschwader's efforts could have no effect on the course of the war.

A DREARY AUTUMN

Whenever permitted by the weather, the Geschwader continued its inconclusive but deadly struggle along the Dutch border with the Spitfires of the Second TAF. At around noon on 2 October, the

First Gruppe sprang a successful trap on one section from No. 401 Squadron (RCAF). When the Spitfires bounced a seemingly unwary flight of FW 190s north of Nijmegen, the rest of the Gruppe fell on them from above, and shot down two Spitfires, without loss. Just south of this battle, the Second Gruppe encountered a larger force of Spitfires, as many as fifty, and shot down three without loss to themselves.

The Third Gruppe welcomed the arrival of Hptm. Walter Krupinski, Klaus Mietusch's successor as Gruppenkommandeur. Krupinski was a celebrated Eastern fighter who had been awarded the Knight's Cross with Oak Leaves for his 177 victories in the Soviet Union. He was only 23 years old and was a very popular figure with the young enlisted pilots. It soon became apparent, however, that he held the reins of command very loosely. He made no changes in his four Staffeln but left things to run as they had under Mietusch—and by all the existing evidence this was very chaotically indeed. It is hard to escape the conclusion that when he arrived at JG 26, Krupinski was as weary of the war as the pilots in his new command. The decline of the Third Gruppe continued unabated.

On 4 October, Hptm. Krupinski ordered twenty Bf 109s of his Gruppe up from Boenninghardt. Their mission was a freie Jagd; their likely opponents, the Spitfires along the border. Uffz. Georg Genth of the 12th Staffel was chosen to fly his first combat mission, as wingman to his Staffelkapitaen. The formation assembled without incident and climbed to 10,000 feet without seeing the enemy. After twenty minutes, someone called out "Indians." A formation of Spitfires, equal in number to the Messerschmitts, was flying within a cloud layer only a few hundred feet above them. Georg Genth continues the story:

> I had been weaving industriously and regularly, in order to keep up with where we were, while at the same time keeping a constant eye on my engine instruments. All seemed to be going well, when suddenly my Kapitaen pulled up in a left bank into the cloud above us; so sharply that I could not follow, although I was right beside him. Callously, that tired warrior had abandoned the formation. Uffz. Genth, the poor little sausage, was now in an almost hopeless situation—should I break away, and fly back to base, or should I join up with another element? I climbed through the cloud

layer, which was only 150 meters [500 feet] thick, reached a clear space between layers, with good visibility, and banked in a broad, flat curve, in hopes of spotting my Staffelkapitaen—but that was a vain hope. He had gone, and he stayed gone. Since there was nothing here above the cloud, I decided to search below again. So I dove through it, only to find—scarcely believing my eyes—a lone Spitfire, not sixty meters in front of my 109, flying several meters below me, and in almost the same direction. I was astonished to see an enemy so close to me. By reflex action, I yanked on the stick in order to regain the cloud. The condensation trails at my wingtips told me, "You are about to enter the cloud in a stall! Just relax, and analyze the situation!" I composed myself by hitting my head with my fist, cursing myself for not having attacked the lone aircraft immediately. However, I armed my weapons; perhaps the poor devil had not noticed my appearance.

I was in luck! As I dove out of the cloud layer for the second time, the Spitfire was still sitting there; somewhat farther away, but easy to overtake. I gave it full throttle and drew up on the poor fellow, who had still seen nothing. I opened fire with my two machine guns at about 100 meters. Since the Spitfire was flying on a diagonal course to mine, my first shots went past his tail. I corrected my aim and hit the fuselage behind the cockpit. I saw strikes wander over the cockpit area into the engine. Two short bursts of smoke came from the engine. I then lost my self-control. I was suddenly overwhelmed with the idea that an enemy aircraft was sitting on my tail. My nervous tension was so great that when I yanked the stick back to regain the cloud, my landing gear's restraining bolts sheared, causing the gear to drop. I trimmed out my elevators and decided to fly home. Only there could I sort out the things that were whirling through my head. I remained in the cloud layer for a while, and then turned onto a course to the southeast. After about five or six minutes, I dove to an altitude of only 300 meters, in order to fly back to the field. To my great surprise, I suddenly spotted to my left a 109 flying in my direction, recognizable as my war-weary Staffelkapitaen! . . .

After flying the usual approach curve, I dropped in and landed without any problems. I hadn't the faintest suspicion of having scored a victory until Obfhr. Lohrberg congratulated me and told me that the pilot had bailed out. One important item I had forgotten completely was the existence of our Numbers 3 and 4! Lohrberg was the Rottenfuehrer flying as Number 3 and had kept me in sight after the "loss" of our Staffelkapitaen. In my excitement, I had not realized this. So I, a greenhorn, had scored the only victory of the entire armada, on my first mission, and from a seemingly hopeless situation!

In early October the Third Gruppe replaced its Bf 109G-6 Beulen with the newest model of the Messerschmitt fighter, the Bf 109G-14. It had a new DB 605ASM engine with 1800 horsepower, giving it a greater maximum speed than the G-6 at any altitude. It also featured enlarged main wheels and an extended tailwheel leg, for better ground handling and vision; a clear-vision canopy; and the FuG 16ZY direction-finding radio. These amenities all improved the aircraft's survivability under the poor weather conditions prevalent during the north European autumn and winter, and they were greatly appreciated by the Gruppe's pilots. Later, a few Bf 109G-10s were taken on charge. This model had yet another engine, the DB 605DCM, which had an enlarged supercharger and was intended to be a high-altitude fighter. The G-10 had a service ceiling of 41,000 feet, and was the fastest G-series Bf 109, reaching 426 mph at 24,000 feet. Both the G-14 and the G-10 had an armament of one 20-mm cannon and two 13-mm machine guns, all in the nose. This was an effective armament against fighters, which were now JG 26's most common aerial targets.

The FuG 16ZY was standard equipment in all aircraft reaching the Geschwader from the fall of 1944. This remarkably compact device incorporated a receiver, a transmitter, and a direction-finding loop, and was intended to aid ground-controlled interceptions. Its transmissions provided the ground control organization with both the range and bearing of the aircraft making them. Its two frequencies also facilitated communications among members of a formation. By the time the FuG 16ZY arrived at the front, bomber interceptions in strength were almost a thing of the past. The FuG 16ZY evolved into a navigational aid, used primarily to provide homing information to lost German pilots. It was to save many lives during the last winter of the war.

Air battles along the Dutch frontier continued for a few more days, until it became apparent within Lkdo West that the battle lines had stabilized, and that there was no profit to be gained in continuing its attempts to penetrate Allied airspace. Battles by the First and Second Gruppen on the 6th and 7th of October resulted in victory claims for six Allied fighters, for the loss of five Focke-Wulfs and pilots.

On 6 October, JG 26 and JG 27 were ordered to fly a freie Jagd to the Eindhoven area, followed by a patrol of the fortifications under construction west of Aachen. Major Borris was to lead the combined formation; his deputy was to be Oblt. Fred Heckmann. Of the twenty-one FW 190s that took off from Krefeld, thirteen aborted, including those of both Borris and Heckmann. Leadership of the unit thus passed to Lt. Georg Kiefner. His nine FW 190s contacted ten Spitfires south of Nijmegen, but the resulting combat was inconclusive.

On 8 October, Hptm. Georg-Peter Eder received orders to report to Kommando Nowotny, the first operational Me 262 unit. He was replaced as Kommandeur of II/JG 26 by Major Anton "Tony" Hackl. Hackl was a 30-year-old professional officer with a reputation as an aggressive, intelligent—and most important, lucky—pilot and combat commander. He had served on all fronts and arrived at JG 26 credited with 165 victories. He had been awarded the Swords to his Knight's Cross on 13 July 1944, eleven days after Obstlt. Priller's receipt of the same decoration. Tony Hackl was one of only four recipients of this high award to serve in JG 26; the others were Adolf Galland and Joachim Muencheberg. His leadership style was similar to that of Emil Lang—performance in combat was all that mattered; traditional military courtesies were enforced only to the extent demanded by higher commands. He was just the right commander for the aggressive pilots of the Second Gruppe, which continued to lead the Geschwader in victory claims and victory-to-loss ratio.

Each of the three Gruppen had by now developed its own distinct personality, a reflection in all cases of that of its most influential Kommandeure. Major Karl Borris, the longtime leader of I/JG 26, was a dour, superstitious, outwardly humorless man—a "typical East Prussian," in the opinion of his pilots. His rigid enforcement of all regulations, including those that restricted the employment of his forces, resulted in lower serviceability rates and fewer missions flown than the Second Gruppe. He brought his young pilots along slowly, and thus he prolonged their lives, at least up until the point that they actually entered combat—the Gruppe's overall casualty rate was almost identical to that of the Second

Gruppe. In combat, the Gruppe had no major failures, but few spectacular successes.

The Third Gruppe in the hands of Klaus Mietusch had been a sharp, but very brittle, weapon. By October 1944, it had very little edge left. It had never regained its numerical strength in pilots after its casualties of June 1944. A more serious problem than mere numbers, however, was its shortage of aggressive, successful formation leaders. This lack greatly reduced its combat efficiency. It is not known why Priller let the Gruppe continue to run down. Why, for example, did he let the efficient Hermann Staiger get away from the Geschwader? And why did he not ask General Galland to provide a few Staffelkapitaene from such proven Bf 109 units as JG 3 and JG 11? Combat leadership in the Gruppe fell by default to the most experienced enlisted pilots, who were called "old hares" for the erratic, jerky courses traced by their aircraft while in the combat zone. Some of these survivors, such as Obfw. Hermann Guhl and Obfw. Karl Laub, were excellent pilots; Guhl had been a test pilot. These two men had a reputation for caution and were popular among the Nachwuchs for the concern they showed for the survival of all the pilots in their formations.

Early on the morning of 12 October, the telephones rang in the command posts of the Geschwader's three Gruppen. The orders from Obstlt. Priller were surprising—the entire Geschwader was to go on thirty minutes readiness. They were to expect further orders from Luftflotte Reich. Their mission would be with the Reichsverteidigung—that is, an intercept mission against heavy bombers. JG 26 had not received such an assignment in many months, and few of the pilots then in the unit had ever had the experience of flying against the "dicke Autos." At 0900, heavy bomber formations were reported over the Zuider Zee. The First Gruppe war diary reports that by 1020 twenty-two of that unit's pilots were strapped in their FW 190s' cockpits in their dispersals. At 1028 they took off, flying toward the northeast and climbing to 22,000 feet. Over Hannover they were attacked from above by a large force of P-47s and P-51s and were dispersed. After combats ranging down to ground level, the Focke-Wulfs landed where they could. The survivors reported back to Krefeld from four different fields. Three enlisted pilots were never heard from again. No victory claims were filed by the First Gruppe's pilots; however, Obstlt.

301

Priller, who was probably flying with them, shot down a 357th Fighter Group P-51 south of Wunstorf for his 101st (and last) victory. That evening, Priller's Stab reported a combat strength of two FW 190s; the First Gruppe had twenty-two FW 190s operational out of the thirty-eight with the unit.

The report filed that evening by the Second Gruppe was similar. The Gruppe took off at 1040 and contacted the bomber stream east of Rheine. They too were hit and scattered by Mustangs. Oblt. Glunz stalked the bombers for two hours without finding a gap in the escort screen; he finally landed back at Kirchhellen after 134 minutes in the air. The Gruppe lost four pilots killed; a fifth succeeded in bailing out with minor burns. No victories were claimed. In its evening report, the Second Gruppe listed sixteen FW 190s as operational out of twenty-nine on strength.

The end result of the Third Gruppe's mission was the same. They were vectored to the north of the Focke-Wulf Gruppen, to the coast near Bremerhaven. There they too ran afoul of the ubiquitous Mustangs and lost six Messerschmitts. Two pilots were killed. The pilots of three fighters apparently parachuted without injury; the sixth Bf 109 was piloted by the 12th Staffel's Oblt. Jan Schild, who recalls:

> Fate overtook me on 12 October 1944, over Bremen at about 1130 hours, when I lost my controls after being struck from long range by a single Mustang above 11,000 meters [35,000 feet] altitude. After many futile attempts to leave the aircraft, I was able to bail out at low altitude. I landed in the Teufelsmoor. I came to four days later, lay in the hospital for two months, and resumed my military career in December 1944.

Schild returned to the Third Gruppe, but he was restricted at first to ground duties. He did not fly in combat again until the following April. No Third Gruppe victories are known. That night thirteen of its Bf 109s remained operational out of twenty on strength.

Apparently JG 26 was the only Jagdwaffe unit to reach the vicinity of the bomber stream on the 12th. A thorough search of the remaining Luftwaffe records has turned up no appropriate claims or losses for any other Lkdo West or Luftflotte Reich fighter unit. The American fighter escorts' nineteen confirmed victory claims are in fairly close agreement with JG 26's fourteen losses.

The most noteworthy performance by an American fighter pilot on 12 October was that of Lt. Charles "Chuck" Yeager of the 357th Fighter Group. Yeager had been given the air command of his entire forty-nine plane group formation that day, despite his very junior rank. Although his current victory total was only 1½, his keen eyesight and obvious tactical sense had attracted favorable attention within the leadership of the 357th. After Yeager had positioned two squadrons of his group on the flanks of the bombers, which had reached Bremen without incident, he led his own squadron, the 363rd, 100 miles ahead of the stream. He spotted specks far in the distance, at the P-51s' altitude of 28,000 feet. The Mustang squadron closed rapidly on the bogies. Yeager identified them as twenty-two Bf 109s, circling while awaiting the arrival of the bombers. Yeager, in the lead, closed to within 1,000 yards of the last two Messerschmitts, which were lagging behind the formation. Just as he reached firing range, both German pilots half-rolled their planes and jumped out, one behind the other. Both Americans and Germans now dropped their tanks, and a wild melee began. Yeager's first gunfire hit a 109 in the cockpit and engine, and it fell away streaming coolant. His next target exploded, and the last was hit with a high-deflection burst of fire after attempting to turn with Yeager; the American then watched the 109 dive away making uncontrolled snap rolls, until its pilot finally escaped.

Lieutenant Yeager's five victories gave him the coveted status of ace-in-a-day. The rest of his flight claimed three more 109s. The other two squadrons of his group were shut out, since Yeager didn't vector them to the combat. His rejoinder back in England was, "There just weren't enough . . . to go around." His opponents were undoubtedly from III/JG 26, and his last victim was, in all probability, Oblt. Schild. The other American units to claim victories on the 12th were the 56th and 78th Fighter Groups, flying Thunderbolts, and the 364th Group, whose Mustang pilots claimed 8-1-1 German fighters near Bremen. These three fighter groups provided the day's opposition for the rest of the Geschwader.

Following the debacle of the 12th, the Geschwader returned to its usual task of patrolling the battle lines. The critical area was now

Aachen, which was under attack by the American First Army. On the 13th, the First Gruppe's field was too boggy to permit takeoffs, but the Second Gruppe flew a successful freie Jagd to Aachen. The Gruppe's major combat was with Lightnings and Thunderbolts from the 474th and 368th Fighter Groups. One FW 190 pilot was killed. Two P-47s were claimed by the German pilots; three were in fact lost. Oblt. Glunz shot down a P-38 in a dogfight and then found himself in a tight spot. His oil pressure suddenly dropped to zero; his engine immediately seized up. Addi Glunz recalls the incident:

> Despite a stationary engine, I was able to escape the attacks of two Thunderbolts by means of tight banks and an almost vertical dive into a cloud bank. I then made a clean belly landing in a beet field.

The source of Glunz's engine trouble was later traced to a broken oil line. This was the closest the lucky Glunz came to losing an aircraft in combat during the entire war.

The weather once again became the airmen's worst enemy. Little combat was seen for the rest of October. Several missions were flown to Aachen, where they engaged the 474th Fighter Group's Lightnings in several inconclusive combats. Action over the city died down after the 20th, when it became the first German city to fall to the Allies. On 22 October, the 8th Staffel's Oblt. Wilhelm Hofmann was injured in a freak ground accident. He was examining a dismounted machine gun when the bolt closed suddenly, injuring his eye. He retained his sight but lost the ability to focus the eye. He refused hospitalization and returned to his unit wearing an eyepatch. Hofmann insisted on flying combat missions, but the job of leading his 8th Staffel in the air was assigned temporarily to a pilot loaned from the 5th Staffel. Two days after his accident, Oblt. Hofmann was awarded the Knight's Cross, the first such decoration received by a Geschwader pilot since the previous June.

On 28 October, a rare clear day, the First and Second Gruppen both flew full-strength anti-Jabo missions to the Dutch border. The First Gruppe saw no combat. Over Venlo, however, the Second Gruppe spotted and attacked several Typhoons of No. 182 Squadron. One Typhoon fell in flames. On the return flight, the Gruppe was bounced by No. 412 Squadron (RCAF). After a lengthy battle, one German pilot was shot down and killed. The Canadian

Spitfire pilots suffered no losses and returned to the Geschwader's territory only an hour later. On their second mission they attacked the Third Gruppe's field at Lette. Two Messerschmitt pilots were killed over the field, and two injured pilots had to force-land their damaged Bf 109s. The Spitfires again returned to their Belgian base without loss.

The Geschwaderstab and the First Gruppe lost their battle with the mud of Krefeld, and on 29 October moved seventy miles to the northeast, to a clearing in a forest outside the village of Greven. It was a poor choice. The Dortmund-Ems canal was nearby and ran in a concrete channel several feet above ground level. The canal was bombed several times by the British, each time causing the inundation of the surrounding countryside. Bedeviled by these un-natural floods and the autumn rains, the men soon found them-selves in deeper mud than they had experienced at Krefeld.

Next it was the turn of the Third Gruppe to move. Their new field was at Plantluenne, thirty miles north of Lette. Plantluenne, code-named Plantenspeck (vegetable fat), was a fully equipped pre-war air base with a large grass landing ground of irregular shape. The long axis was roughly west-east, corresponding to the prevailing wind direction; it was 4,500 feet long, with an additional 1,500-foot overrun. Its width was 2,800 feet. The field was comfortably large and had been used by an experimental bomber unit earlier in the war. It had both Freya and Wuerzburg radars, and it was defended by at least three flak towers, equipped primarily with light 20-mm guns. Most of the antiaircraft crews were schoolboys from the nearby towns. Instead of conventional hangars there were covered repair stations. These had concrete foundations, brick or wooden walls, and flat wooden roofs covered with tar and camouflaged with bushes and small trees. The aircraft were parked under small trees, or in camouflaged tents. All large trees had been cut down to minimize the danger from fire. Sheep from a nearby farm trimmed the grass on the well-drained landing ground. All personnel lived in barracks at the field. The pilots and ground crews of III/JG 26 settled into these relatively comfortable surroundings for the winter. Their stay was to last four months.

November 1944 was the peak month of the Allied strategic bombing campaign against German oil production. On the 2nd, 1,100 B-17s and B-24s bombed oil and rail targets in Germany, escorted by 968 fighters. The First and Second Gruppen were ordered to attack this armada, but could not take off because of the presence of enemy fighters in the area and aborted the mission. The fighters of Luftflotte Reich flew 305 sorties. Seventy German pilots were killed, and another twenty-eight injured. Only forty American bombers were brought down, some by antiaircraft fire, and sixteen American fighters were lost. The recriminations from Hitler's headquarters over the failure of the Jagdwaffe were even more pointed than usual. Goering made a three-and-one-half-hour speech attributing Germany's problems to the cowardice of his fighter pilots. He had the speech recorded and sent excerpts to the fighter units for the edification of the pilots and the betterment of their morale.

The First Gruppe struggled to operate from Greven for several days. Ground accidents increased. Lt. Heinz Kemethmueller, the Kapitaen of the 4th Staffel and a holder of the Knight's Cross, overran the field and flipped his FW 190 over on his return from a sortie on 4 November. He suffered severe injuries and was replaced as Staffel leader by Lt. Vladimir Soeffing. The morning of 6 November found the aircraft of the Geschwaderstab and the First Gruppe mired up to their axles in mud. They were bogged in, and completely out of action. Jagdkorps II suggested that Major Borris should leave his aircraft there until winter froze the ground and pick up new aircraft at Fuerstenau, the new field assigned to his Gruppe. Borris refused to abandon his aircraft, and instead dismantled them. A crew of Italian laborers was drafted to hand-carry the wings and fuselages across the field to the nearest hard-surfaced road. There they were loaded onto trucks and sent on their way to Fuerstenau. On 25 November, the first six of the Gruppe's twenty-eight Focke-Wulfs were reported operational.

Fuerstenau was a war-constructed base that had until recently seen service only as a decoy field. It had a small, L-shaped, but reasonably well-drained landing ground, and the Gruppe's personnel welcomed the opportunity to pass the winter on firm ground. Lodgings were located in nearby villages; the Gruppe ground staff moved into a Catholic girls' school, the Kloster Handrup.

The Second Gruppe abandoned Stevede and concentrated at Kirchhellen. The few missions flown were at low strength. On 6 November, Uffz. Hans Borreck, one of the most promising of the Nachwuchs pilots, led a flight from his 5th Staffel on a mission against artillery spotters. These were not found, but the three Focke-Wulfs encountered P-47s southwest of Dueren; Borreck shot one down for his sixth victory. During the low-level combat, the Germans were taken under fire by light antiaircraft guns, and their formation zoomed for cover in the clouds. Borreck was never seen again.

The Second Gruppe received orders to withdraw to Reinsehlen, south of Hamburg, for re-equipment with Kurt Tank's latest fighter, the inline-engined FW 190D-9. It was to be the second Gruppe to receive the new plane, after III/JG 54. On 19 November, the pilots of II/JG 26 flew their last full-scale missions in their radial-engined FW 190As. That afternoon, a large formation led by the 5th Staffel's Lt. Vogt struck the Canadian Spitfires of No. 412 Squadron, which were on a ground-attack mission. Vogt claimed his 46th victory in this combat, and his Staffel comrades claimed three more; three Spitfires were in fact lost. That evening, the last Second Gruppe pilots in Kirchhellen boarded trucks for Reinsehlen, while the Gruppe ground crews proceeded directly to their next operational base, Nordhorn. The Gruppe's FW 190As were turned over to the First Gruppe, which on the 27th reported its highest aircraft strength of the war, sixty-four FW 190As, although very few of these were operational. In early December, the First Gruppe began to receive its own FW 190D-9s. Borris's outfit was not afforded the luxury of withdrawing from the front but had to train in their new equipment while remaining on combat status in Fuerstenau. It was planned to re-equip each Staffel of the First Gruppe in turn, to minimize the disruption to operational flying.

The Focke-Wulf Gruppen's base movements left the Third Gruppe temporarily the strongest fighter unit in the area. The pilots' routine at Plantluenne was typical for the last period of the war. Their service day began with sunrise and continued until darkness. After breakfast in the pilots' Casino, or common room, they went to their Staffel's dispersal. They were informed about weather conditions and waited there at readiness. The operational aircraft were assigned to the pilots on duty; this late in the war, few pilots had their own aircraft assigned to them.

The Gruppe had received a number of examples of the last version of the Bf 109 to see service, the Bf 109K-4. This variant was very similar to the G-10, but a number of features that had been introduced in stages were standardized. Among these were a clear-vision canopy, an enlarged wooden tail assembly, a retractable tail wheel, and a 30-mm MK 108 or MK 103 nose cannon. The 30-mm cannon were extremely potent weapons, but they had a tendency to jam, and apparently all of the K-4s supplied to III/JG 26 were also equipped with 20-mm guns in the hated underwing tubs. Uffz. Georg Genth's regular aircraft was a G-10, but on occasion he flew a K-4. He preferred the G-10 as a dogfighter, as the K-4's bulky armament sharply reduced its maneuverability. Moreover, at high altitudes, above about 28,000 feet, the K-4 began to float. Genth found that during formation flight at high altitudes it was unnaturally sensitive and gave him the same signals that most aircraft give shortly before a stall. Formation flight had to conform to the speed of the lead aircraft, and a small change in its speed caused the pilots to start "swimming" in space in the very thin air at high altitudes.

On 27 November, a high-altitude mission in a K-4 almost cost Genth his life. The First and Third Gruppen were ordered to intercept heavy bombers. The Third Gruppe's Bf 109s flew with those of JG 3 and JG 27. At 32,000 feet, Genth's canopy iced over. He could see only straight ahead, through the thick, armored glass panel. Georg Genth remembers well the events of the next few minutes:

> I cleared a small aperture in my left canopy pane, a few centimeters in diameter, by exhaling on it. I could then see behind me to my left. The canopy was otherwise covered in a thick layer of ice. As usual, my tactical position was at the rear of the formation, in the place of honor! I observed two Thunderbolts banking toward our formation. In my condition I could not fight them. Being totally unable to defrost my canopy with my heater, I reported my condition over the radio, and dove in a split-S into the cloud layer only a few hundred meters below. I remembered just in time that I had not switched on the artificial horizon. I did it while diving, since it was clear to me that I would have no chance to align the gyro properly in the clouds.
>
> What should I do? I had escaped the immediate danger of being shot down, but I would have no chance to regain control of my aircraft in a cloud thousands of feet thick. I attempted to reduce my speed—about 600 km/h [360 mph] indicated—by pulling on the stick. To my discomfort, however, my speed kept increasing—the

indicator now hit 750 km/h! I realized that I was in an inverted bank and now pushed the stick forward. My speed dropped immediately. I attempted to slow down to about 500 km/h, so that I could make visual contact with the ground. However, this was very difficult. Just as the indicator hit the desired mark, I left the cloud in a 60-degree inverted bank, about 500 meters [1,600 feet] above the ground. The canopy had now warmed up and defrosted, and I could see again in all directions. Control forces were so great that I could not center the stick, so I clenched both hands together and struck the side of the stick as hard as I could. The unbelievable happened—the brave old 109 flipped over into a normal steep descent attitude, from which I could then pull out with the help of the trim wheel! At my terminal speed, the engine cowling panels had torn off, and oil lines had split open from overpressure, but I could see again, and had my bird under control. I flew to Rheine, about three or four minutes away, without touching the throttle, my speed decreasing slowly.

I landed my oil-smeared bird smoothly, and returned to Plantluenne by "Kuebelwagen," a kind of jeep. Probably my good friend Helmut Lohrberg had had similar problems with icing, and had not been as lucky as I. He had been missing since this flight. As I stood on the landing ground at Rheine after landing, I heard three aircraft crash with overstraining engines, all right around Rheine! To this day, I have not been able to strike these ghastly noises from my memory.

There were other casualties in addition to Obfhr. Lohrberg. A second pilot was killed, and two men were shot down by P-51s and bailed out with injuries. In the meantime, only four First Gruppe Focke-Wulfs had gotten off the ground; they struggled up to 32,000 feet, well above their normal ceiling, and were taken under attack by P-51s, which shot down one of them. The three remaining 190s made it back to Fuerstenau. The pilots' comment that the Mustangs were much faster than their own fighters above 29,000 feet was not news, but was duly noted in the combat diary.

No successes were claimed on this mission by the Geschwader's pilots. It was another disastrous day for the Reichsverteidigung; the defensive force's aircraft losses totaled fifty-two destroyed, nine missing, and sixteen damaged. None of the 530 American heavy bombers dispatched were lost; claims by the American fighter pilots totaled 98-4-11, against fifteen losses.

During the Second Gruppe's absence from the front, the First

and Third Gruppen continued to fly whatever missions were assigned them. On 3 December, the First Gruppe flew a rare ground
support mission to Linnich and received an even rarer expression of
gratitude in the form of a commendatory signal from Gen. Man-
teuffel's headquarters, which was of course recorded in the Gruppe
diary.

Two days later, twenty-five First Gruppe pilots returned to
Fuerstenau from an anti-Jabo mission to find Obst. Hannes Trautloft, Inspector of Day Fighters, waiting for them. He was there to
decorate Major Borris with the Knight's Cross. While Trautloft was
in the command post, messages began coming in telling of a major
American raid on Berlin. Trautloft decided to try his hand at tactical
command and ordered I/JG 26 to take off and attack straggling
bombers. Only five Focke-Wulfs could be made ready. They took
off at 1325, led by Major Borris himself. Ten minutes later came the
report, "Abschuss!" It was the Major. He had caught an isolated
B-17 over Lohnerfeld and dispatched it, resulting in the first
Geschwader victory over a heavy bomber since July. As always, Karl
Borris could be relied upon to carry out his orders to the letter. The
bomber, from the 452nd Bomb Group, had been struggling to reach
England on one engine. Only one member of its crew succeeded in
bailing out after Borris's attack.

The Bf 109 Gruppen in northern Germany had now been
assigned to fly patrols over the Me 262 bases in the area, to help
protect the valuable jets during takeoff and landing. On 14 December it was the turn of III/JG 26. Uffz. Heinz Gehrke received the
assignment prized most highly by the 11th Staffel's wingmen—he
would fly with Obfw. Karl "Karlchen" Laub. Near Rheine, Laub
and Gehrke were attacked from above and behind. Heinz Gehrke
recalls:

> Laub took in the situation immediately, began a split-S—
> unfortunately, very near the ground—and attempted to escape the
> hail of shells by coming around onto a reverse course. Always cog-
> nizant of my duty as a Rottenflieger, I turned with him. It was very
> difficult to regain control before hitting the ground. We were not
> very high—below 600 meters [2,000 feet]. During the split-S we
> naturally built up a great deal of speed. I saw very clearly that a wing
> fairing on Laub's aircraft had come loose. It didn't fly off, however,
> because it was secured by a cable. This circumstance led to Laub's

crash. He could no longer counter the forces involved, and rushed straight toward the ground. I was no more than sixty meters from him, and saw him crash. I pulled my aircraft up to determine the exact location, and my 109 was hit. A shell ripped through my canopy and instrument panel. There was a horrible noise, and I was suddenly outside the aircraft. I hung from my chute for only a few seconds, and then I was on the ground for the fourth time. Fortunately, I had received only a few splinters in my legs. A friendly neighbor brought me back the few miles to Plantluenne by motorcycle. Here I was able to report the fate of Obfw. Laub. I was not able to hide my tears, which streamed down my cheeks; my nerves were shot. Ask any member of the 11th Staffel—Karlchen Laub was one of the best in the Third Gruppe.

The fighters responsible for downing Laub and Gehrke were new Hawker Tempests belonging to No. 56 Squadron. A third Bf 109 was shot down by the Tempests; its pilot's body was not found until the following month. The ever-eager Canadians of No. 412 Squadron joined in the battle, and one of its Spitfire pilots shot down another Third Gruppe Bf 109K, whose pilot was able to bail out. The Allied units suffered no losses in this combat.

THE BATTLE OF THE ARDENNES

Early in the morning of 16 December, strong German armored forces attacked the thinly held American front lines in the Ardennes region of southern Belgium and northern Luxembourg. The "Battle of the Bulge" had begun. Heavy snowstorms prevented flying by either side on the 16th—which was undoubtedly the way the German Army preferred it. Much of General Galland's precious reserve of fighters had been brought west to support the drive. Genlt. Dietrich Peltz, Galland's counterpart as General of the Bomber Arm, and a favorite of both Hitler and Goering, had been given operational control of Jagdkorps II; at that moment Adolf Galland realized that his last opportunity to influence the course of the war had passed.

On the afternoon of the 17th, nineteen FW 190As of the First Gruppe took off from Fuerstenau, amid scattered snow showers. Fred Heckmann led the formation; Hans Kukla led the 4th Staffel's contingent of four aircraft. Over the Eifel they spotted a small formation of Lightnings strafing ground targets and attacked. Four of the eight P-38s fell, including three from the cover flight, which was the target of Kukla's Schwarm. Kukla shot down his first airplane, but he had no witness, so did not bother to file a claim. His wingman was not so bashful, however, and claimed (and was awarded) two—and to this day, Hans Kukla believes that one of these was his. No FW 190 was as much as damaged in the encounter. The P-38s belonged to a frequent opponent of the Geschwader, the 474th Fighter Group's 428th Squadron. The four Americans that returned filed claims for 3-3-3 FW 190s, a clear case of overclaiming by a unit caught in an unfavorable tactical situation. They were ultimately awarded credits for 1-4-1.

On 18 December, the entire Third Gruppe, about forty Bf 109G-14s and K-4s, took off on a combat mission under the leadership of Oblt. Peter Reischer. After assembling over Plantluenne, the small armada headed east. The pilot of the designated control aircraft played a prominent role in the mission and its aftermath. He tells this strange, sad tale:

> A special transmitter, a FuG 16ZY, had been installed in my crate, to be turned on upon orders from ground control. As we climbed, I received the proper codewords, "Otter Hans, you will be the locomotive," over the radio, and turned the thing on.
>
> For over an hour we flew around over Lower Saxony. No enemy, no heavies, no Thunderbolts or Mustangs. After landing at Plantluenne, the pilots asked each other what in the world the mission was supposed to have accomplished. All our forty aircraft had done was burn fuel.
>
> Immediately after landing, I was summoned to the telephone. Krupinski asked me, "Hans, where did you go? Did you remain with the Gruppe?" I could only answer, "Yes, sir!" Krupi thanked me and I was dismissed. Just as we were getting ready to head for our quarters, new orders for cockpit readiness were received. Our aircraft were refueled in great haste, and we were soon ready for another mission.
>
> Shortly before the order to take off, Reischer arrived on the field in a staff car. We were all seated in our aircraft waiting for the takeoff flare. My aircraft was beside Reischer's, and as he climbed into his cockpit I could see that his face was flushed and his head was unsteady. I thought to myself that he must have had a few cognacs. We took off immediately; this time we flew to the west.

We soon contacted the enemy and, as we said, "went around with the trumpets and kettledrums." We landed some twenty or thirty minutes later. One aircraft was missing—that of the 11th Staffel's Kapitaen, Oblt. Reischer. Somewhat later, we learned that he had crash-landed his 109 on the other side of the field. We were later told in confidence that Reischer had shot himself with his pistol. Reischer remained sitting in his aircraft after his belly landing— shot in the head.

Still later, I learned that after our first mission Reischer had reported that the Gruppe attacked armor around Aachen, and later fought an air battle—which Krupinski knew had not taken place [because of the transmissions of my FuG 16ZY].

This story is part of the folklore of the Third Gruppe. It cannot be found in the official casualty record, which states that Reischer fell on a mission over Holland before reaching the enemy and did not bail out. He was buried in the Lingen military cemetery, on 21 December 1944, and remains there today. His identification tag was recently found on the airfield site at Plantluenne. It showed no sign of crash damage; neither had it been broken in two at its serration, which was standard practice for any crash victim. So the story of his suicide is probably true in its essentials. Reischer apparently suffered a total failure of nerve on the morning mission. Such failures were not an uncommon experience in the Geschwader, but this one involved an entire Gruppe. Reischer tried to lie his way out of the situation and was caught by the evidence of the FuG 16ZY. Krupinski probably offered him the options of flying an immediate, successful (or fatal) second mission, or standing trial for cowardice in the face of the enemy—the penalty for which was the firing squad. The Gruppe's second mission was inconclusive, and Peter Reischer found and took a third option.

After making their last practice flights from Reinsehlen, the pilots of II/JG 26 headed back to the combat zone, their numbers bolstered by twenty brand-new pilots. The men landed their FW 190D-9s at Nordhorn on 18 December, just before the weather closed in. They were unable to fly their first combat mission in their new mounts for several days. The pilots' opinions of the "long-nosed Dora," or Dora-9, as it was variously nicknamed, were mixed. The new model was intended to correct the FW 190's most glaring weakness, its poor high-altitude performance. What came out of

313

Kurt Tank's shop was a compromise. Tank did not like the liquid-cooled Jumo 213A engine, but it was the best choice available. The long in-line engine had to be balanced by a lengthened rear fuselage to maintain the proper center of gravity, making the FW 190D four feet longer than the FW 190A. The new airplane lacked the high turn rate and incredible rate of roll of its close-coupled radial-engined predecessor. It was a bit faster, however, with a maximum speed of 426 mph at 21,650 feet. Its 1750 horsepower, which methanol/water injection boosted to 2240, gave it excellent acceleration in combat situations. It also climbed and dove more rapidly than the FW 190A, so proved well suited to the dive-and-zoom ambush tactics favored by the Schlageter pilots. The armament of the FW 190D-9 was much lighter than that of the FW 190A-8. The planned engine-mounted cannon had not materialized, and the standard D-9 was armed with two 13-mm MG 131 machine guns above the engine and two 20-mm MG 151/20 machine cannon in the wing roots.

The Second Gruppe's winter home at Nordhorn-Clausheide was 21 miles southwest of the Geschwaderstab and the First Gruppe at Fuerstenau and had the best facilities of the Geschwader's three airfields Clausheide had been built originally in 1928 as a private airfield for the Krupp organization, and had been in constant use since then, first as a civil airfield, and since 1939 as a Luftwaffe base. Its landing ground was carpeted with heath over sand and was usable in the worst weather. The field was approximately 3,250 feet long by 1,300 feet wide; its long axis was aligned with the prevailing westerly wind. The 5th Staffel dispersal was at the west end of the field; the 6th, 7th, and 8th, at the east end. The 5th served as the alert Staffel. On Gruppe missions the 5th always took off first, from west to east, and made a gentle left turn away from the field. The 6th, 7th, and 8th Staffeln then took off to the east, joining the 5th Staffel over the town of Nordhorn. The Gruppe could be assembled very quickly in the air. There were few permanent revetments for the aircraft, only parking spaces, which were very well hidden within the dense forest found on three sides of the field. The field was well defended by five flak towers. The pilots were quartered in private homes in Nordhorn. This proved very beneficial to morale; the citizens were very supportive of "their" pilots, and a number of romances bloomed. The pilots breakfasted in their quarters before coming to the field in the mornings. Dinner was on the base; supper, in a restaurant in town that was used as a pilots' mess.

The weather improved just sufficiently on 23 December to permit aerial activity by both sides. Twenty-three FW 190As of the First Gruppe's 2nd and 3rd Staffeln took off from Fuerstenau at 1114. Their orders were to fly to the tip of the Ardennes salient, there to defend the Panzers of Army Group B against attacks by Allied bombers. Their first challenge was to avoid P-47s in the vicinity of the airfield. Six Focke-Wulfs successfully drew away the Thunderbolts, then sighted an Allied artillery spotter, which was shot down. The rest of the German force proceeded to the ordered patrol zone and attacked a formation of B-26s, claiming the destruction of two. The P-47 escorts then arrived and treated the FW 190s very roughly. Four were shot down. Their pilots were first carried as missing, but all proved to have been killed. By 1200, the pilots of the Gruppe were landing wherever they could; most chose Krefeld. Five aircraft made crash landings, all of them with some injury to their pilots.

The Second Gruppe flew its first Dora-9 mission on the 23rd. Nineteen of the "long-nosed Doras" left Nordhorn at 1152 and headed southwest to intercept a heavy bomber formation nearing the Ruhr. Major Hackl's Gruppe fought its way through an escort force of RAF Mustangs, which shot down one German fighter and damaged another severely. Tony Hackl downed one Mustang, for his 167th claim. The bombers then came into view—a small force of Lancasters and Mosquitoes. The first victim of the fighters' attack was the leading Lancaster; it was followed by five more Lancs and one Mosquito. The German fighters were untouched by the British bombers' return fire. The RAF mission was a total disaster; its leader was rewarded with a posthumous Victoria Cross.

The skies over western Europe dawned clear on the following day, permitting the Eighth Air Force to mount its largest air strike operation of the war. More than 2,000 heavy bombers were escorted by 853 fighters to a number of airfields and communications centers in western Germany. The first combat mission for the First Gruppe's new FW 190D-9s was an interception of this armada. It was not a success. Eighteen fighters, most from the 1st Staffel, took off from Fuerstenau at 1114, led by Oblt. Heckmann. Eight planes aborted immediately. A ninth pilot made off on his own, chasing an Auster artillery spotter. The nine airplanes left in the formation attacked between sixty and eighty B-17s, and their heavy escort, northwest of Luettich. The surviving Dora-9s straggled back to Fuerstenau after 1600, having made intermediate landings at other fields. Their pilots claimed the destruction of one P-38 and damage to one B-17, but four Focke-Wulfs never returned. Two had suffered engine failure. Both of their pilots made successful forced landings, but one was captured behind the Allied lines. The third pilot was also captured, and the fourth has not been found to this day.

The Second Gruppe's intercept force on the 24th did not succeed in reaching the bombers, but it had some success against the escort. Five P-47s were claimed shot down over Liege. The Gruppe took casualties as well—three pilots failed to return (one is still missing), and one bailed out with severe injuries inflicted by a P-47. It was later determined that one of the missing pilots had been shot down by a Bf 109, probably from JG 27.

The Geschwader's pilots flew a variety of small missions on 25 December, claiming two victories against three losses. The day is noteworthy for the return to the combat zone of the Green Hearts of III/JG 54, led by Hptm. Robert Weiss, a member of JG 26 back in its glory days at Abbeville. His Gruppe was put under the command of JG 26, and it is thus appropriate to summarize its story in this history. Its new base was near the village of Varrelbusch, thirty miles northeast of Fuerstenau. On the 25th, Obstlt. Priller welcomed the assembled pilots back to the front, shaking each man's hand. The unit had been built up to its full strength of sixty-eight FW 190D-9s. The Staffelkapitaene were all experienced, successful pilots. Oblt. Willi Heilmann led the 9th Staffel; Lt. Peter Crump, the 10th; Lt. Hans Prager, the 11th; and Lt. Hans Dortenmann, the 12th. Most of the other pilots were fresh from the training schools' final classes. The first mission for the reconstructed Gruppe was an important one—a cover flight for the Me 262 base at Rheine. It was unsuccessful; the Gruppe was scattered by a surprise attack by Allied fighters. Worse was to come.

The 26th of December saw 4/JG 26 debut its new FW 190D-9s. The First Gruppe Stab and the 2nd and 3rd Staffeln were now off operations, training in their new fighters; the fifteen 1st and 4th Staffel aircraft that took off at 1018 formed the entire combat strength of the Gruppe. Oblt. Hans Hartigs of the 4th Staffel led the

force. The mission was intended to be a ground-controlled interception, but when Hartigs' FuG 16ZY failed, he changed the mission to a freie Jagd, since he did not trust any other pilot of the
formation with command of the unit. Hartigs reached the tip of the
Ardennes salient and spotted the leading Panzer units but saw that
they had been abandoned, apparently from lack of fuel and/or ammunition. He had carried out his original instructions as best he
could, but he had not seen any Allied aircraft. Since his unit was
under standing orders not to return from a mission without contacting the enemy, he turned his twelve remaining Focke-Wulfs to
the south and began to climb, knowing full well that he would be
detected by Allied radar, which would vector fighters to attack the
intruders.

Hans Hartigs's wish for combat was soon fulfilled. The Mustangs of the Eighth Air Force's 361st Fighter Group had moved
from England to France on 23 December, to reinforce the air forces
available to resist the German push. On this day, the Group's 376th
Squadron was flying a sweep near Trier at 17,000 feet when a dozen
Focke-Wulfs crossed its course, 2,000 feet below, and then turned
and climbed toward them. A general dogfight ensued, in which the
American pilots emerged as the clear winners. Lt. George van den
Heuvel, who was flying as ass-end Charlie, engaged an FW 190 that
was attacking his element leader. He hit the fighter squarely with a
20-degree deflection shot, and it dove into the ground. He zoomed
up, looking for more action, and spotted two fighters on the deck.
These proved to be an FW 190 and a pursuing P-51, the latter
piloted by the American formation leader. He was out of ammunition and asked van den Heuvel to take over. The Focke-Wulf was
already smoking and took very little evasive action as the American
closed to 200 yards. At the first burst of fire, the German fighter
half-rolled and its pilot dropped out. George van den Heuvel retains
an image of the German pilot's "beautiful leather outfit trimmed in
white."

That splendidly dressed pilot was Oblt. Hartigs, wearing his
fighter pilot's leather coveralls. He bailed out when his oil pressure
dropped and his canopy filmed over with oil. The first thing he saw
when he landed was the body of one of his pilots, lying on his
parachute; he had been shot in the head at close range. Hartigs had
no way of knowing the depth of feeling of the American infantry

317

against any and all Germans as a result of the SS massacres at Malmedy and elsewhere in the Ardennes. He feels today that his clothing may have saved his life. He was wearing no decorations or badges of rank and confused his captors for a few minutes by speaking in "broken Dutch." The Oberleutnant thus survived the critical first few minutes after his capture, and he did not produce his pilot's identity card until he was safely inside an American command post. Hartigs spent his first night of captivity in a pigsty, under the close guard of Belgian resistance fighters.

Hans Kukla was a 4th Staffel Schwarmfuehrer on this mission. His recollections of this battle follow:

> I unfortunately cannot say much. I engaged in a turning battle with Mustangs at an altitude of about 3,000 meters [10,000 feet]. In order not to be shot down, I spun out. I came out of the spin at about 500 meters and saw a Mustang in front of me, in a right bank. I immediately positioned myself behind it and opened fire, but did not hit it. The Mustang pulled up, still in its right turn. I followed it, but it was much faster and escaped.

The Americans were awarded six victory credits for this engagement. True German losses were five; three pilots of the 4th Staffel were killed, and a member of the 1st Staffel was taken prisoner. No P-51s were lost, although the surviving German pilots filed two claims.

The loss of Oblt. Hartigs left Uffz. Kukla as the senior pilot in the 4th Staffel. The Staffelkapitaen, Lt. Soeffing, had run his automobile into a tree shortly before Christmas and had been taken off combat status. Although Kukla had flown no more than a dozen combat sorties himself, he was entrusted with the leadership of his Staffel in the air. On 27 December, he led eleven Dora-9s on a mission from Fuerstenau. According to the Gruppe diary, things did not go well. Three planes aborted, and the remainder got split up without contacting the enemy. The eight Focke-Wulfs to fly the mission landed at four different fields.

III/JG 54 RETURNS TO COMBAT

Despite its long absence from the front for training, there were still doubts as to the combat-worthiness of III/JG 54. On 27 December, a familiarization flight was ordered for all four of its Staffeln over the Muenster basin. Lt. Peter Crump's 10th Staffel served as high cover, at 26,000 feet. Ground control reported the presence of eight Indians above them. Hptm. Weiss then reversed course unexpectedly, putting Crump's Staffel in a most precarious position, with both the sun and the unseen enemy to its rear. On the turn, and despite Crump's express warning, two of the Nachwuchs dropped back—to be shot down immediately by Tempests, which came plummeting down out of the sun. Lt. Crump shot a Tempest off his wingman's tail, then caught and shot down another British fighter in a dive. A disillusioned Peter Crump later summed up the battle as follows:

> The final result—eight Tempests took on more than sixty of the newest German aircraft in a surprise attack; for two enemy losses, five of our own fell. It was discovered after landing that I was the only pilot to have gotten off a single shot. Because of the "word salad" over the radio, Hptm. Weiss had not been able to find us. . . .

The Tempests belonged to No. 486 Squadron, which claimed 4-1-1 of the FW 190Ds. Only one Tempest was lost; apparently Crump's first target escaped. The Hawker Tempest was the newest British fighter to reach the front. It was introduced into Second TAF specifically to fill the air superiority role, and it was one of III/JG 54's (and JG 26's) most frequent opponents for the rest of the war. The Tempest was remarkably similar in concept to the FW 190D-9, and its published performance figures are almost identical to those of the German fighter. Victory in their combats thus tended to go to the better pilot—which meant that the few experienced German pilots did very well in encounters with the RAF fighters, but the Nachwuchs generally came out the losers.

The 29th of December was III/JG 54's "schwarze Tag" (black day). The Gruppe's morning orders called for a mission by successive Staffeln against British fighter-bombers in the area of Osnabrueck, Muenster, and Rheine. Altitude was specified as 6,000 feet. The orders came from the 3rd Jagddivision, which would exercise tactical control using the FuG 16ZY. Hptm. Weiss knew that it was foolish to fly in small Staffel packets rather than as a concentrated Gruppe, and that the specified altitude was well below the normal patrol height of Second TAF's Tempests and Spitfires. However, contrary to the usual German practice, the mission commander, Weiss, was not allowed to offer any input as to the employment of his Gruppe.

The Staffeln were ordered to take off one hour apart. Lt. Crump's 10th Staffel, still recovering from the 27th, did not take part in the mission. Oblt. Heilmann led his 9th Staffel up from Varrelbusch at around 0900. As the Staffel approached the Rheine area at its ordered altitude, it was hit from above by the Spitfires of No. 411 Squadron, which quickly killed six of the German pilots; several more took to their parachutes. The few survivors landed at Varrelbusch one by one, incoherent from shock. Hptm. Weiss could not get a good feel for what had happened and led his Stabs-schwarm and the 11th Staffel off the ground at the scheduled time of 1000, determined to carry out the mission as ordered. None of Weiss's Schwarm returned. The 11th Staffel's Fw. Fritz Ungar was the sole returnee able to shed any light on the Kommandeur's fate. His combat report reads:

> The Staffel and the Stabsschwarm flew in a combat formation led by the Kommandeur, Hptm. Weiss. At 1045, while in quadrant HP [southwest of Rheine] at 1,500 meters [5,000 feet], we made contact with enemy Typhoons and Thunderbolts. In several minutes of combat, several aircraft were shot down, both the enemy's and our own. I myself shot down a Typhoon. After this battle, at about 1050, I saw two FW 190D-9s flying north at low altitude. I was alone, and attached myself to them. A fourth FW 190D-9 joined us, and we all flew on in a generally northerly direction. The Schwarmfuehrer was Hptm. Weiss; I did not recognize the other two. I flew in the far right position.
>
> We were in quadrant GP-3 [west of Rheine], when three air-craft were observed approaching from directly behind us. I watched them closely. At about 200 meters distance, the leftmost airplane banked to the right in order to place itself behind me. At that point I made a positive identification of it as a Spitfire. Immediately, Hptm. Weiss and the other two broke sharply to the right. I contin-ued to fly straight ahead at minimum altitude, since if I had broken right I would have flown right into the core of fire of the turning Spitfire. I was followed briefly, but was soon able to shake it off.

The Typhoon shot down by Fw. Ungar belonged to No. 439 Squadron; its Canadian pilot was taken prisoner by the German

Army. The "Thunderbolts" reported by Ungar were really the Tempests of No. 56 Squadron. Tempests and Thunderbolts, which had similar wing planforms and canopy shapes, were frequently confused by the Germans. The Tempests and Spitfires shot down and killed a total of seven pilots from the Stab and the 11th Staffel.

Back at Varrelbusch, Oblt. Dortenmann and his 12th Staffel were still scheduled to take off at noon. By interviewing the few returnees and listening to the radio transmissions in the command post, Dortenmann formed a picture of the situation—the entire Muenster basin was filled up to an altitude of 16,000 feet with dozens of enemy air formations of all types, primarily Spitfires. Dortenmann made his decision. He led his twelve Dora-9s off the ground, formed up east of the field, and headed for the battle zone in a steady climb, finally leveling off at 20,000 feet. Dortenmann heard the ground controller's order to drop to 6,500 feet and attack Thunderbolts and heavy bombers over Muenster, but he stayed where he was. West of Osnabrueck, he sighted twenty-two Spitfires 3,000 feet below, made a clean bounce, and shot down two fighters. One German pilot was lost, but Oblt. Dortenmann led his remaining eleven planes back to Varrelbusch in formation.

After Dortenmann's return, Obstlt. Priller informed him that the 3rd Jagddivision had ordered him to be court-martialed. Priller advised him to stay calm and keep a low profile, and the next day he instructed Dortenmann to take over the administrative command of III/JG 54. Nothing more was heard of a court-martial.

The Green Hearts lost fourteen pilots killed and at least seventeen aircraft destroyed on the 29th. The popular Robert Weiss, a Knight's Cross recipient with 121 victories at the time of his death, was not replaced for two months. In the opinion of III/JG 54's survivors, the unit never fully recovered from his loss.

By New Year's Eve, the German drive through the Ardennes had been stopped, and the Americans were pressing in on the salient from both sides. Only the youngest and most naive of JG 26's men retained any hopes of Germany's ultimate victory. The successful defense of the western borders that autumn had, however, kept alive the men's hopes for a separate peace with the Western Allies. The Geschwader had performed well since its return to Germany, in that its aerial victories had exceeded its losses. More than 125 victories were claimed, while the Geschwader lost 75 pilots killed in combat and another six in accidents. Seven men had been taken prisoner, and at least forty-nine had been injured. Few pilots spent any time thinking of the Geschwader's record or status. The largest unit to which the typical pilot felt loyalty was the Gruppe, and his Gruppe's successes were not as important to him as questions of survival—for himself, his Staffel comrades, and his family.

Nevertheless, orders reaching the Gruppe command posts on the afternoon of 31 December brought a brief resurgence of hope and pride to the pilots. The code words "Varus-Teutonicus" were received at 1430. This brought all flying to an immediate stop. As many aircraft as possible were to be brought to operational status for a maximum-strength mission. The customary New Year's Eve celebrations were forbidden; the pilots were ordered to their quarters early. While the pilots slept, the ground crews worked in the snow to prepare the largest force of German fighters ever to take to the air. The Luftwaffe High Command had thrown the dice for the last time. The ultimate fate of the Jagdwaffe would be determined in the morning.

13
UNTERNEHMEN BODENPLATTE—THE ATTACK ON ALLIED AIRFIELDS
1 January 1945

JG 26 GETS THE WORD

OBSTLT. PRILLER STARED AT THE CODED MESSAGE IN DISBELIEF: "VARUS 1.1.45. TEUTONICUS." The mission it referred to, Unternehmen Bodenplatte (Operation Baseplate), had been planned before the Ardennes offensive began. On 14 December Priller and his three Gruppenkommandeure had joined Genlt. Peltz's other fighter commanders at Altenkirchen. There they had worked out the details of a massed simultaneous attack on the airfields of the Allies' hated tactical fighters. As many as 1,500 German fighters would be available—the largest concentration of German airpower since 1940. Priller had not known of his army's planned Ardennes attack at the time, but it was now obvious that the air and ground attacks had been intended to coincide. However, the weather had proved unsuitable for large-scale air operations, and Priller had assumed that the air plan had been scrapped. To revive it now seemed foolish—the ground offensive had stalled, and the air fighting of the past two weeks had cost the Germans several hundred precious fighters and pilots. But Priller now held in his hands a piece of paper containing the first two of the enabling code words. Varus set the date for the very next day; Teutonicus authorized the pilots to be informed and called for extraordinary measures to be taken to prepare all possible aircraft for the operation. Priller allowed himself a wry chuckle at the thought of a surprise attack on New Year's morning, when his opponents would have thick heads from the previous night's festivities. He summoned his Gruppenkommandeure to a quick conference in his command post at the Fuerstenau middle school. Their first task would be to ensure that their own pilots' New Year's Eve celebrations were postponed.

Priller's meeting with Borris, Hackl, and Krupinski was brief. Little time was spent discussing their targets for the following day. These were the familiar Brussels airfields of Evere and Grimbergen, both of which had been occupied by the Geschwader four months previously, on its retreat from France. The length of the mission required the use of 300-liter auxiliary fuel tanks, so no bombs would be carried. The armorers would be busy, however, re-belting ammunition. A large proportion of incendiary shells would be carried. In an unprecedented measure, briefing cards were to be prepared for each pilot. These were to contain a map showing checkpoints, turning points, and targets. The pilots would write in further details at their own briefings. Every healthy pilot, however inexperienced, was to take part. The mission would be flown by independent Gruppen, in close formation at low altitude. Each Gruppe would be led across the battle lines by guide aircraft—Ju 88 night fighters, which had been standing by on the Geschwader's three fields.

The course of each JG 26 Gruppe would be west, across the southern tip of the Zuider Zee. After passing Rotterdam, the fighters would turn south in a broad arc and approach Brussels from the north. After the attack they were to return on a reciprocal course; however, the pilots were not to worry too much about this leg of the mission. In case of problems, they were to fly due east. Every emergency airfield in western Germany was to be alerted to receive them. In addition, checkpoints and the front lines would be indicated by smoke shells and "golden rain" flares. The plan appeared sound. Pips Priller would once again be leading his Schlageter Geschwader in the air, for the first time as a full Oberst—his promotion had been announced for the following day. His battle-hardened commanders could not help but feel a surge of enthusiasm as they left his headquarters on the afternoon of 31 December to return to their own Gruppe command posts.

I/JG 26 AND III/JG 54 ATTACK GRIMBERGEN

Major Karl Borris's headquarters was only a short drive away. He and his staff were lodged in the Kloster Handrup, a Catholic convent and girls' school near the Fuerstenau airfield, which his First Gruppe shared with Priller's Geschwaderstab. At 1600, as his own pilots gathered, twenty FW 190D-9s began landing on the small strip. These planes represented the entire fighting strength of III/JG 54, which had been placed under Borris's command for the operation. After seeing to their fighters' servicing, the Green Heart pilots joined the assembly at Handrup.

The pilots waited expectantly in one of the convent's classrooms, which seemed a suitable setting for a briefing by the ascetic Major Borris. Borris entered and told his men and the Green Heart pilots of their mission for the next day. Their target would be the field at Grimbergen. Borris was a man of few words, not given to bombastic speeches, but his emphasis on the overall strength of the mission and the obvious care devoted to its planning made a deep, favorable impression on the pilots. Their route was discussed orally; maps would be given out the next morning. The time of takeoff was not yet fixed, but all pilots were to be in bed by 2200, in anticipation of an early awakening. Consumption of alcohol was strictly forbidden.

In accordance with Luftwaffe procedure, each pilot was then given his specific formation assignment. The 4th Staffel was well up to strength in aircraft, with thirteen Dora-9s. Leutnant Vladimir Soeffing, the unit's only officer, was off duty because of an injury, however, and Uffz. Hans Kukla's name had been written in as Staffel leader for the mission. Kukla summoned up all his courage and refused his orders. His combat experience totaled but one dozen missions, and he felt that the responsibility was too great. Major Borris agreed and designated Obfw. Erich Schwarz of the 3rd Staffel to lead the 4th.

One last pilot straggled in at midnight, displaying the effects of New Year's Eve. Lt. Hans Prager, the II/JG 54 Staffelfuehrer, had aborted his Gruppe's transfer flight because of a bad engine and had then drunk in the New Year in the Green Hearts Casino. Much to his surprise, he had been fetched from Varrelbusch by auto. Oberst Priller prevented an ugly confrontation with Borris by pulling Prager aside and appointing him to lead the formation's cover Schwarm, an insultingly simple assignment for a pilot of Prager's seniority.

Shortly after midnight, the last part of the Bodenplatte order was received in the command posts—"Auftrag HERMANN 1.1.45. Zeit: 09.20 Uhr." All targeted airfields were to be hit simultaneously at the designated time of 0920. Each unit then had to calculate backward to arrive at its own schedule. In the case of I/JG 26, reveille was at 0430. Breakfast was served in the Staffel's common rooms—for the 4th Staffel, this was in the post office in Ohrte, the village where they were lodged. The pilots of III/JG 54 probably ate with Borris's Gruppenstab and II/JG 26 at the Kloster. In his book *Alarm im Westen*, Willi Heilmann, former Kapitaen of 9/JG 54, claims that breakfast consisted of "cutlets, roast beef, and wine, followed by sweet pastries and fragrant coffee." The pilots were given their maps and listened to the final briefing. Takeoff would be aided by canister lights alongside the flying strip. Radio silence was mandatory, and close formation flying was stressed. The men were then issued emergency rations and, in the case of JG 26's pilots, life jackets.

By 0600, the pilots had reached their dispersals. The aircraft had already been pushed to their takeoff positions by the ground crews. Many of the Jumo 213A engines would not start in the cold, and much last-minute juggling of assignments took place. The two Ju 88 navigation aircraft took off at 0813, but the last Focke-Wulf did not get off the ground until 0832. Oberst Priller led the unit. He was accompanied by his longtime wingman Uffz. Heinz Wodarczyk. Next came Major Borris. He was followed by twelve aircraft of Oblt. Fred Heckmann's 3rd Staffel, twelve of Oblt. Franz Kunz's 2nd, ten of Lt. Georg Kiefner's 1st, and ten from the 4th, led by Obfw. Schwarz. Seventeen III/JG 54 pilots brought up the rear. Without their own ground crews, the Green Heart pilots had had great difficulty in getting their aircraft ready to fly the mission. They borrowed several aircraft from I/JG 26, but three III/JG 54 pilots had to stay behind. At least two ferry pilots belonging to Flueg 1 did fly the mission. Oblt. Hans Dortenmann had brought them with him from Varrelbusch, selecting them in preference to his own men because of their greater experience. The eight aircraft of Lt. Peter Crump's 10/JG 54 were positioned last in the formation. The leader of his second Schwarm, Lt. Theo Nibel, had trouble starting his engine, and was the last to take off. It took a long time to catch the formation, but Nibel trailed it toward the target without difficulty.

All but the last few aircraft formed up in the crystal-clear sky over Fuerstenau and then dove for the ground, heading for the Zuider Zee at an altitude of about 100 feet. The planned formation of three shallow vees could not be maintained, because it was impossible to keep station in the ground mist. The individual Schwaerme, which were flying in line abreast formation, kept together, and the Gruppe formation resolved itself into a long, strung-out line of Schwaerme.

Soon after passing the Zuider Zee en route to Rotterdam, the pilots were greeted, not with German flares but with flak. Their route was taking them over one of the most heavily defended areas on the Continent—the V-2 launching sites around the Hague. The Luftwaffe planners had made a serious error. The pilots were accustomed to being fired on by their own flak, and some even recall being briefed to expect it on this mission, but none suspected the presence of such a heavy concentration of defensive fire. They had no room to maneuver and barreled onward through the curtain of tracers. The Focke-Wulf of the 2nd Staffel's Kapitaen, Oblt. Kunz, was among the first to be hit. He turned back, was forced to bail out, and was taken to a private clinic in Gouda with severe injuries. Two Focke-Wulfs made forced landings; a First Gruppe pilot made it back to Fuerstenau uninjured on 5 January, while a pilot of the Green Hearts suffered severe facial burns when his plane ignited on impact and was taken to a Rotterdam hospital.

The formation had by now been reduced to forty-seven aircraft. Fourteen aircraft returned early to Fuerstenau with equipment defects or damage from German flak. The rest made their turn to the south and were then taken under fire by Allied ships in the Scheldt. Two pilots from III/JG 54 were now shot down; one was killed, and the other was taken prisoner.

Just past the Scheldt, Major Borris sighted a formation of a dozen Spitfires, which he thought turned away without attacking. However, this or another unseen formation brought down two of his planes. One pilot crash-landed in an orchard, while the other succeeded in bailing out; both were quickly taken prisoner.

The remaining Focke-Wulfs climbed to 700–1,000 feet on their approach to Grimbergen. They drifted a little to the west of the field, putting it in the glare of the rising sun. Lt. Peter Crump saw that they were about to miss the field entirely, and took the initiative:

> I was assigned with my decimated Staffel of eight aircraft to the suppression of the flak at our target. My unit was thus the last in the entire formation. When we neared the target, the formation, to my astonishment, flew west past Grimbergen. I seized the moment and made the initial attack on the field with my aircraft, primarily to take advantage of surprise.

Highly visible at the takeoff point on the field was a large white diagonal cross, the international symbol for a non-operational airfield. The Thunderbolt unit that the pilots had been briefed to expect was nowhere to be seen. Crump's first pass was made at 0922, according to the British defenders—two minutes later than the ordered time of attack. He strafed a four-engined bomber at the south edge of the field and set it on fire. Then Crump, seeing no sign of any flak that needed suppressing, led his flight in shooting up everything they saw standing around, including trucks, construction equipment, sheds, and barracks.

Although there were no heavy antiaircraft guns at Grimbergen, the field was by no means defenseless. Three units of the RAF Regiment, which was responsible for airfield defense, were present, and their airmen began blazing away at the attackers with Bren guns. Lt. Theo Nibel had eventually caught up to his Schwarm and led it across the field on its assigned task. Nibel recalls:

> The Schwarm that I led had the mission of silencing the flak at Grimbergen airfield. We flew a total of three attacks on the flak, which returned fire strongly. When I pulled up after the third attack, my engine quit. I suspected a flak hit in the engine. I had reached an altitude of 100 meters [325 feet] and had to decide quickly between a parachute jump or a crash landing. I lost height quickly, and was forced to make a belly landing. I found a freshly turned field beside a farmhouse, and made a perfect landing.

Nibel was brought down not by Bren gun fire, but by a partridge strike, which knocked a hole several inches in diameter in his fighter's radiator. Nibel's aircraft, "Black 12," was the first near-whole FW 190D-9 to fall into Allied hands, and Royal Air Force personnel made the most of their opportunity to examine Kurt Tank's new fighter. One British air intelligence report archly attributed the fighter's loss to a Free Belgian partridge. After its declassification, the report was translated into German and used as source material by German historians. At some point it was retranslated into English; the poor partridge has not been transformed in some accounts into a "Belgian resistance fighter, loosing off a rifle bullet into Nibel's radiator"!

Major Borris's pilots made numerous slow firing passes across the field. They noted the presence of four four-engined bombers, one twin-engined bomber, and one Mustang, and claimed the destruction of all—destruction confirmed by British sources. In addition to the preceding aircraft, twelve trucks, two tankers, and two hangars were set on fire; several hangars were seriously damaged; and one antiaircraft position was silenced.

The Bren gunners of the RAF Regiment had ample time to study the German pilots' flight patterns and corrected their aim accordingly. They kept up their fire and began to hit their targets. One First Gruppe pilot was making his second pass when his aircraft caught fire, presumably a result of gunfire. He had climbed to an altitude of 650 feet, and he bailed out without injury.

Fw. Guenther Egli of 11/JG 54 had had an eventful flight before he ever arrived at Grimbergen. German flak near Rotterdam had ignited his auxiliary tank, but he had managed to jettison it successfully. Over Grimbergen he was hit by small-arms fire and had to force-land in the middle of the airfield. He told his captors that he was a pilot in the Einsatzstaffel (operational Staffel) of JG 104, an advanced training unit, and that the Staffel's three pilots had volunteered for, and participated in, Bodenplatte. This was duly recorded in the interrogation report prepared by his British captors. After the declassification of this report, JG 104 began to appear in British historians' accounts of Bodenplatte. A few years later, the report made its way across the Channel, and German histories of Bodenplatte now invariably take note of JG 104 and its brave instructor pilots, even though the unit appears in none of the original German records of the operation. In fact, there was no "JG 104 Einsatzstaffel." Guenther Egli had previously served in JG 104 as a student and later as an instructor, but he had joined JG 54 in March 1944 and was a member of the Green Hearts until his capture. Egli freely admits today that he fabricated the JG 104 Einsatzstaffel as a "white lie" to keep from revealing his true unit to his captors. He succeeded in fooling not only his original captors, but an entire generation of British and German aviation historians.

The ten Focke-Wulfs of 4/JG 26 were apparently the last to reach Grimbergen. It is not known why they had fallen behind III/JG 54. According to Hans Kukla:

> When we arrived over the field, the other machines had already left. We saw from its white cross that the field was not operational. Since we could find no targets on the field, we made three attacks on the hangars, without great effect. Our return flight retraced our earlier course, but at an altitude of 3,000 meters [10,000 feet]. At 1130 seven of us landed at Quakenbrueck on our last drops of fuel.

The last Focke-Wulf to be shot down by the Grimbergen Bren gunners was that of a 4th Staffel pilot who was flying on his first combat mission. He was hit by antiaircraft fire on his second pass, pulled up, and bailed out over the field. He succeeded in impressing his captors as a "particularly dim type" and provided them with no information.

The German machine cannon fell silent at 0937, according to the British records, after an attack of exactly fifteen minutes duration. Borris's men were under orders to return to Germany on the reciprocal of their outbound course. The aircraft recognition abilities of the German antiaircraft gunners around Rotterdam had not improved in the previous hour, and they once again took the Focke-Wulfs under fire. At least four more German fighters fell now, killing two pilots. Many pilots simply disappeared, probably on this leg of the flight. One III/JG 54 pilot survived as a prisoner, but Priller's wingman, Uffz. Wodarczyk; three First Gruppe pilots; three members of III/JG 54; and two ferry pilots from Flueg 1 were killed. Some of these men remain missing to this day.

By 1124, most of the returning pilots had landed at Fuerstenau. It was an enraged Oberst Priller who composed his report to Genlt. Peltz that evening. Twelve First Gruppe pilots had failed to return from the mission, one-quarter of the forty-eight who had taken off that morning. Four would eventually turn up, but even eight losses were too many against the worthless target Grimbergen had proven to be. It was for the decimated III/JG 54 that Priller's heart bled, however. Twelve of its seventeen pilots had failed to return—a devastating 70 percent loss.

As a coda to this sad tale, the question of Priller's own performance on the mission must be addressed. The unit history that he authored is silent on his activities after takeoff. According to Peter Crump:

> The reason the formation had initially flown past the target—which was first noticed only by my immediate attack—was related to me by the Kommandeur of I/JG 26 in a confidential conversation after our return. The formation leader, Oberst Priller, had lost the unit when it altered course to the south in the dawn mists over the Zuider Zee, which had led to a certain confusion at the head of the formation.

How could the formation leader, who was, after all, in the lead, lose the formation? For Major Borris to have phrased his comment in this manner implies that there was more to this story than he told Crump. Priller apparently returned to Fuerstenau early, without suffering combat damage. Pips Priller had not flown a mission in several months, was unaccustomed to flying the Dora-9, and may have become disoriented when he lost sight of the ground in the mists. Since all the principals are dead, the complete stories of the Bodenplatte missions of Oberst Priller and his wingman are probably lost to history.

II/JG 26 ATTACKS BRUSSELS-EVERE

The Second Gruppe spent the morning of 31 December on an intercept mission against fighter-bombers, followed by a freie Jagd that failed to contact the enemy. All aircraft returned safely to the Gruppe's base at Nordhorn-Clausheide, and flying ended at noon. Major Tony Hackl returned from Fuerstenau in mid-afternoon and passed the word of the forthcoming mission to his four Staffel-kapitaene. They in turn reached all their pilots before they were dismissed at nightfall, and ordered them to refrain from alcohol that evening, to pack their flight bags for a long mission, and to turn in no later than 2200. Details of the mission would be made available in the morning.

Gefr. Werner Molge of the 8th Staffel spent the morning of the 31st ferrying a replacement Dora-9 from the Gruppe's resupply field at Reinsehlen. At nineteen, Molge was the youngest pilot in the Staffel and was treated somewhat as a mascot. Oblt. Hofmann usually assigned Molge the ferrying and test flight chores, in an attempt to build his flying hours and skills. He had seen little combat flying to date, but since this was to be a maximum-strength effort, Molge was certain he would be taken along. Bodenplatte was to be his most memorable combat mission; his senses heightened, he paid careful attention to the events around him, and he has recorded his impressions in detail. Werner Molge recalls:

> Since the pilots were quartered in private homes in Nordhorn, enforcement of the order prohibiting alcohol was up to the self-discipline of each individual pilot, but most of us obeyed. We had to pack our flight bags so that they could be picked up in the morning. This in itself was unusual, but none of us knew what was up. I packed my bag in my quarters, which were in the home of the widow of the schoolmaster Planert. I laid everything out, and was in bed at 2000.
>
> At 0500 the next morning, the Gruppe orderly went from house to house and awakened the pilots by ringing on the doorbells. At 0600 breakfast was served in the pilots' mess at the Berning Hotel in Nordhorn. The bus which carried us daily to the field at Clausheide pulled out this morning at 0630. On the bus, the "weather frog" gave us the weather forecast for our mission area, as he did daily. For 1 January he predicted a cloudless sky, light winds from the southwest, and a temperature of about minus-5-degrees Centigrade.
>
> When we turned in at the field, a fantastic sight spread out in front of our eyes. The aircraft of all the Staffeln had been taxied from their dispersals by the ground crews and were lined up around the field, as if for a parade inspection. Fifty FW 190D-9s glistened in the last light of the moon. The mechanics had worked all night to get them ready; several were still being attended to.
>
> The bus did not take us to the readiness shacks at the various dispersals, as usual, but rather to the Gruppe command post. Inside, our three-man band was playing hot rhythms to get us stirring. At the mission briefing we were finally informed of our orders and the target—"Low-level attack on the airfield at Brussels-Evere." The

maps we were given had the course from the German border to the target marked, as well as the return course to the border.

I received for the first time in my career as a pilot a one-man life raft, a life jacket, and emergency rations. We also had to take wrist compasses, flare ammunition, Pervitin stimulant tablets, et cetera, with us. Then we went out to our aircraft, which had their props turning over and their brakes applied. The crew chiefs helped buckle us in and left the engines running.

Takeoff was at 0800, into the reddish glare of the now-rising sun. It was without incident, although the Schwaerme of four aircraft threw up fountains of snow that greatly hampered visibility. Takeoffs at close spacing were always dangerous due to the prop-wash, which threw us about unexpectedly. Also, there were four to six inches of snow on the ground, which made things even more difficult.

The two Ju 88G-6 pathfinders from II/NJG 6 were first off the ground. Major Hackl was next up, leading a full four-aircraft Stabs-schwarm. Next came Oblt. Gerhard Vogt and the 5th "alert" Staffel. There followed, in order, Oblt. Wilhelm Hofmann's 8th Staffel, Oblt. Addi Glunz's 6th Staffel, and Oblt. Waldi Radener's 7th Staffel. It was intended that each Staffel formation should contain twelve aircraft; two 7th Staffel pilots were assigned to Hofmann to make up his dozen. The individual Staffeln made a large circuit around the field and assembled in Gruppe formation, according to their normal procedure. The Ju 88s then led them off on course at an altitude of 150 feet. A few pilots whose balky engines were slow to start straggled along behind.

Other fighter formations were visible in the clear early morning air, flying on the same course. Some pilots remember keeping loose formation with Major Borris's First Gruppe, but no Second Gruppe pilot's memoir mentions sighting the Messerschmitts of Hptm. Krupinski's Third Gruppe—this is somewhat surprising, as both formations flew the same course en route to the same target, Brussels-Evere. The Second Gruppe's flight proceeded smoothly, in total radio silence, until the Zuider Zee checkpoint was reached. They were then suddenly engulfed in a wall of flak, which shot down three Focke-Wulfs. Two pilots were killed; the third survived his bailout but suffered numerous injuries.

The formation made its turn at Rotterdam and then proceeded

across the Scheldt, still at low altitude. They were taken under fire by Allied ships, which cost the unit one more Focke-Wulf; its pilot was taken prisoner. Over land once more, Hackl's pilots could see Brussels in the distance. The leading Ju 88 took a severe flak hit and turned back; it made a successful one-wheeled landing back at Nordhorn. After one more course change, Hackl's Focke-Wulfs climbed to their attack altitude of 2,000 feet, dropping their auxiliary tanks as they neared Evere.

Evere, unlike Grimbergen, was a fully operational airfield of the British Second Tactical Air Force. The field was the base for the forty Spitfires of No. 127 wing (RCAF), whose air commander was the famous Wing Cdr. "Johnnie" Johnson, the RAF's top-scoring fighter pilot in the ETO. The Spitfires were arrayed in a single row along the eastern edge of the field. They were parked close to the perimeter track, as the ground was soft and boggy. The wing had not even bothered to unpack its camouflage netting, since a number of unpainted bombers and transports were parked conspicuously on the other side of the airfield. Among the transports were a Beechcraft assigned to Prince Bernhard of the Netherlands, and a luxurious RAF Dakota belonging to a visiting VIP. Antiaircraft defense was the responsibility of two squadrons of the RAF Regiment. One had eleven Bofors 40-mm guns, while the other had nothing heavier than the ubiquitous Bren gun.

No. 127 Wing's customary dawn flights had been delayed by the necessity to sand the field's only hard-surfaced runway. A thin layer of ice had formed on it overnight, imperiling takeoffs. Shortly before 0900, four Spitfires from No. 403 Squadron got off on a weather flight. No. 416 Squadron was called to readiness for a twelve-fighter patrol. As their Spitfires crept along the perimeter track, the sound of many aircraft engines was heard. Just as the first flight of Spitfires started down the runway, sixty Focke-Wulfs and Messerschmitts screamed across the field. The Canadian mission leader made it off the ground, only to be shot down and killed by a German pilot before reaching combat speed. The three Spitfires behind him burst into flames as their pilots jumped out and ran for their lives. The Second and Third Gruppen of JG 26 had arrived.

Oblt. Hofmann's well-disciplined 8th Staffel split into Schwaerme to begin its assigned task of flak suppression; the other German attackers pounced on the numerous ground targets, displaying no vestige of order or plan. The four taxiing Spitfires were attacked by both Focke-Wulfs and Messerschmitts. Four Second Gruppe pilots were credited with their destruction, but after the mission several pilots from the Third Gruppe put in claims for the same Spitfires. After a single pass by Hofmann's men, the antiaircraft guns fell silent. According to Johnnie Johnson, they had run out of ammunition. No JG 26 aircraft was shot down over Evere by antiaircraft fire, despite the defenders' claims for three German fighters destroyed and ten damaged. Several Focke-Wulfs were seriously damaged, however, including that of the 6th Staffel's Uffz. Norbert Risky, who recalled:

> During my second attack my aircraft shuddered—a flak hit! Oil blinded me. I tried to wash the oil off without success. To the side of the field a large plume of smoke was rising. Fleeing into this, I tried again to clean my canopy—still no luck. Escape was now uppermost in my mind. My engine was running somewhat roughly, but its power and the instruments were all right. I set course over the roofs of Brussels. . . . About ten minutes later I saw aircraft in front of me. I stalked them slowly; as soon as I could identify them as our own, I breathed easier. It was Oblt. Glunz with four or five planes. Hopefully my engine would keep running until I reached our lines. I was slowly losing oil; the oil temperature crept upward. I flew over the ocean at low altitude and was again taken under fire by the picket boats. This obstacle was overcome at full throttle. . . . Oil was flowing everywhere; it turned to smoke whenever it hit hot metal. My comrades disappeared slowly over the horizon. Alone, I crossed the meadows.
>
> Suddenly my oil pressure dropped away to zero; there was a loud noise, and a long flame came out from under the cowling. The hot metal began to crackle. Things looked bad—I was too low to bail out and had too little speed to climb. Beneath me, only trees. . . . Ahead was some flat ground suitable for a crash landing. I tightened my straps, put my head down, and braced for the crash. Unfortunately, the landing site had some holes; one wing broke off, and the engine likewise. It began to get hot in the cockpit. Just as I emerged, the hot ammunition started to go off, and I had to hit the ground. A half hour later, an army Volkswagen picked me up and brought me to Zwolle. By late evening, I was back in Nordhorn.

Gefr. Werner Molge, a wingman in Lt. Gerhard "Bubi" Schulwitz's 8th Staffel Schwarm, dove with it to attack the suspected antiaircraft installations. The flight was then released to join in the general attacks. Molge recalls:

> The first attack silenced all of the flak. We then were free to fire on the many parked aircraft, which were drawn up in neat rows for us. During my second attack flames were visible on the ground, and clouds of smoke began to rise. The third attack was almost suicidal, because I had to dive into thick smoke and could only see my targets at the last second. On my fourth attack I had difficulty leveling out, I was so close to the ground. At that I gave up, and took up a course for my home field.

The four No. 403 Sqd. Spitfires in the air returned to Evere and attempted to intervene. They were engaged by the highest Schwaerme of Focke-Wulfs and Messerschmitts, which were probably serving as cover flights. Three of the Spitfire pilots claimed a total of 3-0-0 FW 190Ds and 3-1-0 Bf 109s before running out of ammunition and fleeing for their lives. In fact, only one JG 26 aircraft was lost to Allied fighters over Evere. This 6th Staffel Focke-Wulf was seen by ground witnesses to strike a tree after an engagement with fighters. The fighter then hit the ground and burst into flames, trapping the pilot inside.

The German pilots continued their attacks on the now-defenseless airfield until, in their opinion, no undamaged targets remained. Major Hackl flew seven attacks; Oblt. Glunz, nine. Addi Glunz claimed the definite destruction by fire of five aircraft, heavy damage to two, and the destruction of one truck. He was able to shoot up a twin-engined aircraft through the open door of a hangar. On his next pass he attempted once again to take the hangar under fire, but it could no longer be seen through the smoke.

After all of the British aircraft were either ablaze or masked by the smoke, the German pilots strafed six tanker trucks and the barracks on the northern edge of the field. They then left Evere as suddenly as they had arrived, leaving behind them a black cloud of smoke that ultimately reached an altitude of 13,000 feet and was clearly visible later that morning from the Gruppe's base at Nordhorn.

Wing Cdr. Johnson had a safe position on the ground from which to observe the attack and gave it his expert evaluation. The

German fighters had made their runs in ones and twos, very slowly—seemingly at no more than 150 mph. They wasted their fire on hangars, rather than on more profitable targets. One comment in his report would have been a severe blow to the pride of the once-notorious Abbeville Kids, had they known of it: "The shooting was atrocious, and the circuit at Evere reminded us more of a bunch of beginners on their first solos than pilots of front-line squadrons."

As soon as possible, Johnson ordered a strong formation of Spitfires to take to the air to guard against a return attack. He then surveyed the damage. His wing had lost one pilot and one ground crewman killed, and nine more enlisted men injured. Despite the spectacular smoke and flames, only eleven of his Spitfires had been destroyed, and another twelve damaged. His unit had come out of the attack incredibly lightly. Across the field, a number of transports and bombers were ablaze; these included both the Prince's Beechcraft and the VIP Dakota.

Soon after leaving Evere, the engine of one of the Gruppe's rookie pilots burst into flames, forcing him to bail out into captivity; his first mission had proved to be his last. At about this time, a Gruppe pilot claimed the destruction of a stray P-47 in the air between Brussels and Antwerp. The Allied shipping in the Scheldt was fully alerted for the returnees and put up a solid curtain of light antiaircraft fire. Two Focke-Wulfs were hit. One pilot bailed out, and the other made a belly landing; both were picked up quickly by Canadian troops. At least one pilot, Uffz. Walter Stumpf of the 7th Staffel, had ammunition remaining, and fired it off at the ships as he passed them.

There was one last gauntlet to be run—the German flak belt between Rotterdam and The Hague. It claimed one victim from the Gruppe, who attempted a forced landing, but broke his neck when his aircraft overturned on uneven ground. In common with several other Geschwader pilots, he had been on his first combat sortie.

Most of the Gruppe pilots had landed at Nordhorn by 1045. Eleven pilots were missing; three of these men would eventually return. The Schlageter Geschwader's claims for ground victories at Evere were broadcast in the OKW communiqué that evening. These totaled twenty B-17s and B-24s, twenty-four twin-engined aircraft, and sixty fighters, all destroyed by strafing. Major Hackl's report singled out for praise Oblt. Hofmann, for his combat leadership, and Oblt. Glunz, for the destruction he had wrought in his nine low-altitude attacks. This had been Addi Glunz's 238th combat sortie, and it proved to be his last. He flew no missions during the rest of January, and in early February he was ordered to Lechfeld for training on the Me 262. The German collapse in April prevented him from returning to a combat unit.

One of the eleven missing pilots showed up unexpectedly at 1700 that evening—Gefr. Werner Molge. After leaving Evere, he flew alone for about fifteen minutes. He then joined up with four Second Gruppe Focke-Wulfs but unaccountably lost them again. Werner Molge continues his narrative:

> I lost sight of my companions, and suddenly found myself alone above the plain. At least I did not encounter any flak on the return. I flew past my field at Nordhorn without seeing it. I landed after two hours and fifty minutes in the air, literally with my last drops of fuel, on III/JG 6's airfield. I had to be towed in from the landing field by a half-track, as my engine had run dry.
>
> I was forbidden to take off, because this was prohibited while enemy aircraft were over the Reich; also, I had trouble getting fuel. Since this was a Bf 109 field, it had only B4 fuel. The FW 190D required C3 gasoline, which had to be brought in in barrels. That afternoon I received fifty-five gallons of gasoline and flew back over Fuerstenau to Nordhorn. I was pounced on in the Berning Hotel pilots' mess, where New Year's was being celebrated belatedly. My comrades had already written me off as missing. My landing report from Bissel was either never received in the general confusion of the morning, or was not passed along.
>
> So we had a proper celebration, but our spirits were not fully in it, as so many of our comrades had lost their young lives in Unternehmen Bodenplatte. All of us were between 18 and 25 years old.

III/JG 26 ATTACKS BRUSSELS-EVERE

Although the Third Gruppe's route and target were the same as those of the Second Gruppe, Hptm. Walter Krupinski's men flew an entirely independent mission. Krupinski's New Year's Eve orders to his pilots at Plantluenne were the same as Major Hackl's at Nordhorn—no alcohol, and lights out at 2200. The next morning, about forty Bf 109K-4s and Bf 109G-14s were prepared for takeoff. The Gruppe had sixty fighters on strength, but there were not enough pilots to fly them all. It is known that the 12th Staffel was led by its Kapitaen, Oblt. Karl-Hermann Schrader; it is assumed that on this maximum-strength mission the other Staffeln were led by their Kapitaene as well. These were Oblt. Gottfried Schmidt of the 9th, Hptm. Paul Schauder of the 10th, and the newly commissioned Lt. Hermann Guhl of the 11th Staffel. As always, there is little documentary evidence of the activities of this Gruppe.

Hptm. Krupinski described the Third Gruppe's mission for Priller:

> We wanted to assemble the entire Gruppe in a single 360-degree circuit. But that went out the window, so the Stab flight and I followed the first pathfinder aircraft, and the rest of the Gruppe flew about a half mile behind us, with the second pathfinder. Our flight path was the same as the rest of the Geschwader's—south edge of the Zuider Zee, wheel past Rotterdam, over the flooded region, and then from the Initial Point northwest of the airfield, straight to the field.

The German flak belt west of the Zuider Zee opened fire on Krupinski's formation and shot down one airplane, killing its pilot. The Messerschmitts apparently made it across the Scheldt without further damage. They then hurtled across a Canadian Army encampment at an altitude of thirty feet, coming under fire by small arms and Bofors light antiaircraft guns. One pilot took a hit in his engine and had to make an immediate belly landing. Hptm. Krupinski's aircraft was also hit, as he related to this author:

> Flying over the front lines, I was hit by light flak on the hinge of the left cowling panel, which popped open, forcing me to zigzag across the countryside. In my initial fright I wanted to turn back, but after it became apparent that the thing was still flying I stayed with the formation, although I was unable to fire my weapons.

At some point Krupinski had to turn back; he ordered Uffz. Georg Genth of the 12th Staffel to accompany him back to Plantluenne. The remaining Messerschmitts reached Evere at 0920, right on schedule. Uffz. Heinz Gehrke of the 11th Staffel struck one of the No. 416 Sqd. Spitfires as it was taking off, and he watched it smash flaming into the ground. He then strafed two twin-engined aircraft, which he identified as Mosquitoes, and saw them burst into flames. After nearly fifteen minutes of unopposed strafing attacks, he and the other Bf 109 pilots joined up in loose formation and headed north on their return flight. All apparently went well until the German flak belt was reached. Two aircraft disappeared without a trace at this time, and two more made successful crash landings.

It was an enthusiastic group of pilots that landed back at Plantluenne. Heinz Gehrke recalls buzzing the field while happily and vigorously rocking his wings, signaling his victory at Evere. Only six pilots were missing, and two of them returned later. Hptm. Krupinski called a quick meeting of all of his pilots and praised them for their highly successful mission.

The Third Gruppe's claims for the destruction of aircraft on the ground at Evere could not be separated from those of the Second Gruppe, and no serious attempt was made to do so. Heinz Gehrke recalls that the aerial victory claims of the two Gruppen totaled between six and eight; subtracting the five known claims of the Second Gruppe leaves from one to three for the Third Gruppe, of which one was Gehrke's Spitfire. His claim was to his knowledge never confirmed, despite witnesses, but he was shortly thereafter awarded the Iron Cross First Class, in part for his successful Bodenplatte mission.

THE BALANCE

Unternehmen Bodenplatte has been analyzed in great detail by many historians. Their opinions are nearly unanimous, and the consensus can be summarized briefly here. German planning for the mission was thorough, and nearly flawless. Only the targeting of one non-operational field (Grimbergen) and the inexplicable failure to route the northernmost Jagdgruppen around the known V-2 flak area marred the concept. But the mission lost all its strategic purpose once the Ardennes offensive had been checked and should have been canceled by Genlt. Peltz. Adolf Galland bears no share of the blame for Bodenplatte. The disgraced General of the Fighter Arm had gone on leave in late December, prior to his formal relief, and had no role in the operation.

Bodenplatte weakened the Jagdwaffe past any last hope of rebuilding. It had sacrificed itself in a single grand, insanely futile gesture. Of the 900 German fighters that took off at daybreak on New Year's Day, 300 failed to return to their bases. Pilots made their way back individually over the next few days, but a total of 214 were killed, taken prisoner, or remained missing. Counted among the casualties were nineteen formation leaders—three Geschwaderkommodoren, six Gruppenkommandeure, and ten Staffelkapitaene. About 150 pilots had taken off under the command of JG 26. Thirty-two of them were killed or taken prisoner. The JG 26 casualty rate was thus slightly less than the average for the entire attacking force.

In their embarrassment at being taken completely by surprise, the Allied air commanders failed to compile a comprehensive list of their losses, but as many as 300 RAF and USAAF aircraft were destroyed or damaged beyond repair. Few Allied pilots were lost, however, and all units were back up to strength in aircraft within a week. The effect of the German fighter pilots' self-sacrifice on the course of the war was thus nonexistent.

The planners at Altenkirchen had attempted to take into account the limited skills of their fighter pilots, but it was the poor quality of those pilots that ultimately doomed the operation. Thirty-three Jagdgruppen and one Schlachtgruppe flew the mission. Their targets were sixteen tactical airfields in the Netherlands, Belgium, and eastern France. Of the thirty-four Gruppen, ten never found their assigned targets at all; their missions were total failures. Nine Gruppen made ineffectual, low-strength attacks on their targets. Two Gruppen, I/JG 26 and III/JG 54, flew missions that must be described as "technical successes"—all went well until their targeted airfield was discovered to be nonoperational. Only one-third of the force, or eleven Gruppen, which included II/JG 26 and III/JG 26, made their attacks entirely according to plan—on time, in strength, and with complete surprise, against airfields that contained the desired targets, Allied tactical aircraft. And even in these cases, the German success was much less than it should have been, and much less than the pilots themselves believed it to have been. Quoting from Johnnie Johnson's book *Wing Leader*, Unternehmen Bodenplatte "was a bold stroke, but we saw for ourselves that the average German fighter pilot was not equal to the task."

14
THE FINAL BATTLES
January–May 1945

ATTRITION CONTINUES

THE WEATHER PERMITTED LITTLE FLYING IN EARLY JANUARY, allowing the Geschwader's pilots a brief period to celebrate their own successes on New Year's Day and to give some thought to the twenty Schlageter pilots who had not returned. The First Gruppe's pilots moved out of their private lodgings and joined the Gruppe ground staff in the girls' school at Handrup, apparently to economize on transportation. Six to eight pilots bunked in each classroom. Luftwaffe servicewomen were also lodged in the school; Borris addressed the fraternization problem by painting a line down the hallway and forbidding his pilots to cross it. However, as one wag put it, the line was invisible after dark.

The Geschwader's pilots were ordered into the air on every flyable day. JG 26's task for the remainder of the war would be to provide support for the German armies defending the northern sector of the Western front against the Canadian First Army, the British Second Army, and the northernmost of the American armies. The Gruppen flew ground-controlled intercept missions and freie Jagden against Allied tactical aircraft; armed reconnaissance, strafing and bombing missions; escorts for other units flying ground support missions; and defensive patrols of the airfields of the jet bomber unit KG(J) 51, to protect its Me 262s during takeoffs and landings. Never again would JG 26 be ordered to attack American heavy bomber formations. This job was left to the few FW 190 and Bf 109 Gruppen remaining in the home defense organization, and to the new jet fighter units.

By noon on 4 January, the weather around the Geschwader's bases had cleared to a light ground haze, and the First Gruppe scheduled a training mission. Twenty-three Dora-9s took off from Fuerstenau, led by Oblt. Fred Heckmann. The 4th Staffel, which was still being led in the air by Obfw. Erich Schwarz, took off last, lost the rest of the formation in the haze, and headed east, toward a formation of Allied fighter-bombers reported near Osnabrueck. Uffz. Hans Kukla's engine caught fire, and he bailed out. The rest of Schwarz's small formation was ordered to reverse course and attack a new formation near Rheine. They climbed to 16,000 feet, crossed the Dutch border, and spotted eight Typhoons beneath them, escorted by from ten to fifteen Spitfires. The German bounce was fended off by the Spitfires, and a turning combat ensued, in which the Allied aircraft held the advantage. Three Focke-Wulfs crashed, killing one pilot. The Canadian pilots of No. 411 Squadron claimed six victories in this engagement and suffered no losses. The fifteen aircraft that had stayed with Oblt. Heckmann made no contact and returned to Fuerstenau without incident.

The Second Gruppe also ordered up a small formation, consisting primarily of aircraft from the 8th Staffel. Shortly after takeoff from Nordhorn, apparently while still forming up on the Dutch side of the nearby border, the Focke-Wulfs were hit by the Spitfires of another Canadian squadron, No. 442. The German formation scattered. The Canadian pilots filed claims for one probable and one damaged. Their "probable" in fact crashed, carrying Lt. Wilhelm Mayer to his death. Although a member of Gerhard Vogt's 5th Staffel, Mayer has frequently led the 8th Staffel in the air since Wilhelm Hofmann's eye injury, and he was flying an 8th Staffel aircraft on this mission. Mayer was one of the most successful pilots in the Gruppe, with twenty-seven victories, and was awarded a posthumous Knight's Cross two days after his death.

At Nordhorn that evening, the Second Gruppe's adjutant, Oblt. Guenther Bloemertz, filled in Mayer's casualty report—an especially painful chore, since the two pilots had joined the Geschwader together back in 1942. Bloemertz had been shot down and severely burned in 1943 and, after a year's hospitalization, had returned to his old Gruppe in a non-flying capacity. It was Bloemertz's fate to watch from the ground as his old Abbeville comrades took off and, one by one, failed to return. The sensitive Bloemertz brooded on the effect this latest death would have on Mayer's closest friend, Gerhard Vogt. Vogt and Mayer were inseparable on the ground, and Bloemertz felt certain that Vogt would soon join Mayer in death. After the war, Guenther Bloemertz expunged his feelings of guilt over his own survival by writing a novel, *Dem Himmel am Naechsten*. It was based on his experiences in II/JG 26 and was meant as a tribute to the fallen fighter pilots of his Gruppe. The book, which appeared in English in 1953 as *Heaven Next Stop*, proved quite successful, and it was translated into several languages.

On 12 January, the Russians began a major offensive along the Vistula River. Twenty Gruppen of single-engined fighters were sent east from the Western front to bolster the German defenders. These units were the remnants of Galland's one-time strategic reserve, which had been brought west for Unternehmen Bodenplatte. The aerial defense of the skies over Germany's western borders was now left to the same four Geschwader that had had the task the previous autumn—JG 26, JG 27, JG 2, and JG 53.

The next day with flyable weather was 14 January. Heavy ground fog persisted up to 1,000 feet, but the skies above were clear. All three JG 26 Gruppen were assigned missions, despite signs of a large heavy bomber raid, which according to the current standing orders was sufficient reason to keep the Geschwader's planes on the ground. But the army, in retreat in the Ardennes, needed relief from the American fighter-bombers, and so shortly before 1100 the Second and Third Gruppen began taking off, under orders to attack Jabos at St. Vith. At this moment, the van of a massive Eighth Air Force bomber formation was crossing the coast at Ostend. Most were en route to bomb oil industry targets in central Germany, but the 187 B-17s of the 1st Air Division were headed for the Rhine bridges at Cologne, closely escorted by forty-two P-51s, and preceded by a sweep of sixty-two P-47Ms from the 56th Fighter Group. This armada was on a collision course with the small German force of Focke-Wulfs and Messerschmitts. The Second Gruppe was led by Major Tony Hackl, who was flying with Oblt. Hofmann and the 8th Staffel. Hackl was apparently not able to form up the Gruppe because of the weather, so ordered them south as a string of independent Staffeln. The 5th was led by Oblt. Vogt; the 6th, by Oblt. Glunz; and the 7th, by Oblt. Radener. Glunz turned back shortly after takeoff, and command of the 6th was assumed by his deputy, Lt. Siegfried Sy.

When about halfway to their assigned patrol zone, Major Hackl spotted the American escort formations, and led the 8th Staffel on a successful bounce. Two straggling 56th Group Thunderbolts went down. Hackl then led his small unit on a wide left turn to the east of Cologne, in hopes of reaching a position from which the oncoming bomber stream could be attacked. The German formation had been picked up by American radar on the Continent, and twenty-five P-51s from the 78th Fighter Group were vectored to meet them. The trailing Staffeln of Hackl's Gruppe, along with the Bf 109s of the Third Gruppe, were spotted three miles southwest of Cologne. The twenty fighters appeared to the American pilots to be disorganized, as though they were just in the process of forming up. The Mustangs' attack apparently caught the Germans by surprise. Four FW 190Ds, three from the 6th Staffel and one from the 7th, went down immediately, killing all four pilots.

Oblt. Vogt's 5th Staffel formation was broken up by the American attack. Vogt himself attempted to escape on the deck. Ground witnesses southeast of Cologne heard gunfire in the clouds, followed by the crash of an aircraft, which proved to be Vogt's. The Knight's Cross recipient had been killed in his cockpit; he thus followed his friend Wilhelm Mayer in death by only ten days, fulfilling Gunther Bloemertz's prediction. His final record stood at forty-eight victories, gained in 174 missions.

A second 5th Staffel pilot escaped to the northeast, but he was shot up by four Spitfires. He was unable to find a landing field and, when he ran out of fuel, force-landed with injuries near Minden. Another member of the 5th Staffel fled the combat to the southwest, but at 1245 was shot down west of Frankfurt by German flak. He was pulled from his burning Dora-9 by two Russian POWs. A fourth member of the 5th Staffel who was lost at this time was still carried as missing in 1990.

The battle moved eastward. The swirling fighters dropped to the deck, where combats continued in and out of the thick clouds. Three Third Gruppe Messerschmitts crashed, killing their pilots. A fourth pilot bailed out and returned to Plantluenne two days later. Hackl led the 8th Staffel back into the action and claimed victories over one P-47 and one P-51. The 8th Staffel got split up in this combat, and one Rotte was pursued back to Cologne by P-51s. The American pilots saw one of these two Focke-Wulfs crash-land on Cologne-Wahn airfield; its pilot was killed in the crash.

The 78th Group pilots filed claims for 6-0-3 FW 190s and 6-0-3 Bf 109s. Actual JG 26 losses in the Cologne area were seven FW 190s and four Bf 109s, in close agreement with the American claims. No P-51 was shot down in this battle, although three Mustang pilots had to make emergency landings on the Continent.

Back at Fuerstenau, the First Gruppe had been at readiness since 1000. Their orders finally came through; they were to fly a defensive patrol of KG(J) 51's airfields in the Rheine-Hopsten area. Thirty-one Dora-9s took off at 1525, led by Major Borris. Three aborted; shortly thereafter Borris's remaining twenty-eight planes engaged a Spitfire formation of the same size, which was en route to its own patrol of the Rheine airfields. Major Borris claimed one Spitfire, for his 43rd victory. Two more Spitfires were claimed; one of these collided with a Focke-Wulf, taking both aircraft down in flames. Two German pilots were shot down and killed. Six Focke-Wulfs were pursued to the Dortmund area, where they landed when low on fuel. Borris carried out his ordered patrol with his last dozen aircraft. His scattered force landed back at Fuerstenau between 1545 and 1630 hours. The Spitfire pilots, who belonged to Second TAF's two Norwegian squadrons, claimed the destruction of four German fighters and lost only one of their number.

After the bitter fighting on the 14th, which cost JG 26 thirteen pilots killed and three injured, the Geschwader was grounded for several days. The Third Gruppe was taken off operations for conversion to the FW 190D-9. Lt. Waldemar "Vladimir" Soeffing was named Kapitaen of the 2nd Staffel, replacing the severely wounded Franz Kunz. Soeffing, who had nearly recovered from the automobile accident that had grounded him in December, now had responsibility for both the 2nd and 4th Staffeln.

As German-held territory shrank, and the strength of the combat units continued to decline, many Luftwaffe higher commands became superfluous. Jagdkorps II was disbanded on 15 January. Three Fliegerdivisionen were formed under Luftwaffenkommando

West to control all the Luftwaffe combat units in the west—bomber and reconnaissance units in addition to the day fighters. JG 26 was assigned to the 14th Fliegerdivision, which was responsible for the northern part of the front.

The Geschwader's next combat mission was flown on 22 January. I/JG 26 and III/JG 54 received orders at 1030 to attack fighter-bombers in the area of Rheine-Muenster. Details of the Green Hearts' mission are unknown; they suffered no losses. Thirty First Gruppe aircraft took off at 1100 into a cloudless sky, led by Major Borris. Six aircraft aborted, but the rest flew the ordered mission. At 1117 they encountered Spitfires at 13,000 feet near Rheine. They claimed one victory, but the Spitfires, which were from No. 421 Squadron (RCAF), shot down four Focke-Wulfs, while claiming five. Two German pilots were killed, and one bailed out uninjured. The fourth, Uffz. Hans Kukla, was hit from behind in a dogfight. His engine caught fire immediately, and Kukla bailed out with serious burns, which kept him in the hospital until the beginning of April. Borris's Gruppe landed at various fields between 1129 and 1152 hours.

The next day brought the last missions of the month. Once again it was I/JG 26 and III/JG 54 that got the call. In the morning, I/JG 26 was ordered to fly high escort for JG 27 on an anti-Jabo mission to Muenchen-Gladbach. Oblt. Heckmann led twenty Focke-Wulfs up from Fuerstenau at 0900. The mission orders had spelled out the route and altitude of each Staffel in detail. Because of its low altitude, the Gruppe was successfully bounced from above by Spitfires, which dove through the German formation at high speed and shot down four Focke-Wulfs. Two German pilots were killed; the other two bailed out with injuries. The enemy fighters were Spitfire XIVs from No. 41 Squadron. The British pilots claimed three FW 190Ds destroyed, while one of their own aircraft failed to return. This was the first major air combat for the Griffon-engined Spitfire XIV, which had just begun moving to the Continent after employment in England against the V-1 threat. The Spitfire XIV was a formidable combat aircraft, with a top speed in excess of 450 mph. Fortunately for the Germans, only four squadrons saw service with Second TAF.

The combat scattered the First Gruppe. Oblt. Heckmann led the remnants of his formation back to Fuerstenau at 1000. At 1430 orders were received for another mission. I/JG 26 and III/JG 54 were to cover the jet airfield at Handorf between 1600 and 1630 hours. At 1530, the scheduled time of takeoff, only ten First Gruppe aircraft were ready. Major Borris led them off to meet the Green Hearts. Fifteen minutes into their patrol, contact was made with a dozen Spitfires and eighteen Tempests. For the next thirty minutes, combats took place around Enschede, from 10,000 feet to ground level. At 1630, according to the Gruppe War Diary, Borris changed the mission to a freie Jagd, the assigned patrol having been completed. This made no difference to his pilots, who were at that moment fighting for their lives. His small force lost only two aircraft; one pilot was killed, and the other bailed out with light injuries. III/JG 54 suffered severely, six pilots being killed. The victors were the Canadian Spitfires of No. 421 Squadron, which claimed two of the FW 190Ds, and the Tempests of No. 122 Wing, which claimed 10-1-7 FW 190s for the day without loss to themselves, on what proved to be the Tempest wing's most successful day of the war.

On 28 January, Oberst Josef Priller was relieved of the command of Jagdgeschwader 26. His tour of combat duty had finally ended, after five continuous years on the Western front. He had scored 101 aerial victories in 307 combat sorties. He was to become Inspector of Day Fighters (West), a sinecure that would keep him from further combat flying. Priller's successor was Major Franz Goetz, who assumed the command on his 32nd birthday. Goetz was a prewar enlisted pilot who came up through the ranks, claiming sixty-three victories in more than 700 combat sorties, mostly on the Eastern front. His most recent posting was as a Gruppenkommandeur in JG 53. The weather was too bad to permit a proper change-of-command ceremony. Only the First Gruppe could be paraded for Goetz at Fuerstenau. The next day, Major Hackl received orders to report to JG 300, as its Kommodore. Oblt. Radener took command of II/JG 26; his 7th Staffel command was assumed by Lt. Gottfried Dietze.

In January, JG 26 lost thirty-one pilots killed in combat, and three in accidents. Eight were taken prisoner on New Year's Day, and at least fourteen were seriously injured during the month. III/JG 54, which was a fourth JG 26 Gruppe in all but name, lost fifteen pilots killed on only two missions. For the rest of the war, the only sources of replacement pilots for the Jagdgeschwader would be the hospitals and disbanded fighter units. The training schools had by now closed down. Until the last weeks of the war, JG 26 would continue to receive ample supplies of Germany's best piston-engined fighter in service, the FW 190D. However, the Geschwader had no special claim to pilots, and its operational strength, which was limited by the number of pilots available for duty, declined steadily.

THE SPIRIT OF THE GESCHWADER

The morale of the Geschwader at this point in the war cannot be summarized in simple terms, nor can it be determined merely by interviewing the surviving pilots—each man's opinion is inevitably colored by his *own* morale at the time. All but the youngest and most naive pilots realized that the war was lost. Most of the pilots had grown up under National Socialism, which of course colored their perceptions of Germany and the rest of the world. However, few had any interest in politics as such, and the political officers assigned to the Gruppen by Goering after the July 1944 attempt on Hitler's life were the butts of constant ridicule. The Second Gruppe under Lang, Eder, and Hackl fostered the spirit and individuality of its pilots by reducing formal military discipline to a minimum; they sponsored dances and maintained a jazz band, both of which were officially forbidden under the state of emergency proclaimed in 1944. Major Borris's First Gruppe, on the other hand, observed all military courtesies with the greatest rigidity—even in POW camp after the war—and this technique seemed to work also. The two Gruppen flew missions daily, weather permitting, until the armistice of 5 May brought the war on their front to an end. In early 1945, Hptm. Krupinski's Third Gruppe was by far the weakest of the three. The men of the other Gruppen had a low opinion of the Third. Many of its surviving enlisted pilots remain bitter about conditions in that unit. Pilots of the Third Gruppe would occasionally find a reason to drop in on Nordhorn or Fuerstenau at mealtime; they claimed that their supply officer, a brother of one of the Geschwader's "names," was selling their own rations on the black market.

None of the Geschwader's 1945 Staffelkapitaene were professional officers. All had been promoted from the enlisted ranks, and none had had any form of officers' or formation leaders' training.

They had not been promoted because of their abilities as leaders, and these abilities varied widely. A few glory-hungry officers were still striving for decorations and promotions, while others flew as little as possible and returned early from those missions they could not avoid. A third category tried conscientiously to fulfill the role of combat leader that had been thrust upon them. The introspective Peter Crump summarizes the motivations and feelings of this last group of officers:

> The morale of most pilots at this point in the war was not bad, despite all adversities. Naturally, the rapidly worsening war situation, especially in the East, was oppressive and forced individuals to give more and more thought to their uncertain fates after the war. But imbued with a sense of military duty, and bolstered by our comrades, we flew our missions. The weaker were supported by the stronger, the stronger looked up to those with more flying experience, and those in authority who were playing at formation leaders—meaning myself and the other formation leaders—hid their doubts and fears behind a feigned outward composure. My knowledge of the weaknesses of each of my young, inexperienced pilots, who looked with anxious glances for me, with my combat experience, to set an example, motivated me as a formation leader, and gave me the strength to overcome my own inadequacies.

The enlisted pilots did not have the luxury of choosing their own missions—they flew when they were ordered, and early returns for mechanical failures, although very common, were always scrutinized carefully. These men flew until they were killed or seriously injured. Some surviving pilots will still not talk about this horrible period in their lives, at least not to outsiders. So any interviews are to an extent preselected, and their results are to some extent predetermined. Nevertheless, the statements of two of the survivors appear to cover the range from "lowest" to "highest" morale, and they will be quoted here. Since they are meant to represent the many, the pilots will not be identified. First, from a former Unteroffizier of the Second Gruppe:

> How was our morale? It was all the best, as far as the young pilots were concerned. We of course gave some thought to the progress of the war, but still hoped for victory. The V-weapons were

still not fully deployed. We, the V-1, and the V-2 would surely bring about the turning point—so we thought—and so we had been trained. We began at age ten in the Jungvolk; continued at age fourteen in the Hitler Youth; and it was no different at age seventeen, in the German Labor Service. My father, a very old man and a confirmed social democrat, had told me where Adolf Hitler was leading us, but what could [such men as my father] accomplish against the overwhelming propaganda?

How things were with the older pilots I don't know. There were not very many of them left alive. All in all—we flew and asked not why. We had our homeland to protect, and often during missions I could see my home city of Hamburg. I remembered, of course, the old Hamburg from the times before the great bomb attacks by the Allies in July and August of 1943—and now I saw only a huge field of rubble.

I believe that I still wanted to win the war in April 1945—what a delusion! Probably other comrades felt the same way, especially those whose homeland is now part of Poland, Czechoslovakia, et cetera. That our leaders had known the war was lost for a long time was in no way known to us.

Representing the opposite point of view is a former Unteroffizier from the Third Gruppe:

One must keep in mind that after the Normandy invasion it was clear to any level-headed German serviceman that the Germans would lose the war. Each death that was suffered now was morally indefensible. Naturally, our officers knew this; even the young Unteroffiziere and Feldwebel knew it. The question was—how can I keep from being killed tomorrow? Our officers naturally had it much easier—they could hide behind administrative duties. We, on the other hand, had to carry on. And so there was a terrible bloodletting of the best young men. What could one do? We lived in a strict dictatorship that had no regard for its citizens, who killed and died without knowing that it was a madman who was guiding their destinies. I freely admit that often after a combat sortie I considered simply flying off in the wrong direction—that is, to the west—and surrendering myself. But then there were my relatives, and the knowledge that my mother would have to endure the bomb raids on Braunschweig, while I like a coward had fled to security. My younger brother, a student, stood duty at night as a flak helper until his death in January 1945. How would he have reacted? For myself, then, it became a matter of ignoring the means of escape at my disposal, and remaining in mortal danger.

The few pilots who survived fall into two categories. The first group continued to do their duty, although they lacked their previous eagerness for action and could not be spurred to greater performance. The second group put their own survival first, whatever the cost. It was clear to them as well as to the greater part of the first group that this war was lost, and that even if the leadership did not end the madness, they wanted nothing to do with prolonging the war. Realistically speaking, that was the situation from the fall of 1944. Unfortunately, that was just when I arrived at the front, with exactly 143 hours of flying experience; I nevertheless was determined to do my best to fend off the terror sweeping the homeland in the form of day and night attacks by the Allies. Only what was the use of taking this position, when others, for reasons of war-weariness, thought entirely otherwise? Thus the whole had to collapse into its parts, which was exactly what happened within the Third Gruppe.

BREAKUP AND CONSOLIDATION

The weather continued unfit for combat flying for the first two weeks of February. On the ground, the American First and Third Armies squeezed out the last of the "Bulge," restoring the battle lines in the Ardennes to their mid-December location. During the few flyable hours, the Geschwader's pilots made test and training flights. The technical officers attempted to find solutions for the problems that were cropping up in their Dora-9s, but serviceability rates would continue to drop for the rest of the war.

The Geschwader's first mission of the new month was ordered early in the morning of 14 February. I/JG 26 and III/JG 54 were the Gruppen called upon. The mission was to be another protection flight for Rheine; this time III/JC 54 would be the high cover. Major Borris took off at 0745 with his twenty-four Focke-Wulfs. He met the III/JG 54 contingent, which was led by Lt. Crump, and was soon over Rheine. The Focke-Wulfs orbited at low altitude, which was not a wise maneuver under the circumstances. Seven No. 41 Sqd. Spitfire XIVs dove through both formations and shot down three Focke-Wulfs, two from III/JG 54 and one from I/JG 26. The two Green Heart pilots were killed. In return, one Schlageter pilot claimed a Spitfire. The British pilots claimed one confirmed and two probable victories over the "long noses," while one Spitfire failed to return.

On 15 February, III/JG 54 finally received a Kommandeur—Hptm. Rudolf Klemm, who had commanded IV/JG 54 until its recent dissolution. JG 26's 8th Staffel was disbanded on the 15th; its nine surviving pilots were transferred to the other three Staffeln of the Second Gruppe. The 8th's Oblt. Hofmann, still flying with only one good eye, took over the leaderless 5th Staffel. On the next day, 4/JG 26 was disbanded; its eleven pilots were split up among the rest of the First Gruppe. On the 19th, it was the turn of 12/JG 54; its pilots went to the rest of III/JG 54. The Kapitaen of the 12th Staffel, Oblt. Dortenmann, took command of 11/JG 54, while the latter unit's Staffelfuehrer, Lt. Prager, moved to 9/JG 54 as a Schwarm-fuehrer.

On 21 February, the Second Gruppe flew its first full-scale mission in more than a month. About twenty Focke-Wulfs took off from Nordhorn at 1515 on a freie Jagd. While in the air, the Gruppe was ordered to intercept a formation of medium bombers. To the pilots' amazement, they reached the Marauders without contacting enemy fighters. One box of 394th Bomb Group B-26s had strayed off course after losing one bomber to flak over their target, the railroad bridge at Vlotho. The Focke-Wulfs struck the loose formation east of Arnhem and brought down three bombers, while seriously damaging four others. Uffz. Walter Stumpf of the 7th Staffel saw the crew bail out of his target. He was given credit for a "final destruction"—his first victory. Other claims were filed for five bombers destroyed and one separated from its formation. Un-usually, all claims were filed by junior pilots rather than formation leaders, and it has not been possible to determine who led this successful mission, which proved to be the Geschwader's last bomber interception.

The time was nearing for the Third Gruppe to return to com-bat in its new FW 190D-9s, despite what many pilots considered grossly inadequate conversion training—Georg Genth's comprised three touch-and-gos at Plantluenne, and one half-hour formation flight. Heinz Gehrke of the 11th Staffel compared his new mount with the Bf 109:

The Dora-9 was a wild bird. Everything was electric. Landing gear, flaps, trim tabs needed only the press of a button. And the bird was fast! In the 109 we could hit 500–520 km/h [300–315 mph] at low altitude, fully armed and equipped—the D-9 was a good 50–60 km/h [30–35 mph] faster. However, for pure flying, I preferred the Messerschmitt, despite all of its problems during takeoff and landing.

On the afternoon of 22 February, four Third Gruppe pilots flew a short test hop from Plantluenne, to run in their Focke-Wulfs' engines. One of the four was Heinz Gehrke, who recalls:

> After about forty-five minutes, we prepared to land. I had to pull up to avoid another plane, which dropped in and landed in front of my nose. I flew on for a while, and suddenly noticed antiaircraft fire. Then I spotted a Spitfire. There was a dogfight, and I received the worst of it. I tried to disappear in an inversion layer, but scarcely was I in it than I reappeared on the other side, and hung there in a sky full of more Spitfires. I was fodder for their cannons. After being hit, my engine caught fire, and I had to bail out. Canopy off and out. I was caught on the diving airplane, but finally broke free. My chute unfurled, and I found myself sitting on the ground. My aircraft had crashed and exploded not one hundred meters away. The inhabitants of a nearby house were my saviors. They summoned a doctor, who treated me. I was brought to the hospital in Lingen. I am thankful that I survived, with second and third degree burns on the face and hands, multiple splinters in both legs, and a shell wound in the left foot—an unhappy toll for an enthusiastic 22-year-old pilot. That was my last flight in the Second World War; I was in the hospital until 12 November, 1945.

No Spitfire unit is known to have claimed Gehrke; in fact, his official casualty report credits his downing to a Tempest, at 1745. Another member of his Gruppe was shot down and killed at the same time by a Tempest. At just this time, Sqd. Ldr. D. C. "Foob" Fairbanks, an American, led his No. 274 Sqd. Tempests in an attack on a small number of Dora-9s near Rheine. Fairbanks shot down two of them and must therefore be given credit for taking Heinz Gehrke out of the war.

Soon after Major Tony Hackl arrived at JG 300, he asked for Oblt. Waldi Radener to join him as a Gruppenkommandeur. The transfer was approved on 22 February; Radener would receive the Knight's Cross on 12 March for his service in JG 26. On 23 February, Hptm. Paul Schauder of the 10th Staffel was given command of the Second Gruppe; Oblt. Jan Schild, who had not yet returned to flying status after his injury the previous October, was made Staffelfuehrer of the 10th Staffel.

On the 24th, one of the most dependable Third Gruppe pilots, Fw. Wolfgang Polster of the 11th Staffel, was strafed by fighters after landing at Plantluenne and was wounded. Polster had been preoccupied with instructing his wingman during the landing. Wolfgang Polster's war flying was over; he was credited with five victories during his 107 combat sorties. His determination and sense of duty never wavered during the last year of the war and its bitter aftermath. According to Heinz Gehrke, Polster flew more missions during this period than any other Third Gruppe pilot.

On the 25th of February, the battered Third Gruppe of JG 54, which had lost at least fifty FW 190D-9s since returning to combat the previous December, officially became part of JG 26, as its Fourth Gruppe. 9/JG 54, with ten pilots commanded by Oblt. Heilmann, became 15/JG 26. 10/JG 54, whose nine pilots were led by Lt. Crump, became 13/JG 26. Oblt. Dortenmann's 11/JG 54 and its twelve pilots became 14/JG 26. IV/JG 26 continued to base at Varrelbusch, under the command of Hptm. Klemm.

The entire Geschwader was ordered on the 28th to fly a freie Jagd to the area of Muenchen-Gladbach, to attack fighter-bombers supporting the American advance on that city. The Third Gruppe, flying its first FW 190D-9 mission, was the first up; Hptm. Krupinski led them off from Plantluenne at around 0730. Shortly after 0800, they were hit at 5,000 feet by six Tempests of No. 274 Squadron, led by Sqd. Ldr. Fairbanks. The Focke-Wulfs proved more than willing to mix it up, and the Allied pilots, badly outnumbered, were soon fighting for their lives. One German plane crash-landed during the battle, and its pilot later died of his injuries, but two Tempests went down, including that of Fairbanks. Foob Fairbanks was the highest-scoring Tempest pilot of the war, with eleven confirmed victories while flying the type. Both RAF pilots survived as prisoners of war.

This successful battle, which could have gotten the Third Gruppe off to an excellent start in their new aircraft, had a disastrous conclusion. Two FW 190Ds collided while in the landing circuit above Plantluenne. Both crashed in flaming balls of fire, which Georg Genth of the 12th Staffel recalls passing over on his own return. The two pilots, Hptm. Bernhard Wollnitz of the Third Gruppe Stab and his wingman, were, of course, killed. The 33-year-old Wollnitz was a dedicated National Socialist; his service to the Nazi party dated back at least to 1931, when he had joined the Sturmabteilung (SA). He was not a successful air fighter, but was considered one of the best pure pilots in the Gruppe. The accident occurred as Wollnitz was making a tight bank around a farmhouse on the border of the field; he was showing off for his girlfriend, whom he had brought to Plantluenne and installed in the house. The horrible scene was witnessed by everyone on the base and set the unit's morale back once again.

The crash of one Tempest had been reported by ground witnesses. Krupinski called the pilots together to establish who had shot it down. According to Georg Genth:

> Krupinski asked us who had had the opportunity to fire. Oblt. Kraus and I spoke up. Kraus's account placed him in a position in which his fire could not have hit the Tempest. My report, however, must have matched up, for the victory was credited to me; however, I never received the confirmation from Berlin—either because the uncertain mail no longer reached Plantluenne, or because no one told me when it arrived. I was myself certain, however, that I had hit the Tempest from a somewhat difficult position (passing flight from right to left in a tight bank) and had seen my fire strike in the wing region. It flew right through my cone of fire.

Since two Tempests failed to return, it appears that the claims of both Kraus and Genth were valid, and that one of them brought down the top-scoring Tempest pilot.

The First Gruppe put up twenty-one aircraft at 1145, but Major Borris ordered them to return to Fuerstenau when they encountered a solid cloud front near Rheine. The Fourth Gruppe got off at the same time as the First and apparently carried out a patrol of its assigned area, but without making contact. The Second Gruppe was the only unit of the Geschwader to carry out its mission according to plan. Oblt. Wilhelm Hofmann's 5th Staffel reached the Muenchen-Gladbach area shortly after noon. Hofmann quickly spotted a formation of P-47s and led a successful attack that resulted in claims for two P-47s destroyed, for the loss of one of Hofmann's pilots. The P-47s were from the 406th Fighter Group, which claimed 1-1-1 FW 190 in this combat and lost one Thunderbolt.

The Geschwader's orders for 1 March were the same as those of the past few days—support the German Army in its retreat to the Rhine by attacking American fighter-bombers in the Muenchen-Gladbach area. The combat zone was some distance south of the Geschwader's airfields, and reaching it through the curtain of patroling Second TAF aircraft was difficult. The Third Gruppe failed to make an appearance over the battle zone. Part of the Fourth Gruppe got there, but they had no luck. Lt. Peter Crump's 13th Staffel reached Muenchen-Gladbach at 0930 and engaged P-51s without loss or apparent success. The 14th Staffel was intercepted by Spitfires near Dortmund; one German pilot was killed, and the remaining Focke-Wulfs scattered.

The other two Gruppen reached Muenchen-Gladbach in strength at about 0930, and both engaged P-47 formations in fierce and prolonged combat. Major Borris led twenty-four aircraft up from Fuerstenau at 0835. He and seven other pilots had to abort because of radio or landing gear difficulties, and the sixteen remaining planes were led to the combat zone by Oblt. Heckmann. When they arrived, they engaged about forty P-47s and P-51s in and beneath the clouds at 1,500 to 3,000 feet. The Gruppe's War Diary comments that the Thunderbolt pilots were experienced and were able to turn with the Focke-Wulfs. The Germans were badly defeated. Five pilots failed to return; all were killed. The survivors landed at a number of fields, and they claimed no victories. Their opponents were a squadron of 406th Fighter Group, which had jettisoned its bombs when bounced by more than a dozen "very aggressive" fighters. The Thunderbolt pilots claimed 2-0-2 FW 190s and 2-0-2 Bf 109s, while losing none of their number. (The difficulty of identifying aircraft types under combat conditions leads to vexing problems for the air war historian. Allied pilots frequently identified long-nosed FW 190Ds as Bf 109s; German pilots had problems telling Tempests from P-47s or Spitfires.)

The Second Gruppe's freie Jagd was more successful. The Gruppe's three Staffeln left Nordhorn at 0810 and reached the battle zone in good order. Oblt. Hofmann spotted eight P-47s pulling up from their bomb runs and led a bounce. The two flights of Thunderbolts immediately split up into pairs and fled into the low overcast. The pilots of both sides took quick deflection shots at enemy aircraft as they suddenly appeared from the clouds. Four P-47s were shot down in the battle zone. A fifth crashed on the return flight; its pilot bailed out uninjured. The Thunderbolt pilots, who were from the 366th Fighter Group, had claims for 1-0-1 FW 190s confirmed. The American pilots, and their comrades who did not return, apparently did better than they claimed—three Second Gruppe pilots were killed in the area. Some may have been lost to American antiaircraft fire, however; at least one Focke-Wulf, that of Uffz. Walter Stumpf, suffered damage from that source. The Gruppe's pilots claimed five P-47s destroyed, exactly matching the American losses.

Only the Third Gruppe engaged the enemy on 2 March. They apparently were ordered to patrol the Rheine airfields, together with the Bf 109s of JG 27. Two Spitfire XIV squadrons, on their own patrol of Rheine, attacked the German fighters. No. 350 Squadron's Belgians hit the Messerschmitts, while No. 130 Squadron attacked the Focke-Wulfs. III/JG 26 lost one pilot, but it otherwise acquitted itself well, shooting down two of the "long-nosed Spits."

On 7 March, the Third Gruppe was ordered to fly a freie Jagd to the Netherlands. As was frequently the case in that Gruppe, no experienced formation leader was available; Obfw. Willi Zester of the 9th Staffel was ordered to lead the mission. After sitting at cockpit readiness for some time, eight or nine pilots took off from Plantluenne at about 1500. Uffz. Genth of the 12th Staffel flew as Zester's wingman. Georg Genth recalls:

> We quickly reached the battle zone at an altitude of 3,000 meters [10,000 feet]. We were to determine the amount of enemy activity around Enschede. Typhoons were busy attacking motor convoys. Spitfires could be seen banking to one side, but they did not spot our formation. Then we saw several flights of Tempests below us. This was very dangerous, as our best combat altitude, at which the FW 190D-9 was superior to the Tempest, began at 5,000 meters [16,000 feet]. Thus it probably happened that the Tempest flights were able to approach our formation without being noticed, using their superb rate of climb at 3,000 meters.
>
> We were still climbing in loose formation when I looked behind me routinely, and realized that Zester and I were alone. There

was nothing to be seen of the others. This was remarkable, since not a word had been said on the radio, either to warn us of an attack or to indicate that a dogfight had begun. While I was still considering the possibility that my radio had failed, I reported by observations to Zester. He acknowledged with a nod. About six Tempests had come up unnoticed in our dead angle beneath. Two of them were now very near to me, and preparing to open fire. I saw Zester bank away in what was in my opinion the wrong direction, and had to slug it out with the Tempests by myself. I later learned that he was also shot down. Had I followed Zester in his defensive maneuver, I would have found myself in exactly the right firing position for the Tempests following me. I thus flew in the opposite direction, and turned on the methanol injection. My engine was now at full power, and my speed increased to about 600 km/h [360 mph]. I must have broken an oil line at that point, since I noticed a large stream of oil coming from the engine. My windshield became covered in oil. However, I could still see to the side. About two miles away was a cloud layer that promised me salvation. I had to reach this cloud layer and dive into it, or there was no way I was going to come out of this situation in good health. My oil leak would permit me to stay in the air for only a few more minutes. The oil now swept over my left wing in thick waves. My engine still ran quietly, nonetheless.

I had seen Tempests above me, I could see them beside me, and new Tempests were approaching from beneath. My only chance lay in evading them until I could reach the cloud layer. So I tore off at top speed toward the cloud, jinking to the left and right with the rudder. This deceived the enemy behind me as to my direction of flight, and the more rapidly I trod on the rudder pedal the more difficult it was for the reflex sights behind me to show the right deflection. As a result, the fire of the Tempests missed to the side, since the pilots relied on the views in their sights. The trick worked well. I reached the cloud and attempted a zoom climb, intending to come around into a head-on firing pass at the Tempests, breaking up their attack. This was not to happen, since (as I was told later) a Tempest below me could see me in the thin cloud and reported my direction of flight to my pursuers. Thus a Tempest was waiting to attack me when I left the cloud, and struck my wounded bird in the tail area. After a sharp blow, which I could feel through the control stick, my elevators failed. It was time to get out.

I jettisoned the canopy at about 600 km/h, released my harness, and was sucked from the cockpit of my FW, which was now standing on its nose. I was hurled upside down along the fuselage, and the fin struck my left arm so hard that it broke it, ripping the sleeve from my leather jacket. I felt only a sharp, painless blow to my upper arm. I had taken one last glance at the speedometer as I was preparing to leave; it read 650 km/h [390 mph]. It was obvious that I could not open my chute at that speed, as it would tear apart; so I started to count. Only after I realized that my arm was broken did I shift my body so that I could grasp the handle with my right hand. When I then pulled the handle, after tumbling between fifteen and eighteen times, my chute opened at a very low altitude. I was startled when I hit the ground after only a few seconds. The shock of the chute's opening severed the radialis nerve in the broken part of my arm, the dead weight of which was supported by the muscle. Nevertheless, I was overjoyed that for me this senseless war was over, and relatively lightly.

Only half of the Focke-Wulfs returned to Plantluenne. Obfw. Zester and Uffz. Genth bailed out with injuries, and two pilots were killed in their aircraft. The Tempests had been up in full force that morning; aircraft from five squadrons took shots at the Third Gruppe's eight or nine Focke-Wulfs. Uffz. Genth was shot down by a Greek pilot from No. 3 Squadron, Flt. Lt. B. M. Vassiliades. Vassiliades saw a Focke-Wulf flying alone and began to pursue it. He scored one strike, which caused the German pilot to take violent evasive action in and out of several clouds. The Tempest pilot followed below for nearly ten minutes, and when the aircraft finally emerged, got on its tail and hit it in the cockpit area. The German pilot then jettisoned his canopy and bailed out, landing two miles southeast of Enschede. Pieces of Genth's aircraft were excavated from this crash site some forty years later. Vassiliades was to live for only two more weeks after this battle; he was shot down and killed by antiaircraft fire on 21 March.

The Geschwader was given yet another top priority target on the 7th, when the First American Army's 9th Armored Division captured a Rhine bridge at Remagen. Although far to the south of their usual combat zone, the Gruppen were several times assigned targets in the rapidly expanding Remagen bridgehead. They are not known to have flown a successful mission to this area, however. In every case they were turned back, either by unfavorable weather or by premature encounters with Allied aircraft. At 1455 on the 9th, Major Borris led seventeen aircraft up from Fuerstenau and headed south. But a solid cloud front blocked their path, and Borris changed the mission to a hunt for RAF fighter-bombers. They contacted a squadron of Typhoons but could not carry out an attack because of the weather. A little later, at 1620, the Second Gruppe got twenty-four fighters away from Nordhorn. They made it as far south as Wesel, which was in front of the advancing American Ninth Army. At 7,000 feet over Wesel, the Gruppe made a head-on attack on a squadron of P-47s. II/JG 26 had once again encountered part of the 366th Fighter Group. The Gruppe claimed the destruction of four P-47s, but three German pilots failed to return. One was killed; another bailed out with severe wounds. The third pilot to go down was Uffz. Walter Stumpf of the 7th Staffel, who recalls:

> I dove through a cloud and emerged directly in front of three Thunderbolts. Behind them were 190s—I learned this later from one of the pilots, who saw me. The lead P-47 destroyed my rudder with his first shots, leaving my plane uncontrollable. The other two P-47s were shot down by the 190s. I saw one of the American pilots in his chute, after I had escaped my plane. The enemy had been attacking a partially destroyed bridge near Wesel, which was serving a German bridgehead. Both the Thunderbolt pilot and myself landed directly behind the front, in what was still German-held territory.

The shaken American pilots reported that their opponents had been "aggressive"—this was noteworthy, because many German formations at this stage in the war avoided contact—and filed claims for 6-0-3 Focke-Wulfs. Their own losses amounted to two P-47s, which were seen to crash during the combat; another made a forced landing on an advanced base, and two others returned with major combat damage.

Only a small fraction of a fighter pilot's career is spent in combat. The German pilots spent more time in the air on test, training, transfer, and ferry flights than they did on combat missions. Such mundane activities are rarely worth reporting. However, by this stage of the war any flight could encounter the enemy; and as shall be seen in the following account, even an *attempt* to make such a flight could be an adventure.

II/JG 26 boasted that in its long retreat across western Europe it never abandoned a flyable airplane to the enemy. Thus, when in

early March word was received in Nordhorn of a Gruppe aircraft on
the field at Cologne-Wahn, it was imperative that it be flown out
immediately, since it was just across the Rhine River from the
approaching American army. The assignment was given to Ogfr.
Werner Molge. Molge's account:

> It was the noon break at Nordhorn. The orderlies had just
> served dinner in the 7th Staffel's readiness room. There was a noise
> at the entrance; the command post officer, Hptm. Groos, stepped in,
> and said to the Staffelkapitaen, Lt. Gottfried Dietze, "One pilot has
> to go to Cologne-Wahn and bring back an FW 190, which force-
> landed there and has now been repaired."
>
> Everyone ducked over their soup plates and busily shoveled in
> their chicken soup—as did I. The thought of traveling to Cologne
> had no charm for anyone, as the half of the city on the left bank of
> the Rhine was already occupied by the enemy. The rattling of the
> spoons in the plates suddenly stopped, and I looked up. All eyes were
> turned on me. It was the same as usual. The youngest had the best
> legs; there was no getting around it.
>
> After their meal, the other pilots returned to their lounge chairs
> outside of the readiness room; in our section of the woods, it was
> almost like summer. I reported to the Gruppe command post, where
> I received my travel papers, aircraft retrieval orders, ration ticket, et
> cetera. Back in the readiness room, I packed my parachute in its
> carrying bag, along with the radio harness, flare pistol, maps, et
> cetera—everything I needed to have with me when I climbed into
> the airplane.
>
> There were no regulations covering our traveling uniforms for
> such occasions, so I headed out in full warpaint—that is, in my
> customary leather flying suit and fur boots. The good wishes from
> my comrades on my departure were partly in earnest and partly in
> jest. A Geschwader car brought me to the Osnabrueck train station,
> from where I was to take the train to Cologne. I was told that this was
> only possible by taking detours. The main tracks were impassable,
> due to shot-up cars and bombed-out rails. I arrived late that evening
> in Gummersbach, after several stops for air-raid alarms. This was the
> railroad's final destination. Truck convoys took ammunition, equip-
> ment, and rations from here to the front. I could go on from here
> only on foot, or as a passenger in a truck. Regulation of transfers was
> carried out from an MP vehicle. After my papers were examined, I
> was allowed to look for a means of transportation. I heard someone
> say in passing, "There is artillery fire a little farther on." My spirits

were not exactly lifted by this news. I was horrified at the thought of traveling on foot. Straight as an arrow, I made for the nearest truck. After I reported to the driver, I made myself comfortable on the fender. There was sufficient room there for my parachute pack. The column started moving slowly, and Ogfr. Molge went with it. For safety's sake, I was always ready to jump for the roadside ditches, in case the "comrades from the other field post office" [the enemy] had something bad in mind for me.

The entire column traveled without lights; even the brake lights were disconnected. Allied aircraft hummed above the roads, trying to disrupt the supply lines. They located the blacked-out convoy by a dirty trick. They scattered flares across the landscape, and the glare hurt our eyes, which were accustomed to the night's blackness. Red rings and spots danced in front of my eyes the whole time. The truck drivers were no better off. One of them was so uncertain of the road that he blinked his headlights briefly, to keep from running off the road into the ditch. It was only a short time, but too long. A twin-engined enemy aircraft (the type was not recognizable) dove on us, and with a short burst of fire ignited the truck. The trucks behind it stopped under cover, as far as was possible, until the burning truck could be pushed into the roadside ditch. My driver's fatalistic comment was, "Thank God. Now we can at least see a little in the firelight." However, my own knees were shaking.

The column crept along through the night, and finally reached the outskirts of Cologne. We then went along the bank of the Rhine, shielded from view from the other bank by a row of houses—or what was left of them. I was aching from the journey on the fender, which was not quite wide enough for me. I took comfort from the fact that I was coming near to my goal. The convoy suddenly stopped at a gap in the row of houses, which left it visible to the enemy. The trucks were sent across one at a time and at irregular intervals, under fire by machine guns and 20-mm flak. I asked the Feldwebel who was controlling the departures whether I had to cross there to get to Cologne-Wahn. There was no other route—shit!

Then it was our turn. Like a monkey, I held tightly to the hood and fender—on the side away from the enemy, naturally—and secured my pack. Then we were off. The engine roared, and we got up to 80 km/h [50 mph] before reaching the last wall. The open stretch—about 300 meters long—was passed quickly, without drawing a single round of fire—at any rate, none that I noticed, as I had enough to do to keep my grip.

Just beyond the gap, again under the protection of ruined

houses, I had to turn right to get to Wahn. I joined two infantrymen who were heading the same way. The area was within range of enemy artillery. Shells passed over us; each time, I would throw myself on the ground. The two soldiers remained on their feet, and I saw them grinning at me. "You do that very well, flyboy!" one said, and the other continued, "But you might as well stop it. They are firing inland."

So I went on, courageously upright, and tried to ignore the howling of the artillery shells. Suddenly there was a sharp, loud explosion, and a fountain of earth erupted to our right. Startled and deafened by the loud noise, I saw the two soldiers getting up from the ground. They had apparently dropped with the speed of lightning. When they were again upright, one of them said sweetly, "You see, if it whistles that briefly, you must throw yourself down."

From then on I sought cover or flattened out at each unknown suspicious noise, much to the amusement of my two companions. I soon reached the airfield of Cologne-Wahn, worn completely out, but still in good health. To my amazement, the flight control unit was still in existence, as was a servicing unit. After showing my aircraft retrieval orders, I learned that the FW 190D-9 "Black 6" was on the opposite side of the field. As it was already 0200 hours, I spent the rest of the night in the flight control building's cellar. I notified the field of my intent to take off in the light of early dawn.

About two or three hours later, still in total darkness, I crossed the field to look over the aircraft. It was a total disaster. An artillery shell had ripped off one wing and filled the fuselage with holes. I would now have to make my previous journey all over again, in the reverse direction. The flight control unit confirmed the destruction of the aircraft, and I made ready for the return trip. But there in the room stood my fate, in the form of two MPs. "No one goes to the rear from here. This is the front, and everyone who shows up here is needed!"

As the crowning blow to this ill-starred journey, I was now to be recruited into the army. My morale sank to zero. Thank God, I was permitted to contact my Geschwader. I reached my Komman-deur, Hptm. Schauder, explained my situation, and turned over the receiver, as ordered, to one of the MPs. The shouting from the other end could be heard two meters from the phone. The "hero-snatcher" said not a word in reply.

I received my marching papers for the return journey, and had to face the same shit all over again. I reached Nordhorn three days later, to be greeted cheerfully by my comrades. I was dead-tired from an experience I would gladly have foregone—but that's the way it went in the service.

Between the 10th and 18th of March, the Geschwader flew only small-scale missions. It was difficult to get off the ground without drawing the attention of the hovering Spitfires and Tempests. On 19 March, JG 26 had its last large-scale encounters with the Eighth Air Force. Nearly seven hundred P-51s swept across the continent in advance of 1,200 heavy bombers, which by now had no industrial targets left to attack and were reduced to bombing railroad yards and airfields. The 78th Fighter Group was assigned the task of neutralizing the airfields around Osnabrueck, which included all of JG 26's and JG 27's bases. The forty-seven Mustangs reached the area at 1230. I/JG 26 was on the ground after an inconclusive early-morning combat with Tempests. IV/JG 26 was returning from a freie Jagd to Muenster. The Messerschmitts of JG 27 were up and were punished severely by the Americans, losing twelve aircraft. II/JG 26 took off into the midst of the action and engaged P-51s in a dogfight right over Plantluenne airfield. Obfhr. Johann Spahn's ship was hit, and he bailed out, only to be shot to death while hanging in his parachute. Spahn had flown as Wilhelm Hofmann's wingman since the latter had lost the use of one eye. He had served as Hofmann's "eyes," taking off and landing alongside him to aid Hofmann in judging his distance from the ground. The Fourth Gruppe reached the area in time to join the combats and claimed at least three P-51s, for the loss of one pilot. Five 78th Group P-51s failed to return from this mission. Details are available of one of the American losses; the victor was Lt. Peter Crump of 13/JG 26. Crump recalls:

> I was returning from a mission around Muenster—attempting to reach my home field at Varrelbusch at low altitude—when I spotted a Mustang. I followed the unsuspecting pilot and caught up to him near my airfield. When the Mustang came within firing range, I surprised the pilot with a tight bank in the opposite direction. Unnerved, he immediately tried to take flight, and I was able to shoot him down without much resistance. He bailed out successfully, with moderate burns to his neck and head. At Varrelbusch that evening, I was able to congratulate him on his survival.

The Mustangs left the area at 1330. On their return to England, the pilots claimed 25-2-11 Bf 109s and 5-1-1 FW 190s. Since the only two Luftwaffe units in the area were JG 26 and JG 27, and their losses are known, these claims appear to be more than twice the actual German losses.

Later in the afternoon, the First and Fourth Gruppen drew the assignment of airfield coverage for the jet base at Handorf. Rather than the expected Tempests and Spitfires, the Focke-Wulfs encountered Eighth Air Force P-51s, making their last sweep of the day. At 1630, the fourteen First Gruppe FW 190Ds engaged eight Mustangs from the 479th Fighter Group, led by Major Robin Olds. After a brief turning battle, the P-51s broke away, leaving behind them the wreckage of two Focke-Wulfs. Both pilots bailed out, but one was killed when his parachute failed to open. In return, the Germans could claim damage to only one Mustang.

The dawn of 22 March brought a cloudless sky and perfect visibility. The First Gruppe stood by at fifteen minutes readiness starting at 0605 but did not receive mission orders until 1539. The Gruppe was to take off immediately and attack a B-26 formation near Rheine. Fourteen FW 190Ds took off, led by Major Borris. Borris soon turned back with a defective radio, passing the lead to Oblt. Heckmann. Heckmann also had radio problems, but he continued the mission. Southeast of Duemmer Lake, he saw twenty-two P-47s, and soon thereafter a small formation of eight B-26s, escorted by a dozen fighters. Heckmann avoided combat and led his unit back to Fuerstenau; all had landed by 1654. Fred Heckmann's reason for not carrying out his mission, "My pilots were mere boys, and I had no radio" was entered verbatim into the Gruppe diary, in an unusual example of candor in an official Wehrmacht document.

The Second Gruppe was also kept on the ground until mid-afternoon, when it apparently drew the patrol duty over Rheine. A dozen of its aircraft—possibly the entire patrol—were caught near Lingen by two squadrons of Tempests. The British pilots quickly shot down five Focke-Wulfs. Four of the German pilots were killed; the fifth bailed out cleanly but broke a leg on landing. Two Tempests were claimed shot down, but none in fact were lost. No. 56 Squadron claimed 3-0-1 FW 190Ds and No. 80 Squadron claimed 2-0-2, in exact agreement with the Gruppe's actual losses.

THE DEFENSES BREAK

On the morning of 24 March, every airfield in northwestern Germany whose location was known to Allied Intelligence was attacked by American heavy bombers. The attacks were in support of Operation Varsity, the assault crossing of the lower Rhine River by the British Second Army and the American Ninth. All four JG 26 airfields were pounded into moonscapes. Fuerstenau received 133.5 tons of bombs; Nordhorn, 121.7 tons; Plantluenne, 328.5 tons; and Varrelbusch, 339.2 tons. It is known that no aircraft were destroyed on the ground at either Fuerstenau or Nordhorn. The other two airfields, which received double the bomb loads, may have suffered more severely. All fields were operational again by the following morning. Narrow runways were filled in with the aid of nearby labor units, a convalescent company, and, in the case of the Second Gruppe, the citizens of Nordhorn—"anyone who could lift a shovel." Nevertheless, the airfields' auxiliary services had been knocked out, and it was time to move on. Field Marshal Montgomery's armies were across the Rhine in force, and only seventy miles from Nordhorn. Three of JG 26's Gruppen received orders to move out on the morning of the 25th. For the Third Gruppe, however, there would be no tomorrow—the unit was to be disbanded, effective immediately. Hptm. Krupinski was to leave the Geschwader and join General Galland's new Me 262 unit, JV 44. The only Third Gruppe Staffelkapitaen to be given a new Staffel command was Oblt. Gottfried Schmidt, who left the 9th Staffel to take over the 6th from Lt. Siegfried Sy. The Third Gruppe's aircraft and pilots were split among the three remaining Gruppen. In its daily report, I/JG 26 listed a strength of thirty-eight pilots and thirty-eight aircraft. Numbers this high would never again be attained.

The Stab and the First Gruppe were to move to Drope, only seven miles northwest of Fuerstenau. The Second and Fourth Gruppen went to Bissel, a ten-minute flight northeast of Varrelbusch. The Geschwader's new fields were very much makeshifts, to be used until permanent facilities farther to the rear could be made ready. Siegfried Sy, serving his last day as Fuehrer of the 6th Staffel, describes the events at Nordhorn on the morning of the 25th:

> We ate breakfast together, as we did every day, and then went to the field in our bus. Today it was somewhat darker than usual. We

wanted to be on our new base before the "comrades from the other field post office" started their daily activities. We stowed our packs in our FW 190Ds and made ready to take off. There was not much time to lose. Everything was talked over in detail, to minimize accidents. There was probably no one on the field who was not excited; the pilots were affected the most, because they knew what it meant to speed through a field of craters, or into the pine forest. Takeoff in an FW 190D was bad enough, because there was no visibility to the front, and one had to take off practically blind. Shortly before time for takeoff, the Kommandeur restricted permission to the older pilots. The young ones had to wait until the last. This was to minimize the chance of a crash on the field, which would block the takeoff of the rest.

The 5th Staffel was to be first to take off. Leutnant Gerd Schulwitz, in the lead, taxied to the takeoff position. All of the command post personnel and ground crews surrounded the field to watch. Everyone's face showed the tension. I stood near my machine beside the command post, to learn what I could from Gerd's takeoff. The second aircraft was already taxiing to the takeoff point. Schulwitz gave his the gas. The engine howled, but the crate didn't move; he was still standing on the brakes. Now it began to roll. The aircraft gained speed smoothly. All eyes were fastened on it. After coming near the small red flag that marked the edge of the strip, the heavy FW 190D lifted abruptly from the ground and stayed in the air. He had made it. The second pilot was now rolling down the strip at high speed. He was almost to the woods before he yanked his aircraft into the air. As everyone's eyes turned back to the third aircraft, there was an explosion in the air, and a single dark-red fireball floated to earth. A huge piece of iron struck the ground not five meters from me, and rolled onto the takeoff strip. It was an engine.

What had happened? Where was the second aircraft? The questions followed in rapid succession. By and by things became clear. Some of the ground crewmen had seen everything. As Gerd Schulwitz made a left turn at close to stalling speed, the other aircraft approached him from the side and rammed him. This accident could be attributed to the poor light, and probably also to the second pilot's inattention.

Further takeoffs were prohibited. The airstrip and the 6th Staffel dispersal were covered in fragments of metal and human flesh. The ground crews began to clean the debris from the takeoff strip, while the pilots stood around in a state of shock—"Bubi"

Schulwitz had been one of the most popular pilots in the Gruppe. His watch was found in 1985 by Gert Poelchau, Nordhorn's unofficial historian; it established the time of his crash as 0557. An hour later, takeoffs were resumed. The 6th Staffel took off last, with Lt. Sy leading. He continues his narrative:

> I gave my weak heart a blow with my fist, and climbed into my mill. My mechanic stood on the wing and helped me with my straps. There was never much to say while waiting for takeoff, but today it was quieter than usual. I was ready, and drew on a cigarette in my open cockpit. Then it was time. I taxied from my revetment onto the narrow taxi strip. My eyes flew over the instrument panel one more time. Now was no time for a mistake, with everyone watching.
>
> Two green flares shot upward from the command post, as the signal to take off. I stood on the brakes with both feet and opened the throttle slowly. The engine roared, and I felt pressure on the stick. I was now completely at peace, with the engine hammering in my ears and the vibrations of the aircraft passing through my body. I took my feet from the brakes and started to roll. I pushed the throttle all the way forward with my left hand, and held it tightly. The speedometer passed the 200 mark; there was the red flag. I calmly lifted my good old Focke from the ground. I flew over the town at low altitude, made a tight bank over the Montblanc Hotel, and turned onto my course.
>
> It was a short flight to our new airfield at Bissel. The landing cross had already been laid out. On the same day that our field had been bombed, an advance party had been placed on the march for this place. I dropped in immediately; landing gear down, gas off, flaps all the way down, and I was quickly on the ground. A white flare came up from one end of the field; that meant that I should taxi down there.
>
> The aircraft, which now appeared every few minutes, were quickly hidden from view from the air. But we had made a bad exchange of fields. The dispersals were a long way from the edge of the landing ground. Due to the present situation in the air, that was very bad. We had learned at Nordhorn what it meant to be surprised during takeoff. And there was neither a command post, nor a ready room for the pilots. There was a barracks, but that was all. It became very clear that things got worse for us each time we changed bases.

The First Gruppe completed its short transfer hops by 0625 and reported itself operational. Shortly after noon, it received orders to attack fighter-bombers in the area of Bocholt. On takeoff from the unfamiliar field, one pilot hit a tree and crashed to his death. Fifteen Focke-Wulfs got off the ground, but several, including that of Major Borris, had to return immediately because of high oil pressure. Eleven were forming up northeast of Drope at 6,500 feet when they were hit from above by Tempests. After a dogfight, two Focke-Wulfs crashed. One pilot bailed out without injury, but the second was killed in his aircraft. As the victorious Tempest pilots headed west, one flight encountered another small group of FW 190Ds, this one from 15/JG 26. Oblt. Heilmann led this formation; his wingman was Fw. Gerhard Kroll. Kroll recalls:

> As we circled and climbed near the Dutch border, we saw three Tempests following us. They climbed better than our D-9s, and would soon overtake us. Suddenly Heilmann reversed direction from a right to a left turn and dove away steeply. I had had it—if I stayed put I would have to battle the three Tempests alone, and if I followed Heilmann I would cross directly in front of their guns. A moment later, I felt my plane shudder from shell strikes. It caught fire instantly. I was at about 7,000 meters [23,000 feet]. I tried to bail out, but my canopy was jammed. Something exploded in front of me, and I received a face full of instruments. Eventually, I cranked the canopy open about a foot. The slipstream ripped it off, and I was sucked from the plane, having previously unbuckled my harness. I let myself fall until the trees looked huge. After I pulled the cord there was the opening shock, one swing— and I was down. I must have opened the chute at about 150 meters [500 feet]. I had now been burned for the third time, and swore at the top of my lungs.

Kroll's injuries took him out of the war. The Tempest pilots, from No. 222 Squadron, suffered no losses and claimed a total of seven victories—the three JG 26 FW 190Ds and four JG 27 Bf 109s.

The Second Gruppe was not assigned any combat missions on the 25th, and was given the rest of the day to settle in at Bissel. Lt. Sy saw to the arrangements for his 6th Staffel and took a few minutes to contemplate the future. He was not happy with the most recent changes in the leadership of the Gruppe. Sy was a prewar veteran of the Wehrmacht who had taken part in the Polish campaign in an engineering company. He did not become a pilot until

1943, and he had then joined the II/JG 26 on the Kanalfront. As a professionally trained officer, he was a rarity in the Gruppe, and his advancement should have been rapid, but circumstances intervened. For one thing, he was a Nazi party member, which was not looked on with favor in the Second Gruppe. And while Sy was a competent pilot, he was a poor shot, who did not claim his first victory until 1 January 1945, on the Bodenplatte mission. He served as second-in-command of Oblt. Glunz's 6th Staffel for many months, leading more and more missions as Glunz's own flying hours tapered off in late 1944. When Addi Glunz left the Geschwader for jet training in early February, Sy was given the command, but as a Fuehrer, not as a formally designated Kapitaen. Now he had been displaced by a man two years younger than he, whose combat record was no better than his. His replacement's main qualification for the job seemed to be his friendship with the new Second Gruppe Kommandeur.

After the war, Siegfried Sy was unable to get clearance from the de-Nazification boards to enter a profession, and while training as a carpenter converted his wartime notes into a memoir, into which he poured out his bitter feelings. Thus sated, Sy put his writing aside, and made no attempt to publish it. It is now seeing print for the first time. His bitterness and jealousy undoubtedly color his writing, but his basic description of the situation in the Second Gruppe at this time appears to be accurate.

Siegfried Sy's story continues on the 26th:

> After morning coffee, the pilots of the individual Staffeln assembled as usual at their dispersals, to get their assignments from the Staffel leaders. We of the 6th Staffel waited in vain for our chief. He was considerate enough to call us from the pilot's mess, where he was eating with the Kommandeur, to tell us that he would not come today. I was to make the assignments and lead the Staffel on the mission. He had to see the doctor on account of his stomach.
>
> That's how it began, and that's how it would continue. To be honest, I was already prepared for this. I quickly made the assignments and passed them on to the command post. As always, Albrecht handled the telephone. "Who is leading the Gruppe?" I asked. Oblt. Hofmann would lead the Gruppe, since the Kommandeur had to attend a conference. Always the same song.
>
> The first mission was flown in the morning. It was a freie Jagd

over our own territory. We were to take this opportunity to become familiar with our new surroundings, so that we could find our field as quickly as possible after each mission. After we had driven around in the air for a good hour without seeing a single Indian, we landed.

The pilots of the 5th Staffel, still shaken by the loss of Bubi Schulwitz, received another shock on the afternoon of the 26th. After all three Gruppen had flown early-morning missions without contacting the enemy, fifteen Second and Fourth Gruppe aircraft had to land at the First Gruppe's base at Drope in order to refuel. At 1432, orders were received for the First and Second Gruppen to fly a combined anti-Jabo mission to the Wesel-Bocholt area. Four Focke-Wulfs from the First Gruppe and four from the Second took off at 1500, led by the 5th Staffel's Kapitaen, Oblt. Hofmann. There was solid cloud cover at ten thousand feet. Visibility below the clouds was restricted to less than a mile by the flames and smoke from destroyed Wehrmacht installations. Hofmann's small force encountered a formation of B-26s near Muenster, and he led a bounce of the escort, nine Tempests of No. 33 Squadron. Hofmann shot down one of the British fighters, for his 44th victory, but the other planes of the victim's flight got the upper hand in the ensuing dogfight and shot down three of the four First Gruppe aircraft. Only one of these three pilots survived.

Wilhelm Hofmann did not return from this, his 260th mission. The crash of his aircraft was not observed in the smoky haze. Back at Drope, the only First Gruppe pilot to return was arrested for shooting Hofmann down. The next day he stood trial at the headquarters of the 14th Fliegerdivision and was acquitted. There was apparently no further investigation at that time, but it can now be said that Hofmann was shot down on the return flight to Bissel by his own wingman, when Hofmann's aircraft loomed up suddenly through the haze. Hofmann's body was not found until 2 April. It was in a forest, a half-mile from the wreckage of his aircraft. He had bailed out, but at too low an altitude, and his parachute had not opened. He was buried in a field grave in the forest. Hofmann's body was exhumed after the war and buried in a military cemetery, but in the prevailing postwar chaos its identity was lost. Not until 1988, after a lengthy investigation by Gert Poelchau, was Hofmann's identity officially confirmed. Wilhelm Hofmann's name could only then be removed from the list of pilots missing in action. Siegfried Sy's comments are a fitting eulogy:

> Oberleutnant Hofmann had been the last member of the Second Gruppe to hold true to the old Schlageter spirit. This spirit disappeared with his death. . . . The news of Hofmann's tragic end was a heavy blow to the hearts of everyone. Wilhelm Hofmann, who knew no other duty but to fly and fly again, even with one eye, and who had never turned back in the face of the enemy, had now had his glorious and soaring career brought to earth.

Wilhelm Hofmann's replacement as Kapitaen of the 5th Staffel was Oblt. Fred Heckmann of the 3rd Staffel. Heckmann had been the most steadfast formation leader in the First Gruppe. Since the unit's return to Germany, he had led more Gruppe missions than had Major Borris himself. His mature good judgment had frequently enabled the First Gruppe to carry out its ordered missions with a minimum of losses. He was very popular with the Gruppe's younger pilots for his accessibility, and for the fact that he rarely lost a wingman—wingmen notice such things! It is probable that Heckmann's failure to carry out his mission orders on the 22nd had made him expendable to Borris. His steadying influence was much needed in the Second Gruppe at this time.

The Geschwader was greatly hampered by shortages of fuel at its new bases. Only the Fourth Gruppe flew a mission on 28 March. Its orders were to attack fighter-bombers that were supporting the American Ninth Army's advance from their Rhine bridgehead. While flying east of Muenster at 1130, before reaching the battle zone, the fifteen or so FW 190Ds were bounced by eight No. 130 Sqd. Spitfire XIVs, which shot down and killed two pilots. While making his escape at low altitude, another Fourth Gruppe pilot hit a row of trees and crashed; his remains were not found until 1988. The Spitfire pilots claimed 7-1-2 FW 190Ds, but only three casualties were suffered by JG 26. The only German successes on this mission were gained by two of the Fourth Gruppe Staffelkapitaene. Oblt. Dortenmann claimed a Tempest; Lt. Crump downed a P-47, for his 23rd victory. Peter Crump recalls:

> My unit scattered, returning alone to my airfield after a mission to Cologne, I encountered near Muenster a formation of between

ten and twelve Thunderbolts, strafing a freight yard. . . . When I saw the Thunderbolts, I sent my wingman home. I wanted a success, and could only carry out my plan alone. Two Focke-Wulfs could possibly have been spotted too soon; also, I did not want to endanger my wingman. . . . Utilizing sun and clouds—there was an inversion layer, with clear visibility and a thick cloud cover—I snuck into the attackers' circle, shot one down, and disappeared into the cloud layer. A second attempt misfired, since the enemy had been awakened from his unconcern, and I had to seek my salvation in flight. This was easy to accomplish in the clouds.

According to the American records, a pilot of the 406th Fighter Group was hit from behind at 3,000 feet by Crump's quick bounce and spun out, still carrying his bombs. After two turns, he got out of his P-47, and made a successful parachute descent into the railroad yard. His companions were unable to catch the lone FW 190D, which had disappeared into the cloud layer.

On the morning of the 29th, the last flyable Second Gruppe FW 190D-9 was ferried from Nordhorn to Bissel, the last load of spare parts was loaded onto the Gruppe's few trucks, and the airfield's fuel inventory—16,000 gallons of aviation gasoline—was turned over to the retreating German Army. Except for a brief period the previous autumn, the Geschwader had up to now rarely had to restrict operations for lack of fuel—adequate supplies were simply a matter of good staff work, and the Geschwader's supply officers, most of whom had been together since before the war, were apparently among the best. The Second Gruppe had been especially fortunate at Nordhorn, in that its source of supplies was the nearby Ems-Vechte Canal rather than the vulnerable railroad. The canal was used only at night. Before dawn, the barges were re-moored in their previous locations and the canal was drained. The Allies never realized that the canal and its barges were operational, so never attacked them.

Oblt. Heckmann's replacement as Kapitaen of the 3rd Staffel reported to the First Gruppe on the 29th. He was Oblt. Hans Dortenmann, formerly of 14/JG 26. Of all the Geschwader officers still flying, Dortenmann was considered one of the most ambitious and eager for combat, qualities that undoubtedly endeared him to Major Borris. Lt. Hans Prager took over Dortenmann's former Staffel.

HIMMELFAHRTSKOMMANDOS—MISSIONS TO HEAVEN

The Allies had broken through the thin defenses along the Rhine and were beginning to surge across Germany with a speed reminiscent of their race across France the previous summer. The most important tasks for JG 26 were now reconnaissance and Jabo attacks on the Allied columns. Reconnaissance was especially important, because there were no German defensive lines as such. The best the army could do was block the roads being used by the Allied spearheads. Each of the three Gruppen was called upon to fly two or three combat missions per day. These flights, which generally contained between four and twelve fighters, were known to the pilots as "Himmelfahrtskommandos," which can be translated loosely as "missions to heaven." There was a slow but steady loss of pilots by the three already depleted Gruppen.

The 1st of April was a typical day. One 1st Staffel Schwarm took off from Drope at 0620 to reconnoiter the highways in the Rheine-Greven area. The flight, led by Lt. Georg Kiefner, located the leading enemy armor between Greven and Ladbergen, and later in the day the 14th Fliegerdivision authorized awards of Iron Crosses to the four pilots for their successful mission. That afternoon, all three Gruppen received orders to mount Jabo attacks by independent Schwaerme in the area between Rheine and Ibbenbueren. Four missions were flown; three were able to carry out successful attacks, and one aircraft was lost to ground fire.

One transfer order that was received on 1 April had to have lifted the spirits of the Second Gruppe's enlisted pilots. Fw. Heinz Gomann was the longest-serving pilot in the Gruppe. He had gotten off to a very good start in 1942 but he had had nothing but bad luck since then; he had suffered three serious injuries in 1943 and 1944. Gomann was now ordered to join JG 7, a jet fighter Geschwader. It was highly unlikely that Gomann's conversion training could be completed in time for him to return to combat before the war's inevitable end. The more analytical of the Geschwader's pilots realized that there were only two sure ways to survive the war—suffer a severe wound, or transfer to jets. Up until now, the latter had been the gentleman's route, restricted to officers. It was good to think that someone in Berlin was looking out for the enlisted pilots' interests as well—perhaps it was their own Pips!

On about 3 April, the Geschwader lost a Staffelkapitaen, when Oblt. Willi Heilmann failed to return from a mission. Other Fourth Gruppe pilots saw him land on the airfield at Muenster-Handorf, his aircraft apparently undamaged. Unfortunately, the field had been captured by the British several days before, a fact that was well-known to Heilmann and the other German pilots. There appears to have been an official cover-up of the circumstances of Heilmann's loss. His 15th Staffel was disbanded immediately, and its pilots were reassigned to the 13th and 14th Staffeln. No reason for this is given in Priller's history; Heilmann himself simply disappears from the record on this day. In his 1951 memoir *Alarm im Westen*, published in the US as *I Fought You From the Skies*, Willi Heilmann claimed that his departure from the war was preceded by a solemn ceremony in which he discharged his entire Staffel to return to their homes. He strongly implies that this took place only days before the end of the war. This part of his story is, of course, rubbish. German veterans draw a sharp distinction between "desertion" and "honorable surrender"; Heilmann's action took place one month too soon to come under the latter category.

From now until the end of the war, II/JG 26 specialized in bombing attacks. Apparently only this Gruppe's FW 190Ds were equipped with bomb racks, giving the unit additional punch for its Jabo missions. Werner Molge describes the ordnance carried by his Gruppe:

> We carried either 250-kg or 500-kg high-explosive bombs, or droppable containers. The latter held a number of 2-kg fragmentation bomblets. We weren't happy about carrying these things, because it was dangerous to land with them—which happened often, due to engine failure. You couldn't jettison the container in an emergency, because the small bombs in it all had impact fuses. The regular bombs, on the other hand, had electric fuses that were energized through the release gear, and could thus be jettisoned on "safe."

On 4 April, the First Gruppe's early morning reconnaissance flight could not get off the ground because of its boggy condition. That evening a court-martial officer came from the 14th Fliegerdivision to Delmenhorst to question Major Borris and Lt. Soeffing about this failure, but the Gruppe's diary makes no further mention of the investigation. A First Gruppe freie Jagd later that day was more successful. Sixteen Focke-Wulfs took off at 1905, led by Lt. Soeffing. Seven aborted, but the others jumped a small formation of Allied fighter-bombers near Diepholz, downing two. In the meantime, Hptm. Schauder had led twenty-eight aircraft of his Second Gruppe in an attack on Canadian armor near the Gruppe's old base at Nordhorn. Only one of his FW 190Ds failed to return. Its pilot was Lt. Sy, who was leading the 7th Staffel in place of the ill Lt. Dietze. Siegfried Sy's memoir describes this mission:

> My things were sent to the 7th Staffel dispersal, and I got ready. I would fly Feldwebel Gomann's mill, "Brown 9." As the senior pilot of the Gruppe, he certainly wouldn't have had a bad aircraft. Takeoff went smoothly. Scarcely had all the planes taken the air, when my own Staffelkapitaen, Oblt. Schmidt, notified us that he was returning to base because of engine problems. By this time I had gotten to know him well, and was not at all surprised. I herded my flock together, and positioned the 7th Staffel to the right of the Kommandeur.
>
> We were lucky, and reached Nordhorn before contacting the enemy. We had crossed the entire stretch at low altitude. Now we were over the target. We saw the tanks bunched together on a large field not far from our former airfield, showing their white stars. The Kommandeur quickly pulled up, dropped his bomb, and turned back. We now faced an unbelievable curtain of flak. Many of us dropped our bombs wildly, missing their targets but taking no hits. I dropped my bomb between two tanks. We were now supposed to strafe the rest of the brothers. But where was the Kommandeur? Had he already gone home? Was this to be all, especially today, with conditions so uniquely favorable? We had to take advantage of this opportunity to score a great success!
>
> "From Sy!" I cried on the radio, "One more of the same! We will show the enemy that we are still flying!" I had already turned around, and approached the tank formation at low altitude for a second time. But of the twenty-eight aircraft, only three came with me—my own Schwarm. The rest were far distant.
>
> In these seconds, I was entirely in my element. I reached the field again, and pulled up a little in order to take the individual tanks under fire from above. I could clearly see my strikes on the tanks. But were they causing any damage? I had my doubts. They were also firing from down below. Rounds of light flak went right through the

wings, both left and right—but the old Focke-Wulf could take those. What was that? A hit in the tail—I noticed that immediately. The rudder was shot through. The clouds were very high above me, and I was headed toward enemy territory. This could be dangerous. I had to fly straight ahead, whether I wanted to or not. My mill took more and more hits. Maybe I should bail out? The thought lasted only a fraction of a second. I had already pulled up. I saw a large cloud in front of me. Would the Focke be able to reach it? I had to try—I had a dread of imprisonment. But now that I was climbing and had little speed, I made an even better target. Forty-millimeter flak began to fire at me from the left. My engine was hit solidly, and quit. My mill shuddered, and the first flames showed from beneath the cowling. There was now only one thing to do—bail out. It was high time; the fuel tank could explode. I beat like a wild man on the canopy release lever, but in vain. In less than a second, my hands became wet with sweat, and my right one went numb from my blows. The canopy still would not come off. I attempted to sideslip by yanking the ailerons to the right and kicking the rudder to the left, although that did little good because of the damage to the controls. I had to reach the ground as quickly as possible. There was no time to think; neither were there any options. The engine was no longer running, although the prop was still turning.

I was now over an open field, and approaching a forest. I had to get down quickly to stay out of the pine trees. There was a tremendous crash. There wasn't time to think—the crate could go up at any second. And then—where was I exactly? I naturally hadn't worried about my bearings in some time, but from the direction of my attack I could assume that I was still behind the enemy lines.

I forced the canopy open with my hands, which was not difficult, thank God, now that I was on the ground. One knob and I had released my parachute. I had heard more than once in my fighter pilot's training that in case I landed behind the enemy lines, the first thing to do was blow up my airplane. The enemy was not to gain possession of it. But why not? Would they really want to fly it? There was no reason; the Spitfire was better than our old Focke, even though not as fast. They probably had as many of our crates as they wanted already.

No, I needed first to look after my own security, if I did not want to fall into the hands of the enemy. I took my pistol out, released the safety catch, and trotted toward the forest as quickly as my flying boot-weighted legs would let me. If they wanted me, they would have to work at it, and find me first.

It took Siegfried Sy only twenty-four hours to return to his unit, but he had a number of adventures on his mini-odyssey. Sy jogged for several hours in the forest. After nightfall he slowed to a walk, following the stars toward the north. At daybreak, he came across a group of German soldiers eating breakfast in a ditch beside a road. A brief conversation established that the men intended to wait there for the Canadians' arrival, in order to surrender. Sy moved onto the road and began passing Dutch civilians, who told him with a laugh that the German defenders had pulled back several days before. He reached the border crossing, which was manned by a single guard, who was under orders to stay put and who had no means of communication or transport to offer him. Back on German soil, Sy finally reached a German defensive unit—but this proved to be an SS detachment engaged in rounding up stragglers. They were firmly convinced that Sy belonged in that category and offered him the option of joining a tank-hunting unit or facing a firing squad. His pilot's pass, which was supposed to guarantee priority treatment, brought only the retort, "Your Luftwaffe no longer exists!" Sy escaped this nightmare by persuading the Leutnant in command of a passing antiaircraft unit to smuggle him aboard a truck. The convoy passed near Bissel, and Lt. Sy was able to report back to Hptm. Schauder in mid-afternoon, to the latter's great surprise.

THE LINES CLOSE IN

After a few days in the Bremen-Delmenhorst area, the Geschwader made a long rearward jump, to Celle and Hustedt. They were required to move again almost immediately. Lt. Sy bypassed Hustedt entirely, leading Bissel's last seven FW 190Ds directly to Uetersen, north of Hamburg, on 6 April. Sy attempted to prepare the base for the arrival of the rest of the Gruppe, but he had difficulty controlling his own rambunctious men—the base contained a large number of servicewomen, who had taken over many of the mechanics' jobs on air bases behind the front. On the next day, the First Gruppe transferred to Stade, a major Home Defense airbase across the Elbe River from Hamburg. The Fourth Gruppe moved to Neumuenster, where on the 11th they received orders to prepare to disband. On 9 April, the Stab and the Second Gruppe joined Sy in Uetersen. The Geschwader's new fields were not stocked with fuel, and few missions could be flown. Whenever possible, however, the Second Gruppe flew bombing missions against the oncoming British armor, while the First Gruppe engaged in their own specialty, armed reconnaissance. The First Gruppe had a remarkable string of successes against the British Tempests. On 12 April, Oblt. Dortenmann led twelve aircraft in a bounce of eight Tempests north of Uelsen. The German pilots returned to Stade to report the destruction of five Tempests, for the loss of one Focke-Wulf and its pilot. No. 33 Squadron in fact lost two Tempests, although a third was written off after its return. The British pilots in their turn claimed three Focke-Wulfs.

On 13 April, the First Gruppe moved east to Suelte, near Schwerin. The transfer proved to be Uffz. Hans Kukla's last flight in a Focke-Wulf. Upon his return to the Gruppe after his injury in January, he had found only one pilot whom he knew from his time in Fuerstenau—Fhr. Gerhard von Plazer. Von Plazer had a strong premonition that he would not survive the war, and he was not very good company. One of Kukla's burned eyelids had not healed properly, and the Gruppe surgeon mercifully ordered him into the hospital. Hans Kukla's war was over; Gerhard von Plazer's would last for one more week.

The Fourth Gruppe flew its last combat mission on 14 April and stood down prior to disbanding. On this day, two of the Geschwader's most stalwart Staffelkapitaene received orders to join General Galland's "Jet Unit of the Aces," JV 44—Lt. Georg Kiefner of the 1st Staffel and Oblt. Fred Heckmann of the 5th. On the 17th, the Fourth Gruppe's pilots arrived at Suelte and Uetersen to join their new units. Oblt. Karl-Hermann Schrader led ten pilots into the First Gruppe. Lt. Peter Crump and nine pilots joined the combat Staffeln of the Second Gruppe. Eight more pilots, including Fw. Gerhard Kroll, Fw. Wolfgang Polster, and Fw. Willi Zester, joined the Second Gruppe's "convalescent Staffel," which contained pilots who were off flying status while recovering from injuries. Oblt. Schrader left shortly thereafter for JV 44, while Lt. Hans Prager went to EJG 1. Lt. Crump took command of the 5th Staffel, but he was too ill to fly. The available records do not list Major Klemm's assignment after the breakup of his Gruppe.

At 1110 on the 17th, Oblt. Dortenmann led eighteen First

Gruppe Focke-Wulfs up from Suelte on an anti-Jabo sweep. South of Luebeck, the Tempests of No. 80 Squadron were met at 6,500 feet, and a furious battle ensued, after which the German pilots claimed the destruction of three Tempests. Six Focke-Wulfs were lost, but only two pilots. The British squadron claimed 2-0-2 FW 190s, for the loss of only one pilot.

On 20 April, Oblt. Dortenmann was awarded his Knight's Cross, to the joy and the probable relief of his 3rd Staffel pilots. This was to be the last major decoration received by a member of the Geschwader. The Wehrmacht's infrastructure was rapidly disintegrating. The American Ninth Army had already reached the Elbe River northwest of Berlin, and within a few days Germany would be cut in two by the American and Russian Armies. The Luftwaffe no longer made a distinction between the Western and Eastern fronts. All air units in the north now came under Genobst. Stumpf's Luftflottenkommando Reich. JG 26 remained the only day fighter unit in the 14th Fliegerdivision, which became one of Lkdo Reich's subordinate units.

Hans Dortenmann was not called on to fly on the 20th, probably in recognition of his decoration, and Major Borris led the First Gruppe's main mission of the day. Eleven Focke-Wulfs took off at 1540 on an anti-Jabo sweep to Lueneburg. As the unit was forming up north of Suelte, Griffon-engined Spitfires were reported attacking the field. Borris led his fighters back and found about a dozen Spitfires. Lt. Soeffing shot one down over the airfield. Fhr. von Plazer shot down another, for his first victory, but was then shot down himself and killed. The Second Gruppe lost two pilots in the Berlin-Soltau area, over the former Eastern front. The Geschwader would fly many bombing and strafing missions against the Russians during the next ten days.

On the 21st, both Gruppen flew missions against the British, who were advancing on Hamburg from the south. At 1515, nine First Gruppe aircraft under Dortenmann's command attacked six Spitfires at 5,000 feet over Buchholz and downed three without loss. Late in the evening, the Second Gruppe found British fighters northwest of Perleberg and downed two, but one Focke-Wulf failed to return.

The First Gruppe flew against the Russians for the first time on 24 April. Oblt. Dortenmann led seventeen aircraft up from Suelte to strafe Russian truck convoys in their salient at Oranienburg, just north of Berlin. They encountered eight Yak-3 fighters at 8,000 feet north of Spandau and shot down three, without loss. They then landed at the Luftwaffe Experimental Station at Rechlin to refuel. They were delayed in taking off by Tempests over Rechlin, but finally arrived back at Suelte at 2040.

The Second Gruppe's mission on the 24th, an attack on the advancing British Army, was a notable success. Siegfried Sy tells the story:

Each morning we had to fly a so-called reconnaissance in force to the Lueneburg Heath, to determine the forward positions of the enemy. This flight took off just at dawn, and returned before the day's normal duties began. We had to fly over the exact positions of the enemy, at low altitude. Because of the constant fog over the heath, the ground could not be seen from above 200 meters [650 feet]—so the flight had to be made very near the ground! The worst thing was the Allied four-barreled flak. We lost a number of men on these flights, which had to be made by a Schwarm. It was frequently the case that of the four aircraft that took off, only two would return to base.

Today it was Lt. Dietze's turn to make the recon flight with the 7th Staffel, but since he had to see the doctor and was thus unable to fly, I flew the mission. Based on the results of the reconnaissance, which could be reported by radio if necessary, Lt. Schramm was prepared to take off immediately with the 6th Staffel. I had just passed Harburg when I saw a solid line of vehicles stretching back across the heath. Our four machines could not do much, since our only weapons were our guns, which were inadequate for a target of this size. The location was easy to find, so I notified ground control immediately by radio. I quickly reversed course, crossed the front at Lueneburg, and then followed the twin-tracked railway line back. Just as I flew over the field at Uetersen with all four of my aircraft, Lt. Schramm took off on his morning mission, loaded with bombs. I shouted for joy when I saw how well things were going, and how tightly the pilots of the 6th Staffel closed up on Schramm. The target couldn't be missed, for it was on the only major highway in the region. And when he found it, a major success was assured.

When they had all taken off, my flight prepared to land. One plane after another settled to the ground. As soon as I had stopped,

I unbuckled myself and jumped from the aircraft. I called to the line chief to refuel me immediately and load me with bombs. I corrected myself; load all of the mills with bombs. Now I had no more time; I had to make my report in person—I didn't want to give it over the phone. I jumped on the nearest bicycle and went to the command post. They were waiting impatiently. Uffz. Albrecht had already called the field twice from the command post, inquiring after me. Even our old operations officer, Hptm. Groos, had a pleased look on his face. As quickly as I gave my report to Uffz. Albrecht, it was passed along to Division. Shortly afterward came the order—Prepare to take off against the known target! In the meantime, I had taken care of detailing the 5th and 7th Staffeln. Three Schwaerme would fly the mission. It wasn't long until all was ready. I quickly returned to my machine. The crew chief tightened my harness once more, and we prepared to move out. The command post fired a single red flare; that meant for us to taxi to takeoff position. Takeoff was forbidden to all other aircraft on the field. One mill after another taxied into position. We hadn't much time to lose, since Lt. Schramm would be returning soon with the 6th Staffel. All twelve aircraft were at the takeoff point. Two green flares came up from the command post. Slowly I pushed the throttle forward. The good old FW 190D accelerated over the grass. It took somewhat longer to lift off carrying a bomb than it did clean. Now the moment came when it was free of the ground, and securely in the air. Press forward, and make the first turn. My Schwarm was in close behind me. Now the other two Schwaerme lifted off, and I could set course. I stayed right beneath the cloud deck, to protect myself from any attack from above. It was a real pleasure to see how the three Schwaerme held tight formation in the air. But what was that over there to the left? Was our little Stumpfl reporting something? Yes, those were aircraft. Hopefully not Spitfires, for we would have to dodge them, since we didn't want to drop our bombs over this territory. No, they couldn't be Spitfires, since they weren't in their usual orderly formation! When they had come somewhat nearer, we recognized them as Focke-Wulfs. It had to be Lt. Schramm and his men. The flak had undoubtedly split up their formation a little bit. But after we had recognized them as our own fighters, they were of no further concern. We flew over Hamburg, then left, past Harburg; everything in order! A little farther straight ahead and we would hit the highway.

Still the pilots displayed no signs of nervousness. All flew calmly—a beautiful sight, as the twelve aircraft moved as one in the air. The highway stretched to the left in front of us. We could clearly see truck after truck. But nothing was moving; they had apparently not yet overcome the shock of the first fighter attack. There were so many targets that we didn't know where to begin. We made a shallow turn to the left, and could now take the entire road under fire. My bomb unfortunately missed its target by a few meters, not striking the road itself, where it was aimed, but rather the ditch beside it. But it wasn't dropped to no purpose! Until now I had seen only trucks on the road beneath me. I now noticed for the first time that the flak had been invited to the party—but this was not the first time we had been taken under fire from such a low altitude. We now jinked to the left and the right along the road. One truck after another burst into flames. To the left, beside the ditch, was a twin-barrel antiaircraft gun. Gently I stepped on the rudder pedal and pressed the firing button. The gun ceased fire immediately. Then in front of me, a truck; it was made a believer also. One after another, in the same manner. The other pilots were firing as well. Here and there an FW 190D flew along gracefully, dipping its snout to graze again and again from the highway. Now, however, it was enough. I banked to the left; behind me, the others were still at work. I gave the recall on the radio, and we ended the bloody business. Most of us had used up all our ammo. Lt. Kraft had received a hit in the engine, but he made it back to base with his damaged crate. No one else received any damage to speak of. Some had a few shell holes, but nothing affecting flying ability.

I happily made ready to land. It was a beautiful feeling to have had one more success. It was a slight compensation for all the successes that our opponents had had recently. While taxiing in, I counted the approaching aircraft. All twelve had returned. After such an outstanding mission, a double pleasure. Now I went with the other pilots to the command post, for each had to report for himself. The rest of the Gruppe were there, listening to the reports of the 6th Staffel. Schramm and his men had also returned without loss. His success was considerably greater, for during the first attack, which had gained total surprise, not a single shot had been fired by the flak. By the time we arrived, the flak was better prepared. All faces were smiling, as each waited to give his report.

In the meantime, our Kommandeur had entered the command post, vigorously expressing his regrets that his military duties had prevented him from flying the mission. Our good old Hptm. Groos, who carried all of the worries of the Gruppe on his shoulders, celebrated with us. Our Gruppe was not called on again that day by Division. We were released from duty earlier than usual, and could return to our lodgings.

The 25th saw both Gruppen staging through Rechlin and flying over Berlin. The First Gruppe brought down two Yak-3s, while
Lt. Sy claimed a P-39. Sy's victory was the 902nd and last of the war
for the Second Gruppe. The First Gruppe's pilots remained overnight in Rechlin, while the Second Gruppe returned to Uetersen—
they had a rendezvous to keep.

The Second Gruppe's successful mission on the previous day
was sufficient reason to throw a party in the pilots' mess that night.
The ground staff decorated the room. The resourceful Hptm. Groos
came up with adequate supplies of alcohol and tobacco. Dancing
was forbidden, and the men of the Gruppe, who were considered
interlopers and troublemakers by Uetersen's permanent staff, did
not press the issue but looked forward to the presence of a large
number of women who would compensate for the lack of dancing.
According to his memoir, Siegfried Sy busied himself previewing
the speeches and skits planned by the men—he was afraid that their
comments about their Kommandeur would be too pointed. This is
the memoir's only reference, as veiled as it is, to Sy's second job—as
political officer of the Second Gruppe. Siegfried Sy's description of
the party is worth quoting at length:

> The pilots' evening was very successful. The pilots assembled,
> their girls sitting beside them. Most of the pilots had lit a small flame
> on the base, for there were numerous long-haired creatures here.
> Those who had none were assigned one for the evening. I myself had
> a small blondie from the Sudetenland sitting next to me, a fine girl.
> First there was singing, then skits by the pilots and a speech by the
> Kommandeur. After a while the effect of the alcohol became no-
> ticeable in our reddened faces. We all became louder and more
> talkative. As a rule I had little to say, but now I showed another side.
> I had partaken freely of the cognac, and at midnight began to make
> a speech to the assembly. The next morning I couldn't remember
> what I had said. I do remember standing on a table, testing the
> durability of several cognac glasses with my feet as I spoke, and
> dropping the ashes of my sweet-tasting cigarette into the bowl of the
> chandelier hanging in front of me. It was an evening unlike any we
> had had in a while, and it would not be repeated in this war.

On the 26th, Obfw. Fritz Ungar of the 2nd Staffel made his
first flight to Rechlin. The mission that followed proved to be one
of his most memorable. Fitz Ungar's story:

At about 0550 on 26 April, we took off on a freie Jagd, landing at about 0710 at Laerz, the Rechlin airfield. Rechlin was well known to us as the Luftwaffe test facility. We were curious. What were we to do in Rechlin? The day passed in uncertain tension. It wasn't until late afternoon that we received the order to fly an escort mission to Berlin, determining while there whether the East-West Axis (a large, broad street in the center of Berlin) was usable as a landing strip, or whether the Russians had already taken it under artillery fire.

We were not told whom we were to escort. We heard from the communiqué that the Russians were already pressing forward into the city. We took off at 1805—twelve FW 190D-9 "long noses"— under the leadership of Oblt. Dortenmann. The sixty miles to Berlin was not a great distance for us. We flew south in combat formation. We had no need to ask where Berlin was; we could see the great wall of smoke. As we approached the city at ten thousand feet, almost all of Berlin was seen burning. An indescribably overwhelming sight. We were able to orient ourselves easily, and could see shell bursts on the East-West Axis.

There was a war on, and the Russians showed us that we were over enemy territory. Light flak took us under fire, and suddenly there came a surprise—the sky around us was full of tracers! In the last few minutes we had climbed to 4,000 meters [13,000 feet]. Based on our experience in the West, only single-shell antiaircraft guns could reach this altitude. But we were now surrounded by strings of pearls. This was rapid fire!

"Achtung! Flak! Dodge it!" Dortenmann shouted over the radio. Hell was upon us! And we began to dance. We could actually see the shells and tracers looping upward, and could avoid them. It was a larger caliber than typical light flak. The shells rose more slowly. We were lucky—all twelve of us came through it. We gradually came out of this zone on a northerly course. We were now north of Berlin, and could see other aircraft in the sky. There, to the east of us and beneath us, were about ten small aircraft. They swarmed like bees. We concluded that they had to be Russian fighters. Up until now we had had nothing to do with them; we had always flown in the West. We continued to watch them. When we had descended to about 2,000 meters [6,500 feet], they flew off.

A minute later Dortenmann's voice came over the radio— "Damn it, we are now thirteen. That is one too many!" And he banked sharply right. Our right halfback was a Russian. We all turned toward him, but he was lucky. He disappeared into a nearby cloud, and we never saw him again.

We then landed at Rechlin, our orders fulfilled. The East-West Axis was under fire. We had seen Berlin from above, several days before the end of the Second World War—nothing but rubble, fire, and smoke.

Fritz Ungar never learned the full story of this flight. Oblt. Jan Schild of the 1st Staffel was one of the dozen pilots, and his logbook indicates that it was indeed an escort mission. There were thirteen FW 190Ds on the flight from Rechlin. Crammed into the thirteenth were Genobst. Ritter von Greim and the test pilot Hanna Reitsch, making their lunatic odyssey to the Fuehrerbunker. Van Greim dropped away from the formation and landed at Berlin's Gatow airport, from where the duo continued to the inner city in a trainer. Russian fire hit the small airplane and nearly severed von Greim's foot before he could put the craft down on the East-West Axis.

For the next two days, the First Gruppe staged out of Rechlin, flying armed reconnaissance missions and escorting FW 190F Panzerblitze, which attacked Russian armor with rockets. Oblt. Dortenmann downed two Yak-3s, for his 37th and 38th victories, while the rest of the Gruppe shot down two more. Its base at Suelte was now in danger from both British and Russian tanks, and the unit withdrew to the northwest late on 28 April, to a field near Neumuenster.

Lt. Sy led a strengthened armed reconnaissance mission of two Second Gruppe Schwaerme up from Uetersen early on the morning of the 29th. They were vectored while in the air toward a formation of Tempests near Lauenburg. The Tempests, from No. 486 Squadron, had attacked a formation of FW 190Fs from SG 151 and had shot down four. SG 151 was the training wing for the Schlachtflieger (attack units) and had been made operational to combat the armor approaching its base at Lauenburg. Sy's force was also treated roughly by the Tempests. Two of his pilots were shot down and were still carried as missing in 1991. No Tempests were lost.

At 1230, Lt. Soeffing led six First Gruppe aircraft off to attack the leading British armor near Lauenburg. In a battle with Spitfire XIVs, Soeffing shot down one, but the unit lost Fw. Helmut Walter. Walter was the last of 763 JG 26 pilots to be killed in the course of the war. Later in the afternoon, Soeffing led seven aircraft in an escort mission for fourteen SG 151 FW 190Fs. The Tempests of

No. 486 Squadron had returned to the area and were attacked by Soeffing's formation. Soeffing reported shooting down one Tempest, for his 34th victory, but was unable to prevent the Tempests from shattering the formation of attack planes. Three SG 151 aircraft went down. Soeffing could not re-form the attack unit and led his own Doras back to base.

On the 30th, the Second Gruppe joined the First in the Neumuenster area. Both Gruppen spent the day attempting to attack British armor while avoiding Second TAF fighters. Uffz. Walter Stumpf of the 7th Staffel, who was flying daily and who had become an accomplished Jabo pilot, made a successful bombing attack in the Lauenburg area and was promoted to Feldwebel. In the last command shake-up of the war, by which Major Goetz hoped to strengthen both Gruppen, Lt. Crump moved from the Second Gruppe's 5th Staffel to take over the First Gruppe's 1st Staffel, while Oblt. Schild left the 1st Staffel to take command of the 5th. The exchange worked; both men began their new assignments with renewed vigor.

The Second Gruppe lost its Kommandeur on 1 May. During a mission that did not find its way into the official records, Hptm. Paul. Schauder was shot down near Lauenburg by British antiaircraft fire and taken prisoner, injured. On the same day, Lt. Guhl of the 2nd Staffel claimed the probable destruction of a Spitfire; this was the First Gruppe's 817th claim and would prove to be the Geschwader's last victory claim of the war. The First Gruppe reported having thirty-eight pilots on strength but only fourteen aircraft. The next day the Gruppen had to move once more, to fields in Schleswig, pressed against the Danish border. On 2 May, Peter Crump, finally promoted to Oberleutnant, led nine First Gruppe aircraft in an interception of eight Typhoons over his own airfield. Oblt. Crump damaged one, but the rest evaded combat in the clouds. Lt. Conrad lost his formation and was shot down by Tempests, but he bailed out without injury. His Focke-Wulf was the First Gruppe's last combat loss.

Heavy rains would restrict flying for the rest of the war. On 3 May Uffz. Werner Molge took off from Husum on a reconnaissance mission. At 1,000 feet there was an explosion, and his engine caught fire. He landed by parachute, very near the airfield. Molge was uninjured, and his Focke-Wulf was the last aircraft lost by the

Second Gruppe. The cause of the explosion—enemy aircraft, flak, maintenance defect, or sabotage—was never determined.

Both Gruppen put up missions on 4 May, despite the rain. Oblt. Schild led a small force away from Husum at 1310 on a freie Jagd. After sweeping the combat zone, they landed again at 1420. This was Jan Schild's 222nd and last combat sortie. The Geschwader's last combat mission was a freie Jagd to the area of the Kiel Canal; it was flown by nine aircraft of the First Gruppe, led by Oblt. Dortenmann. When they landed at Flensburg at 1824, the combat history of Jagdgeschwader 26 "Schlageter"—the Abbeville Kids—had come to a close.

The new head of the Luftwaffe, Generalfeldmarschall Ritter von Greim, had ordered the Geschwader to relocate to Prague. Von Greim had received his promotion and appointment while in the Fuehrerbunker. His nonsensical order would have required a flight of several hundred miles over Allied-held territory, and the abandonment of the Geschwader's ground echelon. However, on 4 May, Generalfeldmarschall Keitel signed an armistice for the northwestern front, to go into effect on the morning of the 5th. The pilots of the Second Gruppe, without a Kommandeur, argued among themselves as to their course of action. About half decided to stay where they were and surrender to the British when they arrived at Husum. The rest were not yet ready to give up, although Germany was only two days away from surrendering unconditionally. Lt. Sy led a dozen Focke-Wulfs to Aalborg, Denmark, before surrendering. Oblt. Schild made it as far as Norway with six aircraft before conceding the inevitable. He destroyed his 190s and joined JG 5 to await the arrival of occupation troops.

The First Gruppe had been held together for almost two years by the strict authority of Karl Borris. However, when Borris informed the pilots that they would be going to Prague—since "orders were orders"—they apparently rebelled. If the Major wanted to go to Prague, he could go by himself. Major Borris looked for a way to maintain his authority. His eyes fell on Uffz. Josef Niesmak, a longtime pilots' orderly in the Gruppe. Josef Niesmak recalls:

> Major Borris tried to convince me to accompany him to an airfield near Prague. He could not win me over to his plan, although I could not actually refuse the order. I tried to talk him out of it, but

it was not a simple task. Luckily the fog did not lift, and we were grounded because of the weather conditions. This was our great fortune. For us the war had come to an end. If everything had gone as Major Borris planned, and we had landed in Prague, we would have immediately been taken prisoner by the Russians. As a souvenir, I kept the large screwdriver used to open the hatch to the fuselage baggage compartment, in which I would have made the flight.

On 6 May, Major Borris paraded his men and aircraft and made a short speech in which he thanked his Gruppe for their sacrifices for "Volk und Vaterland." That evening he turned the Flensburg airfield over to the Royal Air Force, then led his men into a POW camp near the town. The war was over. As one bitter pilot put it in the final entry in his logbook, "Das war das Ende aller Traume"—"That was the end of all our dreams."

SOURCES

THE ORIGINAL INSPIRATION FOR THIS BOOK CAME FROM JOSEF PRIL-
ler's pioneering unit history, *JG 26: Geschichte eines Jagdgeschwaders*. Although it was written too soon after the war to be
objective and made almost no use of Allied records, his book remains a classic of its type. It provided me with the indispensable
chronological framework upon which to hang the results of my
own research.

I have attempted to base this work to the greatest extent possible
on primary source material. The archives and veterans I consulted
have been acknowledged previously. The quotations in this work
from the writings of Karl Borris, Joachim Muencheberg, and Norbert Risky were translated from Priller's book; all other quotations
that are not attributed in the text have been taken from official
documents or were provided by the veterans themselves. The basic
facts surrounding all of the first-person narratives were corroborated
from independent sources; memories sometimes play evil tricks.

The principal source for the history of any military unit should
be that unit's war diaries. In JG 26 these diaries were maintained by
the Gruppen. Nearly all of them were destroyed at the end of the
war, on orders from above. The only JG 26 unit diaries that have
been located belonged to the First Gruppe, and they cover that
Gruppe's operations from 5 October 1944 to 7 May 1945. The
pilots' logbooks were also ordered destroyed; only a pitiful few sur-

vived the bonfire. The official sources available include a brief
Geschwader history written in the unit in 1942; casualty reports for
each pilot lost; and the victory lists of the First and Second Gruppen. The Third Gruppe's victory list did not survive the war, but
lists for many of that Gruppe's most successful pilots have been
pieced together from other sources. We are fortunate in having a
complete list of the 7th Staffel's victories through mid-1941. These
were documented on two plaques that stood outside the Staffel's
command post. The plaques were photographed in late 1941 by
Matthias Buchmann, an armorer in the Staffel, who thus preserved
this invaluable data for posterity.

Recourse to published works was necessary. My bibliographic
database contains nearly one thousand references; my favorites
among them follow.

Aders, G. *History of the German Night Fighter Force 1917–1945*. London:
Jane's, 1978.

Aders, G., and Held, W. *Jagdgeschwader 51 "Moelders."* Stuttgart: Motorbuch, 1985.

Anonymous. *The Air Battle of Malta*. London: His Majesty's Stationery
Office, 1944.

Anonymous. *Ultra & the History of the USSAFE vs. the GAF*. Frederick,
MD: University Publications of America, 1980.

Baker, E.C.R. *The Fighter Aces of the RAF*. London: Wm. Kimber, 1962.

Barbas, B. *Planes of the Luftwaffe Fighter Aces Vols. 1 & 2*. Melbourne,
Aust.: Kookaburra, 1985.

Beaman, J., and Campbell, J. *Messerschmitt Bf 109 in Action Part 1*.
Carrollton, TX: Squadron/Signal, 1980.

Beaman, J. *Messerschmitt Bf 109 in Action Part 2*. Carrollton, TX:
Squadron/Signal, 1983.

Bekker, C. *The Luftwaffe War Diaries*. New York: Doubleday, 1964.

Bendiner, E. *The Fall of Fortresses*. New York: G.P. Putnam's, 1980.

Bennett, R. *Ultra in the West*. New York: Chas. Scribner's Sons, 1979.

Bishop, C. *Fortresses of the Big Triangle First*. Bishops Stortford, UK: East
Anglia Books, 1986.

Bledsoe, M. *Thunderbolt—Memoirs of a World War II Fighter Pilot*. New
York: Van Nostrand, 1982.

Bloemertz, G. *Heaven Next Stop*. London: Wm. Kimber, 1953.

Blue, A. *The Fortunes of War.* Fallbrook, CA: Aero Publishers, 1967.

Bowman, M. *Fields of Little America.* Norwich, UK: Wensum, 1977.

————. *Castles in the Air.* Wellingborough, UK: Patrick Stephens, 1984.

Bowyer, M.J.F. *Two Group R.A.F.: A Complete History, 1936–1945.* London: Faber & Faber, 1974.

Brickhill, P. *Reach for the Sky.* New York: W. W. Norton, 1954.

Brown, J. *Eagles Strike: South African Forces in WWII.* Vol. 4. Capetown, South Africa: Purnell, 1974.

Campbell, J. *Focke-Wulf FW 190 in Action.* Carrollton, TX: Squadron/Signal, 1975.

Carson, L. *Pursue & Destroy.* Granada Hills, CA: Sentry, 1978.

Clostermann, P. *The Big Show.* New York: Ballantine, 1951 (reprint).

Collier, B. *The Defense of the United Kingdom.* London: Her Majesty's Stationery Office, 1957.

Collier, R. *Eagle Day: The Battle of Britain August 6–September 15, 1940.* New York: E. P. Dutton, 1966.

Constable, T., and Toliver, R. *Horrido! Fighter Aces of the Luftwaffe.* New York: Ballantine, 1968 (reprint).

Cooper, M. *The German Air Force 1933–1945.* London: Jane's, 1981.

Craven, W., and Cate, J. *The Army Air Forces in World War II: Plans and Early Operations.* Vol. 1. Chicago: University of Chicago Press, 1948.

————. *The Army Air Forces in World War II: Europe—Torch to Pointblank.* Vol. 2. Chicago: University of Chicago Press, 1949.

————. *The Army Air Forces in World War II: Europe—Argument to V-E Day.* Vol. 3. Chicago: University of Chicago Press, 1951.

Davies, A. *The 56th Fighter Group in World War II.* Washington, DC: Infantry Journal Press, 1948.

Deere, A. C. *Nine Lives.* New York: Beagle Books, 1959 (reprint).

Dezarrois, A. *The Mouchotte Diaries, 1940–1943.* London: Staples Press, 1956.

Ethell, J., and Price, A. *Target Berlin—Mission 250: 6 March 1944.* London: Jane's, 1981.

Farnol, L. *To the Limit of Their Endurance.* Manhattan, KS: Sunflower University Press, 1944 (reprint).

Fleuret, A. *Luftwaffe Camouflage 1935–1940.* Melbourne, Australia: Kookaburra, 1981.

Foreman, J. *Battle of Britain: The Forgotten Months.* Surrey, UK: Air Research, 1988.

Forrester, L. *Fly for Your Life*. New York: Bantam Books, 1956 (reprint).

Franks, N. *The Greatest Air Battle: Dieppe, 19th August 1942*. London: Wm. Kimber, 1979.

———. *The Air Battle of Dunkirk*. London: Wm. Kimber, 1984.

———. *The Battle of the Airfields: 1st January 1945*. London: Wm. Kimber, 1984.

Freeman, R. *The Mighty Eighth*. New York: Doubleday, 1970.

———. *Mustang at War*. New York: Doubleday, 1974.

———. *B-17 Fortress at War*. New York: Chas. Scribner's Sons, 1977.

———. *Thunderbolt: A Documentary History of the Republic P-47*. New York: Chas. Scribner's Sons, 1978.

———. *Mighty Eighth War Diary*. London: Jane's, 1981.

———. *Mighty Eighth War Manual*. London: Jane's, 1984.

———. *The Hub: Fighter Leader*. Shrewsbury, UK: Airlife Publishing, 1988.

Fry, G., and Ethell, J. *Escort to Berlin*. New York: Arco, 1980.

Galland, A. *The First and the Last*. London: Methuen, 1955.

Girbig, W. *Six Months to Oblivion*. New York: Hippocrene, 1975.

———. *Mit Kurs auf Leuna*. Stuttgart: Motorbuch, 1980.

———. *Vermisst*. Stuttgart: Motorbuch, 1986.

———. *Im Anflug auf die Reichshauptstadt*. Stuttgart: Motorbuch, 1975.

Godfrey, J. *The Look of Eagles*. New York: Ballantine, 1958 (reprint).

Goodson, J. *Tumult in the Clouds*. New York: St. Martin's Press, 1983.

Green, W. *Augsburg Eagle*. New York: Doubleday, 1971.

———. *Warplanes of the Third Reich*. New York: Doubleday, 1972.

Groh, R. *The Dynamite Gang*. Fallbrook, CA: Aero, 1983.

Hall, G. *One Thousand Destroyed*. Dallas, TX: Morgan Aviation Books, 1946 (reprint).

Hardesty, V. *Red Phoenix*. London: Arms & Armour Press, 1982.

Hastings, M. *Bomber Command*. New York: The Dial Press, 1979.

Hawkins, I. *Muenster: The Way It Was*. Anaheim, CA: Robinson Typographics, 1984.

Heilmann, W. *I Fought You from the Skies*. New York: Award Books, 1951 (reprint).

Held, W. *Adolf Galland: Ein Fliegerleben in Krieg und Frieden*. Friedberg, Germany: Podzun-Pallas-Verlag, 1983.

Held, W., and Trautloft, H. *Die Gruenherzjaeger*. Friedberg, Germany: Podzun-Pallas-Verlag, 1985.

Hess, W. *P-47 Thunderbolt at War*. New York: Doubleday, 1976.

Hillary, R. *Falling Through Space*. New York: Dell, 1942 (reprint).

Hitchcock, T. *Gustav: Messerschmitt 109G*. Parts 1 and 2. Boylston, MA: Monogram, 1977.

Hodgkinson, C. *Best Foot Forward*. New York: W. W. Norton, 1957.

Hoseason, J. *The Thousand Day Battle*. Lowestoft, UK: Gillingham, 1979.

Houart, V. *Lonely Warrior*. Feltham, UK: Hamyln, 1956 (reprint).

Johnson, C. *History of the Hell Hawks*. Anaheim, CA: Southcoast Type-setting, 1975.

Johnson, J. *Wing Leader*. New York: Ballantine, 1956 (reprint).

———. *Full Circle: The Tactics of Air Fighting 1914–1964*. New York: Ballantine, 1964.

Johnson, R., and Caidin, M. *Thunderbolt*. New York: Ballantine, 1958 (reprint).

Jones, I. *Tiger Squadron*. New York: Award Books, 1954 (reprint).

Knocke, H. *I Flew for the Fuehrer*. New York: Henry Holt, 1953.

Kurowski, F. *Der Luftkrieg ueber Deutschland*. Munich: Wilhelm Heyne, 1977.

Marshall, B. *Angels, Bulldogs & Dragons*. Mesa, AZ: Champlin Fighter Museum, 1985.

Mason, F. *Battle Over Britain*. New York: Doubleday, 1969.

McKee, A. *Strike from the Sky*. London: Souvenir Press, 1960.

Middlebrook, M. *The Schweinfurt-Regensburg Mission*. New York: Chas. Scribner's Sons, 1983.

Mitcham, S. *Men of the Luftwaffe*. Novato, CA: Presidio, 1988.

Murray W. *Luftwaffe*. Baltimore, MD: Nautical & Aviation Publishing, 1985.

Nowarra, H. *Die Bomber Kommen*. Friedberg, Germany: Pallas, 1978.

———. *Die Luftschlacht um England*. Friedberg, Germany: Pallas, 1978.

———. *Geleitzug: Schlachten im Mittelmeer*. Friedberg, Germany: Pallas, 1978.

———. *Die 109*. Stuttgart: Motorbuch, 1979.

———. *Focke-Wulf FW 190—Ta 152*. Stuttgart: Motorbuch, 1987.

Olmsted, M. *The Yoxford Boys*. Fallbrook, CA: Aero, 1971.

Olynyk, F. *USAAF (European Theater) Credits for the Destruction of Enemy Aircraft in Air-to-Air Combat in World War 2.* Bound photocopy available from the author, Aurora, OH, 1987.

Page, G. *Tale of a Guinea Pig.* New York: Bantam Books, 1981.

Payne, M. *Bf 109: Into the Battle.* Surbiton, UK: Air Research Publications, 1987.

Payne, M., and Kit, M. *Les Messerschmitt dans la bataile d'Angleterre.* Paris: Editions Atlas, 1980.

Peaslee, B. *Heritage of Valor.* New York: J. B. Lippincott, 1964.

Potter, J. *Breakout.* New York: Bantam Books, 1970.

Price, A. *Battle Over the Reich.* London: Ian Allen, 1973.

———. *World War II Fighter Conflict.* London: Macdonald and Jane's, 1975.

———. *The Bomber in World War II.* New York: Chas. Scribner's Sons, 1976.

———. *Luftwaffe Handbook.* New York: Chas. Scribner's Sons, 1977.

———. *Focke-Wulf 190 at War.* London: Ian Allen, 1977.

———. *The Hardest Day: The Battle of Britain, 18 August 1940.* New York: Chas. Scribner's Sons, 1979.

Priller, J. *JG 26: Geschichte eines Jagdgeschwaders.* Heidelberg: Kurt Vowinckel Verlag, 1956.

Ramsey, W. *The Battle of Britain Then & Now—Mk. III.* London: Battle of Britain Prints International, 1985.

Rawlings, J. *Fighter Squadrons of the Royal Air Force and Their Aircraft.* London: Macdonald and Jane's, 1969.

Richards, D. *Royal Air Force 1939–1945: Vol. 1: The Fight at Odds.* London: Her Majesty's Stationery Office, 1974.

Richards, D., and Saunders, H. *Royal Air Force 1939–1945: The Fight Avails.* Vol. 2. London: Her Majesty's Stationery Office, 1975.

Ries, K. *Luftwaffen Story 1935–1939.* Mainz, Germany: Verlag Dieter Hoffmann, 1974.

———. *Luftwaffe Embleme 1935–1945.* Mainz, Germany: Verlag Dieter Hoffmann, 1976.

Ring, H., and Girbig, W. *Jagdgeschwader 27.* Stuttgart: Motorbuch, 1971.

Robertson, B. *Lancaster.* London: Harleyford, 1964.

Robinson, A. *Royal Air Force Fighter Squadrons in the Battle of Britain.* London: Arms & Armour Press, 1987.

Rust, K. *The Ninth Air Force in World War II.* Fallbrook, CA: Aero, 1967.

————. *Eighth Air Force Story*. Temple City, CA: Historical Aviation Album, 1978.

————. *Ninth Air Force Story*. Temple City, CA: Historical Aviation Album, 1982.

Rust, K., and Hess, W. *The Slybird Group*. Fallbrook, CA: Aero, 1968.

Ryan, C. *The Longest Day*. New York: Simon & Schuster, 1959.

————. *A Bridge Too Far*. New York: Simon & Schuster, 1974.

Salisbury, H. *The 900 Days*. New York: Harper & Row, 1969.

Saunders, H. *Royal Air Force 1939–1945: The Fight is Won*. Vol. 3. London: Her Majesty's Stationery Office, 1975.

Scutts, J. *Lion in the Sky*. Wellingborough, UK: Patrick Stephens, 1987.

Sharp, C., and Bowyer, M.J.F. *Mosquito*. London: Faber & Faber, 1967.

Shores, C. *Second Tactical Air Force*. Reading, UK: Osprey, 1970.

————. *Duel for the Sky*. Garden City, NY: Doubleday, 1985.

————. *Malta: The Hurricane Years*. London: Grub Street, 1987.

Shores, C., Cull, B., and Malizia, N. *Air War for Yugoslavia, Greece, & Crete*. London: Grub Street, 1987.

Shores, C., and Ring, H. *Fighters over the Desert*. London: Neville Spearman, 1969.

Shores, C., and Williams, C. *Aces High*. London: Neville Spearman, 1966.

Shores, C., Ring, H., and Hess, W. *Fighters over Tunisia*. London: Neville Spearman, 1975.

Sims, E. *American Aces*. New York: Ballantine, 1958 (reprint).

————. *The Greatest Aces*. New York: Ballantine, 1967 (reprint).

————. *The Aces Talk*. New York: Ballantine, 1972 (reprint).

Skawran, P, *Ikaros*. Steinebach, Germany: Luftfahrt-Verlag W. Zuerl, 1969.

Smith, J., and Creek, E. *FW 190D*. Boylston, MA: Monogram, 1986.

Smith, J., and Gallaspy, J. *Luftwaffe Camouflage & Markings*. Vols. 2 and 3. Melbourne, Australia: Kookaburra, 1976.

Spick, M. *Fighter Pilot Tactics*. Cambridge, UK: Patrick Stephens, 1983.

Steiner, E. *King's Cliffe*. Kittanning, PA: 20th Fighter Group Association, 1947 (1983 reprint).

Steinko, J. *The Geyser Gang*. Minneapolis, MN: ROMA Association, 1986.

Swanborough, G., and Green, W. *The Focke-Wulf FW 190*. New York: Arco, 1976.

Thom, W. *The Brotherhood of Courage*. New York: 305th Bomb Group Memorial Association, 1986.

Thomas, C., and Shores, C. *The Typhoon & Tempest Story*. London: Arms & Armour Press, 1988.

Townsend, P. *Duel of Eagles*. New York: Pocket Books, 1971 (reprint).

Vickers, R. *The Liberators from Wendling*. Manhattan, KS: Aerospace Historian, 1977.

Williams, M. *U.S. Army in World War II: Chronology 1941–1945*. Washington, DC: Office of the Chief of Military History, Department of the Army, 1960.

Wood, D., and Dempster, D. *The Narrow Margin*. New York: Paperback Library, 1961 (reprint).

Wood, T., and Gunston, B. *Hitler's Luftwaffe*. London: Salamander, 1977.

Wykeham, P. *Fighter Command*. London: Putnam, 1960.

Yeager, C., and Janos, L. *Yeager*. New York: Bantam Books, 1985.

Ziemke, E. *Stalingrad to Berlin: The German Defeat in the East*. Washington, DC: Office of the Chief of Military History, Department of the Army, 1968.

Zijlstra, G. *Diary of an Air War*. New York: Vantage Press, 1977.

TABLE OF EQUIVALENT RANKS— GERMAN AIR FORCE, U.S. ARMY AIR FORCE, AND ROYAL AIR FORCE

THE SIMILARITIES AND DIFFERENCES AMONG THE RANK STRUCTURES for the three services should be apparent from an examination of the table. The rank abbreviations are those used in the text. They should not be taken as official. The Luftwaffe made extensive use of officer candidate titles, frequently hyphenated with another rank. These titles have been simplified in the text. The philosophy of the Luftwaffe with regard to granting pilots automatic officer's commissions differed from the USAAF and was similar to that of the RAF—a commission was not needed to drive an airplane. Commissioned officers *were* needed for leadership positions, however, and here the Luftwaffe suffered a chronic shorage. In 1939 about one-third of Germany's fighter pilots were commissioned officers. The fraction dropped steadily during the war, until it became common for a Staffel to have no more than one officer on flying status.

TABLE OF EQUIVALENT RANKS

GERMAN AIR FORCE—UNITED STATES ARMY AIR FORCE—ROYAL AIR FORCE

GAF Title	GAF Abbr.	USAAF Title	USAAF Abbr.	RAF Title	RAF Abbr.
COMMISSIONED OFFICERS					
Reichsmarschall					
Generalfeldmarschall		General (5 star)	Gen.	Marshal of the RAF	
Generaloberst	Genobst.	General (4 star)	Gen.	Air Chief Marshal	
General der Flieger	Gen. der Flg.	Lieutenant General	Lt. Gen.	Air Marshal	
Generalleutnant	Genlt.	Major General	Maj. Gen.	Air Vice Marshal	
Generalmajor	Genmaj.	Brigadier General	Brig. Gen.	Air Commodore	Air Cdre.
Oberst	Obst.	Colonel	Col.	Group Captain	Gp. Capt.
Oberstleutnant	Obstlt.	Lieutenant Colonel	Lt. Col.	Wing Commander	Wing Cdr.
Major	Maj.	Major	Maj.	Squadron Leader	Sqd. Ldr.
Hauptmann	Hptm.	Captain	Capt.	Flight Lieutenant	Flt. Lt.
Oberleutnant	Oblt.	First Lieutenant	1st Lt.	Flying Officer	Flg. Off.
Leutnant	Lt.	Second Lieutenant	2nd Lt.	Pilot Officer	Plt. Off.
WARRANT OFFICERS					
Stabsfeldwebel	Stabsfw.	Flight Officer	Flt. Off.	Warrant Officer	Wt. Off.
Oberfaehnrich	Obfhr.	(Sr. Off. Candidate)			

GAF Title	GAF Abbr.	USAAF Title	USAAF Abbr.	RAF Title	RAF Abbr.
NONCOMMISSIONED OFFICERS					
Oberfeldwebel	Obfw.	Master Sergeant	MSgt.	Flight Sergeant	Flt. Sgt.
Faehnrich (Fahnenjunker)	Fhr.	(Officer Candidate)			
Feldwebel	Fw.	Technical Sergeant	TSgt.	Sergeant	Sgt.
Unterfeldwebel	Ufw.	Sergeant	Sgt.		
Unteroffizier	Uffz.	Corporal	Cpl.	Corporal	Cpl.
ENLISTED MEN					
Hauptgefreiter	Hptgefr.			Leading Aircraftsman	
Obergefreiter	Ogfr.			Aircraftsman 1st Cl.	
Gefreiter	Gefr.	Private 1st Class	PFC.	Aircraftsman 2nd Cl.	
Flieger	Flg.	Private	Pvt.		

GLOSSARIES

1. ABBREVIATIONS (NON-GERMAN)

AEAF: Allied Expeditionary Air Force.

ASR: Air-Sea Rescue.

CO: commanding officer.

e/a: enemy aircraft.

ETO: European Theater of Operations.

FAA: Fleet Air Arm.

IFF: Identification—Friend from Foe

POW: prisoner of war.

RAF: Royal Air Force.

RCAF: Royal Canadian Air Force.

SAAF: South African Air Force.

TAF: Tactical Air Force (RAF).

TO: technical officer.

USAAF: U.S. Army Air Force.

2. AVIATION TERMS

(#-#-#): (destroyed-probable-damaged) air claims.

Lufbery: a defensive formation in which two or more aircraft follow each other in a circle for mutual protection. Used generally for any circling combat.

Scramble: a rapid takeoff to intercept enemy aircraft.

Split-S: a half-roll followed by a dive; results in a reversal of direction and the loss of a great deal of altitude. A common means of breaking off combat.

3. AIRCRAFT TYPES

Albacore: Fairey carrier-based biplane torpedo bomber; in British service 1940–1944.

Anson: Avro twin-engined general reconnaissance aircraft; the first RAF monoplane.

Ar 65: Arado biplane fighter; the Luftwaffe's first warplane.

Ar 66: Arado biplane primary trainer; the standard Luftwaffe trainer 1939–1942.

Ar 68: Arado biplane fighter; in first-line Luftwaffe service 1936–1938.

Auster: Taylorcraft lightplane; in service for British army cooperation 1941–1945.

B-17: Boeing four-engined heavy bomber; the Flying Fortress. In USAAF service 1941–1945; Eighth AF mainstay 1942–1945.

B-24: Consolidated four-engined heavy bomber; the Liberator. In USAAF service 1942–1945. The most-produced US airplane (18,500 built).

B-26: Martin twin-engined medium bomber; the Marauder. In USAAF service 1942–1945.

Battle: Fairey single-engined light bomber. A major component of the Royal Air Force in 1940. Underpowered and underarmed. Suffered extremely heavy losses in France and was withdrawn from service as rapidly as possible.

Beaufighter: Bristol twin-engined night fighter and tactical fighter. The RAF's first successful night fighter, and a mainstay of RAF Coastal Command's strike units 1941–1945.

Bf 109: Messerschmitt single-engined fighter (also called Me 109). Most advanced fighter in the world in 1938. 30,000 built. Equipped all of JG 26 from 1938–1941. III/JG 26 was again equipped with Bf 109s between early 1943 and January 1945.

Bf 110: Messerschmitt twin-engined heavy fighter (also called Me 110). Decimated by RAF in Battle of Britain; Luftwaffe withdrew it from Western front.

404

BH 33E: Avia biplane fighter; supplied to Yugoslavia by Czechoslovakia.

Blenheim: Bristol twin-engined light bomber; in RAF service 1938–1942.

Boston: Douglas twin-engined light bomber; produced first for France, RAF; later for USAAF as A-20. Served in Second TAF and US Ninth AF until V-E day.

D 520:   Dewoitine single-engined monoplane fighter; newest French fighter in 1940.

Dakota: Douglas twin-engined transport. RAF version of the USAAF C-47 (military DC-3).

Defiant: Boulton-Paul single-engined monoplane fighter; sole armament a four-gun turret. RAF day service 1939–1940.

Do 17:   Dornier twin-engined medium bomber; in Luftwaffe service 1939–1942.

Do 18:   Dornier twin-engined flying boat; served in Luftwaffe from 1935. Used extensively for air-sea rescue.

Do 217:   Dornier twin-engined medium bomber developed from Do 17; in Luftwaffe service 1942–1945.

FW 190:   Focke-Wulf single-engined fighter. Best fighter in the world when JG 26 introduced it into service in August 1941. Equipped JG 26 1941–1945; 19,500 built.

G-1:   Fokker twin-engined heavy fighter. 1937 Dutch design; 23 in service in 1940.

Gladiator: Gloster single-engined biplane fighter; in RAF home units 1937–1940. Served in the Fleet Air Arm as the Sea Gladiator.

Hawk 75A: Curtiss single-engined monoplane fighter; French export version of USAAF P-36.

He 51:   Heinkel biplane fighter; in Luftwaffe service 1936–1939. Many served in Spain.

He 111:   Heinkel twin-engined medium bomber; in Luftwaffe service 1936–1945.

Hs 123:   Henschel biplane close-support aircraft. Produced to 1938; served Luftwaffe on Eastern front to 1944.

Hs 126:   Henschel single-engined tactical reconnaissance aircraft. Luftwaffe's standard aircraft for this purpose from 1939–1942.

Hurricane: Hawker single-engined monoplane fighter; in RAF home units 1937–1943. The RAF's predominant fighter during the Battle of Britain.

I-15: Polikarpov single-engined biplane fighter. A standard Russian fighter 1935–1939; saw extensive use in Spain.

I-153: Polikarpov single-engined biplane fighter; an improved I-15. USSR used 1939–1941.

I-16: Polikarpov single-engined monoplane fighter; innovative in 1933. Standard USSR fighter 1935–1943.

Il-2: Ilyushin single-engined monoplane ground attack aircraft; the *Shturmovik*. Heavily armored; in USSR service 1941–1945. Greatest production of any aircraft in history; 36,000 built.

Ju 52: Junkers tri-motor transport; standard Luftwaffe transport throughout war.

Ju 87: Junkers single-engined dive-bomber. The Luftwaffe's dreaded Sturmkampfflugzeug (Stuka). Withdrawn from West after Battle of Britain.

Ju 88: Junkers twin-engined medium bomber. Successful as night fighter. In Luftwaffe service 1940–1945; 15,000 built.

Kl 35: Klemm single-engined trainer; a standard Luftwaffe primary trainer.

La-5: Lavochkin single-engined monoplane fighter. Low-altitude; USSR service 1942–1945.

LaGG-3: Lavochkin single-engined monoplane fighter. In USSR service 1941–1942. Unsuccessful.

Lancaster: Avro four-engined heavy bomber. Best RAF heavy bomber; in service 1942–1945.

Lysander: Westland single-engined army cooperation aircraft. Suffered heavy losses in France in 1940. Used thereafter for utility and special purposes, including the dropping of agents and supplies to resistance fighters in Occupied Europe.

Maryland: Martin twin-engined reconnaissance bomber. Produced for France, RAF; served in Mediterranean theater to 1942.

MB 152: Bloch single-engined monoplane fighter; limited French service in 1940.

Me 163: Messerschmitt rocket-propelled fighter; the "Komet."

Me 262: Messerschmitt twin-engined jet fighter; the first operational jet aircraft; in Luftwaffe service as bomber and fighter 1944–1945.

Me 410: Messerschmitt twin-engined heavy fighter; in limited Luftwaffe service 1943–1944.

MiG-3: Mikoyan-Gurevich single-engined monoplane fighter; in first-line USSR service 1941–1942. Unsuccessful as an interceptor.

Mosquito: De Havilland twin-engined bomber. Of wooden construction; highly successful as bomber, fighter, reconnaissance aircraft; in RAF service 1941–1945.

MS 406: Morane-Saulnier single-engined monoplane fighter. Standard French fighter in 1940; markedly inferior to Bf 109.

Mustang: North American single-engined monoplane fighter; the P-51. Early version ordered by the RAF; became successful low-altitude reconnaissance fighter.

O-52: Curtiss single-engined monoplane observation aircraft. A few sent to the USSR; no USAAF combat service.

P-38: Lockheed twin-engined monoplane fighter; the Lightning. Failed as a US Eighth AF escort fighter because of engine problems; some in Ninth AF in tactical role to V-E day.

P-39: Bell single-engined monoplane fighter; the Airacobra. Unsuccessful in the USAAF; over half of production was sent to the USSR, where it was a popular low-altitude fighter.

P-40: Curtiss single-engined monoplane fighter; the Warhawk in the USAAF, Tomahawk and Kittyhawk in the RAF. Standard early-war USAAF fighter; some sent to USSR.

P-47: Republic single-engined monoplane fighter; the Thunderbolt. The US Eighth AF's first American escort fighter, it won air supremacy over western Europe before being supplanted by the longer-ranged P-51; it then served the Ninth AF as its principal tactical aircraft.

P-51: North American single-engined monoplane fighter; the Mustang. Entered service in US Eighth AF in late 1943 as a long-range escort fighter; arguably the best all-around performance of any piston-engined WW II fighter.

Pe-2: Petlyakov twin-engined dive-bomber. A mainstay of USSR tactical units 1941–1945.

Skua: Blackburn ship-based monoplane dive-bomber. In British service 1939–1940.

Spitfire: Supermarine single-engined monoplane fighter. In first-line RAF service throughout the war, it equaled the Luftwaffe's best except from mid-1941 through 1942, when it was outmatched by the Bf 109F and the FW 190A; 20,000 built.

Stirling: Short four-engined heavy bomber; the RAF's first monoplane heavy bomber. It served as a bomber 1941–1943, later as a transport and glider tug.

Sunderland: Short four-engined general reconnaissance flying boat; in British service 1938–1945.

Swordfish: Fairey carrier-based open cockpit biplane torpedo bomber; in British service 1936–1945.

T-V: Fokker twin-engined medium bomber. Modern Dutch design; only 16 built.

Tempest: Hawker single-engined monoplane fighter; air superiority fighter in British Second TAF from late 1944–1945.

Tomahawk: Curtiss single-engined monoplane fighter; the P-40B. Saw much RAF use in North Africa; limited use in UK as reconnaissance fighter 1941–1942.

Typhoon: Hawker single-engined monoplane fighter; served in low-altitude intercept role in UK 1942–1944. It became the standard Second TAF close-support aircraft.

Ventura: Lockheed twin-engined light bomber. Developed from Hudson reconnaissance bomber/transport. Used by RAF in UK as light bomber 1942–1943; unsuccessful.

Wellington: Vickers twin-engined medium bomber. Best RAF early-war bomber; served 1939–1943.

Yak-3: Yakovlev single-engined monoplane fighter. High-altitude variant of the Yak fighter series. Probably best USSR fighter; in service from late 1943.

Yak-7b: Yakovlev single-engined monoplane fighter. Low-altitude fighter and fighter-bomber; in front-line USSR service 1942–1944.

4. GERMAN TERMS

Abschuss: "shootdown"—an air victory.

Alarmstart: scramble.

Ami: slang for American.

Blitzkrieg: "lightning war"—the highly mobile form of warfare practiced by the Wehrmacht between 1939 and 1941; featured close cooperation between armored and air forces.

dicke Autos: "fat cars"—enemy heavy bombers.

Einsatzfreude: love of combat.

Einsatzstaffel: operational Staffel (of a training unit).

Endausbildungsstaffel: operational training squadron.

endgueltige Vernichtung: final destruction of an already-culled aircraft.

Ergaenzungsgruppe (ErgGr): advanced training group.

Ergaenzungsstaffel (ErgSt): advanced training squadron.

Erprobungsgruppe (EprGr): operational test group.

Erprobungsstaffel (EprSt): operational test squadron.

Experte: a fighter pilot proficient in aerial combat; the Allied "ace."

Fliegerdivision (FD): air division—a higher command containing several types of flying unit.

Fliegerfuehrer (Flifue): aircraft command/control unit or its commander. In the case of isolated theaters, the theater air commander.

Fliegerkorps (FK): air corps—a higher command containing several Fliegerdivisionen.

Flugzeugfuehrer: pilot.

freie Jagd: "free hunt"—a fighter sweep without ground control.

Fuehrer: leader.

Fuehrungsstaffel: leader's squadron.

Fuehrungsverband: lead formation.

General der Jagdflieger (GdJ): General of the Fighter Arm; a staff position in the RLM. Werner Moelders and Adolf Galland were the most prominent holders of the position.

Geschwader: wing (pl. **Geschwader**)—the largest mobile, homogeneous Luftwaffe flying unit.

Geschwaderkommodore: wing commodore—usually a Major, Oberstleutnant, or Oberst in rank.

Gruppe (Gr): group (pl. **Gruppen**)—the basic Luftwaffe combat and administrative unit.

409

Gruppenkommandeur: group commander— usually a Hauptmann, Major, or Oberstleutnant in rank.

Herausschuss: "shoot-out" (cull)—to damage a bomber sufficiently to separate it from its formation.

Himmelfahrtskommando: "mission to heaven"—a suicide mission.

Holzauge: "wooden eye"—the last airplane in a formation.

Horrido: hunters' or pilots' cry of victory. St. Horridus was the patron saint of hunters and fighter pilots.

Indianer: "Indians"—enemy fighters.

Jabostaffel: fighter-bomber squadron.

Jaeger: originally, a hunter, now also a fighter pilot.

Jaegerschreck: "fear of fighters"—a derogatory term coined in Goering's headquarters.

Jagdbomber (Jabo): fighter-bomber.

Jagddivision (JD): fighter division; could command one or more Jafue or Jagdgeschwader.

Jagdflieger: fighter pilot(s).

Jagdfliegerfuehrer (Jafue): fighter command/control unit or its commander. The Jafue originated as administrative units but evolved into operational control units during the war.

Jagdgeschwader (JG): fighter wing, commanding three or four Gruppen. The authorized strength of JG 26 ranged from 124 to 208 fighters during the war.

Jagdgruppe (JGr): fighter group, containing three or four Staffeln. The authorized strength of a JG 26 Gruppe ranged from forty to sixty-eight fighters during the war.

Jagdkorps (JK): fighter corps; commanded one or more Jagddivisionen.

Jagdschutz: "fighter protection"—generally, a patrol of a section of front, rather than an escort mission.

Jagdstaffel: fighter squadron, originally containing twelve aircraft (three Schwaerme). Its authorized strength was increased to sixteen aircraft in 1943.

Jagdverband (JV): fighter unit. The term was only used for JV 44, the Gruppe of jet fighters commanded by General Adolf Galland in 1945.

Jagdwaffe: fighter arm or fighter force.

Kampfgeschwader (KG): bomber wing.

Kanalfront: the (English) Channel front.

Kanalgeschwader: the Geschwader serving on the English Channel (JG 2 and JG 26).

Kanaljaeger: fighter pilot(s) based near the Channel.

Kapitaen: "captain"—a Staffel command position rather than a rank.

Katschmarek: a slang term for a wingman—originally a derogatory term for a dim-witted infantry recruit.

Kette: flight of three aircraft.

Kommandeur: "commander"—a Gruppe command position rather than a rank.

Kommodore: "commodore"—a Geschwader command position rather than a rank.

Luftflotte (LF): "air fleet"—corresponded to a numbered American Air Force.

Luftwaffe: "Air Force"—refers to the German Air Force.

Luftwaffenkommando (Lkdo): air command—a small or downgraded Luftflotte.

Nachtjagdkommando: night fighting detachment.

Nachwuchs: "new growth"—a late-war replacement pilot.

Oberwerkmeister: line chief.

Pulk: combat box—an American heavy bomber formation.

Reich: "empire"—Hitler's Germany was the Third Reich.

Reichsluftfahrtministerium (RLM): German Air Ministry; Goering's headquarters, it controlled all aspects of German aviation.

Reichsverteidigung (RVT): organization responsible for the air defense of Germany.

Rotte: tactical element of two aircraft.

Rottenflieger: wingman; the second man in a Rotte.

Rottenfuehrer: leader of an element of two aircraft.

Schlageter: JG 26's honor title; commemorated Albert Leo Schlageter.

Schnellkampfgeschwader (SKG): fast bomber wing (contained Bf 110, Bf 109, and/or FW 190 fighter-bombers).

Schwarm: flight of four aircraft (pl. **Schwaerme**); all German fighter formations were made up of units of Schwaerme.

Schwarmfuehrer: flight leader.

Schutzstaffel (SS): "protection squad"—originally Hitler's body-guard, the SS grew into an army of 600,000 men (the Waffen SS), totally independent of the Wehrmacht.

Sitzkrieg: "sitting war"—the "phony war" in western Europe between September 1939 and April 1940.

Stab: staff.

Stabsschwarm: staff flight.

Staffel (St): squadron (pl. **Staffeln**).

Staffelfuehrer: squadon leader (temporary or probationary).

Staffelkapitaen: squadron leader—usually a Leutnant, Oberleutnant, or Hauptmann.

Stukageschwader (StG): dive-bomber wing.

Sturmabteilung (SA): storm troopers—Hitler's private military force; downgraded (violently) after Hitler became president of Germany in 1934.

Tommy: German slang for Englishman.

Valhalla: a large formation of aircraft.

Wehrmacht: armed forces—refers to the German Armed Forces.

Zerstoerer: "destroyer" (heavy fighter)—Bf 110 or Me 410 twin-engined fighter.

Zerstoerergeschwader (ZG): heavy fighter wing.

Zerstoerergruppe (ZGr): heavy fighter group.

JG 26 TABLES OF ORGANIZATION

JAGDGESCHWADER 132 "SCHLAGETER"—ORGANIZATION AND ESTABLISHMENT
8 JANUARY 1939

Unit & Commander	Base	Aircraft Type	Aircraft* Auth	Aircraft* Str	Aircraft* Serv	Pilots† Auth	Pilots† Str	Pilots† Avail
Stab Obst. Eduard von Schleich	Duesseldorf							
I. Gruppe Hptm. Gotthardt Handrick	Koeln-Ostheim	Bf 109E Bf 109B	39 19	24 19	24	39	39	34
1st St. Oblt. Franz Hoernig 2nd St. Oblt. Walter Kienitz 3rd St. Oblt. W. von. Houwald								
II. Gruppe Hptm. Werner Palm	Duesseldorf	Bf 109E Ef 109D	42 27	7 24	6	42	37	27
4th St. Oblt. Eduard Neumann 5th St. Oblt. Herwig Knueppel 6th St. Oblt. Alfred Pomaska								

* Aircraft Auth, Str, Serv: Aircraft Authorized, On Strength, Serviceable
† Pilots Auth, Str, Avail: Pilots Authorized, On Strength, Available for Duty

413

JAGDGESCHWADER 26 "SCHLAGETER"—ORGANIZATION AND ESTABLISHMENT 30 SEPTEMBER 1939

Unit & Commander	Base	Aircraft Type	Aircraft			Pilots		
			Auth	Str	Serv	Auth	Str	Avail
Stab Obst. Eduard von Schleich	Bonn-Odendorf	Bf 109E	3	3	3	3	3	3
I. Gruppe Maj. Gotthardt Handrick	Bonn-Odendorf	Bf 109E	48	42	36	39	36	35
1st St. Oblt. Franz Hoernig 2nd St. Oblt. Fritz Losigkeit 3rd St. Oblt. Johannes Seifert								
II. Gruppe Hptm. Herwig Knueppel	Boenninghardt	Bf 109E	48	39	36	39	36	28
4th St. Oblt. Karl Ebbighausen 5th St. Oblt. H. von Bonin 6th St. Oblt. Alfred Pomaska								
III. Gruppe Hptm. Walter Kienitz	Werl	Bf 109E	39	45	20	39	34	27
7th St. Oblt. Georg Beyer 8th St. Oblt. Eduard Neumann 9th St. Oblt. Gerhard Schoepfel								
10th (Nacht) Staffel Oblt. Johannes Steinhoff	Bonn-Hangelar	Bf 109D Ar 66	12 6	14 6	12 3	12	11	11

JAGDGESCHWADER 26 "SCHLAGETER"—ORGANIZATION AND ESTABLISHMENT
29 JUNE 1940

Unit & Commander	Base	Aircraft Type	Aircraft			Pilots		
			Auth	Str	Serv	Auth	Str	Avail
Stab Maj. Gotthardt Handrick	Dortmund	Bf 109E	4	2	0	4	2	2
I. Gruppe Hptm. Kurt Fischer	Boenninghardt	Bf 109E	39	29	22	39	37	22
1st St. Oblt. Franz Hoernig 2nd St. Oblt. Fritz Losigkeit 3rd St. Oblt. Johannes Seifert								
II. Gruppe Hptm. Erich Noack	Dortmund	Bf 109E	39	35	16	39	34	30
4th St. Hptm. Kurt Ebbighausen 5th St. Oblt. H. von Holtey 6th St. Oblt. Walter Schneider								
III. Gruppe Hptm. Adolf Galland	Muenchen-Gladbach	Bf 109E	39	32	25	39	34	30
7th St. Oblt. Georg Beyer 8th St. Oblt. Kuno Wendt 9th St. Oblt. Gerhard Schoepfel								

415

JAGDGESCHWADER 26 "SCHLAGETER"—ORGANIZATION AND ESTABLISHMENT 28 SEPTEMBER 1940

Unit & Commander	Base	Aircraft Type	Aircraft			Pilots		
			Auth	Str	Serv	Auth	Str	Avail
Stab Maj. Adolf Galland	Audembert	Bf 190E	4	4	2	4	3	1
I. Gruppe Hptm. Rolf Pingel	Audembert	Bf 109E	39	32	27	39	30	24
1st St. Oblt. Eberhard Henrici 2nd St. Oblt. Fritz Losigkeit 3rd St. Oblt. Johannes Seifert								
II. Gruppe Hptm. Erich Bode	Marquise	Bf 109E	39	34	26	39	31	20
4th St. Oblt. Kurt Ebersberger 5th St. Oblt. Wolfgang Kosse 6th St. Oblt. Walter Schneider								
III. Gruppe Hptm. Gerhard Schoepfel	Caffiers	Bf 109E	39	31	26	39	24	20
7th St. Oblt. J. Muencheberg 8th St. Oblt. Gustav Sprick 9th St. Oblt. Heinz Ebeling								

JAGDGESCHWADER 26 "SCHLAGETER"—ORGANIZATION AND ESTABLISHMENT 28 JUNE 1941

Unit & Commander	Base	Aircraft Type	Aircraft			Pilots		
			Auth	Str	Serv	Auth	Str	Avail
Stab Obstlt. Adolf Galland	Audembert	Bf 109E-4/N Bf 109F-2	4 0	2 3	1 0	4	4	3
I. Gruppe Hptm. Rolf Pingel	St. Omer-Clairmairais	Bf 109E-7	40	21	19	40	33	25
1st St. Oblt. Josef Priller 2nd St. Oblt. Martin Rysavy 3rd St. Hptm. Johannes Seifert								
II. Gruppe Hptm. Walter Adolph	Maldegem	Bf 109E-7	40	30	23	40	32	25
4th St. Oblt. Kurt Ebersberger 5th St. Oblt. Wolfgang Kosse 6th St. Oblt. Walter Schneider								
III. Gruppe Hptm. Gerhard Schoepfel	Liegescourt	Bf 109F-2	43	39	16	40	27	24
7th St. Oblt. J. Muencheberg 8th St. Oblt. Gustav Sprick 9th St. Oblt. Kurt Ruppert	(N. Africa)							

417

JAGDGESCHWADER 26 "SCHLAGETER"—ORGANIZATION AND ESTABLISHMENT 27 DECEMBER 1941

Unit & Commander	Base	Aircraft Type	Aircraft			Pilots		
			Auth	Str	Serv	Auth	Str	Avail
Stab Maj. Gerhard Schoepfel	Audembert	FW 190A-2	4	4	3	4	5	4
I. Gruppe Hptm. Johannes Seifert	St. Omer-Arques	FW 190A-2 Bf 109F-4	40	41 29	7 24	40	50	29
1st St. Oblt. Josef Haiboeck 2nd St. Oblt. Christian Eickhoff 3rd St. Oblt. Walter Otte								
II. Gruppe Hptm. Joachim Muencheberg	Abbeville-Drucat	FW 190A-2	40	36	28	40	46	31
4th St. Oblt. Kurt Ebersberger 5th St. Oblt. Wolfgang Kosse 6th St. Oblt. Otto Brehens								
III. Gruppe Hptm. Josef Priller	Coquelles	FW 190A-2	40	33	27	40	38	38
7th St. Oblt. Klaus Mietusch 8th St. Oblt. Karl Borris 9th St. Oblt. Kurt Ruppert								

JAGDGESCHWADER 26 "SCHLAGETER"—ORGANIZATION AND ESTABLISHMENT 31 DECEMBER 1942

Unit & Commander	Base	Aircraft Type	Aircraft			Pilots		
			Auth	Str	Serv	Auth	Str	Avail
Stab Maj. Gerhard Schoepfel	St. Omer-Wizernes	FW 190A-4	4	5	5	4	4	2
I. Gruppe Hptm. Johannes Seifert	St. Omer-Ft. Rouge	FW 190A-4	40	34	23	40	43	27
1st St. Oblt. Franz Nels 2nd St. Oblt. Fuelbert Zink 3rd St. Oblt. Rolf Hermichen								
II. Gruppe Hptm. Conny Meyer	Abbeville-Drucat	FW 190A-4 Bf 109G-4	40	33 11	26 7	40	53	28
4th St. Hptm. Kurt Ebersberger 5th St. Oblt. Wilhelm Galland 6th St. Oblt. Hans Naumann								
III. Gruppe Hptm. Josef Priller	Wevelghem	Bf 109G-4 Bf 109G-1/R2 FW 190A	40	2 1 35	2 0 29	40	48	35
7th St. Hptm. Klaus Mietusch 8th St. Oblt. Karl Borris 9th St. Hptm. Kurt Ruppert								
10th (Jabo) St. Oblt. Paul Keller	St. Omer-Wizernes	FW 190A-4/U3	15	14	13	15	13	12
11th (Hoehen) St. (1 December) Oblt. Hans Westphal	N. Africa	Bf 109G-1	15	12	8	15	10	0

JAGDGESCHWADER 26 "SCHLAGETER"—ORGANIZATION AND ESTABLISHMENT
31 DECEMBER 1943

Unit & Commander	Base	Aircraft Type	Aircraft Auth	Str	Serv	Pilots Auth	Str	Avail
Stab Obstlt. Josef Priller	Lille-Nord	FW 190A-6	4	4	3	4	3	2
I. Gruppe Hptm. Karl Borris	Florennes	FW 190A-6	68	38	27	68	63	42
1st St. Oblt. Artur Beese 2nd St. Oblt. Karl Willius 3rd St. Oblt. Heinrich Jessen 4th St. Hptm. Wolfgang Neu								
II. Gruppe Hptm. Wilhelm Gaeth	Cambrai-Epinoy	FW 190A-6	68	32	20	68	65	38
5th St. Hptm. Johann Aistleitner 6th St. Hptm. Horst Sternberg 7th St. Hptm. Hans Naumann 8th St. Hptm. Rudolf Leuschel								
III. Gruppe Hptm. Klaus Mietusch	Muenchen-Gladbach	Bf 109G-6	68	26	18	68	54	25
9th St. Hptm. Hans-Georg Dippel 10th St. Hptm. Paul Schauder 11th St. Hptm. Paul Steindl 12th St. Hptm. Hermann Staiger								

JAGDGESCHWADER 26 "SCHLAGETER"—ORGANIZATION AND ESTABLISHMENT 30 JUNE 1944

Unit & Commander	Base	Aircraft Type	Aircraft Auth	Str	Serv	Pilots Auth	Str	Avail
Stab Obstlt. Josef Priller	Chaumont	FW 190A-8	4	3	1	4	4	2
I. Gruppe Hptm. Hermann Staiger	Boissy le Bois	FW 190A-8	68	24	10	68	50	39
1st St. Oblt. Max Groth 2nd St. Oblt. Franz Kunz 3rd St. Oblt. Alfred Heckmann 4th St. Lt. Heinz Kemethmueller								
II. Gruppe Hptm. Emil Lang	Guyancourt	FW 190A-8	68	14	6	68	43	23
5th St. Hptm. Walter Matoni 6th St. Oblt. Adolf Glunz 7th St. Lt. Gerhard Vogt 8th St. Lt. Wilhelm Hofmann								
III. Gruppe Maj. Klaus Mietusch	Villacoublay	Bf 109G-6	68	31	18	68	55	36
9th St. Oblt. Viktor Hilgendorff 10th St. Hptm. Paul Schauder 11th St. Oblt. Peter Reischer 12th St. Oblt. Karl Schrader								

JAGDGESCHWADER 26 "SCHLAGETER"—ORGANIZATION AND ESTABLISHMENT 31 DECEMBER 1944

Unit & Commander	Base	Aircraft Type	Aircraft Auth	Aircraft Str	Aircraft Serv	Pilots Auth	Pilots Str	Pilots Avail
Stab Obstlt. Josef Priller	Fuerstenau-Handrup	FW 190A-8 FW 190D-9	4	1 2	0 1	4	4	1
I. Gruppe Maj. Karl Borris	Fuerstenau-Handrup	FW 190A-8 FW 190D-9	68	3 49	0 32	68	52	41
1st St. Lt. Georg Kiefner 2nd St. Oblt. Franz Kunz 3rd St. Oblt. Alfred Heckmann 4th St. Lt. Waldemar Soeffing								
II. Gruppe Maj. Anton Hackl	Nordhorn-Clausheide	FW 190D-9	68	39	32	68	50	41
5th St. Oblt. Gerhard Vogt 6th St. Oblt. Adolf Glunz 7th St. Oblt. Waldemar Radener 8th St. Oblt. Wilhelm Hofmann								
III. Gruppe Hptm. Walter Krupinski	Plantluenne	Bf 109G-14 Bf 109K-4 FW 190D-9	68	14 29 1	7 13 1	68	40	29
9th St. Oblt. Gottfried Schmidt 10th St. Hptm. Paul Schauder 11th St. Lt. Hermann Guhl 12th St. Oblt. Karl Schrader								

| | | | Aircraft | | | | Pilots | |
			Auth	Str	Serv	Auth	Str	Avail
III/JG 54 (no Kommandeur) 9th St. Oblt. Willi Heilmann 10th St. Lt. Peter Crump 11th St. Lt. Hans Prager 12th St. Oblt. Hans Dortenmann	Varrelbusch	FW 190D-9	68	49	32	68	51	44

JAGDGESCHWADER 26 "SCHLAGETER"—ORGANIZATION AND ESTABLISHMENT
9 APRIL 1945

| Unit & Commander | Base | Aircraft Type | Aircraft | | | Pilots | | |
			Auth	Str	Serv	Auth	Str	Avail
Stab Maj. Franz Goetz	Uetersen	FW 190D-9	4	4	3	4	4	n/a*
I. Gruppe Maj. Karl Borris 1st St. Lt. Georg Kiefner 2nd St. Lt. Waldemar Soeffing 3rd St. Oblt. Hans Dortenmann	Stade	FW 190D-9	52	44	16	52	34	n/a
II. Gruppe Hptm. Paul Schauder 5th St. Oblt. Alfred Heckmann 6th St. Oblt. Gottfried Schmidt 7th St. Lt. Gottfried Dietze	Uetersen	FW 190D-9	52	57	29	52	n/a	n/a
IV. Gruppe Maj. Rudolf Klemm 13th St. Lt. Peter Crump 14th St. Lt. Hans Prager	Kleinskummers- felde	FW 190D-9	36	35	15	36	29†	21†

* n/a = data not available
† data for 20 April

JAGDGESCHWADER 26
VICTORY CLAIMS

A STATISTICAL
SUMMARY

RESEARCH INTO LUFTWAFFE VICTORY CLAIMS IS HAMPERED BY A LACK
of official records. At the end of the war, the Luftwaffe destroyed its
master list of victory confirmations. JG 26 filed about 2,700 claims
with the RLM for enemy aircraft destroyed or separated from formation. It frequently took more than a year for confirmations to be
awarded by Berlin, and the system apparently broke down entirely
early in 1945. Based on the available data, 10 to 20 percent of the
claims received by the RLM were rejected. However, as is made
clear in the text, JG 26's claims were for the most part quite accurate. Thus the graph has been based on "claims" rather than "confirmed claims." We are fortunate in having the claims lists for the
First and Second Gruppen for the entire war, and nearly all of the
claims of the Geschwaderstab. Although details of several hundred
Third Gruppe claims are available, no complete list exists for the
Gruppe, and no post-1940 claims totals for the Gruppe have been
located. However, "milestone" claims totals for the Geschwader (for
example, 2,000, 2,500) were widely reported, and these have been
used to estimate the Third Gruppe's claims totals for the graph.

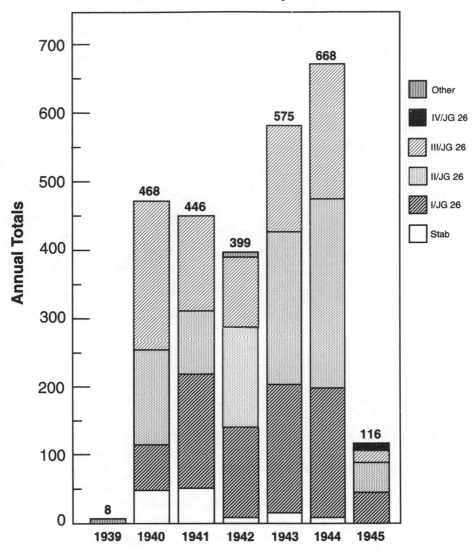

JAGDGESCHWADER 26 "SCHLAGETER"
1939-1945 Air Victory Claims

Other=10(Nacht)/,10(Jabo)/,11(Hoehen)/JG26

JAGDGESCHWADER 26 CASUALTIES

A STATISTICAL SUMMARY

THE RECORDS OF THE WEHRMACHT'S WORLD WAR II CASUALTIES are maintained by the Deutsche Dienststelle, the German personnel bureau in Berlin, and are fairly complete. The files of men still carried as missing are kept open, and they are corrected as remains are located and correctly identified. According to the official records, Jagdgeschwader 26 lost 763 pilots killed or missing in the war; another sixty-seven pilots were captured. Of the fatalties, 631 were lost in combat and 132 were killed in accidents. Records of injuries are less comprehensive, but it is known that more than 300 JG 26 pilots were wounded in combat, and more than 100 were injured in flying accidents. Some of these men were put back on flying status within days, but many never returned to combat.

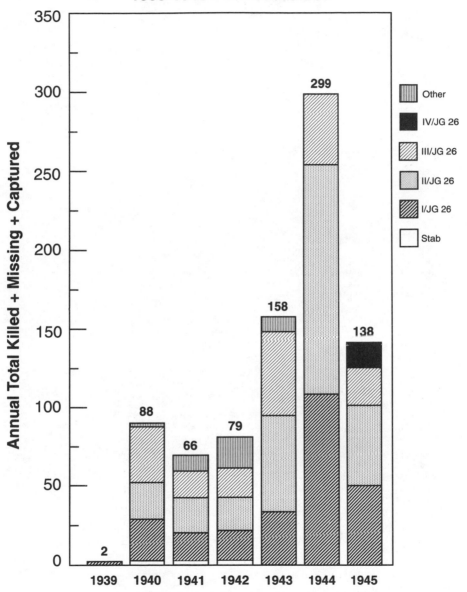

JAGDGESCHWADER 26 "SCHLAGETER"
1939-1945 Pilot Casualties

Other=ErgSt/,10(Jabo)/,11(Hoehen)/JG26

INDEX

Abbeville Kids, *see* JG 26 (Schlageter)
Adlerangriff (Eagle Attack), 35–59
  Adlertag in, 35–41
  Black Thursday in, 41–45
  Defiants air battle in, 50–53
  "hardest day" of, 45–50
  onset of, 35–37
  III Gruppe's role in, 53–59
Adlertag, 38–41
Adolph, Hptm. Walter, 66, 99, 101
Air Ministry, German (RLM), 84, 164,
  180, 183, 225, 236, 243, 275
Albrecht, Uffz., 372, 384
Aldecoa, Lt. Manual, 206
Allen, Plt. Off. Johnny, 32
Arado Ar 65, 2, 3, 6–7
Arado Ar 66, 11
Arado Ar 68, 3, 11
Ardennes offensive, 311–16, 353
Argument, Operation, 219–26
Ark Royal, 75, 76, 78
Armstrong, Brig. Gen. Frank, 168
Ash, Flt. Lt., 51
Austin, Capt. James, 278–79
Avia BH 33E, 76
Avro Lancaster, 258
Ayerle, Uffz. Hermann, 296

Babenz, Fhr. Emil, 232–33
Bader, Douglas, 100–101
Bartels, Oblt. Werner, 32
Baseplate, Operation (Unternehmen
  Bodenplatte), 323–42

assessment of, 340–42
first Evere attack in, 331–37
Grimbergen attack in, 325–31
preparation for, 323–24
second Evere attack in, 338–40
Battle of Britain, 29–71
  JG 26 victories and losses in, 69–71
  turning point of, 61–62
  see also Adlerangriff
Battle of the Bulge, 311–16, 353
Battmer, TO. Ernst, 156, 284
Beckham, Capt. Walter, 199, 217
Beese, Oblt. Artur, 178, 219
Behrens, Oblt. Otto, 98, 99
Belgian Air Force, 16, 116
Bell P-39 Aircobra, 145
Berg, Hptm. Ernst Freiherr von, 11,
  26–27
Berkeley, 127
Berlin raids, 226–31
Beyer, Oblt. Georg, 49, 52
Beyer, Lt. William, 291–92
Big Week, 219–26
Binnebose, William, 186
Bismarck, 86
Black Friday, 279
Black Thursday, 41–45
Blitz Week, 181–84
Bloch MB 152, 16–17, 18
Bloemertz, Oblt. Guenther, 344–45
Blume, Oblt. Walter, 47
Bock, Genobst. Fedor von, 17, 19, 22
Bode, Hptm. Erich, 45, 58, 66

Boeing B-17 Flying Fortress, 126
  fighter tactics vs., 139–41
  survivability of, 133–34
  typical interception of, 131–33
Bomber Command, RAF, 13–14, 29, 111,
  197
Borreck, Uffz. Hans-Joachim, 281–283,
  306–7
Borris, Maj. Karl, 21, 66, 132, 140–41,
  165, 178, 181, 196, 211, 216, 224,
  231, 254, 257, 260, 287, 294–95,
  306, 343, 347, 349, 350, 353, 357,
  361–62, 367, 371, 374, 375, 377, 382
  Baseplate Operation and, 324–25, 326,
  327, 329–30, 331, 333
  downing of, 20–21, 172
  8th Staffel command given to, 102
  I Gruppe command given to, 174
  FW 190 evaluated by, 98–99
  Knight's Cross awarded to, 310
  missions described by, 20, 38–39
  personality of, 185, 300–301
  at war's end, 390–91
Boulton Paul Defiant, 19–20, 21, 24–25
Bristol Beaufighter, 81
Bristol Blenheim, 15, 87, 98, 156
British Expeditionary Force (BEF), 18, 19,
  23
Broadhurst, Air Vice Marshal Harry, 214
Brooke, Gen. Alan, 129
Brooks, Lt. George, 267
Buchmann, Matthias, 79, 81
Buerschgens, Lt. Joseph "Jupp," 11–12,
  15, 27–28, 33, 36, 43–44, 49, 57–58,
  71
Buffalo, Operation, 147
Busch, Oblt. Erwin, 153

Carpenter, Maj. George, 222
Causin, Hptm. Viktor "Pappi," 25
Channel Dash, 110–13
Churchill, Winston, 115, 116
Circus missions, 87, 98, 116
  fighter deployment in, 88–89
  No. 1, 87
  No. 14, 88
  No. 29, 93
  No. 108A, 102
  No. 110, 103
  No. 178, 117
  No. 200, 123
Clark, Capt. McCauley, 281
Coastal Command, RAF, 88
Cobra, Operation, 260
Conrad, Lt., 389
Consolidated B-24 Liberator, 131

  fighter tactics vs., 139–141
Cramer, Lt. Daniel, 282–83
Crossley, Sqd. Ldr. Mike, 47
Crump, Oblt. Peter, 123, 127, 160,
  205–6, 238, 316, 353, 356, 381
  B-17 downed by, 172
  B-24 attacked by, 161–62
  Baseplate Operation and, 326, 327–28,
  331
  Big Week and, 220–23
  Dieppe raid witnessed by, 124–25
  in double victory incident, 157–59
  Dueren raid and, 202–3
  life in JG 26 described by, 121–22
  missions recollected by, 162–63, 366,
  374–75
  on morale, 351
  Spitfire downed by, 130
  transferred to JG 54, 256
  Typhoon downed by, 196
Curtiss Hawk 75A, 11, 17, 18–19, 22
Curtiss O-52 Owl, 147
Curtiss P-40B Tomahawk, 81
Curtiss P-40C Tomahawk, 144, 145

D-Day, 242–53
Deere, Sq. Ldr. Al, 42, 43, 118–19
de Havilland Mosquito, 156, 204–5
Demyansk salient, 144–45, 147
Dewoitine D520, 16
Dieppe Raid, 124–29
Dietze, Lt. Gottfried, 349, 363, 378, 383
Dinort, Hptm. Oskar, 1, 2, 3
Dippel, Hptm. Hans-Georg, 186–87,
  239
Doering, Obst. von, 17
Doolittle, Lt. Gen. James, 214–15, 218,
  228, 239
Dornier Do 17, 25, 36–37
Dornier Do 18, 54
Dornier Do 217, 125, 126, 128
Dortenmann, Lt. Hans, 316, 321, 326,
  354, 356, 374, 375, 381–83, 387,
  388, 390
Douglas, Air Marshal Sholto, 86, 94, 98,
  104, 114, 116, 119, 125
Douglas Boston, 107, 156
Dowding, Air Chief Marshal Hugh, 30–
  31, 48, 59, 61
Dueren raid, 202–4
Dunkirk evacuation, 23–26
Dutch Air Force, 16, 21

Eaker, Gen. Ira, 215
Ebbighausen, Oblt. Karl, 21, 22, 24, 33,
  37, 38, 39–40, 44–45, 71

429

Ebeling, Oblt. Heinz, 48, 53–54, 57, 65, 71
Ebersberger, Oblt. Kurt, 103, 178, 204
Eder, Hptm. Georg-Peter, 274, 285, 350
Egli, Fw. Guenther, 329–30
Eisenhower, Gen. Dwight D., 214, 239
Ellenrieder, Lt. Xaver, 146, 295
Esmonde, Lt. Cmdr. Eugene, 112–113

Fairbanks, Sqd. Ldr. D. C. "Foob," 355, 356
Fairey Albacore, 61
Fairey Swordfish, 112–13
Falling Through Space (Hillary), 58
Fighter Command, RAF, 34, 52, 60, 86–87, 114, 129–30, 152, 157, 213
  as Adlerangriff objective, 35, 38, 42, 50
  declining combat skill of, 100, 115
  Dunkirk evacuation and, 23–25
  formations employed by, 31, 88
  Luftwaffe intelligence and, 68
  Market Garden Operation and, 290
  pilot overclaims and, 68, 94
  pilot shortage of, 59
  summer offensive of, 115–19, 123–24
  "finger four" formation, see Schwarm formation
Fink, Obst. Johannes, 30, 33, 34, 36
1st Airborne Division, British, 293
First and the Last, The (Galland), 64–65, 90–91
First Army, Canadian, 343
First Army, U.S., 304, 353, 361
1st Guards Fighter Air Corps, Soviet, 145
1st Parachute Brigade, Polish, 293
Fischer, Hptm. Kurt, 28, 37, 39, 49
Fleet Air Arm, RN, 112, 113
Focke-Wulf FW 190, 98, 101, 128, 138
  armament of, 102–3, 213, 245, 314
  Bf 109 compared with, 354–55
  equipment of, 138–39
  IFF equipment of, 115
  performance of, 213, 254–55, 314
  production of, 102, 244–45
  production variants of, 138–39
  RAF capture of, 328–29
  Spitfire Vb contrasted with, 120
Focke-Wulf FW 190A-1, 99, 103, 115
Focke-Wulf FW 190A-2, 102, 104, 115
Focke-Wulf FW 190A-3, 120, 138
Focke-Wulf FW 190A-3/U3, 114
Focke-Wulf FW 190A-4, 138–39
Focke-Wulf FW 190A-4/U3, 150–51
Focke-Wulf FW 190A-4/U4, 135
Focke-Wulf FW 190A-5, 143
Focke-Wulf FW 190A-6, 213

Focke-Wulf FW 190A-7, 244, 245
Focke-Wulf FW 190A-8, 244–45
Focke-Wulf FW 190A-8/R4, 245
Focke-Wulf FW 190D-9 Dora, 307, 313–14
Focke-Wulf FW 190F Panzerblitze, 388
Fokker, Anthony, 16
Fokker G-1, 21
Fokker T-V, 21
Franco, Francisco, 4
freie Jagd mission, 19, 143
French Air Force, 16–17, 18, 28

Gaeth, Hptm. Wilhelm, 212, 218–19
Galland, Genmaj. Adolf, 36, 40, 45, 49, 52, 54, 61–64, 66, 69, 70, 88, 89, 98, 103, 131, 141, 142, 148, 149, 151, 155, 193, 196, 300, 301, 311, 345, 381
  Bader episode and, 100–101
  Baseplate Operation and, 341
  becomes top scoring pilot, 67
  BF 109 armament experiments of, 101
  Black Thursday and, 42–43
  casualty rates reported by, 237
  Channel Dash planned by, 110–13
  decorations awarded to, 35, 97
  Defiant fighter action recollected by, 51
  downing of, 90–91
  in first combat over England, 32–33
  Goering and, 60, 104
  "great blow" planned by, 294
  "Jaegerschreck" term used by, 236
  joins JG 26, 26–27
  Moelders replaced by, 104
  Muencheberg's correspondence with, 79–80
  "nonstop offensive" and, 90–91
  "private excursions" of, 85–86
  promoted to wing commander, 48
  Schoepfel's replacement of, 104
  in Spanish Civil War, 4–5
Galland, Lt. Paul, 136, 155
Galland, Oblt. Wilhelm-Ferdinand "Wutz," 102, 124, 127, 130, 138, 159, 161, 163, 165, 167
  death of, 190–91, 193–94
  first victory of, 97
  Knight's Cross awarded to, 180
  II Gruppe commanded by, 155
Garvin, Sqd. Ldr., 51
Gehrke, Uffz. Heinz, 229–31, 235–36, 247–48, 258–59, 269–70, 273, 310–11, 340, 354, 355, 356
Geisshardt, Hptm. Fritz, 155, 165, 168

Genth, Uffz. Georg, 297–99, 308–9, 340, 354, 357, 359–60
Girbig, Werner, 218
Gloster Gladiator, 16, 72
Glunz, Oblt. Adolf "Addi," 102, 103, 108, 167, 191, 201, 208, 220, 231, 246, 253, 302, 304, 346
    Baseplate Operation and, 333, 335, 336, 338
    decorations awarded to, 180, 193, 256
    early success of, 98
    Mosquito destroyed by, 204–5
    named 5th Staffel commander, 219
    named 6th Staffel commander, 227
Gneisenau, 85, 110
Goering, Hermann, 2, 19, 26, 35, 45, 48, 59, 64, 131, 197, 237, 294, 311, 350
    combat leaders' flights limited by, 257
    fighter pilots assailed by, 306
    fighter restrictions ordered by, 170, 190
    Galland and, 60, 104
    ground support missions limited by, 296
    "Jaegerschreck" term used by, 236
    Jagdwaffe punished by, 68–69
Goering, Peter, 102
Goetz, Maj. Franz, 349, 389
Gomann, Fw. Heinz, 376, 378
Gottlob, Oblt. Heinz, 91–93
Grabmann, Obst. Walter, 3, 184, 187, 189–90, 198
Great Britain, 21, 29, 59–60, 62, 113
Great London Raid, 150–52
Greim, Genobst. Ritter von, 388, 390
Groos, Hptm., 363, 384–86
Gross, Lt. Alfred, 257, 281–83
Gross, Uffz. Paul, 221–22
Guhl, Lt. Hermann, 301, 339, 389

Hackl, Maj. Anton "Tony," 300, 315, 324, 331, 334, 336, 338, 339, 345–46, 347, 349, 350, 355
Hafer, Lt., 37
Hager, Fw. Robert, 266, 267
Haiboeck, Oblt., 53, 54, 56, 104
Handrick, Obst. Gotthardt, 4, 9, 28, 38, 48
Hartigs, Oblt. Hans, 224, 316–18
Hasselmann, Oblt., 25–26
Hawker Hurricane, 16, 18, 22, 23–25, 27, 87
Hawker Hurricane I, 72, 73
Hawker Hurricane II, 75
Hawker Hurricane IIb, 117
Hawker Tempest, 311
Hawker Typhoon, 114, 156, 213
Heaven Next Stop (Bloemertz), 345

Heckmann, Oblt. Alfred "Fred," 143, 224, 293, 300, 311, 315, 326, 344, 348–49, 367, 374, 375, 381
Hegenauer, Obfw., 90
Heilmann, Oblt. Willi, 316, 320, 326, 356, 371, 377, 386
Heim, Dr., 91, 97
Heinkel He 51, 1–2, 3, 4, 6–7
Heinkel He 111, 24, 26, 128
Henrici, Lt. Eberhard, 21, 40–41, 49, 66, 71
Henschel Hs 123, 5
Henschel Hs 126, 11, 146
Hermichen, Hptm. Rolf, 143, 180
Herzog, Fw. Gerhard, 19
Heuvel, Lt. George van den, 317
Hilgendorff, Oblt. Viktor, 239, 259–60
Hillary, Plt. Off. Richard, 58
Hitler, Adolf, 2, 4, 59, 62, 63, 67, 97, 110, 135, 144, 197, 234, 262, 311, 350
Hoch, Lt. Hermann, 151
Hoeckner, Hptm. Walter, 143, 145
Hofmann, Oblt. Wilhelm, 255, 262–63, 264, 266, 271–72, 286, 287, 289, 293, 304, 332, 333, 334–35, 338, 344, 345, 354, 357–58, 366, 372, 373–74
Holland, Sqd. Ldr., 36
Hoppe, Lt. Helmut, 191, 196, 208
Horten, Oblt., 25–26, 38, 49–50, 51–52, 63
Houwald, Lt. Wolf-Heinrich Freiherr von, 4

I Fought You From the Skies (Heilmann), 326, 377
Illustrious, 72
Ilyushin Il-2 Shturmovik, 144, 145

Jaeckel, Fw. Ernst, 96–97
"Jaegerschreck," 236
Jagdschutz mission, 19
Jauer, Lt. Erich, 147
Jenkins, Lt. Col. Jack, 207
Jeschonnek, Genobst. Hans, 197
JG 26 (Schlageter):
    "Abbeville Kids" epithet of, 67, 119
    Adlerangriff and, 35–36, 38–41
    assigned to 14th Fliegerdivision, 348
    Battle of Britain and, 53, 54, 57–61, 65, 66, 69–71
    Battle of the Bulge and, 311–16
    Baseplate Operation and, 323–41
    Berlin raids and, 226–31
    Big Week and, 219–20, 223, 226

JG 26 (Schlageter) (cont.)
  Black Thursday and, 42, 44
  Blitz Week and, 181–84
  Channel Dash and, 110–13
  command network of, 115–16
  D-Day and, 242–53
  declining combat efficiency of, 178–79
  defensive reorganization of, 196–98
  Dieppe Raid and, 124–29
  Dueren raid and, 202–4
  Dunkirk evacuation and, 23–26
  in first combat over France, 22
  first major air battle of, 18
  in first mission to England, 32
  first victory of, 11
  formation doctrine of, 5–6, 31, 89, 156, 218
  fuel shortage and, 374, 375
  Galland's departure from, 104–5
  Galland's leadership of, 48–49
  Glunz's departure from, 338
  Great London Raid and, 150–52
  "hardest day" and, 45, 47
  Hitler's visit to, 67
  invasion of Poland and, 9, 10
  joins Jagddivision 4, 192–93
  Knight's Cross recipients of, 180
  last bomber interception by, 354
  last fatality of, 388
  last large scale encounter of, 366
  last victory of, 386
  last victory claim of, 389
  Market Garden Operation and, 290–96
  morale in, 350–53
  Muenster raid and, 198–200
  1943 victory credits of, 210
  "nonstop offensive" and, 89–105
  official establishment of, 6–7
  pilot attrition in, 241
  pilot quality of, 119–20, 219
  political officers in, 350
  predecessor units of, 2–4, 6–7
  Priller named commander of, 142
  Priller's departure from, 349
  reconnaissance missions by, 376–380
  reequipped with FW 190, 83–84, 95
  RAF summer offensive and, 116, 119–20, 123–24
  "St. Omer Boys" epithet of, 119
  Schoepfel's departure from, 142, 153–54
  Schweinfurt-Regensburg raid and, 184–91
  second Schweinfurt raid and, 200–202
  Sitzkrieg and, 14–15
  in Spanish Civil War, 4
  2000th victory claim of, 225

  typical bomber interception by, 131–33
  "vengeance attacks" and, 135–38
  Western campaign and, 17–25
  West Wall defense and, 284–85
JG 26, I Gruppe, 30, 86, 88, 90, 91–92, 102, 107, 108, 117–18, 123, 136, 137, 160, 192, 193, 207, 209, 211–14, 216, 217, 232, 233, 237, 238, 240, 262, 274–75, 276, 281, 287, 296–97, 299–300, 302, 304, 309–10, 315–16, 333, 344, 347–49, 353, 357, 366–67, 370–71, 373, 377–78, 382–83, 386, 388
  Adlerangriff and, 35–39
  airfields of, 285, 314, 343, 368, 380
  Battle of Britain and, 35–36, 37, 38, 39, 41, 44, 49, 54, 56, 61, 66, 69
  Berlin raids and, 227–29, 231
  Big Week and, 220
  Blitz Week and, 181–82, 183
  Channel coast bases of, 86, 109, 212
  command changes in, 148, 257
  D-Day and, 242, 244, 245
  Dieppe raid and, 125, 126
  Dunkirk evacuation and, 23–24
  on Eastern Front, 142–45
  French campaign and, 17, 22
  Grimberger airfield attacked by, 325–31
  invasion of Poland and, 9
  last combats of, 389
  Market Garden Operation and, 293, 295, 296
  military discipline in, 350
  Muenster raid and, 198
  Paula Operation and, 26
  reequipment of, 83, 84, 104, 115, 307
  replacement pilots in, 266, 381
  retreat to Germany and, 280, 285
  rocket mortars carried by, 260
  in return from Eastern Front, 174, 177
  Schweinfurt raids and, 184, 186, 189, 201
  Staffels redesignated in, 196
JG 26, II Gruppe, 90, 102, 107, 108, 118, 119, 122, 133, 136, 137, 139, 157, 160, 161, 165, 170–75, 193, 195–96, 207, 209, 213–14, 216, 217, 233, 236, 237, 257, 274–76, 280, 299–300, 302, 304, 316, 344, 345–46, 354, 357, 358–59, 362–63, 366–67, 371, 373, 375–78, 382, 383, 388
  Adlerangriff and, 35–37, 38, 39–40
  airfields of, 212, 285–86, 306, 314, 380
  Battle of Britain and, 33, 35–36, 37, 38, 39–40, 44, 45, 49, 54, 56, 58, 59, 66, 69–70

Berlin raids and, 227–29, 231
Big Week and, 219–21, 223
Black Friday and, 278–79
Blitz Week and, 181–83
Channel coast bases of, 86, 109
command changes in, 123, 256, 262–63
D-Day and, 242, 244–46, 249, 253
Dieppe raid and, 125–26, 127
Dueren raid and, 202
Dunkirk evacuation and, 23–26
Evere airfield attacked by, 331–38
French campaign and, 17–19, 22
Great London Raid and, 151
invasion of Poland and, 9
under Jafue Brittany, 239–40
Lang's death and, 283
last aircraft lost by, 389–90
last victory of, 386
Market Garden Operation and, 293,
    295, 296
military discipline in, 350
Muenster raid and, 198
Paula Operation and, 26
reequipment of, 98–99, 101, 138, 307
reorganization of, 196–97
replacement pilots in, 262–63, 313, 381
in retreat to Germany, 260, 280,
    285–86
Schweinfurt raids and, 187–90, 201
Sperrle's inspection of, 159–60
Staffels redesignated in, 196–97
trainees incorporated into, 261–69
U.S. 56th Fighter Squadron vs., 193–94
Vitry move of, 154
JG 26, III Gruppe, 90, 102, 103, 107,
    112, 117, 123, 134, 135, 137, 161,
    165, 177–78, 207, 208–9, 216, 231,
    233, 236, 239, 240, 255, 258, 259,
    262, 276, 287, 302, 303, 308–10,
    333, 346–47, 359
Adlerangriff and, 35–37, 39, 40, 53–59
airfields of, 212, 260, 272, 286
Battle of Britain and, 32–36, 37, 39, 40,
    42–44, 48–51, 53–54, 56, 59, 62,
    66, 70
Berlin raids and, 227–29, 231
Big Week and, 219–20, 223
Blitz Week and, 183
Channel coast fields of, 86, 109, 116,
    154
command changes in, 26, 104, 148,
    154, 155
D-Day and, 242, 244, 245, 248, 249
decline of, 297, 301, 350
Dieppe raid and, 125, 126
disbanding of, 368

Dunkirk evacuation and, 23–26
Evere airfield attacked by, 338–40, 341
first FW 190D mission of, 356–57
formation of, 10–11
French campaign and, 17–19, 22
Great London Raid and, 151–52
Gruppe swapping and, 15–16
as "light" Gruppe, 212–13
Lille move of, 171, 192–93
low morale of, 254, 263, 350, 357
Market Garden Operation and, 290,
    293, 295–96
Mietusch appointed commander of, 148
Muenster raid and, 200
Plantluenne move of, 305
Priller named commander of, 104
reequipment of, 85, 212–13, 299, 308,
    354
Reischer incident in, 312–13
reorganization of, 196–97
replacement pilots in, 260
in retreat to Germany, 280–81
Schoepfel named commander of, 48
Schweinfurt raids and, 185, 187, 189,
    190, 200
Staffels redesignated in, 197
JG 26, IV Gruppe, 357, 366, 367, 368,
    373, 380
creation of, 356
last combat mission of, 381
JG 26, Geschwaderstab Staffel, 19, 26, 38,
    55, 104, 109, 160, 185, 192–93, 197,
    212, 260, 263, 276, 279, 280, 305,
    306, 314, 368, 380
JG 26, 1st Staffel, 11, 40–41, 91, 125,
    178, 196, 240, 315, 316, 326, 376
command changes in, 49, 66, 104, 154,
    389
JG 26, 2nd Staffel, 11, 19, 93, 96–97,
    125, 151, 176, 183, 196, 218, 232,
    281, 315, 316, 326, 327
command changes in, 347
JG 26, 3rd Staffel, 11, 67, 125, 147, 177,
    178, 196, 238, 315, 316, 326, 382
command changes in, 180, 375
JG 26, 4th Staffel, 11, 21, 98, 99, 133,
    134, 164, 165, 170, 178, 192, 246,
    267, 311–12, 316–17, 325, 326, 330,
    344
command changes in, 45, 161, 204,
    347
disbanding of, 354
redesignation of, 196–97
JG 26, 5th Staffel, 11, 20, 33, 39, 99,
    124, 130, 137–38, 151, 159, 165,
    178, 207, 208, 263, 277, 285, 293,

JG 26, 5th Staffel (*cont.*)
306–7, 314, 333, 346, 357–58, 369,
373, 381, 384
command changes in, 157, 219, 225,
354, 374, 381, 389
redesignation of, 196–97
JG 26, 6th Staffel, 11, 33, 39, 99, 101–2,
104, 151, 152, 165, 172, 178, 205,
220–21, 263, 274, 285, 314, 333,
346, 369, 370, 371, 383, 384
command changes in, 225, 227, 368
redesignation of, 196–97
JG 26, 7th Staffel, 11, 27, 33, 56, 59, 71,
99, 100, 135, 143, 154, 155, 165,
178, 209, 217, 262, 263, 264, 267–
68, 285–86, 287, 289, 314, 333, 346,
383, 384
Balkan campaign and, 76
command changes in, 49, 101, 349
on Eastern Front, 146–48
Malta campaign and, 73–78
North Africa campaign and, 78–82
redesignation of, 196–97
JG 26, 8th Staffel, 11, 88, 102, 136, 165,
178, 181, 185, 194, 205, 262, 263,
266, 274, 285–86, 287, 289, 304,
314, 333, 334–35, 344, 345, 347
command changes in, 100
disbanding of, 354
reorganization of, 196
JG 26, 9th Staffel, 11, 65, 112, 134, 140,
146, 154, 161, 164, 165, 178, 239,
244, 272–73, 286, 316, 339, 368
command changes in, 48
redesignation of, 97
JG 26, 10th Staffel, 165, 173, 178, 244,
254, 275, 286, 316, 339
redesignation of, 196–97
JG 26, 10th (Jabo) Staffel, 114, 127, 137,
150, 152
JG 26, 10th (Nacht) Staffel, 12–13, 14
JG 26, 11th Staffel, 165, 178, 187–88,
197, 244, 253, 273, 286, 316, 339
JG 26, 11th (Hoehen) Staffel, 121, 123,
125, 136–37, 232
JG 26, 12th Staffel, 165, 178, 197, 217,
244, 286, 316, 321, 339, 357
command changes in, 180–81, 229
JG 26, 13th Staffel, 356, 366, 377
JG 26, 14th Staffel, 356, 375, 377
JG 26, 15th Staffel, 356, 371
disbanding of, 377
Johnson, Wing Cdr. J. E. "Johnnie," 67,
237, 276, 334, 335, 342
Evere attack criticized by, 336–37
Johnson, Lt. Robert, 173, 175, 199, 208

Jubilee, Operation, 124–29
Junck, Genlt. Werner, 154, 239–40
Junkers Ju 52, 2, 4
Junkers Ju 87 Stuka, 20, 24, 31, 33, 36,
38, 39
Junkers Ju 88, 50, 125, 324
Junkers Ju 88G-6, 333

Kehl, Lt. Dietrich, 194
Keitel, Generalfeldmarschall Wilhelm, 390
Kelch, Hptm., 148
Keller, Oblt. Paul, 152–53
Kemen, Fw. Gerhard, 40–41
Kemethmueller, Lt. Heinz, 146–47, 183,
185, 187, 306
Kempf, Lt. Karl-Heinz, 281
Kepner, Maj. Gen. William, 215
Kesselring, Genobst. Albert, 17, 30, 35,
36, 45, 50, 52–53, 61, 62, 63, 69
Kestler, Uffz., 79
Kette formation, 5–6
Kiefner, Lt. Georg, 300, 326, 376, 381
Kienzle, Hptm. Walter, 63–64
Klein, Uffz. Erich, 287
Klemm, Hptm. Rudolf, 354, 356, 381
Klemm Kl 35, 11
Knueppel, Lt. Herwig, 4, 9, 22
Kostenko, Maj. Gen. F. A., 145
Kraft, Fw. Werner, 186
Kraft, Lt., 385
Kraus, Oblt., 357
Kroll, Fw. Gerhard, 371, 381
Krug, Lt., 37, 39–40
Krupinski, Hptm. Walter, 297, 312–13,
324, 333, 338–40, 356, 357, 368
Kruse, Uffz. Ottomar, 261, 262–66, 271–
72, 274–75, 277–80, 286–89
Kukla, Uffz. Hans, 266–67, 311–12, 318,
325, 330, 344, 348, 381
Kunz, Oblt. Franz, 326, 327, 347

Lamberton, Flt. Sgt. W. M., 96
Lang, Hptm. Emil, 256, 257, 261, 263,
264, 267, 272, 276–77, 281–83, 300,
350
Langer, Hptm., 106–7
Laub, Fw. Karl "Karlchen," 230, 240,
258, 301, 310–11
Lavochkin La-5, 145
Lavochkin LaGG-3, 145, 146, 147
Leigh-Mallory, Air Marshal Trafford, 86,
114, 116, 125, 128
Leykauf, Oblt. Erwin, 171, 180–81
Lockheed P-38 Lightning, 169, 202
armament of, 214
Lockheed Ventura, 156

Lohrberg, Obfhr. Helmut, 298, 309
London, Capt. Charles, 182
Longest Day, The (Ryan), 243
Ludewig, Lt. Wolfgang, 18
Luftwaffe, 2, 7, 25, 30, 34, 35, 36, 62,
  127, 128, 382
  Adlertag and, 38–41
  air defense system of, 87, 115
  air-sea rescue (ASR) service of, 32, 53
  Black Thursday of, 41–45
  Canterbury raid by, 136
  casualty rate in, 237
  Condor Legion of, 4–6
  declining aggressiveness of, 236–37
  defense in-depth commitment of, 183
  four-Staffel Gruppe standard of, 197
  Gruppe-switching policy of, 15–16
  intelligence staff of, 68–69
  invasion defense plan of, 243–44
  Jabostaffeln units formed by, 113–14
  London targeted by,59–60
  offensive components of, 10
  officer shortage of, 178
  pilot attrition in, 241
  pilot victory claims and, 40, 68–69
  point system of, 179–80
  shortage of leaders in, 219
  tactical doctrine developed by, 5,
    156
  transfers between units in, 97–98
  weakness in equipment of, 31
Luftwaffe units:
  Luftflotte 1, 143
  Luftflotte 2, 17, 26, 30, 35, 42, 45, 46,
    47, 48, 62, 63, 88
  Luftflotte 3, 26, 35, 47, 48, 52, 62, 63,
    85, 88, 108, 109, 113, 192, 197–98,
    212, 234, 237, 256, 284, 285, 290,
    292, 294
  Luftflotte Reich, 197, 212, 237, 296,
    301, 303, 306, 382
  Luftwaffenkommando West (Lkdo
    West), 294, 295, 296, 299, 303,
    347–48
  Fliegerkorps II, 243–44
  Fliegerkorps X, 72–73, 76, 78
  Fliegerdivision 14, 373, 376, 377, 382
  Erprobungsgruppe 210, 36, 41, 43, 66
  Erprobungsstaffel 190, 98, 99
  Jadgwaffe, 2, 6, 218, 223, 231
  Jagdkorps I, 197, 207
  Jagdkorps II, 192, 198, 212, 253, 256–
    57, 260, 262, 273, 276, 279, 284,
    285, 290, 292, 295, 296, 306, 311,
    347–48
  Jagddivision 3, 154, 319, 321

Jagddivision 4, 192, 198, 256–57
Jagddivision 5, 240, 242, 244, 254,
  256–57
Jagddivision 8, 48
Jagdgeschwader:
EJG 1, 381
JG 1, 13, 110, 156, 184, 185, 198, 260,
  262, 274
JG 2, 14, 48, 66, 88, 89, 91, 93, 100,
  104–5, 110, 112, 114, 116, 120, 121,
  125, 127, 128–29, 136–37, 140, 150,
  152, 154, 161, 164, 206, 207, 212,
  236, 237, 285, 345
JG 3, 17, 19, 22, 24, 45, 66, 206, 262,
  266, 301, 308
JG 4, 153
JG 5, 262, 390
JG 6, 153
JG 7, 376
JG 11, 301
JG 26, *see* JG 26 (Schlageter)
JG 27, 27, 48, 66, 79, 80, 285, 300,
  308, 316, 345, 359, 366, 367
JG 51, 17, 34, 35, 42, 45, 47, 66, 137,
  153
JG 52, 42, 45, 193
JG 53, 14–15, 28, 48, 49, 67, 130,
  233, 285, 345, 349
JG 54 (Green Hearts), 42, 45, 48–49,
  61, 70, 142 43, 144, 115, 146,
  152, 154, 155, 156, 165, 248,
  249, 253, 256, 257, 262, 281, 307,
  316, 318–21, 325–26, 329–30,
  353–54
JG 77, 67, 123
JG 104, 329–330
JG 132 (Richthofen), 2, 7–8
JG 134 (Horst Wessel), 1, 2–3, 7
JG 234, 1, 3, 6–7, 95
JG 300, 349
JV 44, 368, 381
Jafue 2, 2, 7, 28, 62, 86, 178
Jafue 3, 21
Jafue Brittany, 239–240
Kampfgeschwader:
KG 1, 45
KG 2, 30, 36, 47
KG 3, 42
KG 30, 60
KG (J) 51, 343–44, 347
KG 53, 47
KG 76, 45
Lehrgeschwader:
LG 1, 12
Nachtjagdgeschwader:
NJG 6, 333

435

Luftwaffe units (cont.)
Schlachtflieger:
SG 151, 388, 389
Schnellkampfgeschwader:
SKG 10, 153
Stukageschwader, 10
StG 2, 74
Zerstoerergeschwader:
ZG 26, 10, 11, 16, 17, 19, 45, 47, 67

McCollom, Maj. Loren, 187
Mahurin, Capt. Walker "Bud," 190
Malan, Sq. Ldr. "Sailor," 36, 67
Malta, 72, 73–76
Market Garden, Operation, 290–96
Martin B-26 Marauder, 176–77
Martin Maryland, 81
Mason, Flg. Off. E. M. "Imshi," 75, 76
Matoni, Oblt. Walter, 224, 225
Matuschka, Oblt. Graf, 155
Mayer, Hptm. Egon, 139
Mayer, Fw. Wilhelm, 182, 344, 346
Menge, Obfw. Robert, 67
Messerschmitt, Willy, 3, 84
Messerschmitt Bf 109, 5, 7, 10, 13–14,
    18–19, 21, 22, 24–25, 35, 42
  armament of, 3–4, 14, 29, 84, 95, 101,
    139, 212–13, 308
  Bf 110 contrasted with, 16
  British fighters compared with, 23–24,
    60, 87
  close escort mission and, 60
  as fighter-bomber, 64–66
  first production version of, 3–4
  FuG 16ZY equipment in, 299
  FW 190D-9 compared with, 354–55
  Galland's experiments with, 101
  limited combat radius of, 31–32
  performance of, 8–9, 29–30, 212–13, 299
  production of, 120–21
  production variants of, 138–39
  standard equipment in, 307–8
  structural problems of, 83–84
Messerschmitt Bf 109B, 3–4, 5
Messerschmitt Bf 109C, 3, 11, 12, 13
Messerschmitt Bf 109D, 3
Messerschmitt Bf 109E, 20, 24, 32, 52
Messerschmitt Bf 109E-1, 11, 14, 30, 36
Messerschmitt Bf 109E-3, 14, 16, 20, 29
Messerschmitt Bf 109E-4, 29, 30, 84
Messerschmitt Bf 109E-4/B, 64
Messerschmitt Bf 109E-4/N, 29–30
Messerschmitt Bf 109E-7, 65, 73, 83, 84,
    85, 88, 99
Messerschmitt Bf 109F, 84, 144
Messerschmitt Bf 109F-1, 83, 84

Messerschmitt Bf 109F-2, 83, 84, 93, 94,
    95
Messerschmitt Bf 109F-3, 95
Messerschmitt Bf 109F-4, 95, 96, 97, 102,
    108
Messerschmitt Bf 109F-4/R1, 114
Messerschmitt Bf 109G, 120, 125, 138,
    144, 244
Messerschmitt Bf 109G-1, 121, 138
Messerschmitt Bf 109G-4, 139
Messerschmitt Bf 109G-5, 101
Messerschmitt Bf 109G-6, 212, 299
Messerschmitt Bf 109G-10, 299, 307–8
Messerschmitt Bf 109G-14, 299
Messerschmitt Bf 109K-4, 307–8
Messerschmitt Bf 110, 10, 13, 19, 26, 31,
    35, 36, 63, 199, 200
  Bf 109 contrasted with, 16
Messerschmitt Me 262, 32, 294, 300, 310,
    316, 338, 343–44, 368
Messerschmitt Me 410, 199, 200
Meyer, Hptm. Conny, 133, 138, 155
Meyer, Obfw. Walter, 122
Mietusch, Maj. Klaus, 76, 135, 147, 148,
    152, 180, 183, 207–8, 225, 228–29,
    231, 248, 249, 253, 254, 255, 275,
    286, 290, 297
  aggressiveness of, 135, 185–86
  background of, 292
  death of, 291–92
  downing of, 27, 358–59
  injured, 146, 233
  named 7th Staffel commander, 101
  in North Africa, 79–81
  Tippe and, 250–51
Mikoyan MiG-3, 145
Moelders, Obst. Werner, 5–6, 14–15, 31,
    34, 103–4, 153
Molge, Ogfr. Werner, 332–33, 335–36,
    338, 363–66, 377, 389–90
Montgomery, Field Marshal Bernard, 368
Morane Saulnier MS 406, 17, 18, 19, 21,
    22
Mueller-Duehe, Lt. Gerhard, 43–44, 47, 71
Muencheberg, Hptm. Joachim, 15, 25,
    34, 40, 43, 49, 54, 56, 59, 61, 100,
    101–2, 103, 108, 119, 292, 300
  in Balkan campaign, 76
  at Eastern Front, 123
  in Malta campaign, 73–75, 76
  in North African campaign, 79–82
Muenster Raid, 198–200

Naumann, Hptm. Johannes, 131–32, 194,
    196, 219, 255, 256
Netherlands, 10, 17–18, 21, 22

Neu, Hptm. Wolfgang, 234
Neumann, Hptm. Edu, 79, 80
Nibel, Lt. Theo, 326–29
Niesmak, Uffz. Josef, 390–91
Nine Lives (Deere), 42
9th Armored Division, U.S., 361
Ninth Army, U.S., 362, 368, 374, 382
Noack, Hptm. Erich, 26, 33
"nonstop offensive," 89–105
North American Mustang I, 125, 157
North American P-51B Mustang, 209, 214

Oesau, Maj. Walter, 89
Olds, Maj. Robin, 367
Osterkamp, Obst. Theo, 85, 86, 89, 91

Palm, Hptm. Werner, 9
Park, Air Vice Marshal Keith, 30–31, 59,
    61, 65
Paula, Operation, 26–28
Peltz, Genlt. Dietrich, 311, 323, 330, 341
Petlyakov Pe-2, 145, 147
Pflanz, Oblt. Rudi, 121, 123
Philipp, Hptm., 106–7, 108, 146, 242
Pingel, Hptm. Rolf, 49, 61, 88, 94–95
Plazer, Fhr. Gerhard von, 381, 382
Poelchau, Gert, 370, 373
Polikarpov I-16, 147
Polikarpov I-153, 147
Polster, Fw. Wolfgang "Poldi," 249, 356,
    381
Prager, Lt. Hans, 262, 264, 265, 268–69,
    316, 325–26, 354, 375, 381
Priller, Obstlt. Josef "Pips," 92, 96, 100,
    103, 117–18, 134, 136, 152, 161,
    165, 167, 171, 174, 175, 177, 233,
    245, 247, 256, 292, 301–2, 316, 321,
    377
  background of, 153–54
  Baseplate Operation and, 323–26, 330–31
  decorations awarded to, 66, 95, 300
  at Jafue 2, 178, 212, 231
  leaves JG 26, 349
  mission described by, 249–50
  named 1st Staffel commander, 66
  named JG 26 commander, 142
  named III Gruppe commander, 104
  Sword Beach strafed by, 242–43
  trainees and, 155–56
Prinz Eugen, 110

Radener, Oblt. Waldi, 224, 236, 333,
    346, 349, 355–56
Red (Soviet) Air Force, 143, 144, 146
Regenauer, Lt. Hans-Werner, 37
Regensburg Raid, 184–88

Reischer, Lt. Peter, 253, 254, 312–13
Reitsch, Hanna, 388
Rentsch, Werner, 3
Republic P-47 Thunderbolt, 168, 169
Republic P-47D Thunderbolt, 214
"Rhubarb" missions, 87
Richthofen, Manfred von, 50
Risky, Uffz. Norbert, 335
"Roadstead" missions, 87
Roberts, Maj. Eugene, 182
Roberts, Plt. Off. Ralph, 44
"Rodeo" missions, 87
Roosevelt, Franklin D., 135
Rotte formation, 5, 31
Royal Air Force (RAF), 9, 10, 24, 28, 31,
    33, 34, 35, 57, 59, 88, 89, 109, 125,
    128, 228, 391
  air doctrine of, 131, 168
  Air Fighting Development Unit of, 94–
    95, 120
  Battle of Britain losses of, 70
  Channel Dash and, 111–12
  FW 190D-9 in hands of, 328–29
  leaflet raids by, 12
  Malta command of, 73, 74
  mission code names of, 87
  "nonstop offensive" by, 89–105
  pilot overclaims and, 68, 94
  pilot training in, 261
  summer offensive by, 116–19, 123–24
  See also Bomber Command, RAF; Cir-
    cus missions; Coastal Command,
    RAF; Fighter Command, RAF; Sec-
    ond Tactical Air Force, RAF
Royal Air Force Wings:
  Biggin Hill, 207
  Debden, 117–18
  Hornchurch, 117, 118, 120
  No. 122, 349
  North Weald, 118
Royal Air Force Groups:
  No. 2 (Bomber), 117
  No. 10, 35
  No. 11, 19, 31, 35, 37, 39, 42, 45, 46,
    50, 52, 53, 58, 59, 65, 86, 88, 89,
    91, 93, 97, 114, 125, 128, 151
  No. 13, 53
  No. 83, 295
Royal Air Force Squadrons:
  No. 2 (Bomber), 89, 98
  No. 3, 228, 361
  No. 7 (Bomber), 94
  No. 15 (Bomber), 97
  No. 17, 66
  No. 32, 40, 41, 47
  No. 33, 373, 381

Royal Air Force Squadrons (*cont.*)
No. 41, 34, 348, 353
No. 54, 32, 33–34, 37, 42
No. 56, 37, 53, 321, 367
No. 64, 33, 37, 44, 66, 120, 123
No. 65, 32, 40
No. 66, 20
No. 74, 34, 36, 67
No. 75, 66
No. 80, 367
No. 85, 53
No. 88 (Bomber), 101
No. 91, 85
No. 92, 62, 66
No. 130, 359, 374
No. 133, 133
No. 137, 295
No. 139 (Bomber), 102
No. 151, 36, 43
No. 182, 188, 192, 304
No. 185, 78
No. 213, 25
No. 222, 371
No. 235, 61
No. 249, 78
No. 253, 66
No. 257, 34, 66
No. 261, 73, 75, 76, 78
No. 264, 19–20, 50–51
No. 266, 44–45
No. 274, 356
No. 315 (Polish), 275
No. 340 (Free French), 151
No. 350, 359
No. 411, 238–39, 320
No. 442, 344
No. 485, 204
No. 486, 319, 388–89
No. 501, 36, 42, 45–46
No. 603, 53, 58
No. 609, 151
No. 610, 33, 40
No. 615, 40
Royal Canadian Air Force Wings:
No. 127, 276, 334
No. 144, 237
Royal Canadian Air Force Squadrons:
No. 401, 297
No. 403, 118–19, 191, 334, 336
No. 411, 344
No. 412, 304–5, 307, 311
No. 414, 253, 255
No. 416, 334, 340
No. 421, 348
No. 439, 320
No. 443, 252

Royal Navy (RN), 23, 34, 113, 127
Bismarck sunk by, 86
Rundstedt, Genobst. Karl von, 17, 18, 19, 22
Ruppert, Hptm. Kurt, 133–34, 165, 173
Ryan, Cornelius, 243
Rysavy, Oblt. Martin, 93

Salomon, Uffz. Heinz, 263, 264, 270
Scharnhorst, 85, 110
Schauder, Hptm. Paul, 172, 254, 339, 356, 365, 378, 380, 389
Scheyda, Obfhr. Erich, 238–39
Schild, Oblt. Jan, 183–84, 231, 232, 275, 291, 302, 303, 356, 388, 389, 390
Schilling, Maj. David, 199
Schlageter, Albert Leo, 7–8
Schleich, Genlt. Edward Ritter von, 7, 9, 15
Schmid, Hptm. Johannes, 99–100, 102
Schmidt, Oblt. Gottfried, 339, 368, 378
Schmidt, Oblt. Johannes, 121, 125
Schneider, Oblt. Walter, 99, 101, 104
Schoepfel, Maj. Gerhard, 61, 62, 80, 102, 106–8, 114, 131, 139
in Battle of Britain, 53–56
Channel Dash and, 110–12
Galland succeeded by, 104
Knight's Cross awarded to, 60
leaves JG 26, 142, 153–54
mission described by, 45–46
promoted to command III Gruppe, 48
Schrader, Oblt. Karl-Hermann, 339, 381
Schramm, Lt. 383–85
Schroedter, Oblt. Rolf, 84, 103
Schulwitz, Lt. Gerhard "Bubi," 335, 369–70, 373
Schumacher, Obstlt. Carl, 13–14
Schwarm formation, 6, 31, 218
Schwarz, Obfw. Erich, 325, 344
Schweinfurt Raids, 184, 188–91, 200–202
Sealion, Operation (Unternehmen Seeloewe), 62, 63
Second Army, British, 343, 368
Second Tactical Air Force, RAF, 208, 209, 214, 251, 295, 319–20, 334, 347, 389
Seelos, Robert, 167
Seifert, Gerhard, 148
Seifert, Hptm. Johannes, 95, 103, 108, 117–18, 119, 142, 144, 148, 196, 205–7
Seiler, Maj. "Seppl," 155
Short Stirling, 94, 98
Sitzkrieg (Sitting War), 12
Smythe, Plt. Off. R. F., 41

Soeffing, Lt. Waldemar "Vladimir," 181, 233–34, 306, 318, 325, 347, 377, 378, 382, 388–89
South African Air Force, 79, 80–81
Spaatz, General Carl, 239
Spahn, Obfhr. Johann, 366
Spanish Civil War, 4–5
Speck, Uffz. Hermann, 21
Sperrle, Generalfeldmarschall Hugo, 62, 159–60, 234, 253
Sprick, Gustav "Micky," 54, 56–57, 65–66, 80, 93
Staiger, Hptm. Herman, 181, 183, 229, 231, 234–36, 254, 255, 257, 260, 301
Stammberger, Oblt. Otto "Stotto," 134–35, 137, 140, 161, 164, 166–67, 170
Staschen, Lt. Arno, 147–48
Stein, Lt., 268
Steinhoff, Oblt. Johannes, 12
Sternberg, Oblt. Horst, 124–25, 157, 159, 160, 221–22
Stumpf, Fw. Walter, 261, 262–63, 267–69, 270, 279, 337, 354, 359, 362, 382, 384, 389
Stumpf, Genobst., 197
Supermarine Spitfire, 9, 16, 19, 20, 21, 23–24, 169, 213
  Bf 109 compared with, 23–24, 60, 87
  communications equipment of, 44
  FW 190 contrasted with, 120
  shortcomings of, 168
Supermarine Spitfire II, 87
Supermarine Spitfire V, 87, 95
Supermarine Spitfire Vb, 115, 120, 123
Supermarine Spitfire IX, 117, 120, 123, 125, 133
Supermarine Spitfire Mk IXB, 188
Supermarine Spitfire XIV, 348, 353, 359, 374, 388
Sy, Lt. Siegfried, 346, 368–74, 378–80, 383–86, 388, 390

Taylor, Flg. Off. Eric, 74
Tank, Kurt, 98, 99, 138, 307, 314, 329
Teichmann, Gefr. Alfred, 218
Third Army, U.S., 353
Thran, Gefr. Hans, 262
Tippe, Uffz. Erhard, 240–41, 248–49, 250–52
Torch, Operation, 129
Trautloft, Obstlt. Hannes, 4, 6, 48, 61, 152, 259, 310

Ubben, Maj. Kurt, 237
Udet, Genobst. Ernst, 103

Ultra organization, 31, 62, 68, 94, 129, 244, 253, 257, 294
Ungar, Obfw. Fritz, 320–21, 386–88
U.S. Army Air Force:
  aerial superiority attained by, 226
  Berlin raids by, 226–31
  Big Week of, 219–26
  Blitz Week campaign of, 181–84
  close escort policy of, 214–15
  largest operation of, 315
U.S. Army Air Forces:
  8th, 130–31, 135, 139, 140, 148, 162, 168–75, 191, 192, 200, 205, 214–15, 236, 290, 294
  9th, 209, 227, 228, 254, 262, 267, 276, 290
  12th, 137
  15th, 226
U.S. Army Air Force Commands:
  8th Bomber, 126, 131, 133, 156, 160, 165, 168, 189, 192, 198, 208, 209, 231, 237
  8th Fighter, 156, 193, 215, 229, 231
U.S. Army Air Force Divisions:
  1st Bomber, 198, 208, 216, 345
  2nd Bomber, 198, 207, 216, 233
  3rd Bomber, 198, 207, 208, 216, 218
U.S. Army Air Force Wings:
  1st Bomber, 160, 168, 171, 183, 188, 194, 198
  4th Bomber, 171, 173, 184, 188, 198
U.S. Army Air Force Bomber Groups:
  2nd, 156–57
  44th, 162, 217
  91st, 139–40
  92nd, 133
  93rd, 135, 164
  95th, 186
  97th, 126, 133
  100th, 199
  305th, 160–61, 163, 164, 165
  306th, 134, 166, 168
  351st, 172
  386th, 176
  392nd, 250–51
  394th, 354
  445th, 233
  452nd, 310
  492nd, 250
U.S. Army Air Force Fighter Groups:
  4th, 156, 169, 174, 181, 182, 183, 189, 209, 221–22, 275
  20th, 207, 217, 218, 227
  38th, 281–82
  50th, 289
  55th, 205, 207, 246, 248, 255, 281–82

U.S. Army Air Force Fighter Groups
  (*cont.*)
  56th, 169, 173, 174, 175, 182, 190–91,
    192, 193–94, 199, 205, 208, 209,
    293, 303, 345, 346
  77th, 207
  78th, 169, 172, 173, 174, 182, 189,
    192, 207, 209, 222–23, 248, 303,
    346, 347, 366
  352nd, 198–99, 210, 229, 295
  353rd, 184, 187, 191, 199, 200, 201,
    217, 293
  354th, 209, 259, 272, 279
  355th, 199, 240
  356th, 231, 237, 241
  357th, 224, 292–93
  358th, 211–12, 257
  361st, 232, 291, 317
  363rd, 267
  364th, 303
  365th, 227, 253
  366th, 359, 362
  367th, 287
  368th, 254, 262, 304
  370th, 289
  373rd, 259, 269
  406th, 358, 375
  474th, 278, 304, 312
  479th, 367
U.S. Army Air Force Transport Groups:
  38th, 293
  46th, 293
U.S. Army Air Force Fighter Squadrons:
  56th, 311
  79th, 217, 218
  83rd, 222
  335th, 221–22
  355th, 182
  363rd, 303
  367th, 211

376th, 291, 317
428th, 278–79, 312
429th, 278–79

Varsity, Operation, 368
Vassiliades, Flt. Lt. B. M., 361
"vengeance attacks," 135–38
Vickers Wellington, 13
Vieck, Obst., 178, 211
Voelmle, Lt., 259–60
Vogt, Lt. John, 194
Vogt, Oblt. Gerhard, 158–59, 182, 194,
    255, 261, 277–78, 293, 295, 307,
    333, 344, 345, 346

Walter, Fw. Helmut, 388
Way, Flt. Lt. B. H. "Wonky," 33
Webster, Lt. Lee, 267
Weiss, Hptm. Robert, 253, 316, 319–21
Wiegand, Lt. Gerd, 194–95, 204, 209–10,
    227
  downing of, 181–82, 228
  mission described by, 216, 246–47
Wilkinson, Sqd. Ldr., 44–45
Willius, Lt. Karl "Charlie," 147, 176–77,
    218, 219, 224, 225–26, 232
Wing Leader (Johnson), 342
Witt, Obst. Hugo, 15, 25, 26, 28, 38
Wodarczyk, Uffz. Heinz, 242–43, 326,
    330
Wollnitz, Hptm. Bernhard, 357

Yakovlev Yak-1, 147
Yakovlev Yak-3, 383
Yakovlev Yak-7b, 145
Yeager, Lt. Charles "Chuck," 303

Zemke, Col. Hubert "Hub," 173, 190–91,
    192, 193, 194, 208
Zester, Obfw. Willi, 359–61, 381